AF497383

'HEBREW' EXERCISE-BOOK.

'HEBREW' EXERCISE-BOOK

(HEBREW-ENGLISH AND ENGLISH-HEBREW EXERCISES)

WITH

PRACTICAL GRAMMAR OF THE WORD-FORMS

AND AN

APPENDIX

CONTAINING

ANALYSIS OF THE VERB-FORMS IN GEN. I-III, & XII, AND LIST OF ALL THE FORMS
OF THE SO-CALLED 'DOUBLY-IRREGULAR' VERBS IN THE BIBLE;

ALSO

FULL AND EXTENSIVE TABLES.

(SECOND EDITION)

BY THE REV.

P. H. MASON, M.A.,

PRESIDENT, TUTOR AND HEBREW LECTURER,
LATE SENIOR DEAN OF ST JOHN'S COLLEGE, CAMBRIDGE.

CAMBRIDGE. J. HALL & SON.
LONDON:
SIMPKIN, MARSHALL & Co., AND WHITTAKER & Co.
1883.
[Entered at Stationers' Hall.]

ADDRESS TO THE READER.

It is gratifying to have to bring out now a Second Edition[*]
of the 'First Part of the Exercise-book,' and also of the
'Continuation.' The author was anxious to complete the
whole work before having to spend time on a new Edition of
any Part; and therefore no part of the Exercise-book has
been advertised at all as yet in the Papers or Reviews. He
desires however to express his best thanks to those who have
caused such a re-issue to be necessary now, although it is
required rather earlier than he anticipated. And perhaps he
may trust that the expenditure of time and labour demanded
for going carefully over every page in the preparation of the
re-issue may be kindly taken into consideration as offering
some excuse for the delay in the completion of the work.

He is very glad to be enabled to put forth now the whole
work complete in one volume—with 'INDEX OF HEBREW

---

[*] The 'First Part of the Exercise-book' was published at the beginning of the
year 1872. A new Edition of it was really required about a year ago; and there
was then issued what might have been called a Second Edition of it. This issue
was not so called because it was only intended to serve temporarily. The 'Continuation' was published in May, 1873; and what might have been called a Second
Edition of it was required and issued some months ago.

WORDS' (so far as was thought necessary), and an 'INDEX OF MATTERS.' A 'Vocabulary' of some Hebrew words which are sometimes not given (after Exercise XX) in the Notes to the Exercises may be found useful; as also the very brief English-Hebrew Vocabulary following it. Generally all the necessary help is given in the 'Notes to the Exercises.'

The purpose of the author is to enable Students to learn to know this language as a MEANS FOR THE EXPRESSION OF THOUGHT. The great variety of the forms of words in the Bible may well seem likely to perplex a Student unless they be carefully classified for him, and unless he be familiarised with them as so classified. In this book therefore it is endeavoured not only to classify the forms intelligibly, and to present them for study in their several Classes one after the other, but moreover TO ILLUSTRATE THE FORMS BELONGING TO THE SEVERAL CLASSES in Exercises specially devoted to those Classes severally,—so that the Student may gradually be familiarised with them all and may be able TO EMPLOY THEM freely and unhesitatingly in rendering English into Hebrew.

All the Exercises are wholly taken from The Hebrew Bible, and they furnish the Student with a series of passages containing EXAMPLES OF ALL THE LEADING GRAMMATICAL FORMS in the Language. They are arranged progressively, from the very simplest expressions and sentences, which the Beginner may master without any difficulty, to passages involving very intricate forms. By help of the remarks which precede the several sets of Exercises the Student will gradually be able not only to recognize and understand such grammatical forms when he meets with them in his reading,

but moreover he may become so familiar with them as to
form them himself and write them down at once with ACCURACY
as well as with ease and confidence.   Let him spare no pains
in attaining ACCURACY OF ELEMENTARY KNOWLEDGE.   To
encourage him in patient endeavours to attain such accuracy
it may be well perhaps to add that during an extensive and
varied experience of now nearly a quarter of a century of
active work in guiding and training Students to attain a
familiarity*, with this Language, the author has had impressed
upon him—and continually more and more strongly impressed
upon him—that time and patient care devoted to elementary
work are always found by the Student to be time well spent
and care well bestowed ;—that the toil (it may be) of working
conscientiously through the Exercises, till thorough familiarity
with the principal forms of all the great Classes of words
shall have been gained by him, is toil which he will find to
involve great and unfailing reward ;—and that so a good
solid foundation will be laid on which may be raised a secure
building of sound knowledge that can stand firm against
fiercest assaults of the floods and storms of conflicting
opinions.

P. H. M.

St John's College, Cambridge,
October 9, 1876

---

* And of course far beyond the extent covered by this present book, which is
necessarily but elementary.

[The 'Preface' which follows, is that of the First Edition.]

PREFACE.

The object of this Work is to present in an EASY form the leading features of what is usually called the 'Hebrew' Language. The supposition that this is an exceedingly difficult language is caused, to some extent, by attempts to explain it on foreign principles, fundamental principles of its own being ignored. For instance, what we call 'First Person'—viz., 'I'—is not First in Hebrew, but 'He' is First. Herein lies a fundamental difference of Bible-Thought from Thought in which each one refers all to himself as the Centre cf reference. And is it very reasonable that each one of us should reckon himself as 'Number One'? That it is *natural* for one to start from himself as First, is merely an evidence of the need of education for the correction of natural errors to which each of us is liable. There are not as many 'FIRSTS'—Originating Centres of all Time and Space—as there have been, are, and will be, individual men. GOD is the only True Centre of reference. He, The Unseen, is 'FIRST.' It is not too much to say that the conflicting Doubts and Difficulties in modern thought regarding the Bible, arise, in great measure, from misapprehensions caused by non-recognition of this great Principle. [And the mind itself, groping after Truth, seems to shew its want of this by its vain efforts to rise out of mere individual-self made in high Philosophy and in Scientific Thought,—in the mighty conception of the Transcendental 'Ego,' and in the thought of the 'Self of Humanity.'] As, in regard to the planetary world, so long as the Earth was reckoned as the centre of the visible Universe, there were strange confusions and perplexities in human speculations, which have vanished,—which have given way to the recognition of Unity, and grand Simplicity, and beautiful Order, since the Sun was perceived to be the Centre of our System; so, but much more grandly (for the above is but an imperfect illustration), the recognition of the TRUE CENTRE OF BEING removes vast confusion from our self-centred speculations regarding the world of sense and sight and thought and being. We gain great advantage, if we gain only the recognition of this, from study of 'Hebrew' IN ACCORDANCE WITH ITS OWN PRINCIPLES. This study has been neglected.

The endeavour here is to state simply the facts of the Language (without discussing, at present, how they came to be such),—and, as far as possible, in what may be called a *Concrete form* rather than 'Abstract'-ly.

My best thanks are due to those friends who have kindly and carefully Revised the Proof-sheets, and favoured me with many valuable observations, viz., Dr. CHANCE, of Trinity College, Cambridge (and of Burleigh House, Sydenham Hill, London), also the Rev. E. T. LEEKE, M.A., Fellow of Trinity College, and Vicar of Barnwell, and the Rev. F. WATSON, M.A., Fellow of St. John's College, Cambridge.

P. H. M.

ST. JOHN'S COLLEGE, CAMBRIDGE,
    December, 1871.

PREFACE TO THE CONTINUATION.

———

THE endeavour of the writer, in this as in the preceding part of the 'Exercise-book,' is TO STATE FACTS. Controversy is excluded here.

The accompanying pages follow the plan of the 'Exercise-book,' as far as p. 166. After that, pp. 167–178 contain a Sketch, merely, of the remaining Sections. That Sketch is given in order that the Student may be enabled to proceed at once (with the help of the corresponding Tables) to read The BIBLE itself. Pressure of time caused this variation of plan. The Reader will probably be very glad of it, whatever may have caused it. 'Exercise'-work is indeed very helpful to Hebrew Students—one might say even necessary for them. But a somewhat long experience as a lecturer and teacher has made the writer aware of that eager and not unnatural desire to "begin The BIBLE," which many Students shew as soon as they have acquired a certain familiarity with the principles of the Language. This desire the writer endeavours to comply with here, rather earlier than he would, by

giving in the 'Sketch' the chief features of the further information which is needful to the Student, and by some full
Tables.

The elaborate TABLES given in this work (pp. I–XLIII) have
cost much trouble and pains,—which the writer does not regret
having bestowed, as he is sure that these Tables will be found
more and more useful to the Student in his onward progress.

In the body of the work, and in several of the Tables,
ACCENTS are given. They have been so given for the convenience of the Student. But they have been purposely
omitted in some few of the Tables, because the Student should
learn to know the position of the Accents without seeing
them, and must be able to do without them at the earliest
moment. Scholars never accentuate their Hebrew Composition. See, for instance, N. Herz Weisel's שִׁירֵי תִפְאֶרֶת
and Eichenbaum's קוֹל זִמְרָה. The Accentuation of The BIBLE
is a different matter. It is a very important subject, which
must be dealt with at some length elsewhere:—here it would
be out of place.

The several Exercises in this Continuation have been put
together on a plan: *i.e.* the disconnected sentences illustrating
Verb-forms have an underlying connection in thought. The
thought running through an Exercise is not, however, always

to be perceived easily. The writer has sometimes amused himself by illustrating* Rabbinic thought and allusion—to be recognized, it may be, by those only who are in the secret of the method. But sometimes the thought running through an Exercise may be easily seen at once. The Student need not, however, trouble himself at all with this; but may limit his attention, at present, to the Verb-forms. Also he is not expected to parse or analyze any word of which the full meaning is given in the Notes.

Any Verb mentioned in the Notes, or elsewhere, is supposed to be of the First Voice (*Kal*), unless some other Voice-mark is attached to it.

After a time the Student may learn TO KNOW WORDS for himself. Some few words are therefore not given in the Notes sometimes. It will be found useful to write out in a list those marked 'not to be given again,' and those in the Short Vocabularies I–VI; and moreover to combine them all Alphabetically. This will make much easier the first use of a Lexicon.

A few Abbreviations have sometimes been used, which will be recognized without trouble;—as 'fr.' for 'from,' 'r.' for 'root,' etc.

---

* As, for instance, in the latter part of Exerc. XX (*last few lines of* p. 92).

The Reader need not trouble himself, at first, with what is IN SMALL PRINT—except when such is specially referred to.

The many cross References (to other §§) will be found very useful to the careful Student. Much trouble has been bestowed upon them.

The Contents will supply the want of an Index* temporarily, and may advantageously be read along with Sections XI–XIII as an ANALYTICAL SUMMARY so far—which is afterwards unnecessary.

The writer is glad of this opportunity for repeating his thankful acknowledgments to Dr. Chance, of Trinity College, Cambridge (and of Burleigh House, Sydenham Hill, London), the Rev. E. T. Leeke, M.A., Fellow of Trinity College, Cambridge, and Vicar of Barnwell, and the Rev. F. Watson, M.A., Fellow of St. John's College, Cambridge. He does not know how to thank them enough for their kind and careful Revision of the Proof-sheets, and for the valuable suggestions with which they have favoured him.

St. John's College, Cambridge,
  May, 1873.

---

* To be supplied at the earliest opportunity.

PREFACE TO THE 'CONCLUDING PART.'

AFTER rather more than a year of severe work, and not a little ill health, the writer of these pages is enabled to put forth this 'Concluding Part of the Exercise Book.'

First, it has been found necessary to give some ADDITIONAL EXERCISES exemplifying forms of the important Classes of Verbs in Tables XXI–XXIII, and of those Verbs which belong to more than one of the Seven Classes mentioned in § 186, and of Verbs with Pron.-Affixes. To the Exercises are prefixed some brief remarks (in the form of OBSERVATIONS on those several sets of Verb-forms).

Those Students who are wise enough to work through these

additional Exercises, with careful study of the Verb-forms illustrated therein, will hereafter find themselves amply rewarded for their pains by the much greater ease and pleasure with which they will be able to read The Bible.

Secondly, an Appendix has been added in order to supply some aid which the Student is likely to want at his first attempt to read The Bible itself. As a means of not only enabling him to recognize more easily the various forms of Verbs, but also of familiarizing him (by references) with several Tables and Sections in which such forms are classified and mentioned, we give on pages 226–266 an ANALYSIS OF THE VERB-FORMS in chapters i.-iii. and xii. of the Book of Genesis—with a few Notes on some points of interest which we will briefly speak of again at the close of this Preface.

Thirdly, on pages 267–314 the Student will find a List of what some call 'Doubly Irregular' Verbs, which we would speak of rather as Verbs belonging to more than one of the Seven Classes in § 186 (page 124), which might perhaps for convenience be termed briefly 'MIXED' Verbs.

On pages 315–380 we mention some matters and forms and words of importance or of special interest as means of fixing the attention on some principle (see, for instance, pages 360–364). These need not be dwelt upon in detail here. We may therefore now conclude this Preface with a remark or two about the few Notes offered, perhaps somewhat unnecessarily, on some passages in the opening chapters of the Book of Genesis.

The brevity of some of these Notes might possibly cause misapprehension of our meaning, if we were to neglect to give this preliminary notice that we have been content here and there to mention some opinions without entering into any discussion of them. Thus, we very much prefer to render Gen. i. 20 in accordance with what is said in the brief Note upon that verse on page 230; but we have not troubled the Reader with the discussion which would have been necessary had we attempted to give the reasons for our preference.

So in the Note on Gen. i. 5 (p. 227) we have held aloof from the controversy as to the signification of the word 'day';— nor have we there touched upon the signification of the words for 'evening' and 'morning.'—And we beg leave to be allowed to hold aloof from the tumult of that controversy still. But, although a quiet remark of one who will not join in the fray can hardly be expected to be listened to amid the din of conflict, we may perhaps just observe in passing that the

Hebrew word here used for 'evening' involves the notion of a 'Mixing up,' and that the word for 'day' cannot rightly be limited to a twentyfour hours' day, as some wish to limit it.* Also we may venture to express the hope that our own use of the English words 'evening' and 'morning' and 'day' in our little Note on page 227 may not be misunderstood. We do not there mean merely a 'twentyfour-hours' day, with its evening after the daylight and its morning after the night. We use there common words. All of us use common words. And may we not sometimes use common words as a vehicle for rather more meaning than we want them for ordinarily?— For many years past Gen. i. has spoken to us of successive 'Mixings up' followed successively by grand breakings of 'Morning' after 'Morning' not to be confounded with those of ordinary 'day.' We know too that we English people ourselves can have our English word 'day' used indefinitely in such expressions as "the DAY of salvation," and "the passing DAY of this our mortal life." And so with regard to our

---

* It will be seen that we are speaking of what is stated by the Book itself. We object, as strongly as any one, to all attempts to bend and alter and reduce the statements of the Book in order to suit what we might adopt as results of scientific research or any speculations or theories of our own. And as we would not limit it, so also we would not have it made to say more than it says. We may not add thereto, any more than we may diminish therefrom. We hope that the Reader will not misinterpret our Note on Gen. i. 21 (p. 230) to carry more than the corresponding words of this Preface on page vii.

English word 'morning' in such an expression as "we are looking for the dawn of the MORNING of the great Day of Life—the Day of Eternity—which shall be closed in by no evening, and shall know no setting Sun."

*   *   *   *   *   *

And may we, without descending into the arena of controversy, be permitted to say a word or two about a very common mistake? In our short Note on Gen. i. 21 (p. 230) we call attention to what all who will may see for themselves to be the fact, *viz.* that 'CREATING' is mentioned in ONLY THREE VERSES of Gen. i. It is said in *v.* 1 that

"GOD CREATED the heavens and the earth."

But then no mention is made any more of 'Creating' until, after the introduction of animal life had been ordered (*v.* 20), it is said in *v.* 21

"And GOD created" [certain forms].

Again, 'Creating' is mentioned in *v.* 27. Three times in this verse the expression is used. And, as said on p. 230,

The making of man in (or *into*) the Image of GOD is spoken of as an act of Creation.

Is it too much then to say that all objections and difficulties and doubts which rest upon the supposition that the Book of

Genesis speaks of either "Six days of 'Creation,'" or "'Creation' of 'Species,'" fall at once to the ground?—The Book does not so speak,* as all may see who will.

But it is true that the Book is opposed to Materialism, is opposed to Pantheism. It is true that it declares

"GOD CREATED the heavens and the earth."

And after the grand exordium of the opening verse,—it tells of OPERATION OF GOD, ordered production and evolution at the

---

* It will be seen that we are merely stating facts. We have been endeavouring also to be brief.

It is possible that some may think that we attach too much importance to the fact that the word for 'creating' is not used except as we have stated. It is also very commonly supposed that the word for 'making' is 'all the same' as the word for 'creating.' And we own that some have given 'creating' in a few places as the sense of the word to which they allow the sense of 'making' in many other places, and some seem to have no notion of accuracy in the use of the two Roots. In accordance with our general plan of avoiding controversy as much as possible, we will but observe here that—

(i.) The two Roots are not identical, but different;—

(ii.) The usage of the two Roots is not exactly the same, [it is even less so perhaps than is the usage of the English words 'create' and 'make'; and most will allow that to 'make' a box (for instance) is not necessarily the same as to 'create' one];—

(iii.) It is distinctly the Root for 'making,' NOT the Root for 'creating,' which is used in Exod. xx. 11, where the six days of 'making' are spoken of thus:—"For [during] six days The-LORD made (or *wrought*) the heavens and the earth, the sea and all that [is] in them," etc.

It cannot be wrong to observe the fact of the Roots being different. And perhaps we may fairly doubt whether the case against a passage is necessarily a strong one, so far, at least, as the case rests upon the supposition that *it does not matter which one of two different words is used* in the passage. We allow however that we have not in this Footnote dealt with the controversy about those two different words. We shall be glad to have an opportunity for dealing with it fully,—in a more fit place than this.

WORD OF GOD, and HIS Resting after 'Creating' man in the Image and after the Likeness of GOD.

Enough, for the present.

*　　*　　*　　*　　*　　*

We would add a remark about the danger of limiting the Original by our Translations. The substitution of *"the first day"* by Translators, in Gen. i. 5, for the expression in the Original which signifies literally *"one day,"* is perhaps hardly a fair instance of this,—because the facts which we have endeavoured to state in the Note on pages 234–236 scarcely allow us to speak of the renderings *"the first"* and *"one"* as equally admissible renderings of the word which occurs there.—A better example of the danger of limiting the Original, by the exclusion of a possible rendering, is offered in the Note on Gen. iii. 22 (pp. 253–259). The important difference between such renderings as

"Behold! the man IS BECOME as one of us to know good and evil," and

"Behold the man WAS as one of us with-regard-to-knowing etc.,"

is sufficiently plain. That the second is an admissible rendering,* and that it has some support from antiquity, will we

---

* Of another possible rendering, which we have not mentioned, the principle was partially expressed in the Preface to the First Part of the 'Exercise-book.'

think be seen by the Reader of the Note referred to. We may not dwell upon that further here.

We have the pleasurable duty of repeating our expression of warmest thanks to the Friends who have kindly revised Proof-sheets and favoured us with valuable observations and suggestions, viz. Dr. Chance of Trinity College, Cambridge (and of Burleigh House, Sydenham Hill, London), the Rev. E. T. Leeke, M.A., Fellow of Trinity College, Cambridge, and Vicar of Barnwell, and the Rev. F. Watson, M.A., Fellow and Theological Lecturer of St. John's College, Cambridge.

It is but right to record also our thankful acknowledgments to those who have very kindly made the 'Index of passages in the Bible'—whose names we are not permitted to mention.

P. H. M.

St. John's College, Cambridge,
November, 1874.

CONTENTS

(OF THE PART ISSUED IN 1872)

		PAGE
Sect.	I.—The Prefixes בְּכַל, מ, ה	1–6
	Exercises I., II.	7, 8
Sect.	II.—Personal Pronouns,—Absolute Forms (Tab. I.)	9, 10
	Plan of the Exercises	11
	Exercises III., IV.	11, 12
Sect.	III.—Personal Pronouns,—Affix Forms (Tab. II.-VII.)	13–15
	Exercises V.-X.	16–20
Sect.	IV.—The Relative Pronoun אֲשֶׁר	21–24
	Exercises XI , XII.	25–27
Sect.	V.—Demonstrative Pronouns	28
Sect.	VI —Interrogative Pronouns	29
Sect.	VII.—Nouns-Substantive (Tab. V.-XIII)	30–47
	Exercises XIII., XIV.	47–49
Sect. VIII.—Nouns-Adjective		50–55
	Exercises XV., XVI.	55–57
Sect.	IX.—Pronouns-Adjective	58–59
	Exercises XVII., XVIII.	59–61
Sect.	X.—Numerals.	62–68
Sect.	XI.—Verbs : (I.) Voices, (II.) Tenses, (III.) Arrangement of Table XIV. of the 'Full' Verb	69–
Tables I.-XIV.		I-XV

CONTENTS OF THE CONTINUATION.

	PAGE
Sect. XI continued.—Verbs.—Remarks on Table XIV	77–89
(1) Infinitives Absolute..	77, 78
Construct, and with בכלם [App. (A) to Tab. XIV]	79
With Pron. Affixes [Tab. XV]	80
(2) Past Tense [see also p. 73 & 74]........	81, 82
(3) Participles [App. (B) and (C) to Tab. XIV]....................	82–85
(4) Imperative and (5) Future [see also p. 75 & 76]	85–89
Exercises XIX–XXIII	90–96
Vocabulary I.......................................	91
Observations i–xi	93
Sect. XII.—Verbs continued.—Certain USAGES	97–105
GENERAL usage of the TWO TENSES	97–100
The Tenses with ו pref.	100–102
Brief Summary	102, 103
Imperative, Negative Imper., etc............................	103
Some usages—to be referred to, as occasion may arise...............	104, 105
Vocabulary II.	106
Exercises XXIV, XXV	106–108
Sect. XIII.—Verbs continued —VARIATIONS......................	109–124
I. Pause-forms	109–113
II. Certain necessary Variations.............................	114, 115
III. FIRST Rt-letter ה, ה, or ע [Tab. XVI (1)]	115–120
IV. SECOND Rt-letter א, ה, ה, or ע [Tab. XVI (2)]	120
V. THIRD Rt-letter ה, ה, or ע [Tab. XVI (3)]	120, 121
VI. Verbs with ר in the Root. [For ר as 2ᵈ letter, see also Appˣ to Tab. XVI (2)]...................	121
VII. Verbs whose 3ᵈ Rt-letter is ז or ח	121, 122
VIII. Verbs with any of בגדכפת in the Root	122, 123
IX. A TABLE of 7 other Classes	124
Vocabulary III.	125
Exercises XXVI, XXVII	125–127

PAGE

Sect. XIV.—Verbs whose 1st Rt-letter is א [Tab XVII] ... 128–130
    Exercises XXVIII, XXIX.................................. 131, 132

Sect. XV.—Verbs whose 1st Rt-letter is י [Tab. XVIII]...... 133–139
    Observations XII–XV 139
    Vocabulary IV 140
    Exercises XXX, XXXI 140–142

Sect. XVI.—Verbs whose 1st Rt-letter is נ [Tab. XIX] 143–146
    Vocabulary V 147
    Exercises XXXII, XXXIII 147–149

Sect. XVII.—Verbs whose 2d Rt-letter is ו or י [Tab. XX] 150–163
    Vocabulary VI 164
    Exercises XXXIV, XXXV 164–168

Sects. XVIII–XXIV [Note].
        XVIII. Verbs whose 2d and 3d Rt-letters are the same [Tab. XXI]   169
          XIX. Verbs whose 3d Rt-letter is א [Tab. XXII]   169
           XX. Verbs whose 3d Rt-letter is ה [Tab. XXIII] 170–173
          XXI. Verbs belonging to more than one of the last 7 Classes ...   174
         XXII. Verb-forms with Pron.-Affixes [Tabs. XXIV–XXX]   175
        XXIII. Some other Voice-forms 175–177
         XXIV. 'Compound' or 'Mixed' forms 177, 178

Appx (A), (B), (C) to Tab. XIV, and Tabs. XV–XXX...... XVI–XLIII

CONTENTS OF THE CONCLUDING PART.

	PAGE
Observations XVI–XXII	179, 180
Exercises XXXVI & XXXVII [on Verbs having the same letter for their 2ᵈ and 3ᵈ Rt-letters]	181–184
Observations XXIII–XXV	185
Exercises XXXVIII & XXXIX [on Verbs לˈא]	186–189
Observations XXVI–XXX	190–193
Exercises XL–XLII [on Verbs לˈה]	194–201
Observations XXXI & XXXII	202
Exercises XLIII & XLIV [on what are sometimes called 'Doubly-Irregular Verbs']	203–207
Observations XXXIII–L	208–212
Exercise XLV [on Verbs with Pron-Affs.]	213–215
Psalm XXIII	215, 216
Exercises XLVI–L [General Exercises]	217–220
Appendix	221–382
(I.) A few brief remarks on the significations of Voice-forms	221
(II.) Certain Tense-forms, and Apocopated forms, used with ו Convers., and with אל Deprecative, and in the expression of a Positive wish	222

                                                                    PAGE

(III.) ANALYSIS OF VERB-FORMS in Gen. i.–iii. and xii. 226–266
      Preliminary Note: A few remarks on the ⸱⸱ sometimes given to
        ordinary Prefixes ו and בכל 223–225
      Note on Gen. i. 5 227
      Note on Gen. i. 11 228
      Obs. (i)–(iii) on Gen. i. 14 229
      Note on the use of the Root ברא in Gen. i. (viz. only in vss. 1,
        21, and 27)... 230
      Note on Gen. i. 24 .... 231, 232
      Obs (a) & (β) on "day one" and "second," "third," "fourth,"
        "fifth," but "the sixth,"—in Gen i............................... 234–236
      Note on Gen. ii. 3 (lit. "He created to make") 236, 237
            [For another rendering which is possible see Note (H) on
                  pp. 380–382].
      Preliminary Note on Gen. ii. 4 etc.................................... 237
      Note on Gen. ii. 5 (the use of טרם) 238, 239
      Note on Gen iii. 6 (the signification of לְהַשְׂכִּיל) 246, 247
      Note on Gen. iii. 22 (the passage rendered in the E.V. "Behold
        the man has become as one of us to know good and evil") 252–259

(IV.) LIST OF forms of what are sometimes called 'DOUBLY
      IRREGULAR VERBS,'—or, rather, Verbs belonging to
      more than one of the Seven Classes in § 186 (p. 124) 267–314
          The following may be selected, as being more or
      less important, viz. :—
                  אבה   267
                  אור   268
                  אלה and אות   269
                  אפה   270
                  אתה   271
                  בוא   272–275
                  היה   276–278
                  חיה   278–280
                  יגה   281
                  ידה (I.)   281
                  ידה (II) 281, 282
                  ילל   282
                  ינה   283
                  יפה 283, 284
                  יצא   284–286
                  ירא   286–288
                  ירה 288, 289

	PAGE
נאה	290, 291
נבא	291
נדר	292
נוח (forms given from this R. by some, but from ינח by others)	294
נזה	296
נטה	297
נכה	298, 299
נסה	300
נשׂא	302–304
נשׁא	305
נשׁה	305, 306
עוה	309
צוה	309, 310
קוה	311, 312

Note on HITHPÁ-ÊL forms—
  (I.) Transposition of 1st Rt-letter of Verbs whose 1st Rt-letter is שׂ, שׁ, ס, or צ ... 315
    [For הִתְשׁוֹטַמְנָה (Jer. xlix. 3) see § 246, p. 162].
    The replacing of the ת by ט after צ ... 315
  (II.) The dropping of the ת of הִתְ, and the insertion of Dagesh
    (α) in a 1st Rt-letter ד or ט or ת ... 316
    (β) SOMETIMES in the case of a 1st Rt-letter ז or כ or נ or שׁ ... 316–318
    (γ) also in some 'Mixed Voice' forms ... 318

(V.) FURTHER REMARKS ON VERB-FORMS—
  (1) Some Infin. Absolute forms ... 319
  (2) Some Infin. Constr. forms ... 320–324
  (3) Some Past-Tense-forms ... 324–326
  (4) Some Partic. forms ... 326–330
  (5) Some Imper. & Future forms ... 330–337
  (6) Some *Niph-ăl* forms ... 338–341
  (7) Some *Pĭ-él* forms ... 342–347
  (8) Some *Pŭ-ăl* forms ... 347, 348
  (9) Some *Hiph-ĭl* forms ... 348–355
  (10) Some *Hoph-ăl* forms ... 355–357
  (11) Some *Hithpă-él* forms ... 357–360

PAGE

(V.) FURTHER REMARKS ON VERB-FORMS (*continued*)—

The word נִשְׁתָּוֶה‍ Prov. xxvii. 15 360–364

Note (A) on the Voice-forms פֹּעַל & פֻּעַל 365–368

Note (B) on some Verb-forms with א or ה or ח or ע as
2ᵈ Rt-letter 368, 369

Note (C) on some Verb-forms with ה or ח or ע as
3ᵈ Rt-letter 370–374

Note (D) a remark on §§ 230 & 231 374

Note (E) remarks on §§ 236 (γ) & 237.................. 374–378

Note (F) on some forms of Pron-Affs. to Verbs......... 378, 379

Note (G) Objective Pron-Affs. may be used *Relatively* 380

Note (H) on Gen. ii. 3 380–382

VOCABULARY 383–388

FIRST PART

OF THE

EXERCISE-BOOK.

Page 91, l. 5 of Exercise, *for* שׁ , *read* שׂ .

,, 93, l. 3, *for* 2d & 3d words, *read* נתַן עז .

,, 94, l. 3 of Exercise, *for* to, *read* to[17].

,, 94, Note 13, *for* Note † Obs. 1, *read* Note §.

,, 94, Note 15, *for* נֶפֶשׁ, *read* נפֶשׁ *f*.

,, 95, Note 32, *add* Tab. X. 5.

,, 108, l. 4, *for* to Moses, *read* to[43] Moses.

,, 108, l. 5, *for* that I, *read* that[44] I.

,, 108, *add to Notes*, [43] אֵל .   [44] כִּי .

,, 127, ll. 12, 14 & 15, *for* on, *read* on[28].

,, 127, l. 1 of Notes, *for* [1]עבֵר , *read* [1]עבֵר Fut. (–).

,, 127, l. 4 of Notes, *for* (i.e. etc.) *read* (For the construct
form see p. 84, Note *).

,, 132, l. 1 of Notes, *for* [5] אֵל , *read* [5] אלֹהֵ .

,, 167, l. 12, *for* The Lord, *read* The Lord God.

,, 188, l. 12, *after* lift up, *add* (as in Tab. XXII, the נ not
dropped).

200, l. 11, *for* the spoil of, *read* spoil to the.

[The Hebrew for ' the spoil of heathen-nations '
would be בַּז גּוֹיִם].

,, 201, l. 10, *add an* (*) *at the end of* And thou shalt be.

,, 205, last line, *for* to-give-thanks, *read* to give-thanks.

HEBREW EXERCISE BOOK

The Student is advised to limit his attention at first to
the following §§ and pages of the EXERCISE-BOOK, viz. :

§§ 1–59 (with *a–δ* on p. 38), 65–67, 70–73, 75–98 (with
N.B.), 115–137, 138 A. i (omitting ii–v), 138 B. i (omitting
ii–v), 139–141 γ, 142–144 β, 145, Note I on pp. 89 & 89*,

Observations I–XI on p. 93,

§§ 148–159, 161, 164–167. ii. *a*, pp. 113* & 113**,
pp. 114–130** (omitting iv), pp. 133–222. The rest may be
reserved till the Student is at work on The Hebrew Bible.

ALL THE EXERCISES should be done of course.

---

* *Also, even, that, though, whereas,* etc.—There is also a ‍ן *followed by*
Dagesh, which is prefixed to certain Verb-forms only. This need not be dealt
with at present.

† For ן before a letter bearing an Accented vowel, see hereafter,—Obs. XVI
(p. 179).

HEBREW EXERCISE BOOK.

SECTION I.

CERTAIN PREFIXES.

1. The Student should be familiarized as soon as possible with the use of the following Prefixes:

    (i.) וְ,   (ii.) בְּ כְּ לְ,   (iii.) מְ,   (iv.) ה.

2. As regards the Punctuation of these Prefixes,—

    (i.) The וְ takes ־ְ [see also § 3 (*b*—*d*)],

    (ii.) The בְּ, the כְּ, and the לְ, also take ־ְ [§ 4];

    (iii.) The מְ takes ־ִ *followed by Dagesh* [§ 5].

    (iv.) Of the prefixes ה,—there is
    one which takes ־ַ *followed by Dagesh* [§ 6],
    and one which takes ־ָ [§ 7].

In §§ 3—7 we will deal with these one by one in order.

3. (*a.*) The וְ (*and**) is prefixed thus,

    יָד a *hand*,   וְיָד† AND a *hand*.

But some CHANGE MUST BE MADE when the וְ is prefixed to a word which has a *Shva* under its first letter, because

---

* *Also, even, that, though, whereas, etc.*—There is also a וּ *followed by Dagesh*, which is prefixed to certain Verb-forms only. This need not be dealt with at present.

† For וּ before a letter bearing an Accented vowel, see hereafter,—Obs. XVI (p. 179).

N.B. There can never be two Moving Shvas together.
The changes which are made are as follows :—

(*b*.) Before י*, the ו takes ־ֵ; and with this ־ֵ the י blends
so as to form י־ֵ (*Long-Khîrik*), the ־ of the י being then
dropped ; thus,

יְהוּדָה Juda, וִיהוּדָה AND Juda.

(*c*.) (i.) Before any other letter with ־ְ, וּ (not וְ) is prefixed; thus,

תְּמוֹל yesterday, † וּתְמוֹל AND yesterday.

[(ii.) Also וּ (not וְ) is put before ב and מ and פ even
when these letters have a Vowel; thus,

from בֵּין & מִי & פֶּן, we have וּבֵין † & וּמִי & וּפֶן.]

(*d*.) Before any one of the letters אהחע‡ with a Compound
Shva§, the ו takes

־ַ before ־ֲ, ־ֶ before ־ֱ, ־ָ ŏ before ־ֳ; thus,

אֲנִי I, וַאֲנִי AND I,—and so וַחֲדַר, וְאָמִיץ, וְעֶזוּז, וְחֲלִי, etc.

4. (*a*.) The three בּ *in* or *by*, כְּ *as* or *like*, לְ *to* or *for*, are
prefixed thus,—

בְּיָד IN *a hand*, כְּיָד LIKE *a hand*, לְיָד TO *a hand*.

But some change must be made when one of these is to be
prefixed to a word which has a Shva under its first letter, because
there can never be two Moving Shvas together. The changes
which are made are as follows :—

(*b*.) Before י‖, the בּ or כ or ל takes ־ֵ. With this ־ֵ the י
blends so as to form י־ֵ (the ־ of the י being dropped); thus,

לִיהוּדָה, כִּיהוּדָה, בִּיהוּדָה,—from יְהוּדָה Juda.

---

* But not before The NAME [Pt. I. § 79 (2)],—which may be represented by יְיָ,
—for which אֲדֹנָי is read. Before this NAME the ו takes ־ַ, and the ־ is dropped,
as in וַיְיָ (which is read as וַאדֹנָי).

† For the removal of Dagesh Lene from the תּ see Pt. I. § 51 (iv)

‡ (I.) Before אֲדֹנָי The Lord (and some words from אֲדֹנִים, besides), the ו
takes ־ַ, and the ־ֲ of the א is dropped,—as in וַאדֹנָי AND The Lord, וַאדֹנִי, &c.

(ii.) Before אֱלֹהִים God (and some words from it) the ו takes ־ֵ and
the ־ֱ of the א is dropped,—as in וֵאלֹהִים AND God.

(III.) Euphonic exceptions are וְחָיִיתָם, וְהָיָה, וְהָיִי, וְחָיִיתָ, וִהְיוּ, p. 277—9

(iv.) Before ־ַ or ־ֲ when NOT under one of אהחע, וּ is put; thus וְזָהַב.

§ i.e. one of the three ־ַ, ־ֶ, ־ָ; Pt. I. § 23.

‖ But before The NAME יְיָ, ־ַ is given (the ־ being dropped); thus בַּיְיָ etc.
Comp. Note (*) above.

(c.) Before any other letter with ־ְ , the ב or כ or ל takes a
'*Slight*'-vowel [Pt. I. § 56], generally ־ֲ ; thus,

from פְּרִי *fruit*,—*בְּפְרִי , *בָּפְּרִי , *לְפְרִי .

(d.) Before any one of the letters אהחע† with a Compound
Shva (Pt. I. § 23), the prefixes בכל take

 ־ֱ before ־ֱ , ־ֲ before ־ֲ , ־ָ *ŏ* before ־ֳ ; thus,

בְּעָנִי , לַהֲדוֹם , בֶּאֱמֶת , בַּחֲלוֹם , etc.

(e.) For the בכל with ־ַ *followed by Dagesh‡* (with another
vowel in some cases in which the Dagesh cannot stand),—see
below, § 8.

Note. (a.) These prefixed particles have some other *significations* sometimes,
besides those that are given above. When any instance of this occurs in the
Exercises, due notice will be given.

(β.) The בכל have ־ֵ sometimes; comp. Rule II. on p. 225.

(γ) Besides these *prefixes* בכל, there are also the Prepositions בְּמוֹ *in*,
כְּמוֹ *like*, לְמוֹ *to*.—There is also מָן *from*, as well as the prefix מ of § (5).]

5. (a) The prefix מ (*from*) takes ־ִ *followed by Dagesh§*; thus,
מִיָּד FROM *a hand*, מִבְּכִי FROM *weeping*.

(b.) But the 5 letters אהחע״ר do not receive this Dagesh. And

---

* For the removal of Dagesh Lene from the פ, see Pt. I. § 51 (iv).

† (i) Before אֲדֹנָי (and some words from אֲדֹנִים besides), the בכל take ־ַ
and the ־ֲ of the א is dropped;—thus, בַּאדֹנָי , etc. Comp. Note (‡, i.) on p. 2.

(ii.) Before אֱלֹהִים (and some words from it) the בכל take ־ֵ and the ־ֱ of
the א is dropped;—thus, בֵּאלֹהִים , etc. Comp. Note (‡, ii) on p. 2.

(iii.) Euphonic exceptions are בִּהְיוֹת , לִהְיוֹת , etc., on p. 276 & 277; & לִחְיוֹת
p. 278.

‡ כַּנִּבְרָתָהּ (Is. xxiv. 2) has בַּג׳ irregularly, instead of בְג׳.

§ In a few cases the Dagesh is omitted, where it would be *over a Shva*; as
from the ב of מִבְצִיר , Jud. viii. 2 (where some *have* the Dagesh), from the ג of
מִגְבוּרָתָם Ez. xxxii. 30; from the ל of מְלָאוֹם Gen. xxv. 23. [These instances
are cited by R. D. Kimkhi]

'COMPENSATION* for the Dagesh' is said to be made by lengthening the ⸗ of the מ into ⸗; thus,

מֵרֹאשׁ, מֵעִיר, מֵחוֹל, מֵהוּר, מֵאָדֹם, מֵאָרָם, etc.

(c.) Before יְ† the מ takes ⸗, with which ⸗ the י blends so as to form יֵ⸗ (the ⸗ of the י being dropped and the Dagesh NOT then given after the מ;) thus,

יְהוּדָה Juda, מִיהוּדָה FROM Juda.

6. (a.) The prefix ה bearing ⸗ and followed by Dagesh is the mark for 'the'‡; thus,

יָד a hand, הַיָּד THE hand; קוֹל a voice, הַקּוֹל THE voice.

(b) The 5 letters אהחער do not receive the Dagesh. And

'COMPENSATION for the Dagesh' is said to be made by lengthening the ⸗ into ⸗; thus,

אִישׁ a man, הָאִישׁ THE man,—and so הָעִיר THE city, הָרֹאשׁ THE head.

As a RULE,—this Compensation IS MADE before ר and before א, and generally before ע; but

(c.) N.B. The Compensation is NOT MADE

  (i.) before ח,

  (ii.) before ה, except in a few instances§ :—thus,

---

* This 'Compensation for the Dagesh' is sometimes refused, as in מָחוֹט, and so in מָחוֹץ, but we find מְחֹצוֹת (Jer vii. 34). So מֵעֶצְבָּךְ and מֵרָגְזֶךְ Is. xiv. 3, מִרְדֹּף 1 Sam. xxiii. 28, (& 2 Sam. xviii. 16,) etc. And before ה, as in מִהְיוֹת 1 Ki. ii 27, מֵהְיוֹתָם Hag. ii. 16, 'only when it is with Shva,' as R. D. Kimkhi remarks, who cites these examples. This case (of the ה) is slightly different from the others. For, the simple Shva ⸗ beneath the ה [being quiescent (Pt. I. § 25)] shows that the ה is made to *end the syllable* beginning with the מ. [Obs.— Modern editions are not always to be relied upon in this, and in some other matters.]

† But before The NAME יְיָ, for which אֲדֹנָי is read, the מ takes ⸗, thus מֵיְיָ.

‡ The 'Definite Article', as it is called. This Prefix has some other values also, as will be seen by and by. [For *another prefix* which sometimes appears like this, see § 7 (b, Note).

§ הָהָר THE *mountain* (from הָר), and so הָהָרָה; and so also הָהֵם, הָהֵמָה, הָהֵנָּה, תָּהֵנָּה, from הֵם, הֵמָּה, הֵנָּה,—for which see §§ 9 (a) & 94.

(i.) חֵן *favour,* הַחֵן THE *favour;*   חוֹר *a hole,* הַחוֹר THE *hole* *,

(ii.) הוֹד *majesty,* הַהוֹד THE *majesty,* etc

(*d.*) N.B. Moreover, this Prefix ה (*the*) takes ־ָ

(i.) before words beginning with חָ,

thus, חָג *a feast,* הֶחָג THE *feast,* and so הֶחָי, הֶחָכָם, etc.;

(ii.) before words beginning with UNACCENTED הָ †, or עָ †,

thus הָרִים *mountains,* הֶהָרִים THE *mountains* ‡,

עָרִים *cities,* הֶעָרִים THE *cities;*

  [(iii.) also, but only rarely, before unaccented אָ, as in הָאָמוּר (Mi. ii. 7), according to some].

(*e.*) The ־ָ of the Prefix ה (*the*) is sometimes retained before ע, as in הָעֹזְבִים (Prov. ii. 13) THE *ones-forsaking* (*m.*). But this is somewhat rare except in cases of the 'Contraction' mentioned in § 8.]

[(*f.*) The Dagesh for this Prefix ה (*the*) is generally NOT given to י having *Shva* §; thus הַיְאֹר THE *river,* הַיְסוֹד THE *foundation.* But the Dagesh is given sometimes, as in הַיְּוָנִים *the Greeks* (Joel iv. 6); and so in הַיְּעוּצָה (Is. xiv. 26)].

7. (*a.*) The prefix ה having ־ֲ signifies Interrogation ‖; thus, יֵשׁ *there is,* הֲיֵשׁ *Is there* ‡, יָם *a sea,* הֲיָם WHETHER ¶ *a sea?*

---

* So הַחַי THE *living* (or *that liveth*), for which there is once הָחַי Gen. vi. 19. Comp. הַחַמָּנִים 2 Chr. xiv. 4 (and xxxiv. 4 & 7) with הָחַמָּנִים once,—Is. xvii. 8.

† N.B. The ־ָ here is the Long ־ָ; not the ŏ, K. *Khautuph.*

‡ So in הָרוֹתֶיהָ 2 K. xv. 16, בְּעָרֵינוּ Ezra x. 14.

§ The Dagesh F. is sometimes omitted also from מָ (thus הַמְעַט *the little* Nu. xxxv. 8, etc.);—and in the case of a few other letters with — the Dagesh is not given in a few instances.

‖ Sometimes it serves as a 'Note of Admiration!'

¶ We have no *word* really in English for this ה. Perhaps the word "*Whether?*" may temporarily be used for it where an English word may seem to be necessary. The prefix may sometimes be represented by "*whether*" almost without interrogation.

(*b.*) Before a letter with *Shva* (Simple or Compound), the Interrogative הֲ takes a 'Slight'-vowel ◌ֲ; thus,

הַמְעַט* WHETHER *a little?*, הַאֱמֶת WHETHER *truth?*

(*c.*) The הֲ Interrogative sometimes takes ◌ַ † before one of the letters אהחע (even when having a Vowel); thus,

אֵין *there is not,* הַאֵין *Is there not?;* עוֹד *yet,* הַעוֹד WHETHER *yet?*

[NOTE (i.) This prefix is to be placed before the FIRST word of the Interrogative clause.

(ii.) In some instances the context alone‡ can decide whether the prefix הֹ is a mark of *Interrogation* or for the *Definite Article*.]

8. (*a.*) A CONTRACTION is often made when a word with the 'Definite Article' is to have one of the prefixes בכל,—the ה being left out§, and its vowel given to the prefix; thus,

לַיָּם for כְּהַיָּם ... לָיָם for כְּהַיָּם, בַּיָּם for בְּהַיָּם, בַּיָּם for בְּהַיָּם;

and so,   לֶהָעָנִי for לְעָנִי, כֶּהָחָלָל for כְּחָלָל, בֶּהָחָג for בְּחָג.

(*b.*) N.B. This Contraction is NOT made in the case of the prefixes וֹ & מֹ of § 3 & § 5. In the case of these, the full form must always be written; thus,

וְהַיָּם AND THE *sea,* מֵהַיָּם FROM THE *sea.*

(*c.*) The full forms sometimes occur, with the prefixes בְּ, כְּ, לְ;

thus   לַהַגֵּרִים, כַהַיּוֹם, בְּהַשָּׁמַיִם;

and so   ‖ בַּהַדֶּרֶךְ, כְּהֶחָכָם, כְּהַחַלֹּנוֹת, לְהָעָם, לְהַחוֹמָה, לַהַגָּדוֹד.   But,

(*d.*) The *contracted* forms are the most common, and should always be written in Composition.

---

* This word, with the הֹ thus pointed, is exactly like a word with the 'Definite Article' in Note (§) on p. 5. By the Context alone can it be known in this case whether the prefix הֹ is a mark of interrogation or for *the 'Definite Article'.* Comp. 'Note (ii.)' above.

† And *sometimes* (before an unaccented Long ◌ָ) it takes —; thus הָאָמֹר Ez. xxviii. 9, הָאָנֹכִי Nu. xi 12, Job. xxi 4, הֲהָיְתָה Joel i. 2, הֲהָשֵׁב Gen. xxiv. 5.

‡ The context, however, generally decides without any doubt.

§ This is but one instance of a *not unusual* Contraction (as will be seen hereafter). When הֹ would be preceded immediately by a letter bearing Shva, the הֹ in several other cases is dropped sometimes, and its vowel given to that preceding letter.

‖ All these instances in (*c*) are given by R. D Kimkhi

[To face p. 6.]

TABLE OF THE PREFIXES IN SECTION I.

*** The ⋯ after a letter stand in place of a word.

(i) The וְ, and the בְּ, כְּ, לְ, are prefixed thus :—

    (a) ⋯וְ and ⋯בְּ, ⋯כְּ, ⋯לְ, ordinarily [§§ 3 (a) & 4 (a)].

    (b) ⋯וִי and ⋯בִּי, ⋯כִּי, ⋯לִי, before ⋯יְ [§§ 3 (b) & 4 (b)].

    (c) i. וּ and בְּ, כְּ, לְ, before any other letter with —

        [§§ 3 & 5 (c)], and

      ii. וּ also (instead of וְ) before ב and מ and פ.

    (d)   { וַ and בַּ, כַּ, לַ, before ⁻ᵢ ;

         וָ and בָּ, כָּ, לָ, before ⁻ᵢᵢ ;

         וָ* and בָּ*, כָּ*, לָ*, before ⁻ᵢᵢ.

        [Note.—For וַאדֹנָי, בַּאדֹנָי, etc., and בֵּאלֹהִים, וֵאלֹהִים, etc.,
           see Note (‡) p. 2 and (†) p 3.]

(ii) The מ of § 5 is prefixed thus :—

    (a) ⋯מְ *followed by Dagesh,*

    (b) ⋯מֵ before one of the letters אהחער (Pt. I, § 49),

    (c) ⋯מִי before ⋯יְ.

(iii) The הַ of § 6 is prefixed thus :—

    (a) הַ *followed by Dagesh* ordinarily,

    (b) הָ for ' Compensation,'—but

    (c) הַ is retained before ח generally (and before ה some-
        times),

    (d) הֶ is given before חָ and before *unaccented* הָ and עָ.

(iv) The Interrogative הַ is prefixed thus :—

    (a) הַ ordinarily,

    (b) הֲ before a letter which has a Shva.

---

* The ⁻ᵢᵢ here is *ŏ*.

Exercise II.

(*To be translated into Hebrew.*)

*** The Hebrew words required are given in a foot-note. *Contracted* forms (§ 8) are to be used here.

Harvest.[1] And harvest. In harvest. The harvest. And the harvest. In the harvest. And in harvest. And in the harvest. To harvest. And to harvest. To the harvest. And to the harvest. From harvest. From the harvest. And from the harvest. And from harvest. Whether in harvest? Whether like the harvest?

Fire.[2] The fire. In the fire. As the fire. As fire. And as the fire. And in the fire. From fire. And from fire. In fire. Whether in the fire? To the fire. And to the fire.

Water.[3] And water. And the water. From the water. Whether to the water? And as the water. And in the water.

Sand.[4] As sand. The sand. As the sand. From sand. And the sand. And as the sand. In the sand. And in the sand. And from the sand.

An ornament.[5] As an ornament. To an ornament. From an ornament. And an ornament. And to an ornament. And from an ornament. Whether an ornament? And in an ornament.

Truth.[6] And truth. In truth. To truth. As the truth. From truth. Whether truth? Whether as truth? Whether from truth? And the truth. And in the truth. And to the truth. And in truth.

A bee.[7] In a bee. And in a bee. As a bee. And as a bee. And from a bee. The bee. And to the bee. From a bee. From the bee. Whether a bee? Whether from the bee? And the bee.

[7] דְּבֹרָה [6] אֱמֶת [5] עֲדִי [4] חוֹל [3] מַיִם [2] אֵשׁ [1] קָצִיר

SECTION II.

PERSONAL PRONOUNS.—ABSOLUTE FORMS.

9. (*a.*) The absolute forms of the Personal Pronouns are given *fully* in Table I (at the end of the book). The following are the leading forms:

I אֲנִי (or אָנֹכִי),   *thou (m.)* אַתָּה,   *he* הוּא,

we אֲנַחְנוּ (or נַחְנוּ),   *ye (m.)* אַתֶּם,   *they (m.)* הֵם or הֵמָּה;

besides which there are the Feminine forms,

she הִיא *,   *they (f.)* הֵנָּה,

thou (f.) אַתְּ,   *ye (f.)* אַתֵּנָה.

There are also the 'PAUSE'-forms [Pt. I § 41],

I אֲנִי : (אָנֹכִי),| *thou (m.)* אָתָּה : ,| *thou (f.)* אָתְּ : ,| *we* אֲנַחְנוּ : (נֵחְנוּ)

These may be conveniently arranged in a Tabular form:

TABLE I.

[N.B. p. stands for 'Pause-form', Pt. I. § 41]

SINGULAR.

I {	אָנֹכִי,	אֲנִי	*thou m.* (p. : אָתָּה) אַתָּה	*he*	הוּא
	(אָנֹכִי : p.),	(אֲנִי : p.)	*thou f.* (p. : אָתְּ) אַתְּ	*she* (הוּא*) הִיא

PLURAL

we {	אֲנַחְנוּ,	נַחְנוּ ( )	*ye m.* אַתֶּם	*they m.* הֵם, הֵמָּה
	(אֲנַחְנוּ : p.),	(נֵחְנוּ : p.)	*ye f.* אַתֵּנָה	*they f.* הֵנָּה

(*β.*) These (except *הוּא) are the forms to be used in Composition. Those in the Notes on the *full* Tab. I are given

---

* The form הוּא occurs in the Pentateuch. It is 'read' הִיא [Pt. I. § 79 (3)].

in order that the Student may be able to recognise them when he meets with them in the course of his reading.

(γ.) The words by the side of which the "p." is placed, are forms that occur in "Pause" (Cp. Pt. I., § 41). Those Pronouns for which no 'Pause' forms are specified retain, when in 'Pause,' the form given in Table I.

(δ.) According to a fundamental principle of the Language in the Bible, what we call 'Third Person' is reckoned 'First;' *i e.,* He is First—not I. The corresponding arrangement of the personal Pronouns, in an order so *contrary* to that with which we are all of us familiar, would appear very strange to the English Reader. The arrangement of Table I.*, above, has been devised as a means of introducing the matter gradually. According to this, the Reader may take the Pronouns *I, Thou, He,* etc., from left to right — as he is used to read English. But he may also take the *Hebrew* Pronouns there from right to left, as he will wish to take them when familiar with the Hebrew order of the Pronouns.

[N.B —Since *English words* must be used in the sense which they usually bear *in English,* we must use the *English* terms 'FIRST' Person for *I, Me, We,* etc, and 'THIRD' Person for *He, Him, Them,* etc ,—because this is the English usage. But the Student must remember that the Hebrew usage is just the reverse, as he will know for himself by-and-by.]

10. (*a.*). Only *two* Genders, *Masculine* and *Feminine,* are recognized in Hebrew.

(*b.*). The 'First Person' Pronouns (as they are called in English) are of common gender, *i.e.,* have no different forms for different genders.

[Note.—There being no 'Neuter' Pronouns in Hebrew, we may have to place (*m.*) or (*f.*) by the side of "*it*" sometimes, — thus, *it* (*m.*), *it* (*f.*), — in order to point out the gender of the Hebrew word to which "it" refers.]

---

* And so in some other Tables below.

[11. N.B.—In the Exercises·—

(α) The figures 1, 2, 3, etc., attached to words, refer to Notes below the Exer.
cise, in which Notes all necessary assistance is given.

(β) In the Hebrew Exercises (to be translated into English) the meaning of
each word is put in the Note — so far as it cannot be made out from what has
been previously given.

(γ) Wherever a Hebrew word involves something that has not previously been
explained, the full meaning is always given in the Note.

(δ) The mark + is put in the earlier Exercises to shew the place of ‘the
logical copula,’ or the ‘Substantive Verb’ (as some call it), in any of the various
forms *am, is, was, were, art,* etc. [This mark, (*necessary,* perhaps, at first in
order that the student may know where such words are to be *supplied in English)*
will gradually be dispensed with.]

(ε) The Hebrew Verb generally precedes its Subject, except where there is
emphasis on the Subject. Hence the *order* of the words in English must sometimes differ from that of the Hebrew, but no difficulty (it is hoped) will be caused
by this.

(ζ) In the English Exercises (to be translated into Hebrew), words in the
Notes stand each of them for that *one* English word *simply* to which the figure is
attached. [N B.—All English *words connected by hyphens* are to be *taken as one
word* in regard to this.]

(η) The English words are always *given in the order* in which they are to stand
in the Hebrew rendering. But

(θ) The English words, in the order to be observed in the Hebrew rendering, are
sometimes given within ( ), preceded by the word ‘Hebr.’

·(ι) So, too, when the form of expression required in Hebrew is different from
the English form ; — thus, for example, THINE (*m.*), (Hebr , *to Thee).*

(κ) English words (when there are more than one), which are to be rendered
according to the form within the ( ), are *connected by hyphens.*

(λ) Words within [ ] are *not* to be translated into Hebrew.

(μ) In accordance with (ζ), — The *Hebrew Pronouns* are to be expressed
except where the English Pronoun is joined to the Verb by a *hyphen.*

(ν) יְיָ stands for The NAME, pronounced אֲדֹנָי, Pt. I., § 79 (2).]

EXERCISE III.

(*To be translated into English.*)

יְיָ ¹ הוּא + הָאֱלֹהִים ¹ : וַעֲצַת ³ יְיָ ¹ הִיא תָקוּם ⁴ : אַתָּה

קָרָאתָ ⁵ אֶל ⁶ הַמֶּלֶךְ ⁷ : אֲנִי + עַבְדְּךָ ⁸ : וּבִנְךָ ⁹ + אֲנִי : מִי ¹⁰ +

¹ See (ν) above.   ² אֱלֹהִים God.   ³ עֲצַת [the] counsel of.   ⁴ shall stand.
⁵ hast called.   ⁶ to   ⁷ מֶלֶךְ a king.   ⁸ thy servant.   ⁹ בִּנְךָ thy son.   ¹⁰ who?

אָנֹכִי ׃ אַתָּה + הָאִישׁ [11] ׃ הוּא יִקְרָאֵנִי [12] אָבִי [13] + אָתָּה ׃

יָפָה [14] + אַתְּ רַעְיָתִי [15] ׃ וּבְרוּכָה [16] + אַתְּ ׃ נְבֹכִים [17] + הֵם

בָּאָרֶץ [18] ׃ אַתָּה יָדַעְתָּ [19]⋯כִּי [20] גִּבֹּרִים [21] הֵמָּה + ׃ טֹבֹת [22]

הֵנָּה + ׃ מֵאַיִן [23] + אַתָּם ׃ מֵחָרָן [24] + אֲנַחְנוּ ׃ כֻּלָּנוּ [25] בְּנֵי [26]

אִישׁ אֶחָד [27] + נַחְנוּ כֵּנִים [28] + אֲנַחְנוּ⋯ ׃ וְאַתֵּנָה + צֹאנִי [29]

כֹּה [30] אָמַר [31] אֲדֹנָי [32] יְיָ [33] ׃

[11] אִישׁ a man.　[12] shall call Me.　[13] my Father.　[14] beautiful (*f*).　[15] O my love (E. V.).　[16] בְּרוּכָה blessed (*f*).　[17] entangled (pl. *m.*)　[18] אֶרֶץ (fr. אֶרֶץ) a land.　[19] knowest.　[20] that.　[21] mighty men.　[22] fair (*f*) [E V., Gen. vi. 2]　[23] whence?　[24] Haran (with מ).　[25] as for all us.　[26] sons of　[27] 27 one man.　[28] true men.　[29] My flock.　[30] thus.　[31] hath said.　[32] The Lord.　[33] See Pt I, § 79 (2), and 'Vocabulary' (p. 385).

EXERCISE IV.

(*To be translated into Hebrew.*)

I [was] in the way.[1]　He said[2] to the king.[3]　Who [art] thou (*m.*)?　Who[4] [art] thou (*f.*)?　They (*m.*) said[5] to the man.[6]　Like a queen[7] she [was].　As kings[8] [were] they (*m.*).　It (*f.*) [is] Jezebel.[9]　It (*m.*) [is] the bread.[10]　From Haran[11] [were] they (*f.*).　Ye (*f.*) [are] like queens.[12]　And through[13] our-iniquities[14] we-have-been-given,[15] we and our-kings,[16] into[13] their-hands.[17]　Thou [art] our-Father.[18]　And we will-be-joyous[19] in Thy-salvation.[20].

מְלָכִים [8] ׃ מַלְכָּה [7] ׃ אִישׁ [6] ׃ אָמְרוּ [5] ׃ מִי [4] ׃ מֶלֶךְ [3] ׃ אָמַר [2] ׃ דֶּרֶךְ [1] ׃

עֲוֹנֹתֵינוּ [14] ׃ ב [13] (the prefix).　מַלְכוּת [12] ׃ חָרָן [11] ׃ לֶחֶם [10] ׃ אִיזֶבֶל [9] ׃

נָתַנּוּ [15] ׃ מַלְכֵינוּ [16] ׃ יְדֵיהֶם [17] ׃ אָבִינוּ [18] ׃ נְרַנְּנָה [19] ׃ יְשׁוּעָתֶךָ [20] (Pause-form),

[To face p. 12.]

ABSTRACT OF TABLES II–VI.

A) Pron.-Affix endings in Tabs. V (i) & VI (i), *i.e.* with a SINGULAR NOUN.			(a) Pron.-Affix endings in Tabs. II (i) & III, *i.e.* with certain Particles.			
־ִי my	־ְךָ thy (m.)	־וֹ his	־ִי me	־ְךָ thee (m.)	־וֹ him	Sing. Masc.
־ִי my	־ֵךְ thy (f.)	־ָהּ her	־ִי me	־ֵךְ thee (f.)	־ָהּ her	Sing. Fem.
־ֵנוּ our	־ְכֶם your (m.)	־ָם their (m.)	־ֵנוּ us	־ְכֶם you (m.)	־ָהֶם them (m.)	Plu. Masc.
־ֵנוּ our	־ְכֶן your (f.)	־ָן their (f.)	־ֵנוּ us	־ְכֶן you (f.)	־ָהֶן them (f.)	Plu. Fem.

B) Pron.-Affix endings in Tabs. V (ii) & VI (ii), *i.e.* with a PLURAL NOUN.			(b) Pron.-Affix endings in Tab. IV, *i.e.* with certain Particles.			
־ַי my	־ֶיךָ thy (m.)	־ָיו his	־ַי me	־ֶיךָ thee (m.)	־ָיו him	Sing. Masc.
־ַי my	־ַיִךְ thy (f.)	־ֶיהָ her	־ַי me	־ַיִךְ thee (f.)	־ֶיהָ her	Sing. Fem.
־ֵינוּ our	־ֵיכֶם your (m.)	־ֵיהֶם their (m.)	־ֵינוּ us	־ֵיכֶם you (m.)	־ֵיהֶם them (m.)	Plu. Masc.
־ֵינוּ our	־ֵיכֶן your (f.)	־ֵיהֶן their (f.)	־ֵינוּ us	־ֵיכֶן you (f.)	־ֵיהֶן them (f.)	Plu. Fem.

Note:—(α) For the affix-forms with כ *as* or *like*, and מ *from*, see Tab. II (ii).

(β) The endings in (a) for Tabs. II (i) and III are seen to agree with those in (A) for a SING. Noun—in the main.

(γ) The endings in (b) for Tab. IV are seen to agree with those in (B) for a PLU. Noun—in the main.

(δ) The Pron.-endings with a DUAL are the same as with a PLU. Noun.

[To face p 13]

[Note.

The Tables referred to in the following pages will be found AT THE END of the volume. The remarks on these pages are introductory to and explanatory of the Tables.

N.B. In using the Tables for the English-Hebrew Exercises the Student should prefer THE FORM TO THE RIGHT always,—where more forms than one are given, as in some parts of Tab. II].

SECTION III.

PERSONAL PRONOUNS.—AFFIX-FORMS.

12. Besides the '*Absolute*' Forms (as they are called) of the Peisonal Pronouns, given in § 9 above, there are some *Affix*-forms—consisting of one or more of the letters הכנוים —by which the Personal Pronouns are often iepresented.

13. The Pronoun-Affixes are attached both (*a*) to Particles* and Nouns, and (*β*) also to Verbs†.

14. (1.) Thus, from בְ *in*, we have [comp. Tab. II (1)]—

בִּי *in me,* בְּךָ *in thee m.* (בָּךְ *f.*), בּוֹ *in him* (בָּהּ *in her*),

בָּנוּ *in us,* בָּכֶם *in you m.* (בָּכֶן *f.*), בָּהֶם *in them m.* (בָּהֶן *f*).

(2.) So from לְ *to* or *for*, we have [comp. Tab. II (2)]‡—

לִי *to me,* לְךָ *to thee m.* (לָךְ *f.*), לוֹ *to him* (לָהּ *to her*),

לָנוּ *to us,* לָכֶם *to you m.* (לָכֶן *f.*), לָהֶם *to them m.* (לָהֶן *f.*).

(3.) Of כְּמוֹ (or כְּ) *as, like*, the forms are [Tab. II (3)]—

כָּמֹנִי *like me,* כָּמֹךָ *like thee m.* (כָּמוֹךְ *f.*), כָּמֹהוּ *like him* (כָּמָהָ *f*),

כָּמֹנוּ *like us,* כמכֶם *like you m.* (כמֹכֶן *f.*), כְּמֹהֶם *like them m.* (כָּהֶן *f*).

with some other forms to be seen in Tab. II.

(4.) Of מִן (or מִ) *from*, the forms are [Tab. II (4)]—

מִמֶּנִּי *from me,* מִמְּךָ *from thee m.* (מִמֵּךְ *f.*), מִמֶּנּוּ *from him* (מִמֶּנָּה *f.*),

מִמֶּנּוּ *from us,* מִכֶּם *from you m.* (מִכֶּן *f.*), מֵהֶם *from them m.* (מֵהֶן *f.*)

with some other forms to be seen in Tab. II.

⁎ Where more than one form is given in the Table, the Student may take the RIGHT-HAND form.

Obs. These Affixes for *me, thee,* etc., may stand also for *myself, thyself,* etc.

---

* Including Preposition-*letters*, as in Table II., and *Words* such as those in Tables, III., IV. [The Tables are given at the end of the book,—also in a separate Part by themselves, FOR MOUNTING]

† Independently of, and sometimes in addition to, the inflexion-forms

‡ Also לִי (*to me*) = *mine,* לְךָ (*to thee m*) = *thine,* לוֹ (*to him*) = *his,* etc.

Exercise V.

(To be translated into English.)

יְיָ +¹ לִי לֹא² אִירָא³ : אֱלֹהַי⁴ בְּךָ בָטַחְתִּי⁵ : צָמְאָה⁶ לְךָ
נַפְשִׁי⁷ : בְּי⁸ הָמְכָה⁹ יְמִינֶךָ¹⁰ : אֱלֹהִים¹¹ מִי¹² +כָמוֹךָ : חֹשֶׁךְ¹³
לֹא² יַחְשִׁיךְ¹⁴ מִמֶּךָ : אַל¹⁵ תַּסְתֵּר¹⁶ פָּנֶיךָ¹⁷ מִמֶּנִּי : לֹא²
יִסָּתֵר¹⁸ מִמֶּךָ כָּל¹⁹ דָּבָר²⁰ : מֵעוֹלָם²¹ +אַתָּה : לֹא² תַעֲשׂוּ²²
לָכֶם אֱלִילִם²³* : עֵינַיִם²⁴ +לָהֶם וְלֹא²⁵ יִרְאוּ²⁶ : כְּמוֹהֶם יִהְיוּ²⁷
עֹשֵׂיהֶם²⁸ כֹּל²⁹ אֲשֶׁר³⁰ בֹּטֵחַ³¹ בָּהֶם : הָאֵל³² +לָנוּ אֵל³²
לְמוֹשָׁעוֹת³³ : אֵלִי³⁴ צוּרִי³⁵ אֶחֱסֶה³⁶ בּוֹ : לוֹ עֵצָה³⁷ וּתְבוּנָה³⁸ :
מִמֶּנּוּ יְשׁוּעָתִי³⁹ : מִי כָמֹכָה בָאֵלִם⁴⁰* יְיָ :

[1] See Vocab. p. 385. [2] not. [3] I will fear, [*i.e.* (2 and 3 going together) *I will not fear*]. [4] my God. [5] I have trusted [6] hath thirsted. [7] my soul. [8] the prefix בּ of § 4 here signifies 'on.' [9] hath-taken-supporting-hold. [10] Thy right hand. [11] [O] God! [12] who? [13] darkness [14] will obscure, [the 'not' of the preceding word goes with this word to express '*will not obscure*'] [15] not [This Negative Particle with the Tense after it, in No. 16 ('*Thou wilt hide*'), signifies '*Do not hide*,' deprecatively] [16] [see No. 15]. [17] Thy face. [18] it shall be hid. [19] any. [20] thing. [21] עוֹלָם eternity. [22] ye shall make [23] idols. [24] eyes. [25] לֹא not. [26] they will see. [27] shall be. [28] their makers [29] every one. [30] that. [31] trusteth. [32] אֵל God. [33] for salvation. [34] my God [35] my Rock [36] I will take refuge. [37] counsel. [38] and understanding. [39] my salvation. [40] אֵלִם gods —* See Pt. I., § 12.—Here the בּ stands for *among*.

Exercise VI.

(To be translated into Hebrew.)

To me. To thee (*m.*). To thee (*f.*). To him. To her. To us. To you (*m.*). To you (*f.*). To them (*m.*). To them (*f.*).

In me. In thee (*m.*). In thee (*f.*). In him. In her. In us. In you (*m.*). In you (*f.*). In them (*m.*). In them (*f.*).

Like me. Like thee (*m.*). Like thee (*f.*). Like him.
Like her. Like us. Like you (*m.*). Like you (*f.*). Like
them (*m.*). Like them (*f.*).

From me. From thee (*m.*). From thee (*f.*). From him.
From her. From us. From you (*m.*). From you (*f.*).
From them (*m.*). From them (*f.*).

Thine (*m.*) (Hebr., *to Thee*) [am] I. And His (Hebr., *to
Him*) [are] we. What[1] dost-thou-(*m.*)-here (Hebr., [*is there*]
to thee here[2])? There-is-not[3] one-calling[4] among-them (*m.*)
(Hebr., *in them*). Hath-He-not-also-spoken-by-us (Hebr.,
Whether not[5] *also*[6] *by*[7] *us hath-He-spoken*[8])? There-is-none[3]
like it (*f.*) I-am-as-thou-(*m.*)-art (Hebr., *like me like thee*).
Thou-[art]-mightier-than-we (Hebr., thou-art-mighty[9] *from
us*). No-one-of-us-will-withold-his-sepulchre-from-thee (*m.*)
(Hebr., *any-one*[10] *from-us his-sepulchre*[11] *will-not-withold*[12]
from thee). Thou-(*m.*)-shalt-not-be-afraid[13] of-them (*m.*)
(Hebr., *from them*).

[1] מַה. [2] פֹּה. [3] אֵין. [4] קרא. [5] לֹא. [6] גַם. [7] בְּ (the Prefix). [8] דִּבֶּר.
[9] עָצְמְתָ. [10] אִישׁ. [11] קִבְרוֹ. [12] לֹא יִכְלֶה. [13] לֹא תִירָא.

EXERCISE VII. [AND VIII.].

(*To be translated into Hebrew.*)

Me.[1] Thee (*m.*). Thee (*f.*). Him. Her. Us. You (*m.*).
You (*f.*). Them (*m.*). Them (*f.*).

With[2] me. With thee (*m.*). With thee (*f.*). With him.
With her. With us. With you (*m.*). With you (*f.*). With
them (*m.*). With them (*f.*).

To[3] me. To thee (*m.*). To thee (*f.*). To him. To her.
To us. To you (*m.*). To you (*f.*). To them (*m.*). To
them (*f.*).

Upon[4] me. Upon thee (*m.*). Upon thee (*f.*). Upon him.
Upon her. Upon us. Upon you (*m.*). Upon you (*f.*). Upon
them (*m.*). Upon them (*f.*).

[1] Table III. (1). [2] Tab. III. (2). [Also write these with עִם, Tab. III. (3)] [3] אֶל. [4] עַל.

Exercise VIII.

Thee [1] (*m.*) I-brought [2] unto [3] me. It [1] (*f.*) I-brought [2] upon [4] him. With [5] thee (*m.*) [am] I. What [6] [is] with [5] us? And-they-will-kill [7] me [1] and thee [1] (*f.*) they-will-keep-alive [8]. He-spake [9] with [5] us roughly, [10] and-set-us-down (Hebr., *and-gave* [11] *us* [1]) as spies (E.V.). [12] And-we-said [13] unto [3] him true-men [14] [are] we. And-he-made-himself-strange [15] unto [3] them. And-the-people-set (Hebr., *and-they-set* [16] [viz.] *the people* [17]) him [1] over [4] them (*m.*) for a head [18] and for a chief. [19] And-he-came [20] to [3] them (*m.*). And-he-saw [21] them [1] (*m.*). And-He-hath-set-thee [22] to [23] [be] king [24] over [4] us (*m.*).

1 Table III. (1).   2 הֲבֵאתִי.   3 אֶל.   4 עַל.   5 אֵת [Table III (2)].   6 מָה.   7 וְהָרְגוּ.   8 יְחַיּוּ.   9 דִּבֶּר.   10 קָשׁוֹת.   11 וַיִּתֵּן.   12 מְרַגְּלִים.   13 וַנֹּאמַר.   14 כֵּנִים.   15 וַיִּתְנַכֵּר.   16 וַיָּשִׂימוּ.   17 עַם (הָעָם, with the Def. Art.).   18 רֹאשׁ.   19 קָצִין.   20 וַיָּבֹא.   21 וַיַּרְא.   22 וַיִּתֶּנְךָ.   23 ל (the prefix).   24 מֶלֶךְ.

Exercise IX.

(To be translated into English.)

שְׁמַע[1] יְיָ[2] קוֹלִי[3] : צוּרִי[4] אַל[5] תֶּחֱרַשׁ[6] מִמֶּנִּי : זַמְּרוּ[7]

לַיְיָ[8] חֲסִידָיו[9] וְהוֹדוּ[10] לְזֵכֶר[11] קָדְשׁוֹ[12] : יִשְׁמַע[13] מֵהֵיכָלוֹ[14]

קוֹלִי[5] : אֶת[15] קֹלֶךָ[8] שָׁמַעְתִּי[16] בַגָּן[17] : וַיֹּאמֶר[18] שָׁאוּל[19] הֲקֹלֶךָ[3] +

1 Hear Thou.   2 See Vocab. p. 385.   3 קוֹל a voice.   4 צוּר a rock.   5 not. [This with the next word, No. 6, signifies 'do not be silent'].   6 See in No. 5.   7 sing ye hymns.   8 See No. 2 above, and p. 2 Note (‖).   9 חָסִיד a saint (pl. חֲסִידִים).   10 and give thanks.   11 for a remembrance of.   12 קֹדֶשׁ holiness [with aff. קָדְשִׁי *my...*, etc].   13 may He hear.   14 הֵיכָל a palace-temple.   15 The mark for a 'Definite object.' This word אֵת (or אֶת when unaccented as here) cannot be rendered by any *word* in English: it corresponds with the *Accusative form* in languages which have that form.   16 I heard.   17 גַּן, גָּן, a garden.   18 and he said.   19 *viz*, Saul.

זֶה²⁰ בְּנִי²¹ דָוִד²² עֶצֶם²³ מֵעֲצָמַי²³ וּבָשָׂר²⁴ מִבְּשָׂרִי²⁴ :

וְאָסַפְתָּ²⁵ דְּגָנֶךָ²⁶ וְתִירֹשְׁךָ²⁷ וְיִצְהָרֶךָ²⁸ וַיֹּאמֶר¹⁸ הַגְמִיאִינִי²⁹

נָא³⁰ מְעַט³¹ מַיִם³² מִכַּדֵּךְ³³ וַתְּמַהֵר³⁴ וַתֹּרֶד³⁵ כַּדָּהּ³³ עַל³⁶

יָדָהּ³⁷ גַּם³⁸ לִגְמַלֶּיךָ³⁹ אֶשְׁאָב⁴⁰ דּוֹדִי⁴¹ יָרַד⁴² לְגַנּוֹ¹⁷ :

וַיָּבֹא⁴³ נֹחַ⁴⁴ וּבָנָיו⁴⁵ ……אִתּוֹ⁴⁶ אֶל⁴⁷ הַתֵּבָה⁴⁸ : דַּרְכֵי⁴⁹ צִיּוֹן⁵⁰ +

אֲבֵלוֹת⁵¹ ……כֹּהֲנֶיהָ⁵² + נֶאֱנָחִים⁵³ בְּתוּלֹתֶיהָ⁵⁴ + נוּגוֹת⁵⁵ וְהִיא⁵⁶

מַר⁵⁷ + לָהּ : הִנֵּה⁵⁸ כְּעֵינֵי⁵⁹ עֲבָדִים⁶⁰ אֶל⁴⁷ יַד⁶¹ אֲדֹנֵיהֶם⁶²

כְּעֵינֵי⁵⁹ שִׁפְחָה⁶³ אֶל⁴⁷ יַד⁶¹ גְּבִרְתָּהּ⁶⁴ כֵּן⁶⁵ עֵינֵינוּ⁵⁹ + אֶל⁴⁷

יְיָ אֱלֹהֵינוּ⁶⁶ עַד⁶⁷ שֶׁיְּחָנֵּנוּ⁶⁸ : לֹא⁶⁹ מַחְשְׁבוֹתַי⁷⁰

מַחְשְׁבוֹתֵיכֶם⁷⁰ וְלֹא⁶⁹ דַרְכֵיכֶם⁷¹ + דְּרָכָי⁷² : מֶלֶךְ⁷³ אֱלֹהָיִךְ⁶⁶ :

וְהָיוּ⁷⁴ מְלָכִים⁷⁴ אֹמְנַיִךְ⁷⁵ וְשָׂרוֹתֵיהֶם⁷⁶ מֵינִיקוֹתַיִךְ⁷⁷ לֹא⁶⁹ כְּצוּרֵנוּ⁷⁸

צוּרָם⁷⁹ + בָּרְכִי⁸⁰ נַפְשִׁי⁸¹ אֶת¹⁵ יְיָ² וְאַל⁸² תִּשְׁכְּחִי⁸³ כָּל⁸⁴

גְּמוּלָיו⁸⁵ :

20 this. 21 [O] my son. 22 David. 23 עֶצֶם bone [pl. עֲצָמִים]. 24 בָּשָׂר flesh [with aff. בְּשָׂרוֹ his., etc]. 25 and thou shalt gather. 26 דָּגָן corn [דּ, with Affixes]. 27 תִּירֹשׁ new wine. 28 יִצְהָר oil. 29 let me drink. 30 I pray. 31 a little. 32 water. 33 כַּד a pitcher. 34 and she hasted. 35 and she let down. 36 upon. 37 יָד a hand. 38 also. 39 גָּמָל a camel [pl. גְּמַלִּים]. 40 I will draw. 41 דּוֹד a friend. 42 went down. 43 and he came. 44 viz. Noah [came]. 45 בָּנִים sons. 46 אֵת with [w. aff. אִתִּי with me, etc.]. 47 to, into. 48 the ark. 49 [the] ways of. 50 Zion. 51 mourning. 52 כֹּהֵן a priest [pl. כֹּהֲנִים]. 53 sighing. 54 בְּתוּלָה a virgin. 55 afflicted. • 56 and as for her, 57 bitterness. 58 behold. 59 עֵינֵי eyes of [dual עֵינַיִם eyes]. 60 servants. 61 hand of. 62 אֲדֹנִים (pl.*form of אָדוֹן a master. 63 a woman-servant 64 גְּבִירָה a mistress [also גְּבֶרֶת, with aff. גְּבִרְתִּי my , etc.]. 65 so. 66 אֱלֹהִים God [a plural form]. 67 until. 68 that He pity us. 69 לֹא not. 70 מַחֲשָׁבָה a thought [שׁ, with Affixes]. 71 your (m.) ways. 72 דְּרָכִים ways. 73 hath reigned. 74 and they shall be. 75 viz. kings [shall be]. 76 אֹמְנִים nursing-fathers. 77 שָׂרָה a princess. 78 מֵינִיקָה a nursing-mother. 79 צוּר a rock. 80 bless thou (f.) 81 [O] my soul. 82 (with 83) and forget not [Cp. No. 5, above]. 84 all. 85 גְּמוּל a benefit.

NOTE. לֹא (not) may be remembered now.

---

* A 'Plural of excellence,' as some call it, may be used of one. So, in Ex. XXI. 4 & 6, "his master" has the Plural form.

Exercise X.

(*To be translated into Hebrew.*)

His horse.[1] Thy (*m.*) horse. My horse. Their (*m.*) horse. Your (*m.*) horse. Our horse. His horses. Thy (*m.*) horses. My horses. . Their (*m.*) horses. Your (*m.*) horses. Our horses.

My friend[2] [is] mine (Heb., *to*[3] *me*). In thy (*m.*) friend. Like thy (*f.*) friend. To his friend. From her friend. And from our friend. And to your (*m.*) friend. And like your (*f.*) friend. And to their (*m.*) friend. And in their (*f.*) friend. And my friends. Whether thy (*m.*) friends? Thy (*f.*) friends. His friends. Her friends. Our friends [are] your (*m.*) friends. Among[4] your (*f.*) friends [are] their (*m.*) friends and their (*f.*) friends.

His bride.[5] My bride [is] like her. Like thy (*m.*) bride [is] she. The brides. Their (*m.*) brides. Your (*m.*) brides and our brides.

My riddle.[6] Her riddles. Thy (*f.*) riddles. Their (*f.*) riddles. Your (*m.*) riddle. Our riddle. Their (*m.*) riddle. And in his riddle.

Her lamp.[7] From her lamps. To my lamps. In thy (*f.*) lamps. And like your (*m.*) lamps. Their (*f.*) lamps. Whether[8] his lamps? Whether like our lamps [are] thy (*f.*) lamps?

His eye.[9] In his eyes. Like their (*f.*) eyes. In our eyes. And in her eyes. Thy (*m.*) eye. His eyes. Thy (*f.*) eyes. Her eye. Your (*m.*) eyes.

---

[1] סוּס (Plur. סוּסִים *horses*). [2] דּוֹד (Plur. דּוֹדִים *friends*). [3] לְ (the Prefix). [4] בְ (the Prefix). [5] כַּלָּה (Plur. כַּלּוֹת *brides*). [6] חִידָה (Plur. חִידוֹת *riddles*). [7] נֵר (Plur. נֵרוֹת *lamps*). [8] הֲ (the Interrogative Prefix). [9] עַיִן (w. aff. עֵינִי *my eye*, etc.; Dual עֵינַיִם *eyes*, w. aff. עֵינַי *my eyes*, etc., — Table VII.).

SECTION IV.

The Relative Pronoun אֲשֶׁר.

23. The word אֲשֶׁר stands for the Relative Pronouns *who,* *which, that;* and is the same in form for all Persons, Genders, and Numbers; thus,—

הָאִישׁ אֲשֶׁר בָּא	*the man* WHO *came.*
הָאִשָּׁה אֲשֶׁר בָּאָה	*the woman* WHO *came.*
הָאֲנָשִׁים אֲשֶׁר בָּאוּ	*the men* WHO *came.*
הַנָּשִׁים אֲשֶׁר בָּאוּ	*the women* WHO *came.*
הַדָּבָר אֲשֶׁר רָאִיתָ	*the thing* WHICH (or THAT) *thou sawest.*
הַדְּבָרִים אֲשֶׁר רָאִיתִי	*the things* WHICH (or THAT) *I saw.*

24. The Oblique forms *in whom* (or *which*), *to whom* (or *which*), *from whom* (or *which*), are expressed by אֲשֶׁר *followed* by a *Personal Pronoun attached to a Particle;* thus, for instance, [Is. xlix. 3] "O Israel, IN WHOM [אֲשֶׁר בְּךָ, lit., WHO IN-THEE (*m.*)] I will be glorified;" [Deut. iv. 8] "A nation TO WHICH [אֲשֶׁר לוֹ, lit., WHICH TO IT (*m.*)] there-are-statutes and judgments," etc.; [Ps. xcv. 5] "To WHOM [אֲשֶׁר לוֹ, lit, WHO TO-HIM (*belongs*)] the sea," etc.

[Note—(*a*) This is the *full* expression. The אֲשֶׁר is sometimes omitted. See § 31.

(*b*.) The word involving the Personal Pronoun is *separated* from the אֲשֶׁר very often. See more, below (§ 29). N.B. This separation should always take place in Composition, except where there is Emphasis on the Person.]

25. The full Table for *In whom** (for all Persons, Genders and Numbers) is obtained by simply placing אֲשֶׁר before the several expressions in Table II. (i.), as follows,—

---

* Or, *which.*

	1 pers.	2 pers.	3 pers.
(a.) _In whom_ (or _which_) — Singular.	אֲשֶׁר בִּי	(m.) (p. בָּךְ) אֲשֶׁר בְּךָ (f.) אֲשֶׁר בָּךְ	(m.) אֲשֶׁר בּוֹ (f.) אֲשֶׁר בָּהּ
Plural.	אֲשֶׁר בָּנוּ	(m.) אֲשֶׁר בָּכֶם (f.) אֲשֶׁר בָּכֶן	(m.) אֲשֶׁר בָּהֶם, בָּם (f.) אֲשֶׁר בָּהֶן, בָּהֵן

Similarly, full Tables may be formed (β) for _to whom_ (or _which_), (γ) for _like whom_ (or _which_), and (δ) for _from whom_ (or _which_), by placing אֲשֶׁר before the several expressions in Table II. (2), (3), and (4), respectively. And so, too, in the case of Tables III. and IV.

26. Similarly, Table V. with אֲשֶׁר gives the several forms for WHOSE _song_, and WHOSE _songs;_ and so for any other Noun; thus, [Job v. 5, (E.V.)] "WHOSE _harvest_ [אֲשֶׁר קְצִירוֹ (lit., WHO HIS _harvest_)];" [Deut. viii. 9] "A land WHOSE _stones_ [אֲשֶׁר אֲבָנֶיהָ, lit., WHICH HER _stones_]," etc.; [Jer. xxxii. 19] "Thou WHOSE _eyes_ [אֲשֶׁר עֵינֶיךָ, lit., WHO THINE _eyes_] are-open on all-the-ways-of the-children-of men." So [Ps. xcv. 4] "_In_ WHOSE _hand_ [אֲשֶׁר בְּיָדוֹ, lit., WHO _in_ HIS _hand_] are-the secret-depths of earth," etc.

27. Table III. (1), with אֲשֶׁר, gives the _Objective_ Relative Pronouns _whom_ (or _which_), viz., אֲשֶׁר אוֹתוֹ _whom_ (lit., _who him_), אֲשֶׁר אֹתָהּ _whom_ (lit., _who her_), אֲשֶׁר אֹתְךָ _whom_ (lit., _who thee, m._), אֲשֶׁר אֹתִי _whom_ (lit., _who me_)*, etc. [So, for _with whom, on whom,_ etc.].

---

* Thus Gen. xlv. 4, "I am Joseph your brother WHOM _ye sold_ [אֲשֶׁר מְכַרְתֶּם אֹתִי, lit., WHO _ye-sold_ ME]," etc. So, too, when the Personal Pronoun is expressed by an _Affix attached to a Verb_ (§ 13, β); thus, Gen. xxvii. 27, etc. See more, hereafter.

28. These *Objective* Personal Pronouns are often dropped, and then the אֲשֶׁר by itself stands for *whom* (or *which*) in the several Persons, Genders and Numbers; thus [Gen. xxii. 2] "Take now thy son, thine only-son, *whom* [אֲשֶׁר*] thou lovest," etc., and [Gen. xiii. 15] "all the land *which* [אֲשֶׁר†] thou seest," etc.; and many others.

29. In all the cases of §§ 24—27, the word involving the Personal Pronoun is generally‡ *separated from* the אֲשֶׁר by a word or words — especially by the Verb. — Thus, for instance, [Gen. xxi. 23] "the land IN WHICH *thou-hast-sojourned* [אֲשֶׁר גַּרְתָּה בָּהּ, lit., WHICH *thou-hast-sojourned* IN IT];" and so [Gen. xxviii. 13] "the land ON WHICH *thou art-lying* [אֲשֶׁר אַתָּה שֹׁכֵב עָלֶיהָ, lit., WHICH *thou art-lying* ON IT]," and so [Nu. xxii. 30] "Am not I thine ass ON WHICH *thou-hast-ridden* [אֲשֶׁר רָכַבְתָּ עָלַי, lit., WHICH *thou-hast-ridden* ON ME];" [Job iv. 19] "WHOSE-*foundation is-in-the-dust* [אֲשֶׁר בֶּעָפָר יְסוֹדָם, lit., WHO *in-the-dust* IS-THEIR-*foundation*];" [Is. xlix. 23] "I THOSE-WAITING-FOR-WHOM *shall not be ashamed* [אֲשֶׁר לֹא יֵבֹשׁוּ קֹוָי, lit., WHO *not-shall-be-ashamed* MY-WAITERS]."

30 Similarly, (α) אֲשֶׁר *which*, followed by שָׁם *there*, stands for *where*; thus [Gen. ii. 11] "אֲשֶׁר שָׁם הַזָּהָב WHERE (lit., WHICH THERE) [*there is*] *gold*." But

(β) The אֲשֶׁר and the שָׁם are generally separated (as in § 29) by a word or words — especially by the verb — thus [Gen. xix. 27] "the place WHERE *he stood* [אֲשֶׁר עָמַד שָׁם, lit., WHICH *he stood* THERE]," etc.

. (γ.) So אֲשֶׁר *which* before מִשָּׁם *from there* (or *thence*) stands for *whence*; thus [Gen. xxiv. 5] "unto-the land WHENCE *thou-camest-forth* [אֲשֶׁר יָצָאתָ מִשָּׁם, lit., WHICH *thou-camest-forth* THENCE]," etc.

(δ.) So also אֲשֶׁר *which*, before שָׁמָּה *thither*, stands for *whither*; thus, [Nu. xiv. 24] "and I will bring him into the land WHITHER *he-came* [אֲשֶׁר בָּא שָׁמָּה, lit., WHICH *he-came* THITHER]"

(ε.) The שָׁם, שָׁמָּה, are sometimes omitted; as, for instance, in Nu. xiii. 27.

31. The אֲשֶׁר is often omitted, as [Gen. xlii. 28] "What

---

* Instead of אֲשֶׁר אֹתוֹ.
† Instead of אֲשֶׁר אַתָּה.
‡ Except in the case of *Emphasis* on the Personal Pronoun.

is this, God hath done to us?" instead of "WHICH [אֲשֶׁר] God hath done to us?"; [Lam. iii. 1] "I-am the-man HATH-SEEN affliction," instead of "WHO [אֲשֶׁר] HATH-SEEN," etc.* So [Ps. xviii. 3] "my God, my Strength, IN WHOM *I-will-trust*"(E.V.) אֲשֶׁר לוֹ [אֲשֶׁר אֶחֱסֶה בּוֹ], short for אֶחֱסֶה בּוֹ. So לוֹ for in Ps. xxxii. 1, "TO WHOM [He will not impute iniquity]." And so [Ps. lxxxiii. 19] "Thou WHOSE NAME [שְׁמֶךָ, short for אֲשֶׁר שְׁמֶךָ], etc.", and many others.

Obs. Sometimes *the word with the Pron.-Affix* is omitted too; as "*from it*" in [Isai. li. 1], "the rock ye-were-hewn" [*from*]. Comp. § 29

[Note (*a.*) אֲשֶׁר is often used, like the Conjunction כִּי, for '*that*' (*Conjunctive*), '*for*,' '*because*,' etc Thus [Gen. xi. 7] "THAT [אֲשֶׁר] they may not understand," etc.; [Ex. xi. 7] "THAT [אֲשֶׁר] He will separate," etc., and many others.

(*b.*) Conversely כִּי is sometimes said to have the value of the *Relative* אֲשֶׁר.

(*c*) The prefixes ו ב כ ל ם may stand before אֲשֶׁר; thus,—

(ı) With the *Relative-Pronoun* value of אֲשֶׁר, we have וַאֲשֶׁר, *and who*, etc., בַּאֲשֶׁר (as in Is. lvi 4, lxv. 12, lxvi. 4), כַּאֲשֶׁר (as in Job xxix 25, etc), לַאֲשֶׁר (as in Genesis xliii. 16, etc), מֵאֲשֶׁר (as in Isaiah xlvii. 13, etc.). So אֵת אֲשֶׁר *that* (*Objective*) *which*, and *whatsoever* (*Obj*), *whom*, *whomsoever*, etc.

(ıı) With the *Conjunctive* value of אֲשֶׁר, we have בַּאֲשֶׁר *in that*, כַּאֲשֶׁר, lit., *as that* (very frequently for *as*, *according as*, and *when*), לַאֲשֶׁר *for that*, מֵאֲשֶׁר *from* [*the time*] *that* (= *since*), etc.

(*d*) The prefixes שֶׁ, and שַׁ,† followed by Dagesh Forte, stand for the *Conjunctive* אֲשֶׁר; and the latter, שַׁ (followed by Dagesh Forte), often for the *Relative Pronoun*.

(*e.*) When prefixed to a word of which the first letter does not receive Dagesh, — שַׁ becomes שָׁ; but שֶׁ remains שֶׁ (no compensation being made for the Dagesh).

(*f.*) We have also the compound prefixes בְּשֶׁ (once), and בְּשֶׁ like בַּאֲשֶׁר, and כְּשֶׁ like כַּאֲשֶׁר.

(*g*) The word בְּשֶׁל (Eccles. viii. 17) is generally supposed to be made up of שֶׁ (for אֲשֶׁר) followed by לְ *to*, and preceded by בְּ *in*. So בְּשֶׁלִּי (Jon. i. 12) is taken for בַּאֲשֶׁר לִי; and בְּשֶׁלְּמִי (Jon. i. 7) for בַּאֲשֶׁר לְמִי (Jon. i. 8)].

---

* It will be seen that in the first two examples the אֲשֶׁר understood is that of § 23; and, in the following examples, that of §§ 24 etc   [In English the Relative Pronoun is often left out, when, as in the first example (§ 31), it is the Object; but not often when, as in the second, it is the Subject]

† Supposed by many to be a Contraction for אֲשֶׁר.

EXERCISE XI.

(To be translated into English.)

*** For the plan of the Exercise, see § 11 (a—ε).

אֲנִי + יְיָ[1] אֱלֹהֵיכֶם[2] אֲשֶׁר הוֹצֵאתִי[3] אֶתְכֶם מֵאֶרֶץ[4] מִצְרַיִם[5]׃

הָאָרֶץ אֲשֶׁר אַתָּה + בָּא[6] שָׁמָּה[7] לְרִשְׁתָּהּ[8] לֹא כְאֶרֶץ

מִצְרַיִם[9] + הוּא אֲשֶׁר יְצָאתֶם[10] מִשָּׁם[11]׃ אֶרֶץ אֲשֶׁר יְיָ

אֱלֹהֶיךָ + דֹּרֵשׁ[12] אֹתָהּ׃ אֶרֶץ[4] אֲשֶׁר לֹא בְמִסְכֵּנֻת[13]* תֹּאכַל[14]

בָּהּ לֶחֶם[15] לֹא תֶחְסַר[16] כֹּל[17] בָּהּ׃ אֶרֶץ אֲשֶׁר אֲבָנֶיהָ[18]

בַרְזֶל[19] וּמֵהֲרָרֶיהָ[20] תַּחְצֹב[21] נְחֹשֶׁת[22]׃ אַשְׁרֵי[23] הַגּוֹי[24] אֲשֶׁר יְיָ

+ אֱלֹהָיו[1] הָעָם[25] בָּחַר[26] לְנַחֲלָה[27] לוֹ׃ הַמָּקוֹם[28] אֲשֶׁר אַתָּה +

עוֹמֵד[29] עָלָיו אַדְמַת[30] קֹדֶשׁ[31] הוּא +׃ הָאָרֶץ אֲשֶׁר אַתָּה +

שֹׁכֵב[32] עָלֶיהָ לְךָ אֶתְּנֶנָּה[33]׃ יִשְׂרָאֵל[34] אֲשֶׁר בְּךָ אֶתְפָּאָר[35]׃

יְיָ[1] + אֹתוֹ וְכֹל[36] אֲשֶׁר הוּא + עֹשֶׂה[37] יְיָ + מַצְלִיחַ[38]׃ כָּכָה[39]

יֵעָשֶׂה[40] לָאִישׁ[41] אֲשֶׁר הַמֶּלֶךְ[42] + חָפֵץ[43] בִּיקָרוֹ[44]׃ הֲקִמֹתִי[45]

אֶת בְּרִיתִי[46] אִתָּם לָתֵת[47] לָהֶם ⋯ אֶת אֶרֶץ[4] מְגֻרֵיהֶם[48]* אֲשֶׁר

---

[1] See Vocabulary, p. 385. [2] אֱלֹהִים GOD [a Noun of the Plural form, see Table V. (ii.)]. [3] [I]-brought-out. [4] אֶרֶץ a land, earth, (also *land of*). [With the 'definite article' הָאָרֶץ.] In Pause אָרֶץ. [5] Egypt. [6] coming. [7] thither. [8] to-possess-it. [9] See Table I., Note 1. [10] Ye-came-out. [11] thence (lit., *from there*). [12] caring-for. [13] in-poverty. [14] thou-shalt-eat. [15] bread. [16] thou-shalt-lack (with לֹא, *thou shalt* NOT *lack*). [17] anything. [18] אֲבָנִים stones (fr. אֶבֶן). [19] iron. [20] הָרָרִים mountains (§ 31). [21] thou-mayest-dig. [22] brass (E.V.). [23] blessed-is (lit., O-the-happiness-of!) [24] גּוֹי a nation. [25] עָם (הָעָם with 'definite article') a people. [26] He-hath-chosen (§ 31). [27] for-an-inheritance. [28] מָקוֹם a place. [29] standing. [30] ground of†. [31] holiness. [32] lying. [33] I-will-give-it. [34] Israel. [35] I-will-glorify-Myself. [36] and-everything. [37] doing. [38] making-to-prosper. [39] כָּכָה thus. [40] shall-be-done. [41] אִישׁ a man. [42] מֶלֶךְ a king. [43] delighting. [44] יְקָר honour, glory, brightness. [45] I-have-established. [46] My-Covenant. [47] to-give. [48] their-(*m.*)-sojournings.

---

* For the ⃗, as 'Defective Shurik,' see Pt. I. § 14.
† '*Ground-of* holiness' is a phrase for '*holy ground*.'

גְּרוּ⁴⁹ בָהּ׃ אֲנִי + יְיָ¹ אֲשֶׁר לֹא יֵבֹשׁוּ⁵⁰ קֹוָי⁵¹׃ אֵלִי⁵² צוּרִי⁵³

אֶחֱסֶה⁵⁴ בּוֹ׃ אֲשֶׁר בְּיָדוֹ⁵⁵ מֶחְקְרֵי⁵⁶ אָרֶץ⁴׃ אֲשֶׁר עֵינֶיךָ⁵⁷ +

פְּקֻחוֹת⁵⁸ עַל כָּל־+ דַּרְכֵי⁵⁹ בְּנֵי⁶⁰ אָדָם⁶¹׃ זְכֹר⁶² עֲדָתְךָ⁶³ קָנִיתָ⁶⁴

קֶדֶם⁶⁵׃ אַשְׁרֵי²³ הָעָם²⁵ שֶׁכָּכָה³⁰ לוֹ אַשְׁרֵי²³ הָעָם²⁵ שֶׁיְיָ¹

אֱלֹהָיו²׃

49 they-sojourned. 50 they-shall-be-ashamed (with לֹא *they shall* NOT, etc.).
51 those-waiting-for-Me. 52 my God. 53 my Rock. 54 I will trust. 55 יָד a
hand. 56 [the] secret-depths-of. 57 עַיִן an eye, Dual עֵינַים. * 58 Opened, open.
59 [the] ways of. 60 [the] children-of. 61 Adam, man (generally). 62 remember.
63 עֵדָה a congregation [with Affix עֲדָתוֹ *his*, etc]. 64 Thou didst own (§ 31).
65 of old.

---

* For the — as 'Defective Shurik,' see Pt. I. § 14.

† כָּל־ כֹּל all, as p. 14 (*).

EXERCISE XII.

(To be translated into Hebrew.)

** For the plan of the Exercise, see § 11 (ζ—μ).

Thy (*m.*) sojourner[1] who [is] within[2] thy gates.[3] The
thing[4] which thou (*m.*) [art] doing.[5] A man[6] in-whom-
there-is-Spirit (Hebr., *who Spirit[7] in[8] him*). Ye (*m.*) to-
whom-I-have-given (Hebr., *who I-have-given[8] to[9] you*) the
land.[10] I [am] Joseph[11] whom-ye-sold (Hebr., *who ye-sold[12]
me[13]*). The land[10] from-which-I-came-forth (Hebr., *which I-
came-forth[14] from[15] it (f.)*). A land[10] unto-which-I-will-bring-
you (*m.*) (Hebr., *which I-will-bring[16] you[13] unto[17] it (f.)*).
A land it (*f.*) [is] like-which-there-is-not (Hebr. *which there-*

---

1 גֵּר. 2 ב prefix. 3 שְׁעָרִים (Table V. (II.)). 4 דָּבָר. 5 עֹשֶׂה. 6 אִישׁ.
7 רוּחַ. 8 נָתַתִּי. 9 לְ (Table II.). 10 אֶרֶץ (הָאָ with ' def. art.') 11 יוֹסֵף.
12 מְכַרְתָּם. 13 Table III. (1) 14 יָצָאתִי 15 Table II (4). 16 אָבִיא. 17 Table IV. (1).

is-not [18] *like* [19] *it*). Every-one [20] with-whom-it-was found (Hebr., *who it-was-found* [21] *with* [22] *him*). The horse [23] upon-which-he-rode (Hebr., *which he-rode* [24] *upon* [25] *him*). The land [10] upon-which-thou-art-lying (Hebr., *which thou*art-lying* [26] *upon* [25] *it*). The servants [27] with-whom-he-was-angry (Hebr., *who he-was-angry* [28] *upon* [25] *them (m.)*). The man [6] in-whose-hand-the-cup-was-found (Hebr., *who .was-found* [29] *the cup* [30] *in* [2] *his hand* [31]). Thou (m.) in-whose-hand-the-cup-was-found (Hebr., *who was-found* [29] *the cup* [30] *in* [2] *thy hand* [31]). I in-whose-hand-the-cup-was-found (Hebr., *who was-found* [29] *the cup* [30] *in* [2] *my hand* [31]). I-will-comfort-thee [32] [O] Zion [33] in-whom-I-have-delighted (Hebr., *who I-have-delighted* [34] *in thee (f.)*), unto-whom-shall-come (Hebr., *who there-shall-come* [35] *unto* [17] *thee*) the-wealth-of [36] heathen-nations, [37] and within [2] whose borders [38] shall-no-more-come-any-foe [39]; whose walls [40] they-may-call [41] 'Safety,' [42] whose Saviour [43] I [am], saith [44] thy God [45].

[18] אֵין. [19] Table II. (3). [20] כֹּל. [21] נִמְצָא. [22] Table III. (2). [23] סוּם. [24] רָכַב. [25] Table IV. (2). [26] שֹׁכֵב. [27] עֲבָדִים. [28] קָצַף. [29] נִמְצָא. [30] גָּבִיעַ. [31] יָד. [32] אֲנַחֶמֵךְ. [33] צִיּוֹן. [34] חָפַצְתִּי. [35] יָבוֹא. [36] חֵיל. [37] גּוֹיִם. [38] נְבֻלִים (Table V. (ii)). [39] לֹא יָבוֹא עוֹד כָּל צָר. [40] חֹמוֹת (Table VI. (ii)). [41] יִקְרָאוּ. [42] יְשׁוּעָה. [43] מוֹשִׁיעַ (The 'Furtive' — is dropped when an Affix is added). [44] אָמַר. [45] אֱלֹהִים (See Exerc. XI., Note 2).

---

* Masculine.

SECTION V.

DEMONSTRATIVE PRONOUNS.

32. The Demonstrative Pronouns are—

I.* זֶה *this* (*m.*), זֹאת *this* (*f.*), אֵלֶּה *these* (*m.*), אֵלֶּה *these* (*f.*);

II. הוּא *that* (*m.*), הִיא *that* (*f.*), הֵמָּה or הֵם *those* (*m.*), הֵנָּה *those* (*f.*).

Thus:	זֶה הָאִישׁ *this* [*is*] *the man;*	הוּא הָאִישׁ *that* [*is*] *the man;*	
	זֹאת הָאִשָּׁה *this* [*is*] *the woman;*	הִיא הָאִשָּׁה *that* [*is*] *the woman;*	
	אֵלֶּה הַנְּעָרִים *these* [*are*] *the boys;*	הֵמָּה(or)הֵם הַנְּעָרִים *those* [*are*] *the boys;*	
	אֵלֶּה הַנְּעָרוֹת *these* [*are*] *the girls.*	הֵנָּה הַנְּעָרוֹת *those* [*are*] *the girls.*	

[N.B.—The Demonstrative Pronouns *that, those,* are (as the Reader sees) represented in Hebrew by the 3rd Person-Pronouns in § 9.]

There is an *Adjectival* use of these Pronouns, which will be mentioned in Section IX. on Pronouns-Adjective.

33. זֶה stands sometimes for *such,* and sometimes for *thus.* See more hereafter.

34. (*α.*) With the Prefixes וּבְכָל, we find—

(1) וְזֶה, וְזֹאת, וְאֵלֶּה;

(2) בָּזֶה (once בָּזֹה 1 S. xxi. 10), בְּזֹאת, בָּאֵלֶּה, בָּאֵלֶּה;

(3) כָּזֶה, בָּזֹאת, כְּאֵלֶּה, כָּאֵלֶּה;

(4) לָזֶה, לְזֹאת, לָאֵלֶּה, לָאֵלֶּה.

(*β.*). With the Prefix מ, we have מִזֶּה, מִזֹּאת, מֵאֵלֶּה.

[Note.—No special Exercise need be given on this Section.]

For '*this*' and '*that*' ADJECTIVAL see p. 58.

---

* The less frequent forms הַלָּזֶה *masc.*, הַלָּז (also זוֹ) both *masc.* and *fem.*, and זֹה (also זוּ and הַלָּזוּ) *fem.*, for the Singular, — and אֵל for the Plural, — must be dealt with elsewhere rather than here.

SECTION VI.

INTERROGATIVE PRONOUNS.

35. The Interrogative Pronouns are—

(i.). מִי *who?*, (ii.). מַה (also מָה and מֶה) *what?**

[These Pronouns are sometimes used *non*-interrogatively, also.]

36. These words are *themselves Indeclinable;* but they may receive prefixes; thus,—

(i.). from מִי we have וּמִי† (§ 3. c. ii., above), בְּמִי, לְמִי, מִמִּי,—
(ii.). from מָה, מַה and מֶה we have—

(*a.*) וּמָה, וּמֶה;

(*β.*) בַּמֶּה (and בַּמָּה)‡:

(*γ.*) כַּמֶּה (and כַּמָּה)§;

(*δ.*) לְמָה and וְלָמָה‖ (also לָמֶה).

[Note.—(*a*) For expressing *Whose?*,—either

(1) לְ is prefixed to מִי; thus, [Gen. xxxii. 18] לְמִי אַתָּה *whose art thou?*, or

(ii). A word is placed in *close structural connection* with מִי, — as, for instance, בֶּן in [1 S. xvii. 58] בֶּן מִי *whose son?* (lit, son-of whom, — see below § 52.

(iii.) אֶת מִי stands for *whom?* (Objective), as in 1 S. xii. 3 "*whom have I oppressed?*"—

(*β.*) מַה is often read closely with the next word as in מַח־לִּי Ju. xi. 12 [almost as מַלִּי, comp. the כתיב in Ex. iv. 2 and Is. iii. 15]. And so מָה before א and ר, and מֶה before ח etc., may be said to be as the הָ & הֶ in § 6 (*b—d*). But N.B. מֶה occurs also (as in Ps. iv. 3) before ב, etc.

(*γ.*) No special Exercise need be given on this Section]

---

* Also, מַה stands sometimes for *how!* as in [Ps. cxxxiii. 1] "Behold, HOW good and HOW *pleasant* (מַה טּוֹב וּמַה נָּעִים) is the dwelling of brethren in unity."(*β*)

† Also וָמִי in the phrase מִי וָמִי (lit., *who and who?*) Ex. x. 8.—Compare Obs. XVI, p. 179.

‡ Used for *whereby?* (lit., *in the what?*)

§ Used for *how much?, how many?* (lit., *like the what?*).

‖ Used for *why? wherefore?* Observe the two different positions of the Accent.—Also מַה is sometimes used for *why?*

SECTION VII.

Nouns-Substantive.

37. In regard to 'Gender,' 'Number' and 'Case,' — there are in Hebrew—

(i.). Only the Masculine and Feminine 'Genders' (§ 10);

(ii.) The Singular and Plural 'Numbers,'—also the Dual for *some* Nouns-Substantive;

(iii.). No 'Cases,' properly, according to the usual application of the Term.

38. Names of men, and words expressing males and functions of males, are Masculine.

Names of women, and words expressing females and functions of females, are Feminine.

There is great freedom in regard to the Gender of Nouns-Substantive expressing inanimate things, — there being really no *reason* why such should be limited to either one or the other. The *usage* of the Language in regard to any particular word must, of course, be attended to in Composition. There are, however, certain special Marks for the Masculine Plural, and for the Feminine Singular and Plural; as follows,—

39. (*α.*) In the Singular Number there is no distinguishing mark* for the Masculine Gender. But

(*β.*) for the Plural Masculine the distinguishing mark is the termination ‏ִים‎; thus, (1) (from ‏שִׁיר‎ *a song*) ‏שִׁירִים‎ *songs;* (2) (from ‏כּוֹכָב‎ *a star*) ‏כּוֹכָבִים‎ *stars.*

---

* It may be said that,

(i.) Most Hebrew Nouns, which *have no special Feminine form,* are Masculine. But it must be borne in mind that,

(ii.) There are exceptions to (i).

(γ.) Many words undergo a change of vocalisation on receiving this termination; thus (1) (from דָּבָר *a word*) דְּבָרִים *words;* (2) (from מֶלֶךְ *a king*) מְלָכִים *kings;* (3) (from נַעַר *a boy*) נְעָרִים; (4) (from חֹדֶשׁ *a month*) חֳדָשִׁים.

(δ.) Some undergo still further change; thus, הָ– at the end of the word in the Singular is *replaced by* the ◌ִים for the Plural,—as (from מַעֲשֶׂה *a deed*) מַעֲשִׂים *deeds.*

40. There is a special distinguishing mark for the Feminine in the SINGULAR — viz., the accented termination הָ–; thus,

(α.) (from דּוֹד *an uncle*) דּוֹדָה *an aunt;* (from גְּבִיר *a lord*) גְּבִירָה *a lady.*

(β.) Some words undergo a change of vocalisation on receiving this הָ–; thus, (1) (from פַּר *a bullock*) פָּרָה *a cow;* (2) (from נַעַר *a boy*) נַעֲרָה *a girl.*

(γ.) Some undergo still further change; thus, הָ–, at the end of the Masculine word is *replaced by* the הָ– for the Feminine — as (from רֹעֶה *a shepherd*) רֹעָה *a shepherdess.*

41. The mark for the FEMININE PLURAL is וֹת– (or ◌ֹת), which *replaces* the הָ– of the Singular; thus, פָּרוֹת *cows* [§ 40 (β, 1)]. And some words undergo some change; thus, (1) (from מַלְכָּה *a queen*) מְלָכוֹת *queens;* (2) (from נַעֲרָה *a girl*) נְעָרוֹת *girls.*

N.B.—There are some other terminations for Feminine Singular Nouns; as תֶ–שׁ or תֶ–ַ (p. : תֶ–ִ), and וֹת–, ◌ִית.

42. There are Feminine Nouns which are not formed from the corresponding Masculine Nouns, and have no distinguishing mark; thus, אֵם *a mother* (אָב *a father*); רָחֵל *an ewe* (אַיִל *a ram*).

43. Some Masculine Nouns take the Feminine mark of Plural; thus אָב *a father*, plu. אָבוֹת; שֵׁם *a name*, plu. שֵׁמוֹת.

44. Some Feminine Nouns take the Masculine form of Plural; thus, דְּבוֹרָה *a bee* (also *Deborah*), plu. דְּבוֹרִים *bees;* רָחֵל *an ewe* (also *Rachel*), plu. רְחֵלִים *ewes.*

45. Some Nouns have *both* of the Plural forms; thus, אֲלֻמִּים and אֲלֻמּוֹת *sheaves* (from אֲלֻמָּה *a sheaf*). So *דּוֹרִים and דּוֹרוֹת (from דּוֹר *a generation.*)

46. The mark for the DUAL is ־ַיִם (in Pause ־ָיִם׃), which is the same for both Genders.

(α.) Some Nouns do not change on receiving this termination; thus, (1) (from יָד *a hand*) יָדַיִם *hands;* (2) (from שׁוֹק *a leg*) שׁוֹקַיִם *legs.*

(β.) Some undergo a change: thus, (1) (from עַיִן *an eye*) עֵינַיִם *eyes;* (2) (from רֶגֶל *a foot*) רַגְלַיִם *feet.*

(γ.) The termination ־ָה (in the Singular) is replaced by ־ַת, after which the Dual termination ־ַיִם is added; thus, (1) (from שָׁנָה *a year*) שְׁנָתַיִם *two years — a couple of years;* (2) (from שָׂפָה *a lip*) שְׂפָתַיִם *lips* (the upper and lower).

47. The Dual, in Hebrew, is *chiefly* used as a special Plural (if one may say so) for things 'double' or 'in pairs,'— as *scales-of-a-balance, tongs, ears, eyes, nostrils, hands, wings, feet,* etc. Such generally have no other form for the expression of 'more than one,' and we find therefore the *Dual* form with Numerals other than 'two;' as in *"four feet," "six wings," "seven eyes,"* — and so in [1 S. ii. 13] *"three teeth"* (lit., *a triad of the teeth,* Dual.).

48. Some Nouns that have a *Dual,* have a *Plural in another sense;* thus, (1) (from עַיִן *an eye,* also *a fountain*) עֵינַיִם (Du.) *eyes,* עֲיָנוֹת (Plu.) *fountains;* (2) (from רֶגֶל *a foot*) רַגְלַיִם (Du.) *feet,* רְגָלִים (Plu.) *times.*

---

* Only in the phrase דּוֹר דּוֹרִים, Is. li. 8; Ps. lxxii. 5, cii. 25.

49. But some few have both Dual and Plural forms ; as (1) יוֹם *a day*, Du., יוֹמַיִם, Plu., יָמִים ; (2) פַּעַם *one-time, once,* פַּעֲמַיִם *two-times, twice,* פְּעָמִים *times ;* (3) דֶּלֶת *a door,* דְּלָתוֹת,* דְּלָתַיִם. So, there are the Plurals שָׁנוֹת and שָׁנִים of (1) in § 46 (γ).

50. Some Nouns are used in the Singular only, as אָבָק *fine dust,* זָהָב *gold,* יָרֵחַ *moon ;* — others only in the Dual, as מֹאזְנַיִם *a balance, scales of a balance;* מַיִם *water;* מֶלְקָחַיִם *tongs,* שָׁמַיִם *heaven ;* — others only in the Plural, as אֲהָלִים and אֲהָלוֹת *aloes,* זְקֻנִים *old-age,* נְעוּרִים *youth,* פָּנִים *a face, front,* רַחֲמִים *compassion,* תַּחְתִּיּוֹת *lower-parts,* etc.

51. Hebrew Nouns are *Indeclinable* as regards what are usually called 'Cases.' But

52. Many Nouns undergo a modification of form† when they are 'IN CONSTRUCTION' (as it is called), *i. e.*, when they are in close *structural connection* with what follows. Thus, (1) from דָּבָר *a word* and מֶלֶךְ *a king*, we have דְּבַר מֶלֶךְ WORD OF *a king;* and, (2) from צְעָקָה *a cry*, and דַּל *a poor man* (in Pause דָּל), צַעֲקַת דָּל CRY OF *a poor man ;* etc., etc.

In these two examples the Genitive 'of'‡ is supplied in English *before the Second Noun*, but

N.B.—The occurrence of the 'Construct form' (as it is

---

* Some give this from דָּלֵת (i q. דֶּלֶת).

† Many others are unchanged in form when thus in 'Construction.'

‡ Since this 'of' (when it *can* be supplied) is, in Hebrew, involved in the *First* of the two Nouns (not the Second) we cannot say that the word so involving the 'of' is in the 'Genitive' Case. The Genitive Case of 'a word,' 'a cry,' is not 'word of,' 'cry of,' but 'of a word,' 'of a cry.' The difference of Idiom demands different nomenclature. Moreover, the 'Construct State' (or 'State of Construction') may occur where the 'of' *cannot* be supplied in English. Although there is 'Structural connection' where the Genitive 'of' occurs, it does not follow that the Genitive 'of' is always to be used (or *can be used*) wherever 'structural connection' thus modifies the form. This consideration will be found ·to be of importance hereafter.

called) must not be *limited* to the case in which 'of' can be supplied before the Second Noun.

53. The abbreviation 'i. c.' is used for 'In Construction' (§ 52).

Def.—The term '*Absolute*-form' is used of a word which is (1) *not* 'i. c.,' and (2) *without* any Affix or Prefix whatsoever.

54. The CHANGES OF FORM which some Nouns undergo, (1) when 'In Construction,' and (2) when increased in length by the addition of some termination or Affix, may to some extent be classed under these three heads:

I. The shortening of a Long-Vowel into a Short-Vowel;
II. The replacing of a Vowel by *Shva Moving;*
III.   „   „   „   *Shva Quiescent.*

The Second head will be found to be one of great importance.   But, observe,

55. A Vowel *cannot* be dropped and replaced by Shva Moving,

(α.) if followed by a letter having *Shva* (thus the $-$ in (1) מִשְׁפָּט, (2) שִׁפְחָה*),

(β.) if followed by Dagesh Forte, — which virtually involves a *Shva* [Pt. I. § 53], — (thus the $-$ in גַּנָּב),

(γ.) if followed by a letter which would have Dagesh Forte if it could,† (thus $-$ before ר in פָּרָשׁ, see § 60 (*)),

(δ.) if the Vowel be one which involves a Quiescent letter belonging to the word, Cp. Pt. I. § 36 Note, (thus the $-$ in תּוֹרָה *law*, the $-$ in נֵרוֹת *lamps*, etc.   This will be understood hereafter).

[NOTE —Generally, also, a vowel which *belongs to* a word (or form) is *not* dropped.   But *sometimes it is dropped*, as we shall see.]

---

* The *Plurals* of Nouns like (2) are from another form (§§ 66, 67).
† As, one of the five אהחער which do not receive Dagesh [Pt. I. § 49]

56. For words ' i. c.' the following rules may be given :—

(RULE i.) The Vowel NEXT BEFORE THE ACCENTED VOWEL is generally dropped and replaced by Shva-Moving—*if that Vowel can be so dropped* (§ 55);—as in קְצִיר *harvest of* from קָצִיר *harvest*, and עֲקֵב *heel of* from עָקֵב *a heel*. [Obs. The vowel to be dropped is the PENULTIMATE when the Accent of the word is on the last syllable]. Also

(A.) Monosyllables, and words *Mĭ-l'ră* [Pt. I. § 42],

(Rule ii.) Generally replace Long —, in a *closed** final syllable, by —; thus, (1) יַד *hand of* (from יָד *a hand*); (2) [עֵצִים] חָרַשׁ *an artificer-of* [*wood*], i.e. *a carpenter*, (from חָרָשׁ); (3) לְבַב *heart of* (from לֵבָב);

(Rule iii.) *Sometimes* replace — in a *closed** final syllable, by —; as in (1) בֶּן *son of* (from בֵּן);—more commonly by —, as in (2) זְקַן *an elder of* (from זָקֵן);†—and sometimes (especially in Monosyllables) retain the — unchanged, as in שֵׁם Gen. iv. 17, עֵקֶב Gen. xxv. 26;

(Rule iv.) Replace the ending ה— by ה—; thus, (1) מַעֲשֵׂה *work of* (from מַעֲשֶׂה *a work*); so (2) שְׂדֵה *field of* (from שָׂדֶה): except פִּי *mouth of*, from פֶּה *a mouth*,— רֵעֶה (as well as רֵעֶה) *friend of*, from רֵעֶה, and a few others.

(Rule v.). Replace the ending ה— by ת—; thus, (1) תּוֹרַת *law of* (from תּוֹרָה); (2) עֲדַת *company of* (from עֵדָה).

(Rule vi.) Retain a יַ— (except in the last syllable of the Plural), also a וֹ (or—), and a וּ, unchanged.‡

---

* Pt I. § 21.

† These two Examples (1) and (2) belong to *different* classes. See the Section on Nouns in Pt. II.

‡ There is sometimes, however, a change owing to the *removal of the accent* [Pt. I. § 55 (9, b.)] A word ' i. c.' (§ 53) is often *deprived of Tone-accent*, and joined to the following word by *Makkêph* (־) [Pt. I. § 37 (2)].

(B.) Of words *Mi-l'él*, i.e., whose *Penultimate* is their Tone-syllable [Pt. I. § 42],—

    (Rule vii.) Those of the form פָּעֵל, פָּעֶל, or פֶּעַל,— פֶּעֵל, or פֶּעֶל,— פֹּעֵל* or פֹּעַל† (*i.e.*, whose last two vowels are either ־ָ ־ֵ, ־ָ ־ֶ, or ־ַ ־ֶ, | ־ָ ־ֵ, or ־ַ ־ֵ|, ־ָ ־ֵ, or ־ַ ־ֵ), *undergo no change* when ' i. c.' (§ 53).

    (Rule viii.) Those of the forms (1) פָּוֶל, and (2) פַּיִל, are changed in the manner seen in the following words; (1) תּוֹךְ *midst of* (from תָּוֶךְ *midst*); and (2) עֵין *eye of* (from עַיִן *an eye*).

(C.) (Rule ix.) *Plurals* ending in ־ִים, and DUALS in ־ַיִם, always replace these endings by ־ֵי, when ' i. c.' § 53; thus, (1) שִׁירֵי *songs of* (from שִׁירִים *songs*); (2) כּוֹכְבֵי *stars of* (from כּוֹכָבִים); (3) עֵינֵי *eyes of* (from עֵינַיִם); (4) יְדֵי *hands of* (from יָדַיִם).

57. (α.) As seen in some of the Examples in § 56, and those in § 52, there may be *two* of the changes (above-mentioned) at once.

(β.) Example (2) in § 52 offers a means of introducing an important further change that is often necessitated by Rule i. (§ 56), as may be seen thus. The removal of the vowel ־ָ from the ע of צְעָקָה, and the replacing it by a *Moving Shva* [§ 56, Rule i.], *necessitates* some change that there *may not be two Moving Shvas* together (which *must not* ever be, Pt. I. § 22, Note *). The *first* of the two Shvas is, in such a case, always made to adopt a ' Slight-vowel ' form [Pt. I. § 56]. And, since a *Moving Shva* beneath ע takes a *Compound* form [Pt. I. § 24],

---

* But קֹשְׁטְ *truth* (according to the best opinions) Ps. lx. 6, has קֹשְׁטְ *truth of* Pr. xxii. 21 (which is merely a slightly shortened form).

† Thus we may introduce the use of פ for ' *First* Root-letter,' and ע and ל for ' *Second* ' and ' *Third* Root-letters ' respectively; thus, דָּבָר is said to be of the form פָּעָל, מֶלֶךְ of the form פֶּעֶל, etc. This will be fully explained by-and-by.

the particular *form* for the 'Slight-vowel' here, is determined by the following general Rule :—

N.B.—A *'Slight-vowel'* before a *Compound Shva* mostly *agrees with this latter in form.*

Here, the — beneath the ע in צְעָקָה being replaced by ⸗, the 'Slight-vowel' to be given (instead of the — beneath the צ) is ⸗; and so we obtain the form צַעֲקַת given in § 52 (the ה⸗ being changed into ת⸗, in accordance with Rule v. § 56).

(γ.) Similarly, from the Plural דְּבָרִים *words* § 39 (γ), we have the Construct form דִּבְרֵי. For, the removal of the Penultimate vowel (viz., the — beneath the בּ),—by Rule i. of § 56,— necessitates the appearance of a 'Slight-vowel' form for the — beneath the דּ, in order that there may not be two *Moving Shvas* together [Pt. I. §§ 22, Note(*), and 56].

[Obs. A — (*Short-Kherik*) may be considered as the common form for a 'Slight-vowel,' and as the form to be given when there is no reason for adopting some other Short-vowel. See also Pt. I. § 56, Note (†).]

58. The Classification of Nouns, for the changes of form which many of them undergo when receiving Affixed additions, is a somewhat long and difficult subject with which it is unadvisable to trouble the Student at present. Sufficient help will always be given in the Notes to the Exercises. The general subject must be dealt with elsewhere. There is, however, one application of § 54 (II.) which is of such very great importance for understanding vowel-changes in all parts of the Language that it ought to be mentioned at once, viz. :—

59. A word, when increased in length by the appendage of an additional syllable, generally drops (if it *can** drop) and replaces by *Shva Moving* that vowel which would else stand NEXT BUT ONE BEFORE, or THIRD† FROM THE ACCENTED VOWEL of the word.

---

* See § 55.

† [Reckoning from left to right, and from the Accented Vowel inclusively.] Obs —If this vowel cannot be dropped (§ 55), the preceding vowel is generally dropped,—if there be one, and if it can be dropped. Sometimes the succeeding one.

This will be more easily understood by an Example or two. Thus:—

(*α*.) דָּבָר *a word*, on receiving the appendage ־ִים as the mark of the Plural, drops the ־ָ beneath the ר and takes the form * דְּבָרִים (the ־ְ beneath the ר being reckoned *First*, the ־ָ beneath the ב is *Second*, and the ־ָ beneath the ר, if *not* dropped, would be *Third*). So, as may be seen in the Declension of this word with Pronoun-Affixes [Table IX.], the form for '*his word*' is דְּבָרוֹ (not דָּבָרוֹ, the ־ָ of the ר being dropped as said above). And so all through the Singular of Table IX.

(*β*.) The Hebrew forms for '*his words*,' '*her words*,' etc., are from דְּבָרִים *words;* and there is no vowel *Third* before the Accented vowel. But—

(*γ*.) When we come to the Hebrew for '*their (m.) words*,' the analogy of the preceding words might lead us to expect ־ָ under the ב. Here, however, the Accent being on the הֶם, the ־ָ (if it were to appear under the ב) would be '*Third*' (*before* the Accented vowel reckoned as *First*). It is therefore dropped, as above, and replaced by *Shva Moving*. But this necessitates the appearance of a 'Slight-vowel' instead of the *Moving Shva* beneath the ד [Pt. I. § 56]. And ־ִ is the form which it adopts [§ 57 Obs.].

(*δ*.) The same holds in the Hebrew forms for '*their (f.)*,' '*your (m.)*,' and '*your (f.) words*'† (and for the corresponding parts of Tables IV. and X. (1—6) But in the case of '*our words*,' the Accent of the word being on the syllable רֵי, the ־ָ of the ב is retained—it does not come under the Rule of § 59. Thus we have דְּבָרֵינוּ *our words*. Similarly for the corresponding forms in Tables IV. and X. (1—6).

---

* See § 39 (γ).

† The Pronoun-Affixes for 3 pl. m. and *f*, and 2 pl. m and *f.*, are by many called the '*Heavy* Affixes.' The Accent of the word is on these Affixes.

[To face p. 38.]

Summary of §§ 39–59

(α) The mark for MASC. PLU. is םִ‎ָ‎ ; and

(β) this םִ‎ָ‎ is replaced by יָ‎ 'in Construction.'

(γ) The mark for the FEM. SING. is הָ‎ ; and

(δ) this הָ‎ is replaced by תַ‎ in 'Construction.'

(ε) The mark for the FEM. PLU. is תוֹ‎ or תָ‎ ; and

(ζ) this termination is *unchanged* 'in Construction.'

(η) The mark for the DUAL is םִ‎ַ‎ ; and

(θ) this םִ‎ַ‎ is replaced by יַ‎ 'in Construction.'

(ι) For changes of form of Nouns 'i.c.' see §§ 56 & 57.

(κ) For a GREAT RULE of ordinary change of form, see § 59.

[To face p 89]

INDEX FOR NOUNS WITH PRON.-AFFS.

(*a*) For Nouns which do not change, see Tab. V.

(β) For Nouns ending in הָ־ which change *only the ending*, see Tab. VI.

(γ) For Nouns like דָּבָר which drop the penult. ־ָ, see Tab. IX.

(δ) For Nouns like (A) פָּעֵל & פָּעִיל, (B) פּוֹעֵל (& מִפְעָל) & פּוֹעֵל, (c) פֶּעֱלָה & פַּעֲלָה, see App˟ (A), (B), & (C) to Tab. IX.

(ε) For Nouns in ־ ־, or ־ ־, or ־ ־, or in ־ ־, or ־ ־, see Tab. X.

(ζ) For Nouns in ־ ־, or ־ ־, see Tab. XI.

(η) For Nouns (*fem.*) corresponding to those (*masc.*) in Tabs. X & XI, see Tab. XII; (cp. §§ 66–69).

(θ) For (1) אָב, (2) אָח, (3) בַּיִת, (4) בֵּן, (5) בַּת, (6) פֶּה, see Tab. XIII.

(ι) For Nouns in הָ־, see p. 44.

[Note.—(i) For אֶת (or אֵת) mark of the '*Definite* Object,' see p. 43 (*e–h*).

(ii) For some words before which the 'Def. Art.' הַ must NOT be placed, see § 73.]

60. Some Nouns with $\neg\,\neg$, as שָׁרָשׁ* for example, are *not* of the same form as דָּבָר, and must not be declined like it— as they *do not drop* the $\neg$ of their first letter† [See § 55].

61. (α.) The Declensions of Table X. (1—6) are all the same in character. Such a word as מֶלֶךְ Table X. (1), and נֵדֶר Table X. (2), is said to be of '6-point' form,—and נֶדֶר Table X. (2) of '5-point' form.‡

(β.) The $\neg$ of נֶגַע, and the $\neg\,\neg$ of נַעַר [Table X. (4 and 5)], are because of the guttural letter ע. So the $\neg$ in זֶבַח *a sacrifice*, and the $\neg\,\neg$ in לַחַץ *oppression*, because of ח. [But we *may have* two Segols, though the word has a guttural,— as in לֶחֶם *bread*, etc.]

(γ.) So שׂבַע *fulness*, רֹחַב *breadth*, are of the same Declension as אֹרֶךְ *length* [Table XI.]: the $\neg$ replacing $\neg$ because of the guttural letter.

N.B.—All words like the Nouns in Tables X., XI., have their Accent on the *penultimate*, in the 'Absolute' Singular.

62. The 'DECLENSION-VOWEL' (as it may be called) is seen to be (i.) $\neg$ for the '6-point' Noun in Table X (1), and (ii.) $\neg$ for the '6-point' (as also for the '5-point') Noun in Table X (2). (iii.) Some words, as נֵגֶר, חֵלֶק (for instance), have $\neg$ for their 'Declension-vowel'; thus נֶגְרוֹ, נֶגְרְךָ, נֶגְרִי, etc., חֶלְקִי, חֶלְקָהּ, חֶלְקוֹ, etc. The terms

'*ă*-Decl.' '*ĕ*-Decl.' '*ĭ*-Decl.'

will be found useful as a means of designating these Declensions [viz., those of (i.) (iii) (ii.), respectively]. Similarly the Declension of Table XI. (in which the $\neg$ is *ŏ*) may be called an '*ŏ*-Decl.'

---

* This is really of the form נֶבַּ; but as the five letters אהחער do not receive Dagesh, the $\neg$ is put under the פ to 'Compensate for the Dagesh' which belongs to the ר.

†. Any of these that may occur will be duly mentioned, so that no practical difficulty will arise therefrom.

‡ The *actual* terms in use (in Rabbinic works on Grammar) are '*Nouns of* 6 *points*,' '*Nouns of* 5 *points*,'— the *dots* in the $\neg\,\neg$ and the $\neg\,\neg$ being counted.

63. The following shew the Declensions of—

(α.) (1) דְּבַשׁ [p. : דַּבְּשִׁי] honey, דְּבְשִׁי my…;

     (2) שְׁכֶם [p. : שִׁכְם] a shoulder, שִׁכְמֶךָ, שִׁכְמוֹ, etc. ;

(β.) (1) פְּרִי [p. : פֶּרְי] fruit, פִּרְיוֹ, פִּרְיִי, etc., [פָּרְיְךָ, פֶּרְיְכֶם], פְּרְיָם · and פֶּרְיְהֶם;

     (2) לְחִי [p. : לֶחְי] a jaw, לֶחְיוֹ, Du. לְחָיַם, רֶיַח, רְיֶיךָ, רֶחָיָו לְחָיָו, [לְחֵיהֶם their (m)];

     (3) עֲדִי [p. : עֶדְי] an ornament, עֶדְיוֹ, Plu. עֲדָיִים ;

     (4) חֲצִי [p. : חֶצְי] a half, חֶצְיוֹ, etc ;

(γ.) (1) חֳלִי [p. : חֶלְי] sickness, חֶלְיוֹ, etc , Plu. חֳלָיִים;

     (2) עֳנִי [p. : עֶנְי] affliction, עֶנְיוֹ, etc.

(δ.) From כְּלִי [p. : כֶּלְי] a vessel, etc., כֶּלְיךָ thy (m.)…, the Plural is כֵּלִים [‘i. c.’ כְּלָי, כְּלֵי], כֵּלָיו…, כְּלֵיהֶם;

     64. In § 63, the ‘Construct’ Singular is the same as the ‘Absolute.’

65. The ‘Slight-vowel’ for the ‘Construct State’ of the Plural (§ 57, γ.), and for the *Plural* Noun with the Affixes for the 3 & 2 pl. (*m.*) & (*f.*) (§ 59 γ, δ), is the same generally as the ‘Declension-vowel’ of the Noun. Thus the — in מַלְכִי, the — in חֶלְקֵיהֶם, the — in נִגְעֵי, נְדָרֵיכֶם, etc. See Table X.

66. The Feminine Noun in Table XII. 1, corresponds with the Masculine Noun in Table X. 1; and so the Feminines in Table XII. 2, 3, with the Masculines in X. 2, 5. This observation is important as helping to understand the formation of the Feminine Plurals. Thus, from מֶלֶךְ a *king*, and מַלְכָּה a *queen* (the latter agreeing in form with the *Declension-forms of the Singular* in Table X. 1), we have the kindred Plurals מְלָכִים *kings*, מְלָכוֹת *queens*. So from כֶּבֶשׂ a *lamb* (*m.*), כִּבְשָׂה [and כַּבְשָׂה] a *lamb* (*f.*), we have the Plurals כְּבָשִׂים, (*m.*), כְּבָשׂוֹת (*f.*).

67. Feminine Nouns of this class that have no corresponding *Masculine* kindred-form follow (as might be expected) the law of those that have. Thus, from שִׁפְחָה a *woman-servant*, we have the Plural שְׁפָחוֹת (formed after the analogy of an imaginary *Masculine* Plural שְׁפָחִים from the imaginary Singular שֶׁפַח).

68. Similarly there are some Feminine Nouns (with the ending הַ‑) corresponding to Masculines of the form אֶרֶךְ. Thus עֶצֶם *might* (m.) and עָצְמָה* *might* (f.), the latter agreeing in form with the *Decl.-forms of the Singular* in Tab. XI. And so חֹרֶב *drought, aridity, desolation,* חָרְבָּה† *desolation.* The Plural of this latter is חֳרָבוֹת, the Feminine form analogous to an *imaginary* Masculine חֳרָבִים.

69. (α.) The *Declension* of שִׁפְחָה with Pron. Aff. is the same as that of מַלְכָּה in Tab. XII. 1, with ‑ instead of the ‑ under the first letter there; thus—

$$\text{my}\begin{cases}\text{שִׁפְחָתִי}\\\text{שִׁפְחֹתַי}\end{cases}\Bigg|,\ \text{thy }(m.)\begin{cases}\text{שִׁפְחָתְךָ}\\\text{שִׁפְחֹתֶיךָ}\end{cases}\Bigg|,\ \text{his}\begin{cases}\text{שִׁפְחָתוֹ}—[\textit{woman servant}].\\\text{שִׁפְחֹתָיו}—[\textit{woman-servants}].\end{cases}$$
$$\qquad\text{etc.}\qquad\qquad\qquad\text{etc.}\qquad\qquad\qquad\text{etc.}$$

(β.) The Declension of a word of the foim חָרְבָּה with Pron. Affixes is of corresponding form, but with ‑ (ŏ, *K. Kh.*) instead of the ‑ under the מ in Table XII. 1; thus from חָכְמָה *wisdom,* we have

חָכְמָתִי *my wisdom,* חָכְמָתְךָ, *thy* (m.)..., חָכְמָתוֹ *his...*; and from חֳרָבוֹת *desolations* (i. c. חָרְבֹתָיו — (חָרְבוֹת), חָרְבֹתֶיהָ *his..,* *her..,* חָרְבֹתַיִךְ *thy* (f.).., חָרְבֹתֵיהֶם *their* (m)...

70. Besides the *accented* ending הָ‑ of § 40, there is an ending הַ‑ *unaccented* which is not a mark of Feminine Gender, but merely gives a varying equivalent form for some words; thus לֵיל and לַיְלָה *night,* and so הַמָּוְתָה Ps. cxvi. 15 (=הַמָּוֶת).

N.B.—Sometimes the *Declension-form* of the Noun is used in this case, as אַרְצָה *land of,* Is. viii. 23 (=אֶרֶץ‡), and אָרְצָה *earth* (Pause form) Job xxxiv. 13, and xxxvii. 12.

---

* The ‑ under the ע is ŏ, *K. Kh.*
† The ‑ under the ח ıs seen to be ŏ, *K. Kh.* by Pt. I. § 55 (5 and 10 *a.*).
‡ A Noun of ă-Decl., § 62.

71. (i.) There is another *unaccented ending* הָ— which is of frequent occurrence, signifying *to, towards, into ;* thus חֶבְרוֹן *Hebron,* חֶבְרֹנָה *to Hebron,* — צָפוֹן *north,* צָפֹנָה *northwards ;* — קֶדֶם *east,* קֵדְמָה *eastwards.*

(ii.) This הָ— *to, towards, into* may be attached to—

    (α.) a Noun having the definite ה; thus, הַבַּיִת *the house,* הַבַּיְתָה *into the house,* and

    (β.) a Noun in the State of Construction; thus, בֵּית *house of,* בֵּיתָה פַּרְעֹה *into-[the]-house-of Pharaoh.*

(iii.) Sometimes the *Declension-form* of the Noun is adopted for this, as אַרְצָה* *earth-wards* (אֶרֶץ) (p. ‡) ; and so נֶגֶב [of *ĕ*-Decl.] *south,* נֶגְבָּה *southwards ;* etc.

72. N.B.—There being no 'Genitive,' 'Dative,' 'Accusative' or 'Ablative' Cases in Hebrew,—the 'of,' 'to,' 'from,' etc., are expressed by other means :—

(*a.*) The ordinary 'of' — of connection—is expressed by the 'State of Construction,'† § 52 ;

(*b.*) The 'to,' — of relation,—is expressed by the prefix לְ of § 4 ;

(*c.*) 'From' is expressed by the prefix מִ of § 5, or by the full Preposition מִן ;

(*d.*) The context alone can determine when an *Indefinite* Noun is used *Objectively,* as the word *man* twice in " and he SAW A MAN, an Egyptian, SMITING A MAN, a Hebrew " [Ex. ii. 11], where the word אִישׁ *a man* has nothing to mark it as 'Objective'; but

(*e.*) The Particle אֵת (or אֶת־) is a mark of the '*Definite*

---

* Also *to* or *towards land-of,* frequently; [from אֶרֶץ, p. 41 ‡]. Obs. The context alone can decide, sometimes, between the ה of §§ 70 and 71.

† The 'of' = *from, out of,* is expressed by the Prefix מִ of § 5, or by מִן. [Ju. xiii. 2, 1 S. i. 1, etc.].

Object'; thus in "and he SMOTE THE EGYPTIAN" [Ex. ii. 12] we have אֶת־הַמִּצְרִי *the Egyptian* (*Accus.*, or 'Objective'). So in "God created [אֵת הַשָּׁמַיִם] *the heavens,* [וְאֵת הָאָרֶץ] *and the earth*" [Gen. i. 1], we have אֵת before "THE *heavens*" and before "THE *earth*," marking them as 'Objective.'

(*f.*) This *mark* of the 'Definite Object' is not always expressed, and then the context alone can determine whether the Definite Noun is 'Objective' or not; thus, "And they spoiled [הָעִיר] *the city*" [Gen. xxxiv. 27].

(*g.*) This אֵת (or אֶת־) may stand before a *Definite* 'Objective' word — (i.) which has the 'Definite Article' [§ 6];— (ii.) the 'Proper Name' of a *person* or *place*, as *Noah, Job, Ruth, Athaliah, Makkeda, Babylon,* etc.; — (iii.) in Construction, as in "and he took [אֶת־זִקְנִי] [*the*] *elders of* the city,..... and he taught [אֵת אַנְשֵׁי] [*the*] *men of* Succoth" [Jud. viii. 16]; — (iv.) having a *Pron. Affix* attached to it, as in "they took [אֶת־צֹאנָם] *their flock,*" etc. [Gen. xxxiv. 28].

(*h.*) This אֵת (or אֶת־) may also stand before אֲשֶׁר used Objectively for '*that which*' or '*him, thee, them* (etc.), *who*'*, and in a few other cases to be mentioned elsewhere.

73. Obs.—The ה for the 'Def. Art.' must never be placed before

    (1) a Noun 'i. c.', †
    (2) a Noun with a 'Pron. Aff.', †
    (3) אֲשֶׁר *who, whom,* or *which ;*

[Note.—Nor before Proper Names, as a Rule. There are some exceptions (to be mentioned elsewhere), especially the names of some Places and Rivers.

---

* Thus, "[וְאֵת אֲשֶׁר] *and that which* [*was*] in the city, [וְאֶת־אֲשֶׁר] *and that —which* [*was*] in the field, they took" [Gen. xxxiv. 28].

† A few instances may be cited to the contrary (which must be mentioned elsewhere),—but this great Rule of § 73 MUST ALWAYS BE OBSERVED in Composition.

74. More must be said on the Nouns elsewhere [Pt. II.], but the following Notes may be added here.

Note (*a.*) It need scarcely be said that a Noun,—such as רוּחַ *spirit,* for instance,—having *Furtive-Pathakh* to its last letter, must drop the *Furtive-Pathakh* on receiving any Affix;—thus, רוּחוֹת (Plu.), and so רוּחוֹ *his spirit,* רוּחִי *my...,* etc.

(*b.*) Nouns ending in הֶ drop the ה on receiving Affixes; thus from שָׂדֶה *a field* (i. c. שְׂדֵה) the Declension is—

my שָׂדִי	thy	(*m.*) שָׂדְךָ	his	שָׂדֵהוּ	field.
		(*f.*) שָׂדֵךְ	her	שָׂדֶהָ	

Nouns ending in הֶ generally take the Affix form ֵהוּ for 'his,' as in שָׂדֵהוּ *his field,* מַעֲשֵׂהוּ, *his work.*

[The Plural שָׂדִים of this Noun does not occur, but the Construct form שְׂדֵי occurs. The usual Plural is שָׂדוֹת *fields* (i. c. שְׂדוֹת), with Affixes שְׂדֹתֵיהֶם, שְׂדֹתֵינוּ, etc.]

From מַעֲשֶׂה *a work* (i. c. מַעֲשֵׂה), Plu. מַעֲשִׂים (i. c. מַעֲשֵׂי), we have the Plural Declension—

my מַעֲשַׂי	thy	(*m.*) מַעֲשֶׂיךָ	his	מַעֲשָׂיו	מַעֲשִׂים
		(*f.*) מַעֲשַׂיִךְ	her	מַעֲשֶׂיהָ	works.
our מַעֲשֵׂינוּ	your	(*m.*) מַעֲשֵׂיכֶם	their	(*m.*) מַעֲשֵׂיהֶם	(i. c. מַעֲשֵׂי)
		(*f.*) מַעֲשֵׂיכֶן		(*f.*) מַעֲשֵׂיהֶן	

(*c.*) Besides the ending הֶ, for the Feminine, there are some others (to be mentioned elsewhere). The most important, perhaps, of these is the ending תֶ (p. : תֶ), as in עֹפֶרֶת *lead* (the ת being part of the ending).

(*d.*) This remark (*c.*) will be found to be of great use hereafter when we shall have to give the *forms of Participles.* These have simple Noun-forms, and for the Feminine Singular they have the ending תֶ as well as הֶ; thus, from אָמֵר *one* (*m.*) *saying,* we have both אָמְרָה and אָמֶרֶת *one* (*f.*) *saying.*

(*e.*) Some Nouns have both endings, viz., הָ ֵ and ת ֶ ֶ ; thus, (1) from גְּבִיר *a lord,* we have both גְּבִירָה and גְּבֶרֶת *a lady, a mistress.* So we have (2) both תִּפְאָרָה and תִּפְאֶרֶת *beauty, glory;* etc.

(*f.*) The 'Singular' Declension (including the 'Construct State') of such Nouns as those in (*e.*) is, generally, only that of the ת ֶ ֶ form; thus we have גְּבֶרֶת (the 'Construct' form), and גְּבִרְתָּהּ, גְּבִרְתִּי, etc. (Cp. Tab. X. (2)), and so תִּפְאֶרֶת (the 'Construct' form), and תִּפְאַרְתִּי, תִּפְאַרְתְּךָ, תִּפְאַרְתּוֹ, etc. (Cp. Tab. X. (1)), — גְּבִירָה and תִּפְאָרָה are Indeclinable.

(*g.*) This is so even in certain Nouns of which the 'Absolute' form in ת ֶ ֶ does not occur, as מַמְלָכָה *a kingdom,* מֶמְשָׁלָה *dominion,* מֶרְכָּבָה *a chariot.* Of these the 'Construct' forms are מֶרְכֶּבֶת, מֶמְשֶׁלֶת, מַמְלֶכֶת, respectively, and the Declension-forms are מֶרְכַּבְתּוֹ, מֶמְשַׁלְתּוֹ, מַמְלַכְתּוֹ, etc.

(*h.*) The Plurals of such Nouns are from the הָ ֵ form; thus, from מִלְחָמָה and מִלְחֶמֶת *war, battle* (of which the Declension is of the form of מִלְחַמְתּוֹ), the only Plural is מִלְחָמוֹת.

(*i.*) No separate *Table* is needed for Nouns ending in הָ ֵ which drop the Penult. vowel of their Absolute form; thus, עֵדָה * *an assembly,* i. e. עֲדַת (§ 56, i.), w. affs. עֲדָתִי, עֲדָתְךָ, etc.

(*k.*) Table XIII. (1—6) gives the Declensions of some *special* Nouns, viz.,—

[1] אָב *a father,* [2] אָח *a brother,* [3] בַּיִת *a house,* [4] בֵּן *a son,* [5] בַּת *a daughter,* [6] פֶּה *a mouth.*

(*l.*) The Noun אִישׁ *a man* (also *each-one,* etc.) is declined

---

* Obs.—עֵדָה *a testimony,* RETAINS its ֵ .

in the Singular like שִׁיר [Tab. V.]. The Plural אִישִׁים *is* used, but *not generally*. The ordinary word for '*men*' is אֲנָשִׁים, which is declined like עֲבָדִים [Tab. X. (6)].

(*m.*) The Noun אִשָּׁה *a woman, a wife*, is not declined. But there is a Declension of the corresponding Noun אֵשֶׁת (which occurs in the '*Absolute*,' Deut. xxi. 11, 1 S. xxviii. 7, Ps. lviii. 9, and frequently '*i. c.*'). This is declined אֶשְׁתִּי, אִשְׁתּוֹ, אִשְׁתְּךָ, etc., like נֵדֶר [Tab. X. (2)] — as if it were an ordinary '5-point' Noun (§ 62), — but *only in the Singular*. For the Plural '*women*' or '*wives*' the word is נָשִׁים (i. c. נְשֵׁי) which is declined thus,—.

<table>
<tr><td>my</td><td>נָשַׁי</td><td>thy (m.)</td><td>נָשֶׁיךָ</td><td>his</td><td rowspan="2">נָשָׁיו
נְשֵׁיהֶם</td><td rowspan="2">} wives.</td></tr>
<tr><td>our</td><td>נָשֵׁינוּ</td><td>your (m.)</td><td>נְשֵׁיכֶם</td><td>their (m.)</td></tr>
</table>

(*n.*) The Vocative 'O!' is sometimes marked by the Prefix הַ followed by Dagesh Forte, the same as for the 'Def. Art.' (§ 6); thus, [1 S. xvii 55] "As thy soul liveth [הַמֶּלֶךְ] *O king!*", [1 S. xxii. 20] "According to all the desire of thy soul [הַמֶּלֶךְ] *O king!*", etc.

(*o.*) The Rules of § 6 (*b.*), (*c.*), etc., apply to this Prefix הַ for the Vocative 'O!', as well as to that for the 'Def. Art.'; thus in [Is. xlii 18] [הַחֵרְשִׁים] — "*O deaf men*, hear ye!, and [הָעִוְרִים] *O blind men*, look ye!—that ye may see," etc.

(*p.*) This הַ for the Vocative 'O!' may stand before a word 'i. c.' (§ 53); thus [Lament. ii. 13] "What-thing shall I liken to thee [הַבַּת] *O daughter-of Jerusalem!*" etc.

(*q*) In Table V. (i) the words שִׁירָם and שִׁירָן may be considered to be contracted from שִׁירָהֶם and שִׁירָהֶן. With these latter the Plural words שִׁירֵיהֶם and שִׁירֵיהֶן in Tab. V. (ii.) correspond, as שִׁירֵיכֶם and שִׁירֵיכֶן (*your m.*, and *your f.* SONGS) in Tab. V. (ii.) correspond with שִׁירְכֶם and שִׁירְכֶן (*your m.*, and *your f.*, SONG) in Tab. V. (i.). This being so, the analogy between the Affix-forms in Tab. V. (i.) and those in Tab. V. (ii.) — *i. e.*, for the Sing. and the Plu. Noun respectively, — is seen to be complete.

(*r.*) Similarly in Tab. VI. (i), the words תּוֹרָתָם and תּוֹרָתָן may be considered to be contracted from תּוֹרָתָהֶם and תּוֹרָתָהֶן.

(*s*) The ־ֶ before the Affixes כֶם־ and כֶן־ in the Tables is, of course, Shva *Moving*, because there is no Dagesh Lene in the כ, — Pt. I. § 55 (4).

(*t.*) N.B. There is ־ֵ before the כֶם־ and the כֶן־ instead of ־ֶ in the corresponding places of the other words in these Tables (and ־ְ in יֶדְכֶם *your (m) hand*, from יָד *a hand*, w. Affixes יָדוֹ *his*., etc.). Owing to the *stress* and *emphasis* on these Affixes, the earlier parts of the words having them are shortened as much as possible. The *Short-vowel* followed by the Shva *Moving* admits of *rapid* moving

on to the final syllable, on which the stress and emphasis is laid.   There could
not be *Shva* in the place of this Short vowel, because of the Shva following it.

So, too, in the תּוֹרַתְתְֶם and תּוֹרתתֶן, from which תּוֹרָתָם and תּוֹרָתָן may be
considered to be contracted, Tab. VI. (i), and in דְּבָרהֶם and דְּבָרהֶן, from which
דְּבָרם and דְּבָרָן may be considered to be contracted, Tab. IX. (i.).

(*u*) There is a not unfrequent contraction of the forms תּורוֹתֵיהֶם and תּורוֹתֵיהָן
into תּורוֹתָם and תּורוֹתָן.   This is for the sake of shortness.

(*w.*) The form שֹׁפֵט is 'i. c.' the same (*viz.* שֹׁפֵט),—Plu. שֹׁפְטִים (i. c. שֹׁפְטֵי).

EXERCISE XIII.

(*To be translated into English.*)

יְיָ + מַלְכֵּנוּ² : *יְמֵי³ ‡שְׁנוֹתֵינוּ⁴ : מַלְכֵי² הָאָרָצוֹת⁵ : ‡עֲדַת⁶

אַבִּירִים⁷ : *בְּאֵרֹת⁸ חֵמָר⁹ : צִיּוֹן¹⁰ אַל¹¹ יְרָפּוּ¹² יָדֶיךָ¹³ : ‡כַּנְפֵי¹⁴

יוֹנָה¹⁵ : דְּבָרַי¹⁶ פִּי¹⁷ חָכָם¹⁸ : נֵר¹⁹ לְרַגְלִי²⁰ + דְּבָרֶךָ¹⁶ וְאוֹר²¹

לִנְתִיבָתִי²² : נְדָבוֹת²³ פִּי¹⁷ רְצֵה²⁴ נָא²⁵ יְיָ וּמִשְׁפָּטֶיךָ²⁶ לַמְּדֵנִי²⁷ :

לְמִצְוֺתֶיךָ²⁸ יָאַבְתִּי²⁹ : חִשַּׁבְתִּי³⁰ דְרָכָי³¹ וָאָשִׁיבָה³² רַגְלַי²⁰ אֶל³³

עֵדֹתֶיךָ³⁴ : בַּקְּשׁוּ³⁵ אֶת³⁶ יְיָ³⁶ כָּל³⁷ עַנְוֵי³⁸ הָאָרֶץ⁵ כִּי³⁹

בַּעֲוֺנָם⁴⁰ גָּלוּ⁴¹ : וְיָדְעוּ⁴² עֲבוֹדָתִי⁴³ וַעֲבוֹדַת⁴³ מַמְלְכוֹת⁴⁴ הָאָרָצוֹת⁵ :

יֵבֹשׁוּ⁴⁵ כָּל³⁷ עֹבְדֵי⁴⁶ פָּסֶל⁴⁷ : מַעֲשֵׂה⁴⁸ יְדֵי¹³ חָרָשׁ⁴⁹ : מַעֲשֵׂיהֶם⁴⁸ +

מַעֲשַׂי⁴⁸ אָוֶן⁵⁰ : קֶבֶר⁵¹ פָּתוּחַ⁵² + גְּרֹנָם⁵³ : שְׂפָתַי⁵⁴ חֲלָקוֹת⁵⁵ :

1 See p. 385.   2 Table X. (1).   3 יָמִים days.   4 שָׁנָה year.   5 אֶרֶץ earth,
a land, a country   (see page 25 (Note 4), — Plu. אֲרָצוֹת).   6 עֵדָה a company.
7 אַבִּיר a strong one.   8 בְּאֵרוֹת pits.   9 slime.   10 Zion.   11 not.   12 let them
be slack.   13 יָד a hand (Dual יָדַיִם).   14 כָּנָף a wing (Dual כְּנָפַיִם).   15 a dove.
16 Tab IX.   17 Tab. XIII (6)   18 a wise man.   19 a lamp.   20 רֶגֶל a foot (Dual
רַגְלַיִם).   21 and light.   22 נְתִיבָה a path.   23 נְדָבָה a free-will offering.   24 be
pleased with, accept.   25 I pray.   26 מִשְׁפָּט a judgment.   27 teach Thou me.
28 מִצְוָה a commandment.   29 I have longed, had a great desire   30 I thought
on.   31 דֶּרֶךְ a way.   32 and I made to return.   33 to.   34 עֵדָה a testimony
(the ◌ of this word cannot be dropped).   35 Seek ye.   36 See Exerc. IX. Note 15.
37 כֹּל all (כָּל when unaccented).   38 עָנָו a meek one.   39 for, because.   40 עָוֺן
iniquity.   41 they have gone into captivity.   42 and they shall know.   43 עֲבוֹדָה
service.   44 מַמְלָכָה a kingdom.   45 they shall be ashamed   46 עֹבֵד a worshipper.
47 a graven image.   48 מַעֲשֶׂה a work.   49 a workman, smith.   50 nothingness.
51 a grave, sepulchre.   52 opened.   53 גָּרוֹן a throat.   54 שְׂפָתַיִם lips.   55 smooth-

* § 56 (i. & ix).   † § 59.   ‡ § 74 (i).   § § 56 (ix, 4).

וְהַיָּדַיִם[13] יְדֵי[13] עֵשָׂו[56] : אַל[11] תֶּאֱסֹף[57] עִם[58] הַחַטָּאִים[59] נַפְשִׁי[60]

וְעִם[58] אַנְשֵׁי[61] דָמִים[62] חַיָּי[63] : אֲשֶׁר[13] בִּידֵיהֶם[13] + זִמָּה[64] : אֲשֶׁר

פִּיהֶם[17] דִּבֶּר[65] שָׁוְא[66] : יְיָ[1] הַט[67] שָׁמֶיךָ[68] וְתֵרֵד[69] : שְׁלַח[70]

אוֹרְךָ[71] וַאֲמִתְּךָ[72] , הֵמָּה יַנְחוּנִי[73] : וּפְדוּיֵי[74] יְיָ[1] יְשׁוּבוּן[75] :

וְרִחַמְתִּי[76] כָּל[37] בֵּית[77] יִשְׂרָאֵל[78] וְקִנֵּאתִי[79] לְשֵׁם[80] קָדְשִׁי[81] :

וְקִבַּצְתִּי[82] אֹתָם[83] מֵאַרְצוֹת[5] אֹיְבֵיהֶם[84] : צַדִּיק[85] + יְיָ[1] בְּכָל[37]

דְּרָכָיו[81] וְחָסִיד[86] בְּכָל[37] מַעֲשָׂיו[48] : עֵינֵי[87] כֹל[37] אֵלֶיךָ[88] יְשַׂבֵּרוּ[89]

וְאַתָּה + נוֹתֵן[90] לָהֶם אֶת[85] אָכְלָם[91] בְּעִתּוֹ[92] :

ness, flattery. 56 Esau. 57 (with the preceding word) *do not gather.* 58 עִם with. 59 sinners. 60 נֶפֶשׁ a soul. 61 § 74 Note (*l.*). 62 blood. 63 חַיִּים life (a Plural form). 64 wickedness. 65 hath spoken. 66 vanity. 67 incline Thou. 68 שָׁמַיִם heavens (Dual form). 69 and mayest Thou come down. 70 send forth. 71 אוֹר light. 72 אֱמֶת truth (with aff. אֲמִתּוֹ *his.*, etc.). 73 shall guide me. 74 פָּדוּי a ransomed one. 75 shall return. 76 and I will have mercy upon. 77 See Tab. XIII (3). 78 Israel. 79 and I will be jealous. 80 שֵׁם a name, (the same 'i.c.'). Obs. 'The-*Name-of-My-holiness*' here = *My Holy Name.* 81 קֹדֶשׁ holiness. 82 And I will collect. 83 Tab. III. (1). 84 אֹיֵב an enemy. 85 Righteous. 86 and Gracious. 87 עַיִן an eye (Dual עֵינַיִם). 88 Tab. IV. (1). 89 look with hope. 90 giving. 91 אֹכֶל food. 92 in its season.

EXERCISE XIV.

(*To be translated into Hebrew.*)

*** For the plan of the Exercise see § 11 (ζ—μ).

According-to[1] the word[2] of Elijah.[3] The man[4] with-whom-is-My-word (Hebr., *who My word[2] with[5] him*). And-I-will-put[6] My words[2] in his mouth.[7] The words[2] of wise-men[8] and their riddles.[9] As[1] the flesh[10] of our brethren[11] [is] our flesh.[10] Thy (*m.*) bone[12] and thy flesh[10] [are] we. Your (*m.*) bone[12] and your flesh[10] [am] I. And-as-for-me

1 בְּ the Prefix. 2 דָּבָר a word. 3 אֵלִיָּהוּ. 4 אִישׁ. 5 אֵת Tab. III 2. 6 וְנָתַתִּי. 7 Tab. XIII. 6. 8 חָכָם (*s.*). 9 חִידָה (*s.*). 10 בָּשָׂר Tab. IX. 11 Tab. XIII. 2. 12 עֶצֶם

(Hebr., *and I*) my prayer [13] [is] to your (*m.*) God [14] according-
to [1] your words. [2] For [15] great-is-His-Mercy-towards-us (Hebr.,
mighty-hath-been [16] *over* [17] *us His Mercy* [18]). Thy (*m.*) Countenance [19] make-Thou-to-shine [20] upon [21] Thy servant. [22] Many [23]
[are] my persecutors [24] and my enemies. [25] Let-my-supplication-
come-before-Thee (Hebr., *let-come* [26] *my supplication* [27] *to Thy
Presence* [19]). I-will-extol-thee, [28] my God, [14] O * King [29]; and-
I-will-bless [30] Thy Name [31] for-ever-and-ever. [32] His praise [33]
shall-speak [34] [viz.] my mouth [7]; and-shall-bless [35] [viz.] all-
flesh [36] His-Holy-Name (Hebr., *the Name* [31] *of His Holiness* [37])
for-ever-and-ever. [32]

Tab. X. (1). 13 תְּפִלָּה. 14 אֱלֹהִים (a Noun of Plural form). 15 פִּי. 16 גְּבַר.
17 עַל. 18 חָסַר Tab. X. (1). 19 פָּנִים (a Noun of Plural form). 20 הָאֵר. 21 בְּ
the Prefix of § 4. 22 עֶבֶד Tab. X. (1). 23 רַבִּים. 24 רֹדְפִים. 25 צָר (*s.*).
26 תָּבוֹא. 27 תְּחִנָה. 28 אֲרוֹמִמְךָ. 29 מֶלֶךְ. 30 וַאֲבָרְכָה. 31 שֵׁם (i. c. the same),
with affix שְׁמוֹ *his...*, etc. † 32 וָעֶד לְעוֹלָם. 33 תְּהִלָּה. 34 יְדַבֶּר. 35 וִיבָרֵךְ.
36 כָּל־בָּשָׂר. 37 קֹדֶשׁ, Tab. XI. 1.——— * See § 74 (*n*).

† See Tab. XIII, Note (§, *a*).

SECTION VIII.

Nouns-Adjective.

75. There being no 'Cases' in Hebrew, — and no Gender-forms for other than *Masculine* and *Feminine*, — we have only *four* forms to consider, viz., those for the Masculine and the Feminine in (1) the Singular, and (2) the Plural.*

N.B.—Adjectives should agree with their Substantives in Gender and Number.

76. The forms referred to in § 75 are the usual Noun-forms, — having the termination ‎ים‎ְ‎ for the Masc. Plural (§ 39. β—δ), and ‎ה‎ָ‎ for the Fem. Sing. (§ 40), and ‎ות‎ָ‎ (or ‎ת‎ָ‎) for the Fem. Plu. (§ 41). Thus, for instance,

(iv.)		(iii.)		(ii.)		(i.)	
fem.	masc.	fem.	masc.	fem.	masc.	fem.	masc.
יָפָה ,	יָפֶה	‡§ קְטַנָּה	קָטֹן .	‡† גְּדֹלָה	גָּדוֹל ,	טוֹבָה	טוֹב , Sing.
יָפוֹת ,	יָפִים	§‡ קְטַנּוֹת . §‡	קְטַנִּים	‡† גְּדֹלוֹת ‡†	נְדֹלִים	† טֹבוֹת .	טוֹבִים Plu.
beautiful.		*little.*		*great.*		*good.*	

77. Adjectives may be used 'i. c.'; thus, [Dan. i. 4] " Children...[טוֹבֵי] *good-of* appearance ;" [Gen. xxiv. 16] " the damsel was [טֹבַת] *goodly-of* appearance ;" and so ‖ גְּדֹל (Sing. *m.*) *great-of,* יְפֵה (Sing. *m.*) — and יְפַת (Sing. *f.*) — *beautiful-of,* etc.¶

78. The proper PLACE for the Hebrew Adjective is *after*

---

* There are no *Dual* forms for Adjectives proper.

† For the two forms ‎ו‎ and ‎ֻ‎ for the *same vowel*, see Pt. I. § 13.

‡ For the removal of the vowel that would be *Third* before the Accented vowel (reckoned as *First*), see § 59.

§ The last ‎ָ‎ of קָטֹן is replaced by ‎ַ‎ *followed by Dagesh Forte*, on the נ's receiving a vowel. Cp. Tab. IX. (β). [Of the more common word קָטֹן *little*, there is no other form—except only קְטֹן (i. c) 2 Chr. xxi 17.]

‖ And גְּדָל־ (when followed by *Makkêph*, Pt. I. § 37), in which word the ‎ָ‎ is ŏ. This, in Pr. xix. 19, is *Krî* for גרל Kthiv [Pt. I. § 74 3]. In Na. i. 3, Ps. cxlv 8, the ‎ו‎ of גדול — there 'written' — is 'superfluous.'

¶ There are also the following forms (Masculine), כָּבֵד 'i. c.' כְּבַד, pl. כְּבֵדִים 'i. c.' כבדי ; so, fr. עָנָו עֲנָוִים 'i. c.' עַנְוֵי ; etc.

its Noun-Subst.*; thus, אִישׁ טוֹב *a good man* (lit., *a man good*), אִשָּׁה גְדוֹלָה *a great woman,* מְלָכִים גְדֹלִים *great kings,* בְּתוּלוֹת יָפוֹת *beautiful virgins.*

79. Sometimes Participles are used as Adjectives; as in עַם בֹּטֵחַ *a confident* (or *careless*) *people,* אֵשׁ בֹּעֶרֶת† *a burning fire,* אֲנָשִׁים בֹּעֲרִים *burning men,* בָּנוֹת בֹּטְחוֹת *careless daughters.*‡

80. With DUAL Nouns-Subst., Adjectives (and Participles used as such) take Plural forms; thus שָׁמַיִם חֲדָשִׁים *new heavens,* יָדַיִם רָפוֹת *weak hands,* שְׂפָתַיִם דֹּלְקִים *flaming lips,* בִּרְכַּיִם כֹּשְׁלוֹת *failing knees.*

81. If the Noun-Subst. is ' Definite ' — either (1) having the ' Def. Art.,' or (2) having not that Prefix because it is ' i. c.' (§ 73), or (3) having a Pron. Affix, — the Adjective follows the Subst., and *receives also* the ' Def. Art. ;

------

* (i.) There may be more than one Noun Subst. referred to by one Adjective; thus, "good statutes and judgments," would be חֻקִּים וּמִשְׁפָּטִים טוֹבִים (lit. *statutes and judgments good* ").

(ii.) In a few instances, an Adjective *before* a Subst. is supposed to qualify that Subst.:—this *must not be* in Composition.

† This is a not unfrequent form of the Feminine Participle — instead of בֹּעֵרָה; see hereafter.

‡ (i.) There may be several Adjectives (or Participles used as such) one after another, following the Subst.; thus, [Gen. xli. 23] "ears *withered, thin,* and *blasted,*" etc.

(ii.) In a few instances two Adjectives of *different Gender* refer to the same Subst.; thus, [1 K xix. 11] רוּחַ גְדוֹלָה וְחָזָק *a wind great* (*f*) *and strong* (m.),— the ' wind,' being *without life,* cannot be said to have *any* ' Gender' really.

§ (i.) There may be *more Adjectives than one* so following the ' Definite' Substantive, and having each of them the Prefix ה for the ' Definite Article'; thus, "the high and fenced walls," would stand thus, "the walls the *high-ones and the fenced-ones*" So "the high and fenced walls of a city" would stand thus, "*walls of a city the high-ones and the fenced ones*," and so, "thy high and fenced walls " is "*thy walls the high-ones and the fenced-ones*" (Deut. xxviii. 52).

(ii.) A few instances might be cited in which an Adjective *not* having the Pref. ה is rendered by many as an Adjective qualifying a ' Definite' Substantive. Suffice it to say here, that such a form of expression must never be used in Composition.

thus, הַדָּבָר הַטּוֹב THE *good word* (lit., *the word the good*), דִּבְרֵי דָוִד* הָאַחֲרֹנִים THE *last words of David* (lit., *words-of David the last-ones*), בִּתִּי הַגְּדוֹלָה *my elder daughter* (lit., *my daughter the great-one*), דַּרְכֵיהֶם הָרָעִים *their bad ways* (lit., *their ways the bad*).

N.B.—When the Adjective after a ‘Definite’ Substantive *has not* the Prefix ה for the ‘Definite Article,’ the Adjective generally serves as a ‘Predicate.’ See below § 83, etc.

82. Hebrew Adjectives have no (1) ‘Comparative’ or (2) ‘Superlative forms. An Adjective of ordinary form

(i.) followed by מִן (or by מְ, the Prefix of § 5) serves in the place of the ‘Comparative,’—and

(ii.) with the Prefix ה for the ‘Definite Article,’ and followed by בְּ (the Prefix of § 4), serves in the place of the ‘Superlative ;’ thus,—

(i.) טוֹב מִן הָאַרְיֵה הַמֵּת BETTER THAN *the dead lion* (lit., GOOD FROM, or MORE THAN, *the dead lion*), and טוֹב מִמֶּנּוּ *better than he,* מָתוֹק מִדְּבַשׁ *sweeter than honey.*

(ii.) הַגָּדוֹל בָּעֲנָקִים THE GREATEST OF *the Anakim* (lit., THE GREAT ONE IN, or AMONG, *the Anakim*); and so הַדַּל בִּמְנַשֶּׁה THE WEAKEST OF *Manasseh ;* הַצָּעִיר בְּבֵית אָבִי THE LEAST OF *the house of my father.*

N.B.—These expressions for (i.) the ‘Comparative’ and (ii.) the ‘Superlative’ are often used ‘*Predicatively ;*’ thus, [Ps. lxiii. 4] טוֹב חַסְדְּךָ מֵחַיִּים *Thy Grace* [is] *better than life,* and [Judg. vi. 15] “My thousand [is ... הַדַּל בְּ] *the weakest in* Manasseh, and I [am] the least ” etc.

---

* If, instead of “ David,” we had the expression “ *a great king* ” [מֶלֶךְ גָּדוֹל], we should have for “ *the last words of a great king,*” דִּבְרֵי מֶלֶךְ גָּדוֹל הָאַחֲרֹנִים (lit., *words-of a king great the-last-ones*) ; and if, instead of “ David,” we had the expression “ the great king,” we should have for “ the last words of the great king,” דִּבְרֵי הַמֶּלֶךְ הַגָּדוֹל הָאַחֲרֹנִים (lit., *words-of the king the great-one the-last-ones*).

83. Hebrew Adjectives are often used ‘Predicatively,’* and then some form of the so-called ‘Substantive Verb’ (or ‘logical Copula’) is to be supplied; thus, וּזֲהַב הָאָרֶץ טוֹב *and the gold of the land* [*is*] *good,* וְהָאִישׁ גָּדוֹל מְאֹד *and the man* [*was*] *great exceedingly,* גָּדוֹל שְׁמוֹ GREAT [*is*] *His Name,* טוֹב חַסְדֶּךָ *good* [*is*] *Thy Mercy;* and so צַדִּיק אַתָּה *Righteous* [*art*] *Thou,* טֹבֹת הֵנָּה *goodly they* (*f.*) [*were*], רְחוֹקִים אֲנַחְנוּ *far away* [*are*] *we,* etc. etc.

N.B.—The Adjective when used ‘Predicatively,’ often precedes its Subject as in the last five examples; it is then generally emphatic.

84. An Adjective which *precedes* the Substantive or Pronoun to which it belongs, generally serves as a ‘*Predicate*’ thereto; thus, [1 S. xxvi. 13] רַב הַמָּקוֹם *great* [*was*] *the space* [*between them*]; [Job v. 25] רַב זַרְעֶךָ **׃** *great* (or *abundant*) *thy seed* [*shall be*], etc.: as, also, in the last five examples in § 83.

85. So, also, *after a ‘Definite’* Subject an Adjective that *has not* the Prefix ה for the ‘Def. Art.’ is generally used ‘Predicatively;’† thus, [Judg. vii. 4] הָעָם רָב *the people* [*is*] *great* (or *numerous*), whereas “*the numerous people*” would be הָעָם הָרָב, as [Is. xvi. 14] הֶהָמוֹן הָרָב *the great multitude.*

[Obs.—עַם רָב (or עַם רַב) means “*a numerous people.*”]

86. There are not very many adjectives‡ in Hebrew. But no want of them is particularly felt because there is, in common use, another mode of *defining, describing,* and *qualifying* Substantives,—viz., by placing them in Construction with a

---

* In which case the Adjective *need not* agree with the Subst. in Gender or Number.

A Noun-Subst. may also be used ‘Predicatively’ of another Noun-Subst. or a Pronoun.

† A few instances may be cited in which this seems not attended to. It *must* *always* be attended to in Composition.

‡ *i.e.* Strictly such. Participles are often used Adjectively.

word (or expression § 87, 2) which denotes the *qualification*, or the *describing* or *defining thing* or *quality;* thus, [Pr. xv. 26] אִמְרֵי נֹעַם *pleasant words* (lit., *words-of pleasantness*); [1 K. xx. 31] מַלְכֵי חֶסֶד *merciful kings* (lit., *kings-of mercy*), etc. Moreover,

87. The *second* of two words so connected may have a Pron. Affix referring to the *former* one; thus, (1) [Ps. cxix. 62] מִשְׁפְּטֵי צִדְקֶךָ *Thy righteous judgments* (E.V.),—and so (2) [Is. lxiv. 10] בֵּית קָדְשֵׁנוּ וְתִפְאַרְתֵּנוּ *our holy and beautiful house* (lit., *the-house of our holiness and our beauty*), etc.

88. A less common idiom is the following:—A Noun 'in Construction' with a word after it sometimes qualifies or describes *this second word*, in an Adjectival manner;* thus, [Gen. xvi. 12] פֶּרֶא אָדָם *a wild man* (lit., *a wild-ass-of man*), and so [Deut. xxxii. 41) בְּרַק חַרְבִּי *My flashing sword* (lit., *the-lightning-of My sword,* i.e., *My lightning sword*).

In accordance with this, וְתוֹעֲפוֹת הָרִים (lit., *and the-might-of mountains,* Ps. xcv. 4) seems best understood as equivalent to "*and mighty mountains,*" — we have then the whole verse running thus:

     " In Whose hand [are] the-secret-depths-of earth,

     " And His [are] the mighty mountains."

89. Some Adjectives, chiefly *Gentilic* and *Patronymic,*† have the ending ־ִי for the Masculine, and ־ִיָּה or ־ִית for the Feminine, — in the Singular. These take ־ִים (or ־ִיִּם) for the Plural Masc. and ־ִיּוֹת for the Plural Fem.; thus עִבְרִי *Hebrew* (Sing. *m.*), עִבְרִיָּה (Sing. *f.*), עִבְרִים [עִבְרִיִּם Ex. iii. 18] (Plur *m.*), עִבְרִיּוֹת (Plu. *f.*); and מִצְרִי *Egyptian* (Sing. *m.*), מִצְרִית (Sing. *f.*), מִצְרִים (Plu. *m.*), מִצְרִיּוֹת (Plu. *f.*).

90. It seems hardly necessary to say that 'Comparison,' in the way of *Likeness* and *Similitude* is expressed by the Prefix כּ of § 4 (or the word כְּמוֹ, § 4 Note γ); thus, חָסֹן כָּאֵלוֹנִים *strong as the oaks;* נָבוֹן וְהָכָם כָּמוֹךָ *intelligent and wise as thou;* לִבּוֹ יָצוּק כְּמוֹ אָבֶן *his heart [is] firm as a stone.*

---

* Somewhat as we say *a giant of a man* (for *a gigantic man*), *a fool of a man* (for *a foolish man*).

† There are some others, as אַכְזָרִי *cruel,* — and so הַכְלִילִי Gen. xlix. 12.

91. The כ of Comparison is sometimes used with *two words in succession*, to express "just so much as," or "as much the one as the other;" thus, in [Is. xxiv. 2] קָקְנֶה כַמֹּכֵר *so with the buyer as with the seller;* so כְּמוֹ in the well-known passage* [Ps. lviii. 10] כְּמוֹ חַי כְּמוֹ חָרוֹן *as much quick as on fire.*

92. (*a*) Adjectives (and Participles used as such) may be used *concretely;* thus, צָדִיק *righteous* (*m.*) for *a righteous* [MAN], and טוֹב *good* (*m.*) for *a good* [MAN or THING],—[often so

(β.) when 'Predicative,'—and then they need not agree in Gender and Number with the word to which they refer; thus, [Ps. lxxiii. 28] קִרְבַת אֱלֹהִים לִי טוֹב *the nearness of* GOD *to me* [*is*] *good* (or *a good thing*); [Ps. lxvi. 3] מַה נוֹרָא מַעֲשֶׂיךָ *how awful* [*are*] *Thy works!* etc.],—

(γ) So [Nu. xxii. 18] "to do *little or great* [קְטַנָּה אוֹ גְדוֹלָה, lit. *a little* [thing] or *a great* [thing]], and so some give [Pr. viii. 6] "I will speak *excellent-things*" [נְגִידִים]:

(δ) Especially the Fem. Plu.; thus, (1) גְדֹלוֹת *great* [*things*] Ps. xii. 4, lxxi. 19, etc., (2) נוֹרָאוֹת *terrible* [*things*] Ps. xlv. 5, cvi. 22, etc.:

(ε) And *Adverbially,* as נוֹרָאוֹת *fearfully,* Ps. cxxxix. 14, etc.

93. Besides the forms of Expressing the 'Comparative' and 'Superlative,' which were mentioned in § 82, there are some others which need not be mentioned in a Section on *Adjectives.*

Exercise XV.

(*To be translated into English.*)

*** For the plan of the Exercise, see § 11 (*a*—*ε*).

רָחַשׁ¹ לִבִּי² דָּבָר³ טוֹב⁴: טוֹב⁴ יְיָ⁵ לְעוֹלָם⁶ + חַסְדּוֹ⁷:

לֹא⁸ נָפַל⁹ דָּבָר³ אֶחָד¹⁰ מִכֹּל¹¹ דְּבָרוֹ³ הַטּוֹב⁴: טוֹב⁴ יוֹם¹²

¹ hath uttered. ² my heart. ³ דָּבָר a word†(with Affix דִּבְרִי *my word,* etc.). ⁴ טוֹב good (*m.*), טוֹבָה (*f.*). ⁵ See Exercise IX. Note 2. ⁶ for ever. ⁷ חֶסֶד mercy (with Affix חַסְדִּי *my mercy,* etc). ⁸ not. ⁹ hath fallen. ¹⁰ one. ¹¹ כֹּל all, בָּל־ when unaccented, [Pt. I. §§ 37, 55 (9, *b*)]. ¹² a day.

---

* Perhaps best known in the rendering, "*So let indignation vex him even as a thing that is raw.*" The words חַי *alive* and חָרוֹן *hot,* or *on fire,* refer to אָטָד *a thorn* or *a briar;*—the Psalmist seems to express the wish that there may suddenly and utterly fail all the force and fire required for bringing to maturity the plot which his foes are concocting; and this he expresses in figurative language which refers to a storm-blast's sweeping away a fire of thorn-twigs *partly quick* (*i.e.*, with the sap yet in them) but *partly kindled.*

† Also *a promise,*—and *a matter, a thing.*

בַּחֲצֵרֶיךָ 13 מֵאָלֶף 14 כִּי 15 טוֹב 4 חַסְדְּךָ 7 מֵחַיִּים 16 בָּא 17

עֲלֵיכֶם 18 כָּל- 11 הַדְּבָרִי 8 הַטּוֹב 4 הָאָרֶץ 19 הַטּוֹבָה 4 נָתַן 20

לָכֶם 21 בֵּן 21 חָכָם 22 יְשַׂמַּח 23 אָב 24 וּכְסִיל 25 אָדָם 26 בּוֹזֶה 27

אִמּוֹ 28 זְבוּבֵי 29 מָוֶת 30 מָתַי 31 מִסְפָּר 32 וְהָיָה 33 כָעָם 34

כַּכֹּהֵן 35 אַךְ 36 טוֹב 4 לְיִשְׂרָאֵל 37 אֱלֹהִים 38 לְבָרֵי 39 לֵבָב 40

הָאֵל 41 הַגָּדוֹל 42 וְהַנּוֹרָא 43 חַנּוּן 44 וְרַחוּם 45 הוּא דוֹדִי 46 צַח 17

וְאָדוֹם 48 הַיָּפֶה 49 בַּנָּשִׁים 50 יָפָה 49 כַלְּבָנָה 51 בָּרָה 52 כַּחַמָּה 53

לֹא 6 יִטֹּשׁ 54 יְיָ 5 אֶת- 55 עַמּוֹ 56 בַּעֲבוּר 57 שְׁמוֹ 58 הַגָּדוֹל 42

וְגָאַלְתִּי 59 אֶתְכֶם 60 בִּזְרוֹעַ 60 נְטוּיָה 61 וּבִשְׁפָטִים 62 גְּדֹלִים 42

וַהֲקִמֹתִי 63 עֲלֵיכֶם 18 אֵת 55 דְּבָרִי 8 הַטּוֹב 4 בָּרוּךְ 64 הַבָּא 65

בְּשֵׁם 66 יְיָ 5

13 in Thy courts. 14 אָלֶף a thousand [p : אָלֶף]. 15 for. 16 חַיִּים life. 17 there hath come. 18 עַל upon. 19 אֶרֶץ earth, land (הָאָרֶץ when the 'Definite Article' is prefixed). 20 He gave. 21 a son. 22 wise. 23 will gladden. 24 a father. 25 כְּסִיל a fool. 26 man, a man. 27 despises. 28 his mother 29 זְבוּב a fly. 30 death. 31 מְתִים men. 32 number 33 and it shall be. 34 עַם a people (הָעָם when the 'Definite Article' is prefixed). 35 כֹּהֵן a priest. 36 verily. 37 to Israel. 38 God. 39 בָּר pure (Sing. m) 40 heart. 41 אֵל God. 42 גָּדוֹל great. 43 נוֹרָא awful, to be feared. 44 gracious. 45 and merciful. 46 my beloved. 47 white (E V). 48 and ruddy. 49 יָפֶה beautiful (f). 50 נָשִׁים women. 51 לְבָנָה moon. 52 bright. 53 חַמָּה sun. 54 will forsake. 55 (See Exerc. IX, No. 15). 56 His people. 57 because of. 58 His Name. 59 and I will redeem 60 זְרוֹעַ an arm (f.). 61 stretched out (f.). 62 שְׁפָטִים judgments. 63 and I will establish. 64 Blessed (m.). 65 He that cometh. 66 in [the] Name of.

Exercise XVI.

(*To be translated into Hebrew.*)

[N.B.—The ה for the 'Definite Article' must not be put before a word 'i c'— "Is," "are," and "am," here, are not to be expressed in Hebrew.]

*** For the plan of the Exercise, see § 11 (ζ—μ).

A great[1] city.[2] The great[1] city.[2] The city[2] is great.[1] Great[1] cities.[2] The great[1] cities.[2] The cities[2] are great.[1]

[1] גָּדוֹל § 76 (ii.).   [2] עִיר a feminine Noun (Plur. עָרִים f.).

† The same 'in Construction.

Great[1] and goodly[3] cities.[2]   The great[1] and goodly[3] cities.[2]
The cities[2] are great[1] and goodly.[3]   The great[1] and good[3]
prophet.[4]   The prophet[4] is good[3] and great.[1]   A good[3] and
great[1] prophet[4] he is.   The great[1] and good[3] prophets.
A great[1] crown-of[5] gold.[6]   Is-not (Hebr., *Whether 'not*[8]) her
little[9] sister[10] better[11] than she?   What[12] is sweeter[13] than
honey,[14] and what is stronger[15] than a lion.[16]   The greatest[17]
of the Anakim.[18]   My thousand[19] is the weakest[20] of Manasseh,[21]
and I am the least[22] of the house[23] of my father.[24]   The
most-beautiful[25] [one] of the women.[26]   Thy (*f.*) high[27] and
fenced[28] walls.[29].   The Glorious[30] and Awful[31] NAME.[32]

[3] טוֹב, § 76 (i.).   [4] נָבִיא (*m*).   [5] עֲטָרָת (*f.*)   [6] זָהָב.   [7] § 7.   [8] לֹא   [9] קָטָן
§ 76 (iii).   [10] Tab. XIII. † (*a*).   [11] 'Comparative' of (3).   See § 82 (i.).   [12] מַה.
[13] מָתוֹק sweet.   [14] דְּבַשׁ.   [15] עַז strong.   [16] אֲרִי.   [17] 'Superlative' of (1).   See
§ 82 (ii.).   [18] עֲנָקִים.   [19] אֶלֶף Tab. X. (i) (*m*)   [20] דַּל weak.   [21] מְנַשֶּׁה.   [22] צָעִיר.
[23] בֵּית Tab. XIII. (3).   [24] Tab. XIII. (i.)   [25] יָפָה (*f*) [יָפֶה *m*].   [26] נָשִׁים
(§ 74, *m.*)   [27] נָבֹהַּ high (Sing. *m.*)   [28] בָּצוּר fenced (Sing. *m.*)   [29] חוֹמָה a wall.
[30] נִכְבָּד.   [31] נוֹרָא.   [32] שֵׁם.

Note (*a*).   The phrase "flies of death" (p. 56, No. 29 & 30) stands for "dead flies."

(*b*).   The phrase "men of number" (p. 56, No. 31 & 32) stands for "a few men."

SECTION IX.

PRONOUNS-ADJECTIVE.

94. The Pronouns of Section V. (see p. 28),—viz.
(I.) זֶה *this* (*m*), זֹאת *this* (*f.*), אֵלֶּה *these* (*m. & f.*); (II.) הוּא *that* (*m.*), הִיא *that* (*f.*),
etc.,—may be used ADJECTIVELY thus,

this man	הָאִישׁ הַזֶּה	*that man*	הָאִישׁ הַהוּא†
this woman	הָאִשָּׁה הַזֹּאת	*that woman*	הָאִשָּׁה הַהִיא
these boys	הַנְּעָרִים הָאֵלֶּה*	*those boys*	הַנְּעָרִים הָהֵם† or הָהֵמָּה†
these girls	הַנְּעָרוֹת הָאֵלֶּה	*those girls*	הַנְּעָרוֹת הָהֵנָּה
like these words	כַּדְּבָרִים הָאֵלֶּה	*in those words*	בַּדְּבָרִים הָהֵם or הָהֵמָּה

i.e., these *Pronouns-Adjective* follow the Rule of § 81 (p. 51)
—respecting Adjectives with '*Definite*'‡ Nouns-Subst.

> Obs.—The '*Definite*' Noun-Substantive may be 'i. e.' as in [1 S xvii. 11]
> דִּבְרֵי הַפְּלִשְׁתִּי הָאֵלֶּה *these words of the Philistine* (lit., *words of the Philistine the
> these*); and with a Pron. Aff., thus עַמְּךָ הַזֶּה *this Thy people*.

95. If the '*Definite*' Noun-Substantive has an Adjective
belonging to it, besides one of these Pronouns used Adjectively,—the proper place for this Pronoun is *after the Adjective*§; thus, [Nu. xx. 5] הַמָּקוֹם הָרָע הַזֶּה *this bad place*
(lit., *the place the bad the this*); [Nu. xvi. 26] הָאֲנָשִׁים
הָרְשָׁעִים הָאֵלֶּה *these wicked men* (lit., *the men the wicked the
these*); and so [Deut. i. 19] הַמִּדְבָּר הַגָּדוֹל וְהַנּוֹרָא הַהוּא *that
great and terrible wilderness* (lit., *the wilderness the great and
the terrible the that*), etc.

96. (i.) The Pronouns זֶה (*m*), and זֹאת (*f.*), (especially the latter) are sometimes
used for "*this* [*thing*]"; and אֵלֶּה is sometimes used for "*these* [*things*]." So, also,

(ii.) (*a*) The 3 s. (*m.* and *f.*) and 3 pl. (*m.* and *f.*) Pers. Pronouns of Tables I.,

---

* הָאֵל, sometimes; thus, [Gen. xix. 8] לָאֲנָשִׁים הָאֵל *to these men*.

† For the הָ in הַהוּא, הַהִיא,—and the הָ in הָהֵם, etc., —see § 6 (*c*, ii.) and
Note.

‡ The Nouns to which the '*this*' or '*these*,' '*that*' or '*those*' refer being
'Definite.' But the ה is sometimes omitted, thus בַּלַּיְלָה הוּא *in that night*,
דְּבָרֵי אֵלֶּה *these my words*.

§ There are some instances in which this Rule is *not attended to*. It must
always be observed in Composition.

III. (1) (and in other forms), are sometimes used *Neutrally* as in "Is not IT* [הִיא] written etc.", Josh. x. 13, "IT* [אֹתוֹ] 1 must observe to speak," Nu. xxiii. 12, etc, etc

(β) N.B.—Pronouns of the Third Pers. (Tab. I.), stand sometimes where no corresponding Pronoun is required in English, as in "*These are* [אֵלֶּה הֵם, lit. *these* THEY *(are)*] the sons of Ishmael," Gen xxv. 16; "Knowest thou not *what are these* [מָה הֵמָּה אֵלֶּה, lit. *what* THEY *these*]?" Zech. iv. 5.

97. By reason of an *Ellipsis* of the 'Relative' Pronoun after '*this*,' זֶה and זוּ stand sometimes where a *Relative* Pronoun is required in English; thus, [Ps. civ. 8] "unto the place [זֶה] WHICH (E.V.) Thou hast appointed for them."

98. The Prefix הַ of § 6, — as 'Defining,' or 'Marking,' or 'Pointing out,' *that one who*, or *those who*, or *that which*, and the like, — stands sometimes where the *Relative* Pronoun is required in English; thus, [Gen. xxiv. 43] "the damsel [הַיֹּצֵאת] *who cometh out* (lit., *the-one-coming-out*) and to whom I shall say, etc." Cp. Gen. xix. 15, Deut. viii. 14—16, Josh. x. 24, etc.

[N B.—Henceforth the following words need not be given in the Notes to the Exercises.—

      אַל *not* (generally *deprecatively*).
      אֵת (†אֶת־), see Exercise IX. 15.‡
      כֹּל (†כָּל־) *all.*
      לֹא *not.*
   ⁎ For זֶה, זֹאת, אֵלֶּה, used 'Absolutely,' see p. 28.

EXERCISE XVII.

(*To be translated into English.*)

⁎ For the plan of the Exercise see § 11 (*a—ε*).

אֵלֶּה דִבְרֵי[1] הַבְּרִית[2]: וַיְדַבֵּר[3] מֹשֶׁה[4] אֶת הַדְּבָרִים[5] הָאֵלֶּה:

הֲלֹא[6] תִשְׁמֹר[6] לַעֲשׂוֹת[7] אֶת כָּל דִּבְרֵי[1] הַתּוֹרָה[8] הַזֹּאת

[1] דָּבָר a word, thing.   [2] the covenant.   [3] and spake.   [4] Moses.   [5] § 7 (this varies slightly from the Bible).   [6] thou wilt observe.   [7] to do.   [8] the Law.

---

* Cp. § 10.
† The *Makkêph* is generally not given in the Exercises.
‡ The Student is supposed to be familiar with the rest of Tables I—IV.

הַכְּתֻבִים[9] בַּסֵּפֶר[10] הַזֶּה: הַנֶּה הַמִּצְוָה[11] הַזֹּאת אֲשֶׁר אָנֹכִי מְצַוְּךָ[12]

הַיּוֹם[13] לֹא נִפְלֵאת[14] הִוא מִמְּךָ וְלֹא רְחֹקָה[15] הִוא: כִּי[16]

הוּא חָכְמַתְכֶם[17]: הֲנִהְיָה[18] כַּדָּבָר[19] הַגָּדוֹל[1] הַזֶּה אוֹ[20] הֲנִשְׁמַע[21]

כָּמֹהוּ: וְהִגַּדְתָּ[22] לְבִנְךָ[23] בַּיּוֹם[24] הַהוּא לֵאמֹר[25]: זֶה אֵלִי[26]

וְאַנְוֵהוּ[27]: הֲלוֹא הוּא אָבִיךָ[28] קָנֶךָ[29]: הוּא תְהִלָּתְךָ[30] וְהוּא

אֱלֹהֶיךָ[31] אֲשֶׁר עָשָׂה[32] אִתְּךָ אֶת הַגְּדֹלֹת[19] וְאֶת הַנּוֹרָאֹת[33]

הָאֵלֶּה: הָאֹתֹת[34] וְהַמֹּפְתִים[35] הַגְּדֹלִים[19] הָהֵם: בַּעֲבוּר[36] זֹאת[37]:

מִי שָׁמַע[38] כָּזֹאת[37] מִי רָאָה[39] כָּאֵלֶּה[37]: זֹאת הָעֵצָה[40]

הַיְעוּצָה[41]: וְכַאֲשֶׁר[42] יָעַצְתִּי[41] הִיא תָקוּם[44]: כִּי[16] לִי בְּנֵי[23]

יִשְׂרָאֵל[45]+עֲבָדִים[46], עֲבָדַי[46] הֵם: וְנִשַּׁל[47] יְיָ[48] אֱלֹהֶיךָ[31] אֶת

הַגּוֹיִם[49] הָאֵל[50] מִפָּנֶיךָ[51] מְעַט[52] מְעָט[52]: הָרִאשֹׁנוֹת[53] מָה

הֵנָּה: מִי זֶה בָּא[54] מֵאֱדוֹם[55]: זֶה דוֹדִי[56]: בַּיָּמִים[57] הָהֵמָּה

וּבָעֵת[58] הַהִיא נְאֻם[59] יְיָ[48] יָבֹאוּ[60] בְנֵי[23] יִשְׂרָאֵל[45] הֵמָּה וּבְנֵי[23]

יְהוּדָה[61] יַחְדָּו[62]: כִּי[16] זֹאת הַבְּרִית[37] אֲשֶׁר אֶכְרֹת[63] אֶת בֵּית[64]

יִשְׂרָאֵל[45]: בַּיָּמִים[57] הָהֵם תִּוָּשַׁע[65] יְהוּדָה[61] ...וְזֶה אֲשֶׁר יִקְרָא[66]

לָהּ יְיָ[48] צִדְקֵנוּ[67]:

---

9 כָּתוּב written (See § 98) 10 in the Book. 11 the commandment. 12 commanding thee (*m.*). 13 to-day. 14 (with the מ following) too hard for. 15 far off 16 for. 17 חָכְמָה wisdom (the ָ to the ח is *ŏ*). 18 has there been? 19 גָּדוֹל great (§ 76 (ii.)) 20 or. 21 has there been heard? 22 and thou shalt tell. 23 Tab. XIII. (4). 24 יוֹם a day. 25 saying. 26 אֵל God. 27 and I will glorify Him. 28 Tab. XIII. (1). 29 Who owneth thee (*i.e*, Whose thou art). 30 תְּהִלָּה praise. 31 See Exerc. IX. 66. 32 hath done. 33 § 92 (*δ*, 2). 34 אוֹת a sign (Plu. אֹתוֹת). 35 מוֹפֵת a wonder. 36 on account of. 37 § 96. 38 hath heard. 39 hath seen. 40 עֵצָה counsel (*f*). 41 יָעוּץ counselled (*m.*). For the force of the ה here, see § 98. 42 and according to what (or, *and as*). 43 I have counselled. 44 shall stand. 45 Israel. 46 Table X. 6. 47 and He will expel (or, *pluck away*). 48 See Exerc IX 2. 49 the nations. 50 §94(*). 51 פָּנִים a face (a Noun of Plu. form.) 52 מְעַט מְעָט [by] little [and] little. 53 the former things (*f.*). 54 coming (Sing. *m.*) 55 אֱדוֹם Edom. 56 דוֹד a friend. 57 יָמִים Plu. of 24. 58 עֵת time. 59 saith (E V.). 60 they shall come. 61 Judah. 62 together. 63 I will make (lit, *cut*). 64 house of. 65 shall be saved 66 one shall call. (This word, with the ‘ to her ’ following, signifies “ *she shall be called* ”). 67 צֶדֶק righteousness.

Exercise XVIII.

(To be translated into Hebrew.)

₊ For the plan of the Exercise see § 11 (ζ—μ).

[Obs.—'Is' and 'are,' here, are not to be expressed in Hebrew.]

This house.[1] This is the house. In this house. Is-this (Hebr. *Whether*[2] *this?*) the house? That is the house. These are the houses.[1] These houses. Those houses. This great[3] house. That great city.[4] In this city. In this great city. This is the great city. These cities.[4] Those cities. In these cities. From those cities. Who* are these men[5] with[6] thee (*m.*)? What* is this (*m.*) in thy (*m.*) hand[7]?, and-he-said,[8] A rod.[9] This (*f.*) we-will-do[10] to[11] them (*m.*). Hear-ye[12] this (*f.*) O[13] priests.[14] What is this (*f.*) thou-(*f.*)-hast-done[15]? Is this (*f.*) Naomi[16]? Whose-son (Hebr. *son of*[17] *whom**) is this? Whose daughter[18] is this? That is the man[19] from whom we-heard[20] these good[21] words.[22] At[23] that time.[24] In those days[25] I-will-pour-out[26] My Spirit.[27] On[23] that day[28] shall-be-sung[29] this song[30] in the land[31] of Judah.[32]

---

[1] בַּיִת (*m*), Plu. בָּתִּים. [2] The prefix of § 7. [3] Exerc. XVII. 19. [4] עִיר (*f*), Plu. עָרִים. [5] אֲנָשִׁים. [6] עִם. [7] יָד. [8] וַיֹּאמֶר. [9] מַטֶּה. [10] נַעֲשֶׂה.- [11] לְ prefix. [12] שִׁמְעוּ. [13] § 74 (*n.*). [14] כֹּהֲנִים. [15] עָשִׂית. [16] נָעֳמִי. [17] בֶּן. [18] בַּת (the same 'l.c.'). [19] אִישׁ. [20] שְׁמַעֲנוּ. [21] טוֹב § 76. i. [22] Exerc. XVII. 1. [23] בְּ prefix. [24] עֵת (*f.*). (§ 56 vii.). [25] יָמִים [26] אֶשְׁפּוֹךְ [27] רוּחַ. [28] יוֹם. [29] יוּשַׁר. [30] שִׁיר *m.* [31] אֶרֶץ [32] יְהוּדָה.————* See page 29.

SECTION X.

NUMERALS.

99. The Cardinal Numbers from 1 to 20 are—

Fem.		Masc.		Notation.	
Construct.	Absolute.	Construct.	Absolute.		
אַחַת	אַחַת †	אַחַד	אֶחָד *	א.	1.
שְׁתֵּי	שְׁתַּיִם	שְׁנֵי	שְׁנַיִם	ב.	2.
שְׁלֹשׁ	שָׁלֹשׁ	שְׁלֹשֶׁת	שְׁלֹשָׁה	ג.	3.
אַרְבַּע	אַרְבַּע	אַרְבַּעַת	אַרְבָּעָה	ד.	4.
חֲמֵשׁ	חָמֵשׁ	חֲמֵשֶׁת	חֲמִשָּׁה	ה.	5.
שֵׁשׁ	שֵׁשׁ	שֵׁשֶׁת	שִׁשָּׁה	ו.	6.
שְׁבַע	שֶׁבַע	שִׁבְעַת	שִׁבְעָה	ז.	7.
שְׁמֹנֶה	שְׁמֹנֶה	שְׁמֹנַת	שְׁמֹנָה	ח.	8.
תְּשַׁע	תֵּשַׁע	תִּשְׁעַת	תִּשְׁעָה	ט.	9.
עֶשֶׂר	עֶשֶׂר	עֲשֶׂרֶת	עֲשָׂרָה	י.	10.
אַחַת עֶשְׂרֵה (or עַשְׁתֵּי עֶשְׂרֵה)	אַחַד עָשָׂר (or עַשְׁתֵּי עָשָׂר)			יא.	11.
שְׁתֵּים עֶשְׂרֵה (or שְׁתֵּי עֶשְׂרֵה)	שְׁנֵים עָשָׂר (or שְׁנֵי עָשָׂר)			יב.	12.
שְׁלֹשׁ עֶשְׂרֵה	שְׁלֹשָׁה עָשָׂר			יג.	13.
אַרְבַּע עֶשְׂרֵה	אַרְבָּעָה עָשָׂר			יד.	14.
חֲמֵשׁ עֶשְׂרֵה	חֲמִשָּׁה עָשָׂר			טו.	15.
שֵׁשׁ עֶשְׂרֵה	שִׁשָּׁה עָשָׂר			יו or טו	16.
שְׁבַע עֶשְׂרֵה	שִׁבְעָה עָשָׂר			יז.	17.
שְׁמֹנֶה עֶשְׂרֵה	שְׁמֹנָה עָשָׂר			יח.	18.
תְּשַׁע עֶשְׂרֵה	תִּשְׁעָה עָשָׂר			יט.	19.
עֶשְׂרִים (m. & f.)				כ.	20.

† In pause אֶחָת׃.   * Some few times אַחַד.

100. The expressions for the Cardinal Numbers from 21 to 29 inclusive, are formed by placing the Cardinal Numbers 1—9 (in their *Absolute* forms, *m.* & *f.*) either BEFORE or AFTER עֶשְׂרִים *twenty*, with ו prefixed to the *Second* of the two Numbers; thus,—

(f.)	(m.)	(f.)	(m.)		
אֶחָד (אַחַת) וְעֶשְׂרִים, or [עֶשְׂרִים וְאֶחָד (וְאַחַת)]				כא.	21.
שְׁנַיִם (שְׁתַּיִם) וְעֶשְׂרִים, or [עֶשְׂרִים וּשְׁנַיִם (וּשְׁתַּיִם)]				כב.	22.
שְׁלֹשָׁה (שָׁלֹשׁ) וְעֶשְׂרִים, or [עֶשְׂרִים וּשְׁלֹשָׁה (וּשָׁלֹשׁ)]				כג.	23.
אַרְבָּעָה (אַרְבַּע) וְעֶשְׂרִים, or [עֶשְׂרִים וְאַרְבָּעָה (וְאַרְבַּע)]				כד.	24.
חֲמִשָּׁה (חָמֵשׁ) וְעֶשְׂרִים, or [עֶשְׂרִים וַחֲמִשָּׁה (וְחָמֵשׁ)]				כה.	25.
שִׁשָּׁה (שֵׁשׁ) וְעֶשְׂרִים, or [עֶשְׂרִים וְשִׁשָּׁה (וְשֵׁשׁ)]				כו.	26.
שִׁבְעָה (שֶׁבַע) וְעֶשְׂרִים, or [עֶשְׂרִים וְשִׁבְעָה (וְשֶׁבַע)]				כז.	27.
שְׁמֹנָה (שְׁמֹנֶה) וְעֶשְׂרִים, or [עֶשְׂרִים וּשְׁמֹנָה (וּשְׁמֹנֶה)]				כח.	28.
תִּשְׁעָה (תֵּשַׁע) וְעֶשְׂרִים, or [עֶשְׂרִים וְתִשְׁעָה (וְתֵשַׁע)]				כט.	29.

101. If we replace the עֶשְׂרִים in § 100, (α.) by שְׁלֹשִׁים 30, (β.) by אַרְבָּעִים 40, (γ.) by חֲמִשִּׁים 50, (δ.) by שִׁשִּׁים 60, (ε.) by שִׁבְעִים 70, (ζ.) by שְׁמֹנִים 80, (η.) by תִּשְׁעִים 90, we get the Card. Numbers, (α.) for 31—39, (β.) for 41—49 (γ.) for 51—59, (δ.) for 61—69, (ε.) for 71—79, (ζ.) for 81—89, (η.) for 91—99

102. The word for 100 is מֵאָה ('i. c.,' מְאַת), Plu. מֵאוֹת *hundreds*. The Dual מָאתַיִם (p. : מָאתָיִם) expresses 200. By placing the *Construct Feminine* forms [§ 99] for 3, 4,.. 9, before מֵאוֹת, we have 300, 400,.. 900; thus,

שְׁלֹשׁ מֵאוֹת 300, אַרְבַּע מֵאוֹת 400, חֲמֵשׁ מֵאוֹת 500, שֵׁשׁ מֵאוֹת 600, שְׁבַע מֵאוֹת 700, שְׁמֹנֶה מֵאוֹת 800, תְּשַׁע מֵאוֹת 900.

103. The word for 1000 is אֶלֶף ('i. c.' the same), Plu. אֲלָפִים *thousands* ('i. c.' אַלְפֵי). The Dual אַלְפַּיִם (p. : אַלְפָּיִם) expresses 2000. By placing the *Construct Masculine* forms

[§ 99] for 3, 4, 5,.. 10, before אֲלָפִים (or ‘i. c.,’ אַלְפֵי), we have 3000, 4000, 5000,... 10,000; thus,

חֲמֵשֶׁת אֲלָפִים 3000, אַרְבַּעַת אֲלָפִים 4000, שְׁלֹשֶׁת אֲלָפִים 5000,.. עֲשֶׂרֶת אֲלָפִים 10,000,—for which, viz. 10,000, we have also רְבָבָה *a myriad* (‘i. c.’ רִבְבַת), Plu. רְבָבוֹת *myriads*, רִבּוֹא & רִבּוֹת,רְבָאוֹת [and רִבּוֹא, רִבּוֹ, Plu. רִבֹּאוֹת,(‘i. c.’ רִבְבוֹת), Dual רִבֹּתַיִם, Ps. lxviii. 18].

104. For intermediate Numbers to those in §§ 102, 103, we have—

(i.) מֵאָה וְעֶשְׂרִים 110, מֵאָה וָעֶשֶׂר 120 [and also חֲמִשִּׁים וּמֵאָה 130, שְׁלֹשִׁים וּמֵאָה,[עֶשְׂרִים וּמֵאָה 150, and so שְׁמֹנִים וּמְאַת 180 [*days*], וּמְאַת יוֹם]

שָׁלֹשׁ מֵאוֹת וְשִׁשִּׁים 250, חֲמִשִּׁים וּמָאתַיִם 360, שְׁלֹשִׁים 450, אַרְבַּע מֵאוֹת וַחֲמִשִּׁים 420, אַרְבַּע מֵאוֹת וְעֶשְׂרִים 550; חֲמִשִּׁים וַחֲמֵשׁ מֵאוֹת 530, וַחֲמֵשׁ מֵאוֹת

(ii.) מָאתַיִם שְׁנַיִם וּשְׁלֹשִׁים 127, שֶׁבַע וְעֶשְׂרִים וּמֵאָה 232, שֵׁשׁ מֵאוֹת שִׁשִּׁים וָשֵׁשׁ 318, שְׁמֹנָה עָשָׂר וּשְׁלֹשׁ מֵאוֹת 666, חֲמִשָּׁה וָאָלֶף 675, etc., שֵׁשׁ מֵאוֹת חָמֵשׁ וְשִׁבְעִים 1005, חֲמִשָּׁה וְשִׁשִּׁים וּשְׁלֹשׁ מֵאוֹת וָאֶלֶף 1100, אֶלֶף וּמֵאָה 1365, אֲלָפִים וְאַרְבַּע מֵאוֹת 1400, אֶלֶף וְאַרְבַּע מֵאוֹת 2400, etc.

[Note.—As may be seen in the above, there is *variety* in the order of the several Numerals which make up a Composite Number. Still further variety exists; but notice of it, and of some other matters relating to Numerals, must be deferred at present.]

105. We may mention, as examples of the form of higher Numbers,—

שְׁנַיִם וּשְׁלֹשִׁים אֶלֶף וּמָאתַיִם 32,200, שֵׁשׁ מֵאוֹת אֶלֶף וּשְׁלֹשֶׁת אֲלָפִים וַחֲמֵשׁ מֵאוֹת וַחֲמִשִּׁים 603,550.

This last Example offers an illustration of both the following Rules:

106. (i.) After the Numerals 3, 4,· 5,... 10, a Noun is properly put in the Plural; but

(ii.) After a Number higher than 10 it may be (and commonly is) in the Singular.

Thus, after שֵׁשׁ *six*, we see (in the last Example) מֵאוֹת *hundreds* (Plu); but after the 600 we see אֶלֶף *a thousand* (Sing):—after the 3 we see אֲלָפִים *thousands* (Plu); and after the 5 we see מֵאוֹת *hundreds* (Plu.).

The same may be seen in the Examples of the following § 107, and in many others.

N.B.—There are, however, several examples of Numbers higher than 10 followed by Nouns in the *Plural*.

107. In expressing time, the Numerals are often divided, as in—

תְּשַׁע מֵאוֹת שָׁנָה וּשְׁלֹשִׁים שָׁנָה 930 *years* [lit., 900 *year, and* 30 *year*] Gen. v. 5,

חָמֵשׁ שָׁנִים וּמְאַת שָׁנָה 105 *years* [lit., 5 *years, and* 100 (' i. c.') *year*] ib. 6,

שֶׁבַע שָׁנִים וּשְׁמֹנֶה מֵאוֹת שָׁנָה 807 *years* [lit., 7 *years, and* 800 *year*] ib. 7,

שֶׁבַע וּשְׁמֹנִים שָׁנָה וּמְאַת שָׁנָה 187 *years* [lit., 7 *and* 80 *year, and* 100 *year*] ·ib. 25,

שְׁתַּיִם וּשְׁמוֹנִים שָׁנָה וּשְׁבַע מֵאוֹת שָׁנָה 782 *years* [lit., 2 *and* 80 *year, and* 700 *year*] ib. 26,

תְּשַׁע וְשִׁשִּׁים שָׁנָה וּתְשַׁע מֵאוֹת שָׁנָה 969 *years* [lit., 9 *and* 60 *year, and* 900 *year*] ib. 27.

108. The above are Nouns. Some of them are used sometimes in the same way as Adjectives in §§ 78, 81. This is very frequently the case with אֶחָד and אַחַת *one* (*m. & f.*); thus, מָקוֹם אֶחָד *one place*, Gen. i. 9, שָׂפָה אַחַת *one lip* (or *language*) Gen. xi. 6, הַקֶּרֶשׁ הָאֶחָד *the one board*, Ex. xxvi. 16, הַיְרִיעָה הָאַחַת *the one curtain*, Ex. xxvi. 2, etc. [Cp. §§ 78, 81]. From אֶחָד [*one*] *the same*, we have the Plural אֲחָדִים *the same* (as in Gen. xi. 1), also *a few* (as in Gen. xxix. 20).

109. The Ordinals are—

Plural		Singular		
Fem.	*Masc.*	*Fem.*	*Masc.*	
רִאשֹׁנוֹת	רִאשֹׁנִים	רִאשֹׁנָה	רִאשֹׁון	First
	שְׁנִים	שֵׁנִית	שֵׁנִי	Second
	שְׁלִשִׁים*	שְׁלִישִׁית (‑שִׁיָּה)	שְׁלִישִׁי	Third
	רְבִיעִים	רְבִיעִית	רְבִיעִי	Fourth
		חֲמִשִׁית ‡	חֲמִישִׁי †	Fifth
		שִׁשִּׁית	שִׁשִּׁי	Sixth
		שְׁבִיעִית	שְׁבִיעִי	Seventh
		שְׁמִינִית	שְׁמִינִי	Eighth
		תְּשִׁיעִית	תְּשִׁיעִי	Ninth
		עֲשִׂירִית	עֲשִׂירִי	Tenth.

110. These Ordinals are Nouns-Adjective. The Feminines of some of them may be used to express Fractional parts; thus, §שְׁלִישִׁית *a third* [*part*], ‖רְבִיעִית *a fourth* [*part*], etc.

111. For *a half*, however, we have—

חֵצִי (p. : חֲצִי) Masc., and rarely **מֶחֱצָה ('i. c.' מֶחֱצַת) Fem.

112. 'One of' is expressed either by (1) אֶחָד *m.*, אַחַת *f.*, followed by the prefix מ of § 5 (or מִן *from, of*),—Cp.

---

* The לְ with Defective Long Kherik, see Pt. I. § 12. So in הַשְּׁלִשִׁי Sing. *m.*, and הַשְּׁלִשִׁית (הַשְּׁלִישִׁת D. xxvi. 12) Sing. *f.* [The Sing. *f.* שְׁלִישִׁיָּה is rare.]

† Also חֲמִשִׁי [and חֲמִשִׁי, as in Note (*)].

‡ Also חֲמִשִׁית [and חֲמִשִׁת, as in Note (*)].

§ Or שְׁלִשִׁית, or שְׁלִשִׁת [whence שְׁלִשְׁתָה, Ez. xxi. 19, *the-third-time* (E.V.).]. שִׁלֵּשִׁים *third* [*generations*].

‖ Also רֶבַע, and רְבַע. רְבִעִים *fourth* [*generations*].

¶ 'i. c.' the same. There is also חֲצוֹת *half-of*,—only used with לַיְלָה *night*, to express 'midnight.'

** More often מַחֲצִית *a half*,—only used 'i. c.' and with Pron. Affixes.

Lev. vii. 14, xxv. 48, 2 K. iv. 22 (אֶחָד מִן הַנְּעָרִים *one of the youths*); or by

(2) אֶחָד *m.*, אַחַת *f.*, followed by the prefix מ of § 5 (or מִן *from, of*), — as Lev. xiii. 2, אַחַד מִבָּנָיו *one of his sons,* Cp. Lev. iv. 13; or by

(3) אֶחָד *m.*, אַחַת *f.*, in direct Construction with the word following, as in אַחַד הֶהָרִים *one of the mountains* [Gen. xxii. 2], אַחַת הֶעָרִים *one of the cities* [D. xix. 5].

[Note.—אֶחָד is found as the *Absolute* form some few times, as Gen. xlviii. 22, 2 S. xvii. 22, etc.].

113. There is a Noun עָשׂוֹר which stands for:

(1) *ten,*—as *a decad* [of *days*, or *months*]; — also an *instrument-of*-TEN-*strings ;*

(2) *tenth,* as *tenth day* [of a month].

[Note.—For several other words connected with the Numerals, as מִשְׁנֶה *double,* (*מְשֻׁלָּשׁ *tripled,* *רָבוּעַ and *מְרֻבָּע, etc , *foursquare*), etc., see Pt. II.].

114. The letters of the Alphabet are used to mark Chapters and Verses [and for the ‘reckonings’ at the end of certain Books] in the ordinary Editions of the Hebrew Bible; but they are not so used in the Text itself.

[Note.—(a) As seen in § 99, — (a) the first ten letters in Alphabetical order from א to י stand for the Numbers from 1 to 10; and, (β.) for those from 11 to 19, א to ט stand to the left of י; thus, יא (*i e*, 10 and 1) for 11, יב for 12, יג for 13, יד for 14, but טו (*i.e.,* 9 and 6) for 15, יו (or טז) for 16, יז for 17, יח for 18, יט for 19. כ, the eleventh letter, stands for 20; the next letter ל for 30‡; and so מ for 40, נ for 50, ס for 60, ע for 70, פ for 80, צ for 90, ק for 100, ר for 200, שׁ for 300, ת for 400 [see the Table of the Alphabet in Pt. I].

---

* Each of these is a Participle-form, as we shall see. There are some other *Verb*-forms.

† For, יה are letters of The Name [Pt. I, § 79 (2)].

‡ For the Intermediate Numbers 21 to 29, the letters א to ט are placed to the left of כ; thus, כא 21, כב 22, כג 23,... כה 25,... כט 29. So for the Numbers between 30 and 40, 40 and 50, 50 and 60, 60 and 70, 70 and 80, 80 and 90, 90 and 100, — the letters א to ט are placed to the left of ל 30, מ 40, נ 50, .. צ 90. Similarly the Numbers between 100 and 200 are expressed by ק with the letters for 1 to 99 [in descending order of magnitude from right to left; thus קסז 167. And so the Numbers between 200 and 300, 300 and 400, etc., etc.

(*b*) For 500, 600, etc., to 900, either two or more letters (together making up the sums) are used, or the Final Letters ך for 500, ם for 600, ן for 700, ף for 800, ץ for 900. Then (beginning again) א with some mark (thus, ׳א) was used for 1000.

(*c.*) Since the 22 letters of the Alphabet, with the 5 final letters, together give *Twenty-seven* forms of figures, we have three groups of 9 letters each, — א to ט for *units*, י to צ for *tens*, ק to ץ for *hundreds*. [This is mentioned in the *Masoreth ha-Masoreth* of Elias Levita; see Dr. Ginsburg's ed., with Translation and Notes, p. 136].

(*d.*) There is a very common mode of expressing Numbers by means of a word or expression, of which the letters (or certain selected letters) make up the Number. For instance, in a certain well known place, the letters of the word הנץ (*i.e.*, ה 5 + נ 50 + ץ 900) stand for 955; those of the word חג (*i.e*, 8 + 3) for 11; those of the word יגיד (*i e.*, 10 + 3 + 10 + 4) for 27, etc.; and those dotted in כסא כבוד ינחילם (*i.e.*, ו 6 + ד 4 + י 10 + נ 50 + ח 8 + י 10 + ל 30 + ם 40) stand for 158.

Obs.—The Final letters do not *always* stand for hundreds: thus ם in the last example stands for 40, not 600.]

⁎ No special Exercise need be given on this Section.

SECTION XI.

Verbs. — (I.) Voices.

115. The Hebrew Verb has Seven Voices. The *Outline*
forms of these may easily be remembered by means of Seven
well-devised names for them which we will try to explain :—

116. (*α*.) Most Hebrew words are reducible to three
‘ Root’-letters (as they are called), and

(*β*.) Def. These three letters, in their proper order, stand
for what is called the ‘ Root ’ of the word :

(γ.) Thus, (1) of דְּבָרִים [*words*], the Root is the set of letters דבר, — (2) of
לַמַּלְכָּה [*to the queen*] the Root is מלך; etc.

117. The Verb being contemplated as expressing Action,
— *Past, Present,* or *Future,* — the Hebrew name for it is פֹּעַל
from the Root פעל (which expresses *acting, working,* etc.).
These three letters פ ע ל are used as representatives of
Root-letters generally, — פ for ‘ *First* Root-letter,’ ע for
‘ *Second* Root-letter,’ and ל for ‘ *Third* Root-letter.’

Thus in דָּבָר, ד is the פ, ב is the ע, ר is the ל; so in מלכה, the מ is the פ,
the ל is the ע, the ך is the ל.*]

118. The ‘ 3 s. *m.*’ of the Past Tense, in all the Seven
Voices of the Full † Verb, has no letters besides those
which either belong to the Root or are Characteristic
of the Voice. Hence these ‘ 3 s. *m.*’ forms of the Past Tense
in the several Voices, when expressed in the *general* form by
the letters פ ע ל, may be said to give the general *Outline*

---

* As in Note † to Rule vii., § 56 (p. 36, above)—מַלְכָּה is of the form פֶּעְלָה;
מִשְׁפָּט (having a מ Preformative) is of the form מִפְעָל. So the two Nouns in
§ 74 (*e*) (2), are of the forms תִּפְעָלָה, תִּפְעֶלֶת; and the three in § 74 (*e.*) (1) are
of the forms פְּעָלֶת, פְּעִילָה, פְּעִיל, respectively.

† The term ‘ Full ’ is here used of a Verb which, in all its forms, has its Three
Root-letters each of them in Full Consonantal value, — and so has its whole
Root fully brought out always. [We should prefer the term ‘ Complete,’ if
we might use it *in this sense*]. The term ‘ *Regular* Verb ’ is often used for this.

forms of the several Voices. For instance, of the Root פָּקַד,
the Seven forms of the Past Tense 3 s. *m.* are:—

(D) Reflexive.	(C) Causative.	(B) Intensive.	(A.) Simple.
הִתְפַּקֵּד (vii.)	הִפְקִיד (v.)	פִּקֵּד (iii.)	פָּקַד (i.), Active
	הָפְקַד (vi.)	פֻּקַּד, (iv.)	נִפְקַד (ii.), Passive

(a.)

119. (i.) This will perhaps be more clear if we put 1, 2,
and 3, for the *First, Second,* and *Third* Root-letters; thus,—

$$\text{הִתְ־321 (vii.)} \quad \begin{cases} \text{הִ3·21י (v.)} & \text{321 (iii.)} & \text{321, (i.)} \\ \text{הָ21·3 (vi.)} & \text{321, (iv.)} & \text{נ321, (ii.)} \end{cases} \quad (\beta.)$$

(ii.) Or, with פ, ע, and ל, instead of 1, 2, and 3,—

$$\text{הִתְפַּעֵל (vii.)} \quad \begin{cases} \text{הִפְעִיל (v.)} & \text{פִּעֵל (iii.)} & \text{פָּעַל (i.)} \\ \text{הָפְעַל (vi.)} & \text{פֻּעַל, (iv.)} & \text{נִפְעַל, (ii.)} \end{cases} \quad (\gamma.)$$

or, in descending order,

Pau-ăl	פָּעַל	(i.)	פָּקַד	*he visited*	
Niph-ăl	נִפְעַל	(ii.)	נִפְקַד	*he was visited*	
Pĭ-êl	פִּעֵל	(iii.)	פִּקֵּד	*he diligently visited*	
Pŭ-ăl	פֻּעַל	(iv.)	פֻּקַּד	*he was ... visited*	(δ.)
Hiph-îl	הִפְעִיל	(v.)	הִפְקִיד	*he caused to visit*	
Hŏph-ăl	הָפְעַל	(vi.)	הָפְקַד	*he was....*	
Hithpă-êl	הִתְפַּעֵל	(vii.)	הִתְפַּקֵּד	*he visited himself*	

[Obs.—Here 'diligently' is used for expressing the *Intensity* of signification
of the *Pĭ-êl* Voice. Other means of expressing this may be required for other
Roots. Other forms of rendering may be required also for other Voices. Some
Roots require different English Verbs for their different Voices; thus (from
לָמַד (למד) *he learned,* לִמֵּד *he taught,*—(fr. שבע) נִשְׁבַּע *he sware,* הִשְׁבִּיעַ *he
adjured.* Further remarks on the meaning of the Voices are reserved at present.]

120. (i.) The First Voice is not generally called *Pau-ăl* but *Kal* (קַל *light,* i.e. *not burdened*), because this Voice has no prefix belonging to it, and no Doubling Dagesh [Pt. I. § 49]; for,

N.B.—The dot in the First Root-letter ב is merely Dagesh Lene [Pt. I. § 47], and cannot stand when the Verb does not begin with one of the ב ג ד כ פ ת, — as, for instance, in מָשַׁךְ *he drew,* שָׁלַח *he sent.*

But, excepting the First one, the words to the left of the column of Numerals in (δ) give the Names by which the Voices are known; thus,

(ii.) The Second Voice is called *Niph-ăl* (נִפְעַל), because נ is prefixed, the First Root-letter has ־ִ, the Second has ־ַ;

(iii.) The Third Voice is called *Pĭ-ēl* (פִּעֵל), because the First Root-letter has ־ִ and the Second one ־ֵ;

[N.B.—A Dagesh Forte belongs to this Voice and the next one, — in the *Second* Root-letter.]

(iv.) The Fourth Voice is called *Pŭ-ăl* (פֻּעַל), because the First Root-letter has ־ֻ and the Second one ־ַ;

(v.) The Fifth Voice is called *Hiph-ĭl* (הִפְעִיל), because הִ is prefixed, the First Root-letter has ־ְ and the Second one has י־ִ;

(vi.) The Sixth Voice is called *Hŏph-ăl* (הָפְעַל), because ה with ־ָ (δ) is prefixed, the first Root-letter having ־ְ and the Second one ־ַ;

(vii.) The Seventh Voice is called *Hithpă-ēl* (הִתְפַּעֵל), because הִת is prefixed, the First Root-letter having ־ַ and the Second one ־ֵ.

[N.B —A Dagesh Forte belongs to this Voice, — in the *Second* Root-letter.]

121. There are a few other names and forms, which belong to modifications

of some of the above rather than to special Voices. It is best to reserve the mention of these at present, with the exception of one, viz.:—

Some Verbs take — (*ŭ*) instead of — (*ŏ*) in the *Sixth* Voice, giving thus the form הֻפְעַל *Hŭph-ăl,* instead of הָפְעַל *Hŏph-ăl.* But, as there is no need of a special name for so slight a variation, it is usual to include both sets of forms under the one name *Hŏph-ăl.*

122. For practice, the Student may name the several Voices of the following :—

(1) הִשְׁלִיךְ ,   (2) מָלֵא ,   (3) הָמְלַךְ ,   (4) הָלַךְ ,   (5) הִתְנַדֵּב ,

(6) שָׁלַח ,   (7) נִמְכַּר ,   (8) הִסְגִּיר ,   (9) סָגַּר ,   (10) נִמְשַׁל ,

(11) הִתְכַּבֵּד ,   (12) כָּתַב ,   (13) הָשְׁלַךְ ,   (14) דִּבֶּר :

The Student may now compare the several PERSONS OF THE TENSE-FORMS in the different Voices, as follows :—

(II.) TENSES.

123. The Hebrew Verb has forms for expressing PAST, PRESENT, and FUTURE Action; but only *two* TENSES — or TIME-FORMS — viz., PAST and FUTURE.

124. PRESENT Action is expressed in Hebrew by means of a Participle, — as in the English expressions *I* [am] *writing, thou* [art] *writing, he* [is] *writing;* but, the 'am,' 'art,' 'is,' etc., not being expressed in Hebrew, those three English expressions *without the words within* [ ] give the form of the corresponding Hebrew expressions for Present Action, thus, '*I writing,*' '*thou writing,*' '*he writing,*' [see § 140].

125. The distinguishing Person-forms of the Past Tense are *the same for all Voices**; — so that when once these are known well for one Voice, they are known for all the others.

The same is true of the Future.

(i.) Past Tense.

126. The Past Tense *Kal* (§ 120, i.) of פָּקַד *he visited*, is—

Singular.

	I	כָּקַדְתִּי	thou	*m.*	פָּקַדְתָּ	he	פָּקַד†	
				f.	פָּקַדְתְּ	she	פָּקְדָה	

Plural.

	we	פָּקַדְנוּ	ye	*m.*	פְּקַדְתֶּם‡	they	פָּקְדוּ
				f.	פְּקַדְתֶּן‡	*m. & f.*	

visited.

[Obs.—In Past Tenses, the 3 pl. and 1 s. & pl. are common to both Genders.]

127. From this it is seen that in place of the דַ־, in פָּקַד *he visited*, we have for the other Persons,

in the Singular, the endings

דְתִּי־ | דְתָּ־ | דָה־
דְתְּ־

and in the Plural, the endings

דְנוּ־ | דְתֶּם־ | דוּ־
דְתֶּן־

128. If we put these several endings in place of the דַ־

G

in נִפְקַד *he was visited*, we get the several Persons of the PAST of the ii. Voice *Niph-ăl* [see Tab. XIV.].

129. So, by putting those endings in place of the רֵ in פִּקֵּד *he visited diligently*, and of the רֵ in פֻּקַּד *he was diligently visited*, the רֵ in הֻפְקַד *he was caused to be visited*, and the רֵ in הִתְפַּקֵּד *he visited himself*, we get the several Persons of the Past Tenses of the iii. Voice *Pi-ĕl*, the iv. *Pŭ-ăl*, the vi. *Hŏph-ăl*, and the vii. *Hithpă-ĕl*, respectively [see Tab. XIV.].

130. The same is seen to hold for the v. Voice, *Hiph-il*, excepting only the 3 s. *f.* הִפְקִידָה and the 3 plu. *m.* & *f.* הִפְקִידוּ. In these two forms the יֵ of this Voice appears with the Second Root-letter in place of the ֵ in all the other Voices.

131. For practice, the Student may parse* the following :—

לָמְרוּ, לִמְרוּ, לְמַדְתָּם, לְמֵדְתָּם, אָמַרְתָּ, מָלַכְתָּ, שָׁלַחְתִּי,

שָׁלְחוּ, שָׁלַחְתָּ, שָׁלְחוּ, שְׁלַחְתֶּם, שָׁלְחָה, שָׁלַחְנוּ, הִשְׁלַכְתִּי,

הִשְׁלִיכוּ, הִשְׁלִיךְ, הִשְׁלַכְתָּ, הִשְׁלִיכָה, נִמְלַטְתִּי, נִמְלְטוּ, נִמְשַׁל,

קִבַּצְתִּי, גָּנַבְתִּי, גָּדְלָה, גָּדַלְתִּי, הִתְגַּדַּלְתִּי, קִדֵּשׁוּ, קִדַּשְׁתָּ,

הִקְדַּשְׁתִּי, הִקְדִּישׁוּ, הִקְדִּשָׁנוּ, קִדְּשָׁתֶם, הִתְקַדְּשָׁתֶם, הִתְקַדַּשְׁתִּי,

הָשְׁלַכְתָּ, הָשְׁלַכְתִּי, הָשְׁלְכוּ, הִתְקַדְּשׁוּ, הִתְנַדְּבוּ, הִתְעַבַּרְתָּ,

הִקְדִּישׁוּ :

---

* In this manner: הִתְפַּקַּדְתֶּן is 2 pl. *f.* Past *Hithpă-ĕl* [or (as some prefer) thus, *Hithpă ĕl*, Past, Plu., 2 *f.*], of the Root פקד.

[To face p. 74.]

Table of Past-Tenses (in the Seven Voices of § 120) of פקד to visit.

(VII) Hithpá-êl.	(VI) Hoph-ăl.	(V) Hiph-îl.	(IV) Pŭ-ăl.	(III) Pĭ-êl.	(II) Niph-ăl.	(I) Kal.	
ited himself (hereafter).	was caused to visit.	caused to visit.	was visited (Intens.)	visited (Intens.)	was visited	visited.	
הִתְפַּקֵּד	הָפְקַד	הִפְקִיד	פֻּקַד	פִּקֵּד	נִפְקַד	פָּקַד	he.
הִתְפַּקְּדָה	הָפְקְדָה	הִפְקִידָה	פֻּקְּדָה	פִּקְּדָה	נִפְקְדָה	פָּקְדָה	she.
הִתְפַּקַּדְתָּ	הָפְקַדְתָּ	הִפְקַדְתָּ	פֻּקַּדְתָּ	פִּקַּדְתָּ	נִפְקַדְתָּ	פָּקַדְתָּ	thou (m).
הִתְפַּקַּדְתְּ	הָפְקַדְתְּ	הִפְקַדְתְּ	פֻּקַּדְתְּ	פִּקַּדְתְּ	נִפְקַדְתְּ	פָּקַדְתְּ	thou (f).
הִתְפַּקַּדְתִּי	הָפְקַדְתִּי	הִפְקַדְתִּי	פֻּקַּדְתִּי	פִּקַּדְתִּי	נִפְקַדְתִּי	פָּקַדְתִּי	I.
הִתְפַּקְּדוּ	הָפְקְדוּ	הִפְקִידוּ	פֻּקְּדוּ	פִּקְּדוּ	נִפְקְדוּ	פָּקְדוּ	they (m. & f.).
הִתְפַּקַּדְתֶּם	הָפְקַדְתֶּם	הִפְקַדְתֶּם	פֻּקַּדְתֶּם	פִּקַּדְתֶּם	נִפְקַדְתֶּם	פְּקַדְתֶּם	ye (m.).
הִתְפַּקַּדְתֶּן	הָפְקַדְתֶּן	הִפְקַדְתֶּן	פֻּקַּדְתֶּן	פִּקַּדְתֶּן	נִפְקַדְתֶּן	פְּקַדְתֶּן	ye (f.)
הִתְפַּקַּדְנוּ	הָפְקַדְנוּ	הִפְקַדְנוּ	פֻּקַּדְנוּ	פִּקַּדְנוּ	נִפְקַדְנוּ	פָּקַדְנוּ	we.

[To face p. 75.]

Table of Future-Tenses (in the Seven Voices of § 120) of פקד *to visit.*

(VII) Hithpä-ĕl.	(VI) Hoph-ăl.	(V) Hiph-îl.	(IV) Pŭ-ăl.	(III) Pï-ĕl.	(II) Niph-ăl.	(I) Kal.	
ll v. himself (herself, etc.).	*will be caused to v.*	*will cause to v.*	*will be visited (Intens.)*	*will visit (Intens).*	*will be visited.*	*will visit.*	
יִתְפַּקֵּד	יָפְקַד	יַפְקִיד	יְפֻקַּד	יְפַקֵּד	יִפָּקֵד	יִפְקֹד	he.
תִּתְפַּקֵּד	תָּפְקַד	תַּפְקִיד	תְּפֻקַּד	תְּפַקֵּד	תִּפָּקֵד	תִּפְקֹד	she.
תִּתְפַּקֵּד	תָּפְקַד	תַּפְקִיד	תְּפֻקַּד	תְּפַקֵּד	תִּפָּקֵד	תִּפְקֹד	thou (m.).
תִּתְפַּקְּדִי	תָּפְקְדִי	תַּפְקִידִי	תְּפֻקְּדִי	תְּפַקְּדִי	תִּפָּקְדִי	תִּפְקְדִי	thou (f.)
אֶתְפַּקֵּד	אָפְקַד	אַפְקִיד	אֲפֻקַּד	אֲפַקֵּד	אֶפָּקֵד (or א)	אֶפְקֹד	I.
יִתְפַּקְּדוּ	יָפְקְדוּ	יַפְקִידוּ	יְפֻקְּדוּ	יְפַקְּדוּ	יִפָּקְדוּ	יִפְקְדוּ	they (m).
תִּתְפַּקֵּדְנָה	תָּפְקַדְנָה	תַּפְקֵדְנָה	תְּפֻקַּדְנָה	תְּפַקֵּדְנָה	תִּפָּקַדְנָה (or ק)	תִּפְקֹדְנָה	they (f.)
תִּתְפַּקְּדוּ	תָּפְקְדוּ	תַּפְקִידוּ	תְּפֻקְּדוּ	תְּפַקְּדוּ	תִּפָּקְדוּ	תִּפְקְדוּ	ye (m.).
תִּתְפַּקֵּדְנָה	תָּפְקַדְנָה	תַּפְקֵדְנָה	תְּפֻקַּדְנָה	תְּפַקֵּדְנָה	תִּפָּקַדְנָה (or ק)	תִּפְקֹדְנָה	ye (f.).
נִתְפַּקֵּד	נָפְקַד	נַפְקִיד	נְפֻקַּד	נְפַקֵּד	נִפָּקֵד	נִפְקֹד	we.

(ii.) FUTURE TENSE.

132. The FUTURE TENSE of the First Voice *Kal* has two forms—the one with ــَ or וֹ as יִפְקֹד or יִפְקֹד *he will visit* (etc.) fr. פָּקַד, the other with ־ as יִלְבַּשׁ *he will clothe*[a] (etc.) fr. לבשׁ.

N.B (*a.*) Verbs that have the (ـَ)-form may be called 'Verbs Fut. (ـَ),' and

(β.) Verbs that have the (־)-form may be called Verbs Fut. (־).'

[The (־)-form of Fut. *K*.]			[The (ـَ)-form of Fut. *K*]		
יִלְבַּשׁ	*he will clothe*[a]		יִפְקֹד*	*he will visit*	
תִּלְבַּשׁ†	*she will*	...	תִּפְקֹד†	*she will*	...
תִּלְבַּשׁ†	*thou (m.) wilt*	..	תִּפְקֹד†	*thou (m.) wilt*	...
תִּלְבְּשִׁי	*thou (f.) wilt*		תִּפְקְרִי	*thou (f.) wilt*	..
אֶלְבַּשׁ	*I will*	...	אֶפְקֹד	*I will*	...
יִלְבְּשׁוּ	*they (m.) will*	..	יִפְקְדוּ	*they (m.) will*	
תִּלְבַּשְׁנָה‡	*they (f.) will*		תִּפְקֹדְנָה‡	*they (f.) will*	...
תִּלְבְּשׁוּ	*ye (m.) will*	...	תִּפְקְדוּ	*ye (m.) will*	...
תִּלְבַּשְׁנָה‡	*ye (f.) will*	.	תִּפְקֹדְנָה‡	*ye (f.) will*	..
נִלְבַּשׁ	*we will*	..	נִפְקֹד	*we will*	...

[Obs. In Fut. Tenses, only the FIRST PERSONS (Sing. and Plu.) have forms COMMON TO BOTH GENDERS.]

133. Here, (*α.*) the only added terminations arc

  ִי־ for the 2 s. *f.*,

  וּ for the 3 & 2 pl. *m.*,

  נָה for the 3 & 2 pl. *f.*;

but, (β.) there are Four prefixed letters—אִיתָן, viz,

  י for the 3 *m.*, s. & pl.,

  א for the 1 s., and נ for the 1 pl.,

  ת for all the other forms.

---

* Or יִפְקוֹד, and so תִּפְקוֹד etc., with וֹ instead of ־ַ. a Or, *put on clothes.*
† See § 134 (*e*, 1). ‡ See § 134 (*e*, 2).

134. As may be seen by one glance at the Futures in Tab. XIV.,—

  (α.) What has just been stated (§ 133) holds for *all* the Voices; but

  (β.) the prefix-letters אית‍ן have the following Vowel-points in the several Voices—

   (1.) in *Kal, Niph-ăl, Hithpă-ĕl* each one of the three יתן has —, א has —,

N.B.—(2) in *Pĭ-ĕl,* and *Pŭ-ăl,* the יתן have —, א has —,

   (3) in *Hiph-ĭl* all the four אית‍ן have —, and

   (4) in *Hŏph-ăl,* all the four אית‍ן have — (ŏ), [or — (ŭ) sometimes] ;

  (γ.) in *Niph-ăl,* the נ (Characteristic of the Voice) is dropped, and instead of it Dagesh Forte is put in the First Root-letter, as in יִפָּקֵד [for יִנְפָּקֵד] Cp. Pt. I. § 53. So too in הִפָּקֵד Infin., & Imper. 2 s *m*, etc.

  (δ.) in *Hiph-ĭl* *, there is — (instead of יִ—) in 3 & 2 pl. *f.* Also

    N.B.—there is often — instead of יִ— in other Persons, as in יַרְדְּבּ Ps. xlvii. 4 [instead of יַרְדְּבִיר], תַּגְדֵּל Obad. 12 [instead of תַּגְדִּיל], etc.;

  (ε.) in all the Voices the forms are the same for—

   (i.) the 3 s. *f.* & 2 s. *m.* (marked † in § 132),

   (ii.) the 3 & 2 pl. *f.* (marked ‡ in § 132).

135. For practice, the Student may parse the following (with the help of Tab. XIV.):—

אֲדַבֵּר, דִּבַּרְתִּי, תְּדַבְּרִי, יְדַבְּרוּ, נְדִבְּרוּ, תְּדֻבְּרוּ, תְּדַבֵּר,
דִּבַּרְתֶּם, נְדַבֵּר, תְּדַבֵּרְנָה, יְדֻבַּר, יִכְתְּבוּ, תִּכְתֹּב, אֶכְתֹּב,

---

* N.B. The ה of *Hiph.* is generally dropped in Future and Partic. forms, as in מַפְקִיד & יַפְקִיד (instead of מְהַפְקִיד & יְהַפְקִיד), etc. So also the ה of *Hithpă-ĕl.*—For instances of the ה of *Hiph.* STANDING see § 201. Rarely the ה of *Hoph.* appears, as in מְהָקְצָעוֹת *Hoph.* Partic. pl. *f.* fr. קצע.

יִכָּתֵב, כָּתַבְתָּ, יִגְדַּל, תִּשְׁמַעְנָה, תִּדְבַּק, הִדְבַּקְתִּי, נַמְלִיךְ,
אֶמְלוֹךְ, אַמְלִיךְ, תִּמְלֹךְ, יִמְלוֹךְ, יַפְרִיד, נִפְרְדוּ, יִפָּרְדוּ,
יַשְׁלִיךְ, הִשְׁלַכְתִּי, תַּשְׁלֵךְ, הָשְׁלַכְתָּ, הֻשְׁלְכוּ, תָּשְׁלְכִי, יַשְׁלִיכוּ,
נִשְׁמַרְנוּ, אֶתְמַשֵּׁל, יִמְשְׁלוּ, נִמְשָׁל, נִמְשַׁלְתִּי, תִּמְשׁוֹל:

III. Arrangement of the Table of the Full Verb.

136. In Table XIV. the Seven Voices' stand in seven
columns beginning with (i) KAL on the right, so that all
the corresponding forms in the several Voices may be read
from Right to Left in horizontal lines. The order in the
columns is as follows:

(1) Infinitive, (2) Past Tense, (3) Participle, (4) Imperative, (5) Future.

137. The Infinitive forms are (1) 'Absolute,' (2) 'Construct,' (3) 'With the Prefixes מ ל כ ב,' (4) 'With Pronoun-
Affixes.'

(1). (a.) The 'INF. ABS.' forms* of פָּקַד have the following
values in the Seven Voices:—(i.) KAL, [to]visit; (ii.) NIPH-ĂL,
[to] be visited; (iii.) PĬ-ÊL, [to] visit (Intens.); (iv.) PŬ-ĂL,
[to] be visited (Intens.); (v.) HIPH-ÎL, [to] cause to visit;
(vi.) HOPH-ĂL, [to] be caused to visit; (vii.) HITHPĂ-ÊL, [to]
visit oneself.

(b.) Besides the פָּעוֹל form of the Inf. Abs. Kal, there is
also the פָּעֹל form, as גָּדֹל to be great.

(c.) The Inf. Abs. Niph. is sometimes of the form נִפְעֹל
(with Past Tenses Niph.), as in נִשְׁאֹל נִשְׁאַל 1 S. xx. 6.
Tab. XIV., Note d.

(d.) The Inf. Abs. Hiph. has sometimes '־ֵ, as in הַשְׁמֵיד
Am. ix. 8.

[Obs.—The INF. ABS. is often used for expressing *abstractly* the 'Action' of
the Verb. Thus—

(*a*.) Hos. iv. 2, " [There is] אָלֹה *cursing*, וְכַחֵשׁ *and lying*, וְרָצֹחַ (Pt. I., § 60) *and murdering*, וְגָנֹב *and stealing*, וְנָאֹף *and adultery*." - So Job xv. 35, הָרֹה עָמָל *conceiving trouble*, וְיָלֹד אָוֶן *and bearing mischief*." And where an Inf. may be required in English, as, Is. vii. 15, " מָאוֹס *to refuse* the evil, וּבָחוֹר *and to choose* the good." Also,

(*β*.) before* a ‹kindred› Tense, for Emphasis, as in מָלֹךְ תִּמְלוֹךְ, 1 S. xxiv. 21, *thou shalt surely reign* (lit., *to reign thou shalt reign*); הַקְדֵּשׁ הִקְדַּשְׁתִּי, Ju xvii. 3, *I had wholly dedicated* (E.V.), etc.; and

(*γ*) *Without* the ‹kindred› Tense, for brevity,—a short Emphatic expression— where the *context conveys and supplies* the Tense-value; thus, בָחֹר, 1 S ii. 28 [in וּבָחֹר *and did I choose?* E.V.] after an Emphatic expression in ver 27. So, Nu. xv. 35, " The man shall SURELY be put to death; רָגֹם *stone* him with stones. [shall] all the assembly." And, without any preceding Emphatic form, as, Gen. xli 43, " And he made him ride in the chariot of the viceroy [הַמִּשְׁנֶה, lit., *the second*] which he had; and they cried before him, Bow the knee (E.V.). וְנָתוֹן *and he fully set* him over all the land of Egypt." And so, Deut. xiv. 21, " Ye shall not eat any carcase,—to the sojourner who is in thy gates shouldst thou give it, he would indeed eat it (*i e*, although, if thou shouldst give it to him, he would not mind eating it), or [which] מָכֹר *thou couldst sell even* to the foreigner (*i.e*, which he would not mind *even buying* from thee.—but thou shalt not eat it—), for a holy people art thou, etc "†

(*δ*.) Sometimes there are two Infinitives, הָלוֹךְ *to go*, and another, in certain phrases for *going on continually*,—either (i) with a ‹kindred› Tense and Inf., as in Gen. xii. 9, " And he *journeyed* TO GO and *to journey* (*i.e.*, he went on continually journeying);" Gen. viii. 3, " And the waters *returned* TO GO and *to return* (*i e*., went on continually returning)"; also, Gen. xxvi. 13, " And he *went* TO GO and *to be great;* or, (ii) without any kindred Tense, as in Gen viii. 5, " And the waters *were* TO GO and *to decrease* (*i e*, went on continually decreasing)." The Student cannot parse the Tenses in these four examples, at present.]

---

* (i.) And sometimes *after* the Tense, as in וַיִּשְׁפֹּט שָׁפוֹט Gen. xix. 9, etc. Also,

(ii.) after a ‹kindred› Imperative, as in שִׁמְעוּ שָׁמוֹעַ (Pt. I., § 60), Is. vi. 9,—and after a ‹kindred› Participle, as in אֹמְרִים אָמוֹר, Jer. xxiii. 17.

N.B.—(1) The term ‹kindred› is used here for ‹from the same Root›; (2) the Voice is sometimes *not* the same, as in סָקוֹל יִסָּקֵל, Ex. xxi. 28,—נַקֹּר יְקְּרוּהָ, 1 S. ii. 16. (Pt. I., § 12.—The וּ is *added*, § 145.)

† These are usually said to be instances of ‹The Inf. for a *Finite* part of the Verb› (*i e*., for a part *limited* to Time, or Person, or both). The Student should not confuse this usage with what may, at first sight, *seem like it* in English; as in Jer. xxxii. 44, " They shall buy fields for money, *and write* (וְכָתוֹב) in the book, *and seal* (וְחָתוֹם), etc.;" where the English "write" and "seal" correspond with the " buy," all of them being governed by the auxiliary " shall." There is no such correspondence in the Hebrew.

78*

[To face page 78.]

[Our purpose being to familiarize the Student with the Subject gradually by means of the carefully chosen ILLUSTRATIONS GIVEN IN THE EXERCISES, we recommend him to hasten on now as quickly as possible to the Exercises on pp. 90—96.

Every Verb in the Hebrew Exercises should be carefully parsed,—*except when the full Meaning is given in the Notes.*

The following Index for pp. 77—89 may be useful, for reference

INDEX FOR PAGES 77—89.

§ 137   INFINITIVE forms, pp. 77—81; *viz.*

     (1) Infin.   (1) Absol., pp. 77 & 78,—(2) Constr., p 79, —

     (3) Infin. w. prefixes בכלמ, pp. 79 & 80 [Tab. XIV. 'App . (A) '].

     (4)   (i.) Infin w. Pron-Affs., p. 80 & Tab. XV,

        (ii.) May have the prefixes בכלמ, p (80);

        (iii) Infin w. ה ָ (& ת ָ) at the end, p. 80,

        [(iv.) Various vowels of 1ˢᵗ Rt-letter, pp. 80 & 81]

§ 138 (A).   THREE forms of PAST KAL, and designations, p. 81, viz.

        (i.) The פָּעַל form, as פָּקַד *he visited*,

        (ii) The פָּעֵל form, as חָפֵץ *he had pleasure*,

        (iii.) The פָּעֹל form, as יָכֹל *he was able.*

§ 138 (B).   ה ָ sometimes at the end of Past 2 s *m* (and other forms), p. 82.

        [Also ת sometimes at end of Past 3 s *f.*, (ii γ), p. 82,

        א sometimes (& ן) at end of Past 3 pl., (iv. α & β), p. 82]

§ 139.   PARTICIPLES, pp. 82—85.

     (α) Significations (p. 82),   (β) Tab of forms (p. 83);

     (γ) Partic (1) & Partic (2) *Kal*, p. 83.

     (δ) The   (i.) פָּעֵל and   (ii) פָּעֹל forms of Partic *K.*, p. 84.

     (ε) ' ָ ending sometimes of Sing Partic. p. 84

§ 140   (α & β) Partic. used for (not limited to) *Present* Tense, p. 84,

     (δ—ʒ) Some other usages of Participles, pp. 84 & 85.

§ 141.   (α) The (◌) & (◌) forms of Imper. & Fut. *Kal*, p 85.

     (γ) The ה ָ ending sometimes of Imper 2 s. *m.*, p 86.

§ 142   The Imper. and Fut. are connected, p 87.

§ 143.   The ן ending sometimes of Fut. 3 & 2 pl. *f.*, p. 87.

§ 144.   The ה ָ ending sometimes of Fut. 1 s. & 1 plu., p. 88.

§ 145.   Future-form endings ן (& ן ָ), and י ָ, pp. 88 & 89.

Note I.   The ת of *Hithpā-el* sometimes transposed, changed, or dropped, p 89.

     II. Remarks on Tab XV, p. 89 (**).

(2). The ' Construct ' form of the Inf. [*פָּקֹד or פְּקֹד (of פֹּקֵד) in *Kal*, etc.] is used when it is in close structural connection with what follows (cp. § 52); thus, [Gen. v. 1] " In the day of [בְּרֹא אֱלֹהִים] *God's creating* (lit., *creating-of God*)," so שְׁפֹט [*the*] *judging-of* [the judges], Ruth i. 1, etc.

(3). (a.) The Inf. with the prefixes בּ כּ ל מ has the ' Construct ' form; thus, with the ל,

(i.) Kal, { לִפְקוֹד? / לִפְקֹד } *to visit*, or *for visiting*, or *for* [*the*] *visiting of;*

(ii.) Niph-ăl   †לְהִפָּקֵד *to be visited*, or *for being visited*, or *for* [*the*] *being visited of;*

(iii.) Pĭ-êl,   לְפַקֵּד (Intens.) *to visit*, or *for visiting*, or *for* [*the*] *visiting of;*

(iv.) Pŭ-ăl,   לְפֻקַּד (Intens.) *to be visited*, or, *for being visited*, or, *for* [*the*] *being visited of;*

(v.) Hiph-îl,   †לְהַפְקִיד *to cause to visit*, or, *for causing to v.*, or, *for* [*the*] *causing to visit of;* [†לַעְשֵׂר D. xxvi. 12];

(vi.) Hoph-ăl,   לְהָפְקַד *to be caused to visit*, or, *for being caused to visit*, or, *for* [*the*] *being caused to visit of;*

(vii.) Hithpă-êl,   לְהִתְפַּקֵּד to visit oneself, or, *for visiting oneself*, or, *for* [*the*]..., etc.‡

(b.) So with the בּ, and the כּ, we have for the *Kal*, בִּפְקוֹד (or בִּפְקֹד) *in visiting*, (כּ—) כִּפְקוֹד *as*, or *like, visiting*, (or, *visiting of*, in each case).

(c.) But the מ has either — followed by Dagesh [as in

---

* —, as in שָׁכַב 2 K. xiv. 22, is rare. So לִשְׁכַּב [p. : לְשִׁכְּב].

† The ה is sometimes dropped and its vowel given to the Prefix בּ, or כּ, or ל; thus, בֵּעָטֵף (for בְּהֵעָטֵף, *Niph.*, cp. p. 6, Note ‡; the ֵ instead of ֵ because the ע cannot have Dagesh), Lam. ii. 11; וְלַנְפֵּל (for וּלְהַנְפֵּל, *Hiph.*, Nu. v. 22), לְשָׁמִד (for לְהַשְׁמִיד, *Hiph.*, Is. xxiii. 11), לַשְׁמֵעַ (for לְהַשְׁמִיעַ, *Hiph.*, Ps. xxvi. 7). For the —, see Pt. I., § 12; and for the ע, see Pt. I., § 60.

‡ Other renderings of these are sometimes required,—as we shall see.

מִבְּטֹחַ, Ps. cxviii. 8, *than to trust* (lit., *from trusting*), מִדַּבֵּר, Ex. xxxiv. 33, *from speaking*], or — for compensation (Cp. § 5).

(d.) (i) For other Voices, see *Appendix* (*A*) to Tab. XIV.

(ii.) For the Inf. with endings הָ֒, תָ֒, see (4, iii.).

(4). (i.) In the forms of the ' Inf. with Pronoun Affixes,' mentioned in Tab. XIV., and more fully given in Tab. XV., the Pronouns involved are the Possessive* *my, thy, his,* etc.·

(ii.) These Infinitive forms may have the prefixes בכלמ; thus, בְּמָלְכוֹ *in* (or *on*) *his reigning,* בְּשָׁכְבְּךָ *in* (or *on*) *thy* (*m.*) *lying down,* בְּשָׁלְחִי *in* (or *on*) *my sending,* בַּעֲבָרְכֶם *in* (or *on*) *your* (*m.*) *passing over,* בְּזָכְרֵנוּ *in* (or *on*) *our remembering,* בְּשָׁמְעֲךָ *in* (or *on*) *thy* (*m.*) *hearing,* etc.; כְּשָׁמְעָם *at their* (*m.*) *hearing,* לְמָלְכוֹ *to* (or *with reference to*) *his reigning,* וּמִשָּׁמְרוֹ *and from His keeping,* etc.

So in other Voices; thus, בְּהִשָּׁפְטוֹ (*Niph*) *on his being judged,* בְּכָשְׁלוֹ (for בְּהִכָּשְׁלוֹ, *Niph.,* comp. p. 6, Note ‡); בְּדַבְּרָהּ, כְּדַבֶּרְכֶם† (*Pi-êl*) *on her speaking, on your* (*m.*)...; בְּהַקְרִיבְכֶם (*Hiph.*) *on His...,* בְּהַפְרִידוֹ *on your* (*m.*)..., etc.

(iii) The Infinitive has sometimes the accented termination הָ֒, like a Feminine Noun, as in לְקָרְבָה *to draw near,* לְחֶמְלָה (iv., below) *to have compassion,* לְאַהֲבָה *to love,* לְיִרְאָה *to fear.* This הָ֒ is replaced by תָ֒ in ' direct Construction,' as in מֵאַהֲבַת יְיָ אֶתְכֶם‡ *because the* LORD *loved you* (E.V.) D. vii. 8, [lit., *from loving of,* etc.]; and by תָ֒ when the word has a Pron. Affix, as in בְּקָרְבָתָם *in* (or) *on their* (*m.*) *approaching,* Ex. xl. 32, Lev. xvi. 1. So בְּאַהֲבָתוֹ אֹתוֹ *through his loving him,* 1 S. xviii. 3; and so מִיִּרְאָתוֹ 2 S. iii. 11.

[(iv.) The ָ to the first Root-letter is *ŏ* in Tab. XV (i.). There is also ָ, as in the Pause-form : בְּקָצְרֶךָ, and in

---

* The Affixes for *Objective* Pronouns, *me, thee, him,* etc., will be mentioned hereafter

† The ָ of (בְ) is a ' Slight '-vowel; see Note *⁎*, p. 89.

‡ Here the ֲ is because of the ה, and the ֲ under א is because of the ָ֒.

וּבְקֻצְרְכֶם, Lev. xxiii. 22. There is also —, as in בְּשִׁכְבָהּ* *on her lying down,* בְּפִתְחִי *on my opening,* בִּקְעָם *their (m.) cleaving;* and —, as in מַחְאֲךָ, רָקְעֲךָ, Ez. xxv. 6, וּבְשָׁחֲטָם, xxiii. 39.]

N.B —The forms in (ii.), (iii), (iv), here, are those of Tab XV. with Prefixes, —rather than those of (3), p 79, with Pron. Affixes The reason for this remark will be seen hereafter. Suffice it here to state, merely, that the — under the first Root-letter after the לְ, as in 3 (a, 1), is generally Quiescent.

138 (A). (i) The Past Tense *Kal,* in the first column of Tab. XIV., is of the פָּעַל form. There are two other forms of it, viz., the פָּעֵל and the פָּעֹל.

(ii.) The full Past Tense of the פָּעֵל form need not be given; all the Person-forms are THE SAME as those in the first column (i e, those of the פָּעַל form),— except only that the 2d Root-letter has — in 3 s m., and in the Pause-forms of 3 s. f. and 3 pl., thus זָקֵן† *he was old,* and נָבְרוּ ; קָרְבָה : נֶ֫, ‡ the Pause-forms of קָרְבָה *she drew near,* גָּבְרוּ *they were mighty.*

(iii) The פָּעֹל form of the Past Tense is printed in smaller type in the second column of the *Kal* Voice. As may be seen there, the — of the Second Root-letter is retained in the 2 s. m. & f, and the 1 s & pl (in place of — in the פָּעַל forms); but this — is shortened into — (ŏ) in 2 pl. m. & f., in accordance with Pt. I. § 55 (9, b). The — appears also in the Pause-forms of 3 s f. and 3 pl. See Tab. XIV, Note † β. The ordinary 3 s f. and 3 pl. are the same as in the first column.

(iv) The terms ‹Verba Med. A,› ‹Med. E,› ‹Med O,› (used by some for Verbs of the three Classes in i., ii., iii), are rather awkward; and ‹Verbs *Middle A,*› ‹*Middle E,*› ‹*Middle O,*› (given by others), are not better. Taking ע as general representative of the ‹Second Root-letter› (§ 117), we may say—

(1) ‹Verbs עַ›— for the Verbs in (1), of which the 2d Root-letter has — here,

(2) ‹Verbs עֵ›— for those in (ii), of which the 2d Root-letter has —;

(3) ‹Verbs עֹ›— for those in (iii), of which the 2d Root-letter has —.

(v.) Rarely the 2d Root-letter has —, as in שָׁפַט *he judged,* 1 Sam. vii. 17.

---

* As well as — (ŏ) in בִּשְׁכְבוּ. It may be observed that, in the above Examples, the Short vowel of the first Root-letter is *generally* a ‹Slight›-vowel, wherever the — following it can be Moving. But where this — (being followed by another —) *must* be Quiescent, the ‹Slight›-vowel is made to become a real Short-vowel.

† The פָּעֵל form being the same for the *Kal* 3 s. m. Past, and the s. m. Participle,— the context alone decides which of these a word is. Some Verbs have the פָּעֵל form as well as the פָּעַל. [In a few instances the Inf. Abs. K. has this form, as דָּל Gen. xxvi. 13, קָרֹב 2 S. xviii. 25].

‡ The 3 s. m Past, of each of these Verbs, is of פָּעַל form, viz, קָרַב *he drew near,* גָּבַר *he was mighty.*

138 (B.)   (i.) At the end of the 2 s. *m.* Past, there is some-times an additional ה, as in הָשַׁבְתָּה 2 S. xiv. 13, נִכְסַפְתָּה Gen. xxxi. 30, אֲמַצְתָּה Ps. lxxx. 16, הֶעֱמַרְתָּה Ps. xxxi. 8 (for the הֶעֱ see § 178 (ii.)), etc.

(ii) (α.) Rarely at the end of the 3 s. *m.*, as in שָׁמְרָה Am i. 11 (about which, however, opinions differ); and

(β.) at the end of the 3 s. *f.* (the ה of which is then replaced by ת), as in נִפְלְאָתָה (from נִפְלְאָה) 2 S. i. 26, הֶחְבָּאָתָה (from הֶחְבִּיאָה, for the הֶ see § 178), Josh. vi. 17.

(γ.) The 3 s. *f.* has sometimes ת in place of the usual ה, as in אָזְלַת D. xxxii. 36 (for אָזְלָה).

(iii.) Also we find הִשְׁלַחְתָּנָה, Am. iv. 3 (for הִשְׁלַחְתֶּן).

(iv.) (α.) Rarely the 3 pl. Past has א at the end; thus, הֲלִכְבוּא Josh. x 24 [with הֲ *who* prefixed there, § 98 and § 6 (*d*, ii)]; and

(β.) sometimes וּן, as in יְדָעוּן, D. viii. 3, 16 (for יָדְעוּ).

(v) (α.) In such a word as אָמַר, 1 S. xiii. 19, the ◌ֻ is for *Shūrik* [Pt. I., § 14],—the full *Shūrik* cannot be given because there is no וֹ, the *Kthiv* being אמר, so that the ◌ֻ is the only means of marking the *u* of the *Krî* which is אָמְרוּ [Pt. I., § 76].   So in שְׁפֻּכָה, Ps. lxxiii. 2, the ◌ֻ marks the *Shūrik* of the *Krî*, which is שָׁפְכוּ,—the *Kthiv* being שפכה.   So D. xxi. 7, שפכה *Kthiv*, שָׁפְכוּ *Krî.*

(β) So in such a word as יָרַעְתְ, Ps. cxl. 13, the ◌ִ [Pt. I, § 12] is the only means of marking the *i* of the *Krî* יָדַעְתִּי upon the *Kthiv* ידעת.

(γ.) י is 'superfluous' in רברתי 2 s. *f.* [Jer. iii. 5], etc.   In Jer. xxxi. 21 (or 20) הלכתי is *Kthiv* for הָלָכַת *Krî*, etc. In Ruth iv. 5 קניתי is *Kthiv* for קָנִיתָ *Krî* (2 s. *m* Past *K.*, Tab. XXIII.).

139. (α.) Of the PARTICIPLES the Sing. *m.* forms only are given in Tab. XIV.   The Sing. *f.* and the Plu. *m.* & *f.* are seen in the following list of the Participles signifying :—

'One' (or 'more') (i.) (1) *visiting*, (2) *visited;*

(ii) *being visited;*

(iii.) *visiting* (Intens.);

(iv.) *visited* (Intens.);

(v.) *causing to visit;*

(vi.) *caused to visit;*

(vii.) *visiting himself*, or *herself*, or *them-selves.*

(β). PARTICIPLES [TAB. XIV., APP. B.]

Plu. f.	Plu. m.	Sing. f.	Sing. m.	
פּוֹקְרוֹת*	(פּוֹקְרִי i.c.) פּוֹקְרִים*	(פּוֹקֶדֶת† or) פּוֹקְדָה*	פּוֹקֵד* (1)	(i.) Kal.
פְּקוּדוֹת	(פְּקוּדֵי i.c.) פְּקוּדִים	(פְּקוּדַת i.c.) פְּקוּדָה	פָּקוּד (2)	
נִפְקָדוֹת	(נִפְקְדֵי i.c.) נִפְקָדִים	(נִפְקֶדֶת or) נִפְקָדָה	נִפְקָד	(ii.) Niph.
מְפַקְּדוֹת	(מְפַקְּדֵי i.c.) מְפַקְּדִים	(מְפַקֶּדֶת or) מְפַקְּדָה	מְפַקֵּד	(iii.) Pi-ĕl
מְפָקְּדוֹת	(מְפָקְּדֵי i.c.) מְפָקְּדִים	(מְפָקֶּדֶת or) מְפָקְּדָה	מְפָקָּד‡	(iv.) Pŭ-ăl.
מַפְקִידוֹת	(מַפְקִידֵי i.c.) מַפְקִידִים	(מַפְקֶדֶת or) מַפְקִידָה	מַפְקִיד	(v.) Hĭph.
מָפְקָדוֹת	(מָפְקְדֵי i.c.) מָפְקָדִים	(מָפְקֶדֶת or) מָפְקָדָה	מָפְקָד§	(vi.) Hŏph.
מִתְפַּקְּדוֹת	(מִתְפַּקְּדֵי i.c.) מִתְפַּקְּדִים	(מִתְפַּקֶּדֶת or) מִתְפַּקְּדָה	מִתְפַּקֵּד	(vii.) Hithpă.

[N.B. In the above, — (1) the ◌ֶ of any Sing. m. form is seen to be dropped (and replaced by ◌ְ) in one form of the Sing. f., and in the Plural forms; (2) forms ending in ◌ָד, or ◌ִיד, are UNCHANGED ‘i. c.,’ § 53; (3) those ending in ◌ֵד have ◌ֵד ‘i. c.’; (4) those ending in ◌ָה have ◌ַת (and those in ◌ָדָה have ◌ָדַת) ‘i. c.’;—without further change.]

(γ.) There are two Participles in *Kal*, viz., (1) פּוֹקֵד which is of the form פּוֹעֵל, and (2) פָּקוּד which is of the form פָּעוּל.|| The First expresses *Action in progress*, and refers to an *Agent* (פּוֹעֵל), and is therefore sometimes called the ACTIVE Participle *Kal.* The Second expresses Action *wrought* (פָּעוּל) and refers to an *Object acted on*, and is therefore sometimes called the PASSIVE¶ Participle *Kal.*

Obs.—(i.) For the וּ of (2) there is often ◌ֻ [Pt. I., § 14], as in דָּבָר *m.*, שְׂרָפִים pl. *m.*, etc., נֶצֶרת *f.*, שְׁלֻחָה *f.* (i.c.).

(ii.) The Construct form of פָּעוּל is פְּעוּל or פְּעֻל, as in שְׁתֻם Nu. xxiv. 3.

(iii.) Participles of the Passive Voices (II., IV., VI.) generally retain the ◌ַ of the 2ᵈ Root-letter (except when ‘i.c.,’ and in the ◌ַ ◌ֶ form), as in (β.).

(iv.) The *Hiph.* Partic. sometimes drops the ◌ִי See Sect. XIII.

---

* Or with ◌ֹ for וֹ. This need not be noticed hereafter.

† In Pause, sometimes the same (thus, נֹפֶלֶת, אֹמֶנֶת:); and sometimes ◌ָ ◌ֶת: as in עֹמֶרֶת:, יוֹשֶׁבֶת:.

‡ Also, some few times *without* the מ; thus, אֻכָּל, Ex. iii. 2, לֻקַּח; 2 K. ii. 10.

§ Also מָ instead of מֻ (ŏ).

|| These are often called (1) *Po-ĕl*, and (2) *Pa-ûl*, from (1) פּוֹעֵל, (2) פָּעוּל.

¶ The term ‘PERFECT Participle’ is perhaps not unsuitable to it as expressing FINISHED Action. The *Niph-ăl* Particip. is, rather, a PRESENT Passive Participle.

(δ.) (i.) The Participle יָכֹל *able* (Sing. *m.*) given in Tab. XIV., is the Participle *Kal* of פָּעֹל form, [יְכֹלָה Sing. *f*, יְכֹלִים Plu. *m*, יְכֹלוֹת Plu. *f*], whence

(ii) ('ı c.') פָּעֹל s. *m.*, [פָּעֹלַת s *f.*, פָּעֹלִי pl. *m.*, פָּעֹלַת pl. *f*].

(iii.) There is also the Participle *Kal* of פָּעֵל form, as כָּבֵד *heavy* (Sing. *m.*), [פְּעֵלָה Sing *f.*, פְּעֵלִים Pl. *m.*, פְּעֵלוֹת Pl. *f.*], whence

(iv) ('i.c.') פְּעֵלֹ‡ s. *m.*, [*פָּעֲלַת s. *f.*, *פָּעֲלִי pl. *m.*, פָּעֲלֹת pl. *f.*].

(ε.) The Singular Participle sometimes receives an 'added' י, as in אֹסְרִי *binding* (Sing. *m*) [from אָסַר], Gen. xlix. 11; so in הַמַּשְׁפִּילִי [from מַשְׁפִּיל] Ps. cxiii 6, אֹהַבְתִּי [from אֹהֶבֶת] Hos x 11, and מְלֵאֲתִי [from מְלֵאַת, Constr form of מְלֵאָה (δ. iii)] Is. i. 21; גְּנֻבְתִּי [from גְּנֻבַת (for גְּנוּבַת Pt. I. § 14) Constr. form of גְּנוּבָה] Gen xxxi. 39.

[140. (α.) The Present Tense, — *I am visiting, Thou art visiting, He is visiting*, etc., — is expressed by the Pronouns *I, Thou, He*, etc., with the Participle; thus,

Singular.

פּוֹקֵד† { הוּא He [is] / אַתָּה Thou *m.* [art] / אֲנִי or אָנֹכִי I *m.* [am] } visiting	פֹּקֶדֶת { הִיא She [is] / אַתְּ Thou *f.* [art] / אֲנִי or אָנֹכִי I *f.* [am] } visiting	פּוֹקְדָה or פּוֹקֶדֶת	

Plural.

פּוֹקְדִים { הֵמָּה or הֵם They / אַתֶּם Ye / אֲנַחְנוּ We } *m* [are] visiting	{ הֵנָּה They / אַתֵּנָה Ye / אֲנַחְנוּ We } *f.* [are] visiting	פֹּקְדוֹת	

[N.B.—Third-Person Pronouns are often not expressed.   Cp. (δ.) below.]

(β) Similarly for other Participles.

(γ.) The Hebrew expressions in (α) are, of course, the same whatever be the form of the so-called 'Substantive Verb' or 'logical Copula' to be supplied—such as, *was, may be, might be*, etc.   Hence the above may not be called the PRESENT TENSE in Hebrew.   It is a means of expressing *Present Action*, and may stand for the [strictly] *Present Tense in English*; — but it may stand for much more also, and therefore MUST NOT BE LIMITED to 'Present Tense.'

(δ.) The Participles are often used—

(i.) With Nouns Substantive:— as in צִרְקָתוֹ עֹמֶדֶת לָעַד *His Righteousness* [is] *remaining for-ever*, הַשָּׁמַיִם מְסַפְּרִים *the heavens* [are] *telling*, הַמֶּלֶךְ עֹמֵד *the king was standing*, etc.:

(ii.) with Prefix ה, cp. § 98, as in הוּא הַסֹּבֵב, Gen. ii. 11,

---

* Also [§ 56 (i.)] יְרֵאַת s. *f.* & יְרֵאֵי pl. *m.*, (fr. יָרֵא); so קָצְרִי fr. קָצָר.
† The ב is often without its Dagesh Lene, in accordance with Pt. I., § 48.

lit., *it* [*is*] *the* [*one*] *compassing*, i.e. (as in E.V.) *that* [*is*] *it
which compasseth*, הֵם הָעֹמְדִים, Nu. vii. 2, lit., *they* [*were*] *the*
[*ones*] *standing*, i.e., *they* [*were*] *those who* [*were*] *standing;*
so הָעֹמֵד D. i. 38, xvii. 12; הַמְרַגְּלִים, Josh. vi. 22, 23; etc.;

(iii.) as Nouns;*—thus, שֹׁמֵר *one keeping, watching*, for *a
keeper, a watchman*, עֹזֵר *one helping*, for *a helper*, etc.;

(iv.) 'i. c.'; thus, שֹׁמֵר [*the*] *keeper of*, שֹׁמְרֵי [*the*] *keepers
of*, etc.;

(v.) as Adjectives, § 79, etc.

(ε.) Often a Hebrew Participle is used as a Noun where
the corresponding Noun does not exist in English, as עֹמֵד
one standing, where we cannot say, "a stander," הַכֹּרֵת *the*
[*one*] *cutting*, where we cannot say, "the cutter."† So
Ps. l. 5, כֹּרְתֵי בְרִיתִי (lit., *cutters-of My Covenant*) *those that
made a Covenant with* ME.

(ζ.) Participles may receive Pron. Affixes as Nouns; thus,
אֹיְבִי *my enemy*, etc., from אֹיֵב (Partic. *Kal* of אֹיֵב), etc.].

141. (α.) Two forms of the IMPERATIVE and FUTURE,
Kal, are given in Tab. XIV. (I.), one with ─‡ to the 2ᵈ
Root-letter in פְּקֹד (or פְּקוֹד) *visit thou* (m.), יִפְקֹד (or יִפְקוֹד)
he will visit; (ii.) one with ─§ to the 2ᵈ Root-letter in
לְבַשׁ *put thou* (m) *on* (as clothing), יִלְבַּשׁ *he will put on*, etc.
Some Verbs have the one, and some the other.   Some few
have both forms, as we shall see.

[Note—Sometimes the 2ᵈ Root-letter has (1) ─ [§ 167], as in כַּעֲד (Imper.)
Ju xix. 5, יִצְלַח (Fut.) Ez. xviii. 15; (2) וֹ, as in יִשְׁפּוֹטוּ (Fut.) Ex. xviii. 26].

---

* An interesting example of the double use of a Participle, שֹׁמְרִים, (1) as a Noun
"*watchers*," and (2) as a Present-Tense-Participle "*are watching*," or "*do watch*,"
occurs in Ps. cxxx. 6, which may be rendered " My soul [looks with watching] to
The LORD [מִשֹּׁמְרִים לַבֹּקֶר שֹׁמְרִים לַבֹּקֶר] *more than* WATCHERS *for the morning*
DO-WATCH *for the morning.*   So in the former Grammar, Vol II p. 72.

† The word '*feller*' is, however, admissible in Is xiv 8 (E.V.).

‡ Verbs of this class are called, by some, '*Verbs Fut.-(O).*' Better, '*Fut. (─)*'.

§ Verbs of this class are called, by some, '*Verbs Fut.-(A).*' Better, '*Fut (─)*'.

(β.) In the IMPERATIVE there are only Second-Person forms, viz. for *thou* (*m.* & *f.*) and *ye* (*m* & *f.*). The 2 s. *f.* and 2 pl. *m.* & *f.* have the added terminations ִי, וּ, נָה [cp. § 133 (α.)] attached to the fundamental פְּקֹד or לְבַשׁ for the *Kal.* So for other Voices. But, in the *Kal,*

[Obs.:—the Vowel of the 2ᵈ Root-letter is dropped and replaced by ְ on the addition of the ִי (2 s *f.*) and of the וּ (2 pl. m.); the ְ of the 1st Root-letter must then be changed into a 'Slight-Vowel' (Pt. I., § 56). This 'Slight-Vowel' is generally ְ, as in לְבְשׁוּ, לְבְשִׁי, פִּקְדוּ, פִּקְדִי, (Cp. § 57, Obs.); but sometimes another short-vowel is adopted, as in אֲחֹזִי (or אֶחֱזִי) and in (δ.) below.]

(γ.) The Imper 2 s. m. often has an additional ה; thus, (1) שָׁמְרָה (fr. שְׁמֹר) *keep thou* (*m.*), קָרְבָה (fr. קְרַב) *approach thou* (*m.*), (2) מִכְרָה (fr. מְכֹר) *sell thou* (*m.*), שִׁמְעָה (fr. שְׁמַע) *hear thou* (*m.*),* etc. Sometimes, also, in other Voices; thus, (3) *Niph.* הִשָּׁבְעָה *swear thou* (*m.*); (4) *Pi-él* סַפְּרָה *relate thou* (*m.*); (5) *Hiph.* הַקְשִׁיבָה *hearken thou* (*m.*), etc.

(δ.) Sometimes the Imper. *Kal* has ְ (δ) to the 1st Root-letter in the 2 s. *f*, and 2 pl *m* , thus, מְלְכִי, Ju. ix. 10. [This is also *Krí,* in v. 12, for מלוכי *Kthív.* So, in v. 8, מְלְכָה (2 s. m.) is *Krí,* for מלוכה *Kthív.*]† So חָרְבוּ, Jer. ii. 12, and מָשְׁכוּ, Ez xxxii 20, as well as מִשְׁכוּ, Ex. xii 21.—Cp. (γ. 1), and see more hereafter.

(ε.) שְׁמַעַן, Gen. iv. 23, is an instance of the ־ה of 2 pl. *f.* Imper. being dropped. The word stands for שְׁמַעְנָה. The ־ of the ע is given to aid the enunciation of the עַן.

(ζ.) Sometimes, we find the 3rd Root-letter with Dag. Lene, as in אָסְפִּי, Jer. x. 17, חִשְׂפִּי, Is. xlvii. 2; the vowel beneath the 1st Root-letter is then a Real Short-vowel, having the ְ after it *Quiescent.* [Each of these is 2 s *f* Imper *Kal*]

(η). (i) In זְעָמָה, Nu. xxiii. 7, Imper. *Kal* 2 s. *m.* [with ה, see (γ)], the 1st Root-letter has the Long Vowel ֵ.

(ii.) In נִצְּרָה (i.e נְצֹר, Imper. *Kal*, 2 s. *m.*, with ה) Ps. cxli. 3, the Dagesh in צ is *Euphonic.*—Pt. I., App. C.

(θ.) For רָפָאָה, וּסְעָדָה,—and פְּשֹׁטָה, חַגְּרָה, רְגְזָה,—see Index.

---

* And with ְ, as in עָרְכָה, אָסְפָּה.
† Cp. קָסוֹמִי, with וֹ 'superfluous,' 1 S. xxviii. 8,—for קָסְמִי [Pt. I, App D].

142. The FUTURE is connected with the IMPERATIVE. Thus,

(α.) In *Kal*, (i) the forms תִּפְקְדִי *thou* (*f.*) *wilt visit*, תִּפְקְדוּ *ye* (*m.*) *will visit*, תִּפְקֹדְנָה *ye* (*f.*) (or *they* (*f.*)) *will visit*, consist of תִּ and פִּקְדִי, פִּקְדוּ, פְּקֹדְנָה.

[Obs.—In the Imperative forms פִּקְדוּ, פִּקְדִי, the — of the פ is of course replaced by a 'Slight'-vowel, in order that there may not be two Moving Shvas together; but in the Future the — stands after the formative תּ, after which the — may be (and is) Quiescent.]

(ii.) So in the case of יִפְקְדוּ (Fut.) and פִּקְדוּ (Imp.).

(iii). The remaining Fut. Tense forms, viz., יִפְקֹד 3 s. *m.*, תִּפְקֹד 3 s. *f.* (& 2 s. *m.*), אֶפְקֹד 1 s., and נִפְקֹד 1 pl., all correspond with the fundamental פְּקֹד.

(iv.) Similarly in the case of the Verbs 'Fut (—)' [p. 85].

(v.) The Imper. has generally — in Verbs 'Fut (—)', & (—) in Verbs 'Fut.(—)'.

(β.) In *Niph.* the Future forms תִּפָּקְדִי *thou* (*f.*) *wilt be visited*, תִּפָּקְדוּ *ye* (*m.*).. and יִפָּקְדוּ *they*, (*m.*).., תִּפָּקַדְנָה *ye* (*f.*) or *they* (*f.*).., correspond respectively with the Imper. forms הִפָּקְדִי 2 s. *f.*, הִפָּקְדוּ 2 pl. *m.*, הִפָּקַדְנָה 2 pl. *f.*; and the other Persons of the Future Tense, viz., יִפָּקֵד 3 s. *m.*, תִּפָּקֵד 3 s. *f.* (& 2 s. *m.*), אֶפָּקֵד 1 s., and נִפָּקֵד 1 pl., with the fundamental הִפָּקֵד :—the ה being extruded between the prefix letters א י ת נ and the first Root-letter.

(γ.) Similarly in the case of the other Voices; thus, the Fut. 2 s. *f.*, תִּפַּקְדִי *Pi-él*, תַּפְקִידִי *Hiph.*, תִּתְפַּקְדִי *Hithp.*, correspond with the Imper. 2 s. *f.* פַּקְדִי *Pi-él*, הַפְקִידִי *Hiph.*, הִתְפַּקְדִי *Hithp.*

(δ.) In *Pu-ál* and *Hoph-ál*, which have no Imper.,* there is the corresponding analogy with imaginary Imperative forms.

143. The ה of the נָה, in pl. *f.* Fut., is sometimes

---

* We find, however, once [Ez. xxxii. 19] הָשְׁכְּבָה, Imper. *Hoph.*, 2 s. *m*, *be thou laid* (lit., *caused to lie*); and [Jer. xlix. 8] הָפְנוּ, Imper. *Hoph* 2 pl. *m. be ye made to turn*,—from פָּנָה, see hereafter.

dropped, and the ־ָ given to וֹ, as in לֹא תִזָּכַרְן Ez. iii. 20, xxxiii. 13, *they (f.) shall not be remembered.* So תִּלְבַּשְׁן (as given by many) 2 S. xiii. 18, for תִּלְבַּשְׁנָה which is found in several editions; etc.

144. A הָ ־ָ is often found at the end of the 1 s. and 1 pl. of the Future; thus,—

(*α.*) First Person Sing.:—אֶשְׁמְרָה (fr. אֶשְׁמֹר) Ps. xxxix. 2, אֶשְׁכְּבָה (fr. אֶשְׁכַּב) Ps. lvii. 5, אֲכַבְּדָה (fr. אֲכַבֵּד) Ex. xiv. 4, etc., (אֶתְפַּלְלָה (fr. אֶתְפַּלֵל) אַזְכִּירָה (fr. אַזְכִּיר) Ps. xlv. 18, Dan. ix. 4; and

(*β.*) First Person Plu.:—נִשְׂרְפָה (fr. נִשְׂרֹף) Gen. xi. 3, etc., נִתְחַכְּמָה (fr. נִתְחַכֵּם) Ex. i. 10, etc.

(*γ*) Rarely at the end of the 3 s *m* as * יָחִישָׁה Is. v. 19 [יָחִישׁ Tab. XX], and 3 s *f*.† as תַעְגְּבָה Ez. xxiii. 16 (*Krî*), & 20; also, perhaps, 2 s. *m.* תָעֻפָּה [תָעוּף Tab. XX.] Job xi. 17 ,

(*δ*) And with ־ַ before it, as in יַדְשְׁנֶה Ps. xx. 4.

(*ε*) In (*α.*), (*β.*), etc , above, the vowel of the 2nd Root-letter is seen to be dropped when the additional ה appears. [Cp. for the Imper. § 141 (*γ.*)]. But

(*ζ*) it will be found hereafter [§ 166 (ii.)] that, in Pause, the vowel which was so dropped is either (1) restored if it be Long, or (2) replaced (if it be Short) by the corresponding Long Vowel.

(*η*) Sometimes the Moving Shva of the 2nd Root-letter [in cases of (*ε.*)] has the form ־ָ, as in (1) אֶשְׁקוֹטָה [אֶשְׁקֹט] Is xviii. 4, where the וֹ is noted as ‘superfluous’; (2) אֶפְשְׁעָה [אֶפְשַׁע] Is. xxvii. 4; and

(*θ.*) sometimes the form ־ֶ; as in (3) אֶשְׁקְלָה [אֶשְׁיָקֹל] Jer. xxxii. 9, etc. See Pt. I., App. D.

145. An additional וֹ is often found after those Future forms which end in וּ, viz., the 3 & 2 pl. *m.;* thus, יְלַמְּדוּן D. iv. 10, תִּשְׁמְרוּן D. vi. 17. So יַקְטִרוּן 1 S. ii. 15, 16,

---

* For יקרחה *Kthiv* Lev. xxi. 5, יִקְרְחוּ is *Krî* (whence the ־ָ of יִקְרְחָה, cp. p. 85, v)

† Some give as 3 s *f.*, with נָה added, תִּשְׁלַחְנָה Ju. v. 26; (also 2 s. *m.*, Obad 13).

תִּשָּׁחֵתוּן D. iv. 16, etc. (the ־ֵ standing for the ־ִי of the *Hiph-êl*,—Part I, § 12).   And so יִשְׁכְּבֻן 1 S. ii. 22, יַרְשִׁיעֻן Ex. xxii. 8, (the ־ֻ standing for וּ,—Pt. I, § 14).

146.   Also ן is found some few times after the 2 s. *f.* Future. Thus the 2 s. *f.* Fut. *Kal.* תִּפְקְדִי would, with this ן, be תִּפְקְדִין. So we find תִּדְבָּקִין* Ruth ii. 8 (& 21) [for תִּדְבָּקִי].   So the 2 s. *f.* Fut. *Hithpă-êl* תִּשְׁתַּבְּרִין 1 S. i. 14 [for תִּשְׁתַּבְּרִי, the Pause-form of תִּשְׁתַּבְּרִי—comp. Note (*h, a*) on Tab. XIV and *⁎* below there].

147.   The ן of §§ 145 & 146, as also of § 138 (B) (iv, β), is called by some 'ן PARAGOGIC'.   So the ה of § 144, and that of § 138 (B), is called by some 'ה PARAGOGIC'; and so the א of § 138 (B) (iv, a), and the י of § 139 (e).   Some however consider that י to be a mark of CONNECTION—the 'י *Compaginis*,' as they call it, Comp. p. 232 (lines 6—10).

NOTE I.

(i.) As in the last example cited in § 146, *viz.* תִּשְׁתַּבְּרִין for תִּשְׁתַּבְּרִי Pause-form of תִּשְׁתַּבְּרִי [instead of תִּתְשַׁבְּרִי] fr. שׁבר, the 1st Rt-letter and the ת of the הִת of *Hithpă-êl* change places when the 1st Rt-letter is either †שׁ, or שׂ, or ס; thus we have

---

* For the ־ֵ the Student may refer to § 141 'Note'; but he will understand the matter better hereafter [§ 167 (ii) & § 166 (e)]

† With one exception *viz.* הִתְשׁוֹטַטְנָה Jer. xlix. 3.   For this word see § 246 (p. 162).   It belongs to a Class of Verbs to be dealt with hereafter.

הִשְׁתַּפֵּךְ Infin. *Hithpă-ēl* fr. שפך,

מִשְׁתַּכֵּר Partic. s. *m.* *Hithpă-ēl* fr. שכר,

יִסְתַּבֵּל Fut. 3 s. *m.* *Hithpă-ēl* fr. סבל.

(ii.) When the 1st Rt-letter is צ,—not only does the צ change places with the ת of the הת', but moreover this ת is replaced by ט; thus, from ציד we have הִצְטַיַּדְנוּ Past *Hithpă-ēl* 1 pl. [instead of הִתְצַיַּדְנוּ], and so fr. צדק we have נִצְטַדָּק Fut. *Hithpă-ēl* 1 pl. Pause-form [instead of נִתְצַדָּק].

(iii.) When the 1st Rt-letter is ד, or ט, or ת,—the ת of the הת' is dropped, and Dagesh F. is put into the 1st Rt-letter to represent it.

This matter is briefly mentioned and illustrated in ' Notes on Tab. XIV ' (***) [p. xv of the Tables]. The whole matter will be dealt with a little more fully hereafter, as soon as we shall have gone through all the Great Classes of Verb-forms [see ' Note ' on pages 315—318].

NOTE (II).

In Tab. XV (Infinitives with Pron-Affs.) it may be seen that, except in the
Hiph. forms,

(α) When the 3ᵈ Rt-letter- has a VOWEL, the 2ᵈ Rt-Letter has *Shva*;

(β) When the 3ᵈ Rt-letter has SHVA, the 2ᵈ Rt-letter has

   (a) sometimes ⁻ᵣ [necessarily Quiescent, Pt. I, § 55 (13, a)],

   (b) sometimes a '*Slight*'-*vowel*.

   Obs. The Slight-Vowel in (b) generally agrees with the Vowel which
   the 2ᵈ Rt-letter has dropped; thus we have

     (1) the ⁻ᵣ ŏ of the *Kal* forms פְּקָדְךָ, פְּקָדְכֶם, פְּקָדְכָן, Tab. XV
     Notes (*) & (‡),—where the Vowel which the 2ᵈ Rt-letter
     has dropped is the ⁻ of פָּקֹד;

     (2) the ⁻ᵥ of the *Niph-ăl* forms הִפָּקֶדְךָ etc., from הִפָּקֹד,
     and of the *Pĭ-êl* forms פַּקֶּדְךָ etc., from פַּקֵּד, and of the
     Hithpă-êl forms הִתְפַּקֶּדְךָ etc, from הִתְפַּקֵּד,—where
     the Vowel which the 2ᵈ Rt-letter has dropped is ⁻;

     (3) the ⁻ of the Pŭ-al forms פֻּקַּדְךָ etc., from פֻּקַּד, and of
     the *Hoph-ăl* forms הָפְקַדְךָ etc ,—where the Vowel which
     the 2ᵈ Rt-letter has dropped is ⁻ᵤ.

(γ) Instead of the ⁻ᵣ of פְּקָדְכֶם (Comp. β, b, 2), there is sometimes ⁻ː
as in וּבְפָרִשְׂכֶם Is. i. 15 from פָּרֵשׂ (Infin. Pĭ, like פַּקֵּד, but with
Compensation for the Dagesh which the ר cannot receive).

(δ) In place of the 'Slight'-Vowel, a Long real Vowel is sometimes given
to the 2ᵈ Rt-letter before a Guttural 3ᵈ Rt-letter, as in בְּשַׁלֵּחֲךָ D. xv. 18
from שַׁלֵּחַ. [For the 'Furtive' ⁻ᵣ, see Pt. I (§ 60)].

Exercise XIX.

(To be translated into English.)

*** For the plan of the Exercise, see § 11 (a—ε).

יִשְׂרָאֵל[1] אָהַב[2] אֶת יוֹסֵף[3] : שִׁמְעוּ[4] נָא[5] הַחֲלוֹם[6] הַזֶּה :

*הַמֶּלֶךְ[7] תִּמְלֹךְ[7] עָלֵינוּ : הִנֵּה[8] חָלַמְתִּי[9] חֲלוֹם[6] עוֹד[10] : מָכְרוּ[11]

אֹתוֹ : לְעֶבֶד[12] נִמְכַּר[11] יוֹסֵף[3] : הִפְקִיד[13] אֹתוֹ בְּבֵיתוֹ[14] :

הָנְחַלְתִּי[15] לִי[16] יַרְחֵי[17] שָׁוְא[18] : וַאֲנִי[19] אָמַרְתִּי[20] †בְחָפְזִי[21]

נִגְרַזְתִּי[22] מִנֶּגֶר[23] עֵינֶיךָ[24] אָכֵן[25] שָׁמַעְתָּ[4] קוֹל[26] תַּחֲנוּנַי[27]

†בְּשַׁוְּעִי[28] אֵלֶיךָ : מִבֶּטֶן[29] שְׁאוֹל[30] שִׁוַּעְתִּי[28] : יְיָ[31] יִשְׁמַע[4]

†בְּקָרְאִי[32] אֵלָיו : זָרַח[33] בַּחֹשֶׁךְ[34] אוֹר[35] :

וְלֹא יָכֹל[36] יוֹסֵף[3] לְהִתְאַפֵּק[37] : וְלֹא יָכְלוּ[36] אֶחָיו[38] לַעֲנוֹת[39]

אֹתוֹ : לֹא אַתֶּם שְׁלַחְתֶּם[40] אֹתִי הֵנָּה[41] : דִּבְּרוּ[42] אֶחָיו[38]

אֹתוֹ :

לֹא יַרְעִיב[43] יְיָ[31] נֶפֶשׁ[44] צַדִּיק[45] : מֵאֲשֶׁר[46] יָקַרְתָּ[47] בְעֵינַי[24]

נִכְבַּדְתָּ[48] : נִשְׁבְּרָה[49] קִרְיַת[50] תֹּהוּ[51] : כִּי[52] נִבְקְעוּ[53] בַמִּדְבָּר[54]

מָיִם[55] : וְקוֹל[26] הַתּוֹר[56] נִשְׁמַע[4] בְּאַרְצֵנוּ[57] :

[1] Israel. [2] אהב to love. [3] Joseph. [4] שמע to hear [5] now, *or* I pray. [6] חָלוֹם a dream. [7] מלך to reign. [8] behold. [9] חלם to dream. [10] again. [11] מכר to sell. [12] עֶבֶד a slave. [13] פקד to visit (*Hiph.* to-make-visitor, to-appoint-as-officer). [14] בַּיִת a house, Tab. XIII (3). [15] נחל to possess (*Hoph.* to be made-to-possess, to have-as-one's lot). [16] for myself. [17] months of. [18] vanity. [19] and I. [20] אמר to say [21] חפז to be-in-haste. [22] גרז to cut off. [23] from before. [24] עֵין an eye, Tab. XIII. (3, β). [25] but. [26] voice, voice of. [27] my supplications. [28] שוע *Pi.* to cry. [29] בֶּטֶן (§ 56, vii) a womb, *figur^ly.* a hidden depth. [30] *Sh'ol*, pit, grave, hell. [31] Exerc. IX. (ε). [32] קרא to call. [33] זרח to rise (as the sun). [34] חשֶׁךְ darkness. [35] light. [36] יכל to be able (§ 138 A, iii). [37] אפק *Hithp.* to restrain oneself [38] Tab XIII (2). [39] to answer. [40] שלח to send. [41] hither. [42] דבר *Pi.* to speak. [43] רעב to hunger. [44] soul, soul of. [45] a righteous-one. [46] since. [47] יקר to be precious. [48] כבד *Niph.* to be honoured. [49] שבר to break. [50] קרִיָה a city. [51] emptiness. [52] for. [53] בקע to cleave (*Niph.* to be let break forth). [54] in the wilderness. [55] water. [56] the turtle-dove. [57] אֶרֶץ a land, Tab. X (1).——— * See § 137 (1, Obs β.). † See § 137 (4, i, ii.).

[N.B.—Henceforth the following, and words marked in the Notes with *, need not be given in Notes to the Exercises:—

VOCABULARY I.

1. אֱלֹהִים God, a Noun of Plu. form Tab. V.(ii.).
2. אִם *if.* Also *Interrog.,* and = *or?* after ה (§ 7).
3. בַּיִת (*m.*), Tab. XIII. 3.
4. בַּת (*f.*), Tab. XIII. 5.
5. גּוֹי (*m.*) *a nation*, pl. גּוֹיִם *nations, Gentiles, heathen.*
6. גַּם *also, even.*
7. דָּבָר (*m.*) *a word, thing,* Tab. IX.
8. הוּא Tab. I. (1), & § 32 (II.), § 94.
9. יְיָ Exerc. XI. (1).
10. כִּי *for, because, that.*
11. מַיִם (*m.*) *water,* a Noun of Dual form.
12. נְאֻם *saith*[E.V.], lit., [is] *said of.*
13. נְהִי *wailing.*
14. עַם (*m.*) *a people* (Ex. XV., No. 34), w. aff. עַמּוֹ, etc., pl. עַמִּים.
15. פָּקַד *to visit.*
16. קֹדֶשׁ (*m.*)*holiness,* Tab. XI. 1 & ‡.
17. קוֹל (*m.*) *a voice* (§ 43), i c. the same.
18. שֵׁם (*m.*) *a name,* Tab. XIII. (Note §, *a.*), and § 43.
19. שָׁם *there,* שָׁמָּה *thither.*]

EXERCISE XX.

(To be translated into English.)

₊ The VOCABULARY on pp. 383—388 may be referred to, if necessary.

עַל' נַהֲרוֹת' בָּבֶל' שָׁם יָשַׁבְנוּ' גַּם בָּכִינוּ' בְּזָכְרֵנוּ' אֶת

צִיּוֹן' : כִּי שֶׁבֶר' גָּדוֹל' נִשְׁבְּרָה'' בְּתוּלַת'' בַּת עַמִּי : קוֹל

נְהִי נִשְׁמַע'' מִצִּיּוֹן : אוֹי'' לָנוּ כִּי שֻׁדַּדְנוּ'' : כִּי־בָּגוֹד'' בָּגְדוּ'

בִּי'' בֵּית יִשְׂרָאֵל'' : הֲעַל אֵלֶּה לֹא אֶפְקֹד נְאֻם יְיָ אִם

בְּגוֹי אֲשֶׁר כָּזֶה'' לֹא תִתְנַקֵּם'' נַפְשִׁי'' : הִכָּרֵת'' תִּכָּרֵת''

הַנֶּפֶשׁ'' הַהִוא : מָרַדְנוּ'' בּוֹ'' : אֲהָהּ'' אֲדֹנָי'' יְיָ'' :

---

[1] עַל by, on, on account of. [2] rivers of (fr. נָהָר). [3] Babylon.* [4] יָשַׁב to sit, dwell. [5] we wept. [6] זכר K. to remember, *Hiph.* to mention. [7] Zion.* [8] [with a] breach, breaking. [9] great (*m.*). [10] שבר to break. [11] virgin of (§ 88). [12] woe ! [13] שדד *Pi-él* to devastate [Tab. XIV. Note (†, Obs. 1)]. [14] בגד to deal treacherously. [15] בְּ against. [16] Israel.* [17] § 34. [18] נקם *Hithp.* to avenge one-self. [19] נֶפֶשׁ* (*f.*) soul Tab. X. 1, Pl. נְפָשׁוֹת Tab. XII. 1. [20] כרת to cut, cut off. [21] מרד to rebel. [22] Alas ! [23] O Lord.* [24] Pt. I., § 79 (2).

---

* Words marked thus (*) need not be given in the Notes again.
† See § 137 (1, Obs. *β*).

הַמַּשְׁחִית[25] אַתָּה אֶת כָּל שְׁאֵרִית[26] וְשְׂרָאֵל[16] : לֹא †הַשְׁמִיד[27]
אַשְׁמִיד[27] אֶת בֵּית יַעֲקֹב[28] : אֱלֹהִים בְּאָזְנֵינוּ[29] שָׁמַעְנוּ[30] אֲבוֹתֵינוּ[31]
סִפְּרוּ[32] לָנוּ פֹעַל[33] פָּעַלְתָּ[34] בִּימֵיהֶם[35] : הַזְכִּיר[37] שְׁמָא[ ] הַיִפָּלֵא[36]
יְמֵי דָבָר : הַבִּיטוּ[37] אֶל צוּר[38] הֲצַבְתָּם[39] : כִּי[40] נִשְׁבַּעְתִּי[41]
נְאֻם יְיָ : מִי יְמַלֵּל[42] גְבוּרוֹת[43] יְיָ : סַפְּרוּ[32] בַגּוֹיִם כְּבוֹדוֹ[44] :
הִתְהַלְלוּ[45] בְּשֵׁם קָדְשׁוֹ :

צַדִּיק[46] אַתָּה כִּי נִשְׁאַרְנוּ[47] פְּלֵיטָה[48] : אֲבוֹתֵינוּ[31] בְּמִצְרַיִם[49]
לֹא הִשְׂכִּילוּ[50] נִפְלְאוֹתֶיךָ[36] : אָמַר[51] אוֹיֵב[52] אֶרְדֹּף[53] אַשִּׂיג[54]
אֲחַלֵּק[55] שָׁלָל[56] : נָשַׁפְתָּ[57] בְרוּחֲךָ[58] ... צָלְלוּ[59] כַּעוֹפֶרֶת[60] בְּמַיִם
אַדִּירִים[61] : אַל יִתְהַלֵּל[45] הַגִּבּוֹר[62] בִּגְבוּרָתוֹ[44] : צְעַקְנָה[63] בְּנוֹת[64]
רַבָּה[65] חֲגֹרְנָה[66] שַׂקִּים[67] : זֹאת הָעִיר[68] הָעַלִּיזָה[69] הַיּוֹשֶׁבֶת
לָבֶטַח[70] : פָּקַד עֲוֺנֵךְ[71] בַּת[ ] אֱדוֹם[72] : וּמַלְקוֹחַ[73] עָרִיץ[74] יִמָּלֵט[75] :
לְבֻשִׁי[76] עֹז[77] זְרוֹעַ[78] יְיָ : הֵן[79] בַּעֲוֺנֹתֵיכֶם[71] נִמְכַּרְתֶּם[80]

---

25 שׁחת *Hiph.* to destroy. 26 remnant, remnant of. 27 שׁמד *Hiph* to destroy (with perdition). 28 Jacob.* 29 Tab. VII 30 שׁמע to hear. 31 Tab XIII. 1. 32 סֵפֵּר *Pi* to tell, recount. 33 a work. 34 פָעל to work. 35 § 49 (1). 36 פלא *Niph.* to be wonderful (p. 60, No. 14), *Partic* a wondrous work. 37 look ye 38 a rock* [supply "from which"]. 39 חצב *Pi.* to hew. 40 by myself. 41 שׁבע *N.* to swear. 42 מלל *Pi.* to tell, speak of. 43 גְבוּרה might * 44 His glory. 45 הלל *Pi.* to praise, *Hithp.* to glory [Dagesh Forte often dropped from the ל]. 46 Righteous. 47 שׁאר *Niph.* to remain, to be left. 48 a remnant (that escapes). 49 in Egypt. 50 שׂכל *Hiph.* to regard. 51 אמר to say. 52 איב to be hostile. *Partic.* an enemy. 53 רדף to pursue. 54 I will overtake. 55 חלק *Pi.* to divide, 56 spoil 57 נשׁף to blow. 58 רוּחַ Spirit (also wind) * 59 צלל to sink [ל for ל, Pt. I. § 72 (β.)]. 60 like the lead [§§ 6 (e.), 8 (a.)]. 61 grand (pl. *m*). 62 the mighty one (*m*). 63 צעק to cry out (in pain). 64 Tab. XIII. 5. 65 Rabbah. 66 חגר to gird on. 67 sackloth * 68 the city (*f*) 69 the joyous (*f.*) 70 securely. 71 עָוֺן iniquity (§ 43). 72 Edom.* 73 and the booty of. 74 a terrible one (*m*). 75 מלט *N.* to be delivered. 76 לבשׁ to put on (as clothing). 77 strength. 78 O arm of. 79 lo! 80 מכר to sell

---

* Words marked thus (*) need not be given in the Notes again.
† See § 137 (1, Obs. β).
‡ See Tab. XIII. (Note §, α).

וּבְפִשְׁעֵיכֶם[81] שְׁלָחָה[82] אִמְּכֶם[83] : דִּרְשׁוּ[84] יְיָ בְּהִמָּצְאוֹ[85] : אַתָּה
יְיָ אָבִינוּ[31] גֹּאֲלֵנוּ[86] מֵעוֹלָם[87] שְׁמֶךָ : הָרוֹפֵא[88] לִשְׁבוּרֵי[10] לֵב[89] :
הוּא נָתַן[77] עֹז[80] וְתַעֲצֻמוֹת[91] לָעָם בָּרוּךְ[92] אֱלֹהִים :

[81] פֶּשַׁע* (m.) a trespass, Tab. X. 2. [82] שלח to send, put forth, *Pi.* to send away. [83] your (m.) mother (אֵם). [84] דרשׁ to seek, search for. [85] מצא to find. [86] גאל to redeem, *Partic.* Redeemer. [87] from everlasting. [88] רפא to heal, *Partic.* Healer. [89] heart. [90] נתן to give. [91] and power. [92] ברך *K.* & *Pi.* to bless.

Obs. I.—The Negative Particles לֹא *not*, and אַל *not*, PRECEDE the Tense which is Negatively affected.

Obs. II.—לֹא with a Tense expresses an ordinary Negative; thus לֹא עָמַד *he stood not*, or *did not stand*, or *has not stood*, etc.; also,

Obs. III.—לֹא is used with a Future to express PROHIBITION as in לֹא תִגְנֹב *thou shalt not steal*, לֹא יִמְשֹׁל *he shall not rule*, etc.; but

Obs. IV.—אַל with a Future expresses the DEPRECATIVE ‘ *do not*,’ ‘ *let him not*,’ as אַל תְּדַבֵּר (Is. xxxvi. 11) *do not speak*, אַל יְדַבֵּר (Ex. xx. 19) *let him not speak*, etc.

Obs. V.—Never use a Hebrew Imperative with a Negative Particle (cp. IV.).

Obs. VI.—The prefix לְ is to be used generally for *to*,—unless אֶל, or some other word, be given,—in these Exercises. Also,

Obs. VII.—Personal Pronouns are to be expressed in the Hebrew, if not connected by (-) with the next word in the English.

Obs. VIII.—The Interrogative הַ (§ 7) is to be prefixed to the *first word* of the Interrogative sentence, as in הֲלֹא דִבַּרְתִּי *spake I not* [to thee, saying, etc.?] Nu. xxiii. 26; הַעַל אֵלֶּה לֹא אֶפְקֹד *for these things shall I not visit?* Jer. v. 29.

Obs. IX.—For expressing what *has been and still is going on*, use the PAST Tense.

Obs. X.—For expressing what is *not only going on now but also is expected to go on*, use the FUTURE Tense.

Obs. XI.—“ LET *him do*,” “ LET *her do*, etc., are expressed by the FUTURE, ‘ *He, she*, etc., SHALL (or WILL, *do*).”

---

* Words marked (*) need not be given in the Notes again.

Exercise XXI.

[*.* See ‹Glossary,› for words not in the Notes]

(To be translated into Hebrew. § 11, ζ—μ.)

Ye *(m.)* observed.[1] Thou *(f.)* hast-observed.[1] They *(f.)* have-observed.[1] We observed.[1] Observe-ye *(f.)*. She shall observe.[2] They *(m.)* will-observe.[2] Ye *(f)* will-observe. Observe-thou *(f.)* this-thing *(f.)* [§ 96 (i.)]. Thou *(f.)*-shalt not observe[2] [Obs. III. above]. Did-she-not-observe [Heb., *Whether-not observed*[1]*-she*] the matter[3]? If [Vocab. I. (2)] ye *(m.)*-have not observed, observe-ye now.[4]

Thou *(m.)* hast not kept[1] the covenant[5] of thy GOD. They *(m.)* kept[1] His testimonies.[6] Keep-ye *(m.)* My commandments.[7] We will-keep Thy *(m)* commandments.[7] I kept Thy *(m.)* ordinances.[8] In-order-that[9] I-might-keep[2] Thy *(m.)* word.[3] The Preserver[10] of Israel.[11] Thy *(m.)* visitation[12] hath-preserved[1] my spirit.[13] The-LORD[14] is thy *(m.)* Preserver.[10] HE-will-preserve[2] thy *(m.)* soul.[15]

Exercise XXII.

(To be translated into Hebrew. § 11, ζ—μ.)

Thou *(m.)* shalt not come-near[16] [Obs. III., p. 93] to[17] them *(m)*. And a stranger[18] shall not come-near[16] [Obs. II.] unto[17] you *(m.)*. Come-ye *(m.)*-near[16] to Me. Fearers[19] of THE-LORD,[14] trust-ye[20] *(m.)* in THE-LORD.[14] Who among[21] you *(m.)* is a fearer[19] of THE-LORD?, —... let-him-trust[20]

---

[1] Past *Kal* of שָׁמַר. [2] Fut. *Kal* of שמר ‹Fut. (ـ)› [p. 85 (‡)]. [3] דָּבָר. [4] עַתָּה. [5] בְּרִית. [6] p. 45 (*). [7] מִצְוָה, pl. מצות. [8] פִּקוּדִים (pl). [9] לְמַעַן. [10] Partic. (1) *K.* of שמר [§ 140 (δ., iv), and § 139 (β, N.B 2)] [11] p. 91 (16). [12] פְּקֻדָּה. [13] § 74 (a). [14] [Thus the E.V. for The NAME given in Pt. I § 79 (2). [15] נֶפֶשׁ comp. Tab. X. 1 (for the Sing.). [16] קרב Fut. (—) [141 (a, §)]. [17] אֶל. [18] זָר. [19] יָרֵא (1. c. יְרָא s. m. & יְרָאִי pl. m.). [20] בטח Fut. (—). [21] בְּ.

[Obs. XI.] in The Name[22] of The-Lord[14] and lean[23] on[21] his
God. Cast-ye[24] (*m.*) him into[17] this pit.[25] Only[26] [as regards]
the throne[27] will-I-be-greater-than-thou (Hebr., *Will-I-be-
great*[28] *from thee* (*m.*), cp. § 82. i.). His little[29] brother[30] [§ 81
(3)] shall-be-greater than-he.   Over[31] Edom will-
I-fling[24] my shoe.[32] They (*m.*)- shall-fling[24] each-one[33] his
stone.[34] Thou (*m.*)-hast-been flung[35] from thy grave.[36] Upon[31]
Thee (*m.*) have-I-been-flung.[35] Into[21] Thy (*m.*) Hand [§ 46
(*a.*, 1)] will-I-commend[37] my spirit.[19]

Exercise XXIII.

(To be translated into Hebrew. § 11, *ζ—μ*)

My God be-not-far[38]. [Obs. IV.] from me. I-am-weary[39]
[Obs. IX.] in my groaning.[40] How-long[41] wilt-Thou-hide[42] Thy
face[43] from me? Hear-Thou[44] my prayer.[45] All[46] the day[47]
my disgrace[48] is before[49] me. Fallen-hath[50] the crown[51] of our
head.[52] Many-and-mighty-are[53] [Obs. IX.] my destroyers,[54]
my enemies[55] for-naught (Hebr., *a lie*[56]). Thou-hast-made-
men-to-ride (Hebr., *Thou-hast-caused-to-ride*[57] *weak-man*[58])
over (ל) our head.[52]

Athirst-is[59] [Obs. IX.] my soul[15] for God. For[60] Thou
[art] 'the God of my-Might,[61]...; why[62] in-mourning-garb[63]
should-I-have-so-to-go[64] amid[21] an enemy's[55] oppression?[65] ·Thou-
wilt-destroy[66] the talkers[67] of falsehood.[68] Vanity[69] they (*m.*)-

---

[22] Voc. I. 18.   [23] שֵׁעֵן *Niph.*   [24] שֵׁלֵךְ *Hiph.*   [25] בּוֹר (*m*).   [26] רַק.   [27] כָּסָא.
[28] נֵדֵל Fut. (-֑).   [29] קָטֹן.   [30] Tab. XIII (2).   [31] עַל.   [32] נֵעַל.   [33] אִישׁ
[34] אֵבֵן Tab. X. (B).   [35] שֵׁלֵךְ *Hoph.*   [36] קָבֵר Tab. X. (2).   [37] פֵּקֵר *Hiph.*
[38] רֵחֵק Fut (-֑).   [39] יֵנֵע.   [40] אֵנָחָה w. aff. אַנְחָתוֹ (§ 59).   [41] עַר אָנָה.   [42] סֵתֵר *Hiph.*
[43] Exerc. XIV (10).   [44] שֵׁמֵע Fut. (-֑).   [45] תְּפִלָּה.   [46] (כָּל-)כֹּל.   [47] יוֹם.
[48] בְּלִמָּה.   [49] נֵגֵר § 62 (III).   [50] נָפַל.   [51] עֲטֶרֶת (*f.*).   [52] רֹאשׁ.   [53] עֵצֵם.   [54] צָמֵת
Partic. Hiph.   [55] Exerc. XX (52).   [56] שֶׁקֵר.   [57] רכב *Hiph.*   [58] אֵנוֹשׁ
[59] צָמֵא Past K.   [60] בִּי.   [61] מָעֻזִּי.   [62] לָמָה.   [63] קֹדֵר.   [64] Fut. *Hithp.* of הָלַךְ.
[65] לַחַץ.   [66] אָבַד *Pi-êl.*   [67] pl. *m.* 'l. c.' of דָּבָר (§ 139, β.).   [68] כָּזָב.   [69] שָׁוְא.

will-be-speaking,[70] each-one[33] with[71] his fellow.[72] Thou-hast-destroyed[68] a-wicked-one.[73] And [as for] transgressors[74] they (*m.*)-have-perished[75] together.[76] For[60] not[77] a God[78] taking-pleasure-in[79] wickedness[60] [art] Thou. And they-shall-trust[20] (*m.*) in Thee, that-know[81] Thy Name;[22] for[60] Thou-hast not forsaken[82] [Obs. II.] those-that-seek-to-Thee[83] [O] Lord.

For-ever[84] shall-they (*m.*)-sing-gladly[85] [Table XIV. Note (*c*)]. Of[21] The Name[22] of our God we-will-make-mention.[86] For[60] exalted[87] (*m.*) [is] His Name[22] alone.[88] And [to be] praised[89] exceedingly.[90] [Who] maketh-great[91] the salvation[92] [Plu] of His King.[93] Blessed[94] [is] the man[95] who will-trust[20] in The-Lord. For[60] Thou [expressed] wilt-bless[96] a righteous-one.[97] [As for] those (*m.*)-planted[98] in the house of the-Lord, in the courts[99] of our God shall-they-flourish.[100] As a tree[101] planted[98] by[102] rivers[103] of water.

I-will-hymn[104] Thy Name,[22] [O Thou] Most-High.[105] Sing-ye (*m.*)-hymns[104] to The-Lord [Who] dwelleth[106]-in Zion. We-will-sing-gladly[85] [w. ה, § 144 (β)] through[21] Thy salvation[92]; yea (ו) in The Name[22] of our God will-we-triumph.[107] In The-Lord my-soul-shall-glory (Hebr., *shall-glory*[108] *my soul*).

Hallelujah.[109] [O] my soul [2] * [1] praise-thou[110] The-Lord.

---

[70] דבר *Pĭ-ĕl.* [71] Tab. III. (2). [72] רֵעַ w. the aff. הוּ—, Tab. VIII. [See also § 74 (*a*)]. [73] רְשָׁע. [74] פשע Partic. (1) *Kal*, pl *m.* [§ 139 (γ, 11)]. [75] שמר *Niph.* [76] יַחְדָו. [77] לא [78] אֵל. [79] חפץ Partic. of the form mentioned in § 139 (δ., iii). [80] רְשַׁע. [81] ידע Partic. (1) *K*, pl. *m* 'ı. c.' [82] עזב [83] דרשיך. [84] לעוֹלָם. [85] רנן *Pĭ-ĕl.* [86] זכר *Hiph.* [87] שׂגב *Niph.* [88] לְבַדוֹ. [89] הלל Partic. *Pŭ-ăl.* [90] מְאֹד. [91] גדל Partic. *Hiph* [92] יְשׁוּעָה. [93] Tab. X. (1). [94] ברך Partic. (2) *Kal* [§ 139 (γ, 2)]. [95] גֶּבֶר. [96] ברך *Pĭ-ĕl.* (Compensation to be made for the Dagesh F.). [97] צַדִּיק. [98] שׁתל Partic. (2) *Kal.* [99] חַצרות [the — dropped 'ı. c,' § 56 (ı.)]. [100] פרח *Hiph.* [101] עץ (*m*). [102] עַל. [103] פלג a river [Tab. X. (1)]. [104] זמר *Pĭ-ĕl.* [105] עֶליון. [106] ישׁב Partic. (1) *K.* [107] דֶּגֶל Fut. (—). [108] הלל *Hıthpă-ĕl.* [109] יָה preceded by 2 pl. *m.* Imp. of ([110]). [110] הלל *Pĭ-ĕl* [p. 92 (45)].

---

* (1) (2) are put to mark the order in the Hebrew.

SECTION XII.

Verbs (*continued*). — Certain Usages.

148. As said above (§ 123), there are only two Tenses in Hebrew. These two are the only Tense-forms for expressing such various modifications as "*had*," or "*may*," or "*might*," or "*should*," or "*would*," or "*may have*," might have," etc. Also there are no 'Auxiliary' Verbs. From among the somewhat multitudinous forms of modern expression by which one of these old Tenses may be rendered, very great care is sometimes required for selecting that particular one which is *the* one for bringing out (so far as may be possible) the sense of the original passage. Through neglecting to observe the underlying thought of such a passage, a wrong Mood, or a wrong Auxiliary Verb, may give a wrong turn and lead to an altogether wrong view of the passage. And careful attention to the 'Mood of Thought' (if one may say so) not seldom furnishes a very useful clue, by the help of which the intricacies of some very difficult passages may be safely tracked.

149. Again, the Subordination of Time and Mode of Action is sometimes marked with great accuracy and nicety by the use of different Tense-forms.

[Through neglecting to attend to this, or through mistakes respecting it, some Moderns have succeeded in introducing much strange confusion and misapprehension with regard to the usage of the Hebrew Tenses. The leading principle has often been quite lost sight of. Some have fixed their attention on *one set of* the usages of a Tense, some on another, and so one-and-the-same Tense has been called by some a '*Present*,' by others an '*Imperfect*,' by others an '*Aorist*,' etc. It is amusing to see how happy some appear to be when, not content with an 'Indefinite' name, they succeed in giving an indefinite rendering. To be sure, this seems to betoken too often the absence of definite notions about any Meaning to be conveyed by such a rendering.

Controversy, however, would be out of place here. This only shall be said now:—]

150. (1) It is surely not unreasonable that in a Language which has but two TENSES, these two should have reference to the TWO MAIN DIVISIONS OF TIME. We say MAIN divisions; for, such the 'FUTURE' and the 'PAST' are: the 'PRESENT' is (strictly) but an everchanging instant—a connecting *link between* 'the Future' and ' the Past.'*

(2) Such is not at all unlikely to be the case in the language of a people who were looking forwards from a great Past of Wonders to a Future (in store,—reserved,—prepared) of Good and of Glory such as "eye hath not seen, nor ear heard,"—and who recognised their ' Present' as transitory.

(3) Moreover, the usage of the Language is found to be in accordance with this :—as we hope to shew in the proper place.

151. This, too, ought not to be lost sight of, viz. that—There is a MODE OF RECKONING Past and Future, which is different† from that which may perhaps seem to us to be the only natural one, so long as we refer all to ourselves—as if each one were the Centre of all Time and Space. Familiarity with that which is strange to us—quite foreign, even, to our modes of thought,—can only be acquired after some time, and from much experience of the usage which is thus strange. It would be unwise, therefore, to attempt to enter further into this matter just now. Perhaps we have anticipated too much in venturing to allude to it as we have done.

---

* What is often called "the Present Time" consists really of an undefined portion of Past and Future Time, gathered about the instant Present. Some interesting remarks on the ' Tenses' will appear in Dr. Chance's ' Notes on Job,' pp. 543 & 544.

† Consequent, to some extent, on what was said at the opening of § 9 (δ.).

152. Speaking generally, it may be said that, in Hebrew,

(I.) (*α.*) the Past Tense and the Future Tense, respectively, are used with reference to Action *before,* and *after,* some implied POINT OF TIME, which is

(*β.*) to be looked out for, and may be recognised by means of due consideration of what is being spoken about, but

(*γ.*) which may *or may not* be the ' Present' of a speaker, or narrator ;

(II.) (*α.*) such modifications of PAST-Action (and *Contingent-Past* Action) as we can express by means of *did, was, were, have, had, may have, might have, would have,* etc., are all expressed by the Hebrew PAST-TENSE ;

(*β.*) such modifications of FUTURE-Action (and *Subsequent,* and *Conditional,* and *Dependent* Future-Action) as we can express by means of *will, shall,* and *may, might, should, would,* etc., are all expressed by the Hebrew FUTURE-TENSE ;

(III.) (*α*) that which *has been, and is still going on,* is expressed by the Hebrew PAST-TENSE ; and

(*β.*) that which *is now going on, and is expected to go on in future,* is expressed by the Hebrew FUTURE TENSE.

[Obs. An *Indefinite* Tense, or Mode of Expression, in a Modern Language, may (by reason of *its* indefiniteness) be often* used perhaps in rendering a Tense of an ancient Language. It does not follow that the Tense of an ancient Language is Indefinite.]

---

* But also, very often, such an indefinite expression cannot fairly be used for the Hebrew Tense without great loss of meaning ; and sometimes could not be used at all.

(IV.) The SEQUENCE and CON-SEQUENCE of Actions and Events is sometimes marked by a simple use of the Hebrew Past and Future Tenses, where we (in English) require a different mode of expression.   But in order to bring out the point of the Hebrew expression, so far as this is at all possible sometimes in English, either some Particle must be introduced, or a Periphrasis must be adopted, which contrasts unfavourably with the terse, simple elegance of the Original.

[Obs. (α.) Some may prefer to regard this as a deduction from (I.),—as is

(β.) the use of a Hebrew Future-Tense sometimes after certain Particles of Time, to be mentioned hereafter.]

153. The Principles thus stated will receive illustration as we proceed.   We must be content with the bare statement of them at present, and now pass on to the following important Rules.

154. Rule I. A PAST-Tense, with the prefix וֹ* of § 3, often occurs where the most natural English rendering is by means of a FUTURE or some oblique form of expression. This is said to be a ʻPast with וֹ CONVERSIVE.ʼ   Thus, for example, from נָתַן *he gave*, we have וְנָתַן *and he shall give* [or *make*, as in E.V.] Ez. xxvi. 8; from שָׁפַךְ *he poured-out*, וְשָׁפַךְ *and he shall pour-out*, [or *cast*, as in E.V. (*ib.*)], and, *he shall even pour-out*, Lev. xvii. 13.   So וְשָׁפְכוּ *and they shall pour-out*, Lev. xiv. 41, etc.

---

* In any one of its many values *and, even, that,* etc.   This וֹ is, of course, subject to the same changes of punctuation here as in § 3   [See more in § 155]

Rule II. This prefix וֹ before a FUTURE-Tense is simply CONJUNCTIVE, as in § 3,—the Future-Tense being unaffected by it; *e.g.*, וְיִפְקֹד *and he shall* (or *will*) *visit*, וְתִקְרַב *and she shall* (or *will*) *approach*, etc. But,

· Rule III. a FUTURE-Tense with the prefix וַ *followed by Dagesh F.*, is rendered as a PAST, with *and* (or some other value of the וֹ of § 3), and is said to be a 'Future with וֹ CONVERSIVE.' Thus, for example, from יִשְׁפֹּךְ *he will pour-out*, וַיִּשְׁפֹּךְ *and he poured-out*, 2 S. xx. 10. So, from תִּקְרַב *she shall draw near*, וַתִּקְרַב *and she drew near*, Esth. v. 2; etc. But,

Obs. (1) the א, of 1 Sing. Fut., requires this וֹ to have ָ (instead of the ־),—in order to compensate for the Dag. F. which א does not receive [cp. § 6 (*b*.)]. Thus, from אֶפְקֹד *I will visit*, וָאֶפְקֹד *and I visited*, etc.

(2) The Dag. F., belonging to this prefix, is NOT given to י (*i.e.* a י which has ־). Thus, וַיְדַבֵּר *and he spake*, וַיְדַבְּרוּ *and they (m.) spake*, etc.

155. As need scarcely be said,

(*a*) the prefix וֹ of Rules I. & II. (in § 154) is subject to the same changes of punctuation as in § 3; *viz.*,

(*b*) before a word which (when without the prefix) begins with יְ, we have וִי, as in וִישַׁבְתֶּם *and ye (m.) shall dwell*, Lev. xxv. 18 (from יְשַׁבְתֶּם, Rule I.); וִילַמֵּד *and He will teach*, Ps. xxv. 9 (from יְלַמֵּד *He will teach*, Rule II.); etc.

(*c*) i. before any other letter with ־, we have וּ as in וּלְקַחְתֶּם *and ye (m.) shall take*, וּטְבַלְתֶּם *and ye (m.) shall dip*, Ex. xii. 22 (from טְבַלְתֶּם, לְקַחְתֶּם); וּתְחַדֵּשׁ *and Thou wilt renew*, Ps. civ. 30 (from תְחַדֵּשׁ); etc.

ii. also וּ (not וֹ) before ב, or מ, or פ, even when having a Vowel; thus, וּבָאַשׁ *and it* [viz., the river] *shall stink*, Ex. vii. 18; וּמָחַץ *and he shall smite* Nu. xxiv. 17; וּפָחַד *and he shall fear*, Is. xix. 16; etc.

(*d*) before any one of the letters א ה ח ע with a Compound

Shva, the וֹ takes a 'Slight'-vowel agreeing therewith; as in וַעֲבַדְתֶּם *and ye* (*m.*) *shall serve*, Ex. xxiii. 25; וַאֲהַבְתֶּם *and ye* (*m.*) *shall love*, D. x. 19; וַאֲדַבֵּר *and I will speak*, Ez. ii. 1, etc.

[156 Our avowed endeavour being to familiarise the student with facts and usages of the Language, rather than with speculations regarding them, we hardly venture to say what may, however, be allowed perhaps just in passing, *viz.* that

(1) careful attention to the Sequence of Events and Actions spoken of (or merely understood, it may be) in connection with a Past with וֹ, as in Rule I., enables us sometimes to perceive what may be termed a "Relative Past and Future," which accounts (possibly) for some Past-Tense forms so employed. Some of the instances above cited may be so explained, we think, in accordance with principles stated in §§ 151, 152. But, of course, one may easily deceive oneself in such Speculations. We ought to add, that

(2) sometimes a Future form of expression is NOT wanted in English,—the due Subordination of clauses being marked by means of some introduced Conjunctions, etc. And, moreover, that

(3) there are instances of וֹ before a Past Tense which do not fall under Rule I., inasmuch as the most natural rendering is by means of a *Past*-Tense rather than a Future. In several of such instances a possible rendering (although not, superficially, the most natural one) might be offered, in accordance with what was said above in (1), which would favour the extension of Rule I., so as to embrace these instances also. For practical purposes, the Student had better take the prefix וֹ before a Past Tense to be Conversive, generally. The matter must be treated of more fully in the Syntax.

(4) We have a theory with regard to the prefix of Rule III. But this, too, had better be deferred at present.]

157. It will be found practically useful to have the following brief statement of some of the above and other Usages, to which we may refer as occasion may arise;

(α.) the 'Pluperfect' "*had*" is expressed in Hebrew by the ordinary Past Tense (§ 148);

(β.) the Hebrew Past is used also for expressing (1) "*I would have done* so and so," (2) "*Had I done* so and so, then...," and such like; [see also § 152].

(γ.) The Future is sometimes used for (1) "*I should*, or *would*, etc., *do* ;" (2) "*Should I do* so and so, then...," and such like; [see also Obs. X., XI., p. 93];

(δ.) also, sometimes, where we must say "*then* so and so *took place*," or some such an expression, — Cp. § 151.

(ε.) The Future, with the prefix ו *followed by Dagesh F.*, is used just like a Past,* in any of the senses of the Past; and

(ζ) the Past with the prefix of § 3 [*i.e.* ו, etc.] may practically be used as a Future,* in any of the senses of the Future. Further,

158. there being only Second Persons in the Hebrew Imperative, the 3rd and 1st Person Imperative [as sometimes reckoned,—*i.e.*, "*Let him do* so and so," "*Let me...*"] are expressed in Hebrew by the 3rd and 1st Persons Future. Moreover

159. the *Negative* Imperative is in Hebrew expressed by a Future PRECEDED by a Negative Particle; thus, אַל תִּשְׁלַח *Put not forth* [thy hand], Gen. xxii. 12. So, ‡ וְאַל תִּשְׁמְעוּ *and hearken ye not*, 2 K. xviii. 32; וְאַל יִשְׂמְחוּ *and let them* (*m.*) *not rejoice*, Ps. xxxv. 24. See also Obs. IV., p. 93. And,

N.B.—the Hebrew Imperative must never be used with a Negative Particle.   Also

[(1) The "*thou* SHALT *not*," such as in Exod xx 13—17, has לֹא rather than אַל (Cp. Obs. III., p. 93) And so, of course, "*Ye shall not*;" as in לֹא תִכְרתוּ בְרית *ye* (*m.*) *shall not make a covenant* Ju. ii 2, etc.;

(2) the Particles אַל and לֹא are NOT LIMITED TO the uses here mentioned Other uses of them will be found elsewhere.

(3) The Hebrew Imperative is sometimes used where we want an Indicative in English]

---

* With *and, even, that,* or some other value of ו.   See Examples in Exercise XXIV , etc.

‡ וְאַל may be rendered sometimes—*neither* (or *nor*) as in E V. of וְאַל לְעַד תִזְכֹּר עָוֹן *neither remember iniquity for ever*, Is. lxiv. 8, where the position of לְעַד marks emphasis on the *for ever*, "and do not FOR EVER remember iniquity."

160. When a Past-Tense form which has the Accent on the Penultima receives the prefix וְ, the Accent (if not a Pause-Accent) is generally thrown forwards to the final syllable; thus, שָׁמַרְתָּ 2 s *m.* gives וּשְׁמַרְתָּ [and so וּמָלַכְתָּ, מָלַכְתָּ], הִבְדִּילָה 3 s *f.* (*Hiph.*) gives וְהִבְדִּילָה, etc. But,

(1) except the 1 Plu.;—in this the Accent remains on the Penultima, as in וּלְקַחְנוּ;—also,

(2) except, sometimes, cases such as in § 46 of Pt. I; thus, וַיֵּשֶׁב בָּהּ; D. xxvi. 1; and

(3) except some Verbs of the Classes in Sects. XIX., XX, and a few others to be mentioned hereafter

161 Obs (1) the Past with its וְ Convers., and (2) the Future with its וְ Convers., always precede their Subject (when this is expressed in direct connection therewith); thus, וְיָדְעוּ מִצְרַיִם *and* [*the*] *Egyptians shall know* Ex vii 5, וַיִּפְקֹד דָּוִד* *and David reviewed* (lit., *visited*) the people that were with him 2 S. xviii. 1, וַיִּשְׁלַח דָּוִד *and David sent-forth* (ib 2), וַתַּשְׁלֵךְ אִשָּׁה אַחַת† *and a certain woman cast* Ju. ix. 53, etc. Also (3) the Object may come between the Verb and the Subject; thus, וַיִּפְקֹד אֹתָם מֹשֶׁה *and Moses reviewed them* Nu. iii. 16.

162. Besides the few usages referred to in the Section above, there are many others which must be reserved at present The following may be added here in Notes.

(*a*) Verbs 'Fut (—)' are often said to be 'Intransitive,'‡ and most of them are so; thus, יִגְדַּל *he will be great*, יִשְׁכַּב *he will lie down*, etc. Also,

(*b.*) some Roots have both the 'Fut (—)' and 'Fut (—)' forms, (i) sometimes in the same sense [thus, בגד, *to deal treacherously*, has the 'Fut.(—)' form three times and the 'Fut.(—)' form only once; שבת, *to rest, stop, cease*, has the 'Fut (—)' form nine times and the 'Fut (—)' form twice], and (ii.) sometimes in different senses [thus, קצר, in the sense of '*harvesting*,' etc, has the 'Fut.(—)' form ten times, and in the sense of '*being short*,' has the 'Fut.(—)' form six times and the 'Fut.(—)' form once; חרב, in the sense of '*being dry*,' '*lying waste*,' has the (—) form ten times in the Fut. and once in Imper.,§ and in the sense of '*laying waste*,'‖ has the (—) form once in Imper.]. And,

(*c*) the 'Fut.(—)' form sometimes has an Object; as וַיִּפְשַׁט 1 S xix 24, *and he stripped-off* [his clothes (E.V]¶** But,

N.B.—some of the *forms* referred to in (*b.*), (*c.*), cannot be understood by the Student at present.

---

* See § 162 (*e*, i.).   † See § 162 (*e*, ii).

‡ Also the 'Verbs עַ.' and 'Verbs עֲ' [§ 138 (A) (iv. 2, 3)]

§ The Imper. has generally — for Verbs 'Fut (—),' and — for Verbs 'Fut.—)' Cp § 142.

‖ This may be supposed to be a '*Transitive*' *sense corresponding to* the other.

¶ The (—) form in the same sense occurs in Ez xxvi. 16 [יִפְשֹׁטוּ, see § 165 (ii, 1)].

** The (—) form in Is. ix. 19 (in the sense of '*cutting*,' E.V. margin, *v* 20) has not an Object expressed, but only implied, as in 1 K. iii 26.

(*d.*) (i.) A Tense generally precedes its Subject (when this is expressed in direct connection with it, cp. (ε.) of § 11), unless

(ii) there be some Emphasis on the Subject; thus, כֹּה דִבֶּר אֵלַי הָאִישׁ *thus spake the man unto me*, Gen. xxiv. 30, and " the place אֲשֶׁר דּבר אֹתוֹ שָׁם אלהִים *where* (§ 30) GOD *spake with him*," Gen. xxxv. 15,— but, אֱלֹהִים דִּבֶּר בְּקָדְשׁוֹ GOD *hath spoken in His Holiness*, Ps lx. 8. Cp also יָדַע שׁוֹר קֹנהוּ *an ox knoweth his owner*, with the יִשְׂרָאֵל לֹא יָדַע *Israel doth not know*, etc., Is. i. 3, where for Antithesis there is Emphasis on "*Israel*," and so on "My *people*" following it. Also cp Is. xvi. 13, 14 ; xx 2 ; xxvii. 12, etc, with Is. i 2, 20; xxi. 17; xxiv. 3 ; xl. 5, etc But,

(iii.) the Interrogative מִי *who?* always precedes its Verb.

(*e.*) It is the RULE to have [see also, more fully, p. 222.]—

(i.) the ⸺ (rather than וֹ) for the Fut. *Kal*, (*a*) when with the prefix וֹ Conversive, (β) when with the Deprecative אַל, (γ.) in the expression of a *positive wish* (*i e.*, as in ···יִפְקֹד יְיָ *Let the LORD*, GOD of the spirits of all flesh, *set*, etc. (Nu. xxvii. 16); also—

(ii) the ⸺ (rather than יֵ⸺) for the Fut. *Hiph* in the same three cases ; thus, (*a*) וַיִּפְקֹד *and he appointed*, 1 K xi. 28 ; (β) וְאַל תַּסְתֵּר פָּנֶיךָ *and hide not Thy Face*, Ps. lxix. 18 ; (γ) וְיִפְקֹד, *and let him appoint*, Gen. xli. 34 , but

(iii.) N B —except the 1 s. Fut. *Hiph* ,—in which either ⸺ (Pt. I., § 12) or יֵ⸺ is generally found; thus, וָאֶשְׁלַךְ D. ix. 21, וָאַמְלִיךְ 1 S. xii. 1, וָאַכְחִד Zech. xi 8, וָאֶשְׁלִיךְ *ib* 13.

(iv) Some speak of the FUTURE FORMS WITH ה (§ -144) as the 'Optative, because the Future is often uséd 'Optatively' with that ה. But, (1) it is unwise so to *limit* the 'Future with ה'; for, (2) the ה is used some-times where there is no 'Optative' force ; and, (3) the Future is sometimes used 'Optatively' where there is no ה. See more of this in the Syntax.

VOCABULARY II.

1. אָז *then.*
2. אַיִן (*nothing*), אֵין *there is not,* Tab. XIII, Note (‡, δ.).
3. אִישׁ *a man,* § 74 (*l.*).
4. בֵּן *a son,* Tab. XIII. 4.
5. זֶרַע (*m.*) *seed,* Tab. X. 1.
6. עַיִן (*f.*) *an eye,* i.c. עֵין, with aff. עֵינוֹ, etc., Dual. עֵינַיִם.
7. פָּנִים (pl. Noun) *a face, countenance.*
8. שַׂר *a prince,* Plu. שָׂרִים.

EXERCISE XXIV.

(*To be translated into English*)

*** For the plan of the Exercise see § 11 (*a—ε*).

N.B.—The ... below are put where a sentence is incomplete.

וַיְדַבֵּר¹ יְיָ אֶל מֹשֶׁה² בְּהַר³ סִינַי⁴ לֵאמֹר⁵ : דַּבֵּר⁶ אֶל
בְּנֵי יִשְׂרָאֵל וְאָמַרְתָּ⁶ אֲלֵהֶם... אִם בְּחֻקֹּתַי⁷ תֵּלֵכוּ⁸...
וַאֲכַלְתֶּם⁹ לַחְמְכֶם¹⁰ לָשֹׂבַע¹¹ וִישַׁבְתֶּם¹² בְּאַרְצְכֶם¹³ : וּרְדַפְתֶּם¹⁴
אֶת אֹיְבֵיכֶם¹⁵... : וְרָדְפוּ¹⁴ מִכֶּם חֲמִשָּׁה¹⁶ מֵאָה¹⁷ : וְהִתְהַלַּכְתִּי¹⁸
בְּתוֹכְכֶם¹⁹... : וְאִם לֹא תִשְׁמְעוּ²⁰ לִי... וְשָׁבַרְתִּי²¹ אֶת גְּאוֹן²²
עֻזְּכֶם²³ : וְהִשְׁלַחְתִּי²⁴ בָכֶם²⁵ אֶת חַיַּת²⁶ הַשָּׂדֶה²⁷ וְשִׁכְּלָה²⁸
אֶתְכֶם ... וְהִמְעִיטָה²⁹ אֶתְכֶם : וְנִשְׁאַרְתֶּם³⁰ מְתֵי³¹ מִסְפָּר :

1 דבר *Pi.* to speak.　2 Moses.*　3 in the mountain of.　4 Sinai.　5 saying.
6 p. 92, No. 51.　7 in My statutes.　8 ye (*m.*) shall go.　9 אכל to eat (Pt. I., § 24).
Here וֹ＝*then.*　10 לחם (*m.*) bread, Tab. X. (1).　11 abundantly.　12 p. 91, No. 4.
13 אֶרֶץ,* p. 47, No. 5, Tabs. X. 1, XII. 1.　14 p. 92, No. 53.　15 p. 92, No. 52.
16 five. (This is the ‹Subject› of the sentence, here.)　17 a hundred (the ‹Object›).
18 הלך *K., Pi., Hithp.* to go, walk.　19 in your (*m.*) midst (*i.e.,* in the midst of
you), fr. תָּוֶךְ Tab. XIII. (‡, ε.).　20 p. 90, No. 4.　21 p. 91, No. 10.　22 the
pride of.　23 your (*m.*) strength.　24 שלח *Hiph.* to cause to send, to send.
25 בְּ against.　26 the beast of.　27 § 74 (*b.*).　28 שכל *Pi.* to bereave.　29 מעט *Hiph.*
to make few.　30 p. 92, No. 47.　31 (For this and the next word, see p. 56, Nos.

---

* Words marked (*) need not be given again in the Notes.

עֲזָבוּנִי[32] וַיְקַטְּרוּ[33] לֵאלֹהִים[34] אֲחֵרִים[35] : וַיְחַלְּלוּ[36] אֶת שֵׁם
קָדְשִׁי : וַאֲחַלֵּל[36] שָׂרֵי קֹדֶשׁ : וַיִּשָּׁבְעוּ[37] בְּלֹא‡ אֱלֹהִים§ :
וְאָנֹכִי הַסְתֵּר[38] אַסְתִּיר[38] פָּנַי[39]... : וּפָקַדְתִּי בְשֵׁבֶט[39] פִּשְׁעָם : לֹא
אֲחַלֵּל[36] בְּרִיתִי[40] : וְקִדַּשְׁתִּי[41] אֶת שְׁמִי הַגָּדוֹל§ : בְּךָ נַזְכִּיר[42]
שְׁמֶךָ : וַיִּזְכְּרוּ[42] כִּי אֱלֹהִים צוּרָם : וָאֶזְכֹּר[42] אֶת בְּרִיתִי[40] :
וַאֲבַקֵּשׁ[43] מֵהֶם אִישׁ : וְאֵין דּוֹרֵשׁ[44] וְאֵין מְבַקֵּשׁ[43] : הִנְנִי[45]
בָא[46] וְשָׁכַנְתִּי[47] בְתוֹכֵךְ‖ : וְקָרְאוּ[48] לָךְ עִיר[49] יְיָ : וְיָנַקְתְּ[50]
חֲלֵב[51] גּוֹיִם : וַאֲנִי אֶסְבֹּל[52] וַאֲמַלֵּט[53] : הֲקָצוֹר[54] קָצְרָה[54]
יָדִי[55] מִפְּדוּת[56] : אוֹ תִּפָּקַחְנָה[57] עֵינֵי עִוְרִים[58] : אָז יְדַלֵּג[59] כָּאַיָּל[60]
פִּסֵּחַ[61] : וַיִּזְכֹּר[42] אֱלֹהִים אֶת בְּרִיתוֹ[40] : ...גֹּאַלְכֶם§ קְדוֹשׁ[63]
יִשְׂרָאֵל : וַיִּלְבַּשׁ[64] בִּגְדֵי[65] נָקָם[66] תִּלְבֹּשֶׁת[67] : אַל תִּזְכְּרוּ[42]
רִאשֹׁנוֹת[68] : בַּיְיָ יִצְדְּקוּ[69] וְיִתְהַלְלוּ[70] כָּל זֶרַע יִשְׂרָאֵל :

31, 32). [32] they forsook ME. [33] קטר Pi., to offer incense. [34] to gods (p. 3, Note †). [35] אַחֵר another* (m.). [36] חלל Pi., to profane, break (a covenant). [37] p. 92, No. 41. [38] סתר Hiph., to hide. [39] with a rod. [40] בְּרִית (f.) a covenant. [41] קדש Pi., to sanctify. [42] p. 91, No. 6. [43] בקש Pi., to seek, enquire. [Dagesh Forte is often dropped from the ק]. [44] דרשׁ to search [45] behold I. [46] [am] coming. [47] שכן to dwell. [48] קרא to call [often 'governs' a לְ]. [49] a city, city of. [50] ינק to suck. [51] the milk of. [52] סבל to bear. [53] מלט Pi., to deliver [54] קצר to be short. [55] יָד (f.) a hand, i.c., יַד with aff. יָדוֹ, etc., Dual יָדַיִם, i.c. יָדַי* [56] "that it cannot redeem," E.V., (lit., from redemption) [57] פקח to open (eyes). [58] blind (men). [59] דלג Pi., to leap [60] like the hart. [61] a lame (man). [62] p. 93, No. 86 [§ 140 (δ., iii.)]. [63] The Holy ONE of. [64] p. 92, No. 76. [65] the garments of. [66] vengeance. [67] [as] clothing [68] former things (f.). [69] צדק to be righteous. [70] p. 92, No 45.

---

* Words marked (*) need not be given again in the Notes.
† by [them that are] not.
‡ Vocab. I (1).
§ p. 60 (19).
‖ From תָּוֶךְ, see No. 19.

Exercise XXV.

(*To be translated into Hebrew*, § 11, ζ—μ.).

And God heard*[1] their groaning,[2] and God remembered*[3] His Covenant.[4] Why[5] will the bush[7] not burn[6]? And Moses hid*[8] his face.[9] And Aaron[10] spake*[11] all[12] the words[13] which The Lord spake[11] to Moses. And I will take†[14] you (*m.*) to Me for a people,[15] and ye-shall-know†[16] that I The Lord [am] your God.

And Moses wrote*[17] this Law.[18] In-order-that[19] they (*m.*)-may-hear[1] [Future Tense], and in-order-that[19] they (*m.*)-may-learn[20] [Future Tense], and-that[21] they-may-fear†[22]... and-that[21] they-may-observe†[23] to-do[24] all[12] the words[13] of this Law.[18] And Jeshurun[25] waxed-fat,*[26] and kicked.*[27] And they (*m.*)-forgat*[28] His doings.[29] And they (*m.*)-spake*[11] against[30] God. And He-rained*[31] upon them (*m.*) Manna.[32]

Hear-thou[1] (*m.*) [w. ה, § 141 (γ, 2)], My people, and I-will speak.[11] And I-will dwell†[33] in the midst[34] of Jerusalem,[35] and Jerusalem[35] shall-be-called†[36] the city[37] of the truth.[38] Let your (*m.*) hands[39] (*f.*) be-strong.[40] And proclaim-ye (Hebr. *cause-ye* (*m.*) *to hear*) the sound[41] of His Praise.[42]

---

[1] שָׁמַע (Fut. ־ַ). [2] נְאָקָה. [3] זָכַר (Fut. ־ֹ). [4] בְּרִית [5] מַדוּעַ. [6] בָּעַר (Fut ־ַ). Verb to precede Noun. [7] סְנֶה [8] סתר *Hiph.* [9] פָּנִים, a Noun of Plural form. [10] אַהֲרֹן. [11] דבר *Pi* [12] כָּל. [13] Tab. IX. [14] לקח. [15] עַם. [16] ידע. [17] כתב Fut. (־ֹ) [18] תּוֹרָה [19] לְמַעַן. [20] למד. [21] וְ. [22] ירא. [23] שמר (Fut. ־ַ). [24] לַעֲשׂוֹת. [25] יְשֻׁרוּן. [26] שמן (Fut. ־ַ). [27] בעט (Fut ־ַ) [28] שכח. [29] עֲלִילוֹת. [30] בְּ prefix. [31] מטר *Hiph.* [32] מָן. [33] שכן. [34] תָּוֶךְ Tab. XIII.·(ζ, ε). [35] יְרוּשָׁלַם (*f*) [36] קרא *Niph.* [37] עִיר. [38] אֱמֶת. [39] יָד, Du יָדַיִם. [See § 59 (δ)]. [40] חזק (Fut. ־ַ). The ח has ־ַ and the prefixes have ־ֶ in the Fut. *Kal* of this Verb; thus, יחזק, תֶּחֱזַק, etc. See more in next Section. [41] קוֹל (1 c., the same) [42] תְּהִלָּה.——* Fut. with ו Convers. † Past with ו Convers.

END OF THE FIRST PART OF THE EXERCISE BOOK.

SECOND PART

OF THE

EXERCISE-BOOK.

SECTION XIII.

VERBS.—VARIATIONS.

163. For Variations from Tab. XIV. in regard to some additional endings, see § 147; for נ instead of נָה, see § 143.

There are some other important Variations:

I. PAUSE FORMS.

164. Changes of Vocalization [in some forms] occur in Pause,— *i.e.* at the end of a Verse, a Sentence, or a Clause, where a Stop is made.

> (a.) As said in Pt. 1. § 49, *Silluk* (׃־) and *Ethnakh* (־֑) are especially the 'Pause'-Accents; but

> (β.) Pause-forms are found sometimes with other Accents also [see § 167].

> (γ.) The 2 pl. *m.* & *f.* of all Past Tenses are unchanged in Pause.

> (δ.) The Pause-forms of 'Infs. w. Pron. Affs.' are given in Tab. XV. [The only *change* is with the 2 s. *m.* Aff.].

> (ε.) The Pause-forms of Participles are given in Appendix (B) to Tab. XIV. [The only *change* is in the s. *f.* form ת־ ־ֶ, which sometimes becomes ׃ת־ ־ֵ in Pause. Cp. § 139 (β, †).]

N.B. All words in Tab. XIV (except the Past 2 pl. *m.* & *f.* and Infs. w. Pron.-Affs.) have the ordinary Tone-accent on that syllable in which the 2ᵈ Rt-letter is involved:—whether this 2ᵈ Rt-letter

> (I.) bears a vowel as in פָּקַד, or
> (II.) has ־ *Moving* as in פָּקְדָה.

The Rules for the 'Pause'-forms of words in Tab XIV (and the like) may be given in regard to these two great Classes (I.) and (II.) as follows:

165. (I.) When the 2ᵈ Rt-letter bears a Vowel,

(a.) if that Vowel be Long, as in תִּפְקֹדְנָה, יִפְקֹד, etc., the word is generally unchanged in Pause;

(β.) if that Vowel be Short, as פָּקַד, יִלְבַּשׁ, etc., this Short Vowel is generally lengthened* into the corresponding Long Vowel,† as in יִקְרַב (fr. יִקְרַב), אָכַל (fr. אֹכַל): etc. But

(γ.) the ֲ of a *Niph*. Future (Tab. XIV.) remains in Pause, as in תִּרְמַסְנָה, וַיִּנָּפֵשׁ: etc.; and, more generally, it may be said that

(δ.) [the *simple utterance* ֲ, which is given sometimes for Euphony and Ease of pronunciation, instead of the more precise ֱ, is found (not seldom) in Pause; thus הַמְעַד: Imper. *Hiph*. 2 s. *m.*, Ps. lxix. 24, for הַמְעַד, etc.].

---

* (a). This great General Rule holds also in the forms אָכַלְתָּ, אָכַלְתְּ, אָכַלְתִּי, פִּלַּלְתִּי, הָלַכְתִּי, נֶעְמַת, גִּזְעַרְתִּי, גִּזְעַקְתִּי; נִגְזַרְתִּי; לָקַחְתִּי, נֶעְמַת, וַיִּשְׁבְּתָ, אָבַדְנוּ; הַפָּחַתִּי [Sect. XVI.],—הוֹנַעֲנוּ, הוֹרַעְתָּ [Sect. XV.],—וְהִקְדַּשְׁתִּי; יִשַּׁרְתִּי;—הִתְהַלַּכְתִּי, הִתְהַלַּכְתָּ: etc.

(b). But the ֲ is often retained [see (δ)] not only

(i.) in such forms, thus יָסַדְתָּ Ps. cii. 26, זָקַנְתִּי G. xxvii. 2, etc.; and so in other Voices as מְגֵרְתָה 2 s. m. Past *Pi*. [§ 138 (β), 1.] Ps. lxxxix. 45, שִׁוַּעְתִּי Ps. lxxxviii. 14, נַצַּלְנוּ 1 pl. Past *Niph*. (Jer. vii. 10), הַצַּלְנוּ 1 pl. Past *Hiph*. (1 S. xxx. 22) of נצל [Sect. XVI.], etc.; but also

(ii.) in Fut. forms ending in (ֲ ־נָה) as תִּקְשַׁבְנָה 3 pl. f. Fut. K. (Is. xxxii. 3), and so תַּחֲרַשְׁנָה 3 pl. f. Fut. K. Tab. XVI (1) [Mi. vii. 16], etc., and

(iii.) some others.

† For the great Leading Rules, see Pt. I. § 19.

II. When the 2ᵈ Rt-letter has *Shva*, a Vowel is given* to it in Pause. This Vowel is generally the same as either

(i) the Vowel which the 2ᵈ Rt-letter HAS IN THE FIRST word of the Tense or set [see examples below]; or

(ii) the Vowel which the 2ᵈ Rt-letter TAKES IN PAUSE in the FIRST word of the Tense or set. Thus,

(i.) (a) The Pause-form of יִפְקְדוּ 3 pl. *m.* Fut. *K.* is יִפְקֹדוּ; *i.e.* the Pause-vowel for the 2ᵈ Rt-letter is ‾, this being the Vowel of the 2ᵈ Rt-letter in the first word of the Tense (or set) *viz.* יִפְקֹד 3 s. *m.*;

(b) So in *Niph.* Fut., the Pause-form of יִפָּקְדוּ 3 pl. *m.* is יִפָּקֵדוּ, the first word of the set being יִפָּקֵד 3 s. *m.* So, in *Pi.*, יְפַקְּדוּ 3 pl. *m.*, p. יְפַקֵּדוּ.

(c) So, for the 1 s. & 1 pl. Fut. w. the ה of § 144, the forms are

Kal אֶפְקְדָה 1 s., p. אֶפְקֹדָה;   & נִפְקְדָה 1 pl., p. נִפְקֹדָה; [also ii (b)];

Niph. אֶפָּקְדָה 1 s., p. אֶפָּקֵדָה,   & נִפָּקְדָה 1 pl., p. נִפָּקֵדָה;

etc.,   etc.

(ii) (a) The Pause-form of פָּקְדוּ 3 pl Past *Kal* is פָּקָדוּ, the Pause-vowel being ָ because the 2ᵈ Rt-letter TAKES ָ for its Pause-vowel in the first word of the set (*viz.* פָּקַד 3 s. *m.*, p. פָּקָד);

(b) So in the Fut. *Kal* of the (ַ)-form, the Pause-form of יִלְבְּשׁוּ 3 pl. *m.* is יִלְבָּשׁוּ, because יִלְבַּשׁ 3 s. *m.* (the first word of the set) has the Pause-form יִלְבָּשׁ. So in the 1 s. and 1 pl. w. the ה of § 144, thus אֶלְבְּשָׁה p. אֶלְבָּשָׁה.

N.B. (iii) Sometimes we find the — of the פֵּעֵל form of Past Tense [§ 188 (A)], instead of the ָ for the ַ of the פָּעַל form in ii (a); thus חָדְלוּ, Pause-form of חָדְלוּ 3 pl. Past *Kal* of חדל, has the ֵ [of the unused 3 s. *m.* Past חָדֵל] instead of ָ for the ַ of חָדַל.

166. (a.) Often no further change is made by the Pause. But

(b.) If a SLIGHT-vowel precedes the *Shva* which is to be replaced by a Vowel in Pause, that SLIGHT-vowel disappears (there being no longer any need of it) when this Shva has given place

---

* Except (i.) Infinitives with Affs.; (ii) Participles, see § 164 (b) & (c); and (iii.) a few words the regular Pause-form of which is NOT adopted in Pause.

to a Vowel. The *Shva* (Simple, or Compound), which had given place to the Slight-vowel, then returns; thus,

   (i.) of פִּקְדוּ Imper. *K.* 2 pl. *m.* (fr. פְּקֹד) the Pause-form is פְּקֹדוּ,* and of עִמְדוּ (fr. עֲמֹד) the Pause-form is עֲמֹדוּ: So

   (ii.) of שִׁמְעוּ (fr. שְׁמַע, p. שְׁמָע) we have שְׁמָעוּ. And so

   (iii.) the Pause-forms of קָרְבָה, שָׁמְרָה, [Imper. 2 s. *m.* w. ה, § 141 (ʏ)], would be שָׁמֹרָה: קָרְבָה fr. שְׁמֹר, קְרַב (p. קָרָב:), and

   (iv.) the Pause-form of תַּעַבְרִי [see § 171 (i.)] is תַּעֲבֹרוּ: (fr. יַעֲבֹר); and, of יַחְרְדוּ [§ 171 (ii)], יֶחֱרָדוּ: (fr. יֶחֱרַד).

   (c). The Pause-forms of the *Hithp.* Past,† Imper., & Fut., have ־ַ to the 2d Rt-letter, thus הִתְאַזָּר: 3 s. *m.* Past, הִתְפַּלָּשִׁי Mi. i. 10 (*Kri*) Imper. 2 s. *f.*, אֶתְפַּלָּל: 1 s. Fut., יִתְקַדָּשׁוּ: 3 pl. *m.* Fut., etc.; and consequently, [since

      N.B. generally ־ַ is given before ךָ, for Euphony],‡

   (d). when the 2d Rt-letter is ח, the 1st Rt-letter has ־ַ in these *Hithp.* Pause-forms; thus יִתְנֶחָם: 3 s. *m.* Fut., תִּתְנַחֲלוּ: 2 pl. *m.* Fut., etc.; and so, with 2d Rt-letter ה, we have וְהִטֶּהָרוּ: 3 pl. Past w. וֹ Conv. (of טהר).

   (e). The וֹ of § 145 is often found at the end of Pause-forms also;§ thus, in *v.* 28 of Ps. civ. יִלְקֹטוּן (of יִלְקֹטוּ, fr. יִלְקֹט). So *v.* 22 יִבְרָאוּן (of יְבְרָאוּ, fr. יִרְבְּצוּ p. יִרְבָּץ), in *v.* 30 יִרְבָּצוּן (of יִרְבְּצוּ, fr. יִרְבָּץ), & so *v.* 29 יְבֵהָלוּן, *v.* 22 יַאַסְפוּן וֹ to compensate for the

---

   * This Pause-form occurs Na. ii. 9 with the Accent ־ֵ merely. Cp. § 167 (ii, a).

   † Except, of course, the 2 pl. *m.* & *f.* Past.

   ‡ As in § 6 (*d*); and so אָחִיו fr. אָחִים Tab. XIII. 2, etc.

   § Observe, the Accent is brought then upon the *last* syllable.

Dag. F. of *Niph.*]; *v.* 26 יְהַלֵּכוּן (of יְהַלֵּכוּ׳, fr. יְהַלֵּךְ׳), so *v.* 27 יְשַׁבֵּרוּן׳, etc.   So also in § 146.

167. (i) The Pause-form of a word is generally (but *not* necessarily always)* adopted in Pause.

(ii.) In some Pause-forms a more sonorous pronunciation is given to words.   And, as there seems to be no reason why the more sonorous pronunciation should be limited to a place of Pause, so we find in the Bible several instances of such †

(a). with OTHER DISJUNCTIVE Accents (*i.e.* where there is a stop less than that of a Pause); also, sometimes,

(β). with CONJUNCTIVE Accents (*i.e.* where there is no stop at all, but the contrary).

Thus, for example, (¹) with ◌ as יִשְׁכָּבוּ׳. G. xix. 4, (²) w. ◌ (very often) as יְזָעָק׳ Is. xv. 5, וַיְּהַבָּלוּ 2 K. xvii. 15; (³) with ◌ (often) as יְעָץ׳ Is. xiv. 27, נָפָלוּ ix. 9, יְרָבִּץ׳ xxvii. 10, יְשָׂמֵחוּ׳ lxv. 13; (⁴) w. ◌ as שָׁמַע Ez. xliv. 5, יִשְׁמָע׳ Is. vi. 10; (⁵) w. ◌ (*Pashta*) as יְצָעָן׳ Is. xxxiii. 20, נִמְלָחוּ Is. li. 6, שְׁמָעָה Dan. ix. 19 [fr. שְׁמָעָה § 141 (γ, 2)], etc.;—and (⁶) with Conjunctives, as שָׁפַט 1 S. vii. 17, סָעָד Ju. xix. 5, הֲיִצְלָח Ez. xvii. 15.‡

---

* Thus עַבְדֶּךָ *Thy servant* Ps. cxix. 65 (instead of עַבְדְּךָ as in Ps. cxvi. 16, w. ◌). So נוֹעָדוּ [Sect. XV.] Ps. xlviii. 5, and יְדַכְּאוּ Ps. xciv. 5.—But יִפָּלֵא Ps. xlv. 6 may hardly be reckoned here; because the verse has ◌ in it [Pt. I. § 68], and in that case ◌ not seldom occurs *without* Pause-form (though often also with the Pause-form, as in עָמָד Ps. i. 1, etc.

† For expressing energy, or for energy of expression, or for emphasis, or for rhythmic force, etc.)

‡ The three last forms were just mentioned in §§ 138 (A, γ), 141 (a, Note). The bare mention of them was all that could well be made then.

The Student may now, for Practice, parse the following
Pause-forms. It will be advisable also to write out the SIMPLE
WORDS OF WHICH THESE ARE THE PAUSE-FORMS :—

PRACTICE ON PAUSE-FORMS,

*** The references (I) & (II) are to the main divisions of § 165.

עָמַד: (I, β), שָׁמַעְתָּ [(*) Note ,β .I], אֲכַלְתְּ, בָּגַרְתִּי, וּמָשָׁל:

שָׁמַעְנוּ וּמְרַדְנוּ, יִמְחַץ, (I, β), אֲמַעֵר:, נִסְכַּלְתְּ, נִסְתַּרְנוּ: יְשָׁרַתִּי

וְהִקְדַּשְׁנוּ הִתְהַלַּכְתִּי:, יִתְגַּדְּל:

יִשָׁמְרוּ: [(a) i .II], תִּשָׁמְרוּ:, תִּפְרָצִי, יִלָכְדוּ: [(b) i .II], תִּלָכְדִי

יִלָּמְדוּ, יְלַמְּדוּן: גָּדְלָה: (II i.) שָׁכְלוּ, זַמְּרוּ: דַּבְּרִי, דִּבְּרוּ:

וְרַבְּרוּ: יְדַבְּרוּ, וַיְדַבְּרוּ:, יָלְלוּ: [(iii.) (A) 138 § & ,i .II],

חָפְצָה: [(ii.) (A) 138 § & ,i .II], אֶשְׁמֹרָה:, [(c) i .II], אֶכְבְּדָה:

אֶזְמְרָה: וָאֲזַמְּרָה:, וְנִכְרְעָה: [(b) .ii .II], וַיִּצְטַיְּרוּ: [(ii.) ,(*)89 .p]

מְרַדוּ: [(a) ii .II], אֲכָלָה:, וְשָׁמְרוּ:, וְנִלְכְּדוּ:, יִשָׁכְבוּ: [(b) ii .II],

יִשָׁכְבוּן: תִּשָׁכְּחִי:, תִּלָמְדוּ:, אֶשָׁאֵפָה:, גְּבְרוּ, יִתְלַכְּדוּ: [§166.(c)]

הִתְפַּלְשִׁי:

זְכְרוּ: [(i.) b .166 §], עֶבְרִי:, שֶׁלָחוּ: [(ii.) b .166 §], שָׁמְרָה:,

שְׁמָעָה: [(iii.) b §166.], תַּעֲמֹדוּ: [§166. b (iv.)] יִתְפַּלְּצוּן:, תִּתְנַחֲלוּ:,

יַהֲרֹבוּ:

[The Student may now pass on to the Exercises on pp. 125–127, after looking at the intervening pages sufficiently for him to be able to refer thereto for information which he may require respecting the forms of certain Verbs in the Exercises. References to these pages will be rendered more easy by the following Index.]

Index for pages 113–124.

§ 167 (i.) Pause-forms generally (NOT always) used in Pause . . . . . p 113

(ii.) Pause-forms used also, sometimes, when NOT in Pause . . . p. 113

§ 168 (i) A Long-Vowel, followed by Quiescent Shva, shortened at the end of a word (α) if followed by (־) Makkêph, (β) when the Accent is 'turned back' [Pt. 1, § 46] . . . . p 114

(ii.) 'Furtive' ־ to be under ה, and under ח or ע at the end of a word, after any Long-vowel except ־ָ . . . . p. 114

(iii. β). Table of 'Compensation'-vowels for an omitted Dagesh . p. 115

(iv.) Moving Shva takes a Compound form under any one of the four letters ע ה ח א . . . . p 115

(v.) A 'Slight'-vowel, and a Real Short-vowel, preceding such a Compound Shva, adopt a corresponding form . . . . p 115

§§ 169–179. Verbs having [א], ה, ח, or ע, for 1st Rt-letter . . . pp. 115–120

§ 180. Verbs having א, ה, ח, or ע, for 2d Rt-letter . . . . . p 120

[& Appˣ pp 321 & 322, 368 & 369]

§ 181. Verbs having ה, ח, or ע, for 3d Rt-letter . . . . p. 120

[& Appˣ pp 370 to 374]

§ 182. Verbs having ר in the Root . . . . p. 121

§ 183. Verbs having ן, or ה, for 3d Rt-letter . . . . . pp. 121 & 122

§ 184. Verbs having one of the six letters ב ג ד כ פ ת in the Root . . . . pp 122–124

§ 185. Verb-forms may have Pron-Affs. attached to them . . . pp. 124

§ 186. Table of Seven important Classes of Variations . . . . pp. 124

II. CERTAIN NECESSARY VARIATIONS.

168. The Student knows already from Pt. I. that

(i.) A Long-vowel, followed by Quiescent ָ, is generally shortened if the Accent be removed from it [Pt. I. § 55 (9, *b*)];

    (*a*). for some examples of this Shortening* when *Makkêph* (־) follows the word,† see '[Note]' in the 'Notes on Tab. XIV.'

    (β). As examples of this Shortening when the Accent is 'turned back' [Pt. I. § 46] ‡ we have לְהִסָּ֫תֶר שָׁם *for* [the workers of mischief] *to be hid there* (Job xxxiv. 22, Inf. *N.* for לְהִסָּתֵר), and בַּל־יִפָּ֫קֶד רָע׃ *he shall not be visited by evil* (Prov. xix. 23, 3 s. *m.* Fut. *N.* for יִפָּקֵד), etc.

(ii.) Beneath הּ (*i.e.* ה with *Mappêk*), and beneath ח & ע at the end of a word, ‎ַ must be put after any Long-vowel except ָ; and this ‎ַ is called 'Furtive Pathaḵh,' and is pronounced *before* the letter beneath which it stands; Op. Pt. I. § 60.

    [Obs. We need not say 'at the end of a word' (and so *vowelless*) in the case of הּ; for the dot stands in the ה to show that it is *not Quiescent*, and it is only when ' at the end of a word' § that ה is ever Quiescent] :

(iii.) (*a*). There must be variation from Tab. XIV. by the omission of Dag. F. where it would have to stand in one

---

* For the Vowel to be chosen, in each case, see the great Leading Rules in Pt. I. § 19.

† Thus (fr. תִּגְבָּל) תִּגְבָּל־בָה Zech. ix. 2. But יִנְבּוֹל־אֹתוֹ Josh. xviii. 20, in which ו is not shortened; and so יִגְנֹב־אִישׁ Ex. xxi. 37.

‡ But הוֹלְם פָּעַם Is. xli. 7, in some Bibles;—הוֹלֶם פָּעַם in some.

§ And therefore at the end of a *syllable*, and so *vowelless*.

of the five letters אהחע״ר which do not receive Dagesh [Pt. I. § 49]; and, by reason of this,

(β). 'Compensation' (as it is called), for an omitted Dag. F., is often made

by lengthening $\left\{\begin{array}{l}\text{―} \qquad \text{into } \text{ᵀ} \\ \text{▽ \& ᵀ} \quad \text{into } \text{ᵀ} \\ \text{ᵀ} (ŏ) \& \text{ᵥ} \text{ into } \text{⊥}\end{array}\right\}$ Cp. Pt. I. § 19:—

(iv.) A Moving Shva beneath any one of the four letters אהחע takes a Compound form [Pt. I. § 24]; and

(v.) (a). A 'Slight'-vowel, and (β) A Real Short-vowel, preceding such a Compound-Shva, generally adopts the form which agrees with that Compound-Shva [Cp. §§ 3 (d), 4 (d), & 169 (a, ii)].

[Note. There are some further Variations in the case of Verbs having in the Root one of the four letters אהחע mentioned in (iv.) above.]

III. First Root-letter ה, ח, or ע.

169. [Note. (a.) Verbs having א as 1st Rt-letter (i.e. א׳פ) agree in many parts with those having ה, ח, or ע, as 1st Rt-letter; but, (b.) there are some so important differences between the two sets of Verbs that it is best to give a special Section (XIV.) to the Verbs א׳פ,—and to proceed now with the others only, to § 179].

Verbs having ה, ח, or ע, as 1st Rt-letter have

(a). A Compound Shva under the 1st Rt-letter not only

(i.) where there is Shva Moving in Tab. XIV.; thus, עֲמַדְתֶּם like פְּקַדְתֶּם, etc.; but also

(ii.) sometimes where Shva is Quiescent in Tab. XIV; thus יַעֲמֹד corresponding to יִפְקֹד, and so יַעֲרֹב to יִלְבַּשׁ; prefix-letters generally taking ַ before ֲ, and ⸱⸱ before ⸱⸱, and ⸱⸱ (ŏ) before ⸱⸱. See Tab. XVI (1);—also

(β). simple ⸱ Quiescent, sometimes, under the 1st Rt-letter, with a ⸱ or ⸱ TO THE PREFIX-LETTER AS IN (a, ii.); thus, for example,

(i.) לַחְצֹב, לַחְקֹר, לַחְשֹׁב, לַחְתֹּם, etc., (Inf. *K*. w. לְ),* and

[(ii.) לַחְכֹּם Is. xlvii. 14, for which see §§ 137 (2, Note ⸱) & 164 (β).]

(iii.) יַעְצֹר and יֵעְשָׁן 3 s. *m.* Fut. K., נֶעֱדִר 3 s. *m.* Past and נֶעֱלָם† s. *m.* Partic. *Niph.* [Cp. Tab. XVI (1)], etc.

[Note. The simple ⸱ *often* occurs under ה as 1st Rt-letter].

170. The Fut. *K*. (except the 1 s.) has one or other of the four forms יֵעֲמֹר, יֵעְצַר, יֵעֲרַב, יֵעְשָׁן;—and it may be said that, as in these four words, the prefixes יתן take

(i.) generally ⸱‡ when the 2d Rt-letter bears ⸱, and

(ii.) generally ⸱§ when the 2d Rt-letter bears ⸱. But

(iii.) when, in derived forms, the vowel is removed from 2d Rt-letter, there is sometimes an interchange of these vowels for the יתן, as in (1) נַחְמְרֵהוּ (fr. נַחְמֹד, w. aff. הוּ‑ *him*, Sect. XXII.), (2) יַהְדְּלוּ (fr. יַהְדֹּל).‖

(iv.) N.B. The prefix א takes ⸱ as in Tab. XIV, and the 1st Rt-letter takes sometimes ⸱, sometimes ⸱ ; thus

---

* (a) But we have also לַחֲבֹשׁ, לַחֲגֹר, לַחֲטֹא, לַחֲלֹף, etc., like Tab. XVI (1). Also (b) with בּ we have בַּעֲזֹר 1 Chr. xv. 26.

† For נֶעֱבָד Eccl. v. 8, some have the anomalous נֶעְבָּד.

‡ With a few exceptions, as יֶהְדֹּף Pr. x. 3, יַחֲשֹׂף Ps. xxix. 9, תֶּהְדְּפוּ Ez. xxxiv. 21.

§ The form תֵּהֲלָךְ (3 s. *f.* Fut. *K.* of הלך) Ex. ix. 23, Ps. lxxiii. 9, is rare.

‖ So אֶחְדְּלָה K. Fut. 1 s. (אֶחְדֹּל), w. the ה of § 144.

(1) אֶהְפֹּךְ, אֶהֱלֹךְ, (2) אֶחְבֹּל [אֶחְטָם־, § 168 (i. a)],
אֶעֱמֹד, אֶעֱבֹר, אֶעֱבֹד, (3) אֶחֱבֹשׁ, אֶחְסַר, etc.

[Note. (a) Some Verbs have different senses, or shades of
sense, in the two forms of (i.) and (ii.) above; thus
יַחֲרֹשׁ he will plough, יֶחֱרַשׁ he will be deaf (also he will be
silent).

(b) חפץ has the form יַחְפֹּץ ordinarily, but the other form
יֶחְפָּץ in Pause. So אֶחְפֹּץ & יַחְפְּצוּ, תַּחְפֹּץ,—but
אֶחְפָּץ. & יַחְפְּצוּ: יַחְפְּצוּן: תַּחְפָּץ:

171. A Compound-Shva is always Moving.* Therefore it can
never stand when the following letter is·to have Shva, but
(unless it gives place to a simple ◌ָ Quiescent)† it must always be
replaced by a Slight-vowel. Thus (i.) from יַעֲמֹד 3 s. m. Fut. K.,
we have [Tab. XVI (1)] יַעַמְדוּ 3 pl. m., and so תַּעַמְדִי 2 s. f.,
תַּעַמְדוּ 2 pl. m.; the ◌ֲ being generally replaced by ◌ַ as Slight-
vowel.

(ii.) So, from יַעֲרֹב we have יַעַרְבוּ,—fr. יַחֲרֹד, יַחַרְדוּ, etc.;
the ◌ֲ being generally replaced by ◌ַ as Slight-vowel.
And

[(iii.) so ◌ֳ is replaced by ◌ָ before Shva, in *Hoph.* § 179].

(iv.) So, for 1 s. Fut. K. w. the ה of § 144, we have אֶעֶזְבָה
(fr. אֶעֱזֹב), אֶעֶרְכָה (fr. אֶעֱרֹךְ), אֶעֶלְצָה (fr. אֶעֱלֹץ), ‡ [and,
so אֶחֶרְדָה (fr. אֶחֱרֹד)]. But observe, for the 1 s. Fut.,

(v.) forms in which *simple* ◌ָ *Quiescent* occurs under the 1st
Rt-letter, as אֶעְבְּרָה (fr. עבר), are the same as אֶפְקְדָה (fr. פקד) .

---

* It is only a *Moving* Shva that takes a compound form.

† As in יַעֲלֹצוּ Ps. v. 12 (יַעֲלֹצוּ Ps. xxv. 2, lxviii. 4), יַחֲרְדוּ Ez. xxvi. 18 (יֶחֶרְדוּ
in five other places), etc.

‡ The form אֲחֲרֶנָה G. xxvii 41, with ◌ֲ–◌ֶ is rare.

(vi.) So the 1 pl. Fut. *K.* with the הַ of § 144, has the forms (1) נַעֲבְדָה, נַחְלְמָה, with a Slight-vowel under the 1st Rt-letter; and (2) נַעֲבְרָה, נַחְפְּשָׂה, with the ־ֲ Quiescent.

172. It does not follow from § 171 that a Slight-vowel occurs *only* in such cases. On the contrary, the help of the Slight-vowel is sometimes given in a derived form, although the simple word has ־ֲ Quiescent. Thus, יַעְצֹר occurs only with ־ֲ Quiescent, but we have (w. Aff הוּ ־ֲ *him*,. Sect. XXII.) וַיַּעְצְרֵהוּ 2 Kings xvii. 4.

173. In the Imper. *K.* 2 s. *f.* & 2 pl. *m.* these Verbs generally agree with Tab. XIV, *i.e.* the Slight-vowel for the 1st Rt-letter is generally ־ֲ, as in עָמְרִי, עָמְרוּ. [But we find חֲשֹׂפִּי Is. xlvii. 2, where the ־ֲ is a real Short-vowel, (the ־ֲ Quiescent being followed by Dag. L.)].

174. In all the instances mentioned in §§ 171–173, the 'Slight'-vowel is no longer needed when, the word being in Pause, the 2d Rt-letter has a vowel. The Compound Shva then returns to the 1st Rt-letter; thus,

(*a.*) יַעֲמֹדוּ (Pause-form of יַעַמְדוּ), יַחֲרְדוּ (of יַחַרְדוּ), etc.;

(*β.*) נַעֲבֹרָה (of נַעַבְרָה), אֶעֱלֹזָה (of אֶעַלְזָה), etc.

(*γ.*) And so in the Imperative, עֲבֹרִי (Pause-form of עַבְרִי), עֲמֹדוּ (of עַמְדוּ). * †

---

* A Pause-form sometimes occurs of a word which itself nowhere occurs, thus, חֳרָבִי Is. xliv. 27, for חָרְבִי which does not occur anywhere.

[Obs. (1) The ־ֳ (in this word חֳרָבִי) is Pause-vowel for ־ַ. The Imper. 2 s. *m.* of חרב *to be dry*, would be חֲרַב (like תֶּחֱרַב, יֶחֱרַב). The only 2 s. *m.* Imper. of חרב which occurs is חָרֹב *lay waste*, Jer. l. 21.

(2) The ־ֳ (of the ח) may be supposed to belong to the same class as the ŏ of קָ in קָרְבָה. See more in 'Appendix.'

† So הָדֵלּוּ Pause-form of חִדְלוּ (§ 173) fr. חָדַל 2 s *m.* And so we should have אֲחַרְלָה for אַחְדְּלָה (p. 116, Note ‖), and אֱעֱרְדָה for אֲעַרְדָהוּ (§ 171, iv).

175. Two examples from the *Niph.* Voice were adduced in § 169 (β, iii.).   Here we may add that

In *Niph.* (1) the prefix נ (Past and Partic.) has generally ־ֶ*, but (2) the prefix ה (in the Inf. and Imp.), and the prefixes איתן (in the Fut.) have ־ֵ†; see Tab. XVI (1).   Moreover

176. (i.) the 1st Rt-letter has (*a*) sometimes ־ֱ, as in נֶעֱזָב; and (β) sometimes ־ֲ, as in נֶעְדָּר [Cp. § 169 (β, iii.)].

(ii.) When, however, the 2d Rt-letter has ־ֲ, the 1st Rt-letter *cannot ever* have ־ֱ. It must then have either (1) a *Slight-vowel*, as in נֶהְפְּכוּ, נֶחְרְבוּ, נֶעֶרְמוּ, or (2) a Quiescent ־ֵ, as in נֶחְשְׁבוּ, נֶהְפְּכוּ. But

[N.B. the 'Slight'-vowel of (ii, 1) is not needed in Pause, because then the 2d Rt-letter has a vowel; thus, we have נֶעֱצָרֽה׃ 3 s. *f.* Past *Niph.* in Pause, and so נֶעֱשׂוּ׃ and נֶחֱשָׁבוּ׃ 3 pl. Past].

177. In Pĭ., Pŭ., and Hithp., these Verbs agree with Tab. XIV.

178. In *Hiph.* the 1st Rt-letter has (i.) sometimes ־ֲ (preceded by ־ֶ in Past, and by ־ַ in other parts), as in הֶעֱתִיקוּ, וַיַּעְתֵּק מַעְתִּיק, etc.;—but (ii.) more often ־ֱ preceded by ־ֶ in Past,‡ as in הֶעֱבַרְתִּי הֶעֱבִיר, etc., and (iii.) ־ֲ preceded by ־ַ in Inf., Partic., Imp., & Fut. [Tab. XVI (1)];—also (iv.) sometimes ־ַ preceded by ־ַ in the Past, especially

N.B. in the 2 & 1 sing. and 2 pl. when with the pref. וֹ; thus (הַחֲרַמְתֶּם (but וְהַחֲרַמְתֶּם, (הֶעֱבַרְתִּי (but וְהֶעֱבַרְתִּי, וְהֶעֱמַדְתָּ, etc.;

---

* Also ־ֱ (i) rarely in the Past, as in נֶחְבֵּאתָ 2 s. *m.* (for the א־ֵ see Sect. XIX.); and (ii) sometimes in Partic. forms, as in Sect. XX., and so נַעֲרִץ Ps. lxxxix. 8, and נַחֲרָבוֹת as well as נֶחֱרֶבֶת and נֶחֱמָרִים, etc., and so נַעֲלָמָה, etc.

† To compensate for the Dag. F., which cannot stand in the letters אהחע.

‡ A ־ֲ preceded by ־ֵ, as in הֶעֱבַרְתָּ (2 s. *m.*) Josh. vii. 7, is rare.

but also וְהִתְחֹזַקְתִּי 1 S. xvii. 35 (where the Accent is *not* thrown forward, § 160).

[Note (*a*). From some Roots, *only* — forms occur. So those in (i) and יְעֶתָּק Fut. *K.* And so,

(*b*) בַּעְשֵׂר (Neh. x. 39) Inf. *Hiph.* w. בְ, as in Deut. xxvi. 12 לְעַשֵׂר w. לְ (see p. 79, Note †); and יְעַשֵׂר Fut. *K.*]

179. In *Hoph.* the 1st Rt-letter has — generally* agreeing with the — (ŏ) of the Voice, and this — is replaced by — (ŏ, as a 'Slight'-vowel) when the 2d Rt-letter has —. Tab. XVI (1).

[N.B. The 'Slight'-vowel is not needed in Pause, because then the 2d Rt-letter has a vowel; thus, we have הָהָרְבָה: 3 s. *f.* Past *Hoph.* in Pause.]

IV. Second Root-letter א, ה, ח, or ע.

180. For the purposes of this Exercise-book, the Variations when the 2d Rt-letter is א, ה, ח, or ע, are sufficiently given in Tab. XVI (2). Some additional remarks shall be given in an Appendix.

V. Third Root-letter ה, ח, or ע.

181. The Variations when the 3d Rt-letter is ה, ח, or ע, are sufficiently given in Tab. XVI (3), with the following additions :—

(1.) (*a*) The Furtive — under ה, ח, or ע, at the end of a word, after any Long-Vowel (other than —), is dropped when, by any addition being made to the word, the 3d Rt-letter is no longer at the end. Thus, fr. Inf. Constr. שְׁלֹחַ (Abs. שָׁלֹחַ or שָׁלוֹחַ), we have שָׁלְחִי *my sending*, etc ;—and fr. the Partic. שֹׁלֵחַ s. *m.*, we have שֹׁלְחִים pl. *m.*; & fr. שָׁלוּחַ s. *m.*, שְׁלוּחָה or שְׁלֻחָה s. *f.*, etc.

---

* But we have — also, thus הָהְפַּךְ Job xxx. 15, which is just like הָפַּךְ.

(β) The dot of הּ is no longer wanted when, by any addition being made to the word, the 3ᵈ Rt-letter is no longer at the end. The dot (*Mappêk*) is always dropped then; thus, fr. גָּבַהּ 3 s. *m.* Past, גָּבְהָא Ez. xxxi. 5 (for גָּבְהָה) 3 s. *f.*, גָּבְהְתָּ 2 s. *m.*, etc.

Further remarks will be given in the Appendix.

VI. Verbs with ר in the Root.

182. (i.) Verbs whose 1ˢᵗ Rt-letter is ר agree with Tab. XIV except that, in the *N*φ., the prefixes ה and אירן have ◌ֵ (instead of ◌ִ followed by Dag. F.); thus, הֵרָפֵא Inf. *N*φ., אֵרָפֵא 1 s. Fut., יֵרָפְאוּ 3 pl. *m.* Fut., etc.

(ii.) Verbs whose 2ᵈ Rt-letter is ר agree with Tab. XIV except that, in *Pĭ*, *Pŭ*, & *Hθ*.,

> ‑(a) the Dag. F., for those three Voices, cannot appear; and

> (β) compensation is made by lengthening ◌ִ into ◌ֵ, ◌ַ into ◌ָ, ◌ֻ into ◌ֹ, in accordance with Pt. I, § 19;

[for these Verbs in (ii), see "Appendix to Tab. XVI (2)."]

(iii.) Verbs whose 3ᵈ Rt-letter is ר agree generally with Tab. XIV; but sometimes ◌ֵ occurs (instead of some other vowel) before the ר, as in שֵׁבֵּר 3 s. *m.* Past *Pĭ*, and sometimes ◌ִ as in הִבֵּר 3 s. *m.* Past *Pĭ*. often. But this is not limited to these Verbs; see Tab. XIV Note (e).

VII. Verbs whose Third Root-letter is ו or ת.

183. When in the process of word-forming, a letter would occur twice together and the first one would have ◌ִ Quiescent, this letter with ◌ִ *Quiescent* is dropped; and Dag. F. (as imply-

ing a letter with ⸚ *Quiescent,* before it) is then given* to the next letter. For example,

(α) נָתַנּוּ is 1 pl. Past *K.* of נתן† [for נָתַ(נ)נוּ, like פְּקַדְנוּ],
נִשְׁעַנּוּ 1 pl. Past *Nφ.* of שען [like נִפְקַדְנוּ]. Similarly,

(β) with 3ᵈ Rt-letter ת, כָּרַתְּ Pause-form of כָּרַתָּ [for נִפְקַדְתְּ like כָּרַ(ת)תָּ; נכרת [like כָּרַתִּי [like פְּקַדְתִּי], כָּרַתָּ [like נִפְקַדְתָּ]; so fr. שחת, שָׁחַתָּ, שָׁחַתֶּם [like פְּקַדְתָּ, פְּקַדְתֶּם],—see Tab. XVI (2) (*a,* 3)], הִשְׁחַתִּי [like הִפְקַדְתִּי]; so fr. שבת, הִשְׁבַּתָּ, הִשְׁבַּתִּי, הִשְׁבַּתֶּם; etc.

(γ) So הַאֲזֵנָּה G. iv. 23, Is. xxxii. 9 [given by some with אָ, and by some with נָה‐ instead of נָּה‐ (see Note *).

VIII. Verbs having any of the Six בגדכפת in the Root.

184. The Root פקד has two of these in it. There are reasons for preferring this for Tab. XIV, or it might have been well to choose a Root such as כתב *to write* (of which all the Rt-letters are of those six). For, as the Student knows already [Pt. I, 47], those six letters have Dag. Lene

(i) at beginning of a word (except as in § 48, Pt. I).

(ii) after a *Quiescent* ⸚.

And [N.B.] the Dag. L. cannot stand after aught else than *Quiescent* ⸚.

Hence the presence of these letters is useful to the Student as shewing him at once where a ⸚ preceding one of them is

---

* This Dag. F is sometimes not put in נ; thus תֵּאָמֵנָה Is. lx. 4 [for תֵּאָמֵ(נ)נָה; תָּרַנְּנָה Ps. lxxi. 23, § 165 (I, γ)], תֶּעָגֵנָה Ru. i. 13 [for תֶּעָגֵ(נ)נָה like תִּפָּקֵדְנָה]; [for תָּרֹנֵ(נ)נָה like תִּפָּקֵדְנָה]. So תִּשְׁכֹּנָה given in the margins of several Bibles for תִּשְׁכֹּנָּה [*i.e.* תִּשְׁכֹּ(נ)נָה like תִּפָּקֵדְנָה] Ez. xvii. 23.

† For the forms of this Irregular Verb, see 'Notes on Tab. XIX.'

Quiescent or Moving.. This, so far as regards the 1st & 3d Rt-letters, is sufficiently shewn to him by Tab. XIV. We have therefore to deal here with those Verbs only which have one of those six letters as *Second* Rt-letter. See below, (*a*)–(δ). [In (*a*), the ⟂ is seen to be (1) sometimes Moving, but also once or twice Quiescent, after the prefixes בּ & כּ; and (2) mostly Quiescent, but also sometimes Moving, after the prefix ל.]

(*a*) Inf. *K.* (i) w. בּ,— בְּרָבוֹת, בִּנְפֹּל, בִּכְתוֹב, [Tab. XXIII], בִּשְׁפַל Eccl. xii. 4 [p. 79, Note *]; but also —: בְּשָׁפְךָ, בְּשָׁכְן —

(ii) w. כּ,— כִּקְרֹחַ, כִּפְגֹשׁ, כִּנְפֹּל, כִּנְבֹל, כִּגְבֹהַּ, כִּשְׁכַב (cp. p. 79, Note *); but also כִּזְכֹּר :—

(iii) w. ל,— לִכְתֹּב, לִבְגֹּד twice, לִנְפֹּל four times, and so at least forty others; but also לִשְׁדֹד, לִנְתֹשׁ & לִנְתִּן (each thrice), and לְצָבָא [followed by צָבָא, Nu. iv. 23, viii. 24], but לִצְבָּא Is. xxxi. 4.

[Note. When the 1st Rt-letter is ה or ע, these generally have ⟂ as in Tab. XVI (1). So a 1st Rt-letter ח has often ⟂, but also often ⟂ [see § 169 (β, i)]. Simple ⟂ under ח is followed by Dag. L. in one of these six letters [(Pt. I, § 25].]

(β) Fut. *K.* תִּכְתֹּב, יִכְתֹּב, etc., with Dag. L. in 2d Rt-letter, as in the בּ of תִּלְבַּשׁ, יִלְבַּשׁ, etc., in Tab. XIV; and so others :—

(γ) *N*φ. [of שָׁבַר] Past נִשְׁבְּרָה, נִשְׁבַּר (p. נִשְׁבְּרָה:), etc. Partic. נִשְׁבָּר, etc.; and so others :—

(δ) *H*φ. [of לבשׁ] Inf. הַלְבֵּשׁ (Abs.), לְהַלְבִּישׁ (with ל pref.), Past הִלְבַּשְׁתָּ, הִלְבִּישָׁה, etc., Partic. מַלְבִּישׁ,

(the Imper. would be הַלְבֵּשׁ, הַלְבֵּישִׁי, etc.), Fut. יַלְבִּישׁ
(וַיַּלְבֵּשׁ) תַּלְבִּישׁ (וַתַּלְבֵּשׁ), etc. ; and so others.

IX. Further Variations.

185. (i) Verb-forms of the Voices *Kal*, *Pi-él*, *Hiph-íl*, may have Objective Pronouns in the form of Affixes. For these, and any consequent changes of the Verb-form, see pp. 208–212.

(ii) Pronoun-forms so attached as Affixes to Verbs may serve not only Objectively, but also sometimes where in English we require some Preposition (or other word) after the Verb, and so they occur a few times with Verb-forms of a Passive or Reflexive Voice, and with Intransitive Verbs.

186. There are some important 'Variations' in the case of some Verbs of the following Classes :—

(1) having 1st Rt-letter	א,		פ'א,	as	אָכַל	to eat.
(2) „ „	י,		פ'י,	as	יָשַׁב	to sit.
					יָטַב	to be good.
(3) „ „	נ,		פ'נ,	as	נָפַל	to fall.
(4) „ 2d Rt-letter	ו,		ע'ו,	as	קוּם	to rise.
	(or י,		ע'י,	as	שִׂים	to put.)
(5) „ 2d & 3d Rt-letters the same,	כְּפוּלִים,			as	סָבַב	to go round.
(6) „ 3d Rt-letter	א,		ל'א,	as	מָצָא	to find.
(7) „ „	ה,		ל'ה,	as	גָּלָה	to reveal.

These are dealt with in the following Sections XIV to XX.

[The above is adopted as the least artificial arrangement. We might, however, put the פ'י first. There are some advantages in so doing. But the arrangement adopted above appears to be the simplest and best.]

VOCABULARY III.

1. אֹזֶן (*f.*) *an ear*, Tab. VII.
2. דבר *Pi*, *to speak.*
3. דֶּרֶךְ (*m. & f.*) *a way*, Tab. X (1).
4. עַל Tab. IV (2), *on, upon, over, on account of, against*, etc.
5. רָשָׁע *a wicked man*, Tab. IX.
6. שֶׁמֶשׁ (*m. & f.*) *Sun.*

N.B. The abbreviations *Nφ.*, *Hφ.*, *Hθ.*, are used below for *Niph-ăl*, *Hiph-ĭl*, *Hithpă-êl.*

EXERCISE XXVI

[*To be translated into English*, § 11 (a–e).]

יְיָ מָלָךְ[1] : עֹז[2] הִתְאַזָּר[3] : מַדּוּעַ[4] דֶּרֶךְ רְשָׁעִים[5] צָלֵחָה[6] : בְּגָדִים[7]
בָּגְדוּ[7] : מֵעִיר[8] מְתִים[9] יִנְאָקוּ[10] וְנֶפֶשׁ חֲלָלִים[11] תְּשַׁוֵּעַ[12] : יַקְטָל־עָנִי[13][14]
וְאֶבְיוֹן[15] : סָבִיב[16] רְשָׁעִים יִתְהַלָּכוּן[17] : וִילָדֵיהֶם[18] יְרַקֵּדוּן[19] : וַיֹּאמְרוּ[20]
לָאֵל[21] סוּר[22] מִמֶּנּוּ וְדַעַת[23] דְּרָכֶיךָ[24] לֹא חָפָצְנוּ[25] : עַד[26] מָתַי[27]
רְשָׁעִים[5] יְיָ עַד[26] מָתַי[27] רְשָׁעִים[5] יַעֲלֹזוּ[28] : אַלְמָנָה[29] וְגֵר[30] יַהֲרֹגוּ[31]
וִיתוֹמִים[32] יְרַצֵּחוּ[33] : הֲנֹטֵעַ[34] אֹזֶן הֲלֹא יִשְׁמָע[35] : אֲנִי שָׁמַעְתִּי[35] :
שְׁכַחַתְּ[36] אוֹתִי וַתִּבְטְחִי[37] בַּשֶּׁקֶר[38] : נִאֲצוּ[39] אֶת קְדוֹשׁ[40] יִשְׂרָאֵל:

[1] מלך to reign. [2] [with] strength. [3] אזר to gird. [4] why? [5] רָשָׁע a wicked one (*m.*).* [6] צלח to prosper [§ 165 (II)]. [7] Exerc. XX (14). [8] עִיר a city. [9] men. [10] נאק to groan. [11] חָלָל a wounded one (*m.*). [12] שׁוע *Pi.* to cry out. [13] קטל to kill [§ 168 (i, a)]. [14] a miserable one. [15] and a needy one. [16] round about. [17] הלך *Hθ.* to walk. [18] יֶלֶד a young one (*m.*) [Tab. X. 1]. [19] רקד *Pi.* to dance. [20] And they have said. [21] to God. [22] depart. [23] and [the] knowledge of. [24] דֶּרֶךְ a way* [Tab. X. 1]. [25] חפץ to delight in, to take pleasure. [26] until. [27] when [26 with 27 = "how long?"] [28] עלז to exult, to triumph. [29] widow. [30] and sojourner. [31] הרג to slay.† [32] יָתוֹם an orphan. [33] רצח *K.* & *Pi.* to murder. [34] נטע to plant [§ 140 (δ, iv), (ε)]. [35] שמע to hear [For שָׁמְעוּ see § 165 (II, iii)]. [36] שכח to forget. [37] בטח to trust. [38] שֶׁקֶר falsehood. [39] נאץ *Pi.* to despise. [40] [The] Holy One of.

* Words marked thus (*) need not be given in the Notes again. † *Pu.* to be slain.

וּבְשִׁקּוּצֵיהֶם[41] נַפְשָׁם חָפֵצָה[20] : דִּבַּרְתִּי וְלֹא שָׁמֵעוּ[35] : וְעַל יְיָ יָשָׁעֵנוּ[2] :

צִיּוֹן שָׂדֶה[43] תֵּחָרֵשׁ[44] : תִּתְיַפַּח[45] תְּפָרֵשׂ[46] כַּפֶּיהָ[47] :

דַּרְכֵי[24] צִיּוֹן אֲבֵלוֹת[48] : גַּם הִיא נֶאֶנְחָה[49]† ⋯ כָּל עַמָּהּ[50] נֶאֱנָחִים[48] :

בֵּעָטֵף[51] עוֹלֵל[52] וְיוֹנֵק[53] : שָׁאֲגוּ[54] צוֹרְרֶיךָ[55] : שָׁרְקוּ[56] וַיַּחַרְקוּ[57]

שֵׁן[58] אָמְרוּ[59] בִּלַּעֲנוּ[60] : עַד[28] מָתַי[27] אֱלֹהִים יְחָרֶף[61] צָר[62] יְנָאֵץ[39]

אוֹיֵב[62] שִׁמְךָ לָנֶצַח[64] : זְכָר־[65] זֹאת אוֹיֵב[62] חֵרֵף[61] יְיָ : הוֹרַגְנוּ[31]

כָל הַיּוֹם[66] נֶחְשַׁבְנוּ[67] כְּצֹאן[68] טִבְחָה[69] : קוֹלִי אֶל אֱלֹהִים וְאֶצְעָקָה[70] :

נַחְפְּשָׂה[71] דְרָכֵינוּ[24] וְנַחְקֹרָה[72] : גְּאָלְנוּ[73] יְיָ צְבָאוֹת[74] שְׁמוֹ : בְּטֶרֶם[75]

הָרִים[76] הֻטְבָּעוּ[77] : וּמַיִם לֹא יַעֲבֹרוּ[78] פִּיו[79] : גְּבוּל[80] שַׂמְתָּ[81] בַּל[100]

יַעֲבֹרוּן[78] : יִגְעָשׁוּ[82] עָם וַיַּעֲבֹרוּ[78] : הַכְּפִירִים[83] שֹׁאֲגִים[54] לַטֶּרֶף[84] :

תִּזְרַח[85] הַשֶּׁמֶשׁ יֵאָסֵפוּן[86] וְאֶל מְעוֹנֹתָם[87] יִרְבָּצוּן[88] : יָקֹשְׁתִּי[89] לְךָ

וְגַם נִלְכַּדְתְּ[90] בָּבֶל וְאַתְּ לֹא יָדַעַתְּ[91] : אֶרֶץ רָעָשָׁה[92] : וַיֶּחֶרְדוּ[93]

בָּנִים מִיָּם[94] : קְצוֹת[95] הָאָרֶץ יֶחֱרָדוּ[93] : וְנִשְׁבַּעְתָּ[96] חַי[97] יְיָ ⋯

וְהִתְבָּרְכוּ[98] בוֹ גּוֹיִם וּבוֹ יִתְהַלָּלוּ[99] :

[41] and in their abominations. [42] שען Nφ. to lean. [43] [as] a field. [44] חרש to plough. [45] יפח Hθ. to breathe out [groans]. [46] פרש Pĭ. to spread out. [47] her hands. [48] אבל to mourn [§ 139 (δ, iii)]. [49] אנח Nφ. to sigh. [50] her people. [51] עטף Nφ. to swoon [§ 137 (3, †)]. [52] babe, [53] and suckling. [54] שאג to roar. [55] Thy foes. [56] שרק to hiss. [57] חרק to gnash. [58] a tooth. [59] אמר to say. [60] בלע to swallow up. [61] חרף Pĭ. to blaspheme [§ 168 (i, β)]. [62] an adversary. [63] Exerc. XX (32). [64] for ever. [65] זכר to remember [§ 168, (i, a)]. [66] the day. [67] חשב to think, to reckon. [68] as sheep of (or for). [69] slaughter. [70] צעק to cry out (in pain). [71] חפש to search. [72] חקר to enquire into. [73] p. 93 (No. 86). [74] [God of] hosts. [75] before that. [76] mountains. [77] טבע K. to sink, Hŏ. to be founded. [78] עבר to pass, pass over, to transgress.* [79] His command-ment (lit. mouth). [80] a bound. [81] Thou hast placed. [82] נעש Pĭ. to be troubled (E.V.). [83] the young lions. [84] for the prey. [85] Exerc. XIX. (33). [86] אסף to gather, gather away. [87] מְעֹנָה a dwelling (here "a den"). [88] רבץ to crouch down. [89] יקש to lay a snare. [90] לכד to take. [91] ידע to know. [92] רעש to shake. [93] חרד to tremble. [94] from sea, from [the] West. [95] [the] ends of. [96] שבע Nφ. to swear.* [97] liveth. [98] ברך K. & Pĭ. to bless, Hθ. to bless oneself. [99] Ex. XX. (45). [100] not.

---

* Words marked thus (*) need not be given in the Notes again.   † Cp. § 176 (ii, 1).

Exercise XXVII.

(To be translated into Hebrew, § 11, ζ–μ.)

And Abram[43] passed-over*[1] into[2] the land.[3] And he-moved*[4] thence[5] towards[6] the mountain.[7] Before[8] The Lord's destroying†[9] Sodom[10] and Gomorra.[11] And God remembered *[12] Abraham,[44] and sent-away *[13] Lot[14] from the midst[15] of the overthrow,[16] on[2] overthrowing †[17] the cities[18] in which Lot[14] dwelt.[19]

He-will-bless[20] the fearers[21] of The Lord. The generation[22] of upright-ones[23] (*m.*) shall be blessed.[20] He-that-blesseth-himself[20] [*Hθ.* Partic.] in the earth[24] shall-bless-himself[20] in The God of Truth.[25] For as-heaven-is-high (Hebr. *as being-high-of*†[26] *heavens*[27]) above[28] the earth,[24] mighty-hath-been[29] His Mercy[30] on those-that-fear-Him (Hebr. *His fearers*[21] *m.*). As-a-father-is-merciful (Hebr. *as being-merciful-of*†[31] *a father*[32]) to (Hebr. *on*) children,[33] Merciful-hath-been[31] The Lord to (Hebr. *on*) those-that-fear-Him. And I-will-be-merciful-to‖[31] whom[34] I-will-be-merciful-to.[31] In Thee an orphan[35] shall-find-Mercy (Hebr. *shall be compassionated*[31]). Look-forth[36] from Thy-holy-habitation (Hebr. *from the habitation*[37] *of Thy holiness*[38]) from[39] the heaven,[27] and bless[20] Thy people[40] Israel. For Thou, O-Lord, hast-blessed,[20] and [one is] blessed[41] (*m.*) for-ever.[42]

[1] עבר. [2] ב the prefix. [3] p. 47 (s). [4] עתק ‡ *Hφ.* [5] מִשָּׁם. [6] § 71. [7] הַר, w. 'def. art.' הָהָר. [8] לִפְנֵי. [9] שחת *Pĭ.* [10] סדֹם [11] עֲמֹרָה. [12] זכר (Fut. ◌ֲ). [13] שלח *Pĭ.* to bless, *Pŭ.* to be blessed, *Hθ* to bless oneself. [14] לוֹט. [15] p. 108 (34). [16] הַפֵּכָה. [17] הפך. [18] p. 56 (2). [19] יֵשֵׁב. [20] ברך *Pĭ.* [21] יְרֵאִים (1.c, p. 84, Note *). [22] דוֹר. [23] יְשָׁרִים. [24] p. 47 (6). [25] אָמֵן. [26] גבה (the ה is consonantal). [27] שָׁמַיִם. [28] עַל. [29] גבר. [30] הֶסֶד Tab. X. (1). [31] רחם § *Pĭ* to be merciful, to be merciful to, *Pŭ.* to be compassionated. [32] אָב [33] Tab. XIII (4). [34] אֶת אֲשֶׁר. [35] יָתוֹם. [36] שקף *Hφ* (Imper. 2 s m., w ה). [37] מָעוֹן (§ 56, 1). [38] קֹדֶשׁ. [39] מִן. [40] עַם (p 91, 14). [41] *Pŭ.* Partic. [42] לְעוֹלָם [43] אַבְרָם. [44] אַבְרָהָם.

---

* Fut. w. ו Conv.   † Infinitive Constr.   ‡ § 178 (i)
§ 'Compensation' is NOT made in *Pĭ.* & *Pŭ.*, comp Tab. XVI (2) (β, 111) The *Pĭ.* Past 3 s. m. takes ◌ֵ as in Note (e) on Tab. XIV.   ‖ Past w. ו Conv.

SECTION XIV.

Verbs א״פ, *i.e.* whose First Root-letter is א [Tab. XVII].

187. Many forms are like those of Verbs whose 1st Rt-letter is ה, ח, or ע.

188. (*a*) The Chief Variations from Tab. XVI (1) arise from some prefixes taking ־ֳ, as in the Fut. *K.* forms

(i) יֹאבַד etc., fr. אבד, יֹאכַל etc., fr. אכל, יֹאמַר etc., fr. אמר etc.,; and forms used in Pause, such as יֹאבֵד:, תֹּאבֵד:, etc.,* which are of the following Class (ii) *viz.*

(ii) יֹאחֵז, תֹּאחֵז, etc., fr. אחז; for some other instances of which (־ֵ) form see Tab. XVII.

[(iii) For a few forms of *Nφ*. and *Hφ*. see § 190 (β).]

(β) Some other Variations from Tab. XVI (1) in the *Kal*, are but slight. Thus, (i) ־ֵ in place of ־ֶ, see Tab. XVII; and (ii) some contractions, as תֵּזְלִי Jer. ii. 36 (2 s. *f.* Fut. *K.* of אול), וָאֵחֵר G. xxxii. 5 (1 s. Fut. *K.* of אחר, for אֶאֱחֵר which does not occur), and so in Pause אֹהָב Pr. viii. 17, etc.

⁎ The Student's attention may be specially called to the Great Rule in the following § (189), Variations in accordance with which will be found to occur in some other Classes of Verbs as we proceed.

189. These Verbs (פ א) offer us the first opportunity of bringing forward the following very important

Rule: The ו Convers. of the Fut. has the power of drawing back the Accent from the last to the penult. syllable, as in

---

* The (־ֶ) form also occurs in Pause; thus וַיֹּאבַל: G. iii. 6, etc. But,

N.B. The (־ֵ) form of the Fut. is always adopted when (as in § 165, II) a ־ֲ has to be replaced by a Vowel in Pause; thus יֹאכֵלוּ fr. יֹאכְלוּ, etc.

וַיֹּאחֶז 2 S. vi. 6, fr. יֹאחֶז (and so וַיֹּאמֶר v. 9, fr. the unused
יֹאמֶר, וַתֹּאמֶר 2 K. xix. 23, fr. תֹּאמֶר); but

Obs. (i) NOT so in 1 Sing.; thus וָאֹמֶר G. xx. 13, etc.; also

(ii) NOT if there be a Shva† between the last two Vowels
[thus, וַיִּפְקֹד and וַיֵּאָמֵן remain unchanged]; and

(iii) NOT if the Accent be a Pause-Accent‡; and

(iv) sometimes also NOT, if the Accent be less than the
'Pause'-Accents, in a case of § 164 (β).

Note. (a) The Accent is generally NOT drawn back if there be
more than one vowel between the ו Convers. and the last syllable
[thus we have וַיִּפְקֹד and וַיֶּאֱסֹף], but

(b) it *is sometimes* drawn back in such Nφ. forms, as in וַיֵּאָסֵף
G. xxv. 8, etc.

190. (a) The form הֵאָכֹל of Inf. Abs. Nφ. was mentioned in
'Notes on Tab. XIV (d).' (So הֵאָסֹף 2 S. xvii. 11). The Nφ.
forms generally are as in §§ 175, 176; and those of other Voices
as in the §§ following the two just now cited.

(β) There are a few instances of Nφ. and Hφ. forms having
א Quiescent in — (thus אָ֫), or lost in ו or —; thus

(i) Nφ. Past 3 pl. נֹאחֲזוּ Jos. xxii. 9, וְנֹאחֲזוּ w. ו Conv.
Nu. xxxii. 30 (fr. אחז);

(ii) Hφ. Fut. 1 s. אוֹכִיל Hos. xi. 4 (fr. אכל), אֹבִידָה w. ה
Jer. xlvi. 8 (fr. אבד).

---

* N.B. When, as here, the last letter of the word has Shva (which is *Quiescent*,
being at the end of a word),—a long vowel in the last syllable is shortened on the
removal of the Accent from that syllable [Pt. I, § 55 (9, b)]. So we have the ֶ here
instead of the ֵ in יֹאחֶז, in accordance with Pt. I, § 19.

† Even if it is merely implied by Dag. Forte, as we shall see.

‡ Except וַיֹּאמַר in Job iii. 2, xl. 3, and v. 1 of Job iv, vi, viii, ix, xi, xii, xv,
xvi, xviii–xxiii, xxv–xxvii, xxix, xxxiv–xxxvi, xxxviii, xl, & xlii; but not in xxxii. 6,
nor in Chapters i & ii.

191. The א is sometimes dropped in *Pi.* as in מְלִפֵּנוּ Job xxxv. 11 for מְאַלְּפֵנוּ Partic. s. *m.*, w. Pron. Aff. for 1 pl.; and in *Hφ.*, as in אֲזִין Job. xxxii. 11 for אַאֲזִין, and מֵזִין Pr. xvii. 4 for מַאֲזִין. See more in Appendix.

192. With the exception of (ı) the special (—)-form of the Fut. *K.*, viz: יֹאכֵל:, in Pause,*—and (ıı) the retaining of the ⸗ unchanged in the יֹאמַר form when this is used in Pause,— the Pause-forms of these Verbs פ'א agree generally with §§ 165–167.

[Note. In the above, with Tab. XVII, enough is given for our present purpose. It is unnecessary to give here in detail forms which, as said in § 187, are like some or other of those in §§ 169–179.

For the יָאסֹף form of Fut. *K.*, see Tab. XVII (2, ε, i)]

---

* See Tab. XVII (2, γ) for Pause-forms of the Fut. *Kal.*

ADDITIONAL NOTE.

The form אֹכֵל (or אֹכֶל) *K.* Fut. 1 s. takes the ה of § 144 thus אֹכְלָה (p. אֹכֵלָה:). So, with this ה, the 1 pl. Fut. would be נֹאכְלָה (p. נֹאכֵלָה:).

'Appendix on Verbs פ׳א.

As said in § 187, many forms are like those of Verbs whose 1st Rt-letter is ה, ח, or ע.   But

(i) The Infin. *K.* has not only the forms בֶּאֱכֹל ,אֱכֹל, and so אֱמָר־ (with ◌ָ *ŏ* on account of the removal of the Accent), but also—with אֶ—בֶּאֱחֹז ,בֶּאֱמֹר ,כֶּאֱמֹר ,לֶאֱהֹב*.

Note (*a*) Sometimes the א has ◌ָ as in לֶאְסֹר.

    (β) The common word לֵאמֹר (generally rendered 'saying') is Infin. *K.* fr. אמר [for לְאֱמֹר or לֶאֱמֹר].

(ii) In the Imper. *K.*,

    (*a*) The א has ◌ֱ as in אֱכֹל ,אֱמֹר, and אֱהֹב ,אֱמֹץ (p.: אֱמָץ);

    (β) The Slight-vowel, which the א takes in the 2 s. *f.* and 2 pl. *m.*, is generally ◌ִ as in אֱמְרִי & אֱכְלוּ;

    (γ) But before ◌ֱ the א takes the Slight-vowel ◌ָ, as in אֶחֱזוּ and אֶהֱבוּ.   The Pause-forms of these are אֶהֱבוּ: and אֶחֱזוּ: [§ 166 (*b*, i & ii)].

    (δ) With the ה of § 141 (γ) we have the 2 s. *m.* Imper. *K.* forms (1) אֱכְלָה like שֻׁמְרָה, and (2) אֶסְפָה with אֶ.

Note (1). In אֱחֱזִי 2 s. *f.* Imper. *K.*, Ruth iii. 15, the ◌ֱ refers to the ◌ֲ of אֱחֹז. Some however give there אֲחֱזִי like the 2 pl. *m.* אֲחֱזוּ.

(2). For אֱהֱבוּ 2 pl. *m.* Imper. *K.*, Ps. xxxi. 24, some give אֲהֱבוּ.

(3). For the rare form אֱסְפִּי 2 s. *f.* Imper. *K.*, comp. § 141 (ζ).

---

* For this some give לֶאֱהֹב in Eccl. iii. 8.   From the Root אהב we have often the form with ה, thus לְאַהֲבָה.   The form אַהֲבָה gives, in direct Construction, the form מֵאַהֲבָת ,כְּאַהֲבָת ,בְּאַהֲבָת—in אַהֲבָת.   Comp. § 137 (4, iii) p. 80.   And the same form with Pron-Affixes gives בְּאַהֲבָתוֹ etc., see § 137 (4, iii).

The form כְּאָהֳבָם Hos. ix. 10 (Infin. *K.*, fr. אהב, w. כ pref. and Aff. *their m.*) has ◌ָ (*ŏ*), as in Tab. XV, and the ה has ◌ֳ in agreement with the *ŏ* of the א.

(iii) (a) The Verbs which REGULARLY take ־ֶ to the prefixes of the Future, as in § 188 (i & ii) are אבד *to perish,* אחז *to hold,* אכל *to eat,* and אמר *to say,*—together with the Verbs אבה and אפה, for which see pp. 267 & 270.

(β) Several Verbs פ׳א have Fut. *K.* forms such as

    (a) יַאֲרֹב, תַּאֲרֹב, etc.;

    (b) יֶאְסֹר (as well as יַאְסֹר), and so יֶאְפֹּד Lev. viii. 7;

    (c) יֶאֱמַץ fr. אמץ, תֶּאֱבַל fr. אבל, etc.;

    (d) אשם; נֶאְשַׁם 1 pl., fr. יֶאְשַׁם, תֶּאְשַׁם, יֶאְשְׁמוּ 3 pl. *m.,* and so אלף; fr. אטר, יֶאֱטֹר fr. אלף, תֶּאֱלַף 3 s. *f.* and so תֶּאְטַר.

    (e) יַאַסְפוּ 3 pl. *m.,* etc. So some forms with Affixes have ־ַ.

(γ) Some Verbs have more than one of the Future forms: thus,

    (a) From אסף the usual Future *K.* forms are יֶאֱסֹף, תֶּאֱסֹף, etc.; but we find also once וַיִּסֹף 3 s. *m.* (with ו Convers.) for וַיֶּאֱסֹף, and once תֹסֵף 2 s. *m.* for תֶּאֱסֹף,—which are of the forms יֹאחֵז, תֹאחֵז.

    (b) So from אהב we have not only the usual Fut. *K.* forms תֶּאֱהַב, יֶאֱהַב, and so אֱהַב: (contracted, and in Pause, for אֶאֱהַב 1 s.), etc.; but also אֹהַב (like אֹכֵל), once in וָאֹהַב 1 s. w. ו Convers. and three times w. Pron.-Affs. [§ 185].

    (c) And so, conversely, from אחז we have as Fut. *K.* forms not only

      (1) יֹאחֵז 3 s. *m.,* תֹאחֵז 3 s. *f.,* (and וַתֹּחֶז 2 S. xx. 9 for וַתֹּאחֵז 3 s. *f.* with ו Convers.), אֹחֵז 1 s (and, with ה, אֹחֲזָה), יֹאחֲזוּ 3 pl. *m.* (p. יֹאחֵזוּ:; and, with ן, יֹאחֲזוּן),—but also

      (2) וַיֶּאֱחֹז 3 s. *m.* with ו Convers., and תֶּאֱחֹז 2 s. *m.,* like יַאֲרֹב and תַּאֲרֹב.

      (3) There may be ו in place of ־ֶ; thus, אוֹמְרָה 1 s. Fut. *K.* w. ה, fr. אמר, etc.

(iv) Besides the contracted forms mentioned in § 191, we may mention here the following :—

    (1) לְהָכִיל Infin. *Hφ.* (Ez. xxi. 33), supposed by some to be for לְהַאֲכִיל

    (2) וַיֶּאֱצֵל Fut. *Hφ.* 3 s. *m.* (Nu. xi. 25), for וַיַּאֲצֵל or וַיֶּאֱצֵל;

    (3) וַיֵּרֶב Fut *Hφ* 3 s. *m.* (1 S xv 5), supposed by some to be for וַיַּאֲרֵב;

    (4) יַהֵל (Is xiii. 20), which is taken (a) by some as *Hφ.* Fut. 3 s. *m.* for יַאֲהִיל (Job xxv. 5), and (b) by others as *Pï.* Fut. 3 s. *m.* for יְאַהֵל—which last is possible if we may assume a *Pï-él* Voice of the Root אהל. The *Pï.* of אהל occurs nowhere in the Bible.

Exercise XXVIII.

(To be translated into English, §§ 11. a–ε.)

וַיֹּאמְרוּ¹ אֵלַי הֲלוֹא² יָדַעְתָּ³ מָה הֵמָּה⁴ אֵלֶּה וָאֹמַר¹ לֹא אֲדֹנִי⁵ :

זֶה דְּבַר יְיָ אֶל זְרֻבָּבֶל⁶ לֵאמֹר¹ ... : וַאֲמַרְתֶּם¹ בַּיּוֹם⁷ הַהוּא הוֹדוּ⁸

לַייָ : חִזְקוּ⁹ וַיַּאֲמֵץ¹⁰ לְבַבְכֶם¹¹ : אֶת אֲשֶׁר יֶאֱהַב¹² יְיָ יוֹכִיחַ¹³ : אֲנִי

אֹהֲבִי¹² אֵהָב¹² : וָאֹהַב¹² אֶת יַעֲקֹב : וַתֹּאמְרִי¹ לְעוֹלָם¹⁴ אֶהְיֶה¹⁵

גְּבָרֶת¹⁶ : יֹאחֵז¹⁷ בְּעָקֵב¹⁸ פָּח¹⁹ : וּבְכָל²⁰ אַרְצָהּ יֶאֱנַק²¹ חָלָל²² :

*וְהַאֲכַלְתִּי²³ אֶת מוֹנַיִךְ²⁴ אֶת בְּשָׂרָם²⁵ : וְדֶרֶךְ רְשָׁעִים תֹּאבֵד²⁶ :

אֹמַר¹ לַייָ מַחְסִי²⁷ וּמְצוּדָתִי²⁸ : אָמַר¹ לְנַפְשִׁי יְשֻׁעָתֵךְ²⁹ אָנִי :

הֶאֱמַנְתִּי³⁰ כִּי אֲדַבֵּר : אִמְרוּ¹ בַגּוֹיִם יְיָ מָלָךְ³¹ : טוֹב³² הָאָרֶץ

תֹּאכֵלוּ²³ : אָסֹף³³ אָאֵסֹף³³ יַעֲקֹב כֻּלָּךְ³⁴ : אֹסְפָה³³ הַצֹּלֵעָה³⁵ :

יֹאכְלוּ²³ עֲנָוִים³⁶ וְיִשְׂבָּעוּ³⁷ : אֹכְלוּ²³ רֵעִים³⁸ : אֶהֱבוּ¹² אֶת יְיָ כָּל

חֲסִידָיו³⁹ :

---

¹ אמר to say. ² whether not? ³ ידע to know. ⁴ § 96 (ii, β). ⁵ אֲדוֹן a lord.
⁶ Zerubbabel. ⁷ יוֹם (*m.*) a day. ⁸ render ye thankful acknowledgments, give thanks.
⁹ חזק to be strong. ¹⁰ אמץ to be firm. ¹¹ לֵבָב (*m.*) a heart. ¹² אהב to love. ¹³ He
will correct. ¹⁴ for ever. ¹⁵ I shall be. ¹⁶ a lady (ֶ for ֱ in Pause). ¹⁷ אחז to
take hold. ¹⁸ עָקֵב a heel. ¹⁹ a snare. ²⁰ and throughout all. ²¹ אנק to groan.
²² a wounded one (*m.*). ²³ אכל to eat. ²⁴ thy (*f.*) oppressors, those that afflict thee.
²⁵ בָּשָׂר flesh. ²⁶ אבד to perish. ²⁷ my place of refuge, my trust. ²⁸ and my fortress.
²⁹ thy (*f.*) salvation. ³⁰ אמן *Hiph.* to believe. ³¹ מלך to be king. ³² [the] good of.
³³ אסף to gather. ³⁴ the whole of thee. ³⁵ her that halteth. ³⁶ meek ones (*m.*).
³⁷ שבע to have enough, to be satisfied. ³⁸ רֵעַ a companion, a friend. ³⁹ חָסִיד a pious
one (*m.*), a saint.

---

* A Verb in *Hiph.* has sometimes *two Objects* expressed. So here, Nos. 24 & 25,—
the first Object THOSE CAUSED *to eat*, the second Object THAT WHICH *they shall eat.*

Exercise XXIX.

(To be translated into Hebrew, § 11. ζ–μ.)

N.B. All Verbs פ״א in this Exercise have the Fut. K. as in § 188 (α, i). For Pause-forms, see Tab. XVII. (2, γ) and § 192.

Wicked-ones [1] (*m.*) will-perish [2] [§ 162 (*d*, i)]. By [3] the breath [4] of God [5] they (*m.*)-will-perish [2] [Pause-form [6]]. All [7] my bones [8] shall say [9], Lord, who [10] [is] like [11] Thee? And Zion (*f.*) hath-said,* [9] The Lord hath-forsaken-me [12] [§ 162, (*d*, i)]. Say-thou [9] (*m.*). to [13] the house [14] of Israel, So [15] have-ye-said [9] (*m.*), saying,[16]… What shall-we-say? [9]

Tell-ye [9] (*m.*) a righteous-one [17] (*m.*) that [18] [there is] good,[19] for [18] the fruit [20] of their (*m.*) deeds [21] they-shall-enjoy [22] [Pause-form [6]]. Comfort-ye [23] (*m.*), comfort-ye [23] My people,[24] your (*m.*) God [24] will say [9] [§ 162 (*d*, i)]. And He-said,* [9] Verily [25] My people [24] [are] they (*m.*). I will say [9] to the North,[26] Give-up.[27] And I-have-said :* [9] " my Father! " [28] shalt-thou (*f.*) call [29] Me (Hebr. *to Me*). And we-will not say [9] any-more [30] "our God ! " [24] to the work [31] of our hands.[32] The Glory [33] of Thy Kingdom [34] they (*m.*) shall tell [9] [Pause-form [6]].

---

[1] Exerc. XXVI (5). [2] אבד. [3] מ prefix. [4] נְשָׁמָה, § 56 (i & v). [5] אֶל. [6] § 188 (Note *, N.B.). [7] כָּל. [8] עֲצָמוֹת (*f.*) Tab. XII. 1 (pl.). [9] אמר. [10] מִי. [11] כ prefix. [12] עֲזָבְנִי. [13] אֶל. [14] Tab. XIII (s). [15] כֵּן. [16] Inf. *K.*, w. ל, of אמר. [17] צַדִּיק. [18] כִּי. [19] טוֹב. [20] פְּרִי, i.e. the same. [21] מַעֲלָלִים. [22] אכל. [23] נחם *Pi*, Tab. XVI (2) [β, iii]. [24] Vocab. I. [25] אַךְ. [26] צָפוֹן (*f.*). [27] תֵּנִי. [28] אָב. [29] קרא. [30] עוֹד. [31] מַעֲשֶׂה. [32] יָד a hand. [33] כָּבוֹד. [34] מַלְכוּת (*f*).

---

* Fut. w. ו Convers.

SECTION XV.

VERBS פ״י, *i.e.* WHOSE FIRST ROOT-LETTER IS י [Tab. XVIII].

193. Some forms agree entirely with those in Tab. XIV ; thus (i) the Inf. Abs. and the Past* Tense & Participles *K.*, (ii) a few forms of particular Verbs, (iii) the *Pi.†, Pŭ.*, and *Hθ.‡* forms.

The special VARIATIONS are the following :—

194. The י is *dropped* in (a) the Inf. Constr. *K.*, and (β) the Imper. *K.* ; thus, from יֵשֵׁב,

    (a) INF. K. § שֶׁבֶת, בְּשֶׁבֶת, כְּשֶׁבֶת, מְשֶׁבֶת, but ל w. לְשֶׁבֶת ;

    and w. Pron. Affs. ‖ שִׁבְתּוֹ, שִׁבְתְּךָ, שִׁבְתִּי, etc. ;

    (β) IMPER. K. ¶ שֵׁב, שְׁבִי, etc. ; see Tab XVIII.

---

* Thus (fr ירד) יֵרֵד, יָרְדָה, יָרַדְתָּ, etc. [רֵד, Ju. xix. 11, is given by many as 3 s. *m.* Past *K.* of ירד " by *aphæresis.*" But this is somewhat doubtful]

† Except in some instances of the loss of the י by Contraction, as in וַיִּדּוּ Lam. iii 53 (for וַיְיַדּוּ like וַיִּגְלוּ of גלה, cp. Tab. XXIII), and a few other words.

‡ (a) Thus (נַתְּחַצַּב) תִּתְיַצֵּב, יִתְיַצֵּב, הִתְיַצֵּב Ex. ii, 4, is irreg. 3 s. *f.* with ו Convers.), יֵעַן fr וְיִתְיָעֵצוּ, and so (ל) וַיִּתְיַלְדוּ 3 pl. *m.* Fut. w. ו [of יֵלַד], and יִתְיַצְּבוּ ;

(b) But, in some, י is replaced by ו, as in בְּהִתְוַדַּע Inf. Constr. (w. בְּ) of ידע, יִתְוַכַּח 3 s. *m.* Fut. of יכח, and אֶתְוַדָּע 1 s. Fut. of ידע (Pause-form).

§ (a) In Pause שָׁבֶת :.

  (b) From ידע, בַּעַת (p. רָעַת), בִּבְעַת, לָבַעַת.

‖ (a) But [fr. יֵלֵך] לְכִתּוֹ, etc., forms like those in § 62 (iii). And,

  (b) from ידע, דַּעְתּוֹ, etc., forms like those in Tab. X (1).

¶ (a) w. ה, שְׁבָה. So (fr. יֵלֵך), לְכָה, לֵד, לֵד, לֵך, (p. לְכָה:). Also,

  (b) from ידע, דַּע, דְּעִי, דְּעוּ. And,

  (c) from יהב, הַב *give thou* (m.) [הָבָה (i e. הַב w. ה) is used as an Interjection or " Come !", " Come on !" or such like], הָבִי *give thou* (f.), הָבוּ *give ye* (m.).

195. The ' is (*a*) sometimes Quiescent in '־ֵ [see ¿ 197] as in

Fut. K.   תֵּיטְבִי ,תֵּיטֵב ,יֵיטֵב, etc. (or יֵטֵב, etc., Pt. I, § 12);

(β) sometimes Quiescent in '־ֵ as in the *H*φ. forms יֵיטִיב ,הֵיטִיב ,הֵיטֵב, etc., Tab. XVIII.;

(γ) sometimes *lost* in ־ֵ as in the forms

Fut. K.   תֵּשְׁבִי ,תֵּשֵׁב ,יֵשֵׁב, etc. [see ¿ 198]

(δ) sometimes replaced by וֹ*, either

(i) Consonantal,—as in the *N*φ. Inf., Imper., & Fut., see Tab. XVIII; and in some *Hithpa-ĕl* forms [§ 193, Note (‡, δ)];

(ii) Quiescent in וֹ †,—as in the *N*φ. Past & Partic., and in the *H*φ. הוֹשִׁיב ,הוֹשֵׁב, יוֹשִׁיב, etc.; or

(iii) Quiescent in וּ‡, in the *Hoph-ăl;*

(ε) sometimes dropped, and Dag. F. placed in the 2ᵈ Rt-letter [thus, for instance, in some forms of יצק,—as אֶצָּק & אֶצָּק־ Is. xliv. 3 (1 s. Fut. *K.*), מֻצָּק 1 K. vii. 16 (Partic. *Hoph.* s. *m.*, 'i.e.'); so, from יצב, נִצְּבָה (p. נִצְּבָה:) 3 s. *f.* Past *N*φ., הִצִּיב 3 s. *m.* Past *H*φ., מֻצָּב s. *m.* Partic. *Hŏ.*].

196. These Verbs may be dealt with in the three following Classes:—

I. those that retain the ' as in § 195 (*a*);

II. those that *lose* the ' as in § 195 (γ);

III. those that drop the 1ˢᵗ Rt-letter, and take Dag. F. in the 2ᵈ Rt-letter, as in § 195 (ε).   [But

N.B. a Verb has sometimes forms belonging to more than one of these Classes, and like those in Tab. XIV.]

---

* Some imagine Roots פ'ו for forms having ו thus.

† For which there is ־ some few times.

‡ For which there may be ־ֵ [Pt. I, § 14] as in מְעָדוֹת Ez. xxi. 21.

197. Class I.—(a) The forms יִיטַב ,יִיבֵשׁ (or יִטַב ,יִבֵשׁ, Pt. I,
§ 12), etc., are really the same as יִלְבַּשׁ, etc., in Tab. XIV.

[But the 1st Rt-letter ' becoming Quiescent in the preceding ⸗, the ⸗ is not required beneath it. Pt. I, § 29.]

There are a few varying forms which will be given in the Appendix.

(β) In Pause the 2d Rt-letter has ⸗, as in תִּיבָשׁ, יִיבָשׁ: אִיבָשׁ: ,יִיבָשׁוּ: (or יִבָשׁוּ:, Pt. I, § 12).

(γ) With ו Convers. the Fut. form יִיטַב retains its Accent on the *last* syllable ; thus וַיִּיטַב, and so וַתִּיטַב, etc.   But,

(δ) fr. יְקַץ we have once וַיִּיקֶץ G. ix. 24.   וַיִּיקַץ, however, occurs four times, and וַיְקַץ twice (* וַיָּקַץ once, 1 K. iii. 15). So fr. יְצַר, † וַיִּיצֶר G. ii. 7, and † וַיִּיצֶר *v.* 19.

(ε) The 1 s. & 1 pl., w. ה (§ 144), drop as usual the vowel of the 2d Rt-letter ; thus, (fr. יְעַץ) אִיעָצָה 1 s., and (fr. יְרַשׁ) נִירְשָׁה 1 pl. But, in Pause, these would become אִיעָצָה:, נִירָשָׁה: [§ 165, II, ii. 3].   Thus, וָאִישֵׁנָה Ps. iii. 6, 1 s. Fut. *K.* w. ו Convers.

(ζ) Some of these Verbs retain the ' in the *Hφ.* also ;‡ thus, the *Hφ.* forms fr. יְטַב in Tab. XVIII,—and so (fr. יְנַק) הֵינִיק, תֵּינִיק (or תֵּינַק, Pt. I, § 12), etc.; and so 2 s. *f.* הֵילִיכִי, ‖וַיֵּינִיק, §מֵינִיק Imper. *Hφ.* fr. יְלַךְ. [But the usual *Hφ.* forms from יְלַךְ are like הוֹשִׁיב ,יוֹשִׁיב, etc., in Tab. XVIII.] So also, fr. יְלַל,

---

* This form belongs to Class III.

† In the Bible, the Accent here is ⸢ which stands over the *last letter* of the word. That is the place for the Accent ⸢. But it affects the penult. syllable here.

‡ The 1st Rt-letter ' belonging to these forms is (i) sometimes dropped, as in וַיִּנְקֵהוּ (D xxxii. 13) 3 s. *m.* Fut. *Hφ.* of יְנַק w. Aff. הוּ⸗ *him* [Sect. XXII], and

(ii) sometimes retained consonantally, as in וַיֵּיטִב (Job xxiv. 21) 3 s. *m.* Fut. *Hφ.*

§ Partic. s. *m.*, מֵינַקְת & מֵינִיקָה s. *f.*, etc. [The latter, w. Pron. Affs., has the 1-Decl. (§ 62, ii), thus, מֵינִקְתּוֹ, and [‡, i] מֵנִקְתּוֹ 2 K. xi. 2 & מֵנִקְתָּהּ G. xxiv. 59.]

‖ In the form cited in Note (‡, i).

L

הֵילִילִי (for הֵילִיל) 3 s. *m.* Past, הֵילֵל Imper. 2 s. *m.* and
2 s. *f.* & הֵילִילוּ 2 pl. *m.*, אֵילִילָה 1 s. Fut. w. ה.   But

(η) In some *Hφ.* Fut. forms of ילל the י is retained *consonantally* [cp. page 135, Note (‡, ii)], thus יְיֵלִיל 3 s. *m.*, אֵילִיל 1 s., יְיֵלִלוּ 3 pl. *m.*, תְּיֵלִילוּ 2 pl. *m.* [For יְהֵילִילוּ see § 201.]

(θ) When the Fut. *Hφ.* of form יֵיטִיב has וֹ Convers., the Accent is generally drawn back; and the Long Vowel of the last syllable is then shortened.*   Thus, וַיֵּיטֶב 3 s. *m.*, וַתֵּיטֶב 3 s. *f.*; and so וַתֵּינָק fr. ינק, etc.

(ι) But most Verbs of this Class (I) have *Hφ.* forms like those of יָשַׁב in Column V. of Tab. XVIII. For such forms of Fut. *Hφ.* see § 198 (ε, etc.).

198. Class II.—(*a*) In the forms יֵשֵׁב, תֵּשֵׁב, תֵּשְׁבִי, etc., the 1st Rt-letter י is not written, but is understood and implied in the — of the Prefix-letter.

(β) In Pause, — is given to the 2d Rt-letter of Fut.† forms which have — in Tab. XVIII; thus, תֵּלְכִי 2 s. *f.* Fut. *K.* of ילך is in Pause תֵּלֵכִי, and so יֵלְכוּ gives יֵלֵכוּ, תֵּלְכוּ gives תֵּלֵכוּ, etc. Cp. § 165 (II).

(γ) So fr. ‡אֵלְכָה & נֵלְכָה, the 1 s. & 1 pl. w. ה (§ 144), we have in Pause אֵלֵכָה & נֵלֵכָה.

(δ) With וֹ Convers. (1) the Accent of יֵשֵׁב, תֵּשֵׁב, נֵשֵׁב, is drawn back; and so we have [cp. § 189(*)] וַיֵּשֶׁב 3 s. *m.*, וַתֵּשֶׁב 3 s. *f.* & 2 s. *m.*, וַנֵּשֶׁב 1 pl. [see also (η)]. But (2) the

---

* Cp. § 189 (Note *) [on p. 129].

† So also in the Imper. *K.*; thus, fr. ילך we have לְכִי for לְכִי 2 s. *f.* and לְכוּ for לְכוּ 2 pl. *m.*,—as לְכָה 2 s. *m.* Imper. *K.*, w. ה, is in Pause לֵכָה [§ 194 (β, Note ¶)].

‡ אֵילְכָה, Mi. i. 8, with the 1st Rt-letter י standing.

1 Sing. remains unchanged, thus וָאֵשֵׁב. Also (s) in Pause we have וַיֵּשֵׁב׃, etc., cp. § 189 Obs. i & iii. See also (θ) below. So

(ε) the Fut. *IIφ*. (יוֹשִׁיב, etc.) w. ו Convers. is *וַיּוֹשֶׁב 3 s. *m*., וַתּוֹשֶׁב 3 s. *f*. & 2 s. *m*., †וַנּוֹשֶׁב (=וַנּוֹשֵׁב) 1 pl.

(ζ) With ה, § 144, the '— remains; as in אוֹלִיכָה 1 s. Fut. *Hφ*. fr. ילך, and so נוֹדִיעָה 1 pl. fr. ידע. So אֹסְפָה 2 S. xii. 8, with — for ו and — for '—.

(η) The forms יֵשֵׁב, etc., of the *K*., and יוֹשִׁיב, etc., of the *Hφ*, have the Long-Vowel of the closed Final syllable short-ened into — whenever the Accent is removed from the last syllable [as in (δ) and (ε)]. Thus, יֵשֶׁב־נָא G. xliv. 33, יֵשֶׁב בָּהּ׃ Job xxii. 8; so אֵלֶךְ לִי 1 s. (Song. iv. 6), and so [*Hφ*. Fut. of יסף:] יוֹסֶף לָקַח Pr. ix. 9, ‡אַל־תֹּסֶף Ex. x. 28

(θ) The 2ᵈ Rt-letter has sometimes — in the Fut. *K*. and *Hφ*., especially in Pause; thus (from ילך) וַיֵּלֶךְ Job xxvii. 21, וַיֵּלֶךְ׃ G. xxiv. 61, etc., Fut. *K*.; and וַיֵּלֶךְ Lam. iii. 2, Fut. *IIφ*. and so (fr. יסף) אַל־תּוֹסֶף׃ Job xl. 32.

199. When the 3ᵈ Rt-letter is Guttural,

(a) the Fut § *K*. has — instead of — to the 2ᵈ Rt-letter; thus יֵדַע 3 s. *m*., תֵּדַע 3 s. *f*. & 2 s. *m*., אֵדַע 1 s., נֵדַע 1 pl.,

[(β) of these, the Pause-forms are נֵדָע ,אֵדָע ,תֵּדָע ,‖יֵדָע;

(γ) also, in Pause, — replaces the — of 2ᵈ Rt-letter in 2 s. *f*.,

---

and 3 & 2 pl. *m.* Fut.; thus, תֵּרְעִי Pause-form of תֵּרְעִי, and תֵּרְעוּ of תֵּרְעוּ; and so

(δ) the 1 s. & 1 pl. w. ה, *viz.* אֶרְעָה and נֵרְעָה, are in Pause אֶרְעָה: and נֵרְעָה:. Cp. § 165 (II, ii.)].

(ε) In the *Hφ.* Imper. 2 s. *m.* the 2ᵈ Rt-letter has ⟿ as in יִשַׁע fr. הוֹשַׁע, יכח fr. הוֹכַח, ידע fr. הוֹדַע. But,

(ζ) w. ה, § 144, the י⟿ appears as in הוֹשִׁיעָה) 2 s. *m.* (הוֹשַׁע.

(η) In the *Hφ.* Fut. the 2ᵈ Rt-letter has (1) sometimes י⟿ as in יוֹכִיחַ, יוֹדִיעַ, especially in Pause; but also (2) sometimes ⟿ as in וְיִדַע Nu. xvi. 5, וְיוֹכַח Job xvi. 21, וְיִשַׁע Pr. xx. 22, (3) especially thus, in the expression of a wish, or with אַל *Deprecative*, or with ו Convers. (as in וַיּוֹדַע, וַיּוֹכַח, וַיִּשַׁע & וַיּוֹשַׁע).

(θ) The Rules in Tab. XVI (3) may be referred to, as for several of the above, so also for other forms not mentioned here.

200. The Partic. forms are sufficiently given in Tab. XVIII. The s. *f.* and pl. *m.* & *f.* endings agree with those in § 139 (β). But when the 3ᵈ Rt-letter is Guttural, the s. *f.* form is תַ⟿ instead of תְ⟿ [Cp. Tab. XVI (3)]. Thus, יוֹדַעַת *Kal*, and מוּדָעַת *Höph.*, of ידע; and so נִכַחַת *Niph.* of יכח, (in p. ⟿תַ⟿).

201. The ה of the *Hφ.* Voice sometimes appears, as in יְהוֹשִׁיעַ (1 S. xvii. 47 & Ps. cxvi. 6) 3 s. *m.* Fut. *Hφ.* fr. יֵשַׁע; and so in Ps. lxxxi. 6 בְּיהוֹסָף, where יְהוֹסָף is for יוֹסָף *Joseph* (the same in form as 3 s. *m.* Fut. *Hφ.* fr. יסָף). So in יְהוֹדֻוּךְ (Ps. xlv. 18) 3 pl. *m.* Fut. *Hφ.* fr. ידה [Sect. XXI] with Aff. for *thee* (*m.*). So too in יְהֵילִילוּ (Is. lii. 5) 3 pl. *m.* Fut. *Hφ.* fr. ילל for יֵילִילוּ. [The forms יֵילִיל, etc., were mentioned in § 197 (η)].

202. Class III.—The forms in which the 1st Rt-letter is dropped and implied by Dag. F. in the 2d Rt-letter, as in § 195 (ε), agree with those in the next Section (XVI). Compare § 212.

203. Such forms as הַיְצֵא (G. viii. 17 *Kri*) 2 s. *m.* Imp. *Hφ.* fr. יצא [and so הַיְשֵׁר (Ps. v. 9 *Kri*), w. — for — because of the ר, fr. ישר] agree with Tab. XIV. So וַיִּיחָל (G. viii. 12, 3 s. *m.* Fut. *Nφ.*) is like וַיִּפְקָד, *i.e.* יִפְקָד with the Accent drawn back by ו Convers. And so some others, which need not be given, as they are not *Variations* from the forms of the Verb as given in Sect. XI.

OBSERVATIONS XII–XV.

Obs. XII. The prefix ו (*and*) has sometimes — before a letter bearing an Accented Vowel, especially if the Accent be Disjunctive; thus, וָיַיִן *and wine* G. xiv. 18. The Rule shall be given in the Appendix.

Obs. XIII. The Interrogative ה has sometimes — *followed by Dag.* especially where it could not be mistaken for the 'Def. Art.' . Thus, הַכְמַבַת (Is. xxvi. 7) WHETHER *according-to the stroke of* [מַבַת]?

Obs. XIV. Personal-Pronoun forms are sometimes used with a Verb *Reflexively*, as in לְכוּ לָכֶם *go for yourselves* (i.e. *betake yourselves*), וַתֵּשֶׁב לָהּ *and she sat for herself* (i.e. *and she sat her down*).

Obs. XV. The expression "A son of so-many years" is used for "A person so many years old;" thus, בֶּן שֶׁבַע שָׁנִים *a son-of seven years* (i.e. *seven years old*) [was Jehoash at-his-becoming-king (בְּמָלְכוֹ)] 2 K. xii. 1.

N.B. (i) In NIPH. of פ״י Verbs, the 1st Rt-letter י (which is but rarely retained as in the Fut. form יִיָרֶה p. 288) is mostly replaced by ו which is

    (α) sometimes CONSONANTAL, as in the Infin. and Imper. הִוָּשֵׁב etc., and Fut. יִוָּשֵׁב etc.;

    (β) sometimes QUIESCENT, as in the Past נוֹשַׁב etc., and Partic. נוֹשָׁב etc.

(ii) In HIPH. the ו is

    (α) sometimes itself QUIESCENT, as in הֵיטֵב (Infin. Abs , and Imper. 2 s. *m.*) etc., and

    (β) sometimes replaced by ו QUIESCENT, as in הוֹשֵׁב etc. [Tab. XVIII];

(iii) In HOPH. the י is replaced by ו QUIESCENT, as in הוּשַׁב etc.;

(iv) For the HITHPX-EL see § 193, and Note (‡), on p. 133.

VOCABULARY IV.

1. אָב *a father,* Tab. XIII (1).
2. אָח *a brother,* Tab. XIII (2).
3. יַחְדָּו *together.*
4. לֶחֶם (*m.*) *bread,* Tab. X (1).
5. מֶלֶךְ *a king,* Tab. X (1).
6. עֶבֶד (*m.*) *a servant,* Tab. X (6).
7. עֵשָׂו *Esau.*
8. פֹּה *here.*
9. פֶּן *lest, that not.*
10. פַּרְעֹה *Pharaoh.*
11. רוּחַ (*f.*) *spirit* (Exerc. xxiv. 58).
12. שְׁאוֹל *the pit,* or *grave.*

EXERCISE XXX.

(To be translated into English, § 11. a–e.)

לֶךְ- לְךָ[2] מֵאַרְצְךָ · · · נֵצְאוּ[3] לָלֶכֶת[1] אַרְצָה[4] כְּנַעַן[5] :

נֵרֶד[6] אַבְרָם[7] מִצְרַיְמָה[8] · וּלְאַבְרָם[7] הֵיטִיב[9] · וַיֵּלֶךְ[1] לְמַסָּעָיו[10] :

וּמַלְכִּי־צֶדֶק[11] מֶלֶךְ שָׁלֵם הוֹצִיא[3] לֶחֶם וָיָיִן[12] · יָדֹע[13] תֵּרַע[13] כִּי

גֵּר[14] יִהְיֶה[15] זַרְעֲךָ בְּאֶרֶץ לֹא לָהֶם[16] · הַלְּבֶן[17] מֵאָה[18] שָׁנָה[19]

יִוָּלֵד[20] · וַיֹּאמֶר[21] אַבְרָהָם[22] אֶל נְעָרָיו[23] שְׁבוּ[24] לָכֶם[25] פֹּה עִם

הַחֲמוֹר[26] וַאֲנִי וְהַנַּעַר[23] נֵלְכָה[1] עַד[27] כֹּה[27] : הֲתֵלְכִי[1] עִם הָאִישׁ

הַזֶּה וַתֹּאמֶר[21] [רִבְקָה[28]] אֵלֵךְ[1] : וַתֵּלַכְנָה[1] אַחֲרֵי[29] הָאִישׁ :

וַיֹּאמֶר[21] יַעֲקֹב אֱלֹהֵי אָבִי אַבְרָהָם וֵאלֹהֵי אָבִי יִצְחָק · · · אַתָּה

אָמַרְתָּ הֵיטֵב[30] אֵיטִיב[9] עִמָּךְ[31] : וַיֹּאמֶר[21] [עֵשָׂו] נִסְעָה[32] וְנֵלֵכָה[1]

וְאֵלְכָה[1] לְנֶגְדֶּךָ[33] : הֲיֵלְכוּ[1] שְׁנַיִם[34] יַחְדָּו : אַל תֵּלֶךְ בַּדֶּרֶךְ עִמָּם[31] :

---

[1] יָלַךְ to go. [2] for thee (*m.*) [Obs. XIV, p. 139]. [3] יָצָא to go forth, to go out. [This Verb must be given in Sect. XXI; the form here agrees with Tab. XVIII.] [4] אֶרֶץ § 71 (ii). [5] Canaan.* [6] יָרַד *K.* to go down, go down to, *Hφ.* to bring down, bring down to. [7] Abram.* [8] מִצְרַיִם Egypt.* [9] יָטַב *K.* to be good, *Hφ.* to do good, to deal well, *also* to adorn. [10] for (*or* on) his journeyings. [11] And Melchizedeoh [king of Salem]. [12] יַיִן wine [Obs. XII]. [13] יָדַע *K.* to know, to take notice, *Hφ.* to make known. [14] a sojourner. [15] shall be. [16] theirs, [belonging] to them (*m.*). [17] בֵּן a son [Obs. XIII]. [18] a hundred. [19] a year [§ 106 (ii)]. [20] יָלַד *K.* to bear a child, *Nφ.*

אֶשְׁכְּבָה [35] וְאִישָׁן [36] : הָאִירָה [37] עֵינַי פֶּן אִישַׁן [36] הַמָּוֶת † : וְיוֹסֵף [38] הוֹרַד מִצְרַיְמָה [6] : יְיָ [6] מוֹרִיד [6] שְׁאוֹל וַיָּעַל [39] · · · : לְהוֹשִׁיב [24] עִם נְדִיבִים [40] : וַיִּיקַץ [41] פַּרְעֹה וַיִּישָׁן [36] וַיַּחֲלֹם [42] שֵׁנִית [43] : בְּמֵיטַב [44] הָאָרֶץ הוֹשֵׁב [24] אֶת אָבִיךָ וְאֶת אַחֶיךָ : הַאֵלֵךְ [1] וְקָרָאתִי [45] לָךְ אִשָּׁה [46] מֵינֶקֶת [47] וְתֵינִק [47] לָךְ אֶת הַיָּלֶד [48] : וַתֹּאמֶר [21] בַּת פַּרְעֹה לְכִי [1] : הֵילִיכִי [1] אֶת הַיֶּלֶד [48] הַזֶּה [48] · · · : וַיֵּדַע [13] אֱלֹהִים : וַיֵּשַׁע [49] · · · מִיַּד [50] חָזָק [51] אֶבְיוֹן [52] : וְהָיָה [53] כִּי [54] תֵלֵכוּן ‡ [1] לֹא תֵלְכוּ [1] רֵיקָם [55] : וְנוֹדַעְתִּי [13] בָּם :

נוֹדַע [13] יְיָ [6] : הוֹשִׁיעָה [49] לּוֹ יְמִינוֹ [56] : הוֹדִיעוּ [13] בָעַמִּים [57] עֲלִילֹתָיו [58] : מוֹדַעַת [13] זֹאת : הוֹדִיעַ [13] יְיָ יְשׁוּעָתוֹ [59] : לֹא בְּחֶרֶב [60] וּבַחֲנִית [61] יְהוֹשִׁיעַ [49] יְיָ : וְאֶת דַּכְּאֵי [62] רוּחַ יוֹשִׁיעַ [49] : הוֹשַׁע [49] עַבְדְּךָ אַתָּה אֱלֹהַי : הָאֵר [63] פָּנֶיךָ [64] וְנִוָּשֵׁעָה [49] :

to be born. [21] אָמַר to say * [22] Abraham. * [23] נַעַר a youth, a young-man (Tab X. 5). [24] יָשַׁב to sit, to sit down, *also* to dwell. [25] Obs. XIV. [26] חֲמוֹר an ass. [27] עַד לָה so far, to yonder place. [28] Rebekah. * [29] after. [30] Inf. Hφ. of (9). [31] Tab. III. [32] let us take our journey. [33] before thee (*m*). [34] two. * [35] שָׁכַב to lie down. [36] יָשַׁן to sleep. [37] lighten Thou. [38] יוֹסֵף Joseph. * [39] and He hath brought up. [40] princes. [41] יָקַץ to awake. [42] חָלַם to dream. [43] a second time [44] in the best of. [45] and shall I call? [46] a woman. [47] יָנַק K. to suck, Hφ. to suckle, nurse [a child]. [48] יֶלֶד a child (*m*.). [49] יָשַׁע § Hφ. to save. [50] יָד a hand, i e. יָד. [51] a strong one (*m*.). [52] a needy one. [53] and it shall be. [54] that when. [55] empty. [56] יָמִין a right-hand (*f*.). [57] among the peoples. [58] His doings. [59] יְשׁוּעָה Salvation. [60] חֶרֶב a sword. [61] חֲנִית a spear. [62] crushed ones of. [63] shew Thou the Light of. [64] Thy countenance.

---

* Words marked thus (*) need not be given in the Notes again.

† [In] death; or, as some give, ' [the sleep of] death.'

‡ § 145.　　　　§ Nφ. to be saved.　　** Pt. I, § 12.

Exercise XXXI.

(To be translated into Hebrew, § 11. ζ–μ.)

And the thing [1] was-good*[2] in the eyes [3] of Pharaoh. For-asmuch-as-God-hath-shewed-thee (Hebr. *after*[4] *causing-to-know-of*[5] *God ˙thee m.*) all this,[6] there-is-none[7] [so] prudent[8] and wise [9] as-thou.† And the brethren [10] of Joseph went-down.*[11] By this [6] I-shall-know [12] that true-men [13] ye[are]... .—The lad [14] will-not be-able [15] to leave[16] his father. If your (*m.*) little [17] brother [10] shall not come-down,[11] ye-shall-no-more-see (Hebr. *ye-shall-not add* [18] *to-see* [19]) my face.[20] And-we-said[39]to our father, we-shall not ˙be-able [15] to go-down.[11] If thou (*m.*)-art-not [Tab. XIII (‡, δ)] sending,[21] we-will not go-down.[11] Could-we-certainly-know (Hebr. *whether to-know* [22] *could-we-know*) that he-would-say [Fut.], bring-down [23] your (*m.*) brother?

And-offspring-was-born*[24] to Joseph. And his bow[25] abode*[26] in strength.[27] Come-down-thou (*f.*) [11]˙and sit [26] on [28] dust.[29] Who [is] like the wise [9] [One]? and who knoweth [30] the interpretation [31] of a thing?[1]—And He-hath-brought-down *[23] the might [32] of her confidence.[33] Save,[34] O Lord, Thy people [35].... O-now,[36] Lord, save-Thou,[37] we-pray! [38]

---

[1] דָּבָר ˙*m.* [2] יטב (Class I, § 197). [3] Vocab. II (6). [4] אַחֲרֵי. [5] Inf. *Hiph* of ידע. [6] זֹאת. [7] אֵין. [8] נָבוֹן. [9] חָכָם. [10] Tab. XIII (2). [11] ירד (Class II). [12] ידע § 199. [13] כָּנִים. [14] נַעַר. [15] Fut *Hoph.* of יכל. [16] עזב. [17] קָטֹן. [18] Fut. *Hiph.* of יסף (like that of ישׁב). [19] לִרְאוֹת. [20] Vocab. II (7). [21] שׁלח *Pi.* [22] Inf. Abs. of (12) [followed by the Fut. of (12)]. [23] *Hiph.* of (11). [24] *Niph.* of ילד. [25] קֶשֶׁת (*f.*) decl. like Tab. X (1). [26] ישׁב. [27] אֵיתָן. [28] עַל. [29] עָפָר. [30] Partic. (1) *Kal* of (12). [31] פֵּשֶׁר. [32] עֹז. [33] מִבְטָח. (N.B. Put ־ֲ before the ח when it has ־ָ under it.) [34] *Hiph.* of ישׁע (§ 199, ε). [35] Vocab. I (14). [36] אָנָּא. [37] § 199, ζ. [38] נָא. [39] אמר, § 188 (*a*).

---

* Fut. w. ו Conv. † Hebr. *like thee* (*m.*), Tab. II. ‡ § 198, p. 136. . .

SECTION XVI.

VARIATIONS IN THE CASE OF VERBS פ"נ, *i.e.* WHOSE FIRST ROOT-LETTER IS נ [Tab. XIX].

204. Some forms are like those in Tab. XIV, *viz.* the Inf. Abs., the Past Tense, and Participles *Kal*,—the Infin., Imper., and Fut. *Nφ.*,—and the whole of the *Pĭ.*, *Pŭ.*, & *Hθ.*

205. The chief Variations are the following:

(i) the *disappearance** of the 1st Rt-letter נ (*a*) in the Infinitive Constr. *Kal* [thus, גֶּשֶׁת fr. נגשׁ, the ת being added as in the פ"י Verbs, § 194 (*a*)], and (*β*) in the Imper. *Kal*,—see Tab. XIX;

(ii) the dropping of the נ (when it would have ־ *Quiescent*)† and the placing Dag. F. in the 2d Rt-letter,‡ as in יִגַּשׁ for יִ(נ)גַּשׁ, תִּגַּשׁ for תִּ(נ)גַּשׁ, etc. This is seen [Tab. XIX] to be the case in Fut. *K.*, in the Past & Partic. *Nφ.*, and in the *Hiph.* & *Hŏph.* Voices. Also,

N.B. these Verbs have usually the ־ (or *Hŭph-ăl*) form of the Sixth Voice. Cp. § 121. Thus, הֻגַּשׁ 3 s. *m.* Past *Hoph.* for הֻ(נ)גַּשׁ corresponding to הֻפְקַד, etc.

206. When the 2d Rt-letter is a Guttural,

(*a*) instead of the ת ֶ—ֶ Inf. form,§ as in גֶּשֶׁת, we have ת ֶ—ַ as in לְטַעַת Inf. *K.* of נטע w. ל. [See also Note (*a*) on Tab. XIX.]

(*b*) It scarcely need be said that the Rules of Tab. XVI (3) [cp. § 181] hold for these Verbs also.

---

* Only in the case of some of the Verbs which take ־ to the 2d Rt-letter in the Fut. [Cp. § 207]. See also 'Notes on Tab. XIX'

† Forms in which the נ is *not* dropped agree with Tab. XIV, and therefore do not fall under this head, *viz.* of 'Variations.'

‡ The Dag. F. is sometimes dropped when the 2d Rt-letter has ־; thus, from נסע, יִסְעוּ [instead of יִסְּעוּ for יִנְסְעוּ], and so תִּסְעוּ, etc.

§ So also instead of the ת ֶ ־ in s. *f.* Partic. forms. Cp. Tab. XVI (3) (D).

207. Some Verbs פ"נ have the (–) form of Fut. *K.*; thus יִגַּשׁ, etc., as in § 205 (ii). And, of these, some drop the נ in the Infin. Constr. and Imper. 2 s. *m.* *K.*, as said in § 205 (i). But

208. other Verbs פ"נ have the (–) form of Fut. *K.* These do not take the תֶּת form of Inf. *K.*, and do not drop the נ in the Imper. *K.* [§ 205, i]; thus, fr. נפל (of which the Fut. *K.* is יִפֹּל etc.) we have the Inf. *K.* forms לִנְפֹּל, כִּנְפֹּל, בִּנְפֹּל, and the Imper. נִפְלוּ 2 pl. *m.*; and so נְטֹשׁ 2 s. *m.* Imper. *K.* of נטשׁ (of which the Fut. is יִפֹּשׁ, etc.); etc.

209. Before a Guttural 2ᵈ Rt-letter, the נ is generally not dropped. But

(*a*) it is so dropped, and Compensation (for the Dag.) is made, in the *K.* Fut. תֵּחַת, יֵחַת, and

(*β*) it is so dropped, and Compensation is NOT made, in the *Nφ.* Past נֶחַם, נֶחַמְתִּי, נֶחַמְתֶּם, and Partic. נֶחָם, of נחם; and so in the *Nφ.* Past נֶחֲתוּ of נחת.

210. (*a*) Some Verbs have forms like those in Tab. XIV, besides corresponding forms like those in Tab. XIX; thus, fr. נטר תִּטֹּר, יִטֹּר and also יִנְטֹר.

(*β*) Also some have both the (–) and the (–) form of the Fut. *K.*; thus, fr. נדר both וַתִּדֹּר, תִּדֹּר, יִדֹּר, and also וַיִּדַּר.

211. The 1 s. and 1 pl. Fut. *K.*, w. the ה of § 144, drop the Vowel of the 2ᵈ Rt-letter (except when the word is in Pause). Thus, נִסְעָה* & נִסְעָה† 1 pl. Fut. *K.*; אֶפְּלָה (in Pause אֶפְּלָה:) 1 s., & נִפְּלָה (which would be in Pause נִפְּלָה:) 1 pl.; etc.

---

* In Pause the ס would have –, thus נִסָּעָה:.

† See Pt. I, § 72 (Note *, *e*) for (1) the help given to the pronunciation by dropping the Dag. F., as in § 205, Note ‡, and (ii) the *additional* help sometimes given by a Compound Shva [as in אֶשְּׁקָה, fr. נשק, 1 K. xix. 20].

Similarly, in other Voices, except the *H*φ., in which the *Khĕrik* remains as usual (thus, נְגִידָה ,אַגִּידָה, fr. נגד).

212. As said in § 202, some Verbs whose 1ˢᵗ Rt-letter is ' drop their 1ˢᵗ Rt-letter and take Dag. F. in the 2ᵈ Rt-letter, and so have forms like those of the Verbs פ'נ in Tab. XIX. Thus, from

יצב, *N*φ. Past [נִצַּב], נִצְּבָה, etc.   Partic. נִצָּב, etc. ;

    *H*φ. Inf. (w. ל) לְהַצִּיב, Past הִצִּיב, etc., Fut. יַצִּיב (יַצֵּב ‑יַצֶּב), etc. ;

    *H*ŏ. Partic. מֻצָּב.   So, from

יצג, *H*φ. Inf. הַצֵּג, Past הִצִּיג etc., Fut. יַצִּיג (גֵּ‑), etc.
    *H*ŏ. Fut. יֻצַּג (p. גַ‑:).   So, from

יצע, *H*φ. Fut. יַצִּיעַ, etc.
    *H*ŏ. Fut. יֻצַּע.   So, from

יצת,* *K*. Fut. [יִצַּת], תִּצַּת, etc. ;

    *N*φ. Past יִצַּת, etc., Fut. יִצְּתוּ: Is. xxxiii. 12 (for יִצַּתוּ, the ‑ being resolved into ‑ *followed by Dag.*) ;

    *H*φ. Past הִצַּתִּי, הִצַּת, etc. ; Fut. [יַצִּית], וַיִּצַּת, etc.

213. So ינח† is given by some authorities as a Root which drops its ' and takes Dag. F. in the 2ᵈ Rt-letter in *H*φ. and *H*ŏ.; thus, *H*φ. Inf. לְהַנִּיחַ (w. ל), Past הִנִּיחַ (& הִנַּח) etc., Fut. יַנִּיחַ (& יַנַּח) etc. ; *H*ŏ. מֻנַּח, Partic.—הֻנִּיחָה (Zech. v. 11) 3 s. *f.* Past, is partly *Hŏph.* and partly *Hiph.*

214. Besides the above, there are some occasional forms of Verbs פ'י which are like forms of Verbs פ'נ in Tab. XIX.

---

* As given by some authorities.

† Some, however, discard this Root, and suppose that there are two forms of the *H*φ. & *H*ŏ. of נוח, with different significations.

215. The Verb לקח *to take* drops its ל as the נ is dropped [§ 205, i & ii] in the Verbs פ׳נ.   Also,

N.B. on account of the ח, this Verb has חַ– – in the Inf. *K.* instead of the חַ– – of the form גֶּשֶׁת fr. נגשׁ.   Cp. § 206.

[For this Verb לקח see 'Notes on Tab. XIX,' Column (A).]

216. The Verb נתן *to give*, as seen in 'Notes on Tab. XIX' Column (B), also drops its 3ᵈ Rt-letter *Nun* before ת, and before נ; and Dagesh F. is then placed in the following letter (except in the case of תֵּת* Inf. Constr.).   Thus we have the Infin. תִּתּוֹ *his giving* [instead of תִּנְתּוֹ like גִּשְׁתּוֹ], and תִּתְּךָ *thy (m.) giving*, תִּתֵּךְ *thy (f.) giving*, תִּתִּי *my giving*, etc.; and so in the Past-Tense we have נָתַתָּ [instead of נָתַנְתָּ], נָתַתִּי, נְתַתֶּם, נְתַתֶּן. In all these the 3ᵈ Rt-letter נ is dropped before ת.   So in the 1 pl. Past נָתַנּוּ [instead of נָתַ(נְ)נוּ] it is dropped before the נ of the termination נוּ–.

217. For the Pause-forms of the Verbs פ׳נ, it is sufficient to refer to §§ 165 & 166.

---

* This word has – instead of a *Short-Vowel followed by* Dag. F.

VOCABULARY V.

1. גִּבּוֹר *a mighty one* (*m.*).

2. יְבוּל (*m.*) *produce, increase.*

3. כָּבוֹד (*m.*) *glory*, i.e. כְּבוֹד

4. נָקָם (*m.*) *vengeance.*

5. עַיִן (Vocab. II. 6) is rarely *masc.*

6. שְׁבִי (*m.*) *captivity* (i.e. the same).

EXERCISE XXXII.

(To be translated into English, § 11, a–ζ.)

חֶסֶד[1] וֶאֱמֶת[2] יִצְּרוּ[3] מֶלֶךְ : שְׁמַע[4] בְּנִי וְקַח[5] אֲמָרַי[6] : לָקַחַת[5]

מוּסַר[7] הַשְׂכֵּל[8] : לָתֵת[9] לִפְתָאִים[10] עָרְמָה[11] : אִם תֻּקַּח[5] אֲמָרַי[6]

לַתְּבוּנָה[12] תִּתֵּן[9] קוֹלֶךָ : אָז תֵּלֵךְ[13] לָבֶטַח[14] דַּרְכֶּךָ וְרַגְלְךָ[15]

לֹא תִגּוֹף[16] : תְּנָה[9] בְנִי לִבְּךָ[17] לִי וְעֵינֶיךָ דְּרָכַי תִּצֹּרְנָה[3] :

עֵינֶיךָ לְנֹכַח[18] יַבִּיטוּ[19] : וְדַעַת[20] שְׂפָתֶיךָ[21] יִנְצֹרוּ[3] : לֹא יוֹעִילוּ[22]

אוֹצְרוֹת[23] רֶשַׁע[24] וּצְדָקָה[25] תַּצִּיל[26] מִמָּוֶת[27] : לֶקַח[28] טוֹב[29]

נָתַתִּי[9] לָכֶם : קְחוּ[5] מוּסָרִי[7] : הִנֵּה[30] אַבִּיעָה[31] לָכֶם רוּחִי : הַבִּיטוּ[19]

אֶל אַבְרָהָם אֲבִיכֶם : תְּנוּ[9] לַיְיָ אֱלֹהֵיכֶם כָּבוֹד : יִתֵּן[9] קוֹלוֹ :

וְהָאָרֶץ תִּתֵּן[9] אֶת יְבוּלָהּ : וְאֶל זֶה[32] אַבִּיט[19] אֶל עָנִי[33] וּנְכֵה[34]

---

[1] mercy. [2] אֱמֶת truth. [3] נצר to keep, preserve. [4] שׁמע to hear. [5] לקח to take, to receive; Nφ. & Hŏ. to be taken. [6] אֲמָרִים sayings. [7] מוּסָר instruction. [8] wisdom, intelligence. [9] נתן to give, to set, to give forth or utter [one's voice]. [10] to simple ones. [11] subtlety. [12] תְּבוּנָה understanding. [13] ילך to go. [14] securely. [15] רֶגֶל (*f.*) a foot, Tab. X (i), *Du.* רַגְלַיִם.* [16] נגף to stumble [(so E.V. here); *lit.* to strike, dash, smite]. [17] לֵב (*m.*) a heart, w. aff. לִבּוֹ, etc., pl. לִבּוֹת.* [18] straight forwards. [19] נבט Hφ. to look, to behold. [20] and knowledge. [21] שָׂפָה a lip, *Du.* שְׂפָתַיִם.* [22] יעל Hφ. to profit, to avail. [23] treasures of. [24] wickedness. [25] and righteousness. [26] נצל Hφ. to deliver. [27] from death. [28] doctrine. [29] good * [Adject. *m.*, § 76 (i)]. [30] behold! [31] נבע Hφ. to pour out, to utter. [32] this one, such a one (*m.*). [33] a humble one (*m.*). [34] and one (*m.*) stricken of, (or *contrite*, as E.V.).

* Words marked thus (*) need not be given again in the Notes.

רוּחַ[35] : אֶצֹּק[35] רוּחִי עַל זַרְעֶךָ : וְהִקְרַבְתִּיו[36] וְנִגַּשׁ[37] אֵלַי כִּי מִי

הוּא[38] זֶה[38] עָרַב[39] אֶת לִבּוֹ[17] לָגֶשֶׁת[37] אֵלַי נְאֻם יְיָ : מַגִּיד[61] דְּבָרָיו

לְיַעֲקֹב : וְחֹשֵׁב[40] מַחֲשָׁבוֹת[41] לְבִלְתִּי[42] יִדַּח[42] מִמֶּנּוּ נִדָּח[43] : נָקָם

אֶקָּח[5] : גַּם שְׁבִי גִבּוֹר יֻקָּח[5] : מִי בַעַל[44] מִשְׁפָּטִי[44] יִגַּשׁ[37] אֵלַי :

מִפַּחַד[45] אוֹיֵב תִּצֹּר[8] חַיָּי[46] : וְרוּחַ קָדְשְׁךָ[47] אַל תִּקַּח[5] מִמֶּנִּי :

לֹא יִגַּע[48] בְּךָ רָע[49] : יִפֹּל[50] מִצִּדְּךָ[51] אֶלֶף[52] ⋯ אֵלֶיךָ לֹא

יִגָּשׁ[37] : וְהָיִיתָ[53] מֻצָּק[54] וְלֹא תִירָא[55] :

וָאֶתְּנָה[9] אֶת פָּנַי אֶל אֲדֹנָי[56] הָאֱלֹהִים : וְאֶצְּרָה[3] מִצְוֹת[57]

אֱלֹהָי : חֻקֶּיךָ[58] אֶצֹּרָה[3] : אַתָּה הִצַּבְתָּ[59] כָּל גְּבוּלוֹת[60] אָרֶץ :

הִגִּידוּ[61] הַשָּׁמַיִם צִדְקוֹ[62] : יוֹם[63] לְיוֹם[63] יַבִּיעַ[31] אֹמֶר[64] : גַּע[48]

בֶּהָרִים[65] וְיֶעֱשָׁנוּ[66] : כִּי[67] אֶקַּח[5] מוֹעֵד[68] אֲנִי מֵישָׁרִים[69] אֶשְׁפֹּט[70] :

---

[35] יצק to pour (§ 212). [36] and I will bring him near. [37] נגש *K.* & *Nφ.* to approach. [38] who is this [that]? (cp. § 96, ii. *β*, and § 97). [39] hath engaged, or pledged. [40] חשב to think, devise. [41] devices. [42] in order that not. [43] נדח to banish, expel. [44] *lit.* master of my suit, *i.e.* one in controversy with me. [45] from fear of. [46] חַיִּים (*m.*) life (a Noun of plural form).* [47] Vocab. I (16). [48] נגע to touch, happen (as an evil accident) [with בְּ before the *person* or *thing* affected]. [49] evil (*m.*). [50] נפל to fall. [51] beside thee (*m.*). [52] a thousand, Tab. X (1). [53] and thou shalt be. [54] יצק *Hoph.* to be firm. [55] thou shalt fear. [56] The Lord. [57] [the] commandments [of]. [58] חֻקִּים statutes. [59] יצב *Hφ.* to place, to establish. [60] [the] borders [of]. [61] נגד *Hφ.* to declare. [62] צֶדֶק (*m.*) righteousness*, Tab. X (2). [63] יוֹם (*m.*) a day, pl. יָמִים ' *i.e.* ' יְמֵי*. [64] a saying. [65] הַר (*m.*) a mountain, ' *i.e.* ' הַר, pl. הָרִים ' *i.e.* ' הָרֵי*. [66] עשן to smoke. [67] when. [68] appointed-time. [69] rightly. [70] שפט to judge.

Exercise XXXIII.

(To be translated into Hebrew, § 11. ζ–μ.)

And Jacob vowed *[1] a vow.[2] And Jacob told *[3] to Rachel[4] that[16] the brother of her father he [was]. Tell-thou[5] (*m.*) to me what[6] [shall be] thy reward.[7] Better[8] [§ 82, i.] is my-giving[9] her to thee (*m.*) than my-giving[9] her to another[10] man[11]: abide[12] with-me.[22] And it-was-told *[14] to Laban[15] that[16] Jacob had-fled[17] [§ 152]. And he-took *[18] his brethren with[13] him. Recognize[19] for-thyself[20] (*m.*) what[21] [is thine] with-me,[22] and take[18] [it] to thee.—And he-took *[18] of[23] that-which-came-to-hand (Hebr. *the-coming*[24] *into*[25] *his hand*) a present[26] for Esau his brother. And-he-bowed-himself[27] earthwards[28] seven[29] times[30] until[31] his-approaching[32] unto[31] his brother. And the women-servants[33] approached *[32] . . . . And Leah[34] also approached *[32] . . . . And afterwards[35] there-approached[36] Joseph and Rachel.[4]—And they (*m.*)-journeyed *[37] from Beth-el.[38] And Jacob placed *[39] a pillar[40] over[41] her grave.[42] And Israel journeyed *[37].—And He-conducted *[43], like the sheep,[44] His people.[45] And a new[46] spirit[47] I-will-give[48] within-you.[49] And I-will give †[48] in Zion Salvation[50] for Israel My glory.[51]

That-which thou (*m.*)-shalt-vow,[52] pay-thou.[53]

---

[1] נדר Fut. (ֶ). [See § 210 (β).] [2] נֶדֶר. [3] נגד *Hφ.* [4] רָחֵל. [5] Imper. *Hφ.* of נגד, w. ה. [6] מַה. [7] מַשְׂכֻּרֶת, w. aff. מַשְׂכֻּרְתּוֹ, etc. [8] טוֹב [9] Inf. *K.* of נתן, w. aff. for *my.* [10] אַחֵר [11] אִישׁ. [12] Imper. *K.* of ישׁב, w. ה. [13] Tab. III (3). [14] *Höph.* of (3). [15] לָבָן. [16] כִּי. [17] ברח. [18] לקח. [19] נכר *Hφ.* [20] לָךְ. [21] מָה. [22] עָמָדִי. [23] מִן. [24] הַבָּא. [25] בְּ. [26] מִנְחָה. [27] וַיִּשְׁתַּחוּ. [28] אֶרֶץ § 71 (iii). [29] שֶׁבַע. [30] פְּעָמִים. [31] עַד. [32] נגשׁ. [33] pl. of שִׁפְחָה. [34] לֵאָה. [35] אַחַר. [36] 3 s. *m.* Past *Nφ.* of נגשׁ. [37] נסע. [38] בֵּית אֵל. [39] יצב *Hφ* (§ 212). [40] מַצֵּבָה. [41] עַל. [42] קְבֻרָה. [43] *Hφ* of (37). [44] צֹאן. [45] Vocab. I (14). [46] חָדָשׁ (*m.*). See § 59. [47] רוּחַ (*f.*). [48] נתן. [49] בְּקִרְבְּכֶם. [50] תְּשׁוּעָה. [51] תִּפְאֶרֶת (§ 74, *f.*). [52] נדר Fut. (ֹ). [See also No. 1.]. [53] שׁלם *Pi.*

---

* Fut. w. ֹ Convers.   † Past w. ֹ Convers.

SECTION XVII.

VARIATIONS IN THE CASE OF VERBS עו׳, AND VERBS עי׳
[Tab. XX].

218. There are two great Classes of Verbs whose 2ᵈ Rt-letter
is ו or י, *viz.* those

> (I) in which the ו (or the י) is *Consonantal*,
> (II) in which the ו (or the י) is *Quiescent.*

219. The forms of the First Class agree with those of ordinary
Verbs,* and therefore do not require detailed mention here. But

220. IMPORTANT VARIATIONS take place when the 2ᵈ Rt-letter
is ו (or י†) *Quiescent.*

> (i) The ו is sometimes Quiescent in וּ; as in [see Tab. XX]
>
> > (*a*) *Kal*,—Infin., Partic (2), Imper. and Fut.,
> >
> > (β) *Nφ.*,—Past 2 s. & pl. (*m. & f.*), and 1 s. & pl. But
> >
> > (N.B.) the defective form ֻ may occur for וּ, as in
> > כְּרֻם Ps. xii. 9 for כְּרוּם Inf. *K.* w. בְּ (fr. רום),
> > and so קֻמּוּ for קוּמּוּ 2 pl. *m.* Imper. *K.*, וָאָקֻם for
> > וָאָקוּם 1 s. Fut. *K.* w. וְ Conv., יָקֻמּוּ for יָקוּמּוּ
> > 3 pl. *m.* Fut. *K.*, etc.

---

* Thus, (*a*) when the 2ᵈ Rt-letter is ו *Consonantal*,—we have (1) fr. רוח, רָוַח
3 s. *m.* Past *K.*, יִרְוַח 3 s. *m.* Fut. *K.*, מְרֻוָּחִים pl. *m.* Partic. *Pŭ*; (2) fr. צוח,
יְצֻוְחֻוּ׃ in Pause for יְצְוְחוּ 3 pl. *m.* Fut. *K.*; so (3) fr. חור, יֶחֱוָרוּ׃ 3 pl. *m.* Fut. *K.*
in Pause; (4) fr. נוע, the Inf. *K.* לִגְוֹעַ w. לְ, Past גָּוַע 3 s. *m.*, גָּוְעוּ 3 pl. (in Pause
for נָּוָעוּ), גָּוַעְנוּ 1 pl., also the Partic. גּוֵֹעַ s. *m.*, and Fut. יִגְוַע 3 s. *m.*, etc., (5) fr.
עות, *Pĭ.* Inf לְעַוֵּת w. לְ, Fut. יְעַוֵּת 3 s. *m.*, etc. So, also,

(*b*) when the 2ᵈ Rt-letter is י *Consonantal*,—(6) fr. איב, וָאָיַבְתִּי 1 s. Past *K*;
(7) fr. קים, the *Pĭ* Inf. לְקַיֵּם w. לְ, Past קִיֵּם 3 s. *m*, קִיְמוּ 3 pl., Fut. וָאֲקַיְּמָה׃ Pause-
form of וָאֲקַיְּמָה 1 s. (with ה, and with וְ Convers.), etc.; (8) the *Hθ* forms הִצְטַיָּדְנוּ
1 pl Past of ציד, and וַיִּצְטַיָּרוּ 3 pl. *m.* Fut. (in Pause) of ציר   [For the transposition of the צ and the ת of הת, and for the change of the ת to ט, cp. 'Notes
on Tab. XIV' (*₊*)].

† See §§ 225–228.

(ii) The וֹ is sometimes Quiescent in *Khoulem*; as in

    (α) the Inf. Abs. *K.* קוֹם,

    (β) some other Inf. *K.* forms, as כְּמוֹת, בְּמוֹת, **מוֹת, (and so לְבוֹא, but לָמוֹת), and with Pron. Affs., **מוֹתוֹ his dying*, etc., from מוֹת *to die*,

    (γ) some Fut. *K.* forms, as תֵּשֵׁב יֵשֵׁב, etc., besides the more usual תָּשׁוּב יָשׁוּב, etc.; and

    (δ) throughout the *N*ϕ., except the forms in (i, β).

(iii) The וֹ is sometimes dropped† as in the *K.* Past [קָם 3 s. *m.*, קָמָה 3 s. *f.*, קַמְתָּ 2 s. *m*, etc.], and Partic (1) [קָם s. *m.*, קָמָה s. *f.*, etc.], etc.; see Tab. XX.

(iv) The וֹ is sometimes replaced by יֹ, either

    (α) *written*, as in לְהָקִים Inf. *II*ϕ. with לֹ, and הֵקִים Past 3 s. *m.*, etc., or

    (β) *understood*, as in the Inf. Abs. *H*ϕ. ‡הָקֵם, and the Fut. forms § יָקֵם, תָּקֵם, etc.; and

    (γ) the Long Vowel is sometimes shortened into ◌ֵ as we shall see.

(v) The *Höph-ăl* Voice of these Verbs has the same form as in the Verbs פֵּ״י [see Tab. XVIII]

---

* This, and the like words fr. מוֹת, may however be (as some take them to be) Declension-forms of the Noun מָוֶת *death*, with Pron. Affs. as in Tab. XIII (‡. e). There are also מוֹתִי *my dying*, מוֹתָהּ *her* .., מוֹתֵנוּ (& מֻתֵנוּ) *our* .., and מָתָן *their (f.)* .., like the forms from קוֹם.

† For which a Quiescent-letter is *understood*, generally. But sometimes such a letter *appears*, as the א in קָאם (= קָם 3 s. *m* Past *K.*) Hos. x. 14, etc. So, for יָגֵעַ 3 s *m* Fut. *H*ϕ. of נוּעַ, we find יָנָאַע Eccl. xii. 5 (See, also, p. 295).

‡ Once הָקֵים, Jer. xliv. 25.

§ These ◌ֵ forms are used (rather than the יֹ◌ֵ forms) in the three cases mentioned in § 162 (ε, ii).

(vi) Instead of *Pĭ-ĕl, Pŭ-ăl, Hithpă-ĕl* forms, these Verbs have פּוֹלֵל, פּוֹלַל, הִתְפּוֹלֵל forms, *i.e.* the 2ᵈ Rt-letter is Quiescent (and therefore cannot be doubled by Dag. F.), but the 3ᵈ Rt-letter is *repeated*.   See Tab. XX.

221. The Past Tense forms in the second column of the *Kal* in Tab. XX, מֵת, מֵתָה, מֵתוּ, and the Partic. מֵת, correspond to the פָּעֵל forms of Past-Tense and Partic. *K.* in the 'Full' Verb [see § 138 (A)].   But,

Obs. (i) the ⸗ which, in the 3 s. *f.* and 3 pl. Past of the פָּעֵל form of 'Full' Verbs, appears in the *Pause-forms* only, stands regularly in the forms מֵתָה 3 s. *f.*, מֵתוּ 3 pl. ; also

(ii) the Partic (1) *K.* s. *f.* and pl. *m.* and *f.* are מֵתִים *, מֵתָה, [מֵתוֹת].   But

(iii) the Imper. and Fut. of מוּת are like those of קוּם.

[(iv) The Verb מוּת having ת for its 3ᵈ Rt-letter drops this ת on receiving an additional *syllable beginning with* ת, and this latter receives Dag. F. ; thus, מֵתָּ for מֵ(ת)תָּ, מֵתִּי for מֵ(ת)תִּי, מֵתָּה for מֵ(ת)תָה, מֵתֶּם for מֵ(ת)תֶם, etc.   Cp. § 183 (β)].

222. The Past-Tense forms in the third column of the *Kal* in Tab. XX, *viz.* בֵּשׁ, בֵּשָׁה, etc., and the Partic(1) בֵּשׁ, correspond to the פָּעֵל form of the Past-Tense and Partic. in the 'Full' Verbs [see § 138 (A)].   But,

---

* Thus לֵנִים Neh. xiii. 21, pl *m*, fr. לוּן or לִין.   (The corresponding s. *m.* would be לֵ,—like עֵר Song. v. 2, fr. עוּר.)

Obs. (i) the ־ which in the 3 s. *f.* & 3 pl. Past of the פָּעַל form of 'Full' Verbs appears in *Pause*-forms only, stands regularly in the forms בָּשָׁה 3 s. *f.* and בָּשׁוּ 3 pl.—

(ii) The Partic (1) *K.* s. *f.* and pl. *m.* & *f.* are [בּוֹשָׁה], בּוֹשִׁים, [בּוֹשׁוֹת].

(iii) In the Imper. (the form בָּשׁ corresponds to the form פְּקֹד with ־). The ־ stands regularly in the forms בָּשִׁי 2 s. *f.* and בָּשׁוּ 2 pl. *m.*; but it appears in the corresponding *Pause*-forms, merely, in the case of 'Full' Verbs. So also

(iv) in the Fut. forms תֵּבְשִׁי 2 s. *f.*, יֵבְשׁוּ 3 pl. *m.*, תֵּבְשׁוּ 2 pl. *m.*, and in אֵבְשָׁה 1 s. w. ה;—for

(v) the Fut. forms יֵבְשׁ, תֵּבְשׁ, etc., correspond to the (־) forms יִפְקֹד, תִּפְקֹד, etc., of the 'Full' Verb,—the ־ of the prefix-letters being lengthened into ־ in order to avoid the occurrence of the Short-vowel in an open syllable.

223. Some Verbs have here and there forms such as in § 221 or § 222, as well as others like those fr. קוּם in Tab. XX.

224. Some Verbs have (cp. § 220, ii, γ) Fut. *K.* forms such as יָחֹם (fr. חוּם) Ps. lxxii. 13, תָּחֹם Ez. v. 11, as well as others such as תָּחוּם, יָחוּם.

The forms in Tab. XX, of which the chief features are sketched above, will be sufficient for this Exercise book—with the following additions [§§ 225–248].

225. Some few Verbs have ־י (being ע״י therefore) where the ו occurs in the *Kal* of קוּם [Tab. XX]; thus

  (i) Infin. בֵּין (*Absol.*) of Root בין, שֵׂים (*Constr.*) of Root שׂים(=שׂוּם). So שִׁית, and (w. ל) לָשִׁית, and (w. Aff. ־י *my*) שִׁתִי [=שִׁיתִי, Pt. I, § 12] of Root שִׁית(=שׁוּת), etc.;

  (ii) Imper. שִׂים 2 s. *m.* (and w. ה, שִׂימָה), שִׂימִי 2 s. *f.* (and שְׂמִי Jer. xxxi. 21), שִׂימוּ 2 pl. *m.* (also שְׂמוּ);

  (iii) Fut. יָשִׂים 3 s. *m.* (also יָשֵׂם and יָשֵׂם), *תְּשִׂים, etc.

226. Such Verbs have other forms like those in § 220 (iii); [thus, fr. שִׂים in *Kal*,†

  (i) Past שָׂם 3 s. *m.*, שָׂמָה 3 s. *f.*, שַׂמְתָּ 2 s. *m.*, שַׂמְתְּ 2 s. *f.*, etc.;

  (ii) Partic (1) שָׂם s. *m.*, שָׂמָה s. *f.*, etc. Also

  (iii) there are sometimes ע״ו *as well as* ע״י forms having the same 1st and 3d Rt-letters; thus, שׁוֹם Inf. (Abs.) and לָשׁוֹם, שָׁוֹם, etc., besides שִׂים in § 225 (i); and so יָשׁוֹם Ex. iv. 11, besides the more usual יָשֵׂים, etc., in § 225 (iii). So יְשֻׂשׂוּם Is. xxxv. 1 (3 pl. *m.* Fut. *K.* with Aff. ם— *them m.*, Sect. XXII) from שׁוּשׂ, although the usual Imper. and Fut. forms are from שִׂישׂ]. But

227. there are also a few forms, as רִיבוֹתָ (Job xxxiii. 13) 2 s. *m.* Past, בִּינֹתִי (Dan. ix. 2) 1 s. Past, and הֵיגוּ (in וְדִיגוּם, Jer. xvi. 16, 3 pl. *m.* Past with Aff. ם— *them m.*), which are like *Hiph-il* forms without the ה‡.

---

 * Sometimes ־ occurs as in תָּלֶן Job xvii. 2 (3 s. *f.*, fr. לִין); and, in Pause, אַל תָּלֶן Ju. xix. 20 (2 s. *m.*). But also יָלִין 3 s. *m.*, תָּלִין 3 s. *f.* & 2 s. *m.*, אָלִין 1 s., נָלִין 1 pl.; and וַיָּלֶן, אַל תָּלֶן 2 S. xvii. 16, cp. § 232 (iv).

 † They agree generally with Tab XX in other parts also.

 ‡ The full *Hφ*. forms would be הֲרִיבוֹתָ, הֲבִינֹתִי, and וַהֲדִיגוּם fr. הֵדִיגוּ w. Aff. ם— (Sect. XXII).

[Note. Some have supposed that these forms, and also those in § 225 (i & ii), are really *H*φ. forms without the ה. This may fairly be doubted, especially in regard to the forms in § 225 (i & ii)].

228. The Fut. *K.* forms of שׂים, *viz.* תָּשִׂים יָשִׂים, etc., being exactly the same as the *H*φ. forms תָּקִים יָקִים, etc., the 3 & 2 pl. *f.* would be תְּשִׂמְנָה like תְּקָמְנָה. So we find * תָּגֵלְנָה 3 pl. *f.* Fut. *K.* from גִיל of which the Fut. *K.* forms are תָּגִיל יָגִיל, etc.

[Note. As in § 220 (iv, β), the ִי֖ of these forms is often replaced by ֵ; thus יָשֵׂם for יָשִׂים, etc. Cp. Note (§) on § 220 (iv. β).]

229. Some few Verbs have forms like † יָרֹם 3 s. *m.*, תָּרֹם 3 s. *m.*, from רוּם, as well as the more usual forms תָּרוּם יָרוּם. So יָשֹׁב fr. שׁוּב, as well as the more usual יָשׁוּב, etc. [cp. § 220 (ii, γ)]. And so יָדֹון, Gen. vi. 3, fr. דוּן, but the more usual Fut. is (fr. דִין) תָּדִין יָדִין, etc.

230. Of the 3 & 2 pl. *f.* Fut. *K.* two-forms are given in Tab. XX. The first of these two, *viz.* תְּקָמְנָה, corresponds with the Imper. 2 pl. *f.* קֹמְנָה, as תִּפְקֹדְנָה with פְּקֹדְנָה. And so we have, (1) fr. שׁוּב, תָּשֹׁבְנָה (in וַתָּשֹׁבְנָה 1 S. vii. 14; cp. Ez. xxxv. 9 *Krî*, and תָּשֹׁבְן twice in Ez. xvi. 55). Similarly (2) fr. אוֹר, תָּאֹרְנָה (in וַתָּאֹרְנָה *Krî* for ותראנה *Kthîv*, 1 S.

---

* Like תָּשֹׁבְנָה 3 pl. *f.* Fut. *H*φ. of שׁוּב; and so תָּקָמְנָה in Tab. XX.

† Sometimes such forms are used where there is a positive or negative *Wish*. But it is unsafe to limit the usage to that case. If we might *assume* such forms from Roots which have them not, we might say that the ַ (ǎ) of וַיָּקָם (§ 232) is obtained from the ֵ of יָקֵם [which does not occur] instead of the וּ of יָקוּם. But no advantage is gained by the assumption, and some objections might be raised.

xiv. 27). And (3) fr. בוא, תָּבֹאנָה * (and once תָּבוֹאֶנָה, once תָּבֶאןָ). But

231. several of the 3 pl. *f.* Fut. *K.* forms which *occur* are like תְּקוֹמֶינָה, the second form given in Tab. XX. Thus (1) fr. מוט, תְּמוֹטֶינָה; (2) fr. עוף, תְּעוֹפֶינָה; (3) fr. פוץ, תְּפוּצֶינָה †, and so (4) from שוב, תְּשֻׁבֶינָה once (Ez. xvi. 55); (5) fr. בוא, תָּבֶאנָה occurs once, and תָּבוֹאֶינָה once; but the form in § 230 (3) occurs about a dozen times.

232. The DRAWING BACK OF THE ACCENT by the ו Convers. of the Fut. produces, in the *Kal* and *Hiph.*, some remarkable changes in these Verbs. Thus,

(i) in KAL, יָקוּם has [in accordance with Pt. I, § 55 (9, b)] the Accent on the last syllable. But the ו Convers., as in § 189, draws away the Accent to the Penult. syllable. Consequently the Long-Vowel וּ would then (if left) be unaccented and yet followed by *Shva Quiescent* understood with the ם. To avoid such a breach of the great Rule in Pt. I, § 55 (8), the וּ is shortened into ◌ָ (*δ*) [Pt. I, § 19], and so we have the form ‡ וַיָּקָם. Similarly תָּקוּם gives וַתָּקָם. So, fr. שׁוּב, יָשׁוּב gives וַיָּשָׁב, etc.§ And so

---

* The א being Quiescent, there is no *Shva* beneath it. For the Verb בוא see pp. 272–275.

† Also תְּפוּצֶנָה Zech. i. 17, תְּמוֹתֶנָּה Ez. xiii. 19.

‡ In Pause, the Accent returning to the last syllable then, we have ◌ָ instead of the ◌ָ (*δ*). Thus (for וַיָּעָף) וַיָּעֹף from עוף, and (for וַיָּרָץ) וַיָּרֹץ from רוץ; and so (for וַיָּצָם) וַיָּצֹום, fr. צום, etc. For Pause-forms not in Pause, such as וַיָּמֹת Nu. xxxv. 16, נָחֹמֹג Am. ix. 5, cp. § 164 (β).

§ So שׁוּב נָ 1 pl. Fut. *K.* gives וַנָּשָׁב, which appears in the form וַנָּשׁוּב (with ו 'superfluous') in Neh. iv. 9.—Cp. 2 S. xiii. 8.

(ii) in Hiph. יָקִים gives וַיָּקֶם with ‑ָ in the place of the י—
of יָקִים. Similarly תָּקִים gives וַתָּקֶם. So, fr. שׁוּב,
יָשִׁיב gives וַיָּשֶׁב, and נָשִׁיב 1 pl. gives וַנָּשֶׁב, etc.

[N.B. The Pause-forms of וַיָּקֶם, etc., are וַיָּקֹם:, etc.]

(iii) The Fut. forms in § 225, *viz.* יָשִׂים, etc., are treated like
those in (ii) here. Thus יָשִׂים gives וַיָּשֶׂם, etc.

(iv) Similarly when from any other cause the Accent is
removed from the last syllable of יָקוּם, יָקִים, and
such like, the forms are as above in (ı)–(iii). Thus
† יָרֵב בּוֹ 2 S. xix. 38, יֵשֶׁב־נָא Job xxii. 28, וְיָקָם לָךְ
Ju. vi. 32, ‡ אַל תָּשֵׁב 1 K. ii. 20.

233. In the case‑of the 1 s. Fut., the Accent is not drawn
back by the ו Convers.; and so אָקוּם and אָקִים remain unchanged in וָאָקוּם *Kal* and וָאָקִים *Hφ.*

234. When the 3ᵈ Rt-letter is ח or ע, the 2ᵈ Rt-letter takes
‑ַ instead of ‑ֹ (*ŏ*) in the *Kal*, and also instead of ‑ֵ in the
Hiph. Thus, fr. נוּח *to rest*, the Fut. *K.* יָנוּח 3 s. *m.* gives וַיָּנַח
and he rested, and the Fut. *Hφ.* יָנִיח 3 s. *m.* gives וַיָּנַח *and he
caused to rest* (or *and he gave rest*) ; so that, the two forms being
exactly the same, the context alone can enable us to know
whether וַיָּנַח in any place is *Kal* or *Hiph.*§

---

* If we might say that קִים would have the י‑ replaced by ‑ַ on receiving the ו
Convers., and in the other two cases mentioned in § 162 (*e*, iı), then it would be the ‑ָ
of יְקָם which is shortened into ‑ַ in וַיָּקֶם. [But, as in § 189 (i), the י‑ itself
remains in וָאָקִים, and so in וָאָשִׂים, etc. We have, however, וָאָעֵד as well as
וָאָעִיד, etc]

† So too the Imper. *Hφ* הָרֵם 2 s. *m.* becomes הָרֶם when the Accent is removed
from the last syllable. See 2 K. vı. 7.

‡ The Accent is not always drawn back so after אַל, we find also אַל תָּשֵׁב.
Also fr. רִיב, we find אַל תָּרִיב (*Krı*) Pr. iii. 30 [תרוב *Kthıv.*].

§ An Accented ‑ַ also appears sometimes, as in Tab. XVI (3) (B, β) ; thus יָרַח
for יָרֵח, etc. So יָנַע (for יָנִיע) in אַל יָנַע 2 K xxiii. 18.

Similarly וַיָּנַע fr. נוע may be (so far as form is concerned) either Fut. *K.*, fr. יָנוּעַ, or Fut. *Hφ.*, fr. יָנִיעַ; and the context alone can decide which of the two it is. So, also,

235. when the 3ᵈ Rt-letter is ר, sometimes —ָ— is chosen instead of —ֹ— (ŏ) in the *Kal*, and instead of —ִ— in the *Hiph.* Thus, fr. סוּר *to turn aside* (Intrans.) the Fut. *K.* יָסוּר 3 s. *m.* gives וַיָּסַר *and he turned aside* [to see, etc.] Ju. xiv. 8, and the Fut. *Hφ.* יָסִיר 3 s. *m.* gives וַיָּסַר *and he turned aside* [i.e. *removed* the ashes from his face] 1 K. xx.-41.

So too when the Accent is removed from any other cause, as in יָצַר־ 1 K. viii. 37, אַל תָּצַר D. ii. 9,—but these may, perhaps, not be from צוּר.

236. (*a*) The Fut. 1 s. and 1 pl., with ה, are unchanged. Thus נָקוּמָה 1 s., אָקוּמָה 1 pl., of the *Kal*; and so the *Hiph.* אָבִינָה 1 s. (of כון), נָרִיעָה 1 pl. (of רוע), etc.* And so,

(*β*) the *Hφ.* Imper. 2 s. *m.* with ה; thus (הָרֵם) הָרִימָה from רום, etc.

(*γ*) The *K.* Imper. 2 s. *m.* with ה has not only the Accent Penultimate as in קוּמָה from קום; but also sometimes the Accent is on the *last* syllable as in קוּמָה, which is exactly the same in appearance as the s. *f.* Partic (2) *K.* [The context alone enables us to distinguish, then, between the two words.]

---

* For יָתִישָׁה, 3 s. *m.* with ה, see § 144 (*γ*).

237. The corresponding variation in regard to the position of the Accent is found also in the 2 s. *f.* Imper. *K.* (*קוּמִי), and sometimes in the 3 s. *f.* Past *K.* (קָמָה†); and more often in the 3 pl. Past *K.* (קָמוּ).

[Further remarks on the forms in § 236 (γ) and § 237 will be given in the Appendix.]

NOTES.

238. (i) In the Past *K.* of the Verb בוא, the בּ takes ◌ָ in the place of ◌ַ as in בָּאתָ (& בָּאתָה) 2 s. *m.*, בָּאתִי 1 s., etc. This is because the א (being Quiescent in these forms) has not *Quiescent Shva*, as the מ has in קָמְתָ, קָמְתִי, etc.; and therefore, the syllable being now an '*open*' one, the Short Vowel ◌ַ is lengthened into ◌ָ. Many other instances of this will be found to occur. Comp. Obs. XXIII., p. 185 [For the Verb בוא see pp. 272–275.]

(ii) We find ◌ָ (instead of ◌ַ) in וּפְשַׁתֶּם 2 pl. *m.* Past *K.* from פּוּשׁ with וְ pref. This, as also the ◌ָ in יְרִשְׁתֶּם 2 pl. *m.* Past *K.* of יָרֵשׁ and the ◌ָ in שְׁאֶלְתֶּם 2 pl. *m.* Past of שָׁאַל,‡ are supposed by some to be obtained from the ◌ָ of the פָּעֵל form of Past Tense *K.* This is possible; and thus the ◌ָ would be in analogy with the ◌ָ (*ŏ*) of the 2 pl. *m.* & *f.* of the פָּעַל form of Past Tense. But the statement of § 138 (A) (ii) should

---

* קוּמִי (with the Accent on the last syllable) might be, instead, the Infin. *Kal* with Pron. Aff. *my.* The context alone can decide between the two, when the Imper. 2 s. *f.* is so accented.

† קָמָה (with the Accent on the last syllable) might be, instead, the Partic (1) *K.* s. *f.*, and the context alone can decide between the two, when the 3 s. *f.* Past is so accented.

‡ The ◌ָ occurs also, sometimes, instead of the usual ◌ַ, in some forms with Pronom. Affs.,—as will be seen in Sect. XXII.

be borne in mind by the Student.　This matter must be dealt with by and by.

(iii) The position of the Accent on the last syllable of some Past-Tense forms,—instead of the last but one as in Tab. XX,—must be dealt with hereafter, as said above.　But, moreover,

N.B. the Accent is on the last syllable sometimes, not always, in accordance with § 160.

(iv) It need scarcely be said that לָ֫נוּ (in וַלָּ֫נוּ Ju. xix. 13) is 1 pl. Past K. for לַ(נ)נוּ fr. לִין.　Cp. § 183 (a).

(v) The form וַלָּ֫נָה Zech. v. 4 is 3 s. f. Past K. fr. לִין, with ָ in the place of ָ .

239. In accordance with the great General Rule of § 59, the ָ of יְמוּתוּ disappears when the Accent is on the last syllable (by reason of the ן of § 145) as in יְמוּתוּן 3 pl. m. K. with ן (or יְמֻתוּן, Pt. I § 14).　So תְּמוּתוּן (or תְּמֻתוּן) 2 pl. m.　So also in the *Hiph.*; thus יְקִימוּן 3 pl. m. Fut. Hφ. (with ן) Job iv. 4.

240. In Niph., (a) when the 1st Rt-letter cannot receive Dagesh, we find Compensation made in the Infin. לֵאוֹר (for לְהֵאוֹר) Job xxxiii. 30 fr. אוֹר, and so in the Fut. יֵעוֹר Jer. vi. 22, etc., fr. עוּר.*

(β) Instead of the וּ of נְקוּמֹתֶם 2 pl. m. Past, we have ָ in נְפֹצֽוֹתֶם Ez. xi. 17, נְקֹטֹתֶם Ez. xx. 43.

(γ) Instead of the וֹ in the Partic. Nφ. we have, also, *Shûrik*; thus נְבֻכִים pl. m. Ex. xiv. 3 (Pt. I, § 14).

---

* This form is adopted, in the word נֵעוֹר, Zech. ii. 17, for the *Past Niph.* 3 s. m. Once, also, we find נָמָֽר׃ 3 s. m. Past Nφ., in Pause, for נָמַר (as if fr. מרר, Sect. XVIII).

241. Instead of הֵ in the HIPH. Past we find (*a*) sometimes הֶ as in הֲבִישׁוֹתָ Ps. xliv. 8, הֱקִיצֹתִי Ps. cxxxix. 18; also (*β*) ־ֲ before a Guttural, as in הַעֲדֹתִי Jer. xi. 7.

242. Besides the long forms of the 2 s. & pl. and 1 s. & pl. of the Past *Hφ.* in Tab. XX, there are also a few forms which are more like to הֻפְקַדְתְּ, הֻפְקַדְתִּי, etc., in Tab. XIV.   Thus הֻנַּפְתָּ 2 s. *m.* fr. נוּף Ex. xx. 25, etc.; הֻטַּלְתִּי 1 s. fr. טוּל Jer. xvi. 13. Similarly, from מוּת, הֻמַתָּה 2 s. *m.* with ה, הֻמַתִּי 1 s., *הֻמַתֶּם 2 pl. *m.*, *הֻמַתֶּן 2 pl. *f.*; and, from כוּן, הֻכַנּוּ 1 pl. (2 Chr. xxix. 19) [cp. § 183].

243. 'BORROWED' FORMS.—Some words, belonging to Roots ע"ו in sense, agree in form with those of Tab. XX (פ"נ).   Thus, (1) in the *Hφ.* PAST, הֲסִיתוּךָ 3 pl. with Aff. ךָ † *thee* (*m.*) [instead of הֲסִיתוּךְ (or הֲ), fr. סוּת] Jer. xxxviii. 22; and so (2) in the *Hφ.* PARTIC. מֵסִית s. *m.*, and ‡מַלִּינִם or ‡מַלִּינִים ‡ pl. *m.* [instead of מַלִּינִים fr. לוּן]; (3) in the *Hφ.* FUT. יַלִּינוּ 3 pl. *m.*, ‡תַּלִּינוּ 2 pl. *m.*, [instead of יָלִינוּ, תָּלִינוּ]; (4) the *Hoph.* Past הֻקַם 3 s. *m.* [2 S. xxiii. 1, instead of הוּקַם fr. קוּם]; etc.

244. As other instances of 'Borrowed' forms we may mention here (1) הוֹבִישׁ 3 s. *m.* Past *Hφ.*, הוֹבִישָׁה 3 s. *f.*, הוֹבַשְׁתָּ 2 s. *m.*, הוֹבִישׁוּ 3 pl.,—when used in the sense of 'being ashamed' which belongs to the Root בּוֹשׁ, but the *forms* belong to the Root יָבֵשׁ *to be dry* (Hos. xiii. 15).—So, on the other hand, יָבוֹשׁ in the sense "*he* or *it will be dry.*" This sense belongs to the Root יָבֵשׁ, but the form יָבוֹשׁ belongs to the Root בּוֹשׁ.

.* Observe the ־ֲ here, instead of ־ָ. Further remarks on these, and some other forms, will be given hereafter.

† See Tab. XXV.

‡ In the sense *murmuring.*

Many other instances of 'borrowed' forms will be found to occur. Under this head may be classed the forms referred to in §§ 212, 214. Also the usual *Hoph-al* forms of the Verb עִי are 'borrowed' from the פִּי [cp. § 220 (v)].

So, too, we find forms 'borrowed' from the Verbs dealt with in the next Section (XVIII); as בַּז (for בָּזָה *he despised*) Zech. iv. 10, and so טָח Is. xliv. 18 in the sense of מָח Lev. xiv. 42.

245. The main Rules for Pause-forms [§ 165] hold in the Verbs עִי. And, as in § 166 (c), we have the $-$ in such *IIθ.* Pause-forms as הִתְבּוֹנָן׃ 3 s. *m.* Past, הִתְבּוֹנָנוּ׃ 3 plu. Past, etc., הִתְרוֹעָעִי׃ 2 s. *f.* Imper., יִתְעֹרֵר׃ 3 s. *m.* Fut., etc.

246. The rare form הִתְשׁוֹטַטְנָה, Jer. xlix. 3, may be mentioned here. It is the 2 pl. *f.* Imper. *IIθ.* from שׁוּט, the שׁ being NOT transposed with the ת of הִת—probably to avoid having the תוֹ immediately before the טַטְנָה, as would be the case if the form הִשְׁתּוֹטַטְנָה were adopted.

[Obs. The $-$ of the טַ here is in accordance with the (קַ) form in Tab. XIV (vii)].

247. The following Participle-forms with Pron. Affs. will be recognized at once from Tab. XX; *viz.* קָמַי Partic (1) *K.* those *rising up against me* (lit. *my risers up*). So מְרוֹמְמִי Partic. *Pi.* one *raising me on high* (lit. *my raiser on high*), מִתְקוֹמְמִי one *raising himself up against me* (lit. *my opponent*), etc. And so מֵתֶיךָ *thy* (m.) *dead ones*, from מֵתִים plu. of מֵת, etc. But

248. as these Verbs differ so much from the 'Full' Verbs, it may be well to give here the following

163

TABLE OF PARTICIPLE-FORMS.

Plu. f.	i.c.	Plu. m.	i.c.	Sing. f.	i.c.	Sing. m.	
קָמוֹת	יֵ	קָמִים	תֵ	קָמָה	ַ	קָם *(a) (1)	(ɪ) Kal.
מֵתוֹת	יֵ	מֵתִים	תֵ	מֵתָה		מֵת (β)	
בּוֹשׁוֹת	יֵ	בּוֹשִׁים	תֵ	בּוֹשָׁה		בּוֹשׁ (γ)	
קוּמוֹת	יֵ	קוּמִים	תֵ	קוּמָה		†קוּם (2)	
נְקוֹמוֹת	יֵ	נְקוֹמִים	תֵ	נְקוֹמָה		‡ נָקוֹם נָקוּם (ɪɪ) Niph.	
מְקוֹמְמוֹת	יֵ	מְקוֹמְמִים	תֵ	מְקוֹמְמָה / מְקוֹמֶמֶת		מְקוֹמֵם (ɪɪɪ) Pi.	
מְקוֹמָמוֹת	מֵי	מְקוֹמָמִים	מֵת	מְקוֹמָמָה / מְקוֹמֶמֶת	ם	מְקוֹמָם (ɪv) Pu.	
מְקִימוֹת	יֵ	מְקִימִים	תֵ	מְקִימָה		מֵקִים § (v) Hiph.	
מוּקָמוֹת	מֵי	מוּקָמִים	מֵת	מוּקָמָה	ם	מוּקָם (vɪ) Hoph.	
מְתְקוֹמְמוֹ(ת)	יֵ	מְתְקוֹמְמִים	תֵ	מִתְקוֹמְמָה / מָה, מֶמֶת		מִתְקוֹמֵם ‖ (vɪɪ) Hithp.	

---

* (a) As in Note (†) on § 220, iii, so also an א stands in שָׁאטִים pl. *m.*, and שָׁאטוֹת pl. *f.*, (which are like קָמִים and קָמוֹת in ɪ (1, a), above); and so in רָאמוֹת Pr. xxiv. 7.

(b) The Noun גֵּירִים (2 Chron. ii. 16), is of the form מֵתִים in ɪ (1, β); but with י standing after the ֵ. (We find יֵ in קִימָנוּ Job xxii. 20, *our adversary* according to some.)

(c) Instead of קָמִים pl. *m.*, we find once קוֹמִים (2 K. xvi. 7) like בּוֹשִׁים in ɪ (1, γ).

(d) As Partic (1) forms with וּ (or ֵ) some have taken סוּרָה (Is. xlix. 21), and others such, as שׁוּבִי Mi. ii. 8, חֲשִׁים Nu. xxxii. 17. But these seem to belong rather to ɪ (2).

† With ֵ for וּ (Pt. I, § 14) we find מֵלִים Josh. v. 5.—The word זוֹרָה Is. lix. 5, for זוּרָה s. *f.*, has ֹ for ֻ; cp. § 238 (v)

‡ (a) נָפוֹצֶת occurs as s. *f.* in 2 S. xviii. 8 (נפצות *Kthiv.*),

(b) For נְבָבִים see § 240 (γ).

§ For מָסִית see § 243 (a).

VOCABULARY VI.

1. אֲדֹנָי The Lord, O Lord.
2. אַף (m.) anger, w. Aff. אַפּוֹ his . . . etc.
3. אֶרֶץ (f.) earth, a land, country. In Pause אָרֶץ. See also Exerc. XIII. 5. [See Tab. X (1) for the Sing., and Tab. XII (1) for the Plu.]
4. יָמִין (f.) a right hand [§ 56 and § 59].
5. כֹּחַ (m.) strength [§ 74 (α)].
6. נָא now, I pray, we pray
7. תְּפִלָּה (f.) prayer.

EXERCISE XXXIV.

(To be translated into English, §§ 11. a–e.)

קוּמָה¹ יְיָ וְיָפֻצוּ² אֹיְבֶיךָ³ : נָכוֹן⁴ כִּסְאֲךָ⁵ מֵאָז⁶ :יָדָם⁷ וְנִשָּׂא⁸ שֹׁכֵן⁹

עַד¹⁰ : מַשְׁפִּיל¹¹ אַף¹² מְרוֹמֵם⁷ : מְרוֹמְמִי⁷ מִשַּׁעֲרֵי¹³ מָוֶת¹⁴ : כְּבוֹדִי¹⁵

וּמֵרִים⁷ רֹאשִׁי¹⁶ : וְחֶרְפַּת¹⁷ עַמּוֹ יָסִיר¹⁸ · · · : כּוֹנֵן⁴ לַמִּשְׁפָּט¹⁹ כִּסְאוֹ⁵ :

וְהוּא יָבוּס²⁰ צָרֵינוּ²¹ : יָשׁוּבוּ²² רְשָׁעִים : יֵבֹשׁוּ²³ וְיִסֹּגוּ²⁴ אָחוֹר²⁵ :

אַל יָרוּמוּ⁷ לָמוֹ²⁶ : תָּרֹם⁷ יָדְךָ²⁷ עַל צָרֶיךָ²¹ : וְיָרוּם⁷ אֱלֹהֵי יִשְׁעִי²⁸ :

שִׁיתָה²⁹ יְיָ מוֹרָה³⁰ לָהֶם : תָּרוּם⁷ יְמִינֶךָ : אַתָּה תָקוּם¹ תְּרַחֵם³¹

¹ קוּם K. to arise, rise; Hθ. Partic. one raising himself up against another,—— an opponent. ² פוּץ K. to be scattered, Hφ. to scatter. ³ Exerc. XX (52). ⁴ כּוּן Pĭ. to establish, *also* to prepare; Nφ. & Pŭ. to be established. ⁵ כִּסֵּא a throne (w. Aff. כִּסְאוֹ, etc.). ⁶ from of old. ⁷ רוּם K. to be high, exalted; Pĭ. to exalt, extol; Hφ. to make to be high (*and so* to exalt, raise on high), Hŏph. to be taken away. ⁸ נשׂא (Nφ. Partic.) lofty. ⁹ שֹׁכֵן to inhabit. ¹⁰ eternity. ¹¹ שָׁפֵל Hφ. to make low. ¹² also. ¹³ שַׁעַר a gate (Tab. X, 5). ¹⁴ death. ¹⁵ my Glory. ¹⁶ רֹאשׁ a head (w. Aff. רֹאשׁוֹ, etc Plu. רָאשִׁים).* ¹⁷ and the reproach of. ¹⁸ סוּר K. to turn aside, depart; Hφ. to cause to turn aside, to remove. ¹⁹ for the judgment. ²⁰ בּוּס to tread down. ²¹ צָר a foe, pl. צָרִים. ²² שׁוּב to go back, turn back, turn away, return, repent. ²³ בּוּשׁ to be ashamed. ²⁴ סוּג Nφ. to be turned, turned back. ²⁵ backwards. ²⁶ for them (m.) [Obs. XIV, p. 139]. ²⁷ Exerc. XXIV (55). ²⁸ יֶשַׁע salvation. ²⁹ שִׁית to put, place, appoint. ³⁰ fear. [To " put fear to one" = to " put one in fear"]. ³¹ רחם Pĭ. to compassionate, have mercy on.

---

* Words marked thus (*) need not be given again in the Notes.

צִיּוֹן ... כִּי בָא[32] מוֹעֵד[33] : נָסֹגוּ[21] אָחוֹר[25] : רָמָה[7] קַרְנִי[34] בַּיָי :

יָי יָדִין[35] אַפְסֵי[36] אָרֶץ : וְיָרֵם[7] קֶרֶן[34] מְשִׁיחוֹ[37] : מִמִּתְקוֹמְמַי[1]

תְּשַׂגְּבֵנִי[38] : נָמוּ[39] שְׁנָתָם[40] : וַיָּרֶם[7] קֶרֶן[34] לְעַמּוֹ :

תְּמוֹתֵת[41] רָשָׁע רָעָה[42] : שָׂבְעוּ[43] וַיָּרֵם[7] לִבָּם : אָרוּר[44] הַגֶּבֶר[45]

אֲשֶׁר יִבְטַח[46] בָּאָדָם[47] : וְשָׂם[48] בָּשָׂר[49] זְרֹעוֹ[50] וּמִן יָי יָסוּר[18] לִבּוֹ :

וְעַמִּי הֵמִיר[51] כְּבוֹדוֹ בְּלֹא[52] יוֹעִיל[53] : וְלֹא שָׁב[22] מֵרִשְׁעוֹ[54] :

וַיָּסַר[55] כֹּחוֹ מֵעָלָיו[56] : נָעוּ[57] עִוְרִים[58] : וַיֹּאמֶר יָי גַּם אֶת יְהוּדָה[59]

אָסִיר[18] מֵעַל[60] פָּנַי[61] כַּאֲשֶׁר[62] הֲסִרֹתִי[18] אֶת יִשְׂרָאֵל : וְהִטַּלְתִּי[63]

אֶתְכֶם ... עַל הָאָרֶץ אֲשֶׁר לֹא יְדַעְתֶּם[64] : הָעֵד[65] הַעִדֹתִי[65]

בַּאֲבוֹתֵיכֶם ... סָרוּ[18] וַיֵּלְכוּ[66] : וַיָּפִיץ[2] אֹתָם[67] בַּגּוֹיִם[68] : הוּרָם[7]

הַתָּמִיד[69] : צָקוּן[70] לַחַשׁ[71] : הָרִינוּ[72] חַלְנוּ[73] : כְּבוֹדִי מֵעָלַי[60]

הִפְשִׁיט[74] וַיָּסַר[18] עֲטֶרֶת[75] רֹאשִׁי[16] : כֹּהֲנַי[76] וּזְקֵנַי[77] בָּעִיר[78] גָּוָעוּ[79] :

צָפוּ[80] מַיִם עַל רֹאשִׁי[16] : שַׁתָּה[29] עֲוֹנֹתֵינוּ[81] לְנֶגְדֶּךָ[82] : בֹּשְׁנוּ[23] מְאֹד[83] :

---

[32] hath come. [33] an appointed time. [34] קֶרֶן a horn (Tab. X, 1). [35] דין to judge.
[36] the ends of. [37] His Anointed. [38] Thou wilt defend me. [39] נום to slumber, sleep.
[40] their sleep. [41] מות K. to die,* Pĭ. to kill, Hφ. to cause to die, (and so to kill). [42] evil.
[43] שבע to be satisfied, satiated, to be full. [44] ארר to curse. [45] גֶּבֶר a man (properly,
a mighty man). [46] בטח to trust. [47] in man. [48] שׂים to put, make. [49] flesh. [50] his
arm. [51] מור Hφ. to change. [52] for [that which] not. [53] יעל Hφ. to profit, be of use.
[54] רֶשַׁע wickedness* (Tab. X, 4). [55] K. of No. 18. [56] from him. [57] נוע to wander.
[58] blind (pl. m.). [59] Judah.* [60] מֵעַל from (lit. from upon). [61] My Face, Presence.
[62] as. [63] טול Hiph. to fling, cast; Hŏph. to be cast, cast away. [64] ידע to know.*
[65] עוד Hφ. to testify (followed by ב against). [66] ילך to go, go away. [67] Tab. III.
[68] among the heathen. [69] the continual [sacrifice]. [70] צוק to pour out [§ 138 (B),
iv, β]. [71] a prayer (E.V.). [72] we have conceived. [73] חול (or חיל) to be in pain.
[74] פשט Hφ. to strip. [75] the crown of. [76] כֹּהֵן a priest.* [77] זָקֵן an elder.* [78] עִיר a city.
[79] גוע to expire. [80] צוף to flow. [81] our iniquities. [82] before Thee. [83] exceedingly.

---

* Words marked thus (*) need not be given again in the Notes.

מוֹת [41] נָמוֹת [41] : אָכֵן [84] כְּאָדָם [85] תְּמוּתוּן [41] : סַרְתֶּם [18] מִן הַדֶּרֶךְ :

וּמֵתוּ [41] גְּדֹלִים [66] וּקְטַנִּים [87] : הִתְבּוֹנֲנוּ [88] וְקִרְאוּ [89] לַמְקוֹנְנוֹת [90] :

תָּבֹאנָה [91] לָךְ שְׁתֵּי־אֵלֶּה [92] : תָּכֹן [4] תְּפִלָּתִי : אֲדֹנָי יֵשֵׁב־נָא

אַפְּךָ : עַד [93] יְכוֹנֵן [4] וְעַד [93] יָשִׂים [48] :

לְכוּ† [66] וְנָשׁוּבָה [22] אֶל יְיָ : שׁוּבוּ [22] אֵלַי וְאָשׁוּבָה [22] אֲלֵיכֶם : לֹא

אַחְפֹּץ [94] בְּמוֹת [41] הַמֵּת [41] : הֶהָרִים [95] יָמוּשׁוּ [96] וְהַגְּבָעוֹת [97] תְּמוּטֶינָה [98] :

הִתְעוֹרְרִי [99] הִתְעוֹרְרִי [99] קוּמִי [1] יְרוּשָׁלַם [100] : אַל תִּירָאִי [101] כִּי לֹא

תֵבוֹשִׁי [23] : יְיָ מֵמִית [41] וּמְחַיֶּה [102] : לֹא הַמֵּתִים [41] יְהַלְלוּ [103] יָהּ [119] :

קַמְתִּי [1] אֲנִי לִפְתֹּחַ [104] לְדוֹדִי [105] : שׂוֹשׂ [106] אָשִׂישׂ [106] בַּיְיָ : אָגִילָה [107]

בֵּאלֹהֵי יִשְׁעִי [28] : מִי מִצְעָדֵי [108] גֶּבֶר [45] כּוֹנָנוּ [4] : לֹא יוּטָל [63] :

בַּנְתָּה [88] לְרֵעִי [109] מֵרָחוֹק [110] : רַבַּת [111] אֲדֹנָי רִיבִי [112] נַפְשִׁי : הָרִיעוּ [113]

לַיְיָ כָּל הָאָרֶץ : רוֹמְמוּ [7] יְיָ אֱלֹהֵינוּ : וּנְרוֹמְמָה [7] שְׁמוֹ יַחְדָּו [114] :

אֵל [115] יְיָ וַיָּאֶר [116] לָנוּ : וְקַדְמֹנִיּוֹת [117] אַל תִּתְבֹּנֲנוּ [85] : עַתָּה [118] אָקוּם [1]

יֹאמַר יְיָ :

[84] verily, but. [85] as Adam, *or* man. [86] great. [87] and small. [88] בין *K.* & *Hφ.* to understand, *Hθ.* to consider. [89] קרא to call *. [90] קון *Pi* to mourn. [91] בוא to come [see § 230 (s)]. [92] these two [things] (*f*) [93] עד until [that]. [94] חפץ to take delight. [85] the mountains. [96] מוש to depart (E.V). [97] and the hills. [98] מוט *K.* to be moved. [99] עור *Hθ* to rouse oneself. [100] Jerusalem * [101] ירא to fear. [102] and maketh-alive (E.V.). [103] Exerc. XX (46). [104] פתח to open. [105] for my Love. [106] שׂושׂ or שׂיש to rejoice. [107] גיל to be glad. [108] the steps of. [109] my thought. [110] afar off. [111] ריב to contend, plead. [112] ריב a contention, cause. [113] רוע *Hφ.* to shout, make a joyful cry. [114] together. [115] God. [116] אור *Hφ.* to give light. [117] and former things. [118] now [119] IAH.

---

* Words marked thus (*) need not be given again in the Notes.
† Go to! come!—

Exercise XXXV.

(To be translated into Hebrew, § 11, ζ-μ.)

⁎⁎⁎ All Verbs עֹ״ו here are to be Conjugated as in Tab. XX; and Verbs עֹ״י as in §§ 225–228.

God[1] will-arise,⁎[2] His enemies[3] will-be-scattered.⁎[4] When-God-shall-arise-for-the-judgment (Hebr. on[5] arising-of[2] for[6] the judgment[7] God[1]). Earth[8] shall-greatly-reel⁎[9] like the drunkard,[10] and shall-shake†[11] like the night-lodge.[12] Spare-Thou,‡[13] O-Lord, Thy (Hebr. over[14] Thy) people.[15] Raise-high‡[16] Thy (*m.*) foot-steppings.[17] They-have-made[18] their (*m.*) banners[19] tokens.[19]

I-made-to-turn-away[20] from a burden[21] his shoulder.[22] And Mine eye[23] spared⁎[18] them (Hebr. over[14] them (*m.*)). And I-will-make†[18] all My mountains[24] the-way (Hebr. for[6] the way[25]), and My high-ways[26] shall-be-exalted (*m.*).[16]§

My steps[17] make-Thou (*m.*)-firm.[27] I-have-placed[28] in The-Lord my trust.[29] My heart[30] was-glad,⁎[31] and my glory[32] rejoiced.⁎[33] After-Thee[34] we - will - run.‡[35]—Awake (*f.*),[36] awake,[36] put-on[37] strength,[38] O-arm[39] of The-Lord ! . . . Art-

---

[1] אֱלֹהִים. [2] קוּם [3] Exerc. XX (52). [4] פּוּץ *K.* to be scattered. [5] בְ (prefixed to the Infin. *K.*). [6] לְ (the prefix). [7] מִשְׁפָּט. [8] אֶרֶץ (*f.*) [9] מוּע [the "greatly" to be expressed by the Infin. Absol. before the Tense, § 137 (1, d, β)]. [10] שִׁכּוּר. [11] נוּד *Hθ.* [12] מְלוּנָה (used here for a "lodgement" slung up to a tree, or trees). [13] חוּס. [14] עַל. [15] עַם (עַמּוֹ *his* . . . , etc.). [16] רוּם *K.* to be high (*or* exalted), *Hφ* to make (*or* raise) high. [17] פַּעַם Tab X (5). [18] שׂוּם or שִׂים. [19] אוֹת, pl. אֹתוֹת. [20] סוּר *Hφ.* [21] סֵבֶל. [22] שֶׁכֶם Tab X (2) [23] עַיִן Tab. XIII (3) [24] הַר Exerc. XXXII (65). [25] דֶּרֶךְ. [26] pl of מְסִלָּה. [27] כּוּן *Hφ.* [28] שִׁית. [29] מַחְסֶה. [30] לֵב Exerc XXXII (17). [31] שָׂמַח. [32] Vocab. V (5). [33] גִּיל. [34] אַחֲרֶיךָ. [35] רוּץ. [36] עוּר. [37] לָבַשׁ. [38] עֹז.

⁎ Verb to precede its Noun, or Nouns.   † Past w. ו Convers.
‡ With ה at the end.   § With ו at the end.

not thou (*f.*) the-same[40] that[41] made[18] [3 s. *f.* Past] the sea-depths (Hebr. *depths-of*[42] *a sea*[43]) a way[25] for-redeemed-ones-to-pass-over (Hebr. *for*[6] *passing-over-of*[44] *redeemed-ones*[45] (*m.*)) ? And the-ransomed-of[46] The LORD shall return[47] § and shall-come-to †[48] Zion amid[49] glad-singing,[50] . . . ; rejoicing[51] and joy[52] shall-they-attain-to[53] §, sorrow[54] and sighing[55] [shall] have-fled-away (pl.).*[56]

[39] זְרוֹעַ.   [40] הִיא.   [41] The Prefix ה as in § 6. Cp. § 98.   [42] מַעֲמַקִּים.   [43] יָם.   [44] עבר Infin. *K.*   [45] גָּאַל.   [46] פְּדוּיֵי.   [47] שׁוּב   [48] בּוֹא.   [49] ב (the prefix).   [50] רִנָּה.   [51] שָׂשׂוֹן.   [52] שִׂמְחָה.   [53] נשׂג *Hφ.*   [54] יָנוּן.   [55] אֲנָחָה.   [56] נוּס.

The Student may write out for Practice :—
   (1) the Fut. *K.*, and the Fut. *Hφ.*, of רוּם *to be high ;*
   (2) the same two Futures with ו Conversive.

169

Note.

[Those who are eager to begin to read The Bible itself may proceed to do so now
by help of the following Outline-sketch of the remaining Classes of Verbs and by
continual reference to the corresponding Tables.

But we strongly advise the Student not to do so,—but, instead, to work carefully
through not only these pp. 169–178 but also the Observations XVI-L (on pp. 179,
etc.) and the additional Exercises XXXVI-L. It is scarcely possible to get the
requisite familiarity with some of the remaining Verb-forms without carefully working
through the Exercises upon them.   Wise Students will find themselves well rewarded
for this additional toil.]

(I.) Section XVIII has to deal with 'Variations from Tab. XIV

when the 2ᵈ and 3ᵈ Rt-letters are the same.'   [As, for

instance, in Verbs from the Roots סבב, ‏גדד‎.]   But

   (a) in many forms from such Roots there is no 'Varia-

      tion' from Tab. XIV; and

   (β) for the 'Variations' we may refer to Tab. XXI.

[See also Obs. XVI-XXII, & Exerc. XXXVI & XXXVII, pp. 179–184.]

(II) Section XIX has to deal with 'Variations from Tab. XIV

when the 3ᵈ Rt-letter is ‏א‎.'   The *chief* 'Variations from

Tab. XIV' are :—

   (a) the 2ᵈ Rt-letter has ⼀ followed by ‏א‎ Quiescent,

      (i) instead of ⼀ followed by a letter with Shva-

        Quiescent [see Tab. XXII], and

      (ii) in a few instances, in 3 s. *f.* Past forms, as

        קָרָאת (instead of קָרְאָה), and so הֻבָאת

        G. xxxiii. 11 (instead of הוּבְאָה like הוּקְמָה);

   (β) in the פָּעֵל form of Past *K.*, the — is retained in the

      2ᵈ and 1ˢᵗ Persons,—as in יָרֵאתָ 2 s. *m.*, etc. ;

   (γ) The ‏א‎⼀ form is the common one in the other Voices.

   Obs. Some words, which belong in signification to

      Roots ‏ל'א‎, have forms that are 'borrowed' from

      Roots ‏ל'ה‎, for which see Tab. XXIII.

[See also Obs. XXIII–XXV, & Exerc. XXXVIII & XXXIX. pp 185–189.]

[See also Obs. XXVI–XXX, & Exerc. XL–XLII, pp. 190–201.]

(III.) Section XX has to deal with 'Variations from Tab. XIV when the 3ᵈ Rt-letter is ה Quiescent.' These 'Variations' are many and great, as seen in Tab. XXIII. The Student may observe

(α) the Inf. Constr. endings in וֹת, (we have also רָאוֹת as Inf. Abs. *K.*, Is. xlii. 20 *Kri*, נִגְלוֹת Inf. Abs. *Nφ.*, 2 S. vi. 20);

(β) the endings יתָ, יתִי, etc., (sometimes תָ, תִי, etc.), in Past Tenses;

(γ) the endings ה, and ה, in certain other parts;

(δ) ESPECIALLY,—the Imperative and Future forms *without the 3ᵈ Rt-letter* ה, thus

(i) Imperatives 2 s. *m.*,—as גַּל for גַּלֵה *Pi.*, הֶרֶף for הַרְפֵּה *IIφ.* (& הַעַל, fr. עלה), הִתְחַל (p. הִתְחַלֵּה) for הִתְחַלֵּה *Hθ.*

(ii) Futures 3 s. *m.* & *f.*, 2 s. *m.*, and 1 s. & pl.,—as (3 s. *m.*) יִגַל *K.*, | יִגַּל *Nφ.*, | יְגַל *Pi.*, | יַגַל *Hφ.*, יִתְגַּל *Hθ.*, etc.

N.B. Such are often called 'Apocopated forms.'*

(ε) There are several *varying forms*, of which the following may be mentioned here :—(1) יִּשַׁע *K.* fr. שָׁעָה, (2) יַחַר *K.* and יַחֵר *Hφ.* fr. הרה, (3) יֵחַדְּ *K.* fr. (יְהִי (p. יְהִי) corresponding to יֵשֵׁב fr. שבה), (4) יְהִי (p. יְהִי) חדה

---

* These forms are often used with ו Convers. But see also p. 171, Note (‡).

*חיה. fr. *חיה, and so יְחָי (p. יִחְיֶ) fr. חיה*. (5) Also, the *K.* forms יִשְׁל 3 s. *m.* fr. שלה, תִּכֶה 3 s. *f.* fr. כהה, and so תִּתַע fr. תעה, etc.; and (6) יֵפְתְּ 3 s. *m.* Fut. *Hφ.* fr. פתה, etc. [(6) For forms from עלה, עשׂה, and others such, see (ζ).]

(ζ) The Fut. *K.* forms יַעֲלֶה 3 s. *m.*, תַּעֲלֶה 3 s. *f.* & 2 s. *m.*, נַעֲלֶה 1 pl., and their apocopated forms יַעַל, תַּעַל, נַעַל, are the same as those of the Fut. *Hφ.*

Also the 1 s. Fut. *K.* אֶעֱלֶה and the 1 s. Fut. *Hφ.* אַעֲלֶה have, both of them, the same apocop. form אַעַל.

The *Nφ.* forms תֵּעָשֶׂה †, יֵעָשֶׂה, יִגְּלֶה, etc., and so etc., merely lose the ה– when apocopated. Thus וְתֵעֲשׂ 3 s. *f.* (w. ו pref.), and so וַיֵּרֶא, יֵרָא, fr. ראה of יֵרָאֶה.

(η) The 3 s. *m.* Fut. *K.* יִרְאֶה *he will see*, and the 3 s. *m.* Fut. *Hφ.* יִרְאֶה *he will cause to see*, (or *will shew*), have, both of them, the same shortened form וַיַּרְא with ו Convers.‡

N.B. It is only the 3 s. *m.* which has this shortened form from ראה. But we have also וַתֵּשְׁקְ 3 s. *f.* Fut. *Hφ.* fr. שקה.

---

* From היה *to be* the 2 pl *m.* Past *K.* הֱיִיתֶם w. ו pref. becomes וִהְיִיתֶם.
So the 2 pl. *m.* Imper. *K.* הֱיִוּ becomes וִהְיוּ.
But the 2 s *m.* Imper. *K.* הֱיֵה becomes וֶהְיֵה.
Similarly fr. חיה *to live* we have וִחְיוּ, וִחְיִיתֶם, but וְחָיָה.

† Once תִּיעָשֶׂה Ex. xxv. 31 (with ־י instead of ־).

‡ Sometimes forms occur, with ו Convers., not shortened; thus, וָאֶרְאֶה, וַיִּרְאֶה, etc.

(θ) A ׳ Consonantal appears in some forms. Thus,
(1) חָסָיָה 3 s. *f.* Past *K.* and חָסָיוּ 3 pl. from חסה;
and so (2) בְּעָיוּ and אֱתָיוּ 2 pl. *m.* Imper. *K.*;
(3) אֶהֱמָיָה 1 s. Fut. *K.* (with ה also); (4) יִשְׁלָיוּ
3 pl. *m.* Fut. *K.*, and (with ן, § 145) יִבְכָּיוּן, יִרְנָיוּן,
יֶהֱמָיוּן, etc.; (5) תְּרַדְּמִיוּן, 2 pl. *m.* Fut. *Pi.*, etc.

Obs. Such forms may be said to belong to Roots לי׳;
but more must be said on this, elsewhere.

(ι) A ו Consonantal stands in some forms,—from a few
Roots. Thus שָׁלַוְתִּי 1 s. Past *K.* fr. שלה; מְטַחֲוֵי
Pi. Partic. pl. *m.* (i.c.); etc.;—which may be said to
belong to Roots לו׳. For the forms fr. שחה, with
ו introduced at the end, see Tab. XXIII, Notes † to ¶.

(κ) The ending יוֹ— in הִמְסִיוּ Josh. xiv. 8 is Aramæan,
cp. Dan. v. 4.

(λ) The ending הֶ— occurs sometimes where the more
usual הָ— is given in Tab. XXIII; and (rarely)
הָ— instead of הֶ— in the Table.

(μ) No difficulty will be caused by the appearance of
—ָ for —ַ in Pause, or by the ending —ָתָה; for
—ָתָה in 3 s. *f.* Past forms. Cp. also § 167 (iii).—
In Lev. xxv. 21, we find the contracted form
וְעָשָׂת for וְעָשְׂתָה 3 s. *f.* Past *K.* with ו pref.

(ν) The Partic. forms will be sufficiently understood
from the following addition to Tab. XXIII:—

Plu. (f.)	i.c	Plu. (m.)	i.c.	Sing (f.)	i.c.	Sing. (m.)	
גָּלוֹת‡	◌ֶי	גּוֹלִים	◌ֶת	גּוֹלָה†	◌ֶה	גּוֹלֶה* (1)	(I) *Kal.*
יְלֻיּוֹת	◌ֶיְ	גְּלוּיִים	◌ֻיָת	גְּלוּיָה	נְלוּי	גָּלוּי§ (2)	
נִגְלוֹת	◌ֶי	נגלים	◌ֶת	נִגְלָה	◌ֶה	נִגְלָה	(II) *Niph.*

₊ In other Voices the only change from the s. *m.* forms given in Tab. XXIII, is in the endings—which are

Plu. (f)	i.c.	Plu. (m.)	i c.	Sing (f.)	i.c.	Sing. (m.)
◌ָוֹת	◌ָי	◌ָים	◌ֶת	◌ָה	◌ָה	◌ָה

Obs. (i) The Plu. (f.) Partic.-forms are the same in Constr.

(ii) The Partic.-forms *K.* חַי (p. חַיִּ׃) *living* s. *m.*, חָיָה s. *f.*, חַיִּים pl. *m.*, חַיּוֹת pl. *f.*, are "borrowed" from a Root חיי(=חיה), being like סַב s. *m.*, סַבָּה s. *f.*, etc., fr. סבב.

(iii) Also the Past *K.* form חַי (p. חָיִ׃) 3 s. *m.* is "borrowed" from חיי (=חיה), being like סַב 3 s. *m.* Past *K.* of סבב. But

(iv) חָיוֹת Partic. *K.* pl. *f.*, Ex. i. 19, is like שָׁמוֹת from שׂים (§ 226); and so חָיָה Past *K.* 3 s. *f.*, Ex. i. 16.

(ξ) To the forms in (θ) above—we may add here (1) מְמֻחָיִם Is. xxv. 6 *Pŭ.* Partic. pl. *m.* of מחה=מחי in the sense of מחח (some, however, give the ordinary sense of מחה); (2) תֻּגְיוּן Job xix. 2, which is 2 pl. *m.* Fut. *Πφ.* of יגה [cp. § 195 (δ, ii) and Sect. XXI (p, 174, iv, *a*)] with the ן of § 145.

(o) The word כָּסּוּ, Ps. lxxx. 11 and Pr. xxiv. 31, is 3 pl. Past *Pŭ.* of כסה with ◌ֻ(ŏ) instead of ◌ֻ.

(π) There is sometimes א instead of ה; thus יִשְׁנֶא 3 s. *m.* Fut. *K.* of שׁנה, etc.

---

* With א standing for the ה, נָשָׁא s. *m.* 1 S. xxii. 2;—נֹשְׁאִים Neh. v. 7 has א 'superfluous.'

† עֹטְיָה fr. עטה, בּוֹכִיָּה fr. בכה, etc.; cp. (θ) above.—פֹּרָת G. xlix. 22.

‡ אַתִיוֹת, Is. xli. 23, fr. אתה.

§ עָשׂוּ in הֶעָשׂוּ Job xli. 25 (§ 6, *d.* ii). In Job xv. 22 צָפוּי is *Krî* for צפון *Kthîv.*

N.B. As in Pt. I, § 14, we may have ◌ָ for ן.

[See also Obs. XXXI & XXXII, & Exerc. XLIII & XLIV, pp. 202–207.]

(IV.) SECTION XXI is to deal with Verbs belonging to more
than one of the Seven Classes in Sects. XIV–XX.   The
following few examples will sufficiently illustrate this.

(α) From יפה *to be beautiful*, which is both פ״י (Sect.
XV), and ל״ה (Sect. XX), the 3 s. *m.* Fut. K.
would be יִיפֶּה.*   This with ו Convers. becomes
וַיִּיף Ez. xxxi. 7 *and he was beautiful.*

(β) From נטה, which is both פ״נ (Sect. XVI) and
ל״ה (Sect. XX), the 3 s. *m.* Fut. *K.* is יִטֶּה.†   This
gives the apocopated form יֵט in וַיֵּט Zeph. ii. 13,
etc.   And so from תִּטֶּה 3 s. *f.*, & 2 s. *m.*, we
have תֵּט.

(γ) Similarly the 3 s. *m.* Fut. *Hφ.* of נטה is יַטֶּה which
gives יֵט in וַיֵּט; and so תַּטֶּה gives תֵּט, and אַטֶּה
gives אַט (p. אָטֵ).   And so יַכֶּה 3 s. *m.* Fut. *Hφ.*
of נכה gives יַךְ, תַּכֶּה gives תַּךְ, and אַכֶּה gives אַךְ.

(δ) Similarly also for other parts of the Verb; thus,
(i) ‡ הַכּוֹת Inf. *Hφ.* of נכה, and (ii) ‡ הִכָּה 3 s. *m.*
Past *Hφ.*, (iii) ‡ מַכֶּה Partic. s. *m.*, (iv) ‡ הַכֵּה
Imper. 2 s. *m.*; etc.

[Other forms and Verbs must be reserved at present.]

---

* The יְ agreeing with that of יֵיטֵב, etc., in Tab. XVIII,—and the ֶה with
that of יִגְלֶה, etc., in Tab. XXIII.

† The Dag. F. of the ט standing instead of the 1st Rt-letter, as in וַיֵּט Tab. XIX;
and the ֶה being as in Tab. XXIII.

‡ Compare Tab. XXIII.

(V.) Section XXII is to deal with the Verb-forms having Pronom.-Affixes. These will be sufficiently understood from Tables XXIV–XXX, with the help of Observations XXXIII–L which are given in connection with Exercises XLV–L [pp. 208–220].

It is not necessary to trouble the Student with any more Exercises. The remaining pages, including the Appendix, are intended to supply him with some useful help while he is reading The Bible.

(VI.) Section XXIII is to deal with some other Voice-forms :—

In § 220 (vi) the Voice-forms פּוֹלֵל, כּוֹלֵל, and הִתְפּוֹלֵל, were mentioned. There are some other varying forms of *Pĭ-êl*, *Pŭ-ăl*, and *Hithpă-êl*,—chiefly in the case of Verbs such as those in Tabs. XX & XXI, but also in a few forms of other Verbs.

(a) The 1st and the 3d Rt-letters are sometimes both of them repeated, as in

(1) the Infin. כַּלְכֵּל fr. כּוֹל, the Past כִּלְכֵּל 3 s. *m.* (whence the Voice-form is called כִּלְכֵּל,) כִּלְכְּלָה 3 s. *f.*, כִּלְכַּלְתָּ 2 s. *m.*, etc., the Partic. מְכַלְכֵּל s. *m.*, and the Fut. יְכַלְכֵּל 3 s. *m.*, etc.;

(2) the *Passive* כָּלְפַּל (◌ָ, ◌ֳ), corresponding to כִּלְפֵּל as *Pŭ-ăl* to *Pĭ-êl*,—thus the Past כָּלְכַּל, whence כָּלְכְּלוּ 3 pl., fr. כּוֹל;

(3) the *Reflexive* הִתְכַּלְכֵּל, corresponding to כִּלְכֵּל as *Hithpă-êl* to *Pĭ-êl*,—thus הִתְחַלְחֵל, whence the Fut. וַתִּתְחַלְחַל 3 s. *f.* w. ו Convers.

(β) Sometimes also such forms occur from Verbs having
the 2ᵈ and 3ᵈ Rt-letters the same. For these
Verbs,—having the 2ᵈ Rt-letter (the ע, § 117)
repeated as 3ᵈ Rt-letter (*i.e.* as ל, § 117),—the
designation 'Verbs פעע' is appropriate.* Such
forms as those in (*a*), from these Roots which have
the 'ע' in the place also of the 'ל' (§ 117), are פְּעְפַּע
(or הִתְפַּעְפַּע (or פָּעְפַּע (פֻּעְפַּע) (‗ˏ, δ).†

(γ) A form פִּעְפַּע from the Root יפה occurs in Ps. xlv. 3,
viz. יְפִיפִיתָ Past 2 s. *m.*

(δ) In the case of 'Full' Verbs also, sometimes
(*a*) the 3ᵈ Rt-letter is repeated in forms (1) פִּעְלַל
(or לַל—, or פַּעֲ', or פַּעַ'), and (2) פָּעֲלַל;
(*b*) both the 2ᵈ and 3ᵈ Rt-letters are repeated in the
forms (1) פְּעַלְעַל and (2) פָּעֲלַעַל of which the ‗ֲ
(as under the ח in חֲמַרְמָרוּ 3 pl. Past) corresponds
to the ‗ֻ or ‗ֹ (δ) of *Pŭ-ăl.*

(ε) There are a few instances of other Voice-forms; thus,
(*a*) פֹּעֵל (instead of *Pĭ-ĕl*) in לְמִשְׁפְּטִי Job ix. 15,
Partic. s. *m.*, w. ל pref. and Aff. 'ִ‗ for 1 s., fr. שָׁפַט,
(*b*) פֹּפֵל (instead of *Pĭ-ĕl*) in יְעֹעֵרוּ׃ Is. xv. 5, Fut.
3 pl. *m.* fr. עוּר,
(*c*) פָּעְלַע (instead of *Pŭ-ăl*) in מְחֻסְפָּס Ex. xvi. 14,
Partic. s. *m.* fr. חסף,

---

* "ע'ע" is bad. It means, rather, 'having ע as Second Rt-letter.'

† We have also (1) פְּעַפַּע forms in שִׁעֲשַׁע Past 3 s. *m.* and שִׁעֲשַׁעְתִּי׃ 1 s. (in
Pause, (also יְשַׁעֲשְׁעוּ Fut 3 pl. *m*); (2) פָּעְפַּע in תְּשַׁעֲשְׁעוּ׃ Fut. 2 pl. *m.* (in Pause);
and (3) הָתְפַּעְפַּע in אֶשְׁתַּעֲשָׁע (pl ע‗ֵ׃)—And so the Imper. 2 pl. *m.* הִשְׁתַּעַשְׁעוּ,
Is. xxix. 9, may be Imper. 2 pl. *m.* of this form fr שָׁעַע. [Or it may, perhaps, be of a
הָתְפַּע form fr. שָׁעָה].

(*d*) תִּפְעִיל (instead of *Hiph-îl*) in תִּרְגַּלְתִּי Hos. xi. 3, Past 1 s. fr. רגל.

(*e*) Some Mixed-Voice forms, as (1) נִפְעַל (*Nφ.* and *Pŭ*), (2) נִתְפַּעֵל (*Nφ.* and *Hθ.*), (3) הָתְפָּעַל (*Hŏ.* and *Hθ.*), belong to Sect. XXIV.

(ζ) The ה of *IIφ.*, as also that of *Hθ.*, is some few times replaced by א—an Aramaism;—thus, אֶגְאָלְתִּי (for הִגְאַלְתִּי, & in Pause) Is. lxiii. 3, אֶתְחַבַּר (for 'הִתְ) 2 Chr. xx. 35, אֶשְׁתּוֹלְלוּ (for 'הִשְׁ) Ps. lxxvi. 6. The word הַאֶזְנִיחוּ Is. xix. 6 may be said to belong to Section XXIV, being mixed up of the two forms הֻזְנִיחוּ and אָזְ'.

(η) There are words in which MORE THAN THREE Rt-letters appear; thus, פַּרְשֵׁז Job xxvi. 9, Past 3 s. *m.* fr. פרשז; and רֻטֲפַשׁ Job xxxiii. 25, Past 3 s. *m.* fr. רטפש; מְכֻרְבָּל 1 Chr. xv. 27, Partic. s. *m.* fr. כרבל; יְכַרְסְמֶנָּה Ps. lxxx. 14, Fut. 3 s. *m.* with Aff. נָּה‎ *it* (*f.*) fr. כרסם; etc. Some take such Roots as '*Quadriliteral.*' Others consider them as either 'reducible to 3 letters,' or as 'Composite.'

(VII.) SECTION XXIV is to deal with forms which may be said to be 'Compounded' of two Ordinary forms 'mixed up' together. Some instances of 'Compound' or 'Mixed' Voices were noticed in (*e, e*) above. The following is a translation of § 260 in the 5th edition of the Hebrew Grammar [תלמוד לשון עברי] by יהודה ליב בן־זאב;—

"Sometimes there occurs a single word compounded of two VOICE-FORMS; as (1) יְרֹדֵף Ps. vii. 6, which is compounded of

יְרֹדֽף *K.* and יַרְדֵּף *Pi.*; (2) נִגְאָלוּ Is. lix. 3, compounded of נִגְאֲלוּ *Nφ.* and גֹּאֲלוּ *Pŭ.*; (3) * וְנִכַּפֵּר D. xxi. 8, *Nφ.* and *Hθ.*; (4) * הֻכַּבֵּם Lev. xiii. 55 & 56, הִטַּמָּאָה D. xxiv. 4, compounded of *Hoph.* and *Hithp.*; or perhaps they are of *Hothpă-ĕl* form (the ה sometimes having ⸗ (ŏ) and sometimes ⸗ as in *Hoph-ăl*); and [in the last word] the ת [of הת] is swallowed up in Dagesh before ט, and its signification is that 'another was caused to do the action involved in it' (*she has let herself be defiled*).†
And so there is [sometimes] a word which is compounded of two Tenses, as וְיֹלַדְתְּ G. xvi. 11,‡ which is compounded of Past and Present [*or* Participle (for Present)] §; and so (?) מִשְׁתַּחֲוִיתֶם Ez.viii.16. And so there is [sometimes] a word which is compounded of two Gender-forms; as וַיִשַׁרְנָה 1 S. vi. 12, the beginning of which is *m.*, and its end *f.*, so that it is a word partly of one Gender and partly of another (אנדרוגינוס). There are also many such-like abnormal forms; but this is not the place to treat of them at length."

This will suffice for the present.

---

* The ה of הת is dropped here, and Dag. F. is then put in the כ.

† *Sie hat sich verunreinigen lassen.*

‡ The word occurs also in Ju. xiii. 6, 7.

§ *i.e.* compounded of יָלַדְתְּ Past 2 s. *f.* and יֹלֶדֶת Partic. s. *f.*—There are also some other opinions, somewhat different from this,

CONCLUDING PORTION

OF THE

EXERCISE-BOOK.

OBSERVATIONS XVI–XXII.

Obs. XVI. The statement of Obs. XII on p. 139 is a general one,—*viz.* that "The prefix וֹ has SOMETIMES ־ֲ before a letter bearing as Accented Vowel, especially if the Accent be Disjunctive." The cases that come under this statement may be divided into three great Classes, as follows :—

   (1) Simple cases of Obs. XII, as וָאָרֶץ Is. xxvi. 19, and so וָמֵתוּ (with ־ֲ Gen. xxxiii. 13, and with ־ֳ Deut. xxii. 24), etc ; and with a Conjunctive Accent as in וָלַיִשׁ Is. xxx. 6; but this last word, being the second of the 'Couple' לָבִיא וָלַיִשׁ, belongs rather to (2) ;—

   (2) Cases of the second of two words (or *first word of the second group* of two groups of words) forming a "COUPLE"; thus in אָב וָאֵם (*father and mother*) Ez. xxii. 7,—See more on this particular head in Rule I on pp. 223–225,

   (3) Cases of the third of THREE WORDS TAKEN TOGETHER; thus in שׁוֹר וְכֶשֶׂב וָעֵז (*ox and sheep and goat*) Lev vii. 23, גָּדוֹל וָרָב וָרָם (*great and numerous and tall*) Deut. ii. 21, etc.

This is more fully illustrated in Pt. II, § 94.

Obs XVII. Verbs which have the SAME LETTER for their 2d & 3d ROOT-letter are sometimes called כְּפוּלִים *geminata*, because their 2d Rt-letter or ע (§ 117) is repeated in the place of the 3d Rt-letter or ל (§ 117),—so that

Obs. XVIII. They might be said to have the Root-form פֿעֲע, instead of פֿעֲל, and

Obs. XIX. These verbs might therefore be called 'Verbs פֿ״עֲע.'

Obs. XX. The expression 'Verbs עֲ״עֲ,' by which some designate these Verbs, is not a good designation for them—because,

    As the expression 'Verbs עֲ״ו' stands for 'Verbs having ו for their SECOND Rt-letter,'

    and the expression 'Verbs עֲ״י' stands for 'Verbs having י for their SECOND Rt-letter,'

    so the expression 'Verbs עֲ״עֲ' would stand rather for 'Verbs having ע for their SECOND Rt-letter' (such as נָעַר, בָּעַת, טָעַם, etc.), which is an utterly different set of Verbs]

Obs.   XXI. (1) From these Roots (having the 2ᵈ & 3ᵈ Rt-letters the same) there are often forms in which there is no 'Variation' from Tab. XIV, thus, from סבב we have the forms סָבַב 3 s. *m.* and סָבְבוּ 3 pl., Past *Kal*, agreeing with Tab. XIV,—besides the special forms סַבוֹתִי (or סַבֹּתִי) 1 s., and סַבּוּ 3 pl. (in סַבוּנִי and סַבָּנִי, with Aff. *me*), and סַבֹּתֶם 2 pl. *m.* (all of which are Past *Kal*, as in Tab. XXI).

(2) As the 'Special Variation' for this set of Verbs we may mention

(α) the Dropping of the 2ᵈ Rt-letter, and

(β) the occurrence of Dagesh F. in the 3ᵈ Rt-letter (to imply the omitted 2ᵈ Rt-letter), as in סַבְּךָ, סַבּוֹ, etc., the Infin. *K.* with Pron.-Affs.,—and so in the Past-Tense forms (except the 3 s. *m.*) and in the Imper. forms סַבִּי 2 s. *f.*, etc.,—of Tab. XXI.   But

N.B. When the 3ᵈ Rt-letter stands at the end of the word, without a Vowel (and therefore with *Shva Quiescent*), that Dagesh is omitted; and so we have the Infin. סֹב, the Past 3 s. *m.* סַב, the Imper. 2 s *m.* סֹב, and the Fut forms יָסֹב, תָּסֹב, אָסֹב, נָסֹב; and so in other Voices.

Obs. XXII. The forms for *Pi.*, *Pŭ*, and *Hθ*, are the same in Tab. XX (ע'ו) as they are in Tab. XXI (פ'ע'ע or כְּפוּלִים *Geminata*).

[Note. For particular forms in the Exercise, the Notes there given and Tab. XXI, will it is hoped be sufficient.]

EXERCISE XXXVI [on Verbs whose 2ᵈ & 3ᵈ Rt-letters are the same (פֵּעֵ)—Table XXI].

(To be translated into English, § 11. a-ε).

יְיָ מָה[1] רַבּוּ[2] צָרָי[3] ׃ שַׁחוֹתִי[4] עַד[5] מְאֹד[6] ׃ הֲשִׁמּוֹתָ[7] כָּל[8] עֲדָתִי[9] ׃

נָשַׁמָּה[7] כָּל הָאָרֶץ[10] ׃ כִּי[11] יְיָ הֻפַרוּ[12] בְּרִית[13] עוֹלָם[14] ׃ הֲרֵעוּ[15]

מֵאֲבוֹתָם[16] ׃

אָב[16] וָאֵם[17] הֵקַלּוּ[18] בָךְ ׃ וַהֲסִבֹּתִי[19] פָנַי[20] מֵהֶם ׃ וְהוּא יְיָ אֲשֶׁר

לִבּוֹ[21] כְּלֵב הָאַרְיֵה[22] הִמֵּס[23] יִמָּס[23] ׃ יִדַּל[24] כְּבוֹד[25] יַעֲקֹב[26] ׃ דַּלּוֹנוּ[24]

מְאֹד[6] ׃ הִבּוֹק[27] תִּבּוֹק[27] הָאָרֶץ[10] וְהִבּוֹז[28] תִּבּוֹז[28] ׃ כֹּל[8] עוֹבֵר[29] עָלֶיהָ

יִשֹּׁם[7] ׃ חֶרֶב[30] חָרַב[30] הוּחַדָּה[31] ׃ וּבָרוֹתִי[32] מִכֶּם הַמֹּרְדִים[33] ׃ וְשָׂאתָה[34]

יִכַּת[35] שָׁעַר[36] ׃ וּמַדֹּתִי[37] פְּעֻלָתָם[38] רִאשֹׁנָה[39] אֶל חֵיקָם[40] ׃ וְשַׁח[4]

רוּם[41] אֲנָשִׁים[42] ׃

(continued.)

---

[1] how? [2] רבב to be many. [3] צַר a foe. [4] שָׁחַח to bow down, to be depressed, Hθ. to bow oneself down. [5] unto. [6] exceedingly (N.B. 5 and 6 together signify *"very exceedingly"*). [7] שָׁמֵם K. to be waste *or* desolate, Nφ. to be wasted *or* desolated (*also* to be astonied), Hφ. to waste *or* make desolate. [8] כָּל all, כָּל when unaccented. [9] עֵדָה an assembly. [10] אֶרֶץ land *or* earth. [11] for. [12] פרר Hφ. to break, break off. [13] a covenant (the same 'in Construction'). [14] eternity. [Cp. § 86.] [15] רעע Hφ. to do badly (and, with מ following, *"to do worse than"*). [16] אָב a father, Table XIII, 1. [17] אֵם a mother (For the ו see Obs. XVI, p. 179). [18] קלל K. to be of light esteem, to be vile, Hφ. to make light of. [19] סבב K. to go round *or* about, to turn, Hφ. to make to go round *or* turn away. [20] פָּנִים a face (a Plural Noun). [21] לֵב a heart (the same 'in Construction,'—with Affs. לִבּוֹ, etc.). [22] the lion. [23] מסס Nφ. to be melted. [24] דלל to be weak, low, become low. [25] the glory of. [26] Jacob. [27] בקק Nφ. to be emptied. [28] בזז Nφ. to be spoiled, plundered. [29] עבר to pass. [30] a sword. [31] חדד Hoph. to be sharpened. [32] ברר to purge out *or* away. [33] the rebels. [34] and [with] destruction. [35] כתת Hoph. to be smitten, pounded. [36] a gate. [37] מדד to measure. [38] their work. [39] first. [40] their bosom. [41] loftiness. [42] men. [43] מעט to be few, to become few. [44] פֶּשַׁע trespass.

וַיִּמְעֲטוּ[43] וַיָּשֹׁחוּ[4] : כִּי[11] רַבּוּ[3] פְּשָׁעֵיהֶם[44] : שֹׁמוּ[7] שָׁמַיִם[45] עַל[46]

זֹאת : אָכַל[47] אֶת יַעֲקֹב[26] וְנָוֵהוּ[48] הֵשַׁמּוּ[7] : יֵשֵׁב[49] בָּדָד[50] וְיִדֹּם[51] :

דּוֹם[51] אֶל יְיָ וְהִתְחוֹלֵל[52] לוֹ : וַיִּחַן[53] יְיָ עֲלֵיהֶם :

רְאֵה[54] אֹיְבַי[55] כִּי[56] רָבּוּ[3] : וְתֹשֵׁב[19] תְּנַחֲמֵנִי[57] : הָפֵר[12] כְּעַסְךָ[58]

עִמָּנוּ[59] : סֹב[19] דְּמֵה[60] לְךָ[61] דּוֹדִי[62] לִצְבִי[63] · · ·

מַה[64] תִּשְׁתּוֹחֲחִי[4] נַפְשִׁי[65] · · · הוֹחִילִי[66] לֵאלֹהִים[67] : רָנִּי[68] בַּת

צִיּוֹן[70] צַהֲלִי[71] וָרֹנִּי[68] : הָאוֹיֵב[72] תַּמּוּ[73] חֳרָבוֹת[74] לָנֶצַח[75] : הֶחֱלוֹתָ[76]

לִנְפֹּל[77] לְפָנָיו[78] לֹא תוּכַל[79] לוֹ : אָשִׂים[80] קִבְרְךָ[81] כִּי[11] קַלּוֹתָ[18] :

גְּבוּרֵיהֶם[82] יְכַתּוּ[55] : הוּא הֵחֵל[76] לִהְיוֹת[83] גִּבֹּר[82] בָּאָרֶץ[19] : כְּהֵמָּה[23]

דּוֹנֵג[84] מִפְּנֵי[85] אֵשׁ[86] יֹאבְדוּ[87] רְשָׁעִים[88] · · · וְנָמַקּוּ[89] כָּל צְבָא[90]

הַשָּׁמַיִם[45] וְנָגֹלּוּ[91] כַּסֵּפֶר[92] הַשָּׁמַיִם[45] :

---

[45] שָׁמַיִם heavens (m.). [46] at. [47] אכל to eat, devour. [48] נָוֶה a habitation. [49] ישׁב to sit. [50] solitary. [51] דמם to be silent, to be quiet, to look-in-silent-resignation. [52] חול *Hθ.* to hope, to look-with-hope. [53] חנן to be gracious. [54] see Thou. [55] my enemies. [56] for, *or* that. [57] mayest Thou comfort me. [58] כַּעַם anger, vexation, Tab. X, 5. [59] עַם with. [60] be like. [61] ל to *or* for [Obs. XIV, p. 189]. [62] my beloved (E.V.). [63] צְבִי a roe (E.V.) [64] why? [65] my soul. [66] יחל *Hφ.* to wait, look-with-waiting. [67] אֱלֹהִים God. [68] רנן to sing aloud. [69] Tab. XIII. 5 (Note ‖). [70] Zion. [71] צהל to shout joyously. [72] O enemy. [73] תמם to come utterly to an end. [74] destructions. [75] for ever. [76] חלל *Hφ.* to begin. [77] נפל to fall. [78] before him. [79] יבל *K. & Hoph.* to be able (with ל, to prevail *over*). [80] שׂים to put, make. [81] קבר a grave, Tab. X, 2. [82] גְּבוֹר (or גִּבֹּר) mighty *m.*, a mighty one. [83] to be. [84] wax. [85] from the presence of. [86] fire. [87] אבד to perish. [88] wicked ones. [89] מקק *Nφ.* to be dissolved. [90] the host of. [91] גלל *K.* to roll up, *Nφ.* to be rolled up. [92] סֵפֶר a scroll.

Exercise XXXVII [Table XXI].

(To be translated into Hebrew, § 11. ζ-μ.)

*Sinners[1] (*m.*) shall be destroyed*[2]. Unto[3] their (*m.*)-coming-utterly-to-an-end.[4]   And ye (*m.*)-shall-be-consumed-away †[5] through[6] your (*m.*) iniquities.[7]   They-have-come-utterly-to-an-end[8] by-reason-of[9] terrors.[10]   When-once[11] I-have-sharpened[12] My-lightning-sword (Hebr. *the-lightning-of*[13] *My sword*[14]).

And-all-man's-courage-shall-fail (Hebr. *and all*[15] *the heart*[16] *of man*[17] *shall-be-melted*[18]).   And they-shall-be-astonied †[19] one-with-another (Hebr. *each-one*[20] *and his brother*[21]).   And I-will-desolate †[22] earth[23] and all-that-is-therein (Hebr. *its f. fulness*[24]).— Gird-yourselves[25] and be-ye-in-consternation.[26]   The stars[27] of the heavens[28] and their (*m.*) constellations[29] shall-not-make-to-shine[30] their (*m.*) light.[31]

And be-not thou (*m.*)-in-consternation, ‡[26] O-Israel.[32]   *The heathens[33] will-be-in-consternation.[26]   They (*m.*)-have-been-in-consternation[26] and have-been-ashamed.[34]   And-I-will-protect †[35] his-city (Hebr. *over*[36] *this city*[37]).   If[11] ye (*m.*)-shall-break[38] My covenant[39] [with] the day,[40] and My covenant[39] [with] the

<hr>

[1] חַטָּא a sinner.   [2] תמם *Nφ.*   [3] עֵר.   [4] Infin. *K.* of תמם with Pron-Aff.   [5] מקק *Nφ.*   [6] ב the prefix.   [7] עָוֹן, pl. עֲוֹנֹת.   [8] תמם *Kal.*   [9] מֵן.   [10] בַּלָּהוֹת.   [11] אִם.   [12] שָׁנַן *Kal.*   [13] בָּרָק [§ 56 (A, 1. & ii. s)].   [14] חֶרֶב Tab. X, 1.   [15] כָּל (בֹּל when unaccented).   [16] לֵבָב [§ 56 (A, i. & ii. s)].   [17] אֱנוֹשׁ.   [18] מסס *Nφ.*   [19] שמם *Nφ.*, the (ִ)-form.   [20] אִישׁ.   [21] אָח Tab. XIII, 2.   [22] שמם *Hφ.*   [23] אֶרֶץ.   [24] מְלֹא.   [25] אזר *Hθ.*   [26] חתת *Kal.* N.B. (i) The Imper. *K.* is like סֹב, סֹבִי, etc., in the Table. (ii) The Fut. *K.* is like תָּסֹב, יָסֹב, etc ; but Compensation is made for the Dagesh which the ת cannot receive.   [27] כּוֹכָב a star [§ 56 (ix)].   [28] שָׁמַיִם heavens.   [29] כְּסִילִים constellations.   [30] הלל *Hφ.* (Fut. like תָּסֵב, יָסֵב, etc.).   [31] אוֹר.   [32] יִשְׂרָאֵל.   [33] גּוֹיִם.   [34] בוּשׁ in Tab. XX.   [35] גנן *Kal* (Fut. like יָסֹב, etc.).   [36] עַל.   [37] עִיר *f.*   [38] פרר *Hφ.* (Fut. like תָּסֵב, יָסֵב, etc.)   [39] בְּרִית *f.*   [40] יוֹם.   [41] לַיְלָה.

<hr>

* The Tense before the Noun, § 162 (*d,* i).   † Past with ו prefixed.

‡ Obs. IV, p 93.

o

night[41] ... [then] also[42] My *covenant[39] may-be-broken[43] with David[44] My servant.[45]   The-Lord [God of] Hosts[46] will-protect[35] them (Hebr. over[36] them m.).

And I-will-be-gracious-to †[47] whomsoever[48] I-will-be-gracious-to.[47]

[42] נַם.   [43] פרר *Hoph.*   [44] דָּוִד.   [45] עָבַד Tab. X, 6.   [46] צְבָאוֹת.   [47] חנן (the *Kal* Fut. is like יִסֹב, תָסֹב, etc.).   [48] אֵת אֲשֶׁר.

---

* The Tense before the Noun, § 162 (*d*, i).　　　† Past with וֹ prefixed.

OBSERVATIONS XXIII-XXV.

Obs. XXIII. A Long Vowel in an open syllable often takes the place of a Short Vowel in a closed syllable; thus, we have the אָ‑ in מָצָא, מָצָתָ, מָצָאת, etc., of Tab. XXII, corresponding to the ‑דְּ or ‑דְּן of פָּקַד, פָּקַדְתָּ, פָּקַדְתְּ, etc, of Tab XIV.

> N.B. A syllable which ends in a *Quiescent letter* is 'open' [Pt. I, § 21 (3),—for there is no Shva Quiescent, either expressed or understood, under a 'Quiescent' letter [Pt. I, § 29 (3).]

Obs. XXIV. The Fut. *K.* forms יִמְצָא, תִּמְצָא, etc., in Tab. XXII, correspond to the forms יִלְבַּשׁ, תִּלְבַּשׁ, etc, in Tab. XIV.

Obs. XXV. There is an important 'Variation' in the case of the פָּעַל forms of the Past *Kal* of Verbs ל'א. In ordinary Verbs, the 2d & 1st Persons, both Sing. & Plu., are the same as the פָּעַל forms [comp. § 138 (A), ii], thus, from חָפֵץ *he was willing*, we have חָפַצְתָ, חֲפַצְתֶּם, חֲפַצְנוּ: Pause-form of חָפֵצְנוּ. But,

> N B. פָּעֵל forms of Verbs ל'א retain the ‑ֵ in the 2d & 1st Persons both Sing. & Plu.; thus, from שָׂנֵא *he hated*, we have שָׂנֵאתָ, שָׂנֵאת, שָׂנֵאתִי, שְׂנֵאתֶם,—comp. the Past *K.* forms יָרֵא, יָרֵאתָ, etc., in Tab. XXII.

Note. The 3 s. *f.* Past of the Verbs ל'א has sometimes the termination ‑ָאת, as in (a) *Kal* קָרָאת instead of קָרְאָה, and so (β) *Niph.* נִפְלָאת instead of נִפְלְאָה,—and so in the *Hoph.* הֻבָאת instead of הֻבְאָה (or הוּבְאָה) p. 275, l. 17.

EXERCISE XXXVIII [On Verbs ל'א,—Table XXII.]

(To be translated into English, § 11. a–ε.)

בְּרֵאשִׁית[1] בָּרָא[2] אֱלֹהִים[3] אֵת הַשָּׁמַיִם[4] וְאֵת הָאָרֶץ[5] : וַיִּבְרָא[2]
אֱלֹהִים[3] אֶת הָאָדָם[6] בְּצַלְמוֹ[7] : · · · בָּרָאתָ[2] כָּל[8] בְּנֵי[9] אָדָם[10] :
שָׂנֵאתִי[11] כָּל[8] פֹּעֲלֵי[12] אָוֶן[13] : אָמַרְתָּ[14] אַל תִּירָא[15]* : וְאֶת עֵשָׂו[16]
שָׂנֵאתִי[11] : אֵיךְ[17] לֹא יָרֵאתָ[15] לִשְׁלֹחַ[18] יָדְךָ[19] לְשַׁחֵת[20] אֶת מְשִׁיחִי[21]
יְיָ : · · · בְּרָאתִי[2] מַשְׁחִית[20] · · · :

נִטְמָא[22] יִשְׂרָאֵל : תִּמְצָאן[23]† אֹתוֹ רָעוֹת[24] : אֵיךְ[17] תֹּאמְרִי[14]
לֹא נִטְמֵאתִי[22] : נִטְמֵאת[22] בְּגִלּוּלַיְהֶם[25] : אֶת מִקְדָּשִׁי[26] טִמֵּאת[22] :
בְּגִלּוּלַיִךְ[25] אֲשֶׁר עָשִׂית[27] טָמֵאת[22] : מְלֵאָתִי[28] מִשְׁפָּט[29] : מִי[30] יִרְפָּא[31]

---

[1] at first. [2] בּרא to create. [3] Vocab. I (1). [4] the heavens. [5] the earth.
[6] אָדָם man, Adam. [7] צֶלֶם image, Tab. X (1). [8] כֹּל all (כָּל when unaccented).
[9] בֵּן a son, Tab. XIII (4). [10] see No. 6. [11] שׂנא to hate [Past *Kal* like that of ירא
in Tab. XXII]. [12] פעל to work [Partic (1) *Kal* = "a worker."] [13] Vanity, mischief.
[14] אמר to say. [15] ירא to fear [the Past *Kal* is given in Tab. XXII; the Future *Kal*
is like יִמְצָא, תִּמְצָא, etc., in Tab. XXII,—but the 1st Rt-letter ' combines with
the — of the prefs. אית, and so we have יִירָא 3 s. *m.*, תִּירָא 3 s. *f.* and 2 s. *m.*, etc.].
[16] Esau. [17] how? [18] שׁלח to put forth. [19] יָד a hand. [20] שׁחת *Pi.* & *Hφ.* to
destroy. [21] מָשִׁיח an anointed one [§ 56 (A, i)]. [22] טמא *K.* to be unclean, *Nφ.* to
be defiled, *Pi.* to defile, pollute. [23] מצא to find (*also* to come upon), *Nφ.* to be
found. [24] evils (pl. *f.*). [25] גִּלּוּלִים idols. [26] מִקְדָּשׁ a sanctuary. [27] thou *f.* didst
make. [28] one (*f.*) full of [this word is for מְלֵאַת the Construct form of מְלֵאָה s. *f.* from
מָלֵא *K.* Partic. s. *m.* (§ 139, δ, iii), with ' added (comp. 139, ε);—this ' is by some
called the "' Compaginis,' for an example or two of which see p. 232, lines 8–10.
[29] judgment. [30] who? [31] רפא to heal, give healing. [32] נשׂא to take up.

---

* A List of forms from this Root is given on pp. 286–288 below. But this form
will be understood sufficiently from what is said in No. 15 here.

† For the | see § 143.

לָךְ : וְנָשְׂאוּ[32] עָלַיִךְ[16] קִינָה[33] : חֶרֶב[34] יְרֵאתֶם[16] וְהֶרֶב אָבִיא[35]

עֲלֵיכֶם : לְמַלֵּא[36] אֶת דְּבַר[37] יְיָ : לִמְלֹאות[36] שִׁבְעִים[39] שָׁנָה[40] :

מָצָאתִי[23] כֹפֶר[41] : קִנֵּאתִי[42] לְצִיּוֹן[43] : וּבִקַּשְׁתֶּם[44] אֹתִי וּמְצָאתֶם[23] :

וְנִמְצֵאתִי[23] לָכֶם[45] : אֶרְפָּה[46] מְשׁוּבֹתֵיכֶם[47] : וְחַטֹּאת[48] יְהוּדָה[49]

לֹא תִמָּצֶאינָה[23] :

אֵלֶיךָ יְיָ אֶקְרָא[50] : לֵב[51] טָהוֹר[52] בְּרָא[2] לִי אֱלֹהִים[3] : קָרָאתִי[50]

בְּכָל[8] לֵב[51] : הִנְנוּ[53] אֲתָנוּ[54] לָךְ כִּי אַתָּה יְיָ + אֱלֹהֵינוּ[3] : בְּלִבִּי[51]

צָפַנְתִּי[55] אִמְרָתֶךָ[56] לְמַעַן[57] לֹא אֶחֱטָא[58] לָךְ[59] : יְיָ לִי לֹא

אִירָא[60] * :

[33] a lamentation. [34] a sword. [35] בוא *Hφ.* to bring. [36] מלא *K.* to be full of (also, sometimes, *to fill*), *Pĭ.* to fill, to fulfil. [37] דְּבָר a word. [38] [see No. 36, and Note (1, *b*) on Tab. XXII]. [39] seventy. [40] a year [see § 106, ii]. [41] a ransom. [42] קנא *Pĭ.* to be jealous. [43] צִיּוֹן Zion. [44] בקשׁ *Pĭ.* to seek. [45] of you (*lit.* TO you *m.*). [46] רפא to heal [comp. Note (7) on Tab. XXII]. [47] your *m.* backslidings. [48] and the sins of. [49] Judah. [50] קרא to call. [51] לֵב a heart, w. Affs. לִבְּךָ, לִבּוֹ, etc. [52] clean. [53] behold us. [54] [instead of אֶתָאנוּ from אתא *to come*, see Note (2) on Tab. XXII]. [55] צפן to hide, treasure up. [56] Thy word. [57] in order that. [58] חטא to sin [for the ⸺ compare the forms יַעֲרֹב, etc., in Tab. XVI (1)]. [59] against Thee. [60] see No. 15 above.

* See Note (*) on page 186.

Exercise XXXIX [Table XXII.]

(To be translated into Hebrew, § 11. ζ-μ.)

O-Lord, I-have-heard[1] the-report-of-Thee (Hebr. *Thy report*),[2] I-was-afraid.[3] And as-for-me (Hebr. *I*), [I have] not been-called[4] to-come-in[5] unto[6] the King.[7] Call[8]-ye (*f.*) not [Obs. V, p. 93] me (Hebr. *to me*) Naomi,[9] call[8]-ye (*f.*) me (Hebr. *to me*) Mara[10]; for[11] bitterly-hath-dealt[12] The-Almighty[13] with-me (Hebr. *to me*) exceedingly.[14] I-have-adjured[15] you,* O-daughters[16] of Jerusalem,[17] if[18] ye-shall-find*[19] my Love,[20] what[21] ye-shall-tell*[22] Him (Hebr. *to Him*) .... I-will-call[8] to God[23] Most-High.[24] Lo[25] Thou-hast-been-indignant[26] seeing-that[37] we-have-sinned.†[28] We-have-sinned,[29] we-have-done-wickedly.[29] Unto[6] Thee have-I-lifted-up[30] my eyes.[31] I-have-called-on[8] Thy Name,[32] O-Lord. O-God,[33] lift-up[30] Thy Hand.[34] Thou-didst-go-forth[35] (*m.*) for the salvation[36] of Thy people.[37] Thy (*m.*) Right-hand[38] shall-find-out[19] them-that-hate-Thee (Hebr. *Thy haters*[39]). Thou (*m.*)-hast-loved[40] righteousness,[41] and hast-hated†[42] wickedness.[43] My-soul[44] went-forth[35] at (בְ) His speaking.[45]

(continued.)

---

[1] שְׁמַע. [2] שֵׁמַע (declined, with Pron.-Affs., like נֶגַע Tab. X, 4). [3] ירא (see the Past *Kal* of this in Tab. XXII). [4] *Nφ.* Past 1 s. of קרא. [5] לָבוֹא. [6] אֶל. [7] מֶלֶך. [8] קרא. [9] נָעֳמִי. [10] מָרָא. [11] כִּי. [12] מרר *Hφ.* Past. [13] שַׁדַּי. [14] מְאֹד. [15] שבע *Hφ.* [16] בַּת a daughter, Tab. XIII, 5. [17] יְרוּשָׁלַם (p. ־ם). [18] אִם. [19] מצא. [20] דוֹד. [21] מָה. [22] נגד *Hφ.* Tab. XIX. [23] אֱלֹהִים. [24] עֶלְיוֹן. [25] הֵן. [26] קצף. [27] וְ the prefix. [28] חטא [in the Fut. *Kal* of this the prefixes איתן take ־ and the 1st Rt-letter ח takes ־,—as in תֶּעֱרַב, יֶעֱרַב, etc., Tab. XVI (1)]. [29] רשע. [30] נשא. [31] עַיִן an eye (Dual עֵינַיִם). [32] שֵׁם w. Affs. שְׁמוֹ, etc.,—comp. Tab. XIII, 4. [33] אֵל. [34] יָד a hand. [35] יצא. [36] יֶשַׁע (§ 56, vii). [37] עַם w. Affs. עַמּוֹ, etc. [38] יָמִין *f.* (§ 59). [39] שׂנֵא Partic. (1) *K.* plu. *m.* [40] אהב. [41] צָדֶק. [42] שׂנא. [43] רֶשַׁע. [44] נֶפֶשׁ *f.* [Tab. X, 1]. [45] דבר *Pi.* Inf., w. Aff. for 3 s *m.* [46] כֹה. [47] אמר.

---

* The masculine form is used here.   † Future with וְ Convers.

Thus[46] hath-said[47] The-LORD, I-have-given-healing[48] to these waters.[49]   And the waters[49] shall-be-healed. *[50]   And thou (*f.*)-shalt-go-forth *[35] amid (בְ) the dancing[51] of those-that-make-merry.[52]   And thy (*f.*) daughters[16] on (עַל) shoulder[53] shall-be-borne.[54]   Morning[56] hath-come[55] [§ 162 (*d*, i).]   Thou-hast-been-taken,[57] O-Babylon[58] (*f.*), and thou-thyself[59] didst-not (לֹא) know,[60] thou-hast-been-found-out[61] and also[62] hast-been-caught.[63] From The-LORD hath-been[64] this (*f.*), it (*f.*) hath-been-wondrous[65] in our eyes.[31]

[48] רפא *Pi.* [Note (5) on Tab. XXII].   [49] מַיִם.   [50] רפא *Nφ.*   [The א to be 'elided' here, as in Note (3) on Tab. XXII.]   [51] מָחוֹל (§ 56, i).   [52] שׂחק *Pi.* Partic. pl. *m.*   [53] בָּתֵף.   [54] נשׂא *Nφ.*   [55] אתא *K.* Past 3 s. *m.*   [56] בֹּקֶר.   [57] לכד *Nφ.*   [58] בָּבֶל.   [59] אַתְּ.   [60] ידע *K.* Past.   [61] מצא *Nφ.*   [62] גַּם.   [63] תפשׂ *Nφ.*   [64] הָיְתָה.   [65] פלא *Nφ.* Past 3 s. *f.*†

---

* Past with ו Convers.   † As in 'NOTE' on page 185.

OBSERVATIONS XXVI-XXX.

At the risk of some repetition of what has already been said in Note (III) [pp. 170-173] we may perhaps add here the following remarks:—

Obs. XXVI. In the case of Verbs which have for their 3ᵈ Rt-letter a NON-CONSONANTAL (*i e.* QUIESCENT) ה, there are certain forms which are liable to lose this* ה by 'Apocopation.'

The forms that are thus liable to 'Apocopation' are

(α) IMPERATIVE 2 s. *m.* in the following Voices:

Pĭ-ĕl, Hiph-ĭl, Hĭthpä-ĕl,

(β) FUTURE 3 s. *m.* & *f*, 2 s. *m.*, 1 s., and 1 pl., in

Kal & Niph-äl, Pĭ-ĕl [& Pŭ-äl], Hiph-ĭl [& Hoph-äl], and Hĭthpä-ĕl.

Obs. XXVII. (*a*) The 'Apocopated' IMPERATIVE forms are

Pĭ. † גַּל for גְּלֵה,—and so חַל for חַלֵה fr. חלה,—

Hφ. ‡ הֶגֶל for הַגְלֵה,—and so הָרֶף for הַרְפֵּה fr. רפה,—

Hθ. † הִתְגַּל for הִתְגַּלֵּה,—and so † הִתְחַל for הִתְחַלֵּה, fr. חלה.—

(β) The 'Apocopated' FUTURE forms§ are

Kal (*a*) יָגֶל 3 s. *m*, תָגֶל (or ‖ תֵּגֶל) 3 s. *f.* & 2 s. *m.*, נֶגֶל ‖ 1 pl, ‖ אֶגֶל ‖ 1s, also

(*b*) יֵשֵׁב for יֵשְׁבָה fr. שבה, and

(*c*) תֵּבְכֶּה for תֵּבְךְּ, יִבְכֶּה for יִבְךְּ fr. בכה, אֶשְׁתֶּה for אֶשְׁתְּ fr. שתה;

Nφ. יָגֶל 3 s. *m*, תֵּגֶל 3 s. *f.* & 2 s. *m.*, etc. [see Tab XXIII];

Pĭ. ¶ יְגַל 3 s. *m.*, תְּגַל 3 s. *f.* & 2 s. *m.*, etc. [see Tab. XXIII],

---

* N.B. It is only a ה *Quiescent* that is thus dropped. When the 3ᵈ Rt-letter is ה Consonantal, this is not dropped; but we have the forms—

KAL Past גָּבַה 3 s. *m.*, גָּבַהְתָּ 2 s. *m*, etc., Fut. יִגְבַּה 3 s. *m.*, etc.,

HIPH. Fut. יַגְבִּיהַ 3 s. *m.*, etc,

    and so others.

† There may be ⸱⸱ in Pause, instead of the ⸱.

‡ For a 'Variation' when the 1ˢᵗ Rt-letter is 'Guttural,' see Obs. XXVIII (θ).

§ Comp. Tab XXIII & Obs. XXVIII.

‖ This is merely a Form-word,—as also are some few others of the words here given for illustration.

¶ The ⸱ may be lengthened into ⸱⸱ in a Pause-form [comp. § 167 (i) & (ii)].

Hφ. (*a*) יִגָּל 3 s. *m.*, תִּגָּל 3 s. *f.* & 2 s. *m.*, etc. [see
Table XXIII,—also Note (‡), p. 190],

(*b*) יַפָּתְּ for יִפָּתַח fr. פתח, and so יִשָּׁק for יִשָּׁקֶה fr.
שקה, תִּשָּׁק for תִּשָּׁקֶה, etc.;

Hθ. *יִתְגַּל 3 s. *m.*, *תִּתְגַּל 3 s. *f.* & 2 s. *m.*, etc. [see
Table XXIII].

Note (i) ראה *to see* has (with וּ Conversive) וַיַּרְא for both
וַיִּרְאֶה *K.* & וַיֵּרָאֶה *Hφ*, in the 3 s. *m.*, besides the *Kal* forms
(וָאֵרָא &) אֵרָא 1 s., (וַתֵּרָא &) תֵּרָא 3 s. *f.* & 2 s. *m.*, יֵרָא 3 s. *m.*

Note (ii) שחה *Hθ.* *to bow oneself, to worship,* has the following
Apocopated Future Forms:

תִּשְׁתַּחֲוֶה for יִשְׁתַּחוּ* 3 s. *m*, תִּשְׁתַּחֲוֶה for תִּשְׁתַּחוּ* 3 s. *f.*,
comp. Note (†) on Tab. XXIII.—

N.B. וַיִּשְׁתַּחוּ Gen. xxvii. 29 is *Krî* for וישתחו *Kthîv.* The ‑ (which
the Student may see under the וּ in וַיִּשְׁתַּחוּ there) is put as
a *Defective Shurik*, Pt. I, § 14. This is unavoidable, because the
Full Shurik (וּ) could not be written without the וּ.

Obs. XXVIII. When the 1st Rt-letter is ה, or ח, or ע, there are some
'Variations' from Tab. XXIII (corresponding to the 'Variations' in Tab. XVI (1)),
as might be expected; thus;—

(*a*) From עלה, the Fut. *K.* forms† are אֶעֱלֶה, תַּעֲלִי, תַּעֲלֶה, יַעֲלֶה 1 s., etc.,
נַעֲלֶה 1 pl.,
and so from חנה, the Fut. *K.* forms‡ are נַחֲנֶה, תַּחֲנֶה, יַחֲנֶה etc., 1 pl.,—
like תַּעֲמֹר, יַעֲמֹר, etc., in Tab. XVI (1);

(*β*) From חזה, the Fut. *K.* forms are אֶחֱזֶה, תֶּחֱזִי, תֶּחֱזֶה, יֶחֱזֶה 1 s., etc.,
נֶחֱזֶה 1 pl.,
and so from המה, the Fut. *K.* forms are אֶהֱמֶה, תֶּהֱמִי, תֶּהֱמֶה, יֶהֱמֶה 1 s.,
etc., נֶהֱמֶה 1 pl.,—
like תֶּעֱרַב, יֶעֱרַב, etc., in Tab. XVI (1),—

(*γ*) From הגה, the Fut. *K.* is תֶּהְגֶּה, יֶהְגֶּה, etc.,—like יַעֲשֶׂה & יֶחְסַר in Note (*)
on Tab. XVI (1),—and so, fr. חתה, יֶחְתֶּה, etc.

Note. From היה *to be* & חיה *to live* the Fut. *K.* forms are יִחְיֶה & יִהְיֶה,
etc.,—see pages 277 & 279.

---

* The ‑ may be lengthened into ‑ in a Pause-form [comp. § 167 (i) & (ii).
† For the apocopated forms, see (ζ) below.
‡ For ‑ before ה in apocopated forms, see (ζ, *b*) below.

(δ) When the 2ᵈ Rt-letter is ה, or ח, or ע, the only 'Variations' (besides the Compound form adopted by any *Moving Shva* under one of those letters) are in the Apocopated forms; thus,

in the *K.* Fut. 3 s. *m.*, we have יִשַׁע for יִשְׁעֶה (fr. שעה), and so יִמַח for יִמְחֶה (fr. מחה),—corresponding to יִבֶן for יִבְזֶה (fr. בזה), but

(ε) when, by reason of Apocopation, the 2ᵈ Rt-letter ה is made to stand at the end of the word, and without a Vowel after it, this ה has *Mappék* [Pt. I, § 31], because it is not a Quiescent but a Consonantal ה; thus,

in the *K.* Fut 3 s. *f.*, we have

וַתֵּכַהּ and וַתֵּלַהּ (fr. כהה and להה),—

Note. The forms תֵּכַהּ and תֵּלַהּ correspond to the forms תֵּרָא, יִרָא, etc., in Tab. XXIII,—and these correspond to such forms as תֵּשָׁלֶה, יִשָּׁלֶה, etc. (fr. שלה), for תֵּשָׁל, יִשָּׁל, etc.

(ζ) When the forms in (α), (β), (γ), lose by Apocopation their 3ᵈ Rt-letter (ה Quiescent*), then their 1ˢᵗ Rt-letter takes ⁻ and the prefixes איתן take

(a) sometimes ⁻ as in

יַעַל †3 s. *m*, תַּעַל †3 s. *f.* & 2 s. *m.*, אַעַל †1 s., נַעַל †1 pl.,—

and so יַחַל in וַיָּחַל 3 s. *m.* Fut. *K.* of חלה,

תַּחַז 3 s. *f.* Fut. *K.* of חזה, etc., and

נַתַּהַר in מָהַר 3 s. *f.* Fut. *K.* of הרה,—and

(b) sometimes ⁻ (before ח for the 1ˢᵗ Rt-letter), as in

יַחַר fr. חרה, יַחַץ fr. חצה, יַחַן fr. חנה.

Note. The apocop. form יַחַךְ (3 s. *m.* Fut. *K.* of חדה) belongs to the same Class as יֵשֵׁב for יִשְׁבֶה (fr. שבה), the ח taking ⁻ for Euphony as in the 2 s. *f.* Past forms שָׁכַחַתְּ, לָקַחַתְּ, etc.,—Tab. XVI (3) (C).

(η) In the *Hφ.* also there are 'Variations' like those in Tab. XVI (1); thus,

INFIN. הַעֲלֵה, (Absol.), הַעֲלוֹת, בְּהַעֲלוֹת, etc.,

PAST הֶעֱלָה 3 s. *m.*, הֶעֱלִיתָ (or לְ) 2 s. *m*, הֶעֱלִיתִי 1 s., הֶעֱלוּ 3 pl., etc., and

וְהַעֲלָתָה 3 s. *f.*, וְהַעֲלִיתָ (or לְ) 2 s. *m.*, etc., with וְ,—comp. Note (†) on Tab. XVI (1).

PARTIC. (i.e. מַעֲלֶה) מַעֲלֶה s. *m.*, etc,

IMPER. הַעֲלֵה 2 s. *m.*, הַעֲלִי 2 s. *f.*, etc.,

FUT. יַעֲלֶה 3 s. *m.*, תַּעֲלֶה 3 s. *f.* or 2 s. *m.*, תַּעֲלִי 2 s. *f.*, אַעֲלֶה 1 s., etc.,

---

* It is only the *Quiescent* ה that is dropped,—not ה Consonantal.

† The prefixes איתן may have ⁻ in Pause-forms.

(θ) (a) The apocopated form of הַעֲלֵה *Hϕ.* Imper. 2 s. *m.* is הַעֵל (corresponding to
הֶרֶף in Tab. XXIII, for הַרְפֵּה, fr. רפה), and

(b) The apocopated forms of the *Hϕ.* Fut. (corresponding to יֶגֶל, etc., in
Tab. XXIII) are

יַעֲל 3 s. *m.,* תַּעֲל 3 s. *f.* or 2 s. *m.,* אַעֲל 1 s., נַעֲל 1 pl.,

and the Pause-forms of these are

יָעֵל: 3 s. *m.,* חָעֵלִ: 3 s. *f.* & 2 s. *m.,* אָעֵלִ: 1 s., נָעֵלִ: 1 pl.

N.B. These forms of the Fut. *Hϕ.* in (θ, b) are the same as the forms
of the Fut. *K.* in (ζ, a).

(ι) In the *Nϕ.* the Past forms are with $\unicode{x2d0}$ $\unicode{x2d0}$ (rather than with the $\unicode{x2d0}$ $\unicode{x2d0}$ in
Tab. XVI (1)), thus,
from עשה, נַעֲשָׂה 3 s. *m.,* (but נֶעֶשְׂתָה 3 s. *f.,* p. נַעֲשֶׂתָה:), נַעֲשׂוּ 3 pl.; and
so from ענה, נַעֲנִיתִי 1 s ;—
but, from חלה, we have נֶחֱלֵיתִי 1 s., נֶחֱלוּ 3 pl., (with the Partic.-forms
נֶחְפָּה & נֶחֱלָה s. *f.,* נֶחֱלוֹת pl. *f.*; also, from חפה we have נֶחְפָּה
Partic. s. *f.,* and from חרה* we have נֶחֱרִים pl. *m.*).

Note. For the *Nϕ.* of היה see p. 278.

(κ) The only *Hoph.* forms of עלה which occur are irregular, *viz.,*
הֹעֲלָה 3 s. *m.,* הֹעֲלָתָה: 3 s. *f.* in Pause;—
but, from חלה, we have הָחֳלֵיתִי 1 s. with $\unicode{x2d0}$ ($\breve{o}$) under the ה as in
Tab. XXIII.

Obs. XXIX. For the Participles it is sufficient to refer to p. 173. But we
may append here the following general remark:—

Obs. XXX. A word may occur in the Construct form before a Preposition, as in
כָּל חוֹסֵי ב *all that-trust in Him* (Ps. ii. 12), where חוֹסֵי is *Kal* Partic. pl. *m.*
i.e. fr. חסה, etc.—Comp. § 52, N.B.

---

* From חרה we have also the *Nϕ.* Past 3 pl. נֶחֱרוּ.

EXERCISE XL [On Verbs ל,ה—Table XXIII.]

(To be translated into English, with the help of the Glossary at the end of the book.)

רָאָה[1] יְיָ וְהַבִּיטָה[2] ׃ גָּלָה[3] כְּבוֹד מִיְשְׂרָאֵל ׃ גָּלְתָה[3] יְהוּדָה ׃
שָׂרָתִי[4] בַּמְּדִינוֹת[5] הָיְתָה[6] לָמֵס[7] ׃ צִיּוֹן מִדְבָּר הָיָתָה[6] ׃
עֵת[8] לִבְכּוֹת[9] ׃ וָאֶבְכֶּה[9] יוֹמָם[10] וָלַיְלָה[11] ׃ עַרְשִׂי[12] אַמְסֶה[13] ׃
וָאֲצַפֶּה[14] לִרְאוֹת[1] מַה־יְדַבֶּר־בִּי[16,17] ׃ תִּכְלֶינָה[18] עֵינֵינוּ[19] ׃ נֶהֱמָה[20]
כַדֻּבִּים[21] כֻּלָּנוּ[22] וְכַיּוֹנִים[23] הָגֹה[24] נֶהֱגֶה[24] ׃ כִּי נִשְׁבָּה[25] עֵדֶר יְיָ ׃

---

[1] רָאָה *K.* to see, *Nφ.* to be seen, to appear, *Hφ.* to cause to see, to shew.
[2] נבט *Hφ.* to behold [§ 141, γ (δ)]. [3] גלה *K.* to depart, go captive, *Nφ.* to be revealed, to be uncovered, *Pi.* to reveal, to uncover, *Hφ.* to cause to go captive, to take captive, *Hoph.* to be made to go captive, to be taken captive. [4] שָׂרָה (with 'added' י, שָׂרָתִי) a princess. [5] מְדִינָה a province. [6] * הָיָה *K.* to be, also sometimes 'to become,' comp. p. 254 (4, b),—especially when followed by ל, for an example or two of which see the Footnote on p. 255,—*Nφ.* to be done (also *to be done for,* or *destroyed*), to be brought to pass. [7] מֵס tribute (הָיָה לָמֵס *to become tributary.* For the ל comp. Rule II on p. 225). [8] time. [9] בכה to weep. [10] by day. [11] and [by] night. [12] עֶרֶשׂ a couch, Tab. X, 1. [13] מסה *Hφ.* to dissolve, make to melt. [14] צפה *Pi.* to watch, look eagerly. [15] what. [16] דבר *Pi.* to speak. [For the ‌ comp. Pt. I, § 70, and for the ‌ comp. § 168, i.] [17] in my case [or, perhaps, "against me,"—"unto me" (E.V. "in me," in the margin)]. [18] כלה *K.* to come to an end, to fail (when used of the eyes), *Pi.* to finish. [19] עַיִן (*f.*) an eye. [20] המה to make a noise, to roar. [21] דֹּב a bear (root דבב). [22] כֹּל all, every, the whole (כָּל when unaccented),—with Affs. כֻּלּוֹ *the whole of him,* etc., as in Tab. III, 2. [23] and like the doves. [24] הגה † to make a murmuring or moaning noise, to moan. [25] שבה to take captive, *Nφ.* to be taken captive. [26] עָוֹן iniquity (pl. עֲוֹנוֹת).

---

* The forms from this Root are given on pp. 276–278.
† See Obs. XXVIII (β), p. 191.

בַּעֲוֹנָם[26] גָּלוּ[3] : הִרְבּוּ[27] לִמְעֹל־מַעַל[28] כְּכֹל[22] תֹּעֲבוֹת[29] הַגּוֹיִם[30] :

וַיְנַסּוּ[31] וַיַּמְרוּ[32] אֶת אֱלֹהִים עֶלְיוֹן : וַיִּפֶן[33] אֲלֵיהֶם לְמַעַן[34] בְּרִיתוֹ[35] :

וַיֹּסִיפוּ[36] בְּנֵי יִשְׂרָאֵל לַעֲשׂוֹת[37] הָרַע[38] : וַיִּחַר[39] אַף יְיָ בְּיִשְׂרָאֵל :

וַיַּעֲשׂוּ[37] נְאָצוֹת[40] גְּדוֹלֹת[41] : לַמְרוֹת[42] עֲנִי[43] כְּבוֹדוֹ : וַיַּעַשׂ[37] יְיָ

כַּאֲשֶׁר[44] דִּבֶּר[16] : וַיִּחַר[39] עֲלֵי אַפּוֹ : שַׁעֲרוּרָה[45] נִהְיְתָה[6] בָּאָרֶץ :

וְתוֹעֵבָה[29] נֶעֶשְׂתָה[37] בְּיִשְׂרָאֵל וּבִירוּשָׁלַם : נֶחֱרָצָה[46] נֶעֶשְׂתָה[37] :

וַיֶּרֶב[27] בְּבַת[47] יְהוּדָה תַּאֲנִיָּה[48] וַאֲנִיָּה[49] : וַתִּהְיֶינָה[6] צֹאנִי[50] לְאָכְלָה[51]

לְכָל[22] חַיַּת[52] הַשָּׂדֶה[17b] : כִּי הֶעֱוּוּ[53] אֶת דַּרְכָּם[54] : וַיַּעַל[55] עֲלֵיהֶם אֶת

מֶלֶךְ כַּשְׂדִּים[56] : וַיְגַל אֶת מָסַךְ[57] יְהוּדָה : וַתְּהִי[6] נִבְלָתָם[58]

כְּסוּחָה[59] : וַיְגַל[3] הַשְּׁאֵרִית נְבוּכַדְנֶצַּר[60] : הָגְלוּ[3] לְבָבֶל :

---

[27] רבה K. to be many or great, Hφ. to multiply or make many (or great). [28] מעל, followed by the Noun מַעַל perfidy, 'to act very perfidiously' (compare the Note within the [ ] on p. 228,—v. 11 there). N.B. '*to-multiply to-act-very-perfidiously*' = '*to act over-and-over-again very-perfidiously*,' or some other such strong expression. For the $\check{}$(ŏ) comp. § 168, i,—the ו is here 'superfluous.' [29] תּוֹעֵבָה an abomination. [30] גּוֹיִם nations, heathen. [31] נסה Pi. to try, tempt. [32] מרה Hφ. to provoke, rebel against. [33] פנה to turn (followed by אֶל, " to turn to" =" to regard"). [34] because of. [35] His covenant. [36] יסף Hφ. to add (used sometimes with a Verb following it to express " doing so again,"—thus " to add to do evil" =" to do evil again." [37] עשה* K. to do, make, act, Nφ. to be done, made, also to be executed (as punishment). [38] the evil, or that which was evil. [39] חרה †K. to burn or be kindled (used of anger), Hφ. to make to burn, to kindle [wrath] transitively. [40] provocations (E.V.). [41] great, pl. f. [42] No. 32 [comp. § 137 (3), Note (†)]. [43] No. 19,—a ו is dropped here. [44] as. [45] a horrible thing (f.) [46] decreed-punishment. [47] בַּת a daughter (the same 'i.c.'). [48] lamentation. [49] and mourning. [50] צֹאן sheep, a flock (a plur. f. Verb may be used with this as Subject). [51] for food. [52] beast of, beasts of. [53] עוח ‡Hφ. to pervert. [54] דֶּרֶךְ a way (Tab. X, 1). [55] עלה* K. to go up, Hφ. to cause to go up, take up, bring up. [56] Chaldees (with a ו ' superfluous' here). [57] the covering of. [58] נְבֵלָה f. a carcase. [59] torn (E.V.),—" like the dung" (others). [60] Nebuchadnezzar. [61] נטה to stretch out, extend, incline, to slip (of the feet).

---

* See Obs. XXVIII, p. 191, etc.   † (ζ, b) p. 192.   ‡ See p. 309.

וְעוֹד יָדוֹ נְטוּיָה[61] : לְזָרוֹת[62] אוֹתָם בָּאֲרָצוֹת[63] : עַל[64] אֵלֶּה[65] אֲנִי

בוֹכִיָּה[9] : וַתֵּכַהּ[66] מִכַּעַשׂ[67] עֵינִי : וַיְהִי[6] לְאֵבֶל[68] כִּנֹּרִי וְעֻגָּבִי לְקוֹל

בֹּכִים[9] :

עַם תֹּעֵי[69] לֵבָב[70] הֵם : וַיַּקְשׁוּ[71] אֶת עָרְפָּם[72] : וַיִּתְאַוּוּ[73] תַּאֲוָה[74] :

וַיִּשְׁתַּחֲווּ[75] לֵאלֹהִים[76] אֲחֵרִים[77] : וּמֵעֲוֹנֹתֵיהֶם[26] יִתְעַנּוּ[78] :

אוֹי[79] לִי כִּי נִדְמֵיתִי[80] : כְּצֵל[81] כִּנְטוֹתוֹ נֶהֱלָכְתִּי[82] : הִרְאִיתָ[1]

עַמְּךָ קָשָׁה[83] : הֶעֱטִיתָ[84] עָלָיו בּוּשָׁה[85] : וַנְּהִי[6] כַּטָּמֵא[86] כֻּלָּנוּ[22] :

וַתְּכַם[87] עָלֵינוּ[88] בְּצַלְמָוֶת[89] : אֶזְכְּרָה[90] אֱלֹהִים וְאֶהֱמָיָה[20] : ...

יַעֲשֶׂה[37] לִמְחַכֵּה[91] לוֹ :

יְרֵא[1] אֱלֹהֵי אֲבוֹתֵינוּ[92] : שַׁלְמָה[93] אֶהְיֶה[6] כְּעֹטְיָה[94] : מָתַי[95]

אָבוֹא[96] וְאֵרָאֶה[1] פְּנֵי[97] אֱלֹהִים : אַל תֵּפֶן[33] אֶל קְשִׁי[98] הָעָם הַזֶּה :

תְּהִי[6] יָדְךָ עַל אִישׁ יְמִינֶךָ[99] : מַעֲשֵׂי[179] יָדֶיךָ אַל תֶּרֶף[100] : צַוֵּה[101]

---

[62] זרה Pĭ. to scatter. [63] in the lands. [64] on account of. [65] these things. [66] כהה to be weak, to fail (used of the eyes). [67] by reason of vexation. [68] אָבֵל mourning. [69] תעה to err, wander (Partic. pl. m. 'i.c.' = erring of). [70] heart. [71] קשׁח Hφ. to harden. [72] עֹרֶף neck, back of the neck (Tab. XI, 1). [73] אוה Hθ. to lust. [74] [with] lust. N.B. to lust [with] lust = to lust greatly. [75] שׁחה Hθ. to bow oneself, to worship [Tab. XXIII, Notes † to ¶]. [76] to gods. [77] other (pl. m.). [78] K. to be low, Pĭ. to humble, to bring down, Hθ. to humble oneself, to become low. [79] woe! [80] דמה Nφ. to be cut off. [81] like a shadow. [82] הלך Nφ. to be gone. [83] severity, hardship, hard-things (E.V.). [84] עטה * Hφ. to cause to cover as with clothing (and, when followed by עַל, "to clothe one with"). [85] shame. [86] like the unclean thing. [87] כסה Pĭ. to cover, to hide, Hθ. to cover oneself. [88] עַל over. [89] with the shadow of death. [90] זכר to remember. [91] חכה Pĭ. to wait for. [92] אָב a father. [93] (שֶׁ) for (לְמֶה) why? [94] עטה K. to be veiled [p. 173, Note (†)]. [95] when? [96] shall I come? [97] before. [98] the obduracy of. [99] Thy Right-hand. [100] רפה K. *to be weak* or slack, Hφ. to make slack, to stay (also *to let-go-one's-hold-of,*

---

* See Obs. XXVIII, p. 191, etc.

יְשׁוּעוֹת [102] יַעֲקֹב : רַב [103] עַתָּה [104] הֶרֶף [106] יָדֶךָ : אִם תִּבְעָיוּן [105]
בְּעָיוּ [105] שֻׁבוּ [106] אֵתָיוּ [107] :

Exercise XLI [Second Exercise on Verbs ל״ה,—Table XXIII.]

*(To be translated into English, with the help of the Glossary
at the end of the book.)*

וַיֹּאמֶר [109] אֱלֹהִים יְהִי [5] אוֹר וַיְהִי [6] אוֹר : וַיְכַל [18] אֱלֹהִים מְלַאכְתּוֹ
אֲשֶׁר עָשָׂה [37] : הוּא אָמַר [108] וַיֶּהִי [6] הוּא צִוָּה [101] וַיַּעֲמֹד [109] : וַיַּרְא [1]
אֱלֹהִים כִּי טוֹב : וַתֵּרֶא [1] הָאִשָּׁה כִּי טוֹב+הָעֵץ לְמַאֲכָל··· :
וַיִּשַׁע [110] יְיָ אֶל הֶבֶל וְאֶל מִנְחָתוֹ··· : וַיִּחַר [39] לְקַיִן [180] מְאֹד : מָה
עָשִׂיתָ [37]··· : וַיַּעַשׂ [37] נֹחַ כְּכֹל אֲשֶׁר צִוָּה [101] אֹתוֹ אֱלֹהִים בֵּן עָשָׂה [37] :
יַפְתְּ [111] אֱלֹהִים לְיֶפֶת [112] וְיִשְׁכֹּן [113] בְּאָהֳלֵי [114] שֵׁם [115] וִיהִי [6] כְנַעַן [116]
עֶבֶד לָמוֹ : וַיֵּרָא [1] יְיָ אֶל אַבְרָם : וַיִּשְׁתַּחוּ [57] אַרְצָה [117]··· הַמְכַסֶּה [37]
אֲנִי מֵאַבְרָהָם אֲשֶׁר אֲנִי עֹשֶׂה [37] : וַתַּהַר [118] וַתֵּלֶד [119] שָׂרָה לְאַבְרָהָם
בֵּן לִזְקֻנָיו [120] : וַתֵּלֶךְ [121] [הָגָר] וַתֵּתַע [69] בְּמִדְבַּר [122] בְּאֵר שָׁבַע :···
וַתִּשָּׂא [123] אֶת קֹלָהּ וַתֵּבְךְּ [9] : וַתֵּרֶא [1] בְּאֵר מַיִם··· וַתַּשְׁקְ [124] אֶת

and so *to forsake*).   [101] צוה *Pĭ.* to command, *Pŭ.* to be commanded.   [102] salvation of (plu. *f.*).   [103] it is enough.   [104] now.   [105] בעה to inquire [page 172 (θ)].   [106] שוב to return.   [107] אתת (page 271).   [108] אמר to say.   [109] עמד to stand, stand fast.   [110] שעה to look, have regard (*or* respect).   [111] פתה *Hφ.* to give enlargement,   [112] to Japheth.   [113] שכן to dwell.   [114] אהל a tent.   [115] Shem.   [116] Canaan.   [117] § 71.   [118] הרה * to conceive.   [119] ילד to bear (a child).   [120] at the time of his old-age.   [121] ילך to go.   [122] in the wilderness of.   [123] נשא † to lift, lift up.   [124] שקה *Hφ.* to

---

* See Obs. XXVIII ζ (*a*), p. 192.

† The 1st Rt-letter נ is dropped in the Fut. *K.*, as in Tab. XIX, thus יִשָּׂא (for יִנְשָׂא), etc.   For the forms from this Root see pp. 302–304.

הַנַּעַר : הַקְרֵה [125] נָא לְפָנַי [126] הַיּוֹם [127] : וַתְּמַהֵר [128] [רִבְקָה] וַתְּעַר [129]

כַּדָּהּ אֶל הַשֹּׁקֶת [130] : וְהָאִישׁ מִשְׁתָּאֵה [131] לָהּ : וַתִּקַּח [132] הַצָּעִיף [133]

וַתִּתְכָּס [67] : תוֹרֵי זָהָב נַעֲשֶׂה [37] לָּךְ : מַה יָּפִית [134] · · · לֹא יֵבֹשׁוּ [135]

קוָֹי [136] : וָאֵרָא [1] אֶל אַבְרָהָם אֶל יִצְחָק וְאֶל יַעֲקֹב : וַיִּבֶז [137] עֵשָׂו אֶת

הַבְּכֹרָה [128] : וַיְהִי [5] כִּי זָקֵן יִצְחָק וַתִּכְהֶיןָ [139] עֵינָיו מֵרְאֹת [140] : וַיִּגַּשׁ [141]

לוֹ וַיֹּאכַל [142] וַיָּבֵא [143] לוֹ יַיִן וַיֵּשְׁתְּ [144] : הֱוֵה [145] גְבִיר לְאַחֶיךָ וְיִשְׁתַּחֲווּ [75]

לְךָ בְּנֵי אִמֶּךָ : גַּם בָּרוּךְ [146] יִהְיֶה [6] : וּלְכָה [147] אֵפוֹא מָה אֶעֱשֶׂה [37]

בְּנִי : וַיִּשָּׂא [123] עֵשָׂו קֹלוֹ וַיֵּבְךְּ [9] : וַתִּגַּשְׁןָ [141] הַשְּׁפָחוֹת [148] הֵנָּה וְיַלְדֵיהֶן [149]

וַתִּשְׁתַּחֲוֶיןָ [75] : וַיִּרֶב [27] הָעָם וַיַּעַצְמוּ [150] מְאֹד : עָנָה [78] בַּדֶּרֶךְ כֹּחִי :

וַאֲנִי כִמְעַט [151] נָטוּי [61] רַגְלָי : וַיָּקָם [152] מֹשֶׁה · · · וְגַם דָּלֹה [153] דָלָה [153]

לָנוּ וַיַּשְׁקְ [124] אֶת הַצֹּאן : וַיִּחַדְּ [154] יִתְרוֹ עַל כָּל הַטּוֹבָה · · · וַיִּפֶן [33]

וַנִּסַּע [155] הַמִּדְבָּרָה : וַיִּלָּחֶם [156] בְּיִשְׂרָאֵל וַיֵּשְׁבְּ [157] מִמֶּנּוּ שֶׁבִי · · · :

וַנַּעַל [55] דֶּרֶךְ הַבָּשָׁן :

give-drink-to, to water. [125] קרה K. to happen, to occur, Hφ. to cause things to occur, to direct events. [126] before me. [127] to-day. [128] מהר Pĭ. to hasten. [129] ערה Pĭ. to pour out. [130] the drinking-trough. [131] שאה Hθ. to be amazed in oneself. [132] לקח to take, Tab. XIX (A). [133] the veil. [134] *יפה K. to be beautiful, Hθ. to beautify oneself. [For the Dagesh after מה comp. Pt. I, § 70.] [135] בוש to be ashamed, Tab. XX. [136] קוה K. & Pĭ. to wait, wait for, look with waiting for [the K. Partic (1), in the Plu., with Pron-Aff. signifies "those waiting for so and so."] [137] בזה to despise. [138] the birthright. [139] כהה to be dim, or dull. [140] ראה to see [the pref. מ here signifies "so as not" or "so as not to"]. [141] נגש K. to approach, Hφ. to cause to approach, to bring near. [142] אכל to eat. [143] and he brought. [144] שתה to drink. [145] הוה to be (p. 276). [146] blessed (sing.m.). [147] and for thee (m.). [148] שפחה a woman-servant (§ 67). [149] ילד a child (m.), Tab. X, 1. [150] עצם to be numerous, to be mighty. [151] almost, nearly. [152] קום to arise. [153] דלה to draw-water. [154] חדה to rejoice. [155] נסע to journey. [156] לחם Nφ. to fight. [157] שבה to

---

* In the Fut. K., יִפֶּה, תִּיפֶּה, etc., the 1st Rt-letter י becomes Quiescent in ־ , as in יִיטַב, תִּיטַב, etc., in Tab. XVIII (1).

צַו [101] אֶת בְּנֵי יִשְׂרָאֵל : וַיַּעַשׂ [37] כֵּן כַּאֲשֶׁר צִוִּיתִי [101] : וָאֲצַו [101]

אֶתְכֶם : לֹא תַעֲשׂוּ [37] לָכֶם אֱלִילִם [158] : וְלֹא תִשְׁתַּחֲווּ [75] לָהֶם :

הִשְׁתַּחֲווּ לַיְיָ : וְהִשְׁתַּחֲוִיתֶם [75] מֵרָחֹק [159] : אַתָּה אָמַר [108] אֵלַי הַעַל

אֶת הָעָם הַזֶּה : וְהַעֲלֵיתִי [55] אֶתְכֶם מִקִּבְרוֹתֵיכֶם [160] עַמִּי : וּבְהַעֲלוֹתִי [55]

אֶתְכֶם ⋯ וְנָתַתִּי [161] רוּחִי בָכֶם וִחְיִיתֶם [162] :

כֶּרֶם הָיָה לִידִידִי [163] ⋯ וַיְקַו [31] לַעֲשׂוֹת [37] עֲנָבִים [164] וַיַּעַשׂ [37] בְּאֻשִׁים [165] :

וַתַּעְדִּי [166] זָהָב וָכֶסֶף ⋯ וַתִּיפִי [134] בִּמְאֹד מְאֹד : לַשָּׁוְא תִּתְיַפִּי [134] :

קוֹל כְּחוֹלָה [167] שָׁמַעְתִּי [168] : בָּךְ חָסִיתִי [169] אַל תְּעַר [129] נַפְשִׁי : הוֹי

הֲמוֹן גּוֹיִם רַבִּים כַּהֲמוֹת [20] יַמִּים יֶהֱמָיוּן [20] : מַר יִבְכָּיוּן [ʾ] : וְאֶל מִי

תְּדַמְּיוּן [170] אֵל : תַּהֲרוּ [118] חָשַׁשׁ [171] ⋯ : ⋯ יַגִּידוּ [172] לָנוּ אֶת אֲשֶׁר

תִּקְרֶינָה [125] : וְנִשְׁתָּעָה [173] : יִשְׁלָיוּ [174] אֹהֲבָיִךְ [175] : וּמְלָכִים יָרֵךְ [176] :

וְיָרֵךְ [176] מִיָּם עַד יָם : טוֹב+יְיָ : לְקֹו [136] קֹוֵנוּ [136] : נִשְׁתַּחֲוֶה [75]

לַהֲדֹם רַגְלָיו : קַוֵּה [136] יְיָ : קָנִיתִי [136] יְיָ : אַל תִּשְׁתָּע [173] כִּי אֲנִי אֱלֹהֶיךָ :

בָּךְ חָסָיָה [169] נַפְשִׁי : בְּצֵל כְּנָפֶיךָ יֶחֱסָיוּן [169] : יְרַנֵּן [177] מִדֶּשֶׁן בֵּיתֶךָ :

בְּאוֹרְךָ נִרְאֶה [1] אוֹר :

take captive [this, followed by שְׁבִי (p. שֶׁבִי) *a captivity*, stands for "*to take a body of captives*"]. [158] idols. [159] afar off. [160] קְבָרוֹת graves. [161] נתן to give. [162] חיה to live. [163] to my Beloved. [164] grapes. [165] bad-grapes. [166] עדה* to put on as an ornament, to adorn oneself with. [167] חלה to be sick, *or* ill. [168] שמע to hear. [169] חסה* to trust. [170] דמת *Pi.* to liken. [171] stubble. [172] נגד *Hφ.* to tell. [173] שעה *Hθ.* to look at oneself (*also* to become afraid). [174] שלח to prosper. [175] אהב to love. [176] רדה *K.* to have dominion, to subdue, *Hφ.* to cause to subdue. [177] רוה to be abundantly satisfied. [178] שָׂדֶה a field. [179] מַעֲשֶׂה work (p. 44). [180] קַיִן Cain.

* See Obs. XXVIII, p. 191, etc.

Exercise XLII [Table XXII].

(To be translated into Hebrew, § 11, ζ–μ.)

Look-with-waiting[1] (s. *m.*) to (אֶל) The-Lord. I-have-looked-with-waiting-for[1] The-Lord, my soul*[2] hath-looked-with-waiting,[1] and for (ל) His word I-have-hoped.[3] Well[4] hast-Thou-dealt[5] with (עִם) Thy servant,[6] O-Lord, according-to (כְ) Thy word. Make-distinguished[7] Thy loving-kindnesses.[8] In (בְ) Thy doing[9] tremendous-things[10] [which] we-could-not-look-for (Hebr. *not we-could-look-for*[11]).

If[12] The-Lord shall-not build[13] a house,[14] in-vain[15] [will] its builders*[17] have-laboured[16] in (בְ) it. A-spreading-place-of[18] nets[19] she-shall-be[20] in the midst[21] of the sea.[22] And-she-shall-become (Hebr. *and-she-shall-be†*[20] *for*) the spoil[23] of heathen-nations.[24] She-shall-not-be-built[25] any-more.[26] Thy (*f.*) builders[27] had-perfected[28] thy beauty.[29] Thy (*f.*) shame*[31] shall-be-discovered,[30] yea[32] thy disgrace*[34] shall-be-seen.[33] Despised[35] [art] thou (*m.*) exceedingly.[36] According-as[37] thou-hast-done[38] (*m.*) shall-be-done[38] (*m.*) to thee. Heaven*[40] shall-disclose[39] (plu.) his iniquity.[41] ˋThe increase*[43] of his house[14] shall-go-away.[42]

---

[1] קוה *Pi.* [2] נֶפֶשׁ (*f*) Tab. X, 1. [3] יחל *Hφ.* [4] טוֹב. [5] עשׂה. [6] עֶבֶד Tab. X, 6.
[7] פלה *Hφ.* [8] חֶסֶד loving-kindness, Tab. X, 1. [9] Infin. *K.* of No. 5. [10] נוֹרָאוֹת.
[11] Fut. *Pi.* of No. 1. [12] אִם. [13] בנה. [14] בַּיִת (*m.*), Tab. XIII, 3. [15] שָׁוְא.
[16] עמל. [17] Partic (1) of No. 13 (with Pron.-Aff. *his*). [18] מִשְׁטַח. [19] חֲרָמִים.
[20] היה. [21] תָוֶךְ, i.e. תּוֹךְ. [22] יָם. [23] בֵּז. [24] גּוֹיִם. [25] *Nφ.* of No. 13. [26] עוֹד.
[27] Partic (1) of No. 13. [28] כלל Past *K.* ‡ [29] יָפְי (w. Affs. יָפְיוֹ, etc.). [30] גלה *Nφ.*
Fut. apocop. [31] עֶרְוָה. [32] גַּם. [33] ראה. [34] חֶרְפָּה. [35] בזה *K.* Partic (2)
[36] מְאֹד. [37] כַּאֲשֶׁר. [38] עשׂה *K.* to do, *Nφ.* to be done. [39] גלה *Pi.* [40] שָׁמַיִם.
[41] עָוֹן. [42] גלה *K.* Fut. apocop. [43] יְבוּל *m.* [44] אִישׁ. [45] עַם (w. Affs. עַמּוֹ, etc).

* The Verb to precede the Noun.　　　† Past with ו prefixed.
‡ As in Tab. XIV.

Each-one[44] to (אֶל) his people[45] they-shall-turn[46] (*m.*).   And I-will-give-drink-to*[47] the land[48] of thy (*m.*) inundation[49] from thy blood.[50]   And I-will-cover*[51] . . . heaven.[40]   [As-for] that night[52] . . . let-it-not rejoice[53] among the days[54] of a year[55] : . . . let it-look[56] for (לְ) light[57] and there-be-none,[58] and let-it-not-behold (Hebr. *not let-it-look*[59] *at*[60]) the eyelids[61] of a morning-dawn.[62]

And   they-shall-build*[13]   the-old-waste-places (Hebr. *the desolations*[63] *of old-time*[64]).   For-Zion's-sake (Hebr. *because of*[65] *Zion*[66]) I-will-not-be-silent.[67]   And thou-shalt-be[20] (*f.*) a crown[68] of beautiful-glory[69] in the hand[70] of The-Lord.

O-come[71] let-us-worship[72] and fall-down†[73]; let-us-kneel†[74] before[75] The-Lord our Maker.[76]

[18] פנה.   [47] שָׁקָה *Hφ.*   [48] אֶרֶץ.   [49] צָפָה (w. Affs. צָפָתֶךָ, etc.).   [50] דָּם w. Affs. דָּמוֹ, etc).   [51] כסה *Pi.*   [52] לַיְלָה (*m.*).   [53] חדה *K.* Fut. apocop. [p. 170 (ε, 8)].   [54] יוֹם (see Vocab.)   [55] שָׁנָה.   [56] קוה *Pi.* Fut apocop.   [57] אוֹר   [58] אַיִן.   [59] ראה *K.* Fut. (full form).   [60] בְ the prefix.   [61] עַפְעַפַּיִם   [62] שַׁחַר.   [63] חָרְבֹת [see § 69 (β)].   [34] עוֹלָם.   [65] לְמַעַן.   [66] צִיּוֹן.   [67] חשה [the Fut. *K.* has the (— ָ)-form; thus, יָחֱשֶׁה, etc].   [68] עֲטֶרֶת.   [69] תִּפְאֶרֶת.   [70] יָד (i.e. יַד).   [71] בֹּאוּ.   [72] שׁחה *Ho* Fut. [see 'Note' on page 315].   [73] כרע Fut (— ָ), Pause-form.   [74] ברך.   [75] לְפָנֵי.   [76] עֹשֶׂה *K.* Partic (1).

---

* Past with וּ prefixed.   † With the הֵ of § 144.

OBSERVATIONS XXXI & XXXII.

Obs. XXXI. A List of Verbs belonging to more than one of the Seven Classes mentioned in § 186—sometimes called 'Doubly Irregular' Verbs,—is given on pages 267, etc., below.

Obs. XXXII. A few examples of two-fold 'Variations,' in some remarkable instances, are given in Note IV (page 174).

EXERCISE XLIII.

(To be translated into English, with the help of the Glossary at the end of the book).

עַתָּה אֲדֹנָי[1] אֱלֹהֵינוּ אֲשֶׁר הוֹצֵאתָ[2] אֶת עַמְּךָ מֵאֶרֶץ מִצְרַיִם ··· :

הַטֵּה[3] אֱלֹהַי אָזְנְךָ וּשְׁמָע**[4] : תָּבוֹא[5] לְפָנֶיךָ[6] תְּפִלָּתִי : אַל תֵּט[3]

בְּאַף עַבְדֶּךָ : אֵלֶיךָ יְיָ נַפְשִׁי אֶשָּׂא[7] : רְאֵה[8] עָנְיִי וַעֲמָלִי וְשָׂא[7] לְכָל

חַטֹּאותַי[9] : יְיָ הַט[3] שָׁמֶיךָ וְתֵרֵד[10] : אַתָּה[11] נוֹרָא[12] אַתָּה : הָאֵל

הַגָּדוֹל וְהַנּוֹרָא[12] :

קַוֵּה[13] קִוִּיתִי[13] יְיָ וַיֵּט[3] אֵלַי ··· : יְיָ אֱלֹהַי יַגִּיהַּ[14] חָשְׁכִּי[15] : אִם

תֹּאבוּ[16] וּשְׁמַעְתֶּם[4] טוּב הָאָרֶץ תֹּאכֵלוּ[17] :

כִּי לֹא עִנָּה[18] מִלִּבּוֹ וַיַּגֶּה[19] בְּנֵי אִישׁ : עַד[20] אָנָה תוֹגְיוּן[19] נַפְשִׁי :

לַשָּׁוְא[21] הִבֵּיתִי[22] אֶת בְּנֵיכֶם : עַל[23] מֶה תֻּכּוּ[22] עוֹד : הִכֵּיתִי[22] אֹתָם

וְלֹא חָלוּ[24] : וְלֹא יוּכַל[25] יְיָ עוֹד לָשֵׂאת[7] : נִלְאֵיתִי[26] נְשֹׂא[7] : וְאַתָּה

בֶן אָדָם הִנָּבֵא[27] וְהַךְ[22] כַּף אֶל כָּף : וְגַם אֲנִי אַכֶּה[22] כַּפִּי אֶל כַּפִּי :

---

[1] O Lord. [2] יצא *K.* to go out, *Hφ.* to bring out. [3] נטה *K.* to incline, to extend, *Hφ.* to cause to incline *or* extend, to bow, to bow down, *also* to make to turn away (*or* send away, dismiss). [4] שמע *K.* to hear, *Hφ* to proclaim. [5] בוא to come, *Hφ.* to cause to come, to bring. [6] before Thee. [7] נשא *K.* to lift up, to bear, to raise, *also* to forgive (followed by ל). [8] ראה to see.† [9] my sins. [10] ירד to come down, go down. [11] As for Thee [12] ירא *K* to fear, *Nφ.* to be feared. [13] קוה *Pi.* to wait, wait for. [14] נגה (the ה Consonantal) to shine, to be bright, *Hφ.* to make bright, to lighten. [15] my darkness. [16] אבה to be willing. [17] אכל to eat, to enjoy. [18] ענה *Pi.* to afflict. [19] יגה p 281 to grieve. [20] עַד unto. This together with the next word אָנָה "*when?*" = "how long?" [21] in vain. [22] נכה *Hφ.* to strike, to smite, *Hoph.* to be smitten. [23] on, upon. This followed by the word מֶה (*what*) = "why?" "*wherefore?*" comp Nu xxii. [24] חלה to be sick, to be ill [25] יכל *K. & Hoph* to be able. [26] לאה *K. & Nφ.* to be weary. [27] נבא *Nφ.* to prophesy.

---

* For the ⸗ see Pt. I, § 72.　　† Also "*to look,*" followed by ב "*at.*"

הִכָּה[22] אֶפְרַיִם[28] ׃ וָאַט[3] אֶת יָדִי עָלֶיךָ ··· ׃ הִכְּתָה[22] הָעִיר ׃

בַּחוּרֵיהֶם[29]+מִכִּי[22] חֶרֶב בַּמִּלְחָמָה[30] ׃ וַיַּךְ[22] אֹתָם מֶלֶךְ בָּבֶל ···

הִכְבַּדְתְּ[31] עֻלֵּךְ[32] ··· עֲדִינָה[33] ··· וַתָּבֹאנָה[5] לָךְ שְׁתֵּי[34] אֵלֶּה ···

שְׁכֹל[35] וְאַלְמֹן[36] ׃ הִנֵּה אַשּׁוּר[37] אֶרֶז בַּלְּבָנוֹן[38] ··· וַיִּיף[39] בְּגָדְלוֹ ···

וַיֵּצֵא[2] מַלְאַךְ[40] יְיָ וַיַּכֶּה[22] בְּמַחֲנֵה אַשּׁוּר[37] ··· וְהִנֵּה כֻלָּם פְּגָרִים[41]

מֵתִים[42] ׃ וַיְיָ יַפְתְּה[3] יָדוֹ ··· וְיַחְדָּו כֻלָּם יִכְלָיוּן[43] ׃

צֵאוּ[2] מִבָּבֶל ׃ הַטּוּ[3] אָזְנְכֶם וּלְכוּ[44] אֵלַי שִׁמְעוּ[4] וּתְחִי[45] נַפְשְׁכֶם ׃

בָּאתֶם[5] עַד הַר הָאֱמֹרִי[46] ׃ אַל תִּירָא[12] כִּי עִמְּךָ אָנִי ׃ לֹא אִירָא[12]

מֵרִבְבוֹת עָם ׃

וְהוֹצֵאתִי[2] מִיַּעֲקֹב זֶרַע ׃ נֻדוּ[47] מִתּוֹךְ בָּבֶל וּמֵאֶרֶץ כַּשְׂדִּים[48]

צֵאוּ[2] ׃ צְאֶינָה וּרְאֶינָה[8] בְּנוֹת[49] צִיּוֹן בַּמֶּלֶךְ שְׁלֹמֹה ׃ אִתִּי מִלְּבָנוֹן[28]

כַּלָּה[50] אִתִּי מִלְּבָנוֹן תָּבוֹאִי[5] ׃ כִּי אֵיד[51] עֵשָׂו הֲבֵאתִי[5] עָלָיו ׃ בָּאתִי[5]

לְגַנִּי ׃ הִתְקַדִּשׁוּ[52] וּבָאתֶם[5] אִתִּי בַּזֶּבַח[53] ׃ כָּל גּוֹיִם אֲשֶׁר עָשִׂיתָ[54]

יָבוֹאוּ[5] וְיִשְׁתַּחֲווּ[55] לְפָנֶיךָ אֲדֹנָי[57] ׃ מִי כָמֹהוּ מוֹרֶה[58] ׃ אוֹרֶה[59]

שִׁמְךָ כִּי עָשִׂיתָ[54] פֶּלֶא[60] ׃ הוֹדוּ[59] לַייָ כִּי טוֹב כִּי לְעוֹלָם חַסְדּוֹ ׃

[28] Ephraim. [29] their young men. [30] in the battle, *or* war. [31] כבד to be heavy, *Hφ* to make heavy. [32] על a yoke, w. Affs. עֻלּוֹ etc. [33] O luxurious one (*f*). [34] two (*f*). This with the next word = "*these two things.*" [35] bereavement. [36] and widowhood. [37] Assyria. [38] לְבָנוֹן Lebanon. [39] יפה to be beautiful. [40] the angel of. [41] corpses. [42] מות to die, Tab. XX. [43] כלה to come to naught, to be consumed. [44] ילך to go, or to come. [45] חיה to live. [46] the Amorite [47] נוד to move away. [48] Chaldeans. [49] בַת a daughter. [50] a bride. [51] the calamity of. [52] קרש *He.* to sanctify oneself. [53] at the sacrifice. [54] עשה to make, to do, to act. [55] שחה *He.* to worship (followed by ל). [56] before Thee. [57] O Lord. [58] ירה *Hφ.* to teach. [59] ידה *Hφ.* to praise, to render thankful acknowledgments. [60] a wonder, a wondrous thing.

EXERCISE XLIV.

(To be translated into Hebrew, § 11. ζ–μ.)

I-will-lift-up[1] my eyes[2] to (אֶל) the mountains[3]:—
From-whence[4] shall-come[5] my help[6]?—
My help [is] from The-LORD,
The Maker[7] of heaven[8] and earth[9].

Many *[11] shall-see[10], and shall-fear †[12],
And-shall-put-their-trust[13] in The-LORD.
To-be-feared ‡[12] [is] He above (עַל) all[14] [that are called] God[15].
[It is] time[16] to seek[17] The-LORD,
Until-that[18] He-come §[5] and rain §[19] righteousness[20] unto (לְ) you.

THOU-hast-brought[21] [the] day[22] Thou-hast-called-for[23].—

Sit-thou[24] (*f.*) still[25] and enter[5] into (בְּ) the darkness[26].
And there-shall-come[5] (3 *s. f.*) upon thee (*f.*) suddenly[27]
Destruction[28] [which] thou-shalt-not know-of[29].

[It is] good[30] to-give-thanks[31] to The-LORD.

---

[1] נשׂא, pp. 302—304.   [2] עַיִן, Tab. XIII (‡, β).   [3] הָרִים.   [4] מֵאַיִן.   [5] בוא, pp. 272—275.   [6] עֹזֶר *m.* [§ 62 (iii)].   [7] עשׂה Partic. (1) *K.* 'i. c.'   [8] שָׁמַיִם.   [9] אֶרֶץ, Tab. X (1).   [10] ראה.   [11] רַבִּים.   [12] ירא, pp. 286—288.   [13] בטח.   [14] (כָּל) כל.   [15] אֱלֹהִים.   [16] עֵת.   [17] דרשׁ.   [18] עַד.   [19] ירה *Hφ*, pp. 288 & 289.   [20] צֶדֶק.   [21] *Hφ*. of No. 5.   [22] יוֹם.   [23] קרא.   [24] ישׁב Tab. XVIII.   [25] דּוּמָם.   [26] חֹשֶׁךְ.   [27] פִּתְאֹם.   [28] שֹׁאָה *f.*   [29] ידע Tab. XVIII, Note (3).   [30] טוֹב.   [31] ידה *Hφ*. pp. 281 & 282.

---

* The Tense before the Noun.   † Pause-form.
‡ *Nφ*. Partic.   § Future tense.

When-Israel-went-forth (Hebr. *in going-forth-of* ‖[32] *Israel* [33])
    from Egypt[34],
And He-smote[35] ʼall[14] [the] firstborn[36] in their (*m.*) land[9],
Egypt was-glad[37] at (בּ) their (*m.*) departing‖[32];
And He-brought-out[32] Israel[33] from among-them (Hebr. *their
    m. midst*[38]),
And there-went-forth[32] from trouble[39] a righteous-one[40] (*m.*);—

Lightnings*[42] gave-light-to[41] the-world[43],
And He-bowed[44] heavens[8] and-came-down[45].

We-will-not fear[12] though-the-earth-be-moved (Hebr. *in One's-
    removing*[46] *earth*[9]).
Let-us-lift-up[47] our heart[48].

Hear[49]-thou, [O] daughter[50], and see[10], and incline[51] thine ear[52];
Forget[53] also[54] thy people[55] and the house[56] of thy father[57]:
And the King*[59] shall-delight-Himself-in[58] thy beauty[60]:
For[61] He [is] thy Lord[62], and worship[63]-thou Him (Hebr. *to Him*).

Open[64]-ye (*m.*) to me the gates[65] of righteousness[20],
I-will-enter[5] by (בּ) them, I-will-give-thanks-to[31] The-Lord[66].

[32] יצא pp. 284—286.   [33] יִשְׂרָאֵל.   [34] מִצְרַיִם (*m*).   [35] נכה *Hφ*. Fut. apocop., pp.
298 & 299.   [36] בְּכוֹר.   [37] שׂמח *K*. Past 3 *s. m.*   [38] תָּוֶךְ w. Affs. תּוֹכוּ, etc.,—comp.
Tab. XIII, Note (*t*, *ε*).   [39] צָרָה.   [40] צַדִּיק.   [41] אור *Hφ*.   [42] plu. of בָּרָק, Tab. IX.
[43] תֵּבֵל.   [44] נטה *K*. Fut. apocop., p. 297.   [45] ירד [with ⸗ to the 3ᵈ Rt-letter, as in
§ 165 (I. δ)].   [46] מור *Hφ*. Infin.   [47] *K*. Fut. 1 pl. of No. 1.   [48] לֵבָב, w. Affs. לְבָבוֹ
etc.   [49] שׁמע.   [50] בַּת.   [51] *Hφ* of No. 44.   [52] אֹזֶן, w. Affs. אָזְנוּ, etc., Tab. XI. 1.
[53] שׁבח.   [54] ו (to be prefixed to the word "Forget").   [55] עַם, w. Affs. עַמּוֹ etc.
[56] בַּית Tab. XIII. 3.   [57] אָב Tab. XIII. 1.   [58] אוה *Hθ*. Fut. apocop., p. 267.
[59] מֶלֶךְ.   [60] יְפִי, w. Affs. יָפְיוֹ etc, (Comp. § 63 γ).   [61] כִּי.   [62] אָרוֹן pl.   [63] שׁחה *Hθ*.

‖ Infin. *K*.   * The tense before the Noun.

We-give-thanks[31] [Obs. IX, p. 93] unto (לְ) Thee, [O] God[67], we-
   give-thanks[31] [Past];
Yea[68] now[69], our God[67], giving-thanks[31] [Partic.] we [are] untó
   (לְ) Thee;
And Thy Name[70] for-ever[71] we-will-celebrate[31].   Sela[72].

And heavens*[8] shall-celebrate[31] Thy wonders (Hebr. *wonder*[73]),
   [O] Lord.

I-will-praise[31] The-Lord with (בְּ) all[14] my heart[74].

Come[5]-ye before-Him[75] amid (בְּ) glad-singing[76].

[O] give-thanks[31] unto (לְ) The-Lord, for[61] [He is] good[77],
For[61] for-ever[71] [endureth] His Mercy[78].

---

see Note (§) on Tab. XXIII.   [64] פתח.   [65] שַׁעַר (*m.*), Tab. X. 5.   [66] יָהּ.
[67] Vocab. I. 1.   [68] וְ the prefix.   [69] עַתָּה.   [70] שֵׁם, Tab. XIII, Note §.   [71] לְעוֹלָם.
[72] סֶלָה.   [73] פֶּלֶא, Tab. X. 2.   [74] לֵב, w. Affs. לִבּוֹ etc.   [75] לְפָנָיו.   [76] רְנָנָה.   [77] טוֹב
[78] חֶסֶד, Tab. X. 1.

---

* Tense before Noun.

OBSERVATIONS XXXIII—L

Obs. XXXIII. The following is a List of the Tables of Verb-forms with Pron-Affixes ·

Tab. XXIV	Infinitives.
Tab. XXV.	Past-Tense *Kal.*
Tab. XXVI.	Participles.
Tab. XXVII.	Imperative *Kal.*
Tab XXVIII.	Future-Tense *Kal.*
Tab. XXIX.	Some *Pi-êl* and *Hiph-îl* forms.
Tab. XXX.	Forms of Verbs ל״ה.

A few CHANGES OF FORM adopted by Verbs on receiving Pron-Affs. may be mentioned here:—

Obs. XXXIV. In accordance with the Great Rule of § 59, "the vowel which would stand NEXT BUT ONE BEFORE, or THIRD FROM THE ACCENTED VOWEL is generally dropped" (if it can be dropped) and is replaced by *Shva:* thus,

> (a) the ־ָ of פָּקַד is dropped and replaced by *Shva* in פְּקָדוֹ, etc., and so in other Past *K.* forms,—see Tab XXV,—[for the ־ָ of the פ, see Obs. XXXVIII];

> (β) the ־ָ of such forms as יָקִים, etc., Tab. XX, is thus dropped in such forms as יְקִימֵנוּ and יְקִימְהוּ and יְקִימוּ, etc.—But

Obs. XXXV. The vowel which would be thus dropped CANNOT be dropped if it is followed either

> (a) by *Shva*, as in יִפְקֹד, etc., יַהֲרֹג, etc, or

> (β) by *Dagesh F*, as in פִּקֵּד etc., פַּקֵּד etc., יְפַקֵּד etc.;

> (γ) but in order to shorten the word the NEXT VOWEL IS THEN DROPPED (if it can be dropped); and so we have the forms, תַּחְרְגֵנוּ, יִפְקְדֵנוּ, etc, Tab. XXVIII,—and יַהַרְגֵנוּ, יַהַרְגֵהוּ, etc., in which the ־ֲ of יַהֲרֹג, תַּחֲרֹג, is replaced by the Slight-vowel ־ַ [Pt I, § 56]; and so אֶהְרְגֵהוּ etc, with ־ְ, from אֶהֱרֹג;— פְּקֵדוֹ, etc., Tab. XXIX,—and פַּקְדֵהוּ, etc., and יְפַקְדֵנוּ, etc, Tab. XXIX (II, a).

> (δ) For 'Fut. (־ָ)' forms such as יִלְבָּשֵׁנוּ, etc., see Obs XXXIX below.

Obs. XXXVI. Sometimes no vowel can be dropped, and so we have the *Hφ.* forms הִפְקִידוֹ, etc., and יַפְקִידֵנוּ, etc, of Tab. XXIX (I, β) and (II, β)

Obs. XXXVII.   In *Hφ.* forms of some Roots there is no Shva after the first Vowel, and this Vowel can then be dropped; as in such forms as הֲקִימוֹ, etc., from הָקִים, (Tab. XX),—and so in Obs. XXXIV (β) above.

Obs. XXXVIII.   The — of the 'closed' syllable in פָּקַד, etc., is lengthened into ⟨—⟩ when the syllable in which it is becomes 'open' [comp. Obs. XXIII, p. 185]. Thus we have from פָּקַד such forms as פָּקְדוּ, etc., Tab. XXV.

Obs. XXXIX.   Verbs 'Fut. (—)', instead of dropping the — (as the ⟨—⟩ of יִפְקֹד etc., is dropped in Tab. XXVIII), generally lengthen the — into ⟨—⟩ as in Obs. XXXVIII; thus,

> from לבשׁ,—יִלְבָּשֵׁנִי with Aff. *me*, יִלְבָּשֵׁם with Aff. *them (m).*

Obs. XL.   The — in such forms as פְּקָדוּהוּ, etc, is the — of Obs. XXXVIII in an 'open' syllable,—being derived from the — of פָּקַד.

Obs. XLI.   The — of the פָּעֵל form (of Past *K.*) remains with Affs.; thus

> (α) From אהב,—אֲהַבוֹ, אַהֵבְךָ, etc., and
>
> (β) In such forms as אֲהֵבוּךָ *they (m.) have loved thee (m.)*, the — of אָהֵב is given to the 2d Rt-letter in the form for the 3 pl. (אָהֲבוּ) when with the Affix as here.

[See also Notes (α) and (β) on Tab. XXVII, and Notes (α) and (β) on Tab. XXVIII]

Obs. XLII.   In some instances Verb-forms w. Affs. occur with the — of the פָּעֵל form of Past *K*, although the 3 s. *m.* Past *K.* in use is of the פָּעַל form; thus,

> from ירשׁ the 3 s *m.* Past *K.* in use is יָרַשׁ, but we have also — of the פָּעֵל form in
>
> וִירֵשׁוּהָ *K.* Past 3 pl. with וֹ Pref. and Aff. *her,*
>
> וִירֵשׁוּךָ *K.* Past 3 pl. with וֹ Pref. and Aff. *thee m.,*

and from this — it is possible that the — of the following forms may be obtained, *viz.*

> וִירֵשְׁתָהּ *K.* Past 2 s. *m.* with וֹ Pref. and Aff. *her,*
>
> וִירֵשְׁתָם *K.* Past. 2 s. *m.* with וֹ Pref. and Aff. *them m.*

Note (i.) The — occurs also in

> וִירֵשְׁתָם *K.* Past 2 pl. *m.*, with וֹ Pref., [comp. Tab. XXV, Notes (α) and (β)],

but the other parts of the *K.* Past (from this Root ירשׁ) which occur agree with the forms from פקד in Tab. XIV; thus,

> יָרַשְׁתָּ (p. : יְרֵשְׁתָּ) 2 s. *m.*, יָרַשְׁנוּ 1 pl. (and w. Aff. *her* וִירֵשׁנוּהָ).

(ii.) There are other instances of Roots from which both פָּעֵל and פָּעַל forms occur.

Note (iii.) The ⸴ of a פָּעַל form, when followed by ⸴ Quiescent, is shortened into ⸴ *ŏ* on the addition of an Affix removing the Accent from the syllable which contains that ⸴; thus יָכָלְתִּי gives יְכָלְתִּיו *K.* Past 1 s. w. Aff *him*, fr. יכל. This is done in order to get rid of the UNACCENTED LONG Vowel before the QUIESCENT *Shva* under the ל [Comp. Pt. I, § 55 (8)].

Obs. XLIII. The Pron. Affs. for the 2 s. *m.*, and the 2 pl. *m* and 2 pl. *f.*, viz.,

ךָ ⸴ (or כָה ⸴), and כֶם ⸴ and כֶן ⸴,

require a *Shva* under the last letter of the word to which they are affixed, therefore any MOVING *Shva* under the preceding letter must be replaced by a Slight-vowel (but a QUIESCENT *Shva* may of course stand). The Slight Vowel generally agrees with the Vowel that was dropped; thus

(i.) from יִפְקֹד we have יִפְקָדְךָ, יִפְקָדְכֶם, יִפְקָדְכֶן, in Tab. XXVIII, etc.,—where the ק has the Slight-vowel ⸴ (*ŏ*) corresponding to the ⸴ which is dropped in יִפְקְדֵנוּ, etc.; and so,

(ii.) from פָּקַד we have פְּקָדְךָ (Tab. XXIX, I. *a*), etc, and from יִפְקַד we have יִפְקָדְךָ (Tab. XXIX, II. *a*), etc., where the ק has the Slight-vowel — corresponding to the ⸴ which is dropped in פִּקְדוּ etc., and יִפְקְדֵנוּ etc.

(iii.) Instead of the ⸴ in (ii.) there is sometimes ⸴, as in אֲאַמִּצְכֶם (fr. אֲאַמֵּץ) Job xvi. 5.—Comp. Note II (γ) on p. 89.

Obs. XLIV. Before a Guttural letter, as ח, the — of the *Pi-êl* is generally NOT DROPPED except in Pause. Thus we have

אֲשַׁלֵּחֲךָ *I will send thee (m.) away*, from אֲשַׁלַּח, etc.

But in Pause the — is dropped as in אֲשַׁלְּחֶךָּ.

Note. A ⸴ as Slight-vowel, before ⸴ under a Guttural, requires no remark, as that is what the Student would expect of course.

Obs. XLV. The Pause-form of the Aff. ךָ ⸴ *thee (m.)* is not only : ךָ ⸴, but also : ךְ ⸴, as seen in the last-cited example. Comp. Note *ε* (ii.) on Tab. XXVIII.

Obs. XLVI. This is often so in the case of Verbs ל"ה with this Aff. in Pause, as in : אֲצַוֶּךָ Pause-form of אֲצַוְּךָ (Fut. *Pi.* 1 s., fr. צוה), And so in the forms : תּוֹרֶךָ and : אוֹרְךָ on p. 282.

Note But the form : ךְ ⸴ (without the Dagesh) also occurs, as in : יוֹרְךָ on p. 282.

Obs. XLVII. Verbs having for their 3ᵈ Rt-letter ה *Quiescent* drop this ה on receiving Pron. Affs., as seen above and in Tab. XXX.

Obs. XLVIII. By reason of the loss of a syllable thus there is no room for the operation of the great Rule of § 59 [comp. Obs. XXXIV, above], and therefore such forms as עָשָׂתְהוּ, עָשָׂהוּ, etc. [Tab. XXX], retain the vowel of their 1ˢᵗ Rt-letter instead of its being dropped as in פְּקָדַתְהוּ, פְּקָדֻהוּ, etc., Tab. XXV.

Obs. XLIX. For other forms we may refer to the Tables and the Notes thereon.

Note (i.) Verbs ל״ה in the 3 s. *m.* Past take the full Affix הוּ *him*, rather than וֹ; thus,

עָשָׂהוּ *he made him* (fr. עָשָׂה *he made*) Ps. xcv. 5,

קָנָהוּ *he bought it m.* (fr. קָנָה *he bought*) Lev. xxvi. 24.

(ii.) The 3ᵈ Rt-letter ה is dropped even with an Affix having *Shva* before it; thus,

* עָשְׂךָ *He made thee m.* (fr. עָשָׂה) Deut. xxxii 6,

וְנָחֲךָ *and He will guide thee m.* (fr. נָחָה *he guided*, with וֹ pref.) Is. lviii. 11.

(iii.) Special attention may be called to the 3 s. *f.* Past forms with Affixes, such as

עֲשָׂתְהוּ and †עֲשָׂתוּ, †עֲשָׂתָה, etc., in Tab. XXX; and so in

עֲשָׂתְנִי (3 s. *f* Past *K.*, with Aff *me*, Pause-form) Job xxxiii. 4,

הֶעֱלָתַם (3 s. *f.* Past *Hφ.*, with Aff. *them m.*) Josh. ii. 6.

The student will see at once the similarity between the form of the Verb in these words and the shortened form of the 3 s. *f.* Past viz. עָשָׂת‡ instead of עָשֹׂת (like נָלְתָה).

---

* קָנֶךָ Deut. xxxii. 6, is the Pause-form for קָנְךָ,—§ 167 (ii. *a*).

† And so in וּכְלָתּוּ *Pi.* Past 3 s *f.* (כִּלְתָה), with וֹ pref. and Aff. *him*, Zech. v. 4, and צִוַּתָה *Pi.* Past 3 s. *f.* (צִוְּתָה), with Aff. *her*, Ruth iii. 6.

‡ This shortened form was just mentioned in Note III. *μ* (p 172). It is not limited to the *Kal;* for not only do the *Pi-el* words in the preceding Note (†) seem to refer to it, but we have also the

Hφ. Past 3 s. *f.* וְהִרְצָת (fr. רצה), with וֹ pref. Lev. xxvi. 34, and הָלְאָת (fr. לאה), with ◌ֲ for ◌ֳ as in הָגְלָה 3 s. *m* Tab. XXII, Ez. xxiv. 12, and

Hoph. Past 3 s. *f.* הָגְלָת twice in Jer. xiii. 19.

These examples are cited by R. D. Kimk͟hi in the *Michlol.*

Obs. L.　The Rule of § 162 (*e*, ii), viz. that "the ⁓ rather than the ʼ⁓
form" of the Fut. *H φ.* is used in certain cases, must not be
supposed to hold when Pron-Affs are attached. In this
case the the *Long-K͞hirik* is preferred, and is either

(α) *Defective* (Pt. I, § 13), as in such forms as
נִיפָּקְרֵם ,וַתִּפָּקְרֵהוּ etc.,—or

(β) *Full*, as in such forms as
נֵיפָּקִירֵם ,וַתִּפָּקִירֵהוּ, etc.

Note.　Defective *Long-K͞hirik* and Defective *Shurik** [Pt. 1, § 14] occur often
in long Verb-forms—especially when there would otherwise be more than one
Quiescent letter in the word.　Perhaps it may be said that

(i.) This is a matter of כתיב [Pt. I, § 74], and

(ii) The Student had best use the Fᴜʟʟ spelling always.

---

* As in תַּשְׁלִיכָהוּ Ex. i. 22, וַיַּשְׁלִיכֵם Josh. x. 27, יַשְׁמִיעֵנוּ Is. xliii. 9, etc.

EXERCISE XLV.

*(To be translated into English, with the help of the Glossary at
the end of the book.)*

זָכְרֵנִי[1] יְיָ : צְרַפְתַּנִי[2] ... : צְרַפְתָּנוּ[2] כִּצְרָף[3]־כָּסֶף : וַתֹּאמֶר[4]

צִיּוֹן עֲזָבַנִי[5] יְיָ וַאדֹנָי שְׁכֵחָנִי[6] : לָכֵן עֲנַקְתְּמוֹ[7] גַאֲוָה : וּבֹשֶׁת פָּנַי

כִּסַּתְנִי[8] : אֲפָפוּנִי[9] מַיִם עַד נֶפֶשׁ תְּהוֹם יְסֹבְבֵנִי[10] : שַׁתַּנִי[11] בְּבוֹר

תַּחְתִּיּוֹת[12] : כָּל זֹאת בָּאַתְנוּ[13] : וְלִבִּי עֲזָבָנִי[5] : אַל תַּעַזְבֵנִי[5] יְיָ :

בְּיוֹם צָרָתִי אֶקְרָאֶךָ[14] כִּי תַעֲנֵנִי[15] :

מִמַּכּוֹתַיִךְ[16] אֶרְפָּאֵךְ[17] נְאֻם יְיָ : אַהֲבַת[18] עוֹלָם אֲהַבְתִּיךְ[19] :

וְאָנֹכִי לֹא אֶשְׁכָּחֵךְ[6] : הֵן עַל כַּפַּיִם חַקֹּתִיךְ[20] : עוֹד אֶבְנֵךְ[21]

וְנִבְנֵית[21] : וְקִבַּצְתִּים[22] מִיַּרְכְּתֵי[23] אָרֶץ : אוֹלִיכֵם[24] אֶל נַחֲלֵי מָיִם :

---

[1] זכר to remember.   [2] צרף to try (as silver and gold, by melting).   [3] See
the preceding Note. (The word being unaccented here, the ־ָ (*ŏ*) stands instead
of the ־ִ of כִּצְרָף; comp. § 168 (i).)   [4] אמר to say.   [5] עזב to forsake.   [6] שכח
to forget. [The Past *K.* is found with the ־ַ of the פָּעַל form in the following:
—(*a*) the 3 s. *m.* with Aff. *me* in Pause, (*β*) the 3 s. *f.* in Pause (שְׁכָחָה, Prov. ii.
17), and (*γ*) the 3 pl. with Affs. *me* (שְׁכֵחוּנִי and שְׁכֵחָנִי), and *thee f.* (שְׁכֵחוּךְ);
Comp. Tab. XXV, Note (*a*)].   [7] ענק to adorn (as with a chain, or necklace).
[8] בסה *Pi.* to cover.   [9] אפף to encompass.   [10] סבב *K.* to come round, to go
about,   *Pi.* to take about, lead about.   [11] שית to put, place [comp. § 226, and
§ 183 (*β*)].   [12] *lit.* places-below, *i.e.* low-depths. (This word, with the בּוֹר before
it, is an expression for "a pit of low-depths" = "a very deep dungeon pit."
[13] בוא to come, to come upon (p. 272).   [14] קרא to call, to call upon.   [15] ענה to
answer.   [16] מַכָּה a wound, Tab. VI.   [17] רפא to heal.   [18] [with] love of,—see
§ 86.   [19] אהב to love.   [20] חקק   to engrave   [21] בנה *K.* to build, *Nφ.* to be
built   [22] קבץ *Pi.* to collect.   [23] from the recesses of   [24] ילך *K.* to go,   *Hφ.*.

מֹזְרֶה[25] יִשְׂרָאֵל[35] יְקַבְּצֶנּוּ[22] וּשְׁמָרוֹ[26] כְּרֹעֶה[27] עֶדְרוֹ[31] ׃ יִמְצָאֵהוּ[28] בְּאֶרֶץ

מִדְבָּר · · · יְסֹבְבֶנְהוּ[10] יְבוֹנְנֵהוּ[29] יִצְּרֶנְהוּ[30] כְּאִישׁוֹן[31] עֵינוֹ ׃

וְשִׂמַּחְתִּים[32] מִיגוֹנָם[33] ׃ זֶבֶר[1] אֶזְכְּרֶנּוּ[1] עוֹד ׃ בְּחַרְתִּיךְ[34] בְּכוֹר

עָנִי ׃

אֲנִי יְיָ אֱעֶנֵם[15] אֱלֹהֵי יִשְׂרָאֵל לֹא אֶעֶזְבֵם[6] ׃ אֲנִי הַעִירוֹתִהוּ[35]

בְצֶדֶק · · · בָּרוּךְ[36] יְיָ *שֶׁלֹּא נְתָנָנוּ[37] טֶרֶף לְשִׁנֵּיהֶם[38] ׃

בַּצָּר[14] קָרָאתָ וָאֲחַלְּצֶךָּ[39] אֶעֶנְךָ[15] בְּסֵתֶר רָעַם ׃ וָאֶרְמְסֵם[40]

בַּחֲמָתִי[41] וְיִז[42] נִצְחָם[43] עַל בְּגָדַי · · · חֲמָתִי[41] הִיא סְמָכָתְנִי[44] ׃

אֱלֹהִים יְחָנֵּנוּ[45] וִיבָרְכֵנוּ[36] ׃ זֶה אֵלִי וְאַנְוֵהוּ[46] אֱלֹהֵי אָבִי

וַאֲרֹמְמֶנְהוּ[47] ׃ תְּרֹמֹת יְכַסִּימוֹ[48] ׃ עוֹד אוֹדֶנּוּ[49] ׃ תְּבָאֵמוֹ[13]

וְתִטָּעֵמוֹ[50] ׃ יְבָרֶכְךָ[36] יְיָ וְיִשְׁמְרֶךָ[26] ׃ יָאֵר[51] יְיָ פָּנָיו אֵלֶיךָ וִיחֻנֶּךָּ[45] ׃

· · · וָאֹהֲבְךָ[19] וּבֵרַכְךָ[36] וְהִרְבֶּךָ[52] ׃ יְיָ שֹׁמְרֶךָ[53] ׃ יוֹמָם[53] הַשֶּׁמֶשׁ לֹא

to cause to go, to conduct. [25] זרה *Pi.* to scatter. [26] שמר to keep, to guard. [27] רעה to act as a shepherd. N.B. The *K.* Partic(1) s. *m.* is used for a shepherd. [28] מצא to find. [29] בון or בין *K.* to understand, *Pi.* to instruct. [30] נצר to preserve. [31] as the pupil of. [32] שמח *K.* to be glad, *Pi.* to gladden. [33] ינון sorrow. [34] בחר to choose. [35] עור *Hφ.* to rouse up. [36] ברך *K.*† and *Pi.* to bless. [37] נתן to give. [38] שֵׁן a tooth (*Dual.* שְׁנַּיִם). [39] חלץ *Pi.* to deliver. [40] רמס to trample. [41] חֵמָה hot anger, wrath. [42] נזה to be sprinkled, p. 296. [43] נֵצַח used here for *life-blood, strength;*—Tab. X. 2. [44] סמך to uphold. [45] חנן to be gracious to. [46] נוה (see p. 293). [47] רום *K.* to be high, *Pi.* to exalt, to extol. [48] See No. 8, and Tab. XXX [Note β (8)]. [49] ידה *Hφ.* to praise, etc.,—pp. 281 & 282. [50] נטע to plant. [51] אור *K.* to shine, *Hφ.* to make to shine. [52] רבה *K.* to be many, *Hφ.* to make to be many, to multiply. [53] in the day-

---

* For the prefix שֶׁ *who, which, that,* see the latter part of Note (*d*) on p. 24.

† N.B. The KAL in this sense is used only in the Partic (2) of § 139 (γ), & Infin.

יַכֶּכָּה[54] וְיָרֵחַ בַּלָּיְלָה ׃ יְיָ יִשְׁמָרְךָ[26] מִכָּל רָע ׃ יְהַלְלוּהוּ[55] שָׁמַיִם

וָאָרֶץ ׃ יְיָ זִכְרָנוּ יְבָרֵךְ[36] ׃ וּמְשִׁירֵי אֲהוֹדֶנּוּ[49] ׃ אֵלִי אַתָּה

וְאוֹדֶךָ[49] ׃ מִי לֹא יִירָאַךָ[50] מֶלֶךְ הַגּוֹיִם כִּי לְךָ יָאָתָה[57] ׃ יוֹדוּךָ[49]

עַמִּים אֱלֹהִים יוֹדוּךָ[49] עַמִּים כֻּלָּם ׃ יְבָרְכֵנוּ[36] אֱלֹהִים אֱלֹהֵינוּ ׃

אוֹדְךָ[49] בָעַמִּים אֲדֹנָי אֲזַמֶּרְךָ[58] בַּלְאֻמִּים ׃

הוֹרֵנִי[59] יְיָ דַּרְכֶּךָ וּנְחֵנִי[60] בְּדֶרֶךְ מִישׁוֹר[61] ׃ אַתָּה יְיָ עֲזַרְתַּנִי[62]

וְנִחַמְתָּנִי[63] ׃

PSALM XXIII.

(To be translated into English, with the help of the Glossary at the end of the book).

יְיָ רֹעִי[27] לֹא אֶחְסָר[54]

בִּנְאוֹת[65] דֶּשֶׁא יַרְבִּיצֵנִי[66]

עַל מֵי מְנוּחֹת[67] יְנַהֲלֵנִי[68]

נַפְשִׁי יְשׁוֹבֵב[60]

יַנְחֵנִי[60] בְמַעְגְּלֵי[70] צֶדֶק

לְמַעַן[71] שְׁמוֹ

time. [54] נכה *Hφ.* to smite, to strike,—pp. 298 & 299. [55] הלל *Pi.* to praise (Dagesh F. is often dropped from the ל). [56] ירא to fear, p. 287. [57] יאה to be becoming, fitting, suitable,—p. 280. [58] זמר *Pi.* to hymn. [59] ירה *Hφ.* to teach, point out to,—pp. 288 & 289. [60] נחה *K.* and *Hφ.* to guide, lead, (p. 296). [61] right, rectitude,—see § 86. [62] עזר to help. [63] נחם *Pi.* to comfort. [64] חסר to lack. [65] in pastures of,—see § 86 [66] רבץ *K.* to lie down, *Hφ.* to cause to lie down. [67] rest (*lit.* rests). [68] נהל *Pi.* to lead gently. [69] שוב *K.* to return, *Pi* to restore, and to refresh. [70] in the paths of. [71] for the sake of. [72] ילך to go.

גַּם כִּי אֵלֵךְ[72] בְּגֵיא צַלְמָוֶת

לֹא אִירָא[68] רָע כִּי אַתָּה עִמָּדִי[73]

שִׁבְטְךָ וּמִשְׁעַנְתֶּךָ

הֵמָּה יְנַחֲמֻנִי[68]

תַּעֲרֹךְ[74] לְפָנַי שֻׁלְחָן

נֶגֶד צֹרְרָי[75]

דִּשַּׁנְתָּ[76] בַשֶּׁמֶן רֹאשִׁי

כּוֹסִי רְוָיָה[77]

אַךְ טוֹב וָחֶסֶד יִרְדְּפוּנִי[78]

כָּל יְמֵי חַיָּי

וְשַׁבְתִּי[69]* בְּבֵית יְיָ

לְאֹרֶךְ יָמִים :

[73] with me. [74] עָרַךְ to set in order, array, prepare. [75] צָרַר to distress, to be an enemy to. [76] דָּשַׁן Pi. to anoint-richly. [77] fulness;—[a cup of] fulness=the [cup that] "runneth over" of the E. V. [78] רָדַף to pursue, to follow.

* There are various opinions respecting this word:—

The translation "*my abiding, or dwelling*, [shall be] in the etc.", corresponds to the word שַׁבְתִּי (*K.* Infin., שֶׁבֶת, with Aff. 1 s.) from יָשַׁב Tab. XVIII, instead of שַׁבְתִּי. Some suppose that the Root שׁוּב *to return* is used here in the sense of the Root יָשַׁב *to abide* or *dwell.* And some suppose that the word should stand thus—וְיָשַׁבְתִּי (*K.* Past 1 s., with ו, from יָשַׁב) *and I will abide* or *dwell.* The strict sense of וְשַׁבְתִּי as it stands is *and I will return.*

*** The following Exercises are partly taken from the Exercises in the former Grammar.

Note (i) Help required for rendering the English into Hebrew is here given UNDER the several words

(ii) Words connected by hyphens are all comprehended in the Hebrew which stands under them.

(iii.) Some additional help required is occasionally given in Footnotes.

EXERCISE XLVI.

(*To be translated into Hebrew.*)

And he-returned into the house and took the child and restored him*
Hφ. שׁוּב   יֶלֶד   +לקח   בַּיִת   (§ 71)   שׁוּב

to his mother.   And he-turned this-way-and-that and saw that
אֶל   אֵם (see vocab.)   פנה   כּה וָכֹה   רָאָה כִּי

there-was-no man, and he-killed him* and hid him* in the sand.
אֵין אִישׁ   מוּת *Hφ.*   טמן   חוֹל

And the king‡ said 'Fetch-ye (*m.*) me a sword and cut him* into two and
מֶלֶךְ אָמַר לקח   לִי חֶרֶב   גזר§   לְ

give the half to one (*f.*) and the half to the-other.'   And
נתן חֲצִי אַחַת   חֲצִי   אַחַת § 99, Note (†).

I-cried-out and said, 'In-no-wise-kill-him' (Hebr. *to kill* *kill-ye m.*
+צעק   אמר   Infin. Abs. מוּת *Hφ.*

him not*), and they (*m.*)-gave him* to me. · And she-took the child
(Obs. IV. p. 93.)   נתן   לקח   יֶלֶד

and kissed him*,, and she-lifted-up her voice and wept.
נשק+ Tab. XIX.   נשא   קוֹל   בכה (Apocop.)

EXERCISE XLVII.

And I-asked him* saying 'What mayest-thou-be-seeking?'
+שׁאל   Tab. XVII, Note (†, ii).   בקשׁ *Pi.* Fut.

---

* Affix.   + Fut. (--).   ‡ Tense before Noun.   § Fut. (-·-).

and he answered me* that his brethren he [was] seeking. And
עָנָה   כִּי   אָח Tab. XIII.   בקשׁ Pĭ. Partic

they-said to-each-other (Hebr. *a man to his brother*), 'Come-ye and
אמר   אֶל אישׁ   אָח   ילך Tab XVIII.

let-us-slay him*, and let-us-cast-him* into one-of the pits, and-we-will-say
†הרג   שׁלך *Hφ*.   אַחַד ב   בּרות   Past w. ו pref.

An evil beast hath-devoured him*.' But Reuben‡ delivered him* from
חַיָה רָעָה *f.*   אכל   ו רְאובן   נצל *Hφ*.

their hand and said 'We-will-not   smite him* mortally, cast-ye
יָד   אמר   נכה *Hφ*. (p. 299)   נפשׁ שׁלך *Hφ*.

him into this pit,'—in-order to-deliver him from their hand to §restore
אֶל בּור   לְמַעַן נצל *Hφ*.   שׁוב *Hφ*.

him* to his father. · And they-stripped him* as-regards his coat
אֶל אָב Tab. XIII.   פשׁט *Hφ*.   את   ‖כָּתֹנֶת

and they-took him* and cast him into the pit. And Juda‡ said 'Let-us-sell
†לקח   § 71   יְהודָה   †מכר

him*, and our hand let-it-not be upon him.' And they-sold him* to
יָד *f.* Obs. IV. p. 93.   עַל היה   לְ

the Ishmaelites, and they-took-him*-down to Egypt. A king‡ sent
יִשְׁמְעאלים   ירד *Hφ*.   § 71 מִצְרַיִם   שׁלח מֶלֶך

and loosed him*.
נתר *Hφ*. Tab. XIX.

EXERCISE XLVIII.

And he-finished charging-them (Hebr. *to §charge them**), and he-expired
כלה *Pĭ*.   צוה *Pĭ*.   **†גוע

and died. My father adjured me* saying 'In my
מות   שׁבע אָב *Hφ*   Tab. XVII, Note (†, ii).

grave which I-dug for me in the land of Canaan, there (Heb. *thither*)
קֶבֶר Tab. X. 2.   ברה לְ   אֶרֶץ   כְּנַעַן   שָׁמָה

---

* Affix.   † (Fut. (⸗).   ‡ Tense before Noun.   § Infin. w. לְ prefixed.
‖ With Affs., כָּתָנְתִּי etc.   ¶ Fut. (⸗).
** The ו is *Consonantal* here.

shalt-thou-(*m.*)-bury me*.' Go-up and bury-thou (*m.*) thy father as
+קבר עלה כַּאֲשֶׁר

he-adjured thee*. All that I-shall-command thee* (*m.*), thou-shalt-
כָּל אֲשֶׁר צוה ‡*Pi.*

certainly-do (Hebr. *to-do* *thou-shalt-do*) it* (*m.*); and I-will-bless thee*,
Infin. Abs. עשה ברך *Pi.*

and I-will-preserve thee* in all thy ways JAH§ hath-indeed-
+שמר דֶּרֶךְ Tab. X. 1. יה

corrected (Hebr. *to-correct,* *He-hath-corrected*) me*; but to the death
Pi. Infin , (‒) form. יסר *Pi.* מָוֶת ו

He-hath-not given me*.— And I-took ‖ them (*m*) and I-passed-them-over
נתן לקח

(Hebr. *and I-caused-them*-to-pass-over*) the brook; and I-was-left
עבר *Hφ.* נַחַל יתר *Nφ.* (Tab. XVIII).

by-myself, and there-wrestled one with me until the-going-up-of the dawn.
לְבַדִּי אבק *Nφ.* אִישׁ עִם עַד עלה שַׁחַר

And-when he-said 'Let-me-go (Heb. *Send-away-thou m. me**) for the dawn§
ו שלח *Pi.* כִּי

hath-gone-up,' then I-answered-him* 'I-will-not let-thee*-go except thou-
עלה ו ענה שלח *Pi.* כִּי אִם

hast-blessed me*.'
ברך *Pi.*

EXERCISE XLIX.

And these words§ which I [am] commanding thee (*m.*) to-day (Hebr.
דָּבָר (*m.*)

the-day) shall-be ¶ on thy heart. And thou-shalt-impress ¶ them* upon
היה לֵבָב שנן *Pi.* (Tab. XIV).

(Hebr. *to*) thy sons. And-thou-shalt-write ¶ them* on the posts of
בֵּן Tab. XIII. כתב מְזוּזָה

thy house, and at (בּ) thy gates. I will-bring you (*m.*)* into the land of
בַּיִת שַׁעַר בוא *Hφ.* אֶל אֶרֶץ (*f.*)

the nations which (Hebr. *which it**) I-have-given to you to possess it*.
גּוֹיִם (*m*) נתן ירש Tab XVIII.

And I-will-give ¶-them*-up before-you, and ye-shall-smite ¶ them.
נתן פָּנִים w. לְ pref , & Aff. נכה *Hφ.*

---

* Affix. + Fut. (‒). ‡ The ו is *Consonantal* here.
§ Tense before Noun. ‖ Note (A) on Tab. XIX. ¶ Past with ו.

The king‡ of Jericho sought the   men   whom* Joshua sent. And
מֶלֶךְ   יְרִיחוֹ בקשׁ *Pi.*   p. 46 (*l.*)   שָׁלַח יְהוֹשֻׁעַ

the woman‡ said, Pursue-ye (*m.*) quickly after-them that ye-may-overtake
אִשָּׁה   רדף   מַהֵר   אַחֲרִיהֶם כִּי נשׂג *Hφ.*, Tab. XIX.

them*. And she had-taken-them*-up   to   the roof; and she-hid
expressed   עלה *Hφ.*   § 71. ii (*a*)   גָּג   וּטמן

them*, and the mischief‡ did-not come-upon them*.   Ye (*m*) have-
רעה   מצא   expressed

preserved-my*-life.   Flames of fire have-devoured them (*m*)*.
חיה *Hφ.*   לֶהָבָה (*f.*) אֵשׁ   אכל

EXERCISE L.

Draw-Thou me*, after-Thee we-will-run.   The king‡ hath-
וּמשׁך   אַחֲרֶיךָ   רוץ (w. ה at the end.)   מֶלֶךְ

brought-me*-into His chambers. Let-me*-see thy (*f.*) countenance, let-me*-
בוא *Hφ.*   חֶדֶר   ראה   pl. of מַרְאֶה

hear   thy (*f.*) voice. I-have-taken-hold-upon Him*, and I-will-not let-
שׁמע *Hφ.*   אחז

Him*-go.
רפה *Hφ.*

The   watchmen   found‡ me*...; they-smote me* they-wounded
Partic. (1) *K.* of שׁמר   מצא   נכה *Hφ.*   פצע

me*....   Whither turned thy (*f.*) Love? for we-will-seek Him* with thee.
אָנָה פנה   דוֹד (*m.*) וּ   בקשׁ *Pi.*   עִם

Daughters‡   saw   her*, and they (*m.*) called-her*-happy.   Many
בת Tab. XIII.   ראה   אִשֵּׁר *Pi.*

waters shall-not be-able   to-quench Love‖, and floods shall-not
מַיִם   יכל *Hŏph.*   כבה *Pi.* אַהֲבָה (*f.*) נְהָרוֹת (*m.*)

overwhelm it*.   Lo! THE-LORD thy God‡ hath-loved thee (*m.*)*:
וּשׁטף   הִגֵּה   אֱלֹהִים אהב (the — form.)

be-strong, yea (וֹ) be-strong.
חזק (— form.)

APPENDIX.

APPENDIX.

I. Significations of the Voice-forms.

We may give here a few instances of what was mentioned briefly at the foot of page 70, *viz* that other English 'forms of rendering'—more or less different from the main significations of the Voices in general—are sometimes required. Thus,

(*a*) In Gen. i. 4, the Hiph-îl וַיַּבְדֵּל (Fut. 3 s. *m.*) may fairly be rendered "*and He divided*" (or by some such expression, as "*and He made separation*"). The expression "*and He caused to* separate" is not English, and English expressions must of course be used in an English rendering.

(β) So, in Gen. i. 11 תַּדְשֵׁא הָאָרֶץ דֶּשֶׁא is fairly rendered "*let the earth bring-forth grass.*" The Hebrew expression תַּדְשֵׁא דֶּשֶׁא, in which the Verb is from the same Root דשא as the Noun, cannot be rendered *exactly* in English. Similarly in the case of מַזְרִיעַ זֶרַע in the same verse, some such expression as "producing seed" or "yielding seed" must be given.

(γ) In the case of some Roots, as observed at the foot of page 70, *altogether different* English Verbs are required for their several Voices.

(δ) We must be content, at present, to refer the Student to his Lexicon for the renderings of the several Voices of various Roots.

(ε) Also the Lexicon must be referred to as a means of finding what Voices of particular Roots are used. For

N.B. (i) Verbs are not necessarily used in all the Voices; but, on the contrary,

(ii) most Verbs are used in certain Voices only, and not in others.

(II). CERTAIN TENSE-FORMS, AND APOCOPATED FORMS.

(1) As said in § 162 (e), it is the *Rule* to have, in the Future *Kal*, the — (rather than the וֹ) form, *i.e.* יִפְקֹד rather than יִפְקוֹד, in the following three cases:

(a) with וֹ Convers., thus וַיִּפְקֹד *and he visited,*

(β) with אַל Deprecative, thus אַל יִפְקֹד *let him not visit,*

(γ) in a *positive* wish, thus יִפְקֹד *let him visit.*

(2) So also it is the *Rule* to have in *Hiph-il* the — (rather than the יִ—) form, *i.e.* יַפְקֵד rather than יַפְקִיד, in the same three cases, thus

(a) with וֹ Convers., וַיַּפְקֵד *and he caused to visit,*

(β) with אַל Deprecative, אַל יַפְקֵד *let him not cause to visit,*

(γ) in a *positive* wish, יַפְקֵד *let him cause to visit.*

(3) The same holds for other than 'Full' Verbs; and, further,

(4) Verbs ל"ה generally* have the 'Apocopated' forms in these same three cases, thus:

(a) with וֹ Conversive,—וַיִּגֶל from יִגְלֶה (*Kal*),— וַיִּגֶל from יְגַלֶּה (*Pi.*),—וַיֶּגֶל from יַגְלֶה (*Hφ.*), etc.; and so וַיַּעַשׂ from יַעֲשֶׂה, וַיְהִי from יִהְיֶה, etc.; and so in other Persons, as וַתְּהִי from תִּהְיֶה, וַתֵּתַע from תִּתְעֶה, etc.;

(β) with אַל Deprecative,—אַל תְּגַל from תְּגַלֶּה (*Pi.*), אַל תֵּפֶן from תִּפְנֶה (*Kal*),—אַל יְהִי and אַל תְּהִי from יִהְיֶה and תִּהְיֶה, etc.;

(γ) in a *positive* wish,—יִגֶל *let it m. go captive,* from יִגְלֶה,— יְהִי *let it m. be* (or *let there be*), from יִהְיֶה, etc.

[Further remarks on Verb-forms had better be reserved for a subsequent Section of this Appendix. Now we may not delay any longer to give the following]

---

* Not always, see the Note (‡) on p. 171.

(III). Analysis of some Verb-forms.

When the Student first attempts to read the Hebrew Bible, he is likely to find his progress somewhat slow and perhaps wearisome by reason of his inability to analyze at once the Verb-forms with which in such great variety he will meet at every step. It is therefore advisable to offer him some little help, at first, to enable him to recognize more easily the various forms, and to familiarize him (by references) with the several Tables and Sections in which such forms are classified and spoken of. To some extent the Exercises will have already familiarized him with these, class by class. A very little help now will enable him to combine them all. The following Analysis of the Verbs found in the first three, and the twelfth, chapters of the Book of Genesis, will doubtless be amply sufficient for him. With the Prefixes and Affixes to Nouns, etc., he will be sufficiently familiarized already by the Exercises; he will need no help for these now,—with the exception of a word or two, here and there, perhaps. It may however be well to give now the following Rules :—

Rule I. When the Conjunctive ו stands between words, or groups of words, which form a Couple,—if the second word of the Couple, or the first word of the second group, is either

(1) Monosyllabic, or

(2) Dissyllabic with the Accent on the Penultima, the ו generally takes ־ָ;

[N.B. unless the first letter has ־ָ, in the word to which the ו is prefixed] ;—thus,

(i) in Gen. viii. 22 we have

זֶרַע וְקָצִיר וְקֹר וָחֹם וְקַיִץ וָחֹרֶף וְיוֹם וָלַיְלָה *וכו׳ *seed-time and harvest, and cold and heat, and summer and winter, and day and night,* etc.

Here the Nouns are arranged in couples, two and two. And

(α) זֶרַע וְקָצִיר *seed-time and harvest,* the first Couple, has for its second word the Dissyllabic קָצִיר which is accented on the *last* syllable (not on the Penultima) in accordance with Pt. I, § 55 (8, ii) and (9, a). Hence this word does not fall under Rule I above.—For the Accents ـٰ *T'líshá* and ـٰ *Pázêr,* see Pt. I, § 66 (15 & 13). As said in Note (‡) there, the Accent ـٰ stands "always over the first consonant of its word." It affects the *last syllable* here.

(β) קֹר וָחֹם *cold and heat,* the second Couple, has for its second word the Monosyllabic חֹם; before which the וֹ takes ־ָ in accordance with Rule I above.—For the Accents ـٰ *Gêrêsh* and ـٰ *Kadma,* see Pt. I, §§ 66 (16) & 67 (3).

(γ) קַיִץ וָחֹרֶף *summer and winter,* the third Couple, has for its second word the Dissyllabic חֹרֶף accented on the Penultima; before which the וֹ takes ־ָ as above.—For the Accents ־ָ *T'vîr* and ־ָ *Dargá,* see Pt. I, §§ 66 (11) and 67 (4).

(δ) So also יוֹם וָלַיְלָה *day and night,* the fourth Couple, has for its second word the Dissyllabic לַיְלָה accented on the Penultima; before which the וֹ takes ־ָ as above.—For the Accents ־ָ *Tiphkhá* and ־ָ *Mê-r'khá,* see Pt. I, §§ 66 (6) and 67 (6).

But (ii) it is not necessary that the Couple should consist of *two words* only. We have, for instance, in Gen. iii. 22

---

* This וכו׳ signifies "etc." It stands for וְכֻלּוֹ *and the whole of it.*

וְאָכַל וָחַי לְעֹלָם׃ *and eat and live for ever.* Here the COUPLE
consists of two parts (1) וְאָכַל *and eat,* and (2) וָחַי לְעֹלָם *and live
for ever;* and the first word of this second part has ־ָ to the וֹ
prefixed to the accented Monosyllable חַי.—For the Accents
(־ָ׃) *Sillûk Soph-pásûk,* ־ *Mê-r'khá,* and ־ *Tıphkhá,* see Pt. I,
§§ 66 (1), 67 (6), and 66 (6).

This great Rule is not indeed *always* attended to; but it is so
much attended to in the Bible, especially in the case of TWO
WORDS so 'coupled' together, that it is best to observe the Rule
n Composition—in this case of a COUPLE OF TWO WORDS.

This Rule was stated in a very concise form in Obs. XII
on p. 139. There the Rule itself, with even the few examples
given above, would have been out of place.—In a Couplé consisting of *two words,* the second word will mostly have a Disjunctive Accent by reason of the Stop (greater or less) made at
the end of the 'Couple.' It was necessary, as seen in (ii),
not to limit the occurrence to the case of the Accent being
Disjunctive.

[This Rule will be found more fully stated and illustrated in
Pt. II, § 94.]

RULE II. The prefixes בְּכְל also sometimes take ־ָ before an
Accented Vowel, as seen in Pt. II, § 95; thus we have לָמָֽיִם׃
instead of לְמַיִם at the end of Gen. i. 6; and so לָמֵֽת׃ at the
end of Deut. xiv. 1; etc.

Analysis of Verbs in Gen. i–iii.

Gen. i. 1.　בָּרָא * *He created.* Kal Past 3 s. *m.* from בְּרָא.
Tab. XXII.

v. 2.　הָיְתָה † *it f. was* (or *existed in a state of*). Kal
Past 3 s. *f.* from היה.　Tab. XXIII.

מְרַחֶפֶת [was] ‡ *moving* (al. *brooding*).　Cp. Deut.
xxxii. 11.　Pĭ-êl Partic. Sing. *f.* from רחף.
For the Partic. forms see App[x] B to Tab.
XIV, and for the ⸗ retained before ה see
Tab. XVI(2) [β, iii.—page xx.].

v. 3.　וַיֹּאמֶר § *and He said.* Kal Fut. 3 s. *m.* with ו Conversive, from אמר.　Tab. XVII (2, δ).

יְהִי *let there be.* Kal Fut. 3 s. *m.* apocopated for
יִהְיֶה, from היה.　Tab. XXIII (Note 3),
also page 170 (ε, 4).

וַיְהִי § *and there was.* Kal Fut. 3 s. *m.* apocopated
with ו Conversive, from היה (see the preceding word יְהִי).　Cp. p. 222 (4).

v. 4.　וַיַּרְא § *and He saw.* Kal Fut. 3 s. *m.* apocopated,
from ראה.　Tab. XXIII, also page 171 (η).

וַיַּבְדֵּל *and He divided* (or *made separation*).　Hĭph-îl
Fut. 3 s. *m.* with ו Conversive, from בדל.
Tab. XIV.　[For the ⸗ see § 162 (e, ii)
p. 105, and p. 222 (2)]

---

* The Tense here precedes its subject.　Cp § 162 (d, i), p. 105.　This need not be
mentioned after this page.

† The Tense here follows its Subject.　This marks Emphasis on the Subject, as
stated in § 162 (d, ii).　The Emphasis here might perhaps be brought out in English
somewhat thus: " *Now* [*as for*] *the earth, it was a confused and formless mass* ....
And God said, etc."

‡ The 'logical Copula' *was* is to be supplied in the English.　Cp. § 124.　This
need not be mentioned again.

§ See § 161 (2),—page 104.

v. 5. וַיִּקְרָא * *and He called.* KAL Fut. 3 s. *m.* with וֹ Conversive, from קְרָא. Tab. XXII.

קָרָא *He called.* KAL Past 3 s. *m.* from קְרָא. Tab. XXII.

וַיְהִי *. See the third Verb in *v.* 3.

[Note. The literal rendering of the last six words in *v.* 5 is,
as the Student will see at once, "And there was evening, and
there was morning,—one day." This literal rendering seems
plain and clear enough. It tells that, after that great moment,
when

"God said 'Let there be light,—and there was light,"
time went on; and, in due course of time, the light of the day-
time declined towards departure, "and there was evening."
And time went on still continually; and, in due course of
time, day dawned—"and there was morning." And so there
was "one day": *viz.* from the first breaking forth of the light
'offspring of heaven firstborn," to the time when there was
light again—at the breaking forth of the light of the morning.

Obs. Some give "the first day" for יוֹם אֶחָד. For this see
Note' at the end of *v.* 31.]

v. 6. וַיֹּאמֶר *. See the first Verb in *v.* 3.

יְהִי . See the second Verb in *v.* 3.

וִיהִי *and let it be.* KAL Fut. 3 s. *m.* (יְהִי) with
וֹ Conjunctive prefixed [§ 3 (*b*)], from הָיָה.
Tab. XXIII.—See also *v.* 3.

מַבְדִּיל *one m. dividing* (or *making separation*). HIPH-îL
Partic. Sing. *m.* from בדל. Tab. XIV.

v. 7. וַיַּעַשׂ *and He made.* KAL Fut. 3 s. *m.* with וֹ Conversive,
from עשה. See p. 171 (ζ), and Supp^t to Tab.
XXIII.

---

v. 7 (contin.) וַיַּבְדֵּל. See the second Verb in *v.* 4.

וַיְהִי. See the third Verb in *v.* 3.

v. 8. וַיִּקְרָא. See the first Verb in *v.* 5.

וַיְהִי. See the third Verb in *v.* 3.

v. 9. וַיֹּאמֶר. See the first Verb in *v.* 3.

יִקָּווּ *let them be gathered together.* Niph-Āl
Fut. 3 pl. *m.* from קוה. Tab. XXIII.

וְתֵרָאֶה *and let it f. be seen.* Niph-Āl Fut. 3 s. *f.*
with וְ Conjunctive, from ראה. Tab.
XXIII. The ⸗ is instead of ⸗ *followed
by Dagesh,* as in § 182 (i).

וַיְהִי. See the third Verb in *v.* 3.

v. 10. וַיִּקְרָא. See the first Verb in *v.* 5.

קָרָא. See the second Verb in *v.* 5.

וַיַּרְא. See the first Verb in *v.* 5.

v. 11. וַיֹּאמֶר. See *v.* 3.

תַּדְשֵׁא [דֶּשֶׁא] *let it f. bring-forth* [*grass*]. Hiph-îl
Fut. 3 s. *f.* from דשא. § 162 (*e,* ii),
p. 105; & p. 222 (2).

[Note. This use of a Verb and Noun together, from the same
Root, is often found—especially where the repetition of the
Root implies *abundance, multitude, greatness,* or emphasizes that
which the Root expresses. Cp. פָּחֲדוּ פָחַד Ps. xiv. 5 *they were
greatly afraid* (lit. *they feared a fear*), etc.; and so],

מַזְרִיעַ זֶרַע *yielding seed.* Hiph-îl Partic. Sing. *m.*
from זרע.

עֹשֶׂה *yielding* (or *producing,* lit. *making*). Kal
Partic. Sing. *m.* from עשה. Tab. XXIII.

וַיְהִי. See *v.* 3.

v. 12. וַתּוֹצֵא *and it f. brought forth.* Hiph-îl Fut. 3 s. *f.*
with ו Conversive, from יצא. This Verb is both
פ' like ישב in Tab. XVIII, and ל'א like מצא
in Tab. XXI.   The — instead of '— is in
accordance with § 162 (e, ii), and p. 222 (2).

מַזְרִיעַ. See *v.* 11.   עֹשֶׂה. See *v.* 11.   וַיַּרְא. See *v.* 4.

v. 13. וַיְהִי. See *v.* 3.

v. 14. וַיֹּאמֶר. See *v.* 3.   יְהִי. See *v.* 3.

[Obs. (i). The Verb יְהִי is in the Singular, but מְאֹרֹת *lights*
in the Plural. This is often the case when the Verb comes
first, especially when the Verb is used as here in a somewhat
Impersonal manner.   Cp. וִיהִי כֹּהֲנִי בָמוֹת 1 Kings xiii. 33
that there-might-be priests of high-places.   So in Gen. x. 25
וּלְעֵבֶר יֻלַּד שְׁנֵי בָנִים *and to Eber there-were-born two sons,* cp.
Gen. xli. 50.

N.B. A Singular Verb may occur with a Plural Noun in
certain other cases also, to be mentioned elsewhere.

Obs. (ii). The Plural of the Masculine Noun מָאוֹר has the
Feminine form.   Cp. § 43.

Obs. (iii). The word מָאוֹר signifies *a light,* i.e. *a light-giver*
φωστήρ (LXX).   In *vv.* 3–5 the word is אוֹר (φῶς LXX).]

לְהַבְדִּיל *to divide* (or *make separation*). *Hiph-il* Infin.
with ל prefix, from בדל.

וְהָיוּ *and they shall be* (or *let them be*). Kal Past
3 plu. with ו prefixed, from היה.   Tab. XXIII.

v. 15. וְהָיוּ. See *v.* 14.

לְהָאִיר *to give light* (lit. *to cause light*). *Hiph-il* Infin.
with ל prefixed, from אור.   Tab. XX.

וַיְהִי. See *v.* 3.

v. 16. וַיַּעַשׂ. See *v.* 7.

לְמֶמְשֶׁלֶת] is a Noun with ל *for* prefixed, "*for* the govern-
ance of."]

v. 17. וַיִּתֵּן and *He set* (lit. *gave*). KAL Fut. 3 s. *m.* with ו
Conversive, from נתן. Tab. XIX (B).

לְהָאִיר. See *v.* 15.

v. 18. וְלִמְשֹׁל and *to rule.* KAL Infin. with ל prefix, from
משל. Tab. XIV.

וּלְהַבְדִּיל. See *v.* 14.   וַיַּרְא. See *v.* 4.

v. 19. וַיְהִי. See *v.* 3.

v. 20. וַיֹּאמֶר. See *v.* 3.

יִשְׁרְצוּ [שָׁרַץ נ׳ ח׳] *let them bring-forth-abundantly* [*moving* creature
that hath life],—lit. *let them swarm-with* [*a*
swarm of creatures that have life].—KAL Fut.
3 pl. *m.* from שׁרץ. Tab. XIV.

יְעוֹפֵף [that] *may fly* (E.V.) PÏ-ÊL Fut. 3 s. *m.* from
עוּף. Tab. XX.—Cp. § 31.

[Note. Many prefer to render thus:—"And let fowl fly."
The word "Fowl" should then be read with EMPHASIS, because
it precedes its Verb.]

v. 21. וַיִּבְרָא and *He created.* KAL Fut. 3 s. *m.* with ו Conversive, from ברא. Tab. XXII.

[Note. The Root ברא has not occurred since *v.* 1, "In the
beginning (*or* at first) GOD CREATED the heavens and the earth."
It occurs again now in *v.* 21, at the introduction of 'animal
life'; it does not occur again till *v.* 27, "And GOD CREATED
אֶת הָאָדָם, etc." which is subsequent to the "Let us MAKE (*or*
We will MAKE) אָדָם, etc." in *v.* 20. The making of man in
the image of GOD is an act of Creation.]

v. 21 (contin.) הָרֹמֶשֶׂת *that moveth.* KAL Partic. Sing. *f.* (App[x] B to Tab. XIV) from רמש, with the ה of §§ 6 & 98.

שָׁרְצוּ *brought forth abundantly* (or *swarmed with*). KAL Past 3 pl. from שרץ. Tab. XIV.

וַיַּרְא. See *v.* 4.

v. 22. וַיְבָרֶךְ *and He blessed.* PĬ-ÊL Fut. 3 s. *m.* with ו Convers., from ברך. [App[x] to Tab. XVI (2)]. The ⸗ is for the ⸗, because the Accent is removed from the last syllable. Cp. Pt. I, § 55 (9, *b*).

לֵאמֹר *saying.* KAL Infin. with ל, from אמר. Tab. XVII [Note † (ii)].

פְּרוּ *be ye fruitful.* KAL Imper. 2 pl. *m.* from פרה. Tab. XXIII.

וּרְבוּ *and multiply.* KAL Imper. 2 pl. *m.* with ו pref., from רבה. Tab. XXIII.

וּמִלְאוּ *and fill.* KAL Imper. 2 pl. *m.* with ו pref., from מלא belonging to Tab. XXII (but the same here as in Tab. XIV).

יִרֶב *let it multiply.* KAL Fut. 3 s. *m.* apocop. from רבה. Tab. XXIII.

v. 23. וַיְהִי. See *v.* 3.

v. 24. וַיֹּאמֶר. See *v.* 3.

תּוֹצֵא *let it (f.) bring forth.* HIPH-ÎL Fut. 3 s. *f.* from יצא which is a Verb both פ״ו and ל״א. Cp. וַתּוֹצֵא in *v.* 12.

[The word חַיְתוֹ is for חַיַת which is the Constr. form of חַיָּה,

as in חַיַּת הָאָרֶץ in the next verse (25). Some speak of the form חַיְתוֹ as an *Archaic* form. Discussion of this matter must be deferred at present. We may just mention (1) the similar מַעְיְנוֹ מָיִם in Ps. cxiv. 8 for 'מַעְיָן מ, and בְּנוֹ בְעֹר Nu. xxiv. 3 & 15 (in which last, however, some have thought that the *Rt-letter* ה comes out in the וֹ); and (2) likewise the additional ִי— which is attached sometimes to a word (this ִי is termed by some 'ִי *Compaginis*') as in מַלְכִּי צֶדֶק *Melchizedech* Gen. xiv. 18,— instead of מֶלֶךְ צֶדֶק *king of righteousness*;—and so בְּנִי אֲתֹנוֹ *the colt* (lit. *son*) *of his ass* Gen. xlix. 11, instead of בֶּן אֲתֹנוֹ, etc.]

v. 24 (contin.) וַיְהִי. See *v.* 3.

    v. 25. וַיַּעַשׂ. See *v.* 7.   וַיַּרְא. See *v.* 4.

    v. 26. וַיֹּאמֶר. See *v.* 3.

        נַעֲשֶׂה *let us make* (or *We will make*). KAL Fut. 1 pl. from עשׂה. See p. 171 (ζ), and Supp[t] to Tab. XXIII.

        וְיִרְדּוּ *and let them have dominion* (or *and they shall have dominion*). KAL Fut. 3 pl. *m.* with וֹ Conjunctive, from רדה. Tab. XXIII.

[Note. The word בִּדְגַת consists of דְּגַת *the fish of* (Construct form of דָּגָה *fish* collectively) and the prefix בְּ *over*. Since there may never be two Moving Shvas together, the — of the בְּ has to become a 'Slight-Vowel.' Pt. I, § 56. Cp. § 4 (*c*) of the Exercise-book.—The Dag. L. is removed from the בּ here in accordance with Pt. I, § 48.]

        הָרֹמֵשׂ *that creepeth* (E.V.) [Cp. הָרֹמֶשֶׂת in *v.* 21.] KAL Partic. Sing. *m.* from רמשׂ, with the ה of §§ 6 & 98.

v. 27. וַיִּבְרָא. See *v.* 21.   בָּרָא. See *v.* 1.

v. 28. וַיְבָרֶךְ . See *v.* 22.   וַיֹּאמֶר . See *v.* 2.

פְּרוּ וּרְבוּ וּמִלְאוּ . See *v.* 22.

וְכִבְשֻׁהָ *and subdue it.* KAL Imper. 2 pl. *m.* with
prefix וְ and Aff. הָ *it* (*f.*), from כבשׁ.
Tab. XXVII.

וּרְדוּ *and have dominion.* KAL Imper. 2 pl. *m.* with
וְ pref., from רדה . Tab. XXIII.

הָרֹמֶשֶׂת . See *v.* 21.

v. 29. וַיֹּאמֶר . See *v.* 3.

נָתַתִּי *I have given.* KAL Past 1 s. from נתן.
Tab. XIX (B).

זֹרֵעַ [זֶרַע] *bearing* (lit. *seeding*) [*seed*]. KAL Partic. s. *m.*
from זרע . Tab. XIV.

[Note. זָרַע (a little later in this verse) is merely the Pause-
form of זֶרַע . Cp. Tab. X, Note (*).]

יִהְיֶה *it shall be.* KAL Past 3 s. *m.* from היה.
Tab. XXIII.

[Note. לְאָכְלָה *for food* is best taken to be a Noun of the same
form as חָכְמָה *wisdom*, with לְ. (The ◌ָ in the first syllable is *ŏ*).
Some however take לְאָכְלָה to be the 'KAL Infin. of אכל with ה
added' as in § 137 (4, iii) [p. 80]; its meaning then would be
'*to eat.*']

v. 30. רוֹמֵשׂ [כֹל *every*] *creeping* [*thing*]. KAL Partic.
Sing. *m.*, from רמשׂ . Tab. XIV. Cp. *v.* 26.

[Note (i). אֵת כָּל יֶרֶק עֵשֶׂב *all green herb* (lit. *all greenness-of
herb*). Cp. § 88.

(ii). The '*I have given*' of *v.* 29 is carried on in thought
to 'govern' also the words in (i).]

לְאָכְלָה . See *v.* 29.   וַיְהִי . See *v.* 2.

v. 31. וַיַּרְא. See *v.* 4.

עָשָׂה *He made.* KAL Past 3 s. *m.* from עָשָׂה. Tab. XXIII.

וַיְהִי. See *v.* 3.

[Note. יוֹם הַשִּׁשִּׁי lit. *a day* [*which was*] *the sixth.*

Obs. (*a*) The 'Def. Art.' ה has not appeared thus in the case of the preceding "days." The Numerals in connection with יוֹם *day* in *vv.* 5, 8, 13, 19, and 23, are respectively "*one,*" "*second*" (or "*a second*"), "*third*" (or "*a third*"), "*fourth*" (or "*a fourth*"), "*fifth*" (or "*a fifth*"). Whereas in *v.* 31 we have "*day* THE *sixth,*" literally.

(β) Many suppose that יוֹם אֶחָד in *v.* 5 may be rendered, and is to be rendered, "*the first day,*"—although the Numeral is not the word for "*first*" (viz. רִאשׁוֹן) but the word for "*one*" (viz. אֶחָד). They suppose that the word may so be rendered because the expression מֶלֶךְ אֶחָד *one king* in Is. xxiii. 15 has been rendered by some "*the first king.*" But this last rendering is, to say the least, not certainly admissible. Consequently we are not thereby convinced that the preceding supposition is correct. A little more support for that supposition may be claimed from the phrase בְּאֶחָד לַחֹדֶשׁ which occurs several times (as Gen. viii. 5 & 13, etc.), and which stands short for בְּיוֹם אֶחָד לַחֹדֶשׁ *in day* ONE *to the month*, literally (Ezra x. 16 & 17, etc.). But we must bear in mind that it is usual to employ the CARDINAL Numbers with the *day* of the month, and ORDINALS for the number of the month itself, as in Gen. viii. 13 בָּרִאשׁוֹן בְּאֶחָד לַחֹדֶשׁ *in the first* [month] *in* [day] ONE *to the month.* So we have the Ordinal בָּעֲשִׂירִי *in the tenth* [month] Gen. viii. 5; but the Cardinal בֶּעָשׂוֹר *in* [day] TEN (not בָּעֲשִׂירִי *in the* TENTH) in Lev. xvi. 29 בַּחֹדֶשׁ הַשְּׁבִיעִי

בֶּעָשׂוֹר לַחֹדֶשׁ *in the seventh month in the* [day] TEN *to the month*, etc. Such a use of the Cardinal Numbers is not quite the same as this of "*one*," and then "*a second*," "*a third*," "*a fourth*," "*a fifth*," and "THE *sixth*," in Gen. i.

Nor is this quite the same even as the "year-of* ONE" (*lit.*), in Dan. i. 21 (& ix. 1, 2, etc.), which last is in accordance with the "year-of THREE" in Dan. i. 1, and "the year-of FOUR" in 1 K. xxii. 41, and so the "year-of TWO" in 1 K. xv. 25, etc. Nor is it the same even as the "year-of THE FOURTH (וְהָרְבִיעִית)" Jer. li. 59, the "year-of THE SEVENTH (הַשְּׁבִיעִית)" Ezra vii. 8, and the "year-of THE NINTH (הַתְּשִׁיעִית)" 2 K. xxv. 1.†

It has indeed been said that "the first" is properly represented by "one," and then "second," "third," etc., follow as bearing reference to the first mentioned,—and some have thought that "first" could not be said when as yet there was no other.

Perhaps it may be well to have just mentioned here that the word actually employed in Gen. i. 5 is NOT the ordinary word for "first" (viz. רִאשׁוֹן).

It may, however, be thought to be beyond the limits of our proper business here to mention thus the few facts stated above. And we ought perhaps to add that the amount of 'authority' which may be claimed, from the opinions of 'learned' men, for rendering the words יוֹם אֶחָד (Gen. i. 5) "*the first day*" is

---

* Perhaps we may be allowed the use of this expression here, for a moment, although it is not an English expression. We give "*year-of*" as an equivalent of the Hebrew word שְׁנַת, in order to call the Reader's attention to the fact of this word being in the Construct form.

† The 'English' for these would be "the *first, third, fourth,* etc., *year.*"

simply overwhelming. But, nevertheless, these facts remain :—

(i) the words יוֹם אֶחָד strictly signify "ONE DAY,"

(ii) the ordinary Hebrew for "the first day" is a very different expression.]

Gen. ii. 1. וַיְכֻלּוּ *and they were finished.* Pŭ-Xl Fut. 3 pl. *m.*, with וֹ Conversive, from כלה. Tab. XXIII.

v. 2. וַיְכַל *and He ended* [or HAD *ended,* or *finished,* § 157 (*a*) & (*e*)]. Pĭ-êl Fut. 3 s. *m.* apocopated, with וֹ Conversive, from כלה [like יִגֶל in Tab. XXIII].

עָשָׂה *He had made.* KAL Past 3 s. *m.* from עשה. Tab. XXIII.

וַיִּשְׁבֹּת *and He rested* (or *stopped,* 'ceased'). KAL Fut. 3 s. *m.* with וֹ Conversive, from שבת. Tab. XIV.

[Note. It need scarcely be said that the word 'Sabbath (שַׁבָּת)' is from this Root.—But the word is used also in the Bible for other than 'Sabbath'-cessation, sometimes.]

v. 3. וַיְבָרֶךְ . See ch. i. 22.

וַיְקַדֵּשׁ *and He sanctified* (or *hallowed*). Pĭ-êl Fut. 3 s. *m.* with וֹ Conversive, from קדש. Tab. XIV.

שָׁבַת *He had rested* (or *ceased*). KAL Past 3 s. *m.* See *v.* 2.

בָּרָא *He created.* See ch. i. 1.

לַעֲשׂוֹת *to make.* KAL Infin. with לֹ pref. See Suppᵗ to Tab. XXIII, and § 169 (*a*).

[Note. The literal rendering of these last two words is given here. There is some rather needless controversy about the sense of them. We may not enter into that here. The literal rendering seems to bear a sufficiently clear and simple sense. Another rendering is however possible,—as will be seen a little further on in this Appendix (vi. 2, μ).]

v. 4. [Note. A slightly different arrangement in the printing of the Analysis may perhaps be admitted now, as a means of marking more distinctly what many suppose to be the commencement of a new sub-division of the Book.—It will be seen that the NAME of The Almighty (for which the E.V. gives generally "the LORD," cp. Pt. I, § 79 (2)) occurs for the first time in this verse. And it is followed immediately by אֱלֹהִים, throughout this chapt. ii. and in *vv.* 1, 8–24, of chapt. iii. Some Moderns have made what is really a serious mistake in imagining both these alike to be merely Appellative Nouns. The word אֱלֹהִים may be so termed: But the other is the NAME—the 'Proper-NAME,' if the expression may be used.— Here, however, we may but just state what has been said above, and add a caution to the Reader against adopting too hastily certain plausible theories. The thoughtful and unbiassed Student, who can afford to think for himself and to delay his adhesion to other people's theories until he has sufficient education in the subject to be able to form a fair opinion about it, will find too many instances of modern theories resting on a fundamental misconception, which are nevertheless accepted by some as 'latest results of Biblical Criticism.' We would urge the Student to labour for a knowledge of the facts and usages of the language, and we say to him boldly:— "Work your work honestly and carefully and thoughtfully, and resolve to know for yourself the truth of the matter, so far as in you lies, by THOROUGH Work."]

v. 4 (contin.) בְּהִבָּרְאָם *when they were created* (lit. *on their being created*).' NIPH-ĂL Infin. with בְּ pref. and Pron.-Aff. ם‑ָ‑ *their* (*m.*), from ברא.—Tab. XV.

עֲשׂוֹת [the] *making of.* KAL Infin. Constr. from עשׂה. Tab. XXIII and Pt. I, § 24.—This word is here 'in Construction with' the NAME יי (which is followed by the epithet אֱלֹהִים), and the 'Object' of it is אֶרֶץ וְשָׁמָיִם.

v. 5. טֶרֶם [יִהְיֶה *before*] *it was.* KAL Fut. 3 s. *m.* from היה. Tab. XXIII.

טֶרֶם [יִצְמָח *before*] *it grew.* KAL Fut. 3 s. *m.* from צמח (like יִלְבַּשׁ Tab. XIV),—in Pause, § 165 (I, *β*).

[Note. When the word טֶרֶם has a Tense after it, this Tense is generally the Future in Hebrew; probably because the time of the event referred to in the Tense is later than (and therefore yet *future* with regard to) the time to which attention is directed by the word טֶרֶם *before*, or *before-that*. But in English, events are regarded as Past or Future from the point of view of the writer or speaker rather than from consideration of relative order. Hence we have sometimes a FUTURE Tense in Hebrew even where some form of PAST is generally given in English, as in the case of the two Verbs above (and so in יַעֲלֶה *v.* 6), which may best be read on in connection with *v.* 5 thus, "and [before that] a mist went up etc." So in Gen. xix. 4 טֶרֶם יִשְׁכָּבוּ *before they lay down*, and Josh. ii. 8, etc.

N.B. (i) A Hebrew Future after טֶרֶם may of course be also rendered sometimes, in other places, by a Future in English, as in Is. lxv. 24 טֶרֶם יִקְרָאוּ *before they shall call*; and

(ii) A Past occurs a few times after טֶרֶם;—it may be rendered by the Pluperfect form '*had*' (as well as, sometimes, by an ordinary Past) ; thus, Gen. xxiv. 15 טֶרֶם כִּלָּה *before-that he had finished*,*—for which the man in his own account says, *v.* 45, "as-for-me [it was] before *I finished* (אֲכַלֶּה)†, that behold, etc." —See also 1 S. iii. 7 טֶרֶם יָדַע [it was] *before-that he had known*, followed by "*and before-that it-was-revealed* or *manifested* (Fut.)‡." And so also with בְּטֶרֶם, as in Ps. xc. 2 "before-that mountains *had-been-brought-forth* (יֻלָּדוּ Pŭ-Ăl Past 3 pl., in Pause),— Prov. viii. 25 "before-that mountains *had-been-founded* (הָטְבָּעוּ Hoph-Ăl Past 3 pl., in Pause).

(iii) In some instances the Future with טֶרֶם may (perhaps) be rendered in English by means of the Auxiliary "could"; thus, Gen. ii. 5 "before it-could-be" and "before it-could-grow,"— and so in Gen. xxiv. 45 "before I-could-finish," etc. But in some instances a *direct Past* form of rendering seems to be the most natural in English.

(iv) Gesenius' treatment of the word טֶרֶם is unsatisfactory.]

v. 5 (contin.) הִמְטִיר *He had caused rain.* Hiph-îl Past 3 s. *m.*, from מטר. Tab. XIV.

לַעֲבֹד *to till.* Kal Infin. with ל pref., from עבד. Tab. XVI (1).

v. 6. יַעֲלֶה *it went up.* Kal Fut. 3 s. *m.* from עלה, p. 171 (ƒ).

[Note. This verse seems to be best taken in connection with

---

* The Narrative treats his "finishing to speak" as a Past event.

† He marks his "finishing" as subsequent to the act of her coming out.

‡ The "Revelation of the Word of Tho Lord to him" is marked as subsequent to the child's having-knowledge-of The Lord. That Revelation implying an advance in knowledge,—the first 'knowing' is expressed in the Past form, and the 'being revealed' in the Future.

v. 5,—as remarked above. So the emphatic position of the word אֵד *mist,* before its Verb, is allowed for in the rendering.]

v. 6 (contin.) וְהִשְׁקָה *and watered.* HIPH-îL Past 3 s. *m.* with ו pref., from שׁקה. Tab. XXIII.—See the Note on *v.* 5 above.

v. 7. וַיִּיצֶר *and He formed.* KAL Fut. 3 s. *m.* with ו Convers., from יצר. See § 197 (δ).

וַיִּפַּח *and He breathed.* KAL Fut. 3 s. *m.* with ו Conversive, from נפח. Tab. XIX.

וַיְהִי. See ch. i. 3.

[Note. The Verb היה with ל after it, as here, is often used for *to become.*]

v. 8. וַיִּטַּע *and He planted.* KAL Fut. 3 s. *m.* with ו Convers., from נטע. Tab. XIX.

וַיָּשֶׂם *and He put.* KAL Fut. 3 s. *m.* with ו Conversive, from שׂים. See §§ 225 (iii) and 232 (iii).

[Note. Some consider such words to be forms of the *Hiph-îl* Future from the corresponding עו Root,—שׂום here.—Perhaps the Student's safest plan will be to give, when asked, both of these two: thus, KAL Fut. from שׂים, or HIPH. Fut. from שׂום. We prefer the former.]

יָצָר *He had formed.* KAL Past 3 s. *m.* from יצר, in Pause. § 165 (β).

v. 9. וַיַּצְמַח *and He caused to grow.* HIPH-îL Fut. 3 s. *m.* with ו Conversive, from צמח. [Tab. XVI (3) (B, β),—p. xxii.]

נֶחְמָד *pleasant* (E.V.). NIPH-ĂL Partic. s. *m.* from חמד (*to covet*),—like נֶעְלָם in § 169 (β, iii).

הַדַּעַת *the knowing.* KAL Infin. דַּעַת (Tab. XVIII, Note 1) with 'Def. Art.' ה prefixed, from ידע.—This strictly Infin.

form is often used for the Noun "*knowledge*." Here it governs the Object טוֹב וָרָע.

v. 10. יֹצֵא [was] *going out.* KAL Partic. s. *m.* from יצא (like פֹּקֵד in Tab. XIV).

לְהַשְׁקוֹת *to water.* HIPH-îL Infin. with לְ pref., from שקה. Tab. XXIII.

יִפָּרֵד *it was parted.* NIPH-ĂL Fut. 3 s. *m.* from פרד. Tab. XIV·

[Note. The Future Tense here marks that the "being parted" was *subsequent to* the "going out." Cp. § 152 (I). So also in the case of the next word.]

וְהָיָה לְ··· *and it became.* KAL Past 3 s. *m.* with וְ pref., from היה. Tab. XXIII. Cp. the Note at the end of *v.* 7.

v. 11. הַסֹּבֵב *that which compasseth* (lit. *the one-compassing*). KAL Partic. s. *m.* (like פֹּקֵד in Tab. XIV) with הַ prefixed as in § 98, from סבב.

v. 13. הַסּוֹבֵב. The same as הַסֹבֵב in *v.* 11.

v. 14. הַהֹלֵךְ *it-which goeth* (lit. *the one-going*). KAL Partic. s. *m.* (like פֹּקֵד in Tab. XIV) with הַ prefixed, as in § 98.

v. 15. וַיִּקַּח *and He took.* KAL Fut. 3 s. *m.* with וְ Conversive, from לקח. Tab. XIX (A).

וַיַּנִּחֵהוּ *and He put him* (with 'Defective' Long-Khērik, Pt. I, § 12). This word consists of יַנִּיחַ HIPH-îL Fut. 3 s. *m.* with וְ Conversive and the Objective Affix הוּ— *him.*

[Note. There is a difference of opinion as regards the Root of this word, as said in § 213 and Note (†) there. If the Root is ינח, the י is dropped as in § 212; and so we have forms from this Root like those in Tab. XIX. But Moderns generally take

the Root to be נוח and suppose the ־ָ of יָנִיחַ is resolved into
־ַ *followed by* Dagesh so as to give יַנִּיחַ, and similarly in other
forms—thus הַנִּיחַ Infin. (for הָנִיחַ), הֵנִיחַ Past 3 s. *m.* (for הֵנִיחַ),
הַנַּח=הַנִּח Imper. 2 s. *m.* (for הָנִח=הַנִּח). This may be.   But
so may the other, which the Student will we think find reason
hereafter for preferring.   And we think also that he will easily
see that the objections which some urge have not much weight.]

v. 15 (contin.) לְעָבְדָהּ *to dress it* (or *till it*, as in *v.* 5).   KAL
Infin. with לְ prefix and Objective Affix ־ָהּ *it f.*, from עבד.
Tab. XXIV (p. xxxv).

וּלְשָׁמְרָהּ *and to keep it.*   The same as the preceding word in
form, with וּ prefix, from שמר.

v. 16. [וַיְצַו [עַל *and He commanded* (or *laid-a-charge* upon).
PI-ÊL Fut. 3 s. *m.* apocopated, with וּ Conversive, from צוה (like
יִגֶל in Tab. XXIII).

לֵאמֹר.   See ch. i. 22.

אָכֹל *to eat.*   KAL Infin. Absolute from אכל, as in Tab. XIV.

תֹּאכֵל *thou mayest eat.*   KAL Fut. 2 s. *m.* from אכל.   Tab.
XVII (2, γ).

[Note. The Infin. Abs. is here used before the Tense to give
emphasis,—"*thou mayest freely eat,*" as in E.V.—See § 137
(1, Obs. β).]

v. 17. הַדַּעַת.   See *v.* 9.

[לֹא] תֹאכֵל *thou shalt [not] eat.*   The Dag. L. is removed from
תּ here,—(see Pt. I, § 48).   KAL Fut. 2 s. *m.* from אכל.
Tab. XVII (2, a).

אָכְלְךָ *thy eating.*   KAL Infin. with Pron. Aff. ךָ *thy m.* from
אכל.   Tab. XV, Note (*).

v. 17 (contin.) מוֹת *to die.* KAL Infin. Absolute from מוּת. Tab. XX.

תָּמוּת *thou shalt die.* KAL Fut. 2 s. *m.* from מוּת. Tab. XX.

[Note. The Infin. Abs. is here used before the Tense to give emphasis,—"*thou shalt* (or WILT) *surely die*," or "*terribly die.*" See § 137 (1, Obs. β).]

v. 18. וַיֹּאמֶר. See ch. i. 3.

הֱיוֹת [הָאָדָם] *that the man should be* (lit. *the-being-of* the man). KAL Infin. Constr. from היה (like גְּלוֹת in Tab. XXIII, the Moving Shva of the ה taking the Compound form ־ֱ).

אֶעֱשֶׂה *I will make.* KAL Fut. 1 s. from עשה (like אֶגְלֶה in Tab. XXIII, the ע having ־ֱ as in Tab. XVI (1).

v. 19. וַיִּצֶר *and He formed* (with 'Defective' Long-Khērik, Pt. I, § 12). KAL Fut. 3 s. *m.* with ו Conversive, from יצר. See § 197 (δ). Cp. *v.* 7.

וַיָּבֵא *and He brought* (lit. *and He caused-to-come*). HIPH-îL Fut. 3 s. *m.* with ו Conversive, from בוא (like יָקֵם in Tab. XX).

לִרְאוֹת *to see.* KAL Infin. with ל pref., from ראה. Tab. XXIII.

יִקְרָא *he would call.* KAL Fut. 3 s. *m.* from קרא. Tab. XXII.

v. 20. וַיִּקְרָא *and he called.* The same as the preceding, with ו Conversive.

[לֹא] מָצָא *there was* [*not*] *found* (lit. *he found not*). KAL Past 3 s. *m.* from מצא. Tab. XXII.

v. 21. וַיַּפֵּל *and He caused to fall.* HIPH-îL Fut. 3 s. *m.* with ו Conversive, from נפל. Tab. XIX. [§ 162 (*e*, ii).]

וַיִּישָׁן *and he slept.* KAL Fut. 3 s. *m.* with ו Conversive, from ישן. See § 197 (*a* & β).

וַיִּקַּח. See *v.* 15.

v. 21 (contin.) וַיִּסְגֹּר *and He closed.* KAL Fut. 3 s. *m.* with וּ
Conversive, from סגר. Tab. XIV.

v. 22. וַיִּבֶן *and He made* (lit. *built*). KAL Fut. 3 s. *m.* apocopated with וּ Conversive, from בנה [like יִגֶל in Tab. XXIII.]

לָקַח *He had taken.* KAL Past 3 s. *m.* from לקח. Tab. XIV.

וַיְבִאֶהָ *and He brought her* (with 'Defective' *Long*-Khērik,
Pt. I, § 12). HIPH-îL Fut. 3 s. *m.* with וּ Conversive, from בוא.
[יָבִיא being like יָקִים Tab. XX.]

v. 23. וַיֹּאמֶר. See ch. i. 3.

יִקָּרֵא *it shall be called.* NIPH-ĂL Fut. 3 s. *m.* from קרא.
Tab. XXII.

לֻקֳחָה *she was taken.* Pŭ-ĂL Past 3 s. *f.* from לקח [like פֻּקְדָה
Tab. XIV. To help the pronunciation the Dag. Forte is dropped
from the ק, and ﹻ (corresponding to the preceding ﹻ, see
Pt. I, § 22 *end*) is also given. Cp. Pt. I, § 72, Note (*, *e*).].

v. 24. יַעֲזָב (–ŏ) *he shall leave.* KAL Fut. 3 s. *m.* from עזב,
like יַעֲמֹד Tab. XVI (1) but with ﹷ(ŏ) instead of ﹹ because the
Accent is removed from the word (and therefore Makkeph
follows in the Bible). See Pt. I, §§ 37 (2) & 55 (9, *b*).

וְדָבַק *and he shall cleave.* KAL Past 3 s. *m.* with וּ prefix, from
דבק. Tab. XIV. [This Verb is often followed by בּ as here,
where we want "to" in English.]

וְהָיוּ *and they shall be* (or, with the following לְ, *and they shall
become,*—see the Note at the end of *v.* 7). This word is the
same as וְהָיוּ *and let them be* (or *and they shall be*) in ch. i. 15
where the rendering may also very well be "*and let them* BE-
COME" (or "*and they shall* BECOME.")

v. 25. וַיִּהְיוּ *and they were.* KAL Fut. 3 pl. *m.* with וּ Conversive, from היה. Tab. XXIII.

v. 25 (contin.) [וְלֹא] יִתְבּשָׁשׁוּ *and they were* [*not*] *ashamed.*
HITHPA-ÊL Fut. 3 pl. *m.* from בוש [like יִתְקוֹמְמוּ in Tab. XX].
For the — in Pause, see § 245.   The Future Tense here marks
'Sequence' or 'Con-sequence.'

Gen. iii. 1. הָיָה *he was.* KAL Past 3 s. *m.* from הָיה. Tab. XXIII.

עָשָׂה *He had made.* · KAL Past 3 s. *m.* from עשה. Tab. XXIII.

וַיֹּאמֶר *and he said.*   See ch. i. 3.

אָמַר *He hath said.*   KAL Past 3 s. *m.* from אמר.   Tab. XIV.

[לֹא] תֹאכְלוּ *ye shall* [*not*] *eat.* KAL Fut. 2 pl. *m.* from אכל.
Tab. XVII (2, *a*).   [Pt. I, § 48.]

v. 2. וַתֹּאמֶר *and she said.*   KAL Fut. 3 s. *f.* with וֹ Conversive,
from אמר.   Tab. XVII (2, δ).

נֹאכֵל *we may eat.* KAL Fut. 1 pl. from אכל.   Tab. XVII (γ).

v. 3. אָמַר. See *v.* 1.   [לֹא] תֹאכְלוּ. See *v.* 1.

[וְלֹא] תִגְּעוּ *and ye shall* [*not*] *touch.*   KAL Fut. 2 pl. *m.* from
נגע.   Tab. XIX.   [Pt. I, § 48.]—Note. This Verb generally
'governs' a בְ as here.

תְּמֻתוּן *ye die.*   KAL Fut. 2 pl. *m.* from מות; *i.e.* תָּמוּתוּ with
the ן of § 145 (see § 239).

[Note. The Future here marks the 'Subjunctive' after "*lest.*"]

v. 4. וַיֹּאמֶר.   See *v.* 1.

מות.   See ch. ii. 17 and the Note there.

תְּמֻתוּן.   See *v.* 3.

v. 5. יֹדֵעַ *doth know* (lit. *is knowing*).   KAL Partic. s. *m.* from
ידע.   Tab. XVI (3) [A].

אֲכָלְכֶם *your eating.* KAL Infin. with Pron. Aff כֶם *your* (*m.*)
Tab. XV, Note (‡).

וְנִפְקְחוּ *then they shall be opened.*   NIPH-AL Past 3 pl. with וֹ
prefix, from פקח.   Tab. XIV.

v. 5 (contin.) וִהְיִיתֶם *and ye shall be.* KAL Past 2 pl. *m.* with ו prefix, from הִיה. See p. 171, Note (*).

יֹדְעֵי *knowing* (lit. *knowers of*). KAL Partic. pl. *m.* 'i.e.' [*i.e.* the Constr. form of יֹדְעִים,—like פֹּקְדֵי from פֹּקְדִים (App* C to Tab. XIV).]

v. 6. וַתֵּרָא *and-when she saw.* KAL Fut. 3 s. *f.* apocopated, with ו Conversive, from ראה. Tab. XXIII.

וְנֶחְמָד. The same as נֶחְמָד in ch. ii. 9, with ו pref.

לְהַשְׂכִּיל *to make wise* (E.V.). HIPH-îL Infin. with ל pref., from שׂכל. Tab. XIV.

[Note. Some give "to contemplate," or "look at," "*adspicere*," for this. And they may claim the support of some ancient Versions. But we may perhaps observe that the Root occurs nowhere else in this sense throughout the Bible.—The *Hiph-il* occurs indeed in the sense of "considering," "applying the שֵׂכֶל (*thought, intellect*)," but not in the sense of "looking." Also this sense is somewhat unsuitable here, the "looking at" being already expressed by the עֵינַיִם *eyes.* There are three members of the statement, *viz.* that the tree was

     (*a*) good for food,

     (*β*) an-object-of-desire to the eyes,

     and (*γ*) נֶחְמָד לְהַשְׂכִּיל.

If there were no (*a*), then indeed (*β*) and (*γ*) might be supposed to be alike,—if there were no other objection. But, with (*a*) for the first of the three, "delightful to look at" would not add much to תַּאֲוָה לָעֵינַיִם of (*β*). And, moreover, "to give understanding" is a strictly admissible signification of לְהַשְׂכִּיל. It is not often wanted as here, but it occurs in

אַשְׂכִּילְךָ *I will give thee* שֵׂכֶל (*understanding*) Ps. xxxii. 8, and in the sense " to instruct" elsewhere.　And of the (α), (β), (γ), above,—this is the only one that expresses the effect of the seductive promise of *v.* 5 upon the woman, *viz.*

" ye shall be as God, knowing good and evil."

If the meaning "to look at" be assigned to (γ), then there is nothing in all the three members (α), (β), (γ), to express the effect upon her of this tempting promise of *v* 5.　The above-given strictly admissible signification of the word connects *v.* 6. with *v.* 5; and the signification objected to,—and which seems to us really inadmissible,* and of which there is no other instance throughout the Bible,—deprives *v.* 6 of any connection with what appears to be put forward as a main article of persuasion in *v.* 5.

We are therefore unable to adopt what we nevertheless know very well to be a widely accepted and indeed very fashionable opinion.]

v. 6 (contin.) וַתִּקַּח *and she took.*　KAL Fut. 3 s. *f.* with וֹ Conversive, from לָקַח.　Tab. XIX (A).

וַתֹּאכַל *and she ate.*　KAL-Fut. 3 s. *f.* with וֹ Conversive, from אכל.　See § 188 (*a*, i, Note *).

וַתִּתֵּן *and she gave.*　KAL Fut. 3 s. *f.* with וֹ Conversive, from נתן.　Tab. XIX (B).

וַיֹּאכַל *and he ate.*　KAL Fut. 3 s. *m.* with וֹ Conversive, from אכל.　See § 188 (*a*, i, Note *).

---

* We are quite aware that Gesenius gives this as the fundamental sense of the Root.　And so some others also.

v. 7. וַתִּפָּקַחְנָה *and they (f.) were opened.* NIPH-ĂL Fut. 3 pl. *f.* with וּ Conversive, from פקח. [Like תִּפָּקַדְנָה in Tab. XIV.]

וַיֵּדְעוּ *and they knew.* KAL Fut. 3 pl. *m.* with וּ Conversive, from יָדַע. Tab. XVIII.

וַיִּתְפְּרוּ *and they sewed.* KAL Fut. 3 pl. *m.* with וּ Conversive, from תפר. Tab. XIV.

וַיַּעֲשׂוּ *and they made.* KAL Fut. 3 pl. *m.* with וּ Conversive, from עשׂה. [Like יִגְלוּ in Tab. XXIII, but with יַעֲ because of the ע, comp. Tab. XVI (1).]

v. 8. וַיִּשְׁמְעוּ *and they heard.* KAL Fut. 3 pl. *m.* with וּ Conversive, from שׁמע. Tab. XIV.

מִתְהַלֵּךְ *walking* (or *going*). HITHPĂ-ĔL Partic. s. *m.* from הלך. Tab. XIV.

וַיִּתְחַבֵּא *and he hid himself.* HITHPĂ-ĔL Fut. 3 s. *m.* with וּ Conversive, from חבא.

v. 9. וַיִּקְרָא. See ch. i. 8.   וַיֹּאמֶר. See ch. i. 3.

[אַיֶּכָּה *where art thou?* consists of the Particle אַיֵּה *where* and the Pron. Aff. כָה 2 s. *m.* [Pause-form of כָה (= ךָ); see Tab. VIII.]

v. 10. וַיֹּאמֶר. See ch. i. 3.

שָׁמַעְתִּי *I heard.* KAL Past 1 s. from שׁמע. Tab. XIV.

וָאִירָא *and I was afraid* (or *and I feared*). KAL Fut. 1 s. with וּ Conversive, from ירא. [This word has אִי like אִיטַב in Tab. XVIII by reason of the 1st Rt-letter י, and אָ like אֶמְצָא in Tab. XXII by reason of the 3d Rt-letter א.]

וָאֵחָבֵא *and I was hid.* NIPH-ĂL Fut. 1 s. with וּ Conversive, from חבא [like אֶמָּצֵא in Tab. XXII, but with אֵ to compensate for the Dagesh which the ח cannot receive.]

v. 11. וַיֹּאמֶר.- See ch. i. 3.

הִגִּיד *he told.* Hiph-îl Past 3 s. *m.* from נגד. Tab. XIX.

צִוִּיתִיךָ *I commanded thee.* Pi-êl Past 1 s.. with Objective Affix ךָ *thee m.* [צִוִּיתִי is like גִּלִּיתִי in Tab. XXIII.]

אֲכֹל (–ŏ) *to eat.* Kal Infin. from אכל,—for אֲכֹל, the –̣ being shortened into –̣ (ŏ) because the accent is removed from the word (and therefore Makkeph follows in the Bible). See Pt. I, §§ 37 (2) and 55 (9, b).

אָכַלְתָּ *hast thou eaten.* Kal Past 2 s. *m.*, in Pause [for אָכַלְתָּ, like פָּקַדְתָּ in Tab. XIV]. Cp. § 165 (I, β).

v. 12. וַיֹּאמֶר. See ch. i. 3.

נָתַתָּה *Thou gavest.* Kal Past 2 s. *m.* from נתן. Tab. XIX (B), and § 138 (B).

נָתְנָה *she gave.* Kal Past 3 s. *f.* from נתן. Tab. XIX (B).

וָאֹכֵל *and I ate.* Kal Fut. 1 s. with ו Conversive. Tab. XVII (2, γ).

v. 13. וַיֹּאמֶר. See ch. i. 3.

עָשִׂית *thou (f.) hast done.* Kal Past 2 s. *f.* of עָשָׂה. Tab. XXIII.

וַתֹּאמֶר. See *v.* 2.

הִשִּׁיאַנִי *he beguiled me.* Hiph-îl Past 3 s. *m.* with Objective Aff. נִי– *me,* from נשא. [The word הִשִּׁיא *he beguiled* is like הִגִּישׁ. Tab. XIX.]

וָאֹכֵל. See *v.* 12.

v. 14. וַיֹּאמֶר. See ch. i. 3.

עָשִׂיתָ *thou hast done.* Kal Past 2 s. *m.* from עָשָׂה. Tab. XXIII.

אָרוּר *cursed.* Kal Partic. s. *m.* [like פָּקוּד (2) in App[x] B to Tab. XIV, see § 139 (γ) on p 83] from ארר.

v. 14 (contin.) תֵּלֵךְ *thou shalt go.* KAL Fut. 2 s. *m.* from יָלַךְ [like תֵּשֵׁב in Tab. XVIII.]

תֹּאכַל. See ch. ii. 17.

v. 15. אָשִׁית *I will put.* KAL Fut. 1 s. from שִׁית, see § 225; or HIPH-îL Fut., as some say, from שׁוּת. Comp. the Note on וַיָּשֶׂם in ch. ii. 8.

יְשׁוּפְךָ *it shall bruise thee.* KAL Fut. 3 s. *m.* with Objective Affix ךָ *thee m.,* from שׁוּף. Tab. XX.

[Note. The ‑ֹ of יָשׁוּף (like יָקוּם in the Table) is removed when the Affix is put on;—cp. § 59.]

תְּשׁוּפֶנּוּ *thou shalt bruise him.* KAL Fut. 2 s. *m.* with Objective Affix נּוּ‑ *him,* from שׁוּף. Tab. XX.

[Note. The ‑ֹ of תָּשׁוּף (like תָּקוּם in the Table) is removed when the Affix is put on;—cp. § 59.]

v. 16. אָמַר. See *v.* 1.

הַרְבָּה *to multiply.* HIPH-îL Infin. Absolute from רבה. Tab. XXIII. This is an unusual form of the Infinitive. It is given in column V of the Table.—The Infin. Abs. is here used before the Tense to give Emphasis:—"I will greatly multiply," as in the E.V.

אַרְבֶּה *I will multiply.* HIPH îL Fut. 1 s. from רבה. Tab. XXIII.

תֵּלְדִי *thou shalt bring forth.* KAL Fut. 2 s. *f.* from ילד. Tab. XVIII.

יִמְשָׁל (‑ֹ) *he shall rule.* KAL Fut. 3 s. *m.* from משל, like יִפְקֹד in Tab. XIV but with ‑ֹ instead of ‑ֹ because the Accent is removed from the word. See Pt. I, § 37 (2) & 55 (9, b).

v. 17. אָמַר. See *v.* 3.

שָׁמַעְתָּ *thou hast hearkened.* KAL Past 2 s. *m.* from שמע, like פָּקַדְתָּ in Tab. XIV.

r. 17 (contin.) וַתֹּאכַל *and thou hast eaten.* Kal Fut. 2 s. *m.* with ו Conversive, from אָכַל. Tab. XVII (2, *a*).

צִוִּיתִיךָ *I commanded thee.* Pĭ-ĕl Past 1 s. with Objective Affix ךָ *thee m.,* from צָוָה. [צִוִּיתִי being like גִּלִּיתִי in Tab. XXIII.]

לֵאמֹר. See ch. i. 22.

[לֹא] תֹאכַל. See ch. ii. 17.

אֲרוּרָה *cursed.* Kal Partic. s. *f.,* of the Masc. אָרוּר in *v.* 14.

תֹּאכֲלֶנָּה *thou shalt eat* [*of*] *it.* Kal Fut. 2 s. *m.* with Objective Affix ־ֶנָּה *it f.,* from אָכַל. [Without the Affix, the form is תֹּאכַל which has occurred already. For the 'Compound Shva' see Pt. I, § 72:—the ־ֲ here may be said to allude to the ־ֲ of תֹּאכַל. In Ezek. iv. 12 some copies have תֹּאכֲלֶנָה (in which word of *v.* 12, and תֹּאכְלֻנוּ once in *v.* 9 & twice in *v.* 10, some copies have ־ְ—other copies have ־ֲ).]

v. 18. תַּצְמִיחַ *it shall bring forth* (lit. *shall cause to grow*). Hiph-ĭl Fut. 3 s. *f.* from צָמַח. Tab. XVI (3) (Δ).

[Note. This word is generally taken thus as 3 s. *f.* "*it shall cause to grow.*" There is an old difficulty, as some know, with regard to the word לָךְ *to thee* or *for thee* (or *thyself*); it has been urged that "it would have been enough to say merely תַּצְמִיחַ" without the לָךְ.—But, as every one must always have seen, this word תַּצְמִיחַ may also be 2 s. *m.* "*thou shalt cause to grow.*" The לָךְ with this would signify his being himself the cause of hindrances and troubles to himself: and so the two Verbs in *v.* 18 would each have the same Subject "*thou (m.).*" This however is not necessary, as there are many instances of change of Subject. Also the rendering "Thorns and thistles thou shalt (*or* wilt) cause-to-grow (*or* bring-forth, as in E.V.) for thyself," although in itself possible, seems unnatural, and has not the support of Authorities, but it ought perhaps to be mentioned in passing.]

v. 18 (contin.) וְאָכַלְתָּ *and thou shalt eat.* KAL Past 2 s. *m.* with וֹ pref., from אכל. Tab. XIV.

v. 19. תֹּאכַל. See ch. ii. 17.

שׁוּבְךָ lit. *thy returning.* KAL Infin. with Pron. Aff. ךָ *thy m.,* from שׁוּב. [שׁוּב being like קוּם in Tab. XX.]

לֻקָּחְתָּ *thou wast taken.* Pŭ-ĂL Past 2 s. *m.* from לקח, in Pause. [§ 165 (I, *β*).]

תָּשׁוּב *thou shalt return.* KAL Fut. 2 s. *m.* from שׁוּב. Tab. XX.

v. 20. וַיִּקְרָא. See ch. i. 5.   הָיְתָה. See ch. i. 1.

חָי *a living one.* KAL Partic. s. *m.* (in Pause) from חיה=חיי. Sce p. 173, Obs. ii.

v. 21. וַיַּעַשׂ. See ch. i. 7.

וַיַּלְבִּשֵׁם *and He clothed them* (for 'Defective' *Long* Khērik, see Pt. I, § 12). HIPH-ÎL Fut. 3 s. *m.* with וֹ Conversive, and Objective Aff. ם— *them m.,* from לבש [יַלְבִּישׁ being like יַפְקִיד in Tab. XIV.]

v. 22. וַיֹּאמֶר. See ch. i. 3.   הָיָה. See *v.* 1.

[Note.—(1) From the fulness of meaning of Hebrew words it follows that, in the use of a translation (however good it may be), we should be continually on our guard against a possible limitation of the sense of the Original by a rendering which gives but one view of the passage. The greatest care and skill are often required for selecting a form of rendering—from among several forms by which the Original might be rendered. We have here an instance of this. A great difference will be at once perceived between two such renderings as

> · (α) "*Behold! the man* HAS BECOME *as one of us, with-regard-to-knowing, etc.,*" and
>
> (β) "*Behold! the man* WAS *as one of us, with-regard-to-knowing, etc.*"

Without adopting either the one or the other of these two possible renderings, we may perhaps use this passage in illustration of what-was just now stated.

(2) The word הָיָה (KAL Past 3 s. *m.* from הָיָה *to be*) is rendered in the English Authorized Version by several forms of expression. We find

> (i) "*he* (or *it*) WAS,"—in Gen. iii. 1, and in many other places;*
>
> (ii) "*he* (or *it*) HATH BEEN,"—in Gen. xxxi. 5, etc.;
>
> (iii) "*he* (or *it*) HAD BEEN," in Gen. xiii. 3, xxxi. 42, etc.;
>
> (iv) "*he* (or *it*) IS,"—in Nu. ix. 13, Ps. xxii. 14 (Hebr. *v.* 15)†, Ps. lxxxix. 41 (Hebr. *v.* 42), Is. xxxiii. 9,† etc.;
>
> (v) "*he* (or *it*) *is become*,"—in Gen. iii. 22. This sense agrees with (iv).

There are also some other renderings of הָיָה,—with which, however, we need not trouble the Reader just now. And with regard to the renderings in (i)—(v), it is enough perhaps here to observe that

---

* When followed by כ, too, as in 2 S. iv. 10 (margin), 1 K. iii. 12, etc. [See Note (*) on page 254.]

† In this passage the הָיָה is followed by כ. But of course the כ merely expresses the 'Comparison,' and does not at all affect the sense of the Verb—as to whether the Comparison is spoken of as (a) 'having been, in the Past,' or (b) as 'having been, and still continuing,' or (c) as 'yet to be.'

(3) as the word פָּקַד (from פקד *to visit*) may signify, either

     (a) "*he visited*" (or "*he has visited*," *i.e.* the Past of 'Finished Action,'—or "*he had visited*," or "*he might have visited*," etc.),—as in § 152 (II, *a*),—or

     (b) "*he has visited and is still visiting*," — as in § 152 (III, *a*) ;—

(4) so the word הָיָה (from היה *to be*) may signify, either

     (a) "*he was*" (or "*he has been*," or "*he had been*," or "*he might have been*," etc.),—as in § 152 (II, *a*),—or

     (b) "*he hath* (or *is*) *become*,"—as in § 152 (III, *a*).

(5) Hence we see that, of the renderings in (2),

     (a) those in (i) and (ii) and (iii) are included under § 152 (II, *a*) ; and

     (b) those in (iv) and (v) are included under § 152 (III, *a*).

(6) It may therefore be said that each of the two renderings (*a*) and (*β*), in (1) above, is admissible—so far as the word הָיָה in itself is concerned.* But as far as each of them is admissible,

---

* Some have fancied that the הָיָה here is to be rendered "*is* (or *has*) *become*," because it is followed by ב But הָיָה כ' must not be so limited. There are passages in which that expression stands for "*was as* …,'"—not "*has become as* …." For instance, in 2 S iv. 10 David says that the man who told him 'Saul is dead!' הָיָה כמבַשֵּׂר בְּעֵינָיו was *as one-telling-good-tidings in-his-own-eyes* ;—he was so no longer as soon as he heard the king's warrant for his execution. There are indeed several passages in which the Past of היה is used as above [in 1 (iv and v)], when followed by כ. But the Student may be warned here of the mistake which some seem anxious to make of tying down a Hebrew expression too much. Even if there were as much of the phrase-value "*to become*" in היה כ' as there is in היה ל, yet it would be incorrect to LIMIT the former expression to any such phrase-value. There is certainly much less of this phrase-value in היה כ' than there is in היה ל. Even the English Reader may to some extent perceive this by observing that in היה כ' "*to become* AS so and so," the כ of 'Comparison' retains its full value "AS"; whereas when היה ל is used for "*to become* so and so" (lit. "*to be to* or *for* or *into* so and so"), the ל is swallowed up and lost in the English phrase. Thus,

so far the adoption of the other (to the exclusion of that one) may involve the loss of an admissible rendering. This should not be lost sight of. As we are not concerned here to advocate either of them, we need not trouble ourselves to argue at all about 'them from the context or from general considerations. But we may just observe, in passing, that man's being said to have been made and created in "the image" and "likeness" of God (Gen. i. 26 & 27) may to some not unreasonably appear to correspond with the rendering (β) rather than with (a) in (1). And, further, that the rendering

> "*Behold! the man* WAS *as one of us, with regard to knowing good and bad; whereas now*——" he was NOT TO TAKE OF THE TREE OF LIFE,

may to some appear consonant with the warning (ii. 17) "*thou shalt surely die.*"

(7) We may perhaps add that advocates of (*a*) cannot surely intend their rendering to signify (what it certainly seems to signify) that Man became—in some way, or in some sense, or in some regard—like God, through his disobedience and experience of evil !

וְהָיְתָה לְגוֹיִם G xvii. 16 *and she shall become nations,* הָיִיתִי לִשְׁנֵי מַחֲנוֹת G xxxii. 11 (E.V. *v.* 10) *I am* (or *have*) *become two bands,* etc. But although we must fully allow this phrase value of היה לְ *to become,* yet we would also warn the Student most emphatically against supposing for a moment that the expression is limited at all to that phrase-value. היה לְ may have other values: for instance "*to be to* so and so," as in Gen. xxx 30 "It was little that הָיָה לְךָ *was to thee* (or *thou hadst*),"—and "*to be to*" in the sense of "*happening,*" as in 1 S. vi. 9 "An accident it [was that] הָיָה לָנג *was to us* (or *happened to us*),"—and "*to be for*" in the sense "*to be on one's side,*" as in G. xxxi. 42 "Unless the God of my father ... הָיָה לִי *had been for me* (i.e. *had been on my side*)...," etc. We cannot too strongly urge the Student to be on his guard against attempts to limit the sense where it ought not to be so limited.

Also we cannot suppose any one to argue seriously that the false tempter's promise "*ye shall be as* GOD (E.V. *gods*)," in Gen. iii. 5, must needs be true in this instance.

We are aware however that Dr. Kalisch says on this :—"The serpent was degraded, the human pair was ennobled by the glory of intelligence; the former was pressed down nearer to the earth, it was condemned to go upon the belly; the latter rose heavenward on the youthful wings of the mind; the one eats dust, the other became capable of imbibing the dew of eternal truth. Thus man has made a gigantic step beyond the limited sphere of his primitive existence." This is a grandiloquent account of what must have been therefore (if Dr. Kalisch is right) a "Rise"* rather than the "Fall." The Narrative seems to us to be not quite in agreement with it. It cleverly mixes up the opinion expressed by the LXX in

Ἰδοὺ Ἀδὰμ γέγονεν † ὡς εἷς ἐξ ἡμῶν τοῦ γινώσκειν καλὸν καὶ πονηρόν · καὶ νῦν κ.τ.λ.,

with some such a one as that expressed by Maimonides‡ in

הן מין זה של אדם היה יחיד בעולם ואין מין שני דומה לו
בזה הענין שיהא הוא מעצמו § בדעתו ובמחשבתו יודע הטוב
והרע ועושה כל מה שהוא חפץ ‖ וכו׳

---

* As some fancy.

† The following words of Fagius.

    "Ironia est ... Vide quam vera promiserit serpeus, quam factus sis par Deo sciens bonum et malum. Imo nihil minus es,"—

may commend themselves to some; but to others they may perhaps seem rather forced, or even (to some extent) evidence of an effort to escape from something that he could not approve of.

‡ See *Yad kh͞ᵃzdkd* (*Hǐ-l'khoth Tshuvd*, v. 1). See also Dr. Bernard's Selections, pp 55 & 262.

§ The word מִמֶּנּוּ (G. iii. 22) may mean either "*from us*" or "*from him*." Cp. Tab. II. 4.

‖ For וכו׳ see Note (*) on p. 224.

" Lo ! this race (lit. *kind*) *of man has become unique in the world, and there is not any other race* (lit. *kind*) *like to it in this regard,* viz. *that it is, of itself,—by its own mind and by its own thought,—knowing the good and the bad, and doing all that it likes, etc."*

This latter is supposed by many to derive authority from the Targum of Onkelos, viz. :—

הא אדם הוה יחידי בעלמא מיניה למידע טב וביש

which is taken to mean *" Lo! man has-become unique in the world, from himself to know good and bad"*; in which, we may observe, there is nothing whatever about "DOING" or *"doing* ALL THAT HE LIKES,"—and no mention of *" his mind"* and *" his thought"* (which may, however, be supposed to be implied).— We may also mention that there are some objections to such a rendering of the Original passage, as was pointed out long ago by Aben Ezra. We may not here dwell on this.

(8) But it is only fair to mention that there is some ' Hebrew' authority for understanding the הָיָה of Gen. iii. 22 in the sense *" he was."* Thus, in the Midrash Rabba, "R. Berechiah" in the name of R. K̄hanina said

כאליהו מה זה לא טעם טעם מות אף זה לא היה ראוי לטעום
טעם מות וכו׳

*" ' like Elijah.' ' What is this [Elijah]?'—' He tasted not the taste of death:' also this [Adam] was not by-rights to have tasted the taste of death." . . . . " All the time that man was, he WAS as etc." ***

---

* We are merely giving a few evidences of the word הָיָה having been understood in the sense *"was"* in Gen. iii. 22—rather than in the sense *" has become."* We may omit aught which we do not want for our immediate purpose.

On which we read in the Commentary מתנות כהונה—"When man was שָׁלֵם *complete* [*i.e.* in the state in which he was created], he was by-rights to have remained alive, as one who died not, like Elijah; etc."

And similarly a little earlier in the Midrash Rabba we find

תוקף שנתן הק'בה באדם הראשון לנצח לעולם היה כיון
שהניח דעתו של הק'בה והלך אחר דעתו של נחש ...

"*Might which The Holy One, Blessed be He, imparted to the first man was-to-have-been for ever and ever : when he left the Mind of The Holy One, Blessed be He, and went after the mind of the serpent*"—[then the latter half of the verse Job xiv. 20 expresses what resulted to him]. On the "*was-to-have-been for ever*," we read in מתנות כהונה—"By-rights he was to have been so for ever, etc." And a little earlier still in the Midrash we read "When He sent him away He began lamenting over him [in the words of Gen. iii. 22]," on which we read in the Commentary נבחר מפנינים—"It means that He said, by way of lamentation and bewailing, "Ah! how he 'WAS' from the first 'like one of us' in the highest attainment : whereas now he hath-gone-backward 'in-regard-to-knowing good and bad,' and he is expelled from his high-estate, for [it is said] 'lest he put forth his hand and take also of the Tree of Life,' etc. Therefore [it is added] 'and The LORD sent him forth from the garden of Eden.'"

(9) We may add that there are several interpretations given of the words כְּאַחַד מִמֶּנּוּ; and that, as a possible rendering* of

---

* Some may think that The "אַחַד" referred to in the Midrash, and by R. Juda b Simon in ביחודו של עולם, points to the כְּאַחַד מִמֶּנּוּ as taken together thus;— though others dissever the two words.

the words, some might perhaps choose such an English expression as "*like The*-*One *from-Himself*,"—"Behold! man was
like The-One from-Himself (*i.e.* The Self-Originated One) in-
regard-to-knowing good and bad; whereas, now, etc." Cp.
Gen. i. 26 & 27.—What was said in (2–8) above is seen to be
quite independent of this remark in (9).

But we must return to the 'Analysis of Verb-forms.']

v. 22. (contin.) לָדַעַת *to know* (or *for knowing, with-regard-to-
knowing*). Kal Infin. with לְ pref., from יָרַע. Tab. XVIII
(Note 1).

יִשְׁלַח *he put forth.* Kal Fut. 3 s. *m.* from שָׁלַח [like יִלְמַד in
Tab. XIV.]

וְלָקַח *and take.* Kal Past 3 s. *m.* with וְ prefix, from לָקַח.
וְאָכַל *and eat.* Kal Past 3 s. *m.* with וְ prefix, from אָכַל.

וְחַי *and live.* Kal Past 3 s. *m.* with וְ prefix [p. 173, Obs. iii.]
The וְ has — before the 'Accented Syllable' to which it is prefixed,—see p. 225.

v. 23. וַיְשַׁלְּחֵהוּ *and He sent him forth.* Pĭ-ĕl Fut. 3 s. *m.*
with וְ Conversive, and Objective Affix ־הוּ *him*, from שָׁלַח.
Tab. XXIX (II, *a*) [p. xlii.]

לַעֲבֹד. See ch. ii. 5.

לֻקַּח *he was taken.* Pŭ-ăl Past 3 s. *m.* from לָקַח. Tab. XIV.

v. 24. וַיְגָרֶשׁ *and He drove out.* Pĭ-ĕl Fut. 3 s. *m.* with וְ
Conversive, from גָרַשׁ [like יְבָרֶךְ in App[x] to Tab. XVI (2), but

---

* The 'Construct' form marks that the word כְּאַחַד is to be taken in close connection with the following word מִמֶּנּוּ. As it is in 'Construction,' it may not have
the הַ for the 'Def. Art.' We may therefore supply "the" in English, if this be
wanted, before the English word which stands for it.

with — for the — because the Accent is removed from the last syllable,—cp. Pt. I, § 55 (9, b)].

v. 24 (contin.) וַיַּשְׁכֵּן *and He placed* (lit. *caused to dwell*). HIPH-îL Fut. 3 s. *m.* with ו Conversive, from שׁכן. Tab. XIV.

הַמִּתְהַפֶּכֶת *which turned every way* (E.V.,—lit. *which was turning-itself*). HITHPĂ-ÊL Partic. s. *f.* with the ה of § 98 (or merely that of § 6), from הפך [like מִתְפָּקֶדֶת in App[x] B to Tab. XIV].

לִשְׁמֹר *to keep.* KAL Infin. with ל pref., from שׁמר. Tab. XIV.

ANALYSIS OF VERB-FORMS IN GEN. XII.

Gen. xii. 1. וַיֹּאמֶר. See ch. i. 3.

לֶךְ *go thou.* KAL Imper. 2 s. *m.* from ילך. [Like שֵׁב in Tab. XVIII, but with — for — because the Accent is removed— as signified by the (-) in the Bible. Cp. Pt. I, § 55 (9, b).]

[Note. The word לְךָ here is the word signifying *to thee* (*m.*) in Tab. II, and it is used here *Reflexively* as in Obs. XIV (p. 139).]

אַרְאֶךָּ *I will shew thee* (lit. *I will cause thee to see*). HIPH-îL Fut. 1 s. from ראה. [The full form of the *Hiph.* Fut. 1 s. is אַרְאֶה. This, on receiving the Pron.-Aff. would give regularly אַרְאֶךָ (the 3[d] Rt-letter ה being dropped when the Affix is put on). For this latter we have here אַרְאֶךָּ in Pause. For the ךָ— see Tab. XXVIII, Note (ε, ii) on p. xl, and cp. וַאֲבָרֶכְךָ Gen. xxvi. 3 *and I will bless thee* (which is PĬ-ÊL Fut. 1 s. with ו Conjunctive and Objective Affix *thee m.*, in Pause, from ברך); and אֶרְאֶךָּ 2 Kings iii. 14 *I would see thee* (which is KAL Fut. 1 s. with Objective Affix *thee m.*). The *Hiph.* אַרְאֶךָ occurs in Zech. i. 9 with the Accent — merely,—a Pause-form not in Pause, cp. § 167 (ii, *a*).]

v. 2. וְאֶעֶשְׂךָ *and I will make thee.* KAL Fut. 1 s. (אֶעֱשֶׂה) with ו Conjunctive and Objective Affix ךָ *thee m.*, from עשה. Tab. XXX.

וַאֲבָרֶכְךָ *and I will bless thee.* PĬ-ÊL Fut. 1 s. (אֲבָרֵךְ App[x] to Tab. XVI (2)) with ו Conjunctive and Objective Affix ךָ *thee (m.)*, from ברך; like אֶפְקָדְךָ in Tab. XXIX (II, *a*), but with ֶ before the ר to compensate for the Dag. F. which the ר cannot receive.

[Obs. This word has the simple form for which the Pause-form is וַאֲבָרְכֶךָ (mentioned just now in *v.* 1). But in our word the ר has ֶ whereas in the Pause-form the ר has ְ. The ךָ of our word agrees with the קָ of אֶפְקָדְךָ in Tab. XXIX (II, *a*). In each, the ֶ is a Slight-vowel (Pt. I, § 56) masking the Moving-Shva which the 2[d] Rt-letter would have but cannot have when the 3[d] Rt-letter also has ְ. (The ֶ adopted here as the Slight-vowel agrees with the ֶ of the 2[d] Rt-letter in the form אֶפְקֶד without the Affix). But in Pause, the 3[d] Rt-letter receiving then a vowel, and there being no need then for the Slight-vowel, the *Shva* drops its mask (ְ); and thus the 2[d] Rt-letter has ְ as seen in *v.* 1, and so in אֲבָרְכֶךָ Ps. cxlv. 2.]

וַאֲגַדְּלָה *and I will make great.* PĬ-ÊL Fut. 1 s. with ו Conjunctive and the ה of § 144, from גדל.

וֶהְיֵה *and thou shalt be* (lit. *be thou*). KAL Imper. 2 s. *m.* with ו pref., from היה. See p. 171, Note (*).

v. 3. וַאֲבָרְכָה *and I will bless.* PĬ-ÊL Fut. 1 s. with ו Conjunctive and the ה of § 144, from ברך.

מְבָרְכֶיךָ *those blessing thee* (lit. *thy blessers*). PĬ-ÊL Partic. pl. *m.* with Pron.-Affix ךָ *thy (m.)*, from ברך. [This, without the Affix, would be מְבָרְכִים pl. *m.* of מְבָרֵךְ in App[x] to Tab. XVI (2). For the ֶ see Pt. I, § 72.]

v. 3 (contin.) וּמְקַלֶּלְךָ *and him that curseth thee* (or, *thy reviler**). Pĭ-êl Partic. s. *m.* with וּ pref. and ̅Pron.-Affix ךָ *thy* (*m.*), from קָלַל. [The form without the Affix is מְקַלֵּל like מְפַקֵּד in Tab. XIV. The ̤ beneath the ל is a Slight-vowel. Pt. I, § 56.]

אָאֹר *I will curse.* Kal Fut. 1 s. from אָרַר [like אֶסֹב in Tab. XXI].

וְנִבְרְכוּ *and they shall be blessed.* Niph-âl Past 3-pl. with וְ pref. from בָּרַךְ [like נִפְקְדוּ in Tab. XIV].

v. 4. וַיֵּלֶךְ *so he departed* (lit. *and he went*). Kal Fut. 3 s. *m.* with וַ Conversive, from יָלַךְ. See § 198 (δ).

דִּבֶּר *He had spoken.* Pĭ-êl Past 3 s. *m.* from דָּבַר. [For the ̤ see Note (*e*) on p. xv—back of Tab. XIV.]

בְּצֵאתוֹ *when he departed out* (lit. *on his going-out* or *forth*). Kal Infin. with בְּ pref. and Pron.-Affix וֹ *his,* from יָצָא.

[Note. Instead of צֵאת like שֶׁבֶת from יָשַׁב, Tab. XVIII, the Inf. Constr. of יָצָא has the contracted form צֵאת which takes Pron.-Affs. thus:—צֵאתוֹ *his going out,* צֵאתְךָ *thy* (*m.*) *going out,* etc.]

v. 5. וַיִּקַּח. See ch. ii. 15.

רָכָשׁוּ *they had gathered* (or *acquired*). Kal Past 3 pl. in Pause, from רָכַשׁ.

עָשׂוּ *they had gotten* (lit. *made*). Kal Past 3 pl. from עָשָׂה [like גָּלוּ in Tab. XXIII].

וַיֵּצְאוּ *and they went forth.* Kal Fut. 3 pl. *m.* with וַ Conversive, from יָצָא [like יֵשְׁבוּ in Tab. XVIII].

---

* Even this word is a little stronger than the original, which might be rendered "*any one speaking-lightly-of thee.*"

v. 5 (contin.) לָלֶכֶת *to go.* KAL Infin. with ל pref., from יֶלֶךְ [like לָשֶׁבֶת in Tab. XVIII].

וַיָּבֹאוּ *and they came.* KAL Fut. 3 pl. *m.* with וּ Conversive, from בּוֹא.

[Note. The KAL of this Verb has the following forms with *Khoulem*, [see more on pp. 272 & 273] :—

(*a*) Infin. (Absol. & Constr.) בּוֹא; and (with בכלם) בְּבוֹא, מְבוֹא (i.e.), לְבוֹא כִּבוֹא;

Or with –, thus בָּא בְּבֹא, כְּבֹא (לְבֹא (i.e.), מְבֹא.

(β) Imper. בּוֹא or בֹּא (and, with ה, בֹּאָה) s. *m.*, בּוֹאִי or בֹּאִי s. *f*, בֹּאוּ pl. *m.*

(γ) Fut. יָבֹא 3 s. *m.*, תָּבֹא 3 s. *f.* & 2 s. *m.*, תָּבֹאִי 2 s. *f.*, אָבֹא 1 s., יָבֹאוּ 3 pl. *m.*, (תָּבֹאנָה or תָּבֹאן) תָּבֹאֶינָה), 3 pl. *f.*, תָּבֹאוּ 2 pl. *m.*, נָבֹא 1 pl.

Obs. These may have וֹ in the place of the –; thus, יָבוֹא, and so תָּבוֹא, etc.

(δ) So, with the ה of § 144 we have both אֲבוֹאָה & אָבֹאָה 1 s., and נָבוֹאָה & נָבֹאָה 1 pl.]

v. 6. וַיַּעֲבֹר *and he passed over* (followed by בּ *into*). KAL Fut. 3 s. *m.* with וּ Conversive, from עָבַר. Tab. XVI (1).

v. 7. וַיֵּרָא *and He appeared.** NIPH-ĂL Fut. 3 s. *m.* apocopated from רָאָה [like יִגַּל in Tab. XXIII; but with – to compensate for Dag. F., and with א– instead of ל–, cp. p. 169 (II, *a*)].

וַיֹּאמֶר. See ch. i. 3.

אֶתֵּן *I will give.* KAL Fut. 1 s. from נָתַן. Tab. XIX (B).

וַיִּבֶן *and he built.* KAL Fut. 3 s. *m.* apocopated from בָּנָה [like יִבֶן in Tab. XXIII]. The full form of the 3 s. *m.* Fut. *K.*, fr. בָּנָה, is יִבְנֶה.

---

* From רָאָה *to see*; the *N*φ. *to be seen* is used for "*to appear.*"

v. 7 (contin) הַנִּרְאָה *Who appeared* (lit. *The One appearing* or *seen*). Niph-Ăl Partic. s. *m* from רָאה.   Tab. XXIII.

v. 8. וַיַּעְתֵּק *and he removed* (or *moved*). Hiph-îl Fut. 3 s. *m.* with ו Conversive, from עתק. This is like יַפְקֹד in Tab. XIV. Cp. § 178 (i).

[Note. This expresses a Transitive "*removing*" or "*moving*," viz. his goods and things. The English Reader will find no difficulty in this, because the English Verb *to move* is often used for 'to move one's goods and chattels.']

וַיֵּט *and he pitched* (lit. *and he extended*). Kal Fut. 3 s. *m.* apocopated, with ו Conversive, from נטה. The form יִנְטֶה (like יִגְלֶה in Tab. XXIII) becomes יִפֶּה, cp. § 205 (ii), and this by apocopation becomes יֵט.

וַיִּבֶן. See *v.* 7.   וַיִּקְרָא. See ch. i. 5.

v. 9. וַיִּסַּע *and he journeyed.* Kal Fut. 3 s. *m.* with ו Conversive, from נסע. Tab. XIX.

הָלוֹךְ *to go.* Kal Infin. Absol. from הלך. Tab. XIV.

וְנָסוֹעַ *and to journey.* Kal Infin. Absol. with ו prefix, from נסע. Tab. XVI (3) (A).

[Note. The phrase וַיִּסַּע הָלוֹךְ וְנָסוֹעַ, lit. *and he journeyed to go and to journey*, stands for *and he went on continually journeying*,— cp. § 137 (1), Obs. (δ).]

v. 10. וַיְהִי. See ch. i. 4.

וַיֵּרֶד *and he went down.* Kal Fut. 3 s. *m.* with ו Conversive, from ירד. Cp. § 198 (δ).

לָגוּר *to sojourn.* Kal Infin. with ל, from גור. Tab. XX.

v. 11. וַיְהִי. See ch. i. 3.

הִקְרִיב *he drew near.* Hiph-îl Past 3 s. *m.* irom קרב. Tab. XIV.

v. 11 (contin.) לָבוֹא *to come.* KAL Infin. with ל, from בוא.
[See Note (*a*) on וַיָּבֹאוּ in *v.* 5.]

וַיֹּאמֶ. See ch. i. 3.

יָדַעְתִּי *I know.* KAL Past 1 s. from ידע. Tab. XIV.

v. 12. וְהָיָה *therefore it-shall-come-to-pass* (E.V.). KAL Past
3 s. *m.* with וּ pref., from היה.

יִרְאוּ *they shall see.* KAL Fut. 3 pl. *m.* from ראה [like יִגְלוּ in
Tab. XXIII].

וְאָמְרוּ *that they shall say.* KAL Past 3 pl. with וּ pref.,
from אמר.

וְהָרְגוּ *and they will kill.* KAL Past 3 pl. with וּ pref., from הרג.

יְחַיּוּ *they will save alive* (E.V.). PĬ-ĒL Fut. 3 pl. *m.* from חיה
[like יִגְלוּ in Tab. XXIII].

v. 13. אִמְרִי *say thou.* KAL Imper. 2 s. *f.* from אמר [like
פִּקְדִי in Tab. XIV].

יִיטַב *it may be well.* KAL Fut. 3 s. *m.* from יטב [Tab. XVIII].

וְחָיְתָה *and it shall live.* KAL Past 3 s. *f.* with וּ pref., from
היה [like גָּלְתָה in Tab. XXIII].

v. 14. וַיְהִי *and it came to pass* (E.V.). See ch. i. 5.

כְּבוֹא *on the coming of.* KAL Infin. Constr. with כְּ pref., from
בוא. [See *v.* 5, Note (*a*).]

וַיִּרְאוּ *that they beheld.* KAL Fut. 3 pl. *m.* with וּ Conversive,
from ראה.

v. 15. וַיִּרְאוּ *and they saw.* See *v.* 14.

וַיְהַלְלוּ *and they commended.* PĬ-ĒL Fut. 3 pl. *m.* with וּ Conversive, from הלל. The Dagesh F. is often dropped from the ל.
For the — comp. Pt. I, § 72 (Note (*, *e*)).

וַתֻּקַּח *and she was taken.* HOPH-ĂL Fut. 3 s. *f.* with וּ Conversive, from לקח. [Note (A) on Tab. XIX (γ, vi).]

v. 16. הֵיטִיב *he did good.* HIPH-îL Past 3 s. *m.* from יטב [Tab. XVIII].

וַיְהִי *and there were.* See ch. i. 5.

v. 17. וַיְנַגַּע *and He plagued.* PĪ-ÊL Fut. 3 s. *m.* with ו Conversive, from נגע [like יְשַׁלַּח Tab. XVI (3) (B, β)].

v. 18. וַיִּקְרָא *and he called.* KAL Fut. 3 s. *m.* with ו Convers., from קרא.

וַיֹּאמֶר. See ch. i. 3.   עָשִׂיתָ. See ch. iii. 14.

הִגַּדְתָּ *thou didst tell.* HIPH-îL Past 2 s. *m.* from נגד [like הִגַּשְׁתָּ in Tab. XIX].

v. 19. אָמַרְתָּ *thou saidst.* KAL Past 2 s. *m.* from אמר.

וָאֶקַּח *so I might have taken* (E.V.) [or, lit., *and I took*]. KAL Fut. 1 s. with ו Convers., from לקח [Note (A) on Tab. XIX].

קַח *take thou.* KAL Imper. 2 s. *m.* from לקח [Note (A) on Tab. XIX].

וָלֵךְ *and go.* KAL Imper. 2 s. *m.* with ו pref., from ילך [like שֵׁב in Tab. XVIII.—For the ◌ָ see p. 225].

v. 20. וַיְצַו *and he commanded.* PĪ-ÊL Fut. 3 s. *m.* apocopated, with ו Convers., from צוה [like יְגַל in Tab. XXIII].

וַיְשַׁלְּחוּ *and they sent away.* PĪ-ÊL Fut. 3 pl. *m.* with ו Conversive, from שלח.

IV. List of Verbs belonging to more than one of the Seven Classes mentioned in § 186—[sometimes called 'Doubly Irregular' Verbs]

[The Student will perhaps have some little difficulty, at first, in analyzing some of the Verb-forms from Roots belonging simultaneously to *more than one* of the Seven Classes mentioned in § 186. Many of such forms may be recognized without much difficulty, by allowing for each set of 'Variations' separately. But in some of them there are special Variations, and some few of them are irregular,—and some apocopated forms may well seem strange to him. It will, without doubt, be useful to him to have these Verbs all collected together. We therefore give him here the following List, in the Alphabetical order of Roots, with the Verb-forms which occur in the Bible.]

אבה used only in *Kal* (*to be willing*).

Kal

Past and Partic (1) like those of נלה Tab. XXIII, but for אָבוּא (Is. xxviii. 12)—3 pl. Past—cp. § 138 (B) iv, *a.*

Fut. יֹאבֶה 3 s. *m.,* תֹּאבֶה 3 s. *f.* & 2 s. *m.* (once תֹּבֵא Prov. i. 10), יֹאבוּ 3 pl. *m.,* תֹּאבוּ 2 pl. *m.*

אוה used only in *Pi* and *Hθ.* (*to desire, lust*).—The ו is Consonantal always in Verb-forms from this Root.

Pi-êl

Past אִוָּה 3 s. *m.,* אִוְּתָה 3 s. *f.,* אִוִּיתִי 1 s. ;

Fut. [יְאַוֶּה 3 s. *m.*], תְּאַוֶּה 3 s. *f.*

Hithpa-êl

Past הִתְאַוָּה 3 s. *m.,* הִתְאַוִּיתִי 1 s., הִתְאַוּוּ 3 pl. ;

Partic. מִתְאַוֶּה s. *m.,* מִתְאַוִּים pl. *m.* ;

Fut. יִתְאַוֶּה 3 s. *m.* (apocop. יִתְאָו), תִּתְאַוֶּה 3 s. *f.* (apocop. תִּתְאָו), יִתְאַוּוּ 3 pl. *m.*

אוֹן (or אנן) used only in the *Hθ.* (*to complain*). Partic. מִתְאֹנְנִים pl. *m.*, and Fut. יִתְאוֹנֵן 3 s. *m.*

אוּץ used only in the Past and Participle (1) of *Kal* (*to haste*), and Fut. *Hφ.* (*to cause to haste, to urge*) The forms are like those of קוּם in Tab. XX.

אוֹר used only in *Kal*, to be light, *Nφ.* to be lightened, *bright, glorious, Hθ. to make light* or *bright, make to shine.*

PAST אוֹר 3 s. *m.*, אֹרוּ 3 pl. (like בּוֹשׁ, בּשׁוּ, cp. Tab. XX).
PARTIC. אוֹר s. *m.*;
IMPER. אוֹרִי 2 s. *f.* (like בּוֹשִׁי);
FUT. תָּאֹרְנָה 3 pl. *f.* (like תָּקֹמְנָה in Tab. XX). See §230 (1).
NIPH-ÄL
INFIN. לֵאוֹר Job xxxiii. 30 (for לְהֵאוֹר, cp. §137 (3) Note †);
PARTIC. נָאוֹר s. *m.*;
FUT. יֵאוֹר 3 s. *m.* (or Fut. *K.* like יבוֹשׁ).
HIPH-ÎL
INFIN. לְהָאִיר;
PAST הֵאִיר 3 s. *m.*, הֵאִירָה 3 s. *f.*, הֵאִירוּ 3 pl.;
PARTIC. מֵאִיר s. *m.*, מְאִירַת Ps. xix. 9 (Constr. form of מְאִירָה s. *f.*), מְאִירוֹת pl. *f.*;
IMPER. הָאֵר s. *m.* and with ה added הָאִירָה;
FUT. תָּאִיר and יָאִר 3 s. *m.* (with וּ Convers. וַיָּאַר), יָאֵר 3 s. *f.* & 2 s. *m.*, יָאִירוּ 3 pl. *m.*, תָּאִירוּ 2 pl. *m.*

אוֹשׁ (or אשׁשׁ) only in the *Hθ.* הִתְאֹשָׁשׁוּ Imper. 2 pl. *m.* in Pause, Is. xlvi. 8 "*shew yourselves men.*"

אוֹת used only in the Future *Kal* (*to consent*).

KAL

FUT. יָאוֹת 3 s. *m.*, נָאוֹת 1 pl. (and נאוֹתָה with ה,).

> [Note. The forms which are thus like יְבוֹשׁ etc. in
> Tab. XX, are by some taken rather as *N*φ. forms
> —*i.e.* like יָקוֹם or יֵעוֹר etc. in Tab. XX.]

איב *K. to be an enemy,* or *hostile to,* only used in אִיַבְתִּי 1 s.
Past, and in the Partic (1) forms, viz. אוֹיֵב or
אֹיֵב s. *m.* (*an enemy*),—with Affs. (*his*) אֹיְבוֹ,
(*thy m.*) אֹיִבְךָ, etc.,—אוֹיְבִים (or 'א) pl. *m.*,
i.c. אֹיְבֵי (or 'אוֹ),—with Affs. (*his*) אֹיְבָיו, etc.
אֹיַבְתִּי *an enemy* (Mi. vii. 8 & 10) is the Sing. fem.
form אֹיֶבֶת with י, like אֲהַבְתִּי in § 139 (ϵ).

אלה used only in *K. to swear,* etc., *II*φ. *to adjure.*

KAL

INFIN. Abs. אָלֹה and אָלוֹת;
PAST אָלִית 2 s. *f.*;
IMPER. אֲלִי 2 s. *f.*

HIPH-îL

INFIN. לְהָאֲלוֹת (in לְהָאֲלָתוֹ, with Pron.-Aff. וֹ *him*);
FUT. יָאֶל (in וַיֹּאֶל 1 S. xiv. 24). [This is usually taken
thus, as *Hiph.*; but the *form* might very well be
Fut. KAL apocop., the — being like the — in וַיֹּאמֶר.
The אֶת הָעָם following must however be allowed
for, of course.]

אנה (I.) *to mourn*, used only in *Kal* וְאָנוּ Past 3 pl. w. וֹ ; and
(II.) *to occasion*, in *Pĭ.* אִנָּה Past 3 s. *m.*,—*Pŭ.* (*to be occa-*
sioned, to happen), תְּאֻנֶּה & יְאֻנֶּה Fut. 3 s. *m.* & *f.*,—
and *Hithp.* Partic. מִתְאַנֶּה (*one making occasion, or*
seeking occasion) s. *m.*—These forms agree with
Tab. XXIII.

אנן (see אוֹן).

אפה used only in *Kal* (*to bake*), *Nφ.* (*to be baked*)

Kal
     Past אָפָה 3 s. *m.*, אָפִיתָ 2 s. *m.*, אָפִיתִי 1 s., אָפוּ 3 pl ,
     Partic. אֹפֶה s. *m.* (whence אֹפֵהֶם, with Pron.-Aff. הֶם *their*,
         Hos. vii. 6), אֹפִים pl. *m.*, אֹפוֹת pl. *f.* ;
     Imper. אֵפוּ (Ex. xvi. 23) 2 pl. *m.*, instead of אֱפוּ ;
     Fut. וַתֹּפֵהוּ (1 S. xxviii. 24) 3 s. *f.* w. וֹ Conv. and Aff. *him*
         or *for him*—instead of וַתֹּאפֵהוּ,—
         תֹּאפוּ 2 pl. *m.*, יֹאפוּ 3 pl. *m.* ;
Niph-ăl
     Fut. תֵּאָפֶה 3 s. *f.*, תֵּאָפֶינָה 3 pl. *f.*

אפף only in *Kal* (*to compass*) אָפְפוּ Past 3 pl., like פָּקְדוּ in
     Tab. XIV,—and w. Aff. *me* as in Tab. XXV.

ארה only in *Kal* (*to pluck*) Past אָרִיתִי 1 s., אָרוּ 3 pl. (in וְאָרוּהָ
     with וֹ pref. & Objective Aff. הָ *it* (*f.*), Ps. lxxx. 13).

ארר *to curse*, used only in *K.*, *Nφ*, *Pĭ.*, and *Höph*
Kal
     Infin. Abs. אָרוֹר ;

Past אֲרוֹתִי 1 s. (also אֲרוֹתִיהָ with Objective Aff. הָ *her*) ;

Partic (1) אֹרְרֵי pl. *m.* (i.c.), אֹרְרֶיךָ pl. *m.* w. Aff. *thy m.*
  [For the ⁻ see Pt. I, § 72 (β).]

Partic (2) אָרוּר s. *m.*, אֲרוּרָה s. *f.*, אֲרוּרִים pl. *m.* ;

Imper. [אֹר] 2 s. *m.* אָרָה with ה. (Tho ⁻ of the א is ŏ,
  there being no Accent on the word,—Pt. I, § 37),
  אֹרוּ and אוֹרוּ 2 pl. *m.* ;

Fut. תָּאֹר 2 s. *m.*, אָאֹר 1 s.

Niph-ăl

Partic. נֶאָרִים pl. *m.* Mal. iii. 9.

Pï-êl

Past [אֵרֵר] in אֵרֲרָה 3 s. *m.* with Objective Aff. הָ⁻ *her*
  Gen. v. 29. For the ⁻ comp. Pt. I, § 72.

Partic. מְאָרְרִים pl. *m.*

Hoph-ăl

Fut. יוּאָר 3 s. *m.* (in Pause, for יוּאַר).

אתה (or אתא) *to come*, used only in *Kal* and in Imperative IIφ.

Kal

Past אָתָה (and אָתָא Is. xxi. 12), אָתָנוּ 1 pl. from אתא ;

Partic. אֹתִיּוֹת pl. *f.* ;

Imper. אָתָיוּ 2 pl. *m.* ;

Fut. יֶאֱתֶה 3 s. *m.* (וַיֵּתָא Deut. xxxiii. 21, וְיֵאָת Is. xli. 25,
  —and with Aff. נִי⁻ *me*, וְיֶאֱתָיֵנִי Job iii. 25),
  תֵּאתֶה 3 s. *f.* (Mi. iv. 8),
  יֶאֱתָיוּ 3 pl. *m.* (וַיֶּאֱתָיוּן Is. xli. 5), with ן, and
  ו Conversive ;

Hiph-îl

Imper. הֵתָיוּ 2 pl. *m.*

בוֹא used only in *Kal* (*to come, come upon, enter*, etc.), *IIɸ.* (*to cause to come, to bring*), and *Hoph.* (*to be brought*).

KAL

INFIN. (*בְּבֹא*), & בְּבֹאָה 1 K. xiv. 12 with ה, בּוֹא & בֹּא—(מִבֹּא); כְּבֹא, לָבֹא—לִבוֹא in *actual construction*,—with Affs. בֹּאֲכָה & בֹּאֲךָ, בֹּאָה, בֹּאוֹ with ה, etc.

PAST בָּא 3 s. *m.*, בָּאָה 3 s. *f.* (w. Aff. *us* בָּאַתְנוּ Ps. xliv. 18), בָּאתָ 2 s. *m.*, בָּאתָה & בָּאת 2 s. *f.* (For בָּאת, in וּבָאת 2 S. xiv. 3, see Pt. I, § 29, Note (†)).

בָּאתִי 1 s.,

בָּאוּ 3 pl. (also †בָאוּ, perhaps twice),

בָּאתֶם 2 pl. *m.*,

בָּאנוּ 1 pl. (בָּנוּ 1 S. xxv. 8, with the Note 'lacking א');

PARTIC. בָּא s. *m.*, בָּאָה s. *f.*,

בָּאִים pl. *m.* (i.e. בָּאִי), w. Aff. *her* בָּאֶיהָ,—בָּאוֹת pl. *f.*;

IMPER. בֹּא (or בּוֹא, and בֹּאָה with ה) 2 s. *m.*,

בֹּאִי (or בּוֹאִי) 2 s. *f.*, בֹּאוּ 2 pl. *m.*;

FUT. ‡יָבֹא (with ו Conv. ‡וַיָּבֹא, ויבו 1 K. xii. 12 *Kthiv* for וַיָּבֹא *Kri*, ויבאו 1 K. xii. 3 *Kthiv* for וַיָּבֹא *Kri*),—for the 3 s. *m.* 'w. Affs.' see *⁎* next page,—

---

* There may be ו in the place of ־ָ, as in מְבוֹא, לָבוֹא & בְּבוֹא, כְּבוֹא, לָבוֹא & בְּבוֹא, and so מִלְּבוֹא & (*from the entering of*), בּוֹאוֹ *His coming* Mal. iii. 2, בְּבוֹאָה, etc.,—and so בָּאֶן and בֹּאנָה (also בּוֹאֶנָה) *their f. coming.*

† בָאוּ Jer. xxvii 18 is generally taken as Past 3 pl, like בֹּשׁוּ in Tab. XX. Some propose to read יָבֹאוּ (Fut. 3 pl. *m.*). But the *Infin., not the Future*, is mostly used after לְבִלְתִּי. The Future is rare. The Past is also rare, but it occurs in Jer. xxiii. 14 (לְבִלְתִּי שָׁבוּ). [If any *must* emend, they had better propose to read בֹּא—omitting the ו.—They would thus have the Infin. בֹּא after לְבִלְתִּי as usual.] Some have taken בָאוּ Jer l. 5 also as Past 3 pl.

‡ There may be ו in place of ־ָ here.

*תָּבֹא 3 s. *f.* (this with ה would be תְּבֹאָה, from which is †תְּבֹאָתָה Deut. xxxiii. 16 with a re-duplicated ה, and תְּבוֹאָתְךָ Job xxii. 21 with Aff. ךָ *thee m.*),

   with ו Conv. *וַתָּבֹא,—

   for 3 s. *f.* 'w. Affs.' see *** below,—

*תָּבֹא 2 s. *m.*, תָּבֹאִי 2 s. *f.* See also Note (†) for 1 S. xxv. 34 (and Ez. xxii. 4),

*אָבֹא 1 s. (and, with ה,*אָבֹאָה), with ו Conv.*וָאָבֹא,

יָבֹאוּ 3 pl. *m.* (and, with ן, § 239, יְבֹאוּן),

‡תְּבֹאֶינָה 3 pl. *f.*, also תָּבֹאן & *תְּבֹאֶינָה, § 231 (5).

תָּבֹאוּ 2 pl. *m.*,

נָבֹא 1 pl. (and, with ה,*נָבֹאָה), with ו Conv. וַנָּבֹא.

   *** With Pron.-Affs. the forms are :—

3 s. *m.* *יְבֹאֶנּוּ w. Aff. *him*, יְבֹאֵנִי w. Aff. *me*;

3 s. *f.* *תְּבֹאֶנּוּ & תְּבוֹאֵהוּ with Aff. *him*,

   תְּבוֹאֵךְ [p. for תְּבוֹאֶךָ] w. Aff. *thee m.*,—also תְּבוֹאֵנִי, תְּבוֹאָתְךָ see under תָּבֹא 3 s. *f.* above,— w. Aff. *me*;

3 pl. *m.* יְבֹאוּנִי w. Aff. *me* (also וִיבֹאֻנִי with ו pref.).

HIPH-ÎL

INFIN. הָבֵא Absol., הָבִיא (לְהָבִיא, לָבִיא Jer. xxxix. 7, comp. Note † on p. 79);

---

* There may be ו in place of the ◌ֳ here.

† A similar form to this, *viz.* וַתָּבֹאת *Kri* (ותבאתי *Kthiv*), 1 S. xxv 34, is 2 s *f.* Fut. *K.* fr. בוא w. ו Conv.—We also find וַתָּבוֹא as 2 s *f.* Fut. *K.* w. ו Conv. Ez. xvii. 4). Each of these is irregular for וַתָּבֹאִי.

‡ And תָּבֹאֶינָה with י 'superfluous,' 1 S. x. 7. Also, with ו Convers., Esth. iv. 4.

[Hiph-îl contin.]

Past הֵבִיא 3 s. *m.*—w. Affs. (*him*) הֱבִיאוֹ, (*her*) הֱבִיאָהּ,—; (*me*) הֱבִיאַנִי, (*thee m.*) הֱבִיאַךָ—;

הֵבִיאָה 3 s. *f.*;

הֵבֵאתָ 2 s. *m.* (הֵבֵאתָה 2 K. ix. 2,—and הֵבֵיאתָ in הֲבִיאֹתַנִי, הֲבִיאֹתָם, הֲבִיאֹתָנוּ, *i.e.* 2 s. *m.* w. Affs. *me, them m., us*; but there are also, fr. הֵבֵאתָ, the forms הֲבֵאתוֹ, הֲבֵאתָהּ, הֲבֵאתָנוּ, *i.e.* 2 s. *m.* with Affs. *him, her, us*);

הֵבֵאתִי 1 s. (הֵבֵיאתִי Nu. xiv. 31,—and in הֲבִיאֹתִים, הֲבִיאֹתִיךָ, הֲבִיאֹתִיהוּ & הֲבִיאֹתִיו *i.e.* 1 s. w. Affs. *him, thee m., them m.*),—also הֲבֵיאתִיו (Song iii. 4) 1 s. w. Aff. *him.*

הֵבִיאוּ 3 pl.—w. Affs. (*him*) הֱבִיאוּהוּ, (*thee f.*) הֱבִיאוּךְ, (*them m.*) הֱבִיאוּם & ־ֻם Pt. I, § 14;

הֲבֵאתֶם 2 pl. *m.* (הֲבִיאֹתֶם 1 S. xvi. 17);

הֲבִיאֹנוּ in הֲבִיאֹנֻם 1 pl. w. Aff. *them m.*, Nu. xxxii. 17.

Partic. מֵבִיא s. *m.* (מֵבִי *Kthiv* for מֵבִיא *Kri* four times, and הַמֵּבוֹא *Kthiv* for הַמֵּבִיא *Kri* once), מְבִיאִים pl. *m.* (& מְבָאִים, *i.e.* מְבָאִי);

Imper. הָבֵא 2 s. *m.* (once הָבִיא 1 S. xx. 40,—and הָבִיא Jer. xvii. 18, which may however be Infin.,—also הָבִיאָה with ה);

הָבִיאִי 2 s. *f.*, הָבִיאוּ 2 pl. *m.*;

Fut. יָבִיא 3 s. *m.* (& יָבֵא Pt. I, § 12), with וּ Conv. וַיָּבֵא, and once וַיָּבִיא Ez. xl. 3,—With Affs., (*him*) יְבִיאֵהוּ & יְבִיאֶנּוּ, (*her*) יְבִיאֶנָּה & יְבִיאֶהָ, (*thee m.*) יְבִאֲךָ & יְבִיאֲךָ, etc.,—

תָּבִיא 3 s. *f.* & 2 s. *m.*, with וְ Conv. וַתָּבֵא,—

     With Affs., (*him*) תְּבִיאֵנוּ etc., (*them m.*) תְּבִיאֵם

     & תְּבִאֵמוֹ Ex. xv. 17,—

אָבִיא 1 s. (אבי *Kthiv* for אָבִיא *Kri* 1 K. xxi. 29,

     אָבִי ' lacking א ' Mi. i. 15, with וְ Conv. וְאָבִיא

     (& וָאָבֵא), ואביאה *Kthiv* for וְאָבִיא *Kri* Josh.

     xxiv. 8; with Affs , (*him*) אֲבִיאֶנוּ, etc. ;

יָבִיאוּ 3 pl. *m.* (& יְבִיאוּן, יְבִיאוּן with וֹ—§ 239), with

     וְ Conv. וַיָּבִיאוּ) (and וַיָּבֵאוּ),—

     With Affs., (*him*) יְבִאֻהוּ & יְבִיאֻהוּ, (*me*) יְבִיאוּנִי,

     (*them m.*) יְבִיאוּם & יְבִאוּם ;

תְּבִיאֶינָה 3 pl. *f.* ;

תְּבִיאוּ 2 pl. *m.* ;

נָבִיא 1 pl.,—w. Aff. (*them m.*) נְבִיאֵם .

Hoph-Āl

     Past הוּבָא 3 s. *m.*,

         הֻבָאת 3 s. *f.* Gen. xxxiii. 11, and הֻבָאתָה (with ה)

         Ez. xl. 4 [for הוּבְאָה],

         הוּבְאוּ 3 pl. ;

     Partic. מוּבָא s. *m.*, מוּבָאִים pl. *m.*, מוּבָאוֹת pl. *f.* ;

     Fut. יוּבָא 3 s. *m* , יוּבָאוּ Jer. xxvii. 22 Pause-form (not

         in Pause) for יוּבְאוּ 3 pl., comp. § 167 (ii).

[Note. The 2ᵈ Rt-letter is Consonantal in Verb-
forms from the next five roots—except in the
case of certain contracted and apocopated forms
which the Student will easily recognize] :—

דָּוָה only in דְּוֹתָהּ (Lev. xii. 2, *her being weak* or *faint*), Infin.
Kal w. Aff. *her* [like גְּלֹתָהּ from גְּלֹת, of נגלה].

הוּא (?) used only in *K.* (*to be*).

> KAL
>
> > IMPER. הֱוֵא 2 s. *m.*;
> >
> > FUT. יְהוּא 3 s. *m.* (a shortened form, Eccles. xi. 3),—
> > perhaps for יְהוּא with וּ in the place of וְ *i.e.* "the
> > וּ Quiescent—as the וּ in יִשְׁתַּחוּ " for יִשְׁתַּחֲוֶה (as
> > R. D. Kimk͞hi says), or for יְהוֶה or יְהֱוֶה from הוה
> > as יְהִי short for יֶהְיֶה from היה (so the Mendels-
> > sohnian *Bi-ūr hammilloth*).   According to this
> > latter view the א might be 'added' as in אָבוֹא for
> > אָבֹוּ and הָלְכוּא for הָלְכוּ (so Aben Ezra, who takes
> > יְהוּא to be plural, as R. D. K. did at first).
> >
> > Both of the two words above might have been given
> > under the next Root הוה, as R. D. K. gives them.

הוה used only in *K.* (*to be*).

> KAL
>
> > PARTIC (1) הֹוֶה s. *m.*;
> >
> > IMPER. הֱוֵה 2 s. *m.*, הֱוִי 2 s. *f.*
> >
> > > [Note. The form הֱוֵא Imper. 2 s. *m.* with א in the
> > > place of the Quiescent ה, and יְהוּא short for
> > > יְהוֶה or יְהֱוֶה Fut. 3 s. *m.* with א added, were
> > > given under הוּא—see there].

היה used only in *K.* (*to be*), and *Nφ.* (*to be done, etc.*).

> KAL
>
> > INFIN. הָיֹה & הָיוֹ (Absol.), הֱיוֹת (Constr.)—and, with
> > prefixes, מֵהֱיוֹת, לִהְיוֹת, בִּהְיוֹת (or with ◌ְ
> > thus, מֵהֱיֹת, לִהְיֹת, בִּהְיֹת),—and with Pron.-Affs.
> > הֱיוֹתוֹ (*his*), הֱיוֹתָהּ (*her*), etc.,

בִּהְיוֹתוֹ (*at his being,* i.e. *when he was*), וְלִהְיֹתְךָ (*and for thy m. being,* i.e. *and that thou mightest be*), etc.;

Past הָיָה 3 s. *m.,* הָיְתָה (p. וְהָיְתָה) 3 s. *f.* and (with ה Interrogative הֲהָיְתָה) comp. § 7, *c,* Note (†),

הָיִיתָ (also הָיִתָ once, and הָיִיתָה once) 2 s. *m.,*

הָיִית 2 s. *f.* (הָיִיתִי with ' 'superfluous,' Ez. xvi. 31.— For וְהָיִיתָ 2 S. xiv. 2, see Pt. I, § 29, Note †),

הָיִיתִי 1 s.,

הֱיִיתֶם (& הִיתֶם Deut. xxxi. 27) 2 pl. *m.,* and with ו pref. וִהְיִיתֶם,

הָיִינוּ 1 pl.;

Partic (1) הֹוָיָה s. *f.* (Ex. ix. 3);

Imper. הֱיֵה 2 s. *m.* (with ו pref., וֶהְיֵה), הָיִי 2 s. *f.,*

הֱיוּ 2 pl. *m.* (with ו pref., וִהְיוּ).

Fut. יִהְיֶה 3 s. *m.*—apocop. יְהִי (p. וַיְהִי:), and with ו Convers. וַיְהִי (p. וַיְהִי:),—

תִּהְיֶה 3 s. *f.* & 2 s. *m.*—apocop. תְּהִי, & with ו Convers. וַתְּהִי,—

תִּהְיִי 2 s. *f.*—with ו Convers. וַתְּהִי, (also apocop. תְּהִי Nah. iii. 11, & with ו Convers. וַתְּהִי Ezek. xvi. 34),—

אֶהְיֶה 1 s.—apocop. אֱהִי, & with ו Convers. וָאֱהִי,—

יִהְיוּ 3 pl. *m.*—with ו Convers. וַיִּהְיוּ,—

תִּהְיֶינָה or תִּהְיֶין 3 & 2 pl. *f.* (also, twice, תְּהֶיןָ in וַתְּהֶיןָ or וַתִּהְיֶינָה—with ו Convers. וַתְּהֶיןָ),—

נִהְיֶה 1 pl.—with ו Convers. וַנְּהִי & וַנִּהְיֶה.

Niph.

 Past נִהְיָה 3 s. *m.*—with הֲ Interrog. הֲנִהְיָה

   נִהְיָתָה 3 s. *f.* (p. וַנִּהְיֶתָה),

   נִהְיֵיתָ 2 s. *m.*,

   נִהְיֵיתִי 1 s.;

 Partic. נִהְיָה s. *f.*

חוה used only in *Pi.* (*to tell, declare, shew*).

 Pi-ĕl

  Infin. חַוֹּת in מֵחַוֹּת with pref. מ;

  Fut. יְחַוֶּה 3 s. *m.*, אֲחַוֶּה 1 s. & w. Aff. (*thee m.*) אֲחַוְךָ

   (p. אֲחַוֶּךָ).

חיה used in *K.* (*to live*), *Pi.* (*to keep alive, let live, sustain,*
 cherish, enliven, quicken), and *Hφ.* (*to cause to live,*
 to keep alive, etc.).

 Kal

  Infin. חָיֹה & חָיוֹ (Absol.), חֲיוֹת (Constr.) in בִּהְיוֹתָם w. Aff.
   their m. and לִחְיוֹת w. pref. ל;

  Past חָיָה 3 s. *m.*,—the forms חַי 3 s. *m.* (p. חָי), and
   with וְ pref. וָחַי (p. וָחָי), are 'borrowed' from a
   Root חיי;—

   חָיְתָה 3 s. *f.*,—the form חָיָה 3 s. *f.* (in וְחָיָה Ex. i. 16)
   from חיי is like שָׂמָה from שִׂים § 226 (i);

   חָיִיתָ 2 s. *m.*, and with ה at the end in וְחָיִתָה
   Jer. xxxviii. 17;

   חָיוּ 3 pl.,

   חֲיִיתֶם 2 pl. *m.* in וִחְיִיתֶם with וְ pref.

PARTIC (1) [borrowed from a Root חָי [חיי s. *m.* (p. חֵי:),
   חָיָה s. *f.*, חַיִּים pl. *m.*, חַיּוֹת pl. *f.*,—the form חָיוֹת
   pl. *f.* (Ex. i. 19) is like שָׁמוֹת from שִׁים § 226 (ii) ;—

IMPER. חֲיֵה 2 s. *m.* in וֶחְיֵה with ו pref. (Gen. xx. 7, etc.),
   חֲיִי 2 s. *f.* (Ez. xvi. 6),
   חֲיוּ 2 pl. *m.*, וִחְיוּ with ו pref. ;

FUT. יִחְיֶה 3 s. *m.*—apocop. יְחִי (with ו Conjunctive
   וִיחִי & p. וַיְּחִי:), with ו Convers. וַיְּחִי & p. (וַיֶּחִי:),—
   תִּחְיֶה 3 s. *f.* or 2 s. *m.*—apocop. תְּחִי (with ו Con-
      junctive וּתְחִי, with ו Convers. (וַתְּחִי),
   תִּחְיִי 2 s. *f.*,
   אֶחְיֶה 1 s. (with ה Interrogative הַאֶחְיֶה),
   יִחְיוּ 3 pl. *m.*, with ו Convers. וַיִּחְיוּ,
   תִּחְיֶינָה 3 pl. *f.*, & with ה Interrogative הַתִּחְיֶינָה,
   תִּחְיוּן 2 pl. *m.*, & with ן (§ 145) תִּחְיוּן,
   נִחְיֶה 1 pl.

PI-ÊL

INFIN. לְחַיּוֹת with pref. לְ, & w. Affs. (*him*) לְחַיֹּתוֹ,
   (*us*) לְחַיֹּתֵנוּ, (*them m.*) לְחַיֹּתָם ;

PAST חִיָּה 3 s. *m.*,
   חִיָּתְנִי Ps. cxix. 50, 3 s. *f.* w. Aff. *me*—in Pause,
   חִיִּיתַנִי 2 s. *m.* with Aff. *me* (p. נִי:—ָ),
   חִיּוּ 3 pl.,
   חִיִּיתֶם 2 pl. *m.* in הַחַיִּיתֶם, with ה Interrogative ;

PARTIC. מְחַיֶּה s. *m.* ;

IMPER. [חַיֵּה 2 s. *m.*] w. Affs. (*it m.*) חַיֵּיהוּ, (*me*) חַיֵּנִי ;

Fut. יִחְיֶה 3 s. *m.*, with Affs. (*him*) יְחַיֵּהוּ in וִיחַיֵּהוּ with

   ו Conjunctive, (*her*) יְחַיֶּהָ in וַיְחַיֶּהָ with ו Convers.,

   יְחַיֵּנוּ (*us*),

תְּחַיֶּה 3 s. *f.* or 2 s. *m.*,

   w. Affs. (*me*) תְּחַיֵּנִי, (*us*) תְּחַיֵּנוּ,

תְּחַיֶּינִי in Ps. lxxi. 20 is *Kthîv* for תחיינו *Krî*;

וַאֲחַיֶּה 1 s. & with ו Conjunctive אֲחַיֶּה,

יְחַיוּ 3 pl. *m.*, and with ה Interrogative הַיְחַיוּ,—

   with Aff. (*us*) יְחַיֵנוּ,

תְּחַיֶּינָה [3 &] 2 pl. *f.*, & וַתְּחַיֶּין with ו Convers.,

תְּחַיוּ 2 pl. *m.* in תְּחַיוּן with ן (§ 145),

נִחְיֶה 1 pl.

Hiph.

   Infin. הַחֲיֵה (Absol.), לְהַחֲיֹות & לְהַחֲיֹת [Constr. in]

     with ל pref.,—and w. Aff. *him* לְהַחֲיֹתוֹ;

   Past הֶחֱיָה 3 s. *m.*,

     הֶחֱיִתָ 2 s. *m.* in הֶחֱיִתָנוּ 2 s. *m.* w. Aff. *us,*

     הֶחֱיֵיתִי 1 s.,

     הֶחֱיִתֶם 2 pl. *m.*;

   Imper. הַחֲיֵה 2 s. *m.* in הַחֲיֵינִי 2 s. *m.* w. Aff. *me,*

     הַחֲיוּ 2 pl. *m.*

טוא (or טאא) used only in the *Pilpêl* Past 1 s. (טאטאתִי) with

   Objective Aff. הָ *her*, in וְטֵאטֵאתִיהָ Is. xiv. 23.

טוה *to spin*, only in טָווּ (Ex. xxxv. 25, 26) *K*. Past 3 pl.

יאה only in יָאֲתָה (Jer. x. 7) *K*. Past 3 s. *f.* [in Pause, for יָאֲתָה].

יבב only in וַתְּיַבֵּב Ju. v. 28 *and she cried out*, 3 s. *f.* Fut. *Pi.*

   with ו Convers.

יגה used only in *Nϕ. (*to be afflicted*), *Pi.* and *Hϕ.* (*to afflict*).

Niph-Ăl

    Partic., with וּ in place of the usual וֹ, נוּגֵי pl. *m.* in Constr. [from נוּגִים], נוּגוֹת pl. *f.* ;

Pi-Ĕl

    Fut. וַיַּגֶּה 3 s. *m.* with וְ Conversive, Lam. iii. 33, for (וַיְיַגֶּה) (cp. וַיַּדֹּו for וַיְיַדֹּו) ;

Hiph-Îl

    Past הוֹגָה 3 s. *m.* (הוֹגָהּ, with Aff. הָ‑ *her*) ;

    Partic. מוֹגִים pl. *m.* in מוֹגַיִךְ Is. li. 23, with Aff. ‑יִךְ (*thy f.*) ;

    Fut. תֹּוגְיוּן 2 pl. *m.* with ן, Job xix. 2, (instead of תֹּוגוּ).

    [Note. הֻגַּה 2 S. xx. 13 has a form borrowed from this Root, but in signification it belongs to הגה *to remove* (Is. xxvii. 8, Prov. xxv. 4). This הֻגַּה may be *Hiph.* Past 3 s. *m.* of יגה (according to form), "*one caused to remove* [*him*]"="*he was caused to be removed.*" It might perhaps be supposed to be for הָרְגָה *Hoph.* Past 3 s. *m.* of הגה,—or, possibly, for הוֹגָה with ‑ for וֹ as some take הוֹדַע Lev. iv. 23 to be *Hoph.* Past 3 s. *m.* from ידע.]

ידה (I) (*to put forth* or *away, Pi. to cast* the lot) used only in *Kal* Imper. יְדוּ 2 pl. *m.* Jer. l. 14, and *Pi.* Infin. לְיַדּוֹת Zech. ii. 4 & Fut. יַדּוּ for יְיַדּוּ 3 pl. *m.* in וַיַּדּוּ Lam. iii. 53. (But יָדוּ in Joel iv. 3, Obad. *v.* 11, Na. iii. 10, may be supposed to be 'borrowed' fr. a Root ידד,—like סַבּוּ Past *K.* 3 pl. fr. סבב.)

ידה (II) (*to render acknowledgment, confess, praise*), used only in *Hϕ.* and *Hθ.*

Hiph-îl

Infin. (לְהֹדֹת ,בְּהֹדֹת ,הוֹדֹת, (or with — as in בְּהֹדֹת ;
Past הוֹדִינוּ 1 pl., הוֹדוּ 3 pl.;
Partic. מוֹדֶה s. *m.*, מוֹדִים pl. *m.*;
Imper. הוֹדוּ 2 pl. *m.*;
Fut. יוֹדֶה 3 s. *m.* (once יְהוֹדֶה Neh. xi. 17),—w. Aff.
   יוֹדְךָ & יוֹדֶךָּ Pause-form Is. xxxviii. 19,
   (*thee m.*) תּוֹדֶה 3 s. *f.* in תּוֹדֶךָ Pause-form, w. Aff. *thee m.*,
   אוֹדֶה 1 s. (once אֲהוֹדֶה in אֲהוֹדֶנּוּ—with Aff. נּוּ — *him*
   —Ps. xxviii. 7), also w. Affs. (*him*) אוֹדֶנּוּ,
   (p.: אוֹדְךָּ: (*thee m.*),
   יוֹדוּ 3 pl. *m.* (once יְהוֹדוּ in יְהוֹדוּךָ Ps. xlv. 18),
   also w. Aff. *thee m.* יוֹדוּךָ (& יוֹדֻךָ Ps. xlix. 19),
   נוֹדֶה 1 pl.

Hithpä-êl

Infin. וּכְהִתְוַדֹּתוֹ in הִתְוַדֹּות—with prefixes כ and וְ, and
   Aff. וֹ *his*;
Past הִתְוַדָּה 3 s. *m.*, הִתְוַדּוּ 3 pl.;
Partic. מִתְוַדֶּה s. *m.*, מִתְוַדִּים pl. *m.*;
Fut. אֶתְוַדֶּה 1 s., יִתְוַדּוּ 3 pl. *m.*

ילל used only in H♦. (*to howl, utter a loud cry of lamentation*).

Hiph-îl

Past הֵילִיל (for הֵילִל) 3 s. *m.*;
Imper. הֵילֵל 2 s. *m.*, הֵילִילִי 2 s. *f.*, הֵילִילוּ 2 pl. *m.* (הֵילִילִי
   Jer. xlviii. 20 is *Kthiv* for הֵילִילוּ *Kri*);
Fut. יְיֵלִיל 3 s. *m.*, אֲיֵלִיל (& אֵילִילָה with (ה 1 s.,
   תְּיֵלִילוּ (& וַיֵלִילוּ) 3 pl. *m.*, יְהֵילִילוּ 2 pl. *m.*

יָנָה used only in *Kal* and *IIφ.* (*to oppress*).

Kal

> Partic. יוֹנָה s. *f.* (in הַיּוֹנָה, with the ה of § 6, *the oppress-*
> *ing one f.*, Jer. xxv. 38, etc.) ;

> Fut. נִינָם 1 pl. with Aff. ם‑ *them m.* [for ם‑, cp. וַנִּירָם
> and Note (ϵ, vii, 2) on p. xl] according to some. —
> Others take this to be the Noun נִין *progeny* with
> ם‑ *their m.*—Ps. lxxiv. 8.—

Hiph-îl

> Infin. לְהוֹנֹת (in לְהוֹנֹתָם, with Aff. ם‑ *them m.*) ;
> Past הוֹנָה 3 s. *m.*, הוֹנוּ 3 pl. ;
> Partic. מוֹנִים (in מוֹנַיִךְ Is. xlix. 26—with Aff. יִךְ‑ *thy f.*) ;
> Fut. יוֹנֶה 3 s. *m.*, תּוֹנֶה 2 s. *m.* (w. Aff. *him* תּוֹנֶנּוּ),
> יוֹנוּ 3 pl. *m.*, תּוֹנוּ 2 pl. *m.*

יָעָה used only in וְיָעָה (Is. xxviii. 17) *K.* Past 3 s. *m.* with וְ,
" *and it shall sweep away* " (E.V.).

יָפָה used only in *Kal* (*to be beautiful*),—and in *Pî.* (*to beautify*)
once, and once in פָּעְפַּע [comp. p. 176 (γ)] (*to be very*
beautiful), and once in *Hθ.* (*to beautify oneself*).

Kal

> Past [יָפָה 3 s. *m.*], יָפִית 2 s. *f.* (like גָּלִית in Tab. XXIII),
> יָפוּ 3 pl. ;

> Fut. יִיף 3 s. *m.* apocopated—for יִיפֶה—(in וַיִּיף Ez. xxxi. 7),
> תִּיפִי 2 s. *f.* (in וַתִּיפִי Ez. xvi. 13).

Pĭ-ÊL ·

  Fut. יְיַפֶּה 3 s. *m.* in יְיַפֵּהוּ (with Aff. ‎ הוּ‎ — *him*);

פִּעְפַּע

  Past יְפֵיפִיתָ 2 s. *m.*, Ps. xlv. 3.;

Hĭthpă-êl

  Fut. תִּתְיַפִּי 2 s. *f.*

יָצָא (*to go out, go out from*) used only in *Kal*, *Hφ.*, and *Hoph.*

Kal

  Infin. *יְצֹא Abs., צֵאת Constr. (לָצֵאת, כְּצֵאת, בְּצֵאת,
      but לָצֵאת in actual construction—מִצֵּאת, and
      with Affs. צֵאתוֹ, צֵאתְךָ, etc.);

  Past יָצָא 3 s. *m.*, יָצְאָה 3 s. *f.* (p. יָצָאָה׃), יָצָאתָ 2 s. *m.*,
      יָצָאת 2 s. *f.*,
      יָצָאתִי 1 s. (once יָצָתִי, Job i. 21, 'lacking א'),
      יָצְאוּ 3 pl. (p. יָצָאוּ׃,—w. Aff. *me* יְצָאֻנִי Jer. x. 20),
      יְצָאתֶם 2 pl. *m.*, יָצָאנוּ 1 pl.;

  Partic. *יֹצֵא s. *m.*, *יֹצֵאת s. *f.* (הַיּוֹצֵת Deut. xxviii. 57,
      with the Note "lacking א;" comp. § 98)—שֶׁיָּצָא,
      Eccl. x. 1, is for שֶׁיָּצְאָה Partic. *K.* s. *f.* with
      pref. שֶׁ (p. 24, latter part of Note *d*),—
      *יֹצְאִים pl. *m.* (i.c. *יֹצְאֵי), *יֹצְאֹת pl. *f.*;

---

* There may be וֹ in the place of ‎ ֹ‎ here.

IMPER. צֵא 2 s. *m.* (& צֵאָה׃, with ה, in Pause), צְאִי 2 s. *f.*,
  צְאוּ 2 pl. *m.*, p. צֵאוּ׃ (יצאו, Jer. l. 8, is *Kthiv* for
  צֵאוּ *Kri*), צֶאינָה 2 pl. *f.*;

FUT. יֵצֵא 3 s. *m.*, תֵּצֵא 3 s. *f.* & 2 s. *m.*, etc. (like יֵשֵׁב,
  etc., in Tab. XVIII, but)
  תֵּצֶאנָה 3 & 2 pl. *f.* (and תֵּצֶאן 3 pl. *f.*, Ex. xv. 20).
  With ו Conversive the ־ of א־ remains,—thus
  וַיֵּצֵא וַתֵּצֵא, etc.

HIPH-îL
  INFIN. הוֹצִיא, לְהוֹצִיא, etc.,—and, with Affs.,
    (*my bringing out*) הוֹצִיאִי (this is *Kri*, for הוֹצִיא
      Kthiv, in Jer. vii. 22), etc.,
    (*to bring him out*) לְהוֹצִיאֵהוּ, etc.;

  PAST הוֹצִיא 3 s. *m.* (& הוֹצֵא Deut. xxii. 14),—with Affs.,
    (*thee m.*) הוֹצִיאֲךָ & הוֹצִאֲךָ, (*me*) הוֹצִיאַנִי,
    (*them m.*) הוֹצִיאָם, (*us*) הוֹצִיאָנוּ;—
    הוֹצֵאתָ 2 s. *m.*—w. Affs. (*him*) הוֹצֵאתוֹ, etc.,—
    הוֹצֵאת 2 s. *f.*, (for וְהוֹצֵאת 2 s. *f.* 1 K. xvii. 13,
      see Pt. I, § 29, Note †),
    הוֹצֵאתִי 1 s.,—w. Affs. (*them m.*) הוֹצֵאתִים, etc.,—
    הוֹצֵאתָם 2 pl. *m.*; הוֹצִיאוּ 3 pl.;

  PARTIC. מוֹצִיא s. *m.* (& מוֹצֵא once, Ps. cxxxv. 7),—w Affs.,
    מוֹצִיאוֹ, etc., (הַמּוֹצִיאֲךָ *The One bringing thee out*,
      Deut. viii. 14 & xiii. 11),—
    מוֹצִיאִים pl. *m.*, & מוֹצְאִים, i.e. מוֹצְאֵי;

Imper. הוֹצֵא 2 s. *m.* (and הוֹצִיאָה with ה),—also הוֹצִיא
Is. xliii. 8 (which may however be Infin.);—
*הַיְצֵא Gen. viii. 17 is *Krî* for הוֹצֵא *Kthîv*,—w. Affs.,
(*it f.*) הוֹצִיאָהּ, (*me*) הוֹצִיאַנִי, (*them m.*) הוֹצִיאָם,—
הוֹצִיאִי 2 s. *f.*, הוֹצִיאוּ 2 pl. *m.*,—and, with Affs.,
(*him*) הוֹצִיאֵהוּ, (*her*) הוֹצִיאוֹהָ;

Fut. יוֹצִיא 3 s. *m.* (& יֹצֵא Job xxviii. 11),—†וַיֵּצֵא, וַיֹּצֵא
Ju. xix. 25,—also וַיּוֹצֵא),—
w. Affs., (*it f.*) יוֹצִיאָהּ, etc.,—
תּוֹצִיא 3 s. *f.* & 2 s. *m.* (and †תֹּצֵא),—
w. Affs., (*me*) תּוֹצִיאַנִי, (*us*) תּוֹצִיאֵנוּ,—
יוֹצִיאוּ 3 pl. *m.* (also יֹצְאוּ),—
w. Affs., (*him*) יֹצִיאֻהוּ (& †יְצִיאָהוּ), (*them m.*) יוֹצִיאֻם,
תּוֹצִיאוּ 2 pl. *m.*, נוֹצִיא 1 pl.

Hoph-Al

Past [הוּצָא 3 s. *m.*], הוּצָאָה 3 s. *f.* in Pause for הוֹצָאָה;
Partic. [מוּצָא s. *m.*], מוּצֵאת s. *f.*, מוּצָאִים pl. *m.*,
מוּצָאוֹת pl. *f.*

ירא used in *Kal* (*to fear*), *Nφ.* (*to be feared*), and *Pi.* (*to put
in fear*).

Kal

Infin. Constr. יְרֹא Josh. xxii. 25, like פְּקֹד; also לְיִרְאָה
with ה, cp. § 137 (4, iii),—and לֵרֹא 1 S. xviii. 29,—
מִיְרָאתוֹ 2 S. iii. 11 *from his fearing*;

---

* This form is like הַפְקֵד. Similarly, in Ps. v. 9, הַיְשַׁר *Krî* for הוֹשַׁר *Kthîv*
(with — before the ר for Euphony).
† There may be וֹ in place of the — here.

Past יָרֵא 3 s. *m.*, יָרְאָה 3 s. *f.* (p. יְרֵאָה:),

     יָרֵאתָ 2 s. *m.*, יָרֵאתִי 1 s.,

     יָרְאוּ 3 pl. (יְרֵאוּהוּ with Aff. *him*,

       יְרֵאוּךָ w. Aff. *thee m.*, יְרֵאוּנִי w. Aff. *me*),

     יְרֵאתֶם 2 pl. *m.* (יְרֵאתֶם Josh. iv. 24),

     יָרֵאנוּ 1 pl.

Partic. יָרֵא s. *m.* (i.c. יְרֵא), יִרְאַת Constr. form of יְרֵאָה s. *f.*,

     יְרֵאִים pl. *m.* (i.c. יִרְאֵי, and with Affs. יְרֵאָיו, יְרֵאֶיךָ);

Imper. יְרָא 2 s. *m.*, יְראוּ 2 pl. *m.*;

Fut. יִירָא 3 s. *m.*

      (with וַ Convers. וַיִּירָא and sometimes וַיִּרָא),

      w. Affs. (*thee m.*) יִרְאֲךָ Jer. x. 7, (*me*) יִירָאֻנִי,—

     תִּירָא 3 s. *f.* & 2 s. *m.*,

     תִּירְאִי 2 s. *f.* (p. תִּירָאִי:),*

     אִירָא 1 s.,—w. Aff. *him* אִירָאֶנּוּ,

     יִירְאוּ & יִרְאוּ: (& יְראוּ Pt. I, § 44) 3 pl. *m.* (p. יִירָאוּ:,

      also יִרָאוּן: with ן),—

      w. Aff. *thee m.* יִירָאוּךָ & יִרְאוּךָ,—

     תִּירֶאןָ 3 pl. *f.* Ex. i. 17,

     תִּירְאוּ 2 pl. *m.* (p. תִּירָאוּ:, & תִּירָאוּן: with ן),—

      w. Aff. *them m.* תִּירָאוּם and תִּירָאֵם,—

     נִירָא 1 pl.

Niph-āl

Partic. נוֹרָא s. *m.*, נוֹרָאָה s. *f.*, נוֹרָאוֹת pl. *f.* (w. Aff.

     thy m. נוֹרְאוֹתֶיךָ, Ps. cxlv. 6);

Fut. תִּוָּרֵא 2 s. *m.*, Ps. cxxx. 4.

---

* תָּבָאִי 2 s. *f.* Is. lx. 5,—but תָּרְאִי in some Bibles.

PĬ-ÊL

    INFIN. יָרֵא (in לְיָרְאֵנִי *to put me in fear,* לְיָרְאָם *to frighten them*) ;

    PAST יֵרְאוּ 3 pl. (in יֵרְאֻנִי *they frightened me*) ;

    PARTIC. מְיָרְאִים pl. *m.*

ירה used in *Kal, to cast* (*to place* stones for a pillar, also *to shoot, shoot at,*—also *to water*), Nφ. *to be shot,* Hφ. *to shoot* (also *to teach, to point,* and *to cast*).

KAL

    INFIN. יָרֹה Absol., לִירוֹת (and once לִירוֹא 2 Chr. xxvi. 15);

    PAST יָרָה 3 s. *m.,* יָרִיתִי 1 s. ;

    PARTIC.* יֹרֶה & יֹרֶה s. *m.,* יֹרִים & יוֹרִים pl. *m.* ;

    IMPER. יְרֵה 2 s. *m.* ;

    FUT. נִירֶה 1 pl. in וַנִּירָם *and we shot at them,* Nu. xxi. 30.

NIPH-ĂL

    FUT. יִיָּרֶה 3 s. *m. he shall be shot* Ex. xix. 13.

HIPH-ÎL

    INFIN. לְהוֹרֹת,—*w.* Aff. *them m.* לְהוֹרֹתָם ;

    PAST הֹרָה (in הֹרָהוּ *he taught him,* הֹרַנִי *he hath cast me*), הוֹרֵתָ 2 s. *m.* in הֹרֵתַנִי *thou hast taught me* (— for — in Pause),

        הוֹרֵיתִי 1s. (and הֹרֵתִי in הֹרֵתִיךָ Prov. iv. 11 (*I have taught thee*).

---

* This Participle is used as a Noun for the "*early rain*" in Deut. xi. 14, Jer. v. 24. יוֹרֶא Prov. xi. 25 is taken by some as *Hoph.* Fut. 3 s. *m.* from רוה (יוֹרָא for יָרְוֶה — *b*), and by others as *Hoph.* Fut. 3 s. *m.* from ירה (יוֹרָא for יֹרֶה and this for יוֹרֶה—"as הוֹדַע for הוֹדַע," which is somewhat questionable, Lev. iv. 23 & 28). It may perhaps be for the יוֹרֶה "*early rain*" above, this being taken figuratively for a "refreshing beneficent one."

Partic. מוֹרֶה s. m., מוֹרִים pl. m. (מוֹרְאִים 2 S. xi. 24,
  w. א 'superfluous'),—w. Affs. מוֹרֶיךָ thy m. teachers,
  מוֹרָי: my teachers (in Pause);

Imper. הוֹרֵה 2 s. m. (in הֹרֵנִי & הוֹרֵנִי teach me),
  הוֹרוּ 2 pl. m. (in הוֹרוּנִי teach me);

Fut. יוֹרֶה 3 s. m. (וַיֹּור and he shot 2 K. xiii. 17),—w. Affs.,
  יֹרֵם (them m.), יֹרֵנִי (me), יוֹרֵהוּ & יוֹרֶנּוּ (him)
  יוֹרֶנּוּ (us);

  תּוֹרֶה 3 s. f. & 2 s. m. (in תּוֹרְךָ, p. תּוֹרֶךָ, it f. will
  teach thee, תּוֹרֵם thou m. wilt shew them),

  אוֹרֶה 1 s. (w. Aff. thee וְאוֹרְךָ and I will instruct thee
  Ps. xxxii. 8),

  יוֹרוּ 3 pl. m. they shall teach (יֹרוּ they shall shoot,
  and once יֹראוּ 2 S. xi. 24 with א superfluous,
  יֹרֻהוּ Ps. lxiv. 5 they will shoot at him), יוֹרוּךָ they
  shall teach thee m.

ירה (the ה being consonantal) is a Root supposed by some for
  the word תִּרְהוּ Is. xliv. 8, which would then be
  K. Fut. 2 pl. m. for תִּירְהוּ of which they suppose
  the meaning to be *ne stupeatis*. A Metheg might
  have been expected under the ת then, thus תֵּ.—
  Others (as R. D. Kimkhi, and so Fürst) take the
  word to be from a Root רהה in the sense of
  " fearing."

כוה used only in *Nφ.* (*to be burned*).
  Niph.
  Fut. תִּכָּוֶה 2 s. m., תִּכָּוֶינָה 3 pl. f.

לוה used in *K.* (*to stick to, abide with,*—once, Eccl. viii. 15,—
elsewhere *to borrow*), *N*φ. (*to be joined to, united with*),
*H*φ. (*to lend, lend to*).

Kal
  Past לָוִינוּ 1 pl.
  Partic. לוֶֹה s. *m.*
  Fut. יִלְוֶה in יִלְוֶנּוּ 3 s. *m.* w. Aff. *him,*
    תִּלְוֶה 2 s. *m.*

Niph.
  Past נִלְוָה 3 s. *m.* (הַנִּלְוָה with the ה of § 98, Is. lvi. 3),
    נִלְווּ 3 pl. ;
  Partic. נִלְוִים pl. *m.* ;
  Fut. יִלָּוֶה 3 s. *m.*, יִלָּווּ 3 pl. *m.*

Hiph.
  Past הִלְוִיתָ 2 s. *m.* ;
  Partic. מֵלְוֶה s. *m.*
  Fut. יַלְוֶה in יַלְוְךָ 3 s. *m.* w. Aff. *thee m.,*
    תַּלְוֶנּוּ in תַּלְוֶה 2 s. *m.* w. Aff. *him.*

נאה *to be beautiful, becoming* (or *suitable*), used as a Verb only in
  נָאוָה, Ps. xciii. 5, Past 3 s. *m.* (as some say), and
  נָאווּ Is. lii. 7 & Song i. 10, Past 3 pl.
  These words some have taken to be *Kal,* others *Pi-êl,*
  others *Pilêl* [the ו being supposed to stand for the
  repeated 3ᵈ Rt-letter ה,—and so in הִשְׁתַּחֲוָה in
  Tab. XXIII, Note (†)]. The first one has also been
  supposed to be *Niph.* Past 3 s. *m.* of אוה.*

---

* So R. D. K. in his Lexicon; but in his Commentary he connects the word with
נאה, merely mentioning the other as possible.

We might perhaps suppose נָאוּ to be 'compounded' of the two forms נָאוּ and נָוּ (fr. נוה) 'mixed' up together. And נָאֲוָה may be a Noun "*beauty,*" or "*that which is becoming,*" of the same form as גַּאֲוָה from גאה.

Obs. נָאוֶה s. *m.*, and *נָאוָה s. *f.*, are Adjectives.

נבא *Nφ.* and *Hθ.* to prophesy (*Hθ.* also *to offer oneself for prophesying*).

Niph-ăl

Infin. בְּהִנָּבְאוֹ, לְהִנָּבֵא in הִנָּבֵא (w. Aff. *his,* also † Zech. xiii. 4), כְּהִנָּבְאִי (w. Aff. *my*) ;

Past נִבָּא 3 s. *m.*, נִבֵּאתָ 2 s. *m.* (נִבֵּיתָ Jer. xxvi. 9), נִבֵּאתִי 1 s., נִבְּאוּ 3 pl. (p. נִבֵּאוּ) ;

Partic. נִבָּא s. *m.*, נִבְּאִים and נִבָּאִים (i.c. נִבֵּאִי) ;

Imper. הִנָּבֵא 2 s. *m.* ;

Fut. יִנָּבֵא 3 s. *m.*, תִּנָּבֵא 2 s. *m.*, יִנָּבְאוּ 3 pl. *m.*, תִּנָּבְאוּ 2 pl. *m.* ;

Hithpa-êl

Infin. הִתְנַבּוֹת, with מ prefixed 1 S. x. 13 ;

Past הִתְנַבִּיתָ 2 s. *m.*, 1 S. x. 6, הִנַּבֵּאתִי 1 s. (for הִתְנַ׳) Ezek. xxxvii. 10, הִנַּבְּאוּ 3 pl. (for הִתְנַ׳) Jer. xxiii. 13 ;

Partic. מִתְנַבֵּא s. *m.*, מִתְנַבְּאִים pl. *m.*, מִתְנַבְּאוֹת pl. *f.* ;

Fut. יִתְנַבֵּא 3 s. *m.*, יִתְנַבְּאוּ 3 pl. *m.*

נבב used only in *K.* Partic (2) נָבוּב s. *m.* "*hollow,*" i.c. נְבוּב.

---

* For which we find נָוָה, in הַנָּוָה Jer. vi 2.

† Some give this as *Hithpă-ĕl, i.e.* הִתְנַבָּאוֹתוֹ for הִנָּבָ׳.

נגה used only in *K.* (*to shine*), and *Hφ.* (*to cause to shine, to lighten*).

KAL

   PAST נָגַהּ 3 s. *m.*;

   FUT. יִגַּהּ 3 s. *m.*;

HIPH.

   FUT. יַגִּיהַּ 3 s. *m.*

נדד *Kal to move, move away,*—also *to be driven away,* as in *Pŭ.* & *Hoph.*;—*Hφ. to drive away*; *Hθ. to move oneself, move oneself away.*

KAL

   INFIN. נְדֹד;

   PAST נָדְדָה 3 s. *f.,* נָדְרוּ 3 pl. (p. נָדֶדוּ);

   PARTIC. נֹדֵד (or נוֹדֵד) s. *m.,* נוֹדֶדֶת s. *f.,* נֹדְדִים pl. *m.*;

   FUT. יִדּוֹד 3 s. *m.* Na. iii. 7,[*] תִּדַּד 3 s. *f.* G. xxxi. 40, יִדֹּדוּן 3 pl. *m.* (with ן) Ps. lxviii. 13.

Pŭ-ĂL נוֹדַד 3 s. *m.* Tab. XXI (IV).

HIPH-îL יְנַדּוּ 3 pl. *m.* in יְנַדְּהוּ (with Aff. הוּ *him*).

Hoph-ĂL

   PARTIC. מֻנָּד (al. מֻנָד fr. נוד) s. *m.* 2 S. xxiii. 6;

   FUT. יֻדַּד 3 s. *m.*

HITHPĂ-ÊL

   PAST הִתְנוֹדֲדָה 3 s. *f.*;

   FUT. תִּתְנוֹדָד 2 s. *m.* (in pause, cp. § 166 (c)), יִתְנוֹדֲדוּ 3 pl. *m.*

נדה used only in *Pi. to remove as unclean.*

PĬ-ÊL

   PARTIC. מְנַדִּים pl. *m.* (& מְנַדֵּיכֶם with Aff. כֶם 2 pl. *m.*).

---

[*] Comp. § 210 (β).

נהה used only in *Kal* and *N*φ. *to lament.*

Kal

    Past נָהָה 3 s. *m.*;

    Imper. נְהֵה 2 s. *m.*

Niph-ál

    Fut. יִנָּהוּ 3 pl. *m.* 1 S. vii. 2, where some give the Chald. sense *to be congregated.*

נוא used only in *H*φ. *to hold back, to refuse;*—also (in E.V.) *to discourage,* and *to break, to disallow, to make of none effect.*

Hiph.

    Past הֵנִיא 3 s. *m.*;

    Fut. יָנִיא 3 s. *m.* (יָנִי Ps. cxli. 5),

    יָנִיאוּ 3 pl. *m.,* תְּנִיאוּן 2 pl. *m.* (with ן) *Krî* for תנואון *Kthiv* Nu. xxxii. 7.

נוב used only in *K.* (*to flourish, grow, abound, abound with,*) and *Pi.* (*to make to flourish*—E.V. *to make cheerful* or *grow,* Zech. ix. 17),—like קום in Tab. XX.

נוד *to move about,* etc., used only in *Kal, H*φ. & *H*θ.,—like קום in Tab. XX.—For תָּנֹד (Jer. xvi. 5) 2 s. *m.* Fut. *K.,* comp. § 224.

נוה used only in *Kal* (*to remain at home*) and *H*φ. (*to prepare a home,*—or *to glorify,* נוה=נאה,—Ex. xv. 2).

Kal

    Fut. יִנְוֶה 3 s. *m.*

Hiph-íl

    Fut. אַנְוֶה in אַנְוֵהוּ 1 s. with Aff. הוּ— *him.*

נוּחַ *to rest* used only in *Kal*, *Hɸ.* & *Hoph.* (like קוּם in Tab. XX, but comp. also § 234).

[Note. Some give as from this Root the following forms (which are given as from ינח by others, see § 213 and the Note there)—*Hɸ.* *to place, allow, leave, let alone*, etc., and *Hoph.* *to be placed, to be left*:—

Hiph.

Infin. לְהַנִּיחַ

Past הִנִּיחַ 3 s. *m.* (& הִנַּח 1 K. viii. 9),

הִנַּחְתִּי 1 s., הִנַּחְתָּ 2 s. *m.*,

הִנַּחְתֶּם 2 pl. *m.*, הִנִּיחוּ 3 pl.;

Partic. מַנִּיחַ s. *m.*;

Imper. הַנַּח 2 s. *m.* (& הַנִּיחָה with ה),

(הַנִּיחוּ & הַנִּחוּ) 2 pl. *m.*;

Fut. יַנִּיחַ 3 s. *m.* (וַיַּנַּח),

with Affs. (*him*) יַנִּיחֵהוּ & יַנִּחֵהוּ, (*them m.*) יַנִּיחֵם,

תַּנַּח 3 s. *f.* & 2 s. *m.* (short for תַּנִּיחַ),—

with Affs. (*me*) תַּנִּיחֵנִי, (*us*) תַּנִּחֵנוּ,—

אַנִּיחַ 1 s. in שֶׁאַנִּיחֶנּוּ (Eccles. ii. 18) with pref. שֶׁ *that* and Aff. *him*,

יַנִּיחוּ 3 pl. *m.*,—and, with Affs.,

(*him*) יַנִּיחֵהוּ, (*them m.*) יַנִּיחֵם & יַנִּיחוּם.

Hoph-Ăl

Partic. מֻנָּח s. *m.*—(For הֻנִּיחָה, see § 213 end).]

נוּט only in תָּנוּט *Kal* Fut. 3 s. *f.* *it will be moved.*

נוּם *to slumber*: used only in *Kal* [like קוּם in Tab. XX].

נון only in יִנּוֹן (*Krî* Ps. lxxii. 17, *it shall be continued* E.V., for יָנִין *Kthîv*)—Nφ. *Fut.* 3 s. *m.* like יָקוֹם in Tab. XX.

נוס *to flee*: used only in *Kal* and *H*φ.,* like קוֹם in Tab. XX.

נוע *to move to and fro*: used only in *Kal*, *N*φ. and *H*φ., like קוֹם in Tab. XX, but comp. also § 234.

נוף used in *Kal* (only נַפְתִּי Prov. vii. 17, *I have sprinkled*), *Pi.* (only יְנֹפֵף Is. x. 32, *he shall shake*), and *H*φ. *to wave, sift, move backwards and forwards*,—like קוֹם in Tab. XX; but besides the regular Infin. *H*φ. לְהָנִיף we find also לַהֲנָפָה Is. xxx. 28 with לְ prefixed and הָ‑ at the end. The *H*φ. Past 2 s. *m.* is הֲנַפְתָּ (§ 242). The 1 s. however is הֲנִיפוֹתִי Job xxxi. 21. *Hoph.* Past הוּנַף 3 s. *m. it hath been waved*.

נוץ only in *H*φ. *to blossom*.

HIPH-ÎL

PAST הֵנֵצוּ 3 pl.; ·

FUT. יָנֵאץ (Eccles. xii. 5) 3 s. *m.* [Others take this to be from נאץ, *H*φ. *Fut.* 3 s. *m.* for יַנְאִץ, in the sense of "*giving disgust.*"]

[נוק]. 'Borrowed' in form from this Root we find וַתְּנִיקֵהוּ Ex. ii. 9—*H*φ. *Fut.* 3 s. *f.* with וְ Convers.,—in the sense of the Root ינק (*K. to suck*, *H*φ. *to suckle*).

נושׁ only in וָאָנוּשָׁה Ps. lxix. 21, *and I am full of heaviness*, E.V.), *Kal Fut.* 1 s. with וְ Convers. & ה at the end.

---

x

נזה used only in *K.* (*to be sprinkled*, E.V.) and *Hφ.* (*to sprinkle*, E.V.) ;—Gesenius gives "*shall make to jump up*" instead of "*shall sprinkle*" for יַזֶּה in Is. lii. 15. Fürst observes : "nil impedit quominus etiam hoc loco ingenitam verbi significationem retineamus."

KAL

    FUT. יִזֶּה 3 s. *m.*, apocop. יִז (in וְיִז Is. lxiii. 3), and with ו Convers. וַיִּז 2 K. ix. 33 ;

HIPH.

    PAST הִזָּה 3 s. *m.*, הִזֵּיתָ 2 s. *m.*,

    PARTIC. מַזֶּה Constr. form of מַזֶּה s. *m.*,

    IMPER. הַזֵּה 2 s. *m.*,

    FUT. יַזֶּה 3 s. *m.*, apocop. (& with ו Convers.) וַיַּז.

נחה used only in *Kal* and *Hφ.* to *guide, lead.*

KAL

    PAST [נָחָה] 3 s. *m.* (in וְנָחֲךָ *and He will guide thee m.*, נָחַנִי *He hath led me*, נָחָם *He led them*), נָחִיתָ 2 s. *m.* ;

    IMPER. נְחֵה 2 s. *m.* (with Aff., נְחֵנִי *lead me*) ;

HIPH-îL

    INFIN. לְהַנְחֹתָם *to lead them* Neh. ix. 19, & לַנְחֹתָם Ex. xiii. 21 comp. § 137 (3) Note (†).

    PAST הִנְחָה 3 s. *m.* (in הִנְחַנִי *He led me*),

        הִנְחִיתָ 2 s. *m.* (in הִנְחִיתָם *Thou didst lead them*) ;

    FUT. יַנְחֶה 3 s. *m.* (in יַנְחֵנוּ, w. Aff. *him*, יַנְחֵנִי w. Aff. *me*, יַנְחֵם w. Aff. *them m.*),

        תַּנְחֶה 3 s. *f.* or 2 s. *m.*,—

        w. Affs., (*me*) תַּנְחֵנִי, (*them m.*) תַּנְחֵם,—

        אַנְחֶה 1 s. (in אַנְחֵהוּ w. Aff. *him*, and אַנְחֶנָּה w. Aff. *her*),

        יַנְחוּ 3 pl. *m.* (in יַנְחוּנִי w. Aff. *me*).

נטה used only in *Kal* (*to incline, extend, pitch* tent, etc.), *Nφ.*
(*to be extended*, etc.), and *Hφ. to cause to incline*, or
decline, etc.).

KAL

INFIN. נְטוֹת Constr., לִנְטוֹת or לִנְטֹת, etc.,
בִּנְטֹתִי (w. Aff. *my*), כִּנְטוֹתוֹ (w. Aff. *his*) ;

PAST נָטָה 3 s. *m.*, נָטְתָה 3 s. *f.*, נָטִיתָ 2 s. *m.*, נָטִיתִי 1 s.,
נָטוּ 3 pl. (נָטָיוּ Ps. lxxiii. 2, *Krî* for נטוי *Kthiv*) ;

PARTIC (1) נוֹטֶה s. *m.* (or נֹטֶה) and with Aff. *them m.*
נוֹטֵיהֶם ;

PARTIC (2) נָטוּי s. *m.*, נְטוּיָה s. *f.*, נְטוּיוֹת pl: *f. Krî* for
נטווֹת *Kthiv* Is. iii. 16 (comp. 1 S. xxv. 18);

IMPER. נְטֵה 2 s. *m.* ;

FUT. יִטֶּה 3 s. *m.* (apocop. יֵט, and ־יֵט when unaccented),
תִּטֶּה 3 s. *f.* or 2 s. *m.* (apocop. תֵּט),
יִטּוּ 3 pl. *m.*, נִטֶּה 1 pl.

NIPH-ĂL

PAST נִטָּיוּ 3 pl. ;

FUT. יִנָּטֶה 3 s. *m.*, יִנָּטוּ 3 pl. *m.*

HIPH-ÎL

INFIN. לְהַטֹּת or לְהַטּוֹת, w. Aff. *her* לְהַטֹּתָהּ ;

PAST הִטָּה 3 s. *m.*,—w. Aff. *him* הִטָּהוּ,
הִטַּתָּה in הִטַּתּוּ 3 s. *f.* with Aff. *him,*.
הִטִּיתִי 1 s., הִטּוּ 3 pl., הִטִּיתֶם 2 pl. *m.* ;

PARTIC. מַטֶּה s. *m.*, מַטִּים pl. *m.* (i.e. מַטִּי);

IMPER. הַטֵּה 2 s. *m.* (apocop. הַט), הַטִּי 2 s. *f.*, הַטּוּ 2 pl. *m.* ;

FUT. יַטֶּה 3 s. *m.* (ápocop. יֵט),—and, with Affs.,
יַטֵּהוּ & יַטֵּנוּ (*him*),
(*thee m.*) יַטֶּךָ Job xxxvi. 18 (in Pause for יַטְּךָ),
תַּטֶּה 3 s. *f.* or 2 s. *m.* (apocop. תֵּט),—
with Aff. *him* תַּטֵּהוּ,
אַטֶּה 1 s. (apocop. אַט, p. אָט), יַטּוּ 3 pl. *m.*

ניר *to till* only in נִירוּ Imper. *Kal* 2 pl. *m.*

נכא *Nφ. to be crushed*: only in נִכְּאוּ (Job xxx. 8) 3 pl. Past *Nφ.*
[Some give this from נכה (*Nφ.* Past 3 pl., for נִכּוּ).]

נכה used in *Hφ.* (*to smite*), and *Nφ.* & *Pŭ.* & *Hoph.* (*to be smitten*).

NIPH-ĂL
PAST נִכָּה 3 s. *m.*

PŬ-ĂL
PAST נֻכְּתָה 3 s. *f.* (in Pause for נֻכְּתָה), נֻכּוּ 3 pl.

HIPH-ÎL
INFIN. הַכֵּה Absol., (הַכּוֹת, בְּהַכּוֹת, לְהַכּוֹת, מֵהַכּוֹת), and
     with Affs. p. הַכֹּתְךָ: ך_ָ, הַכֹּתָה הַכּוֹתוֹ & הַכֹּתוֹ
     (הַכֹּתָם הַכֹּתִי);

PAST הִכָּה 3 s. *m.*,—and, with Affs.,
     (*him*) הִכָּהוּ, (*thee m.*) הִכְּךָ, (*me*) הִכַּנִי, p. נִי_ָ,
     (*them m.*) הִכָּם,—
     הִכִּיתָ 2 s. *m.* (& הִכִּיתָה with ה, § 138 B. i.),—and,
     with Affs., (*him*) הִכִּיתוֹ, (*me*) הִכִּיתָנִי Nu. xxii. 28
     Pause-form of הִכִּיתָנִי [comp. § 167, ii. (2)],
     (*them m.*) הִכִּיתָם, (*us*) הִכִּיתָנוּ,—
     הִכֵּיתִי 1 s.,—but, with Affs.,
     (*thee f.*) הִכִּיתִיךְ, (*thee m.*) הִכִּתִיךָ, (*him*) הִכִּיתִיו,—
     הִכּוּ 3 pl.,—and, with Affs.,
     (*them m.*) הִכּוּם ו, (*me*) הִכּוּנִי, (*him*) הִכָּהוּ,—
     הִכִּיתֶם 2 pl. *m.*;

PARTIC. מַכֶּה s. *m.* (i.e. מַכֶּה, and with Affs. מַכֵּהוּ *one
     smiting him*, מַכֵּךְ *one smiting thee f.*),
     מַכִּים pl. *m.*, מַכּוֹת pl. *f.*;

Imper. הַכֵּה 2 s. *m.* (apocop. הַךְ, and with Aff. ־ֵנִי *me* (הַכֵּינִי),

הַכּוּ 2 pl. *m.* (with Affs. הַכּוּם, הַכֻּהוּ);

Fut. יַכֶּה 3 s. *m.*, apocop. יַךְ,

with ו Convers. וַיַּכֶּה and וַיַּךְ (p. וַיָּךְ),—

with Affs., (*him*) יַכֵּהוּ & יַכֶּנּוּ (once יַכּוֹ 2 S. xiv. 6,),

(*her*) יַכֶּהָ, (*thee m.*) יַכְּכָה, p. יַכֶּכָּה [כָּה for ךָ,

comp. Note ϵ (iv) on Tab. XXVIII],

(*them m.*) יַכֵּם,

תַּכֶּה 3 s. *f.* or 2 s. *m.*, apocop. תַּךְ, w. ו Convers. וַתַּךְ,

תַּכֶּנּוּ (Prov. xxiii. 13 & 14) 2 s. *m.* w. Aff. נּוּ־ *him*,

אַכֶּה 1 s., apocop. אַךְ,

with ו Convers. וְאַךְ and וְאַכֶּה,—

with Affs. (*him*) אַכֵּהוּ & אַכֶּנּוּ, (*thee m.*) אַכְּכָה

2 S. ii. 22—Pause-form of אַכֶּכָה with the

Accent ־ *Pashta* [כָה for ךָ, comp. Note ϵ (iv)

on Tab. XXVII],—

יַכּוּ 3 pl. *m.*, and w. ו Convers. וַיַּכּוּ,—

with Affs., (*him*) יַכֻּהוּ, (*her*) יַכּוּהָ,

(*thee m.*) יַכּוּךְ, (*them m.*) יַכּוּם,—

נַכֶּה 1 pl., with ו Convers. (apocop.) וַנַּךְ,—

with Affs., (*him*) נַכֵּהוּ & נַכֶּנּוּ, (*them m.*) נַכֵּם;

Hoph-Ăl

Past הֻכָּה 3 s. *m.* (once הוּכָה Ps. cii. 5, cp. Pt. I, § 14, N.B.),

הֻכְּתָה 3 s. *f.*, הֻכֵּיתִי 1 s., הֻכּוּ 3 pl.;

Partic. מֻכֶּה *s. m.* (i.e. מֻכֶּה), מֻכָּה *s. f.*,

מֻכִּים pl. *m.* (i.e. מֻכִּי);

Fut. יֻכּוּ 3 pl. *m.*, תֻּכּוּ 2 pl. *m.*

נלה only in the *Hφ.* Infin. בְּנַלְתְךָ *on thy ceasing* . [for 'כַהֲנ,
cp. § 137 (3) Note (†). The Dagesh of the נ is
Euphonic].

נסה used only in *Pi.* *to tempt, try, adventure,* etc.

PĬ-ÊL

INFIN. נַסּוֹת, לְנַסּוֹת, and with Affs. נַסֹּתוֹ, etc.;

PAST נִסָּה 3 s. *m.* (with ה Interrog. הֲנִסָּה Deut. iv. 34 &
Job iv. 2),—

    with Aff. (*him*) נִסָּהוּ,

נִסְּתָה 3 s. *f.*,

נִסִּיתָ 2 s. *m.,* in נִסִּיתוֹ 2 s. *m.* w. Aff. *him* Deut. xxxiii. 8,

נִסִּיתִי 1 s.,

נִסּוּ 3 pl. in נִסּוּנִי with Aff. *me* Ps. xcv. 9,

נִסִּיתֶם 2. pl. *m.*;

PARTIC. מְנַסֶּה s. *m.*,

IMPER. נַס 2 s. *m.,* and with Aff. *me* נַסֵּנִי;

FUT. יְנַסֶּה 3 s. *m.* in וַיְנַסֵּם with ו Convers. and Aff. *them m.*,

אֲנַסֶּה 1 s.,—and, with Affs.,

    (*him*) אֲנַסֶּנּוּ,

       (*thee m.*) אֲנַסְּכָה Eccl. ii. 1 [כָה for ךָ, comp.
       Note ε (iv) on Tab. XXVIII].

יְנַסּוּ 3 pl. *m.*,

תְּנַסּוּ 2 pl. *m.* (and, with ן, תְּנַסּוּן).

נסם used only in *K.* Partic (1) נָסֵם s. *m.,* and in *Pi.* & *Hθ.*
like סבב in Tab. XXI.

נצא *to fly away* used only in נָצֹא Infin. Absol. *Kal,* Jer. xlviii. 9,
and perhaps in נָצוּ (Lam. iv. 15),. 3 pl. Past *Kal.*
This would then be for נָצְאוּ as כָּלוּ 1 S. vi. 10 for
כָּלְאוּ, etc. But

נצה (I) is generally given as the Root of that נְצוּ (Lam. iv. 15), and by some as the Root of נָצָא Jer. xlviii. 9 (the א being supposed to stand for the ה).

נצה (II) is used in *N*φ. & *H*φ. *to strive* (*Kal* once, Jer. iv. 7, תִּצֶּינָה *they f. shall be laid waste*, E.V.)—[For נְצוּ Lam. iv. 15, see under נצא and נצה (I).]

NIPH-ĂL
    PARTIC. נִצִּים pl. *m.*;
    FUT. יִנָּצוּ 3 pl. *m.*;

HIPH-ÎL
    INFIN. בְּהַצֹּתוֹ & הַצּוֹת in בְּהַצֹּתָם;
    PAST הִצּוּ 3 pl.

נצץ only in נֹצְצִים *sparkling*, *Kal* Partic. pl. *m.*, Ez. i. 7.

נקה used in *Kal* (only once) *to be clear* or *unpunished*, in *N*φ. in the same sense, and *to be cut off*, and in *Pi.* *to clear, to hold guiltless*.

KAL
    INFIN. Absol. נָקֹה Jer. xlix. 12.

NIPH-ĂL
    INFIN. הִנָּקֵה Absol.;
    PAST נִקָּה 3 s. *m.*, נִקְּתָה 3 s. *f.* (p. נִקָּתָה:),
    נִקֵּיתָ 2 s. *m.*, נִקֵּיתִי 1 s.;
    IMPER. הִנָּקִי 2 s. *f.*;
    FUT. יִנָּקֶה 3 s. *m.*, תִּנָּקֶה 2 s. *m.*, תִּנָּקוּ 2 pl. *m.*

PĬ-ÊL
    INFIN. נַקֵּה Absol.;
    PAST נִקֵּיתִי 1 s.;

IMPER. נַקֵּה 2 s. *m.* (in נַקֵּנִי with Aff. ‏נִי‎_ *me*);

FUT. יְנַקֶּה 3 s. *m.*,

     תְּנַקֶּה 2 s. *m.* (in תְּנַקֵּהוּ with Aff. ‏הוּ‎— *him*,

     תְּנַקֵּנִי with Aff. ‏נִי‎_ *me*),

     אֲנַקֶּה 1 s. (in אֲנַקֶּךָ with Aff. ‏ךָ *thee*, in Pause).

נשא used in *Kal* (*to bear, lift up, take away, pardon,* etc.),

     Nφ. (*to be borne,* etc.), Pi. (*to lift up, exalt,* etc.),

     Hφ. (*to cause to bear, to bring*), and Hθ. (*to lift one-*

     self, exalt oneself).

KAL

INFIN. נָשׂוֹא & נָשׂא Absol., נָשׂוֹא & נשׂא & שְׂאֵת Constr.

     (בִּשְׂאֵת, once בִּשׂוֹא Ps. lxxxix. 10,—לִשְׂאֵת,—with

     Affs. שְׂאֵתִי, שְׂאֵתוֹ once מִשְּׂאֵתוֹ Job xli. 17,

     once בְּנָשְׂאִי Ps. xxviii. 2);

PAST נָשָׂא 3 s. *m.*,—and, with Affs.,

     (*him*) נְשָׂאוֹ, (*thee m.*) נְשָׂאֲךָ,—

     נָשְׂאָה 3 s. *f.*,—and with Aff. *me* נְשָׂאַתְנִי,—

     נָשָׂאתָ 2 s. *m.* (& נְשָׂאתָה with ‏ה),—

     with Aff. (*me*) נְשָׂאתַנִי,—

     נָשָׂאת 2 s. *f.* (in נְשָׂאתִים *thou f. hast borne them m.*),

     נָשָׂאתִי 1 s.,

     נָשְׂאוּ 3 pl. (p. ‏נָשָׂאוּ),—once נָשׂוּ 'lacking א'

       Ez. xxxix. 26, and once (as some say) נָשׂוֹא

       Ps. cxxxix. 20,—

     with Aff. *them m.* נְשָׂאוּם,—

     נְשָׂאתֶם 2 pl. *m.*;

PARTIC (1) נֹשֵׂא s. *m.,* & נֹשֵׂאת s. *f.,*

נֹשְׂאִים pl. *m.* (i.c. נֹשְׂאֵי), & נֹשְׂאוֹת pl. *f.;*

PARTIC (2) נָשׂוּי s. *m.* (i.c. נְשׂוּא & נָשׂא,—once נָשׂוּי

Ps. xxxii. 1, a form 'borrowed' from a Root

ל״ה, like גְּלוּי in Tab. XXIII),

נְשׂאִים pl. *m.,* נְשׂאת pl. *f.* in נְשֻׂאֹתֵיכֶם (with

Aff. *your m.*) Is. xlvi. 1;

IMPER. שָׂא 2 s. *m.* (once נְשָׂא Ps. x. 12, and once נְסָה

Ps. iv. 7),—

with Aff. *him* שָׂאֵהוּ,

שְׂאִי 2 s. *f.,*

שְׂאוּ 2 pl. *m.,* and with Aff. *me* שָׂאוּנִי;

FUT. יִשָּׂא 3 s. *m.,*—and, with Affs.,

(*him*) יִשָּׂאֵהוּ, (*her*) יִשָּׂאֶנָּה & יִשָּׂאָהּ, (*thee m.*) יִשָּׂאֲךָ,

(*me*) יִשָּׂאֵנִי, (*them m.*) יִשָּׂאֵם,—

תִּשָּׂא 3 s. *f.* or 2 s. *m.,*—and, with Affs.,

(*him*) תִּשָּׂאֵהוּ, (*me*) תִּשָּׂאֵנִי, (*them m.*) תִּשָּׂאֵם,—

תִּשְׂאִי 2 s. *f.,*

אֶשָּׂא 1 s., and w. Aff. *him* אֶשָּׂאֶנּוּ,

יִשְׂאוּ 3 pl. *m.,*—and, with Affs.,

(*him*) יִשָּׂאֻהוּ, (*thee m.*) יִשָּׂאוּנְךָ Ps. xci. 12, comp.

Note (γ) on Tab. XXVIII,

(*them m.*) יִשָּׂאֻם & יִשָּׂאֵם, (*us*) יִשָּׂאֻנוּ,—

תִּשֶּׂאנָה 3 pl. *f.* (and three times תִּשֶּׂנָה) 'lacking א',

תִּשְׂאוּ 2 pl. *m.* (p. תִּשָּׂאוּ and תִּשָּׂאוּן),

תִּשֶּׂאינָה 2 pl. *f.,*

נִשָּׂא 1 pl.

NIPH-ĂL

INFIN. הִנָּשֵׂא in בְּהִנָּשֵׂא and בְּהִנָּשְׂאָם (w. Aff. for 3 pl. *m.*),

PAST נִשָּׂא 3 s. *m.* (נִשֵּׂאת Zech. v. 7. is Partic. s. *f.*);

PARTIC. נִשָּׂא s. *m.*,

    נִשָּׂאָה s. *f.* (& נִשֵּׂאת instead of נִשֵּׂאת),

    נִשָּׂאִים pl. *m.*,

    נִשָּׂאוֹת pl. *f.*;

IMPER. הִנָּשֵׂא 2 s. *m.*, הִנָּשְׂאוּ 2 pl. *m.*;

FUT. יִנָּשֵׂא 3 s. *m.*, אֶנָּשֵׂא 1 s.,

    יִנָּשְׂאוּ 3 pl. *m.* (p. יִנָּשֵׂאוּ),—also יִנָּשׂוֹא once, Jer. x. 5,

    תִּנָּשֶׂאנָה 3 pl. *f.*,

    תִּנָּשֵׂאוּ 2 pl. *m.* in Pause for תִּנָּשְׂאוּ.

PĬ-ÊL

PAST נִשֵּׂא 3 s. *m.* and נִשָּׂא 2 S. v. 12,—

    with Aff. נִשְּׂאוֹ *he exalted him*;

PARTIC. מְנַשְּׂאִים pl. *m.*;

IMPER. נַשֵּׂא 2 s. *m.* in נַשְּׂאֵם (with Aff. ם— *them m.*);

FUT. יְנַשֵּׂא 3 s. *m.* in וַיְנַשְּׂאֵהוּ and וַיְנַשְּׂאֵם,

    יְנַשְּׂאוּ 3 pl. *m.* in יְנַשְּׂאוּהוּ (with Aff. *him*);

ḤIPH-ÎL

PAST הִשִּׂיאוּ 3 pl.;

HITHPĂ-ÊL

INFIN. בְּהִתְנַשֵּׂא, הִתְנַשֵּׂא;

PARTIC. מִתְנַשֵּׂא s. *m.*;

FUT. יִתְנַשֵּׂא 3 s. *m.* (in Pause, cp. § 166 (*c*)),

    תִּנַּשֵּׂא 3 s. *f.* & תִּתְנַשֵּׂא Nu. xxiv 7

    יִנַּשְּׂאוּ 3 pl. *m.* Dan. xi. 14,

    תִּתְנַשְּׂאוּ 2 pl. *m.*

נָשָׁא (I) used only* in *Nφ.* (*to be deceived*), and *Hφ.* (*to deceive*).

NIPH-ĂL

    PAST נִשְּׁאוּ 3 pl.;

HIPH-îL

    INFIN. הַשֵּׁא Absol.;

    PAST הִשִּׁיא 3 s. *m.*,—and, with Affs.,

        (*thee m.*) הִשִּׁיאֲךָ Obad. *v.* 3—Pause-form not

        in Pause for הִשִּׁיאֲךָ,

        (*me*) הִשִּׁיאַנִי Gen. iii. 13,

        הִשֵּׁאתָ 2 s. *m.*,

        הִשִּׁיאוּ 3 pl. (in הִשִּׁיאוּךְ, with Aff. *thee m.*);

    FUT. יַשִּׁיא 3 s. *m.* (& יַשִּׁא Is. xxxvi. 14),—and

        with Aff. *thee m.* יַשִּׁיאֲךָ,—

        יַשִּׁיאוּ 3 pl. *m.*,   תַּשִּׁיאוּ 2 pl. *m.*

נָשָׁא (II) used only in *Kal* (*to be a creditor*) & *Hφ.* (*to act as a*

    creditor).

KAL

    PARTIC. נֹשֵׁא s. *m.*, נֹשִׁאים pl. *m.* Neh. v. 7—which might

        however be given under נָשָׁה (II), as the א here is

        'superfluous';—

HIPH-îL

    FUT. יַשִּׁיא 3 s. *m.* (יַשִּׁיא *Kri* Ps. lv. 16).

נָשָׁה (I) used only in *Kal* (*to forget*), *Pi.* (*to make to forget*), and

    Hφ. (*to cause to forget*), also (*to put out of mind,* and

    so *forget intentionally*).

KAL

    INFIN. נָשֹׁא Absol. (borrowed from Root נָשָׁא in form);

Past נָשִׁיתִי 1 s. ;

Nɪᴘʜ-ăʟ

Fᴜᴛ. תִּנָּשֶׁה 2 s. *m.* in לֹא תִנָּשֵׁנִי (*thou shall not be for-gotten of Me*, Is. xliv. 21) ;

Pĭ-êʟ

Past נִשָּׁה 3 s. *m.* in נַשַּׁנִי with Aff. *me*, Gen. xli. 51, the נַ to suit perhaps the נַ in מְנַשֶּׁה there. The מְנַשֶּׁה is strictly the *Pĭ.* Partic. s. *m.* of נָשָׁה.

Hɪᴘʜ-îʟ

Past הִשָּׁה 3 s. *m.* in הִשָּׁה (with Aff. הָ — *her*, Job xxxix. 17) ;

Pᴀʀᴛɪᴄ. מַשֶּׁה only used as a Noun (in the Constr. form מַשֵּׁה, Deut. xv. 2) ;

Fᴜᴛ. יַשֶּׁה 3 s. *m.*,

תַּשִׁי 2 s. *f.* Deut. xxxii. 18, borrowed in form from a non-existing Root שהה, perhaps for תִּשְׁהִי, as some think. Some take the word to be *Kal.* Fut. 2 s. *f.*

נשה (II) used only in *Kal* (*to be a creditor*), and Hφ. (*to lend, to act as a creditor*).

Kᴀʟ

Past נָשִׁיתִי 1 s., נָשׁוּ 3 pl. ;

Pᴀʀᴛɪᴄ. נֹשֶׁה s. *m.* (or נוֹשֶׁה),

נשׁים pl. *m.* and נוֹשִׁים in מַנּוֹשַׁי Is. l. 1 (*from* or *of My creditors*) ;

Hɪᴘʜ-îʟ

Fᴜᴛ. יַשֶּׁה 3 s. *m.*, תַּשֶּׁה 2 s. *m.*

[For the Irregular נתן, see Note (B) on Tab. XIX [p. xxvɪ].

סוא A Root imagined by some (and. סאא by others) for the word בְּסַאסְאָה Is. xxvii. 8. There is, however, the undoubted Hebrew Root סאה, from which the word has long been taken and is still taken by many. Thus, for instance, R. D. Kimk͟hi says that

(1) "possibly it is a Noun, in place of סָאָה,—and in it the 1st and 2d Rt-letters are repeated, and the ה at the end is the 3d Rt-letter" (and as an example of the repetition of the 1st and. 2d Rt-letters he cites יְפֵיפִ֫ית in Ps. xlv. 3) ;

(2) that "moreover, one might say that it is an INFINITIVE of an Intensive Voice, and that the 1st Rt-letter only is repeated, as in the word זַרְזִיף from זרף, the first א being the 2d Rt-letter and the second א in the place of the 3d Rt-letter,—and the form of the word therefore בְּפַעְפְלָה."

[Obs. (i) The Dagesh in the ס of בְּסַאסְאָה brings the word into more full agreement with the FORM in (2), by virtually supplying the Quiescent Shva [implied by the Dagesh, Pt. I, § 53, Note (†)] for the close of the syllable after (ـَ),—rather than בְּסָאסְאָה.

(ii) The termination being an unusual one for an Infinitive of a Verb לֹ"ה with pref. בַ, we prefer R. D. K.'s first-mentioned opinion, viz. that the word may be a NOUN of reduplicated form.

(iii) Some think that the word is produced by actual repetition of the Noun סָאָה. So Gesenius says (Thesaurus, p. 932.a) that it is "contracted from

בְּסַאֽה־סָאֽה‎," which he supposes to mean "*ad mensuram, i.e. modice.*" But the sense "*moderately*" is rather questionable. And Dr. Ewald, in Note (2) on p. 182 of his *Ausfuhrliches Lehrbuch der Hebr. Sprache,* has a remark on "die ganz verkehrte ableitung von סָאֽה סָאֽה *mass mass.*" And Fürst on p. 750 of the Concordance writes the words "ejus modi forma composita abhorret a linguæ hebraicæ legibus." It is scarcely necessary to warn the Student against the mistake of supposing that either the Targum or R. D. Kimk͞hi or Aben Ezra or Rashi make any such statement (at least definitely) respecting the form of the word. The technical term כפולה "*reduplicated*" does not necessarily signify the bodily repetition of a word. And we see no need for imagining a new Hebrew Root (whether סוא or סאא), from which the word in Is. xxvii. 8 may be a פלפל or a פעפע form (Infin. w. pref. בֽ and Aff. *her,* as some say) in the sense of "*agitating*" as some suppose, or "*frightening her*" as others fancy, or "*her expulsion*" or "*her foul-dealing*" as others imagine. The reduplicated form from סאה may fairly stand in some such a sense as we might express by "*in measured-measure*" or "*careful measure*" or "*due measure.*" But we may not dwell any longer on this now. A Commentary on the passage would be out of place in this mere LIST of VERB-FORMS.]

In the following Roots the 2ᵈ Rt-letter ו is Consonantal, and
the forms correspond therefore with those in Tab. XXIII :—

עוה used in *K.* (*to be perverse*), *Nφ.* (*to be perverted* or *perverse,
also to be distorted with pain*), *Pĭ.* (*to pervert, turn,
make crooked*), and (*Hφ. to make perverse, pervert, act
perversely*).

KAL

    PAST עִוְּתָה 3 s. *f.*, עִוִּינוּ 1 pl. ;

NIPH-ĂL

    PAST נַעֲוֵיתִי 1 s.,

    PARTIC. נַעֲוֶה s. *m.* found only in the Constr. form נַעֲוֵה;

PĬ-ÊL

    PAST עִוָּה 3 s. *m.* ;

HIPH.

    INFIN. הַעֲוֵה Absol., [הַעֲוֹת Constr.] in בְּהַעֲוֺתוֹ w. pref. ב
        and Aff. *his,*

    PAST הֶעֱוָה 3 s. *m.*, הֶעֱוֵיתִי 1 s., הֶעֱווּ 3 pl., הֶעֱוִינוּ 1 pl.

צוה used only in *Pĭ.* (*to command*) and *Pŭ.* (*to to be commanded*).

PĬ-EL

    INFIN. צַוֹּת in צַוֺּתוֹ w. Aff. 3 s. *m.,*—and w. prefs. בְּצַוֹּת,
        לְצַוֺּת, and בְּצַוֺּתוֹ ;

    PAST צִוָּה 3 s. *m.,*—and, with Affs.,

        (*him*) צִוָּהוּ, (*thee m.*) צִוְּךָ, in Pause צִוָּךְ:
        (*me*) צִוַּנִי, in Pause צִוָּנִי:,
        (*them m.*) צִוָּם, (*us*) צִוָּנוּ,—

        צִוְּתָה 3 s. *f.,*—and with Aff. *her* צִוַּתָּה,—

        צִוִּיתָ 2 s. *m.* & צִוִּיתָה,—and, with Affs.,
        (*me*) צִוִּיתָנִי in Pause, (*us*) צִוִּיתָנוּ,—

        צִוִּיתִי 1 s. (& צִוֵּיתִי),—and, with Affs.,
        (*him*) צִוִּיתִיו & תִּיו, (*her*) צִוִּיתִיהָ, (*thee m.*) צִוִּיתִיךָ,
        (*them m.*) צִוִּיתִים & תִּים,—

Partic. מְצַוֶּה s. *m.* (i.c. ה—ֵ), w. Aff. *thee m.* מְצַוְּךָ, and in Pause ‏‎ ‎‏: ‏‎ ‎‏‎ & ‏‎ ‎‏,

מְצַוָּה s. *f.*

Imper. צַוֵּה 2 s. *m.*, apocop. צַו, צַוּוּ 2 pl. *m.*;

Fut. יְצַוֶּה 3 s. *m.* (apocop. יְצַו, with ו Convers. וַיְצַו and twice וַיְצַוֶּה, which is also *Kri* for ויצוהו *Kthiv* in 2 K. xvi. 15),—and, with Affs.,

    (*him*) יְצַוֵּהוּ, (*thee m.*) יְצַוְּךָ, (*them m.*) יְצַוֵּם, (*us*) יְצַוֵּנוּ,

תְּצַוֶּה 3 s. *f.* or 2 s. *m.*,—and, with Affs.,

    וַתְּצַוֵּהוּ (*and she commanded him*) with ו Convers., תְּצַוֶּנּוּ *thou m. shalt command him,*—

אֲצַוֶּה 1 s., apocop. אֲצַו, with ו Convers. וָאֲצַוֶּה and once וָאֲצַו,—and, with Affs.,

    (*him*) אֲצַוֶּנּוּ, (*thee m.*) אֲצַוְּךָ and in Pause ‏‎ ‎‏: ‎ & ‏‎ ‎‏ ,

יְצַוּוּ 3 pl. *m.*,

תְּצַוּוּ 2 pl. *m.* in תְּצַוֻּנִי *ye shall command me* and תְּצַוֻּם *ye shall command them m.* ;

Pŭ-ăl

Past צֻוָּה 3 s. *m.*, צֻוֵּיתָ 2 s. *m.*, צֻוֵּיתִי 1 s.;

Fut. יְצֻוֶּה 3 s. *m.*

קהה only used in *K.* (of the teeth) *to be dull, blunt, "on edge"* E.V., and *Pi.* *to be very blunt* (Eccles. x. 10).

Kal

Fut. תִּקְהֶינָה 3 pl. *f.*;

Pi-ĕl

Past קִהָה 3 s. *m.* Eccles. x. 10.

קוא used only in *K.* & *Hφ.* *to spew, spew out.*

KAL

    PARTIC (1) קָאָה s. *f.* Lev. xviii. 28. [The Accent being on the last syllable, this word is properly s. *f.* Partic.— like בָּאָה 1 S. xxv. 19 (as R. D. Kimk͞hi says) the s. *f.* Partic (1) *K.* of בוא. The rendering in Lev. xviii. 28 should, in accordance with this, be "*as the land is spewing out . . . .*" The word has however been supposed to be a Past-Tense form.]

  IMPER. קִיא 2 pl. *m.* "borrowed" in form from an unused Root קיה;

HIPH.

    PAST וַהֲקֵאתוֹ 2 s. *m.* with ו pref. and Aff. *it m.*;

    FUT. יָקִיא 3 s. *m.*, with ו Convers. וַיָּקִא, and— with Aff. *it m.* וַיְקִאֶנּוּ,—

        תָּקִיא 3 s. *f.* or 2 s. *m.*, with ו Convers. וַתָּקִא Lev. xviii. 25,—and with Aff. *it f.* תְּקִיאֶנָּה.

קוה (I.) used only in *Nφ.* *to be gathered* or *gathered together* (E.V.), and

קוה (II.) used in *K.* (only in Partic. 1) *to wait* or *wait for*, and *Pi.* *to wait* or *wait for* with an Intensity of signification.

  KAL (of II.)

    PARTIC (1) קוֹיִם pl. *m.* in קוֹיֵ Constr. form "*waiters of*" = "those waiting for," and—

        with Affs. *his,* לְקוָו (with pref. לְ, Lam. iii. 25), *thy m.* קוֶֹיךָ, *my* קוָֹי (in Pause, for קוָֹי) Is. xlix. 23.

Niph. (of I.)

    Past נָקֽוּוּ 3 pl. Jer. iii. 17;

    Fut. יִקָּווּ 3 pl. *m.* Gen. i. 9.

Pi-êl (of II.)

    Infin. קַוֵּה & קַוֹּה Absol.;

    Past קִוְּתָה 3 s. *f.*,

        קִוִּיתִי 1 s.,—w. Aff. *thee m.* קִוִּיתִיךָ,—and קִוֵּיתִי in
        Is. viii. 17.

        קִוּוּ 3 pl.,

        קִוִּינוּ 1 pl.,—w. Affs., (*him*) קִוִּינֻהוּ, (*thee m.*) קִוִּינוּךָ;

    Imper. קַוֵּה 2 s. *m.*;

    Fut. יְקַוֶּה 3 s. *m.* apocop. יְקַו and with ו Convers יַיְקַו;

        אֲקַוֶּה 1 s., וַאֲקַוֶּה with ו, and וָאֲקַוֶּה with ו Convers.,

        יְקַוּוּ 3 pl. *m.*, נְקַוֶּה 1 pl.

רוה used in *K.* (*to be satisfied with, to be saturated with*), *Pi.* (*to
      satisfy, satisfy with, saturate*), and *Hφ.* (*to make
      satisfied or saturated, to give plenteously*).

Kal

    Past רָוְתָה 3 s. *f.*;

    Fut. יִרְוְיֻן 3 pl. *m.*, נִרְוֶה 1 pl.

Pi-êl

    Past רִוְּתָה 3 s. *f.*, רִוֵּיתִי 1 s.;

    Imper. רַוֵּה 2 s. *m.*;

    Fut. אֲרַיְּוֵךְ 1 s. Fut. w. Aff. *thee f.* (Irregular),

        יְרַוֻּךָ 3 pl. *m.* w. Aff. *thee m.*

Hiph.

    Past הִרְוָה 3 s. *m.*,—w. Aff. *me* הִרְוַנִי,—

        הִרְוִיתָ 2 s. *m.* in הִרְוִיתַנִי w. Aff. *me*, in Pause for ‑נִי,

        הִרְוֵיתִי 1 s.;

    Partic. מַרְוֶה s. *m.*

שׁוה used in *K.* (*to be equal,* etc), *Pî.* (*to set, to level,* etc.), *Hφ.* (*to make equal*), and *Nθ.* (*to be alike*), a 'Compound' or 'Mixed' Voice.

KAL
> PAST שָׁוָה 3 s. *m.* ;
> PARTIC (1) שׁוֶה ;
> FUT. תִּשְׁוֶה 2 s. *m.,*
> אֶשְׁוֶה 1 s.,
> יִשְׁווּ 3 pl. *m.*

PĪ-ÊL
> PAST שִׁוָּה 3 s. *m.,* שִׁוִּיתִי 1 s ;
> PARTIC. מְשַׁוֶּה s. *m.* ;
> FUT. יְשַׁוֶּה 3 s. *m.,* תְּשַׁוֶּה 2 s. *m.*

[PU-ĂL given by some for תֻּשְׁוֶה *Kthîv* Job xxx. 22, where the Noun תֻּשִׁיָּה is *Krî.*]

HIPH.
> FUT. אַשְׁוֶה 1 s., תַּשְׁווּ 2 pl. *m.* ;

NITHPĂ-ÊL
> PAST נִשְׁתַּוָּה 3 s.,   —which is in form partly *Nφ.* and partly *Hθ.**

תוה used in *Pî.* (*to mark* or *make marks,* also *to mark out bounds* —and so *Hθ.,* in a borrowed form, as is supposed),— and *Hφ.* *to make a mark,* also *to limit*).

PĪ-ÊL
> FUT. יְתָו 3 s. *m.* apocop. in וַיְתָו 1 S. xxi. 14 [for וַיְתַוֶּה],
> תְּתָאוּ 2 pl. *m.* Nu. xxxiv. 7 & 8, 'borrowed' in form from תאה ;

---

* For the transposition of the ת of הִתְ with the 1st Rt-letter שׁ, see 'Note' on page 315.

Hiph.

Past הִתְוִיתָ 2 s. *m.*,

הִתְווּ 3 pl., Ps. lxxviii. 41,—this has been supposed
to have the sense "*they made to grieve, abhor, or
repent,*" which however is rather doubtful;—

Hithpä-êl

Past הִתְאַוִּיתֶם 2 pl. *m.*, Nu. xxxiv. 10,—'borrowed' in
form from אוה.

NOTE.

(I.) THE TRANSPOSITION OF THE ת of the Prefix הִת (of *Hithpá-él*)
and THE 1ST Rt-LETTER in some instances.

(*a*) When the 1st Rt-letter is (1) שׂ,* or (2) שׁ, or (3) ס, or (4) צ,
the ת of the הִת in *Hithpá-él* forms CHANGES PLACES
with that 1st Rt-letter; and,

(β) Moreover, when [*a* (4)] the 1st Rt-letter is צ, the ת of
הִת is replaced by ט.

As examples of the above, we may give the following forms:—

(1) From שָׁפַךְ,—הִשְׁתַּפֵּךְ, [וַיִּשְׁתַּפֵּךְ], תִּשְׁתַּפֵּךְ,

From שָׁחָה,†—הִשְׁתַּחֲוֵיתִי, הִשְׁתַּחֲוִיתָ, הִשְׁתַּחֲוֹת, etc.,

הִשְׁתַּחֲווּ, הִשְׁתַּחֲוִי, [הִשְׁתַּחֲווֹת], מִשְׁתַּחֲוֶה,

(יִשְׁתַּחֲוֶה), p. יִשְׁתַּחֲווּ (apocop. יִשְׁתָּחוּ), etc.;

(2) From שָׂכַר,—[הִשְׂתַּכֵּר], מִשְׂתַּכֵּר, [יִשְׂתַּכֵּר, etc.];

(3) From סָתַר,—[הִסְתַּתֵּר], מִסְתַּתֵּר, [יִסְתַּתֵּר], and
תִּסְתַּתֵּר: (§ 166, *c*);

(4) From צָדַק,—[הִצְטַדֵּק, וַיִּצְטַדֵּק], נִצְטַדָּק: [Gen. xliv.16
(§ 166, *c*)],

and so, from צִיד formally,‡—הִצְטַיַּדְנוּ [Josh. ix. 12
(Past 1 pl.)],

and, from צִיר formally,—וַיִּצְטַיָּרוּ [Josh. ix. 4,
Fut. 3 pl. *m.*, w. ו Convers. (§ 166 *c*)].

---

* With one exception, see § 246.

† From this Root the forms are given also at the foot of Tab. XXIII, in
Notes † to ¶.

‡ We say ' formally,' because the word here belongs *in form* to the Root צִיד.—
N.B. The ו is here Consonantal.

(II.) The Dropping of the ת of the Prefix הִת (of *Hithpă-ĕl*), and the Insertion of Dagesh F. in the 1st Rt-letter,— in some instances.

(*a*) When the 1st Rt-letter is (1) ד, or (2) ט, or (3) ת, the ת of the הִת in *Hithpă-ĕl* forms is dropped, and Dagesh F. is put in the 1st Rt-letter to stand for an implied * letter instead of the ת; thus,

(1) From דבר,—[הִתְדַּבֵּר], מְדַבֵּר, [יְדַבְּר], etc], ·

(2) From טהר,—[הִטַּהֵר], הִטָּהֲרוּ pl. הִטֶּהֲרוּ: [Nu. viii. 7 (§ 166, *d*)], מְטַהֵר, הִטַּהֲרֵנוּ, הִטַּהֲרוּ (Imper.), and וַיִּטַּהֲרוּ (Fut. w. ו Convers.);

(3) From תמם,—[הִתַּמֵּם], מִתַּמֵּם, [יִתַּמֵּם], and תִּתַּמָּם: [Ps. xviii. 26 & 2 S. xxii. 26 (§ 166, *e*)].

(β) Also the ת of the prefix הִת (of *Hithpă-ĕl*) is dropped, and Dagesh F. is inserted in the 1st Rt-letter to stand for an implied letter instead of the ת, sometimes when the 1st Rt-letter is (1) ז,† (2) כ, (3) נ, and (4) שׁ;

(1) From זכה,—once הִזַּכּוּ Imper. *Hθ.* 2 pl. *m.* [Is. i. 16];

---

* In the case of (3), *i.e.* when the 1st Rt-letter is ת, such a form as הִתַּמֵּם (instead of הִתְתַּמֵּם) is in accordance with the general statement of Pt I, § 55 (12). The occurrence of this form in the case of (1) & (2) may be taken as some evidence of the *likeness in sound* of the letters ד, & ט, and ת,—in old times.

N.B This being only 'sometimes' so in (β) points to some difference between the cases of (*a*) & (β),—a *partial likeness* in the sound (it may be), but also an *unlikeness* which may not be disregarded.

† Once, Is i. 16.—N B. In the 'Chaldee,' as it is called, we find ד (instead of the ת), and transposition of this and the 1st Rt-letter ז; thus הִזְדַּ׳ (Dan. ii 9, *Ktî*), instead of הִתְזַ׳,—comp the Targum (Onk) of Lev. xxv 23, 34, 42,—etc.

(2) (*a*) From כסה,—once תְּכַסֶּה Fut. *Hθ*. 3 s. *f.*
[Prov. xxvi. 26],

> N.B. The ת *stands* in the following forms from this Root כסה, *viz.*
> Partic. מתכסה s. *m.*, מְתְכַּסִּים pl. *m.*,
> Fut. יִתְכַּס 3 s. *m.* & תתכס 3 s. *f.* Pause-form
> (apocop. for תִּתְכַּסֶּה & יִתְכַּסָּה), & יִֽתְכַּסּוּ 3 pl. *m* ,

(*b*) and so, from כון (comp Tab. XX), תִּכּוֹנֵן
Fut. *Hθ*. 3 s. *f.* [Nu. xxi. 27], and the
Pause-forms תִּכּוֹנְנִי 2 s. *f.* [Is. liv. 14], &
יְכוֹנְנוּ 3 pl. *m.* [Ps. lix. 5],

> N.B. the ת *stands* in יִתְכּוֹנָן 3 s. *m.* Pause-form [Prov. xxiv. 3].

(3) (*a*) From נבא,—הִנַּבֵּאתִי *Hθ*. Past 1 s. [Ez. xxxvii. 10]
and הִנַּבְּאוּ Past 3 pl. [Jer. xxiii. 13],

> N.B. the ת *stands* in the following forms from this Root נבא, *viz.*
> הִתְנַבּוֹת *Hθ* Infin. [1 S. x. 13] and הִתְנַבִּיתָ Past 2 s *m.*
> [1 S. x. 6]—both of which are ' borrowed ' in form
> from an unused Root נבה,—
> מתנבא Partic. s. *m.*, מְתְנַבְּאִים pl. *m.*, מְתְנַבְּאוֹת pl *f.*,
> and
> יִתְנַבָּא Fut. 3 s *m.*, יִתְנַבְּאוּ 3 pl. *m.*,

(*b*) and so, from נחם,—הִנַּחֵמְתִּי *Hθ*. Past 1 s.
Pause-form [Ez. v. 13],

> N.B the ת *stands* in the following forms from this Root נחם, *viz.*
> להתנחם Infin , מְתְנַחֵם Partic s. *m.*, and יִתְנָחֵם 3 s. *m.*
> Fut , & אֶתְנֶחָם 1 s. Fut. (Pause-forms),

(*c*) and so, from נשא,—תִּנַּשֵׂא *Hθ*. Fut. 3 s. *f.*
[Nu. xxiv. 7] and יִנַּשְׂאוּ Fut. 3 pl. *m.*
[Dan. xi. 14];

> N B the ת *stands* in the following forms from this Root נשא, *viz.*
> הִתְנַשֵּׂא Infin , מְתְנַשֵּׂא Partic. s. *m* , יִתְנַשֵּׂא Fut 3 s. *m.*
> (Pause-form), תתנשׂא Fut. 3 s. *f.*, תִּתְנַשְּׂאוּ Fut.
> 2 pl *m.*

(4) And so, from שָׁמַם [comp. Tab. XXI], once
תִּשּׁוֹמֵם *Hθ.* Fut. 2 s. *m.* [Eccles. vii. 16],

N.B. the ת *stands* in the following forms from this Root שמם, *viz.*
יִשְׁתּוֹמֵם Fut. 3 s. *m.* and אֶשְׁתּוֹמֵם Fut. 1 s.

Note. So, from רוּם (comp. Tab. XX],—some
give אֲרוֹמֵם [Is. xxxiii. 10] as *Hθ.*
Fut. 1 s. Pause-form, (instead of
אֶתְרוֹמֵם), but it may also be a 'Mixed'
Nφ. and *Pŭ.* form, Fut. 1 s.;

N.B. the ת *stands* in יִתְרוֹמֵם *Hθ.* Fut. 3 s. *m.*

(γ) The ת is also dropped in some 'Mixed Voice' forms; thus,

(1) From יסר,—נוֹסְרוּ 'Mixed' *Nφ.* & *Hθ.* Past 3 pl.
[Ez. xxiii. 48],

(2) From כבס,—הֻכַּבֵּס 'Mixed' *Hoph.* & *Hθ.* Infin.
[Lev. xiii. 55 & 56],

(3) From כפר,—נְכַפֵּר 'Mixed' *Nφ.* & *Hθ.* Past 3 s. *m.*
[Deut. xxi. 8],

N.B. the ת *stands* in יִתְכַּפֵּר *Hθ.* Fut. 3 s. *m.*,

(4) From נאץ,—מְנֹאָץ 'Mixed' *Hθ.* & *Pŭ.* Partic. s. *m.*
[Is. lii. 5].

[The 'Note' just given on pages 315–318 is a fuller statement of a matter which has been already mentioned briefly—see Note (***) on p. xv of the Tables. It was necessary to give to the matter this more full treatment, and to bring it thus more prominently before the Student's attention.

There are also several other 'Verb-forms' on which a few remarks will be at least useful to the Student in his BIBLE-reading. Such we will now give in the following (Vth) Section of this Appendix.]

(V). FURTHER REMARKS ON VERB-FORMS.

CERTAIN INFINITIVE FORMS.

INFINITIVE ABSOLUTE.

(1) The INFIN. ABSOL. KAL has mostly the form פָּעוֹל or פָּעֹל. The פָּעֹל form, as גָּדֹל* G. xxvi. 13, is comparatively rare. Of this latter form we have (with וֹ prefixed) וּבָשֵׁל Ex. xii. 9 (before the Pŭ-ĂL Partic. מְבֻשָּׁל,—the two words together† expressing the "*or sodden at all*" of the E.V.).

[Note. The word וּפָרַח, Hos. x. 4, is supposed by some to be the Infin. Absol. (corresponding to the Infin. Absol. כָּרֹת just before it). If so, it is short for וּפָרֹחַ. Such shortening takes place sometimes in the Infin. Constr., See Tab. XVI (3) (B); but it is rare in the Infin. Absolute. Also this word וּפָרַח, in Hos. x. 4, may very well be the Past 3 s. *m.* with וֹ prefixed—signifying "*and it shall flourish* or *grow*."]

---

* Comp. § 137 (1, b).　　　　† Comp. p. 78, (β) [Note (*) N.B. (2)].

INFINITIVE CONSTRUCT.

(2) (*a*) The INFINITIVE CONSTRUCT KAL has the (–̇)-form
פָּעוֹל or פְּעֹל much more frequently than the (–̄)-form
פְּעַל (as שְׁכַב mentioned in Note (*) on p. 79).   But this
פְּעֹל form, though less common than the other, must
not be lost sight of.   [For לְחֻמָם see § 169 (β) &
§ 167 (ii).

(β) The (–̇)-form of Infin. Constr., with הָ— at the end
[as in § 137 (4, iii)], would in Pause be פָּעֳלָה׃.   And

(γ) The (–̄)-form of Infin. Constr., with הָ— at the end
[as in § 137 (4, iii)], would in Pause be פָּעֳלָה׃.
    Hence,—bearing in mind that

(δ) Pause-forms are *not limited* to places of Pause, but occur
sometimes with Accents other than Pause-Accents [see
§ 167 (ii) and the examples there given],—we see that

(ε) פְּשֹׁטָה and חֲגֹרָה, in Is. xxxii. 11, and so also רְגָזָה (*ib.*),
may—so far as form is concerned—be Infinitive 'Pause-
forms not in Pause'; the former two words like פָּעֳלָה
in (β), and the latter one (רְגָזָה) like פָּעֳלָה in (γ).

    For the sense in which if so they would stand—see
'Note' after (η) below.

(ζ) These three words, of Is. xxxii. 11, are however taken
by some to be Imper. *K.* 2 s. *m.* with ה at the end.
They must, then also, be 'Pause-forms not in Pause';
and we should have the somewhat awkward* construc-

---

* It seems to us rather awkward to have to say " *Shudder-thou* (*m.*), *O ye* (*f*)-
confident-ones" for רְגָזָה בֹּטְחוֹת.   The reference is to the "confident daughters"
בָּנוֹת בֹּטְחֹת of *v.* 9, to whom the Feminine Verb תִּרְגַּזְנָה is applied in *v.* 10.
There is an idiom to which advocates of such a Construction might appeal in support

tion of Singular *Masculine* forms referring to those who are addressed as Plural *Feminine*.

But the three words need not be Imper. 2 s. *m.* at all. They may be Infinitive forms,* as seen above.

(η) Similarly the word עָרָה† (ib.) may be Infin. KAL of עָרַר [like סַב in Tab. XXI] with ה at the end.

[Note. The Infinitive Construct is often used as a Verbal Noun. Thus the three words in (ε) may stand for—רְגְזָה "*shuddering,*" פְּשֹׁטָה "*stripping,*" חֲגֹרָה "*girding on*"; and so עָרָה in (η) for "*baring.*" The rendering would then be of the form "[there shall be] *shuddering, etc.*"

(θ) INFINITIVES WITH 2ᴰ RT-LETTER א *or* ה *or* ח *or* ע.

When the 2ᵈ Rt-letter is either א or ה or ח or ע, the Infin. *K.* with the ה◌ָ of § 137 (4, iii),—as also the Infin. with Pron.-Affs.,—has

(i.) Sometimes ◌ַ under that 2ᵈ Rt-letter, with ◌ָ ŏ under the 1ˢᵗ Rt-letter, as in

לְרַחֲקָה *K.* Infin. w. ל pref. fr. רחק (לִרְחֹק) w. ה◌ָ,

בָּחֳרִי *K.* Infin. w. Aff. *my,* fr. בחר,

מָאֳסָם & מָאֳסְכֶם‡ *K.* Infin. w. Affs. *their (m.)* & *your (m.)* fr. מאס, and

____

of it. But as we think that the Construction is inadmissible here, at least, we need not dwell longer on it. Moreover we cannot venture to argue that רְגְזָה etc. may be SING. *m.* because חָרְדוּ (in Is. xxxii. 11) is PLU. *m.* This last word חָרְדוּ may be said to refer to the Masculine *form* נָשִׁים, with which שַׁאֲנַנּוֹת agrees in Gender.

* Some prefer to consider them as Imper. *K.* 2 pl. *f.*—רְגְזָה for רְגַזְנָה the Pause-form of רְגַזְנָה, and פְּשֹׁטָה for פְּשֹׁטְנָה, חֲגֹרָה for חֲגֹרְנָה.

† If this be taken [as in Note (*)] to be 2 pl. *f.* Imper. *K.,* it must be for עָרֶנָה—a form of 2 pl. *f.* Imper. corresponding to the 3 & 2 pl. *f.* Fut. form תָּסֹבֶּנָה given in Note (5) on Tab XXI.

‡ The ◌ַ is replaced by the Slight-vowel ◌ָ ŏ before the ס with MOVING *Shva.*

לְפָעֳלָם *K.* Infin. w. לְ pref. and Aff. *their m.*, fr. פָּעַל,
[comp. Tab. XV (i)] ;—

(ii.) Sometimes ֲ under the 2ᵈ Rt-letter, with ֲ under
the 1ˢᵗ Rt-letter, as in

לְאַהֲבָה *K.* Infin. w. לְ pref. fr. אהב (לֶאֱהֹב) with
הָ—, and so שְׁחֲטָה *K.* Infin. fr. שׁחט with הָ—,[*]
מַעֲלוֹ *K.* Infin. w. Aff. *his* fr. מַעַל, etc. ;—and

(iii.) Sometimes the 2ᵈ Rt-letter has *Quiescent* ֲ, as in
לְרָחֳצָה *K.* Infin. w. לְ pref. fr. רחץ (לִרְחֹץ) w. הָ—;
זַעֲפוֹ *K.* Infin. w. Aff. *his* fr. זַעַף,
בִּצְעָדֶךָ † *K.* Infin. w. בְּ pref. & Aff. *thy m.* fr. צָעַד,
etc.

(ι) As a rare form of Infin. Constr. *K.* we may mention
here יְכֹלֶת (Nu. xiv. 16, Dt. ix. 28) fr. יכל; and so
יְבֹשֶׁת (Gen. viii. 7) fr. יבשׁ.

> Note (i.) בְּאָבְדָן (Esth. viii. 6) is by some given as
> an Infin. Constr. *K.* with בְּ pref. and
> ן added, and by others as a Noun 'i.e.'
> (and this we think it certainly is).
>
> (ii.) לְדַרְיוֹשׁ (Ezra x. 16) is an anomalous form
> for the usual לִדְרוֹשׁ. -

---

[*] As the Pause-form of such an 'Infin. with הָ—' some give שְׁאָלָה Is. vii. 11
[from an imaginary Infin. שְׁאָל, after the form of שְׁכַב in Note (*) on p. 79.]
But this word שְׁאָלָה is properly the Pause-form of the IMPER *K.* 2 s. *m.* (שְׁאַל)
with הָ—, and there is no reason why it should not be so in Is. vii. 11. There are
several other instances of two Imperatives together where we want an Infin. in
English for the second Verb.—Some prefer to read שְׁאֹלָה to agree with the εἰς ᾅδην
given by Aquila, Symmachus, and Theodotion.

† This is the correct form in Ju v. 4 and Ps. lxviii. 8. Some Bibles have an
incorrect form in Ju. v. 4.

(iii.) לִבְרָם (Eccl. iii. 18) is *K.* Infin. w. לְ pref. and Aff. *them* (*m.*), fr. ברר.—The Infin. form without the prefix and affix would be בַּר, like רַד fr. רדד and like שַׁךְ fr. שכך which are given in Note (1, *a*) on Tab. XXI.

(κ) The ending תָ ָ (instead of the ending הָ ָ for the Infin. w. ה) is mentioned in 'Appendix (A) to Tab. XIV' (*₊*, 3);—בְּצַדְּקָתֵךְ Ez. xvi. 52 being from צַדְּקַת [for צַדְּקָה, Pĭ-ĕl Infin. w. ה] with pref. בְּ, and Aff. *thy* (*f.*).

That ending is found in הֻלֶּדֶת Gen. xl. 20 & Ez. xvi. 5, which is Hoph. Infin. of ילד (instead of הֻלְּדָה, w. ה), comp. § 202,—for which we find הוּלֶּדֶת in Ez. xvi. 4, with וּ for *Kibbuts* as in Pt. I, § 14 (N.B.).

Note (i.) This (תָ ָ)-form is the ordinary form of the *Kal* Infinitive Constr. in the case of Verbs פ״י and Verbs פ״נ, when the 1st Rt-letter is dropped,—see Tabs. XVIII & XIX.

(ii.) Also the (הָ ָ)-form רִדָה occurs in מֵרְדָה [Gen. xlvi. 3] *K.* Infin. w. pref. מ & w. ה, fr. ירד,—instead of the ordinary form רֶדֶת.

(iii.) We find also דֵּעָה (with ֵ) Is. xi. 9 Infinitive *K.* fr. ידע with ה, as in לְדֵעָה (with pref. לְ) Ex. ii. 4.

(iv.) The Infin. Constr. forms ending in וֹת,—as גְּלוֹת, etc., in Tab. XXIII,—are perhaps contracted, as some have supposed, from the (תָ ָ)-form in (ι) above.

(v.) מֵהַרְבַּת (*Kri* for מהרבית *Kthiv*) 2 S. xiv. 11
is *Hφ*. Infin. Constr. fr. רבה,—corresponding to the Infin. Absol. הַרְבָּה [Gen. iii. 16
& xvi. 10 & xxii. 17] which is given in
Column (V) of Tab. XXIII by the side of
the ordinary form ending in ה‑ַ.

(vi.) The irregular form בְּהִשְׁתַּחֲוָיתִי 2 K. v. 18
has ' introduced in a somewhat Aramæan
manner. It is an Infinitive [הִשְׁתַּחֲוָיָה],
from the *Hithpă-ĕl* of שׁחה', with בּ pref.
and Aff. *my*.

SOME PAST-TENSE FORMS.

(3) (*a*) As has already been said [§ 138 (A), ii], the ‑ַ of the
פָּעַל form of PAST KAL occurs in the 3 s. *m.* and in
the PAUSE-forms of the 3 s. *f.* & 3 pl.; but
N.B. Ordinarily the Second & First Person-forms
Singular and Plural, of the Past *K.* פָּעַל, have
‑ַ to the 2ᵈ Rt-letter as in the פָּעַל forms in
Tab. XIV, *viz.* פָּקַדְתִּי, פָּקַדְתָּ, etc.

(*β*) In the case of a few Roots however we find ‑ַ instead
of ‑ַ under the 2ᵈ Rt-letter in such Past *K.* forms;
thus in וִירִשְׁתֶּם (Deut. iv. 1, etc.) the *K.* Past 2 pl. *m.*
with ו pref.,—and so in וִירִשְׁתָּה and וִירִשְׁתֶּם given in
Obs. XLII on p. 209; see also the forms fr. ילד and
fr. שאל in Note (*β*) on Tab. XXV.

Note. R. D. Kimkhi cites also וּפִשְׁתֶּם Mal. iii. 20,—
which word we mentioned above in § 238 (ii).

(γ) Very rarely the 2ᵈ Rt-letter has — in such a form, as
in שְׁאֶלְתֶּם (2 pl. *m.* Past *K.*) 1 S. xii. 13 & xxv. 5,
and Job xxi. 29.

[(δ) As we remarked in § 238 (ii), the — and — in such
forms as those referred to in (β) & (γ) may have been
obtained from the — of the פָּעֵל form of the Past *K.*
So some think. And we may add (as before, in § 238, ii)
that so this — and — would be in analogy with the
—(δ) of יִכְלְתֶם & יִכְלְתֶן the 2 pl. *m.* & *f.* Past *K.* of
the פָּעֵל form, Tab. XV,—as also with the —δ of
Obs. XLII, Note (iii). But we may not omit to
remark also that

(ε) Euphony may be said to have had some concern with
the — and the — in those instances. Also that

(ζ) If we may say that 'in the forms from יל״ד in Note (β)
on Tab. XXV the — of the ל is a mark of the פָּעֵל
form of Past *K.*,' we must also admit that it is the
only trace of such a form from this Root. But
although we fully admit that there is no actual פָּעֵל
form from this Root throughout the Bible, but only
פָּעַל forms, yet we cannot but admit also that possibly
it may be a trace (though the only trace) of such a
form from this Root.]

(η) We find also —, in the place of the more usual —,
some few times in the *Hφ.* Past; thus in
הִשְׁאִלְתִּיהוּ 1 S. i. 28 (*Hφ.* Past 1 s., fr. שָׁאַל, with
Aff. *him*),

and in the following forms from מוּת, *viz.*

הֲמַתֶּם & הֲמַתֶּן (*Hφ.* Past 2 pl. *m.* & *f.*),

וַהֲמִיתִּיו 1 S. xvii. 35 (*Hφ.* Past 1 s. with Aff. *him*), the ִי before the ת being as in Pt. I, § 12, N.B.,—

וַהֲמִתִּיהָ Hos. ii. 5 (*Hφ.* Past 1 s. with Aff. *her*).

N.B. But the only form of the 1 s. Past *Hφ.* (without an Affix) from מוּת is הֵמַתִּי with the ַ.

(θ) So also in the *Hθ.* Past forms וְהִתְגַּדִּלְתִּי וְהִתְקַדִּשְׁתִּי Ez. xxxviii. 23, וְהִתְקַדִּשְׁתֶּם Lev. xi. 44 & xx. 7, the 2ᵈ Rt-letter has ִ in the place of the more usual ַ.

Note. We have some remarks to offer on the Verb-forms, with special reference to those in (β)—(θ). But such remarks would be out of place here. We will but observe that

(i.) The ִ (and the ַ) of the above-mentioned forms, in the place of the usual ָ, occur in UNACCENTED syllables;

(ii.) In (η) the ִ *may* have a relation to the ִי of the הִפְעִיל form; and

(iii.) In (θ) the ִ *may* have a relation to the ֵ of the הִתְפַּעֵל form.

CERTAIN PARTICIPLE FORMS.

(4) Two forms of the Partic (1) *Kal* are given in Tab. XIV, *viz.* the פֹּעֵל form and the פָּעֻל form. There is also the פָּעֵל form of Participle mentioned in 'Appendix B to Tab. XIV' [δ (iii)].

The פָּעֻל and פָּעֵל forms of Participles differ from the פֹּעֵל form in this remarkable particular that

(*a*) Whereas in the Sing. *f.* and the Plu. *m.* & *f.* of the פֹּעֵל
form the vowel of the 1ˢᵗ Rt-letter is retained, and the
vowel of the 2ᵈ Rt-letter is dropped—thus we have [p. 83]
s. m פֹּקֵד, *s. f.* פֹּקֵדֶת (or פֹּקֵדָה), pl. *m.* פֹּקְדִים, pl. *f.* פֹּקְדוֹת,—

(β) Contrariwise, Participles of the פָּעֵל and פָּעֹל forms drop
the vowel of the 1ˢᵗ Rt-letter and retain the vowel of the
2ᵈ Rt-letter in the Sing. *f.* and the Plu. *m.* & *f.* ; thus

(i.) The פָּעֵל forms are [read from right to left]
s. m. פָּעֵל, *s. f.* פְּעֵלָה, pl. *m.* פְּעֵלִים, pl. *f.* פְּעֵלוֹת:—

(ii.) The פָּעֹל forms are [read from right to left]
s. m. פָּעֹל, *s. f.* פְּעֹלָה, pl. *m.* פְּעֹלִים, pl. *f.* פְּעֹלוֹת:—

(γ) (i.) 'IN CONSTRUCTION'—the *s. m.* form פֹּקֵד [in (*a*)]
remains unchanged.* Also the *s. f.* form פֹּקֶדֶת,
and the pl. *f.* פֹּקְדֹת, remain unchanged in Construction.

(ii.) The Constr. form of פֹּקֵדָה *s. f.* is פֹּקֶדֶת,

(iii.) The Constr. form of פֹּקְדִים pl. *m.* is פֹּקְדֵי.

(δ) So the פָּעֵל forms in β (i) are 'in Construction'
s. m. פְּעֵל, *s. f.* פְּעֵלַת, pl. *m.* פְּעֵלֵי, pl. *f.* פְּעֵלוֹת:—

(ε) But the פָּעֹל forms in β (ii) are 'in Construction' somewhat various, as follows :

(i.) (*a*) The Constr. form of the Sing. *m.* is פְּעֹל (as in
חֲסַר fr. חָסֵר, חֲדַל fr. חָדֵל, כְּבַד fr. כָּבֵד,
שְׁבַע fr. שָׂבֵעַ, עֲרַל fr. עָרֵל).

(*b*) We find also כַּאֲבָל־אֵם fr. אָבֵל־, in
·Ps. xxxv. 14. But

---

* With the rare exception of ⸗ in place of the ⸗ thus אֹבֵד D. xxxii. 28
perishing of (or '*void of*') the K. Partic (1) '*i.e.*' fr אבד.

(*o*) N.B. The Sing. *m.* Participle of פָּעֵל form from Verbs לא׳ retains the ◌ֵ 'in Construction,' as in טָמֵא fr. טָמֵא, יְרֵא fr. יְרֵא, מְלֵא fr. מָלֵא, etc.

(ii.) The Sing. fem. Constr. form פְּעֶלֶת, and the Plu. masc. Constr. form פְּעֲלֵי, are sometimes shortened by the removal of their penultimate vowel,—in accordance with § 56 (i).

Thus we have not only the forms

(*a*) טְמֵאַת (fr. טְמֵאָה) s. *f.*, and שְׂמֵחִי, חֲפֵצִי, אֲבֵלִי (from שְׂמֵחִים, חֲפֵצִים, אֲבֵלִים) plu. *m.*,

but also such *shortened* forms as

(*b*) יְרֵאַת (fr. יְרֵאָה) s. *f.*, and כִּבְדִי, יִרְאִי, גִּדְלֵי (fr. כְּבֵדִים, יְרֵאִים, גְּדֵלִים) שְׂמֵחִי, קִצְרֵי, עִמְקֵי (fr. שְׂמֵחִים, קְצֵרִים, עֲמֵקִים) pl. *m.*

(ζ) (i.) Rarely the פֹּעֵל form of Participle has י *Quiescent* (*a*) after ◌ֵ thus סֹבֵיב (fr. סבב) in הַסֹּבֵיב 2 K. viii. 21 *the-one-compassing*, (*b*) after ◌ֵ thus תֹומֵיךְ (fr. תמך) Ps. xvi. 5 *One-supporting*—which some however will not allow to be a Participle, but which they suppose to be Fut. IIφ. 2 s. *m.* fr. an imaginary Root יְמַךְ.

(ii.) Also rarely with Defective *Long-khīrik* instead of ◌ֵ thus יֹוסֵף (fr. יסף) in הִנְנִי יֹוסֵף Is. xxix. 14 & xxxviii. 5 *behold I am adding.*

(iii.) Not to be confused herewith is such a ◌ֵ as that in אֹיִבְךָ (fr. אֹויֵב, r. איב) Ex. xxiii. 4 & 2 S. iv. 8, *thy enemy* (§ 140, ζ), and אֹסִפְךָ (fr. אֹסֵף, r. אסף) 2 K. xxii. 20 & 2 Chr. xxxiv. 28[*] *One taking thee away.* Such a ◌ֵ as these is merely a '*Slight*'-vowel

---

[*] אֹסִפְךָ, as in 1 S xv. 6, IIφ Fut. 1 s. (tr. יֹסֵף). Pt. I. § 44.

(in place of the *Moving Shva* which the 2ᵈ Rt-letter
has in אֹיְבִי, אֹיְבוֹ, etc., but which the 2ᵈ Rt-letter
cannot have when the 3ᵈ Rt-letter also has a *Moving
Shva*. This is the case when the Affix ךָ is
attached).

N.B. Such a '*Slight*'-vowel under the 2ᵈ Rt-letter
when the 3ᵈ Rt-letter has a *Moving Shva* is sometimes ־ as in (iii), sometimes ־ as in נְתָנְךָ, sometimes ־ as in אֲהֵבְךָ.

(iv.) Also before the Affs. כֶם ־ & כֶן ־ the 2ᵈ Rt-letter
cannot have a *Moving Shva*,—as in (iii).

(v.) In such a form as שְׁלֵחֲךָ (fr. שְׁלֵחַ, r. שלח) 1 S. xxi. 3,
the 2ᵈ Rt-letter retains the ־ of שְׁלֵחַ which is
dropped in such a form as שִׁלְחִי, *i.e.* when the Affix
is such that the 3ᵈ Rt-letter has a Vowel.

(η) (i.) The rare form בֹּעֵרָה (accented on the penultima)
Hos. vii. 4, is the Sing. Participle of פֹּעֵל form, with
הָ ־ at the end.

(ii.) The form in (i.) is to be distinguished carefully from
the form פֹּעֲלָה (accented on the last syllable) the
Sing. *Fem.* of the פֹּעֵל Partic. (with ־ in the place
of the more usual ־ under the 2ᵈ Rt-letter). This
form* occurs some few times. Thus we have אֹכְלָה
s. *f.* in Is. xxix. 6 & xxx. 30 & xxxiii. 14, and so
בֹּעֲרָה s. *f.* in Is. xxxiv. 9 (instead of בֹּעֵרָה Is. xxx. 33).

---

* The fact of this form occurring several times in a place of Pause hardly allows
us to speak of it as a *Pause*-form. The Accent BELONGS TO THE LAST SYLLABLE
in each instance.

So also יוֹלֵדָה s. *f.* in Is. xxi. 3, etc., נוֹטֵרָה s. *f.* in
Song. i. 6, and צֹלֵעָה s. *f.* Mi. iv. 6 & 7, etc.

(iii.) The Plural also is found thus, with ֵ in place of
the more usual ֶ, both in the Plu. *Masc.*, as in
שׁוֹמֵמִים* Lam. i. 16 (and, with the termination † יִן ֵ,
שׁוֹמֵמִין Lam. i. 4),—and in the Plu. *Fem.*, as in
תּוֹפֵפוֹת Ps. lxviii. 26.

(iv.) The ֵ stands sometimes (in place of the more usual ֶ)
in other Voices also, thus in the *Pi.* Partic. s. *f.*
מְרַקֵּדָה Na. iii. 2 *jumping*, and in the *Hθ.* Partic. s. *f.*
מִתְנַכֵּרָה 1 K. xiv. 5 & 6 *one feigning herself to be
another.*

(θ) We may mention here also that some Participles of *Pi.* &
Pŭ. occur without the usual prefix מְ; thus some give
שַׁבֵּחַ Eccles. iv. 2 as *Pi.* Partic. s. *m.* for מְשַׁבֵּחַ, and so
מַהֵר Zeph. i. 14 for מְמַהֵר, מָאֵן Ex. vii. 27 etc. for מְמָאֵן,—
and so in the *Pŭ.*, אֻכָּל Ex. iii. 2 for מְאֻכָּל, לֻקַּח 2 K. ii. 10
for מְלֻקָּח.

Note (i.) For some other Participle forms it may be sufficient to refer to 'Appendices (B) & (C) to Tab. XIV.'

(ii.) For Participle-forms with Pron-Affs. see Tab. XXVI.

SOME IMPERATIVE AND FUTURE FORMS.

(5) (*a*) The ֶ-ŏ of the 1st Rt-letter in the form of שָׁמְרָה
K. Imper. 2 s. *m.* fr. שְׁמֹר (r. שׁמר) with ה [§ 141, γ]
is not limited to Verbs which have ֵ to the

---

* From the Root שׁמם we have also שׁוֹמֵמָה & שְׁמָמָה s. *f.*, and שְׁמֵמוֹת pl. *f.*
(i.e. שְׁמֵמוֹת "*desolate* places of").

† This termination יִן ֵ is common in Aramæan for the Plural ים ֵ.

2ᵈ Rt-letter in the Imper. 2 s. *m.*, and in the Fut. Thus the Root קרב has the Imper. 2 s. *m.* קְרַב and the Fut. forms תִּקְרַב, יִקְרַב, etc.; but we have ‑ŏ under the ק of the word קָרְבָה *K.* Imper. 2 s. *m.* fr. קרב w. ה.

(β) Unnecessary confusion and consequent trouble, which have been introduced by some, may be avoided by our bearing in mind that such a ‑ŏ may be considered in direct relation to the ‑ of a GENERALLY-UNDERLYING* form פֻּעַל,—without any 'mediate' reference to the form of the Imper. 2 s. *m.*

[N.B. The form פֻּעַל, from several Roots, stands itself as an UNDEFINED or 'INFINITIVE' form, when this is used not Abstractly or 'Absolute'-ly but as a *Component-part of its sentence—i.e.* 'CON-STRUCT.']

(γ) So also the ‑ of חָרְבִי *be thou f. dry* (2 s. *f.* Imper. *K.* fr. חרב, in Pause) may be and is best considered in direct relation to the ‑ of a *generally-underlying* form corresponding to פֻּעַל—quite independent of the (‑)-form of Imper. 2 s. *m.* [חֲרַב, p. חֲרָב] from which the ‑ of the ר in חָרְבִי is obtained in Pause.

(δ) And so the ‑ of וּסְעָדָה *and refresh* or *have refreshment* (2 s. *m.* Imper. *K.* fr. סְעָד, w. ו pref. and ה at the end, in Pause) 1 K. xiii. 7, as also the ‑ of וּצְעָקִי *and cry out f.* (Pause-form of 2 s. *f.* Imper. *K.* fr. צעק, w. ו pref.) Jer. xxii. 20 may have direct relation to

---

* In the case of some Roots the K͟houlem comes out in certain *Infinitive* forms only.

the ÷ of a *generally-underlying* form corresponding
to פְּעֹל—quite independent of the (⸚)-form of Imper.
2 s. *m.* (סְעָד p.: סַעֲדִ fr. סְעַד, and צְעַק p.: צַעֲקִ fr.
צְעַק) from which the Pause-vowel ⸗ is obtained in
each case.

[(ε) (i.) We ought perhaps to mention the supposition, on the
part of some, that וְסַעֲדָה may be a sort of mixture
of "וְסַעֲדָה and וְסָעֲדָה(??),"—and וְצְעַקִי such a
mixture of "וְצַעֲקִי and וְצָעֲקִי(??)." This seems to
us to be unnecessarily clumsy, and not quite satisfactory, because it does not touch at all upon that
which specially requires consideration, *viz.* the occurrence of a ⸚ bearing reference to an *o*-vowel in
these two Imperative forms, whereas (1) the ⸗ of
the 2ᵈ Rt-letter belongs not to the (÷)-form but
distinctly to the (⸗)-form of the Imperative, and
(2) only the (⸗)-forms of the Imperative and the
the Future are found from the Root צְעַק.*

We do not recognize aught anomalous in the two
words as they stand, because to us the ⸚ seems to
refer directly to a *generally-underlying* פְּעֹל form
[comp. (β) above] †

---

* The *K.* Imper. 2 s. *m.* סְעָד (Ju. xix. 8) may fairly be claimed by those who
wish to claim it as evidence of the (÷)-form of Imper. *K.* from סעד. But as the
accented word סַעֲד [for which see § 141, α, Note (1)] occurs just before (Ju. xix. 5),
and as it is at least possible that these two words so near to each other may be the
same,—*i.e.* the ⸗ in *v.* 8 the same as that in *v* 5,—it may be that we have in Ju. xix. 8
an instance of a *Long*-Vowel (⸗) before *Makkêph* like the two instances of *Khoulem*
before *Makkêph* in Note (†) on p. 114 [comp. Pt. I, § 55 (8, 'Note') If so, there
are only (⸗)-forms of the Imperative and Future found from the Root סעד.

† Some cut the knot by asserting that the ⸗ is merely because of the preceding ٍ,

(ii.) If, instead of assuming an imaginary form involving the same irregularity as that which they have to deal with, and then supposing that imaginary word to be mixed up with the regular form, and so fancying that they had in any degree accounted for an Irregular form—as they regard it,—the advocates of that mixture had said that

(iii.) 'The ⁻ may be regarded as a trace (although the only trace) of a (⁻)-form of Imper. *K.*, even in a word which not only involves a mark of the (⁻)-form but which belongs to a Root (as, for instance, צעק) from which the (⁻)-form alone certainly occurs,'—they would at least have touched upon the important point really involved. We could not have contradicted such a statement, even if we had wished to do so. For]

(ζ) We find sometimes ⁻ in a Future form, where it is either entirely due to Euphony (Pt. I, § 72, γ), or it is the only trace remaining of a (—)-form. Thus, from the Root נשק we find אֶשְׁקָה (1 s. Fut. *K.*, w. ה at the end) 1 K. xix. 20; but elsewhere the Future from this Root has the (⁻)-form as in יִשַּׁק, תִּשַּׁק, etc.* And so from the ל״ע Roots פשׁע and

***

and this supposition is better than that of the above-mentioned mixture. But the assertion cannot be made good. And it does not touch the very similar case of the word חָרְבִי in which we find the ⁻ (in place of ⁻) although there is no ו preceding. This however is asserted to be because of the following ר.

Euphony may indeed have been *partly concerned* in the occurrence. But we cannot credit it with the whole concern in these particular instances.

* For some Verbs having both the (⁻) and the (⁻) forms see § 162 (*b*).

שמע we find אֶפְשְׂעָה (1 s. Fut. *K.*, w. ה at the end)
Is. xxvii. 4, and וָאֶשְׁמָעָה (1 s. Fut. *K.*, w. ו Convers.)
Dan. viii. 13 in some copies.

In these, some impute the ⸗ wholly to Euphony,—
as also the following.

Note (i.) The ⸗ occurs some few times in such forms
from Verbs 'Fut. (—)'; thus in the 1 s. Fut.
K. w. ה fr. שקט and fr. שקל, *viz.* אֶשְׁקוֹטָה
Is. xviii. 4 and וָאֶשְׁקוֹלָה Ezra viii. 25, where
there is in each a 'ו superfluous,'—from
אֶשְׁקוֹט and אֶשְׁקוֹל.   But

(ii.) N.B. The Student should never write such
forms.

(iii.) Somewhat less rare is the occurrence of ⸗ in
some Verb-forms that have Pron.-Affs.; thus
from הדף we find in Nu. xxxv. 20 יֶהְדְּפֶנּוּ
(*i.e.* יֶהְדֹּף *K.* Fut. 3 s. *m.* with Aff. *him*),
and in Josh. xxiii. 5 יֶהְדְּפֶם (*i.e.* יֶהְדֹּף *K.*
Fut. 3 s. *m.* with Aff. *them m.*); also
From יסר we find in Hos. x. 10 וְאֶסְּרֵם
[*i.e.* אֶסֹּר *K.* Fut. 1 s. (comp. § 195, ε
& § 212) with ו pref. and Aff. *them m.*];
and a few others which will be given in the
'Analytical Index.'

(η) (i.) The Student will have observed that the 'ִ⸗ of the
Hiph-îl Voice stands in הַקְשִׁיבָה Imper. 2 s. *m.*
w. ה [§ 141 (γ, ⁵)] fr. קשב, and in אֶזְכִּירָה Fut.
1 s. w. ה [144 (*a*)] fr. זכר;—and so also in
נַזְכִּירָה Fut. 1 pl. w. ה fr. זכר.

(ii.) With the exception of such *Hφ.* forms,—and except also the Pause-forms of other Voices,—

When the Verb-form has at the end of it the ה of § 141 (γ), or § 144, the Vowel is dropped from the 2ᵈ Rt-letter in the case of 'Full' Verbs, and of Verbs פ א and פ י and פ נ. For 'Full' Verbs, see the examples in § 141 (γ), and in § 144; and so in the Imperative forms

אָסְפָה & אָכְלָה corresponding to אֱכֹל & אֱסֹף fr. אכל & אסף,

גְּשָׁה & שְׁבָה corresponding to שֵׁב & גַּשׁ (or גְּשׁ) fr. ישׁב & נגשׁ;

and similarly in Future forms (1 s. & 1 pl.) from such Roots, as in

נֵשְׁבָה & אֵשְׁבָה fr. ישׁב, נֹאכְלָה & אֹכְלָה fr. אכל, and נִפְּלָה & אֶפְּלָה fr. נפל. But

(iii.) We find the following ל"א Verb-forms,

(*a*) רְפָאָה (Ps. xli. 5) Imper. *K.* 2 s. *m.*, w. ה at the end, fr. רפא,

(*b*) *וָאֶקְרָאָה (1 S. xxviii. 15) Fut. 1 s., w. ו Convers. & ה at the end,

in which the 2ᵈ Rt-letter has $\bar{\,}_{\tau}$, as in the forms רְפָא and אֶקְרָא without the ה.

---

* We find sometimes הָֽ thus instead of the more usual הָ at the end of a word. So in יְדַשְּׁנֶה (Ps. xx. 4) *Pĭ.* Fut. 3 s. *m.* fr. דשׁן [comp. § 144 (γ & δ)]. So also in וְהַזּוֹרֶה (Is. lix. 5) *K.* Partic (2) s. *m.* fr. זור—like קוּם in Tab XX—with the pref. ו and the ה of § 98 . So too in וְלָנֶה (Zech v. 4) *K.* Past 3 s *m.* fr. לין (§ 226), and in רְעֶה (as in some Bibles, but רְעֶה in others, w. הֵֽ, Prov xxiv 14) *K.* Imper. 2 s. *m.* fr. ידע.

[The word רְעֶה, as it stands in some Bibles in Prov. xxiv. 14, is by some taken as as a Noun '1.c.' "*knowledge of*,"—as in the E.V.].

This is very rare.   But

Note. In some Noun-forms also the $-$ is not dropped before א; thus we have חֲטָאֵיכֶם from חֲטָאִים, instead of a form corresponding to מַלְכֵיכֶם from מְלָכִים (the great Rule of § 59 even being broken so as to retain the $-$ before א). So also from חֲטָאִים we have the Construct-form חֲטָאֵי,—in which the penultimate vowel $(-)$ is retained,* instead of being dropped as it is in מַלְכֵי from מְלָכִים.

Similarly, [from מוֹצָאִים] we have מוֹצָאֵיהֶם and מוֹצָאֵיהֶן and the Construct form מוֹצָאֵי; and so מוֹצָאֹתָיו from מוֹצָאוֹת.

N.B. Such a $-$ however is sometimes dropped in accordance with the Rules of § 59 and § 56 (i), as in תּוֹצְאֹתָם & תּוֹצְאֹתָיו from תּוֹצָאוֹת, and in the Construct form of it—*viz.* תּוֹצְאוֹת.

(θ) The *ū*-form of Fut. *K.* was just mentioned in the 'Note' at the end of § 141 (*a*), and as an example there was given יִשְׁפּוֹטוּ (Ex. xviii. 26) *K.* Fut. 3 pl. *m.* fr. שפט— for which the usual form is of course יִשְׁפְּטוּ (p. יִשְׁפֹּטוּ).

[Obs. In some Bibles the Accent of יִשְׁפּוֹטוּ is put on the penultima (perhaps for the sake of having the Accent 'drawn back' as in Pt. I, § 46). But the Accent should be on the last syllable, as it is in other Bibles, and as we have given it above.]

---

* Sometimes the $-$ is retained also before ע. Thus in מַטָּעֵי [Constr. form of מַטָּעִים] in Mi. i. 6.   But

N.B. The $-$ of נְטָעִים is dropped in the Constr. form נִטְעֵי Is. xvii. 10—as in Tab. X, 4.

So we have in Ruth ii. 8 תַּעֲבוּרִי *K.* 2 s. *f.* fr. עבר—
for which the ordinary form would be תַּעַבְרִי.

So, with a Pron.-Aff., we have in Prov. xiv. 3
תְּשְׁמוּרֵם *K.* Fut. 3 s. *f.* (some say 2 s. *m.*) w. Aff.
them m. fr. שמר.

N.B. The ו of the 2ᵈ Rt-letter is seen to be
unaccented in all these instances. This is in favour
of the ו being in each instance of *somewhat* the same
class as the ⟨ ⟩ by the side of the ⟨ ⟩ in the ⟨ ⟩ of
(ζ, i) above [comp. Pt. I, § 22 (latter part), and
§ 14, N.B.].

(ι) Rarely, what is usually the form of the 2 pl. *m.* of the
Fut. seems to be used for the 3 pl. *f.*—Thus in
Ez. xxxvii. 7 *וַתִּקְרְבוּ עֲצָמוֹת and bones came-near.
So the word תִּבְטְחוּ in Jer. xlix. 11 is mostly rendered
as 3 pl. *f.*, *let them (f.) trust*; but the word might very
well be rendered literally *ye (m.) should trust* or *must
trust* :—thus, " *Leave thy fatherless-children, I-will-preserve alive ; and as for thy widows, ye-must-trust in Me.*"
The other rendering is however more natural, it may be.

---

* This might perhaps be rendered literally " *and ye-came-together, O bones*"; for
the Noun עֶצֶם *bone* (pl. עֲצָמִים and עֲצָמוֹת), though almost always Fem.,—and so
in this Chapter,—yet is sometimes Masc., as in Ez xxiv. 10, Job xxx. 30. But the
other may certainly be claimed as the more natural rendering.

In this Section V of the Appendix we have hitherto dealt
mainly with Verb-forms of the KAL Voice,—only mentioning a
few others as occasion offered or seemed to require. We will
conclude this Section with a brief mention of some Verb-forms
of the other Voices,—

NIPH-ĀL.

(6) (a) The following are the passages in which we find the
instances of the נִפְעֹל form of Infin. Absol. *Nφ.* which
are given in Note (*d*) on Tab. XIV.

נִכְסֹף נִכְסַפְתָּה *thou didst greatly long,* Gen. xxxi. 30,

אִם נִלְחֹם נִלְחַם *or did he at all fight?* Ju. xi. 25,

נִשְׁאֹל נִשְׁאַל דָּוִד *David earnestly asked,* 1 S. xx. 6 & 28,

וְנִשְׁלוֹחַ סְפָרִים *and letters were sent,* Esth. iii. 13
[comp. p. 78, Obs. (γ)] ;

to which we may now add the following, which is
cited with those above by R. D. Kimk͞hi,

אַךְ נָגוֹף נִגַּף הוּא *surely he is quite smitten,* Ju. xx. 39.

In these instances the נִפְעֹל form stands, for
emphasis, before the *Nφ.* PAST,—with the exception
of the passage from Esther, in which the Infinitive
is used alone (the 'Infinitive' in place of a 'Finite'
part of the Verb, as some say. Comp. Note (†) on
p. 78).

Note (i.) Similarly נֶחְתּוֹם Esth. viii. 8, נֶהֲפוֹךְ Esth. ix. 1, and נַעְתּוֹר 1 Chron. v. 20, may be (as some say) Infin. Absol. *Nφ.* of this form. They may however be (as others say) forms of the Past Tense 3 s. *m. Nφ.*, or of the Participle *Nφ.* s. *m.*

There is no valid reason against their being unusual Participle forms. So R. D. K. in his Lexicon takes the first one, and so the second one may very well be. [Perhaps they are best taken to be—one of them Infin. Absol., another of them the Past 3 s. *m.*, and the other one Partic. s. *m.*]

(ii.) נֶחְבָּה Jer. xlix. 10 is given by R. D. K. as Infin. "like to the Past" of *Nφ.* (for נֶחְבָּא) from חבא.* But it may very well be the Partic. s. *m.*,—the particular form of the so-called 'Substantive Verb' to be supplied in English being here the Infin. '*to be,*' so that the passage may run thus: "*and he shall not be able to be hidden (or a hidden-one).*"

(β) The *Niph.* 'Infin. Absol.' form הִפָּעֵל is the form also of the 'Infin. Constr.' and of the 'Infin. with prefixes,' and it is the form of Infinitive which receives the Pron.-Affs. But

N.B. This form of 'Infin. Absolute' is not used with a PAST Tense or a PARTICIPLE for the purpose of giving Emphasis.

---

* He gives it also as either '*Nφ.* Past or Infinitive' of חבה.

(γ) So also the Absolute forms הִנָּתֹן and הֵאָכֹל in Note (*d*)
on Tab. XIV are used before a Future.   And so also
הֵאָסֹף before יֵאָסֵף in 2 S. xvii. 11, and הַאִדָּרֹשׁ (with
א instead of ה,—probably, as R. D. K. says, to avoid
having to pronounce ה twice consecutively) before
אִדָּרֵשׁ in Ez. xiv. 3.

Note. The rare form כְּהִנְדֹּף, Ps. lxviii. 3, is generally taken as a form of Infin. Constr. *N*φ. corresponding to the form הִפָּעֵל.   It may have been modified
to suit the form of תִּנְדֹּף following.*   It may also be
a 'Compound form' made up of the *N*φ. Infinitive
and the *K*. Infinitive (כְּנְדֹּף) mixed together.   Comp.
pp. 177 & 178.

(δ) We mentioned in Note (†) on p. 79 the dropping of the
ה of the Infin. *N*φ. form הִפָּעֵל after a prefix sometimes, as in בְּעָטֵף for בְּהֵעָטֵף Lam. ii. 11.   So we
have בְּהָרֵג for בְּהֵהָרֵג Ez. xxvi. 15 (with ֵ before
the *unaccented*† הֵ).   And so the ה is dropped in
לְעָנֹת for לְהֵעָנֹת Infin. *N*φ. fr. עָנָה Ex. x. 3, and
לֵרָאוֹת for לְהֵרָאוֹת Infin. *N*φ. fr. רָאָה.

(ε) Instead of נִגְדַּע (3 s. *m.* Past *N*φ., fr. גדע), some Bibles
have נִגְדַּע with ֵ in Jer. l. 22—a form like נֶחְמַד,
נֶעְדַּר, etc.

---

* The Dag. Lene of the ד forbids us to say merely that the form is deduced
directly from הִנְדֹּף by dropping the penultimate vowel. But the form תִּנְדֹּף, or
הִנְדֹּף, so obtained, may perhaps have been altered into כְּתִנְדֹּף in order to suit the
subsequent תִּנְדֹּף.

† The ֵ in the Bible here is reckoned only as a *Metheg*,—see Pt. I, § 44 (e).

(ζ) The ־ָ of the *Nφ*. Partic. is generally retained in the Sing. fem. and the Plu. masc. & fem. ['Appˣ (B) to Tab. XIV' (β)]. But, as R. D. K. observes, we find also, with Shva in place of that ־ָ, נֶחְבָּאִים (Josh. x. 17) *Nφ*. Partic. pl. *m.*, and נִטְמָאִים (Ez. xx. 30 & 31), and הַנִּמְצָאִים in נִמְצָאִים (Esth. i. 5, besides 1 S. xiii. 15 and several other passages). But there is also הַנִּמְצָאִים (Ezr. viii. 25), and נִמְצָאֶיךָ (Is. xxii. 3), and הַנִּמְצָאת and הַנִּמְצָאָה.

(η) The ־ָ is sometimes replaced by, or resolved into, '־ִ followed by *Dagesh*'; thus in *נִכְבַּדִּי *Nφ*. Partic. pl. *m.* 'i.e.,' and נִכְבַּדֶּיהָ *Nφ*. Partic. pl. *m.* w. Aff. *her*,—but נִכְבַּדִּים pl. *m.* & נִכְבַּדּוֹת pl. *f.*,—נִכְבַּדֵּיהֶם pl. *m.* w. Aff. *their* (*m.*).

(θ) It is hardly necessary perhaps to call the Student's attention to the following differences :—

(i.) נִפְקַד *Nφ*. Past 3 s. *m.*⎫ (but, in Pause, each of
נִפְקָד *Nφ*. Partic. s. *m.*⎭ them alike is נִפְקָד׃).

נִפְקַד Constr. form of *Nφ*. Partic. s. *m.*

(ii.) נִפְקְדָה (p. נִפְקָדָה׃) *Nφ*. Past 3 s. *f.*,

נִפְקָדָה (in Pause the same) *Nφ*. Partic. s. *f.*

---

* Thus it is in Is. xxii. 8 & 9. In Prov. viii. 24 נִכְבַּדִּי is given in some Bibles; but the word should be either נִכְבָּדֵי as it is given in some (which is *irregular*), or נִכְבַּדִּי as it is given in others.

PĬ-ÊL.

(7) (a) R. D. Kimḵhi calls attention to the following forms of
the INFIN. PĬ.,—besides the ordinary form פַּקֵּד,—viz.

(i.) פִּקֵּד* (like the Past 3 s. m.), in the נִאֵץ of נִאֵץ נִאַצְתָּ
2 S. xii. 14, and הִלִּיץ† Lev. xiv. 43;

(ii.) פַּקְּדָה (i.e. the ordinary form פַּקֵּד, with the ־ה of
§ 137, 4, iii.), in זַמְּרָה Ps. cxlvii. 1 and לְיִסְּרָה
Lev. xxvi. 18;

(iii.) פַּקֵּד,* in יַסֹּר Ps. cxviii. 18 and קַנֹּא 1 K. xix. 14
and רַפֹּא Ex. xxi. 19,—

(iv.) פִּקֵּד,* in the יִסּוּד of לְיִסּוּד‡ [for לְיִסֹּר] 2 Chr. xxxi. 7.
But, as he adds, this may be the Infin. Kal—for
לִיסֹוד, like לִיסֹד Is. li. 16, the Short-ḵhĭrik followed
by Dagesh being instead of the Long-ḵhĭrik. The
Dagesh may however be (as some think) merely a
Euphonic Dagesh [Pt. I, § 70 (2)].

---

* Used here as a 'form,'—instead of the *proper* one fr. פעל, for reasons too plain to need mention.

† Some however take this to be PAST *PĬ.* 3 s. m.,—the ordinary form. The rendering of אַחַר חִלֵּץ would then be "*after* [that] he hath taken away," as in the E.V., comp. אַחַר הֻכָּה Jer. xli. 16. But the הַקְצוֹת (INFIN. *H*φ. fr. קצה, with הַ in place of the usual הָ), and הַטּוֹחַ (INFIN. *N*φ. fr. טוח), in the same verse, may be taken to support R. D. K.'s opinion.

Note (i.) אַחַר may be followed by the Infin., as well as אַחֲרֵי. So אַחַר שָׁלַח Jer. xl. 1, etc.

(ii.) So וַדְבֵּר Job xlii. 7, after אַחַר, may be Past *PĬ.* 3 s. m. as some give, or it may be the Infin. *PĬ.* as above (with ־ in place of ־) as some give it in Ex. vi. 28, D. iv. 15, and Hos. i. 2; or it may be the Noun דבר (Jer. v. 13) 'i.e.,'—like חֶבֶל and קְטֹר and שָׁלֹם.

‡ A Contraction somewhat similar to that mentioned in § 8 (a). Although the ' is allowed to *remain standing* here, it has lost its power, and the case is one of Pt. I, § 12, N.B. So the Construct Noun יְקַהַת Gen. xlix. 10 occurs (with the ל of § 4) in the contracted form לִיקָהַת (for לְיִקְהַת) Prov. xxx 17—where some however give לִיקָהַת badly.

(v.) פַּקֶּרֶת (instead of פַּקְּרָה, see (ii) above) in בְּצִדְקָתֶךְ already mentioned [p. 323 (κ)].

Note. It is very unusual for a Verb whose 3ᵈ Rt-letter is ה *Quiescent* to have an Infin. Constr. Pĭ-ÊL of the form פַּקֵּד. But וּכְחַכֵּי (Hos. vi. 9) is such* an unusual form of the Infin. Constr. *Pĭ-êl* w. וְ (*and*) & כ (*as*) prefixed, fr. חכה.

(β) (i.) As was mentioned in Note (e) on Tab. XIV, the Pĭ-ÊL Past 3 s. *m.* has

    (a) sometimes ⸗ to the 2ᵈ Rt-letter, as in אִבַּר 2 K. xxi. 3,†—and

    (b) sometimes ⸗ to the 2ᵈ Rt-letter, as in דִּבֶּר and כִּבֵּס and וְכִבֵּם often (though דִּבֵּר‡ and § occur ‖), and in וְכִפֶּר often.

---

* The form חַכֵּי is in principle the same as חַכֵּה (the only difference being that it has ‘ *Quiescent* in place of the ה *Quiescent*). And חַכֵּה agrees in form with פַּקֵּד, which is the SAME FOR THE CONSTRUCT AS FOR THE ABSOLUTE Infinitive *Pĭ-êl*. The usual form is גַּלּוֹת for the Infin. Constr. *Pĭ.* of such Verbs ל״ה. R. Abraham ben Ezra, in his Commentary on Hos. vi. 9, cites as a similar instance (of the פַּקֵּד form of the Infin. *Pĭ.* from such a Verb (ל״ה) לְכַלֵּא Dan. ix. 24 fr. כלה,—with א, like the ‘ here, in place of the Quiescent ה. There is also לְכַלֵּה 2 Chron. xxiv. 10.

† (i.) So in אֵחַר fr. אחר, אֵרֵשׂ fr. ארשׂ, בֵּרֵךְ fr. ברך, etc.,—in which the Compensation is made for the Dagesh of the 2ᵈ Rt-letter; and

  (ii.) So in לָהַט fr. להט, נָחַם fr. נחם, etc.,—in which the Compensation is not made for the Dagesh of the 2ᵈ Rt-letter.

‡ This form, from the Root דבר, may be said to be only used ‘in Pause,’ or ‘as a Pause-form not in Pause’ (§ 167, 2).

§ Once with the Accent ⸗, and once with the Accent ⸗.

‖ Of this form (פַּקֵּד) are, of course,

  (i.) בֵּרֵךְ בֵּאֵר [Nu. xxiii. 20, Ps. x. 3], מֵאֵן, etc.,—in which the Compensation is made for the Dagesh; and

  (ii.) נִאֵר, כִּהֵן, בִּעֵר, etc.,—in which the Compensation is not made for the Dagesh.

(ii.) Instead of the $\bar{\;}$ of the 2^d Rt-letter in the form פָּקַד, Verbs לֹא have of course $\bar{\;}$ in the open syllable אָ $\bar{\;}$ [comp. Obs. XXIII on p. 185]. So, as R. D. K. cites, נִשָּׂא (Pĭ. Past 3 s. m. fr. נשׂא) 1 K. ix. 11 & Am. iv. 2 and דְּכָא Ps. cxliii. 3 and מִלָּא Jer. li. 34.

Note. From נשׂא we have also the ordinary form נִשֵּׂא (Pĭ. Past 3 s. m.) 2 S. v. 12, and from מלא the form מִלֵּא several times. Some Verbs לֹא have only the ordinary ($\bar{\;}$)-form, as might be expected.

(iii.) When the 2^d Rt-letter is either א or ה or ח or ע, any Moving *Shva* of the 2^d Rt-letter must take a Compound form; thus,

> (a) מֵאֲנוּ, מֵאֲנָה, etc.,—in which the Compensation is made for the Dagesh of the 2^d Rt-letter,— and
>
> (b) שִׁחֲתוּ, נִאֲצוּ, מִהֲרָה, etc.,—in which the Compensation is not made.

Note. It is but rarely that the 1st Rt-letter takes $\bar{\;}$, before $\bar{\;}$ under the 2^d Rt-letter, as in אֵחֲרוּ (Pĭ. Past 3 pl., fr. אחר) Ju. v. 28, and יֶחֱמַתְנִי (Pĭ. Past 3 s. f., w. Aff. *me*, fr. חמה) Ps. li. 7.

(γ) For some Pĭ. Participle forms which vary from the ordinary forms see above [4 (η, iv) & (θ), p. 330].

(δ) As in (*a*, i) so also in the Imper. 2 s. *m*. PĬ-ÊL the 2ᵈ Root-letter has sometimes ⸴ [thus פַּקֵּד], instead of the usual form פַּקֵּד (or פַקֵּד when unaccented). So in פַּלֵּג Ps. lv. 10, and so in וְקָרֵב Ez. xxxvii. 17 and כַּתֵּר Job xxxvi. 2.

These forms are represented by the (קֵ) by the side of the form פַּקֵּד in Tab. XIV.

(ε) So in the *Pĭ.* Fut. 3 & 2 pl. *f.*, the forms תִּעְכַּסְנָה Is. iii. 16 and תִּנְאָפְנָה Hos. iv 13 & 14 and תְּרֻטַּשְׁנָה Is. xiii. 18 (with ⸴* under the 2ᵈ Rt-letter) are represented by the (קֵ) by the side of the form תִּפַּקֵּדְנָה in Tab. XIV.

Note (i.) The ⸴ to the 2ᵈ Rt-letter, as in תְּפַלַּחְנָה Job xxxix. 3, etc., is usual before a Guttural 3ᵈ Rt-letter; comp. Tab. XVI (3) 'Note.'

(ii.) The form וַתְּחַלֶּלְנָה Ez. xiii. 19 (with ⸴ under the 2ᵈ Rt-letter) is not represented in Tab. XIV, on account of its rarity.

(iii.) וָאֶעֱנֶּה 1 K. xi. 39 is for וָאַעֲנֶּה *Pĭ.* Fut. 1 s. fr. עָנָה w. ו pref. The א dropping its ⸴ becomes Quiescent in the ⸴ of the ו, as in וָאדֹנָי (for וַאֲדֹנָי) etc., p. 2, Note (‡). This is not usual in the case of the *Pĭ.* Fut 1 s. with ו.

---

* R. D K. mentions these as occurring IN PAUSE. They would then come under § 165 (I, δ). [Hos. iv 14 would come under § 167 (II,).]

(ζ) The Dag. F. of the 2ᵈ Rt-letter is often omitted over Shva, as in אֲהַלְלָה *Pĭ.* Fut. 1 s. (*i.e.* אֲהַלֵל, with ה) etc.;* and the Moving Shva of the 2ᵈ Rt-letter has sometimes a Compound form, as in וַתְּאַלֲצֵהוּ Fut. *Pĭ.* 3 s. *f.* fr. אלץ, w. ו pref. and Aff. *him,* Ju. xvi. 16,—comp. Pt. I, § 72 [Note (*, *e*)].

[(η) It has been asserted by some that when the Dagesh F. (for the *Pĭ.* & *Pŭ.*) is omitted as in (ζ) from the 2ᵈ Rt-letter, the preceding vowel is moreover sometimes lengthened even when the 2ᵈ Rt-letter is not one of the five letters אהחער. In theory this might very well be true, and we might be glad to find some *sure* examples† of it.   We do not know of

---

* So in בְּקַנְאוֹ Infin. *Pĭ.* fr. קנא, w. ב pref. and Aff. *his*, Nu. xxv. 11,
    מִלְאוּ Past *Pĭ.* 3 pl. fr. מלא, Num. xxxii. 11 & 12,
    קִנְאוּנִי Past *Pĭ.* 3 pl. fr. קנא, w. Aff. *me*, Deut xxxii 21,
    וּמְפַלְּטִי Partic. *Pĭ.* Sing. *m.* fr. פלט, with ו pref. and יַ— at the end (§ 139, ε, and p. 232), 2 S. xxii. 2.   The word is there unaccented; but in Ps xviii. 3 the ל has its Dagesh, and the word is accented),
    תְּבַקְשֶׁנָה Fut. *Pĭ.* 2 s. *m.* fr. בקש, w. Aff. *it* (*f.*), Gen. xxxi. 39, etc. etc.

† As examples of this we might fairly claim כהָתֵל [for כְּהַתֵל Infin. *Pĭ.* w. כ pref.] and תִּהָתָלוּ or תְּהָתְלוּ [for תְּהַתְלוּ 2 pl. *m.* Fut. *Pĭ.*] Job xiii. 9, and so יְהָתֵלוּ or יְהָתְלוּ [for יהתלו 3 pl. *m.* Fut. *Pĭ.*] Jer. ix. 4,—like וַיְהַתֵל 3 s. *m.* Fut. *Pĭ.*, 1 K. xviii 27,—if indeed התל be supposed to be the Root of all these words.   The Dagesh in the ל of תְּהָתְלוּ and יְהָתֵלוּ, as given in good Editions, is then Euphonic. So too הִתֵל [for הֵתֵל 3 s. *m.* Past *Pĭ.*] in הֵתֶל בִּי Gen. xxxi. 7, and הֵתַלְתָּ [for הֲתַלְתָ 2 s. *m.* Past *Pĭ.*] Ju xvi. 10 & 13 & 15.   But,

If, instead, the Root is תלל (as some say), the ה of תהתלו and יְהָתֵלוּ is the *Hφ* pref ה appearing as in 9 (ε, i) below.   Then the Dagesh belongs of right to the 3ᵈ Rt-letter ל, to represent the 2ᵈ Rt-letter.   Then also the form יְהַתֵל 1 K. xviii. 27 may be said to be for יהתל [or יתל, like יֵסב Tab. XXI] the — being resolved into

any such examples. One example of it there would be if we could adopt a doubtful reading (mentioned by R. D. K.) of the word מַאֲסְפָיו Is. lxii. 9. Another reading of this word (also mentioned by R. D. K.) would make it of the פֹּעֵל form—see Note (A) below].

PŬ-ĂL.

(8) (a) In the PŬ-ĂL Voice the 1st Rt-letter has sometimes —ŏ in place of the usual —; thus R. D. K. cites *כָּרֻת (Ez. xvi. 4) Past *Pŭ.* 3 s. *m.* fr. כרת, †שֻׁדְּדָה (Na. iii. 7) Past *Pŭ.* 3 s. *f.* fr. שדד, כָּלּוּ (Ps. lxxii. 20) Past *Pŭ.* 3 pl. fr. כלה, and similarly כֻּסּוּ (Ps. lxxx. 11) fr. כסה,—and a little earlier he cites the *Pŭ.* Participle forms מְאָדָּם s. *m.* (Na. ii. 4) and מְאָדָּמִים pl. *m.* (which last occurs in Ex. xxv. 5 and in four other places in Exodus).

(β) To the *Pŭ.* Participle forms without the מְ, which were mentioned above [4 (θ), p. 330], we may add here מוֹרָט (Is. xviii. 2 & 7), which is supposed to be such a *Pŭ.* Partic s. *m.* for מְמוֹרָט from מרט. We may

---

— *followed by Dagesh.* Some may however prefer to say that this latter form is 'borrowed' from a Root התל.

Also, if the Root is תלל, כְּהָתֵל is the regular Infin. *H*φ (like כְּהָסֵב fr. סבב) with כ pref., and הָתֵל 3 s. *m.* Past *H*φ. (like הָסֵב fr. סבב), and הֲתַלְתָּ is "borrowed" in form from an unused Root [תול].

* For the Dagesh in the ר, comp Pt. I, § 49 [latter part of Note (*)].

† This word occurs once, but שְׁדָדָה (with —) occurs three times and the Pause-form שֻׁדָּדָה once; also שֻׁדְדוּ and שֻׁדְּדוּ 3 pl., and the Pause-form שֻׁדַּדְנוּ 1 pl.

also mention the form יוּלָד in הַיּוּלָד (Ju. xiii. 8) which R. D. K. gives as *Pŭ*. Partic.* s. *m.* fr. ילד with the ה of § 98.

[He gives also יוּקָשִׁים (Eccles. ix. 12) as such a *Pŭ*. Partic. pl. *m.*, without the Dag. F. of the 2ᵈ Rt-letter, and מוּעָדֶת (Prov. xxv. 19) Partic. *Pŭ*. s. *f.* fr. מעד—in Pause for מוּעָדֶת†—in which וּ stands for the ־ֻ instead of this being lengthened into ־ֹ to compensate for the Dagesh.]

(γ) R. D. K. cites הַיְחָבְרְךָ (Ps. xciv. 20) as a form of Fut. *Pŭ*. 3 s. *m.* w. ה Interrog. and Aff. *thee* (*m.*), fr. חבר,—shortened from יְחָבַּר (for יְחֻבַּר) with an Affix (§ 185, ii). This is a very unusual contraction, but others also explain the word so.

HIPH-îL.

(9) (*a*) (i.) The HIPH-îL INFINITIVE has generally the form הַפְקֵד (or הַפְקִיד, § 137, 1, d) when Absolute, הַפְקִיד when Construct, and when with one of the prefixes בכלמ, and with Pron.-Affs., and with ה at the end.

---

* Some give it as a *Hoph*. Partic. without the מ. But so the וּ would be on the wrong side of the 1ˢᵗ Rt-letter.—For the וּ before Dagesh in הַיּוּלָד, compare Pt. I, § 14 (N.B.).

† Some however have supposed that this is for מוּעֶדֶת KAL Partic (1) s. *f.*, the וּ being replaced by וֹ. Dr. Ewald remarks (Lehrb. der hebr. spr., p. 440) "dies kann nicht Part. Qal" (i.e. *Kal*) "von מעד seyn."

(ii.) In a few instances however the form הֻפְקַד occurs
in Construction, as in בַּעְשֵׂר * הַלְוִיִם *at-the-tithing-
of* (or *taking-tithes by*) *the Levites*, Neh. x. 39,—
comp. * לַעְשֵׂר Deut. xxvi. 12 which was cited in
§ 137 (3. a. v.); and so בְּהַנְחֵל Deut. xxxii. 8, etc.
[Note. Very rarely the ('–͏)-form occurs with a
prefix as in לְהָפֵיר Zech. xi. 10].

(iii.) Sometimes the Infin. Absol. *H*ϕ. has '–͏ to the
2ᵈ Rt-letter,† in place of the usual –͏. This
occurs chiefly in cases of (iv).

(iv.) Sometimes the prefixed ה of the Infinitive *H*ϕ.
(Absol. or Constr.) has –͏ in place of the usual –͏.
Thus R. D. K. cites as Infin. Absol. *H*ϕ. the הַצֵּיל
and הַמְלִיט of Is. xxxi. 5 [which may however be
the ordinary Past-Tense forms, as some take them],
and the Verb-forms in לְמַעַן הַרְגִּיעַ הָאָרֶץ וְהִרְגִּיזֵ ···
Jer. l. 34 [each of which he says however may
possibly be a Past Tense], and הַדְרִיכָה *to thresh*

---

* Comp. § 178 [Note (*b*)]. The ה of the form הַעְשֵׂר is dropped here, and its
vowel is given to the prefix, as in לַחֲלָק (for לְהַחֲלִיק) Jer. xxxvii. 12 [Pt. I, § 12]
לַרְאֹתְכֶם (for לְהַרְאֹתְכֶם, *H*ϕ. Infin. fr. ראה w. לְ pref. and Aff. *your m.*), etc.;—
comp. Note (†) on p. 79.

† As an instance of this it is quite fair to cite הַעְבִיר Josh. vii. 7. But we should
observe that as the Infin. there *follows* the Tense, the Infin. is perhaps not quite so
much cut off from ' Structural Connection' with the rest of the sentence as it is when
it precedes the Tense.

Again, הָכִין Josh. iv. 3 is generally taken as Infin. Absol. [so Fürst, Concord.
p. 549, and others]. But we ought to observe that the Accentuation in Josh. iv. 3 is
against our taking the word הָכִין there in the same manner as the Infin. Absol.
הָבֵן in Josh. iii. 17. Perhaps therefore the word הָכִין has rather some ' Structural
Connection' with what follows it. It is much *easier* undoubtedly to take it in the
same manner as the word הָבֵן in Josh. iii. 17.

*her** Jer. li. 33, and הִשָּׁמְדָם † *their* (*m.*) *destroying* Josh. xi. 14, and הַשְׁלִכוֹ ‡ *His casting* 2 K. xxiv. 20; also, under the Verbs ל״ה, הַקְצוֹת Infin. Constr. *Hφ.* fr. קצה—which was mentioned in Note (†) on p. 342.

(v.) Instead of the הַ of (iv) there is sometimes הֶ before a Guttural 1st Root-letter. As examples of this R. D. K. cites הֶחֱזִיקִי *My taking-hold* Jer. xxxi. 32. He cites also as Infinitives הֶעֱבִיר Gen. xlvii. 21 and הֶאֱרִיךְ Prov. xix. 11, each of which may very well be Past 3 s. *m.*,—as others give them.

(vi.) We find א (in place of the usual ה) in אַשְׁכִּים (Jer. xxv. 3) *Hφ.* Infin. Absol. fr. שׁכם,—for הַשְׁכֵּים Jer. xliv. 4 and הַשְׁכֵּם Jer. xxvi. 5. R. D. K. cites also the well-known אַבְרֵךְ of Gen. xli. 43, and remarks that some say it is Infin. [Absol. *Hφ.* fr. ברך] with 'interchange of ה with א,' but adds that one might say that the א is the mark of the 1 s. [Fut. *Hφ.*].

(vii.) (*a*) Instead of the usual *Hφ.* vowel we find ־ under the 2d Rt-letter in הִפְצַר (1 S. xv. 23) *Hφ.* Infin. fr. פצר (used as a Noun). This might be both because of the Pause, comp. § 165, I (δ), and for Euphony before the ר.

---

* But the rendering "It is time [that] *one had threshed her*" is quite admissible, in accordance with which the word would be the ordinary Past *Hφ.* w. Aff. *her*.

† Comp. הִשְׁמִידוֹ *His destroying* Deut. xxviii. 48 and הִשְׁמָדְךָ *thy* (*m.*) *destroying* Deut. vii. 24.—But there are also הַשְׁמִידוֹ *His destroying* Josh. xxiii. 15 and הַשְׁמִידָם *to destroy them* (*m.*) Josh. xi. 20, etc.

‡ Comp. הַשְׁלִכוֹ Jer. lii. 3, where some Bibles however have הָ'.

(*b*) Also in הַזְכַּרְכֶם Ez. xxi. 29 *H*φ. Infin. fr. זכר
w. Aff. *your* (*m.*) there is — in place of the
יִ— of the form הַפְקִידְכֶם in Tab. XV (v).   This
may be said to be for Euphony before the ר.

(β) (i.) The Past-Tense forms הִשְׁאִלְתִּיהוּ and הֵמַתֶּם etc.
(with — in place of the more usual —) were
mentioned in 3 (η) [pp. 325 & 326].

(ii.) The form הֶעֱבַרְתָּ was mentioned in Note (‡) on
p. 119.   Comp. the *H*φ. Past 3 s. *m.* הֶעֱלָה
fr. עלה.   [R. D. K. cites both these.]

(iii.) (*a*) In 'Full' Verbs the prefix ה of the *H*φ. Past
has rarely — (in place of the usual —) before a
letter other than one of the four אהחע [§ 178];
thus הִכְלַמְנוּם (1 S. xxv. 7) *H*φ. Past 1 pl.
fr. כלם w. Aff. *them* (*m.*).

(*b*) So, with א in place of the ה—an Aramaism,
אֶגְאַלְתִּי (Is. lxiii. 3) *H*φ. Past 1 s. fr. גאל, in
Pause.

(*c*) So too, with both ה and א, וְהֶאֱזְנִיחוּ (Is. xix. 5)
*H*φ. Past 3 pl. fr. זנח w. ו pref.,—which is
supposed to be mixed up of the two forms, one
with ה and the other with א, "the א after the
manner of the Aramæan tongue and the ה after
the manner of the sacred tongue," as R. D. K.
remarks that some say.

(*i*) But in Verbs ל״ה, the ה of the *H*φ. Past has ־ָ
in several instances. Thus from גלה we have
not only the ordinary forms

הִגְלָה 3 s. *m.* (וְהִגְלָם w. ו pref. and Aff.
them m.),

הִגְלִיתָ 2 s. *m.*, etc., see Tab. XXIII,—
but also הֶגְלָה 3 s. *m.* (w. Aff. *them m.* הֶגְלָם).
So 'from ראה there are forms with הֶ and forms
with הָ, *viz.*

הֶרְאָה 3 s. *m.* (w. Affs., *thee m.* הֶרְאֲךָ,
me הֶרְאָנִי, p. הֶרְאַנִי, *them m.* הֶרְאָם,
(הֶרְאָנוּ *us*),

הִרְאִיתָ 2 s. *m.* (with Affs., *me* הִרְאִיתַנִי,
(הִרְאִיתָנוּ *us*),

once הַרְאֵיתִי* 1 s. (in וְהַרְאֵיתִי w. ו préf.,
Na. iii. 5),—and the 1 s. with Affs.,
thee m. הִרְאִיתִיךָ, *them m.* הִרְאִיתִים and
הִרְאִיתָם Pt. I, § 12.

From לאה the only *H*φ. Past forms which
occur are the following—with הֶ—*viz.*

הֶלְאַנִי 3 s. *m.* w. Aff. *me*, הֶלְאָת 3 s. *f.*
(contracted, like הִרְצָת in Tab. XXIII),
and הֶלְאֵיתִיךָ 1 s. w. Aff. *thee m.*

So הֶחְבָּאַתָה Josh. vi. 17 (for הֶחְבִּיאָה *H*φ. Past
3 s. *f.*) has הֶ as in הֶעְתִּיקוּ § 178 (i), and
an additional ־ָ ה [§ 138, B (ii, β)].
R. D. K. says that it has "two marks of

---

* This form (with הַ) is, as R. D. K. observes, unusual. The ־ַ may be said to
be a Euphonic irregularity.

the feminine, and so in Nouns יְשׁוּעָתָה for יְשׁוּעָה and עֶזְרָתָה for עֶזְרָה‎"; and he adds that the ‎יְ‎ ‎ of הֶחְבִּיאָה vanishes in order to lighten the word—because of the reduplication.

(γ) (i.) The *H*φ. PARTICIPLE has mostly the (‎יְ‎ ‎)-form, as מַפְקִיד etc., in 'Appendix (B) to Tab. XIV.'

(ii.) The (‎ ‎)-form of the s. *m.*, as מַפְקֵד, occurs as a Noun often; thus מַכְתֵּשׁ *a mortar* (as a means of 'pounding,' fr. כתש *to pound*), מַפְתֵּחַ *a key* (as a means of 'opening,' fr. פתח *to open*). But מַסְתֵּר in וּכְמַסְתֵּר Is. liii. 3 is taken by many to be a Participle "*and as* [*one*] *hiding*,"—like מַסְתִּיר in הַמַּסְתִּיר Is. viii. 17.

(iii.) The ‎יְ‎ ‎ is in some few instances altogether dropped as in מַחֲלְמִים Jer. xxix. 8, instead of מַחֲלִימִים (fr. חלם),—in illustration of which R. D. K cites מְעַזְרִים 2 Chr. xxviii. 23 (fr. עזר).

(δ) (i.) The *H*φ. IMPER. 2 s. *m.* has generally the (‎ ‎)-form הַפְקֵד.

(ii.) The ‎ ‎ is of course shortened into — if the Accent be removed, as in הַעֲבֶר־נָא 2 S. xxiv. 10.

(iii.) In a few instances the 2ᵈ Rt-letter has ‎ ‎, as in הַנְחַת (Joel iv. 11) *H*φ. Imper. 2 *s. m.* fr. נחת. So in הַיְשַׁר (*Krî* for הוֹשֵׁר *Kthiv*, Ps. v. 9) *H*φ. Imper. 2 s. *m.* fr. ישר. For the ‎ ‎ of הַרְחֵק Job xiii. 21, instead of הַרְחֵק Prov. iv. 24, etc., the Student may compare § 165 (I, δ) and הַמְעַד there cited. So

Note. The ($-$)-form is common before a Guttural 3ᵈ Rt-letter,—as in הַצְלַח, הוֹשַׁע, etc.,—comp. Tab. XVI (3) (B, β).

(iv.) The 'ִ is not dropped but stands in the 2 s. *m.* Imper. *H*φ. with the ה of § 141 (γ), as in הַקְשִׁיבָה there cited.

(v.) The ('ִ)-form, as הַפְקִיד fr. פקד, may be said (as it is said by some) to stand in a few instances for the IMPER. *H*φ. 2 s. *m.*; thus הוֹפִיעַ Ps. xciv. 1 fr. יפע *may* be Imper. 2 s. *m.* (It would thus suit the IMPER. *N*φ. at the beginning of the next verse, better than if it were taken to be the PAST *H*φ. 3 s. *m.*)

(ε) (i.) The somewhat rare appearance of the ה of *H*φ., after the 'איתן' prefix-letter of the Future-Tense, as in יְהוֹשִׁיעַ fr. ישע, and in יְהֵילִילוּ fr. ילל,—was mentioned in § 201. So we have also the forms יְהוֹדָה and אֲהוֹדֶנּוּ and יְהוֹדוּךְ mentioned on p. 282. And similarly, if fr. תלל*, יְהָתֵלּוּ (for יָתֵלּוּ 3 pl. *m.* Fut. *H*φ.) Jer. ix. 4 and תְּהָתֵלּוּ (for תָּתֵלּוּ 2 pl. *m.* Fut. *H*φ.) Job xiii. 9. Comp. Tab. XXI.

(ii.) For the form יַצְלַח, in place of יַצְלִיחַ or יַצְלֵחַ, when the 3ᵈ Rt-letter is Guttural,—see Tab. XVI (3) (B, β).—So עַ$-$ in יָנַע for יָנֵעַ & תִּרַע for תָּרַעַ.

---

* As some suppose. See Note (†) on p. 346 for a different account of יְהָתֵלּוּ (or יְהָתֵלּוּ, as some give it) and תְּהָתֵלּוּ (or תְּהָתֵלּוּ, as some give it),—as also for the words כְּהָתֵל Job xiii. 9, and הֵתֵל (in הֵתֶל בִּי Gen. xxxi. 7), and הֵתַלְתָּ Ju. xvi. 10 & 13 & 15.

(iii.) The ׳— of the *Hφ.* Voice-form is sometimes altogether dropped, as in the following instances cited by R. D. K.:—וַיְדְרְכוּ Jer. ix. 2, וַיַּדְבְּקוּ 1 S. xiv. 22 & xxxi. 2 (and so in 1 Chr. x. 2, but וַיִּדְבְּיקוּ in Ju. xviii. 22 & xx. 45), יַעְשְׁרֶנּוּ 1 S. xvii. 25 (3 s. *m.* Fut. *Hφ.* fr. עשׁר, w. Aff. *him*), and תְּעַשְׁרֶנָּה Ps. lxv. 10 (2 s. *m.* Fut. *Hφ.* w. Aff. *it f.*). So fr. כתת we have in Nu. xiv. 45 וַיַּכְּתוּם *Hφ.* Fut. 3 pl. *m.* w. ו pref. and Aff. *them* (*m.*) from וַיִּכְּתוּ as in Deut. i. 44. [Comp. γ (iii), p. 353.]

(iv.) וָאֶעְשִׁר Zech. xi. 5 is contracted from וְאַעְשִׁר (or וְאַעְשִׁיר) 1 s. Fut. *Hφ.* fr. עשׁר w. ו prefixed.

N.B. This contraction is very unusual in the case of the 1 s. Fut. w. ו prefix. But there are instances of other words in which such a Contraction takes place—as in הֹטְאִים for הֹחֹטְאִים, etc.

Hoph-ăl.

(10) (*a*) The הָפְּעַל instead of הָפְעַל form of the 5th Voice was mentioned in § 121. Such forms are the following (cited by R. D. K.): הֻשְׁלַךְ Past 3 s. *m.* fr. שׁלך and הֻשְׁלָכָה Pause-form of הֻשְׁלְכָה Past 3 s. *f.*, הֻמְלַחַתְּ Past 2 s. *f.* fr. מלח (corresponding to the form הָפְקְדְתְּ in Tab. XIV).

(β) With this (⸱⸱)-form corresponds the (ו)-form in Tabs. XVIII, XX, & XXI.

(γ) (i.) Instead of the (וֹ)-forms, such as יוּסַב, מוּסַב, הוּסַב, etc., in Tab. XXI, there are some which correspond rather with the *Hoph-ăl* forms in Tab. XIX, —*i.e.* with Dag. F. in the 1ˢᵗ Rt-letter, as in וְהֻמְּכוּ Job xxiv. 24 *Hoph.* Past fr. מכך w. וֹ pref. (on which R. D. K. writes "it ought by rights to be וְהוּמַכּוּ, after the form of וְהוּסַבּוּ, וְהוּמַקּוּ"). The form הֻמְּכוּ is like הֻגְּשׁוּ fr. נגשׁ in Tab. XIX, and so the form might be said to be 'BORROWED' from a Verb פ׳נ.*

So also in the *Hoph.* FUT. 3 s. *m.* יֻכַּת fr. כתת & יֻסַּךְ fr. סכך, and (with וֹ as in Pt. I, § 14, N.B.) יוּסַּב in Pause Is. xxviii. 27 fr. סבב & the Pause-form יוּשַּׁד Hos. x. 14 fr. שׁדד;—and so in the 2 s. *m.* Fut. *Hoph.* תּוּשַּׁד Is. xxxiii. 1 fr. שׁדד.

(ii.) With —ŏ followed by Dagesh we have הֻשַּׁמָּה (Lev. xxvi. 34 & 35 and 2 Chron. xxxvi. 21), *Hoph.* Infin. fr. שׁמם,—w. ה—ָ, which is said by R. D. K. to be for הָ— the Affix *her*. This word with בְ pref. would be בְּהֻשַּׁמָּה, instead of which we have בְּהֻשַּׁמָּה Lev. xxvi. 43 (*Hoph.* Infin. fr. שׁמם).

(iii.) In Job xxi. 5, וְהָשַׁמּוּ with Dagesh in the שׁ has been found in some copies instead of the וְהָשַׁמּוּ which is given in the best editions. The Student must not confuse these two words. הֻשַּׁמּוּ would

---

* Similarly the Fut. *K.* forms יֵסֹב etc., and the Fut. *Hφ.* forms יֻסַּב etc., in Tab. XXI, may be said to be " BORROWED " from Verbs פ׳נ. Comp. § 243.

be *Hoph.* IMPER. 2 pl. *m.* fr. שָׁמֵם [comp. Note (*) on p. 87]; but in הָשַׁמּוּ the $-$ is *Long Kaumets* (or '*Broad Kaumets*,' as R. D. K. calls it), and this latter word therefore is not a *Hoph-ăl* form at all. It is best taken to be Imper. 2 pl. *m.* HIPH-îL fr. שָׁמֵם,—in somewhat the same sense as the *Hφ.* s. *m.* Partic. מֵשִׁמִים fr. שָׁמֵם in Ez. iii. 15.

(iv.) In יְכַתּוּ (p. יִכַּתּוּ) *Hoph.* Fut. 3 pl. *m.* fr. כתת,—instead of יוּכַתּוּ like יוּסַבּוּ in Tab. XXI,—it might be supposed that there is a mixture of the פ'נ form with the ordinary פ'ע form. But

Note. In some of the above-mentioned instances it might have been enough to have said merely that the LONG-vowel of the ordinary form is 'RESOLVED' into a SHORT-VOWEL AND DAGESH.

HITHPÄ-ÊL.

(11) (*a*) As was mentioned in Note (*h, a*) on Tab. XIV,—

(i.) The 2ᵈ Rt-letter often has $-$ instead of $-$ in the *Hθ.* Past 3 s. *m.*, Imper. 2 s. *m.*, and Fut. 3 s. *m.* etc.,—as is marked in the Table by the (ק) given after the ($-$)-forms. Examples are given in that Note.

(ii.) In Pause the 2ᵈ Root-letter has $-$ in *Hθ.** Past and Imper. & Fut. forms (except Past 2 pl. *m.* & *f.*). See examples in Note (*h*) on Tab. XIV.

(iii.) This $-$ of the Pause-forms corresponds with the ($-$)-forms of (i.)

---

* Comp. § 166 (c), N.B. and (d). Also § 245, and Note (iv) on Tab. XXI.

(iv.) Some Roots have (‑)-forms, and moreover Pause-forms corresponding with the (‑)-forms. Thus, fr. הלך we have the (‑)-forms אֶתְהַלֵּךְ and יִתְהַלֵּךְ; but in Pause we have the ‑ of the (‑)-forms, thus יִתְהַלָּכוּ: & יִתְהַלָּךְ:.

(β) The Dag. F. is sometimes omitted from the 2ᵈ Rt-letter when this letter has *Shva*, as in וַיִּתְיַלְדוּ fr. ילד Nu. i. 18, תִּתְהַלָלִי fr. הלל Jer. xlix. 4.

(γ) As seen in Note (*h, β*) on Tab. XIV, the 1ˢᵗ Rt-letter has sometimes ‑ (in place of the ‑ *followed by Dagesh*) as in הִתְפָּקְדוּ (3 pl. Past) in place of הִתְפַּקְּדוּ, and יִתְפָּקֵד 3 s. *m.* Fut. in place of יִתְפַּקֵּד, and יִתְפָּקְדוּ 3 pl. *m.* Fut. in place of יִתְפַּקְּדוּ.

> Note (i.) Although these three are the only *Hithp.** forms which occur from the Root פקד (those given in the Table being merely general Paradigm-forms), yet we may perhaps admit that it is allowable to assume and assert as some do that the ‑‑ [of the forms הִתְפַּקְּדוּ and יִתְפַּקֵּד and יִתְפַּקְּדוּ (which do not occur)] has been lengthened into the ‑ of הִתְפָּקְדוּ and יִתְפָּקֵד and יִתְפָּקְדוּ (the forms which actually occur), the ‑ *followed by Dagesh* being replaced by this ‑. And,

---

(ii.) In support of such an assumption it might be urged that the *Hθ.* forms are generally connected with Pí-êl forms—as may be seen in Table XIV*; and similarly in Tables XX & XXI. But

(iii.) We are bound to admit also that the reverse may possibly have been the order of the actual process of formation—*viz.* that the ־ָ of the פָּקַד (or פָּקַד) & פָּקְדוּ forms may have been resolved into the ־ַ 'followed by Dagesh' of the ordinary forms, and that thus there may have been preserved in these rare forms a hint which may be useful in dealing with the general derivation of Verb-forms from simple forms of the First Voice KAL.

[But we may not indulge ourselves in thus theorizing here].

(δ) The ־ֵ of the 2ᵈ Rt-letter (in place of the usual ־ַ) in some *Hθ.* Past-Tense forms was mentioned under the head of 'SOME PAST-TENSE FORMS,' 3 (θ) above [p. 326].

(ε) For some Pause-forms, with ־ַ before a 2ᵈ Rt-letter ה bearing ־ַ,—and also before הָ,—see § 166 (d).

(ζ) The transposition of the ת of הת and a 1ˢᵗ Rt-letter שׁ† or שׂ, ס, & צ,—and moreover the replacing of

---

* The *Pí.* Infin. form פַּקֵּד is the generally underlying form in the *Hθ.* But the ast and Imper & Fut. *Hθ.* have not only the ־ֵ of the פַּקֵּד form, but also the ־ַ 'a פַּקַד form, whence the ־ַ of the Pause-forms may be said to be obtained.

† For the word הִתְשׁוּמַטְנָה (fr. שׁוּט) Jer. xlix. 3, see § 246.

the ה by ט after a 1ˢᵗ Rt-letter צ,—with some other
Hθ. forms,—were considered too important to be
reserved for this late position at nearly the end of
these 'FURTHER REMARKS ON VERB-FORMS' of which
some are of but rare occurrence. This important
matter was therefore placed in a special Note on
pages 315–318, to which it is sufficient here to refer.

(η) (i.) The word נִשְׁתָּוָה Prov. xxvii. 15 is generally said
to be of 'Mixed' *Nφ.* & *Hθ.* form,—or *Nithpăal,* a
Voice-form which is common in Rabbinic, a kind
of Passive form of *Hθ.*, or having somewhat the
same relation to *Hθ.* that *Nφ.* has to *Kal.*

(ii.) It is also said by some to be a Past-Tense form 3 s.;
but some have said that it is Partic. s. *f.* In each
of these last two cases the Accent should be on
the last syllable, and so some copies have it. But
there is high authority in favour of the Accent
being on the Penultima, and also of the word
being taken to be the Third Pers. Sing. of the
Past Tense. In the מכלל יופי the word is said
to be Past 3 s. *Masc.* (referring to the word דְּלֹף),
but there is added " or it may be Partic. s. *Fem.,*
although the Accent is on the Penult."—which
however appears to be at least doubtful.

(iii.) The word is more generally taken to be 3 s. *Fem.*
Past. But

(iv.) The form is a strange one for the Past 3 s. *Fem.* of
a Verb whose 3ᵈ Rt-letter is ה *Quiescent,* and no

one seems to have thought of explaining how the word can be such a Past 3 s. *Fem.* As. such, fr. שׁוה, it ought to be נִשְׁתַּוָתָה׃ in Pause for נִשְׁתַּוְתָה [for נִשְׁתַּוָתָה—if, as is said, the ־ָ is instead of ־ַ *followed by Dag.* as in (γ) above]. The shortening of such a form into נִשְׁתַּוָה׃ is at least strange. It may perhaps be illustrated by the rare form *תִּתְפַּתָּל׃ 2 S. xxii. 27, for the תִּתְפַּתָּל׃ of the corresponding passage in Ps. xviii. 27. If we may suppose that in. ordinary current speech the ת between the פ and the ל of תִּתְפַּתָּל became transposed so as to be pronounced along with the תִּת, and so תִּתְפַּל (the regular contraction for such a word as תִּתְתַּפָּל) was obtained,†—similarly it might be possible for the second ת of נִשְׁתַּוָתָה׃ to have become transposed so as to be taken with the previous ת. But this is not quite satisfactory; and it would not account for the Accent being under the ת in נִשְׁתַּוָה׃, as it is given by high authority in Prov. xxvii. 15.

(v.) A very easy explanation of the word is possible if we may suppose that there is merely a transposition‡ of the ת and the ו of נִשְׁוָתָה׃, which would

---

* This is sometimes said to be of the Aramæan form *Ittaphal*. But from פתל we might expect rather תִּתְפַּתָּל. It might however be supposed to be " BORROWED " from a Root פלל. But the Root of the word in Ps. xviii. is פתל. The *Tense form* of each is 2 s. *m.* Fut.

† It will be seen that one of the many *t*-letters in the word is thus got rid of.

‡ There are several instances of such ' Transposition' of letters, or ' *Metathesis*' as it is called. Thus we have both כֶּבֶשׂ and כֶּשֶׂב *a lamb*, and both שִׂמְלָה and

be the regular Pause-form of the *Nφ*. Past 3 s. *f.*
[*i.e.* נִשְׁוְתָה] from שׁוה. The *Nφ*. of this Root
does not indeed occur. But perhaps it is not
more objectionable to assume an ordinary Niph-ăl
form with one letter transposed, than it is to
assume an extraordinary Nithpă-al* form—one
which as such cannot be satisfactorily explained
except with great difficulty.

(vi.) Let it be observed that it is נִשְׁתּוָה׃ with the Accent
on the Penultima which demands and is so diffi-
cult† of explanation.

(vii.) If the word be of *Nθ*. form, the ת stands in the
place of the 1st Rt-letter שׁ—in accordance with
'Note I (*a*, i)' on page 315.—The word therefore
belongs to that limited class of Verb-forms in
which the Accent is on the syllable to which the
First Rt-letter belongs. The great principle

שֹׁלְמָה *a robe*, etc. So in Hos. x 9 we have עֲלָוָה instead of the more usual
עַוְלָה *wrong;* and so we have both זְוָעָה Is. xxviii. 19 and זַעֲוָה Deut. xxviii. 25 &
Ez. xxiii. 46 (and in a few other places *Krî*). So also we have both מַלְתְּעוֹת
Ps. lviii. 7 and מְתַלְּעוֹת Job xxix. 17, etc.

Euphony might very well cause the labial ו of נִשְׁוְתָה to be removed FROM BETWEEN
the two *more* kindred letters שׁ and ת. The word נִשְׁתָּוָה is much more euphonious
than נִשְׁוְתָה. But this is merely offered as just possible;—we own that we have no
authority for the conjecture.

* Or 'Mixed' *Nφ*. & *Hθ*. Although this is a common form in Rabbinic, it is
exceedingly rare in Biblical Hebrew. There is a great weight of authority for
taking our word to be of such a *Nθ*. or 'Mixed' *Nφ*. & *Hθ*. form.

† By no means so difficult is נִשְׁתָּוָה׃ with the Accent on the LAST syllable—as some
give the word in Prov. xxvii. 15. This may be *Nθ* Past 3 s *m.* fr. שׁוה [for נִשְׁתַּוְהָה׃],
referring then to the Noun דֶּלֶף;—or it might be *Nθ*. Partic. s. *f.*, referring then
to אִשֶּׁת. But it is best to adopt the more difficult form—*i.e.* with the Accent
PENULTIMATE.

stated in the case of 'Full' Verbs on page 109
[see 'N.B.' at the foot of that page] may be
stated now as a GENERAL PRINCIPLE in the
following terms:—

> N.B. The accent of most Verb-forms is (where
> nothing interferes* with it) on that syl-
> lable in which the SECOND Rt-letter is
> involved or implied, or to which that
> 2^d Rt-letter belongs.

Nothing interferes with this Great Principle in
the case of the 3 s. *m.* and 3 s. *f.* Past $N\phi$.†, and
therefore we should expect the SECOND Rt-letter to
be involved in the syllable תָּ of נִשְׁתָּוֵה׃. This
would require the form to be one which, using פ
and ל for 1st and 3^d Rt-letter (§ 117), we might represent by נִתְפְּלָה׃. This form נִתְפְּלָה׃ can be
explained (as 3 s. *f.* Past $N\theta$. or 'Mixed' $N\phi$. &
$H\theta$.) only in one or other of the two following
ways:—

(*a*) It might correspond with such a form as ‡נִתְקָמָה׃
fr. קוּם. If so, נִשְׁתָּוֵה׃ as 3 s. *f.* Past would
correspond with a 3 s. *m.* form ‡נִשְׁתָּו׃ [as
נִתְקָמָה׃, 3 s. *f.*, would correspond with a 3 s. *m.*
form נִתְקָם׃], and we should have to suppose that

---

* For some cases of interference, see Note (†) on p. 375 below.

† If our word be of 'Mixed' $N\phi$. & $H\theta$. form, the beginning and end are of
$N\phi$. form—with the $H\theta$. part in the middle. So in יָרֹדִף, Ps. vii. 6, the beginning
and end of the word are of *Kal*, and the middle of *Pi.* form.

‡ This is merely a form. There is no such word.

it is "borrowed" from a Root שׁוּו. the 2^d Rt-letter
of which (*i.e.* tho first וּ) is treated like the וּ of
קוּם in Tab. XX.* But as we should thus have
to assume for tho *Nφ*. Past the unusual form
נָקַם†, 3 s. *m.*, instead of the usual form in Tab. ·
XX, if we must adopt ono or other of the two—
i.e. either (*a*) or (*b*),—we should prefer to say that

(*b*) It might correspond with such a form as נִסְתַּבָּה:‡
(Pause-form of ‡נִסְתַּבְּה:) fr. סבב, the ending of
which agrees with that of the usual *Nφ*. forms
נָסַב 3 s. *m.*, נָסַבָּה 3 s. *f.*, in Tab. XX,—which in
Pause would be נָסַב: 3 s. *m.*, נָסַבָּה: 3 s. *f.* ʼ

Thus our word נִשְׁתַּוָה: would stand for נִשְׁתַּוָה:
Pause-form of נִשְׁתַּוָה:,—a form "borrowed" from
a Root שׁוּו having each וּ Consonantal. The Root
in ordinary use is שׁוה.

We have dwelt upon this difficult word at some length, not
on account of the interest attached to itself, but for the sake of
the opportunity offered by it for calling the Student's attention
to some matters of general importance.

We must be content with mentioning some other difficult
words more briefly in the ANALYTICAL INDEX, and will now
conclude this Section with the following NOTES.

---

* This might be illustrated by the form חָיָה Past *K.* 3 s. *f.* (in וַתְּחָיֶהָ: Ex. i. 16)
which is not obtained directly from the common Root חיה but is "borrowed" from
a Root חיי the 2^d letter of which (*i.e.* the first יּ) must for this form be treated as
being like the יּ in שׁים whence the 3 s. *f.* Past *K.* is שָׂמָה § 226 (1). And so
חָיוֹת Partic. *K.* pl. *f.* (Ex. i. 19) must be from חיי, like שָׂמוֹת from שׁים § 226 (ii).

† As נָקַם:, which was mentioned in Note (*) on p. 160.

‡ This is merely a form. There is no such word.

Note (A).

Note on the *VOICE*-forms פֹּעַל (or פּוֹעַל) & פֵּעַל (or פּוֹעֵל).

(*a*) (i.) The Voice-form פֹּעַל instead of פְּעַל is common in Verbs
which have the same letter for their 2ᵈ & 3ᵈ Rt-letter
(פְּעַע, Tab. XXII & Obs. XIX on p. 179). Thus as
R. D. K. observes " וַיְמֹדֶד (whence וַיְמֹדֶד־ Hab. iii. 6)
is of the form יְפֹעַל," *i.e.* of the פֹּעַל Voice-form.

(ii.) The פֹּעַל form of the Verbs in (i),—as עוֹלֵל, Past 3 s. *m.*
fr. עָלַל,—Lam. i. 12, is related to the פֵּעַל form as
the ordinary פְּעַל is related to the פָּעַל form.

(iii.) So, too, the הִתְפֹּעַל form of the Verbs in (i),—as
לְהִתְגֹּלֵל Infin. w. לְ fr. גָּלַל, Gen. xliii. 18, etc.,—is
related to the פֹּעַל form as the ordinary הִתְפָּעֵל form
is related to the פָּעַל form. Comp. (ii) on p. 359.

(*β*) In the case of Verbs עו (Tab. XX), forms such as those in
(*a*) are "borrowed," in place of פָּעַל and פֵּעַל and הִתְפָּעֵל
forms. [But, if reckoned as from Verbs עע, these are פֹּלֵל
and פֹּלַל and הִתְפֹּלֵל forms—the 3ᵈ Rt-letter being reduplicated;—thus קוֹמֵם etc., and קוֹמַם etc., and הִתְקוֹמֵם
etc., from קוּם.]

(*γ*) In the case of "Full" Verbs also, a few פֹּעֵל and פֹּעַל and
הִתְפֹּעֵל forms occur. Thus,

(i.) From שֶׁרֶשׁ we have

(*a*) The פֹּעֵל form שֹׁרֵשׁ (Past 3 s. *m.*) *he hath taken
root*, Is. xl. 24, and

(*b*) The פֻּעַל form שֹׁרָשׁוּ* (Past 3 pl., Pause-form) *they are rooted*, Jer. xii. 2.

(ii.) As other instances of this פֻּעַל form, "according to the opinion of some of the grammarians," R. D. K. cites יוֹדַעְתִּי 1 S. xxi. 3 (E.V. *v*. 2, "*I have appointed*"), Past 1 s. fr. ידע,—but he adds, "some say that the י is instead of the ה of the *Hφ.* הוֹדַעְתִּי,"— and שֹׁפְטָה Ju. iv. 4 *she judged* Past 3 s. *f.* (which may however very well be the Partic (1) *K*. s. *f.*). R. D. K. also cites from שפט the פֻּעַל Partic. מְשֻׁפָּט in לְמִשְׁפָּטִי Job ix. 15 (Partic. s. *m.* w. ל pref. and Aff. *my*).

(iii.) בוֹשַׁסְכֶם Am. v. 11 (Infin. w. Aff. *your m.*) is given by some as a פֻּעַל form from a Root בשׁס. It is perhaps better to take it (as others take it) to be from the Root בוס. If so, the שׁ is in place of the first ס of the form בוֹסַסְכֶם (*Pĭ.* or *Po-lēl* form of Infin. as in Tab. XX—w. Aff. *your m.*). See R. D. K., and Ben Zev, under the Root בוס.

(iv.) As an instance of הִתְפָּעַל form we may cite הִתְגֹּעֲשׁוּ fr. גֹּעשׁ (Past 3 pl.), in וְהִתְגֹּעֲשׁוּ Jer. xxv. 16— corresponding to the form† וְהִתְהֹלְלוּ׃ which follows

---

* This, so far as form is concerned, might be said to be the usual *Pŭ·ăl* Pause-form of Past 3 pl.—the ֻ being lengthened into ֹ to compensate for the Dagesh which cannot be received by the ר. But the sense in Jer. xii. 2 requires the word to be taken as above—*i.e.* as a פֻּעַל corresponding to the פֵּעַל form,—since the פֵּעַל of שרש is used in the sense of "*uprooting*," thus וְשֵׁרֶשְׁךָ Ps. lii. 7 *and He will uproot thee*, *Pĭ.* Past 3 s. *m.* w. ו pref. & Aff. *thee m.*—and the פֻּעַל in the sense of "*being uprooted*," thus יְשֹׁרָשׁוּ Job xxxi. 8 *they m. shall be uprooted*, Fut. *Pŭ.* 3 pl. *m.* in Pause.

       † Past 3 pl., w. ו pref., fr. הלל.

it,—and, from the same Root, יִתְגָּעֲשׁוּ (Fut. 3 pl. *m.*)
Jer. xlvi. 8 although the ordinary form יִתְגָּעֲשׁוּ
occurs just previously, in verse 7.

Note. On מְנֹאָץ (Partic. s. *m.* fr. נאץ) Is. lii. 5,
R. D. K. writes (Shor. נאץ) that "it is properly
מִתְנֹאָץ," *i.e.* of this *Hithpo-él* form. He adds
however "or it is compounded with the *Pŭ-ăl.*"
We prefer this latter. But some object to this,
and prefer to consider the word as of *Hithpo-él*
form.*

(δ) (i.) The ‑ of the פֹּעֵל form is sometimes shortened into ‑ŏ;
thus we have the s. *m.* Partic. form מְלָוְשֵׁנִי fr. לשן
with "ו superfluous" (Ps. ci. 5), and with ׳ at the end
—as in 'App^x (B) to Tab. XIV' (ε).   So in †וְתֹאֲכְלֵהוּ
Job. xx. 26 the ‑ is ŏ, and the word may be (as
R. D. K. gives it) a פֹּעֵל form of Fut. (3 s. *f.* w. Aff.
him) fr. אכל.

(ii.) Some may perhaps think that the rare form יְחָבְרְךָ in
הַיְחָבְרְךָ Ps. xciv. 20 (which is usually taken as a
shortened form of *Pŭ-ăl* Fut., see above, p. 348, γ)
might possibly be a פֹּעֵל, or a פֹּעֵל, form of Fut.—
with ‑ŏ in place of the ‑. The ה in Ps. xciv. 20
is of course the Interrogative prefix, and the ךָ at the
end is the Affix for *thee m.* (comp. § 185, ii).

---

* It should be observed that R. D. K.'s interpretation (which some object to) is
based on the *He.* part, and is therefore only all the stronger if the *Pŭ.* part be
rejected.

† Some may suppose that this word is connected with the common form תֹּאכְלֵהוּ
(Fut. *K.* 3 s. *f.* w. Aff. *him*), with the ‑ŏ of the form תֹא׳ in place of the ‑ of the
form תֹּא׳. Some also may suppose that the converse relation is the true one.

(ε) There are some other פֹּעַל forms,—for instance, הֹרוֹ* וְהֹגוֹ
Is. lix. 13 (Infin. Absol. fr. הרה and הגה) and שׁוֹשֵׂתִי
Is. x. 13 (Past 1 s., fr. שׁסה=שׁשׂה). It will be sufficient
to mention such in the 'Analytical Index.'

(ζ) The word נְגֹאֲלוּ, which occurs in Is. lix. 3 and Lam. iv. 14,
has been supposed by some to be a Passive of the פֹּעַל
form—נִפְעַל corresponding to פֹּעַל as נִפְעַל to פָּעַל or
פֵּעַל § 138 (A).—This may be. But, since properly the
פֹּעַל form has פֻּעַל for its corresponding Passive, perhaps
it is best to say with others that the word is one of
'Compound' or 'Mixed' Voice-form. There are several
instances of such. A few of them are mentioned on
pp. 177 & 178 above.

Note (B).

Some Verb-forms of which the 2ᵈ Rt-letter is א, ה, ח, or ע.

(a) Of these some Infinitives were mentioned in 2 (θ) on
pp. 321 & 322.

(β) (i.) The forms הִשְׁאַלְתִּיהוּ & שְׁאֶלְתֶּם were mentioned on
p. 325, and שְׁאֶלְתִּיהוּ & שְׁאַלְתִּיו in Note (β) on
Tab. XXV.; but, as may be seen there, this occurrence of ⸗ in place of the usual ⸗ is not limited to
Verbs of which the 2ᵈ Rt-letter is א.

(ii.) וְהִזַּרְתֶּם (Lev. xv. 31) Hφ. Past 2 pl. m. w. ו fr. זהר,
is a somewhat rare instance of contraction—for
וְהִזְהַרְתֶּם.

---

* But הָרוֹ in Is. lix. 4 is of the usual פָּעַל form.

(γ) (i.) In מְבַעְתֶּ֑ךָ (1 S. xvi. 15) *Pi.* Partic. s. *m.* fr. בעת w. Aff. *thee* (*m.*), for מְבַעֶ(ת)תֶּ֑ךָ [§ 183 (β)], the

⸺ of the 2ᵈ Rt-letter is merely as in Note (§) on Tab. XXVI [from the form מְבַעֶתֶת like מְפַקֶּדֶת, instead of מְבַעֶתֶת].

(ii.) מָשְׁחָת (Mal. i. 14) has been supposed to be contracted for the *Hoph.* Partic. s. *f.* form מָשְׁחֶתֶת fr. שחת.*

(δ) (i.) For the Imper. forms וְצַעֲקִי, וְסַעֲדָה, see pp. 331 & 332.

(ii.) In שַׁחֲדוּ (Job vi. 22) *K.* Imper. 2 pl. *m.* the 1ˢᵗ Rt-letter has ⸺ (as in פִּקְדוּ) before the ⸺ of the ח. This is unusual, since the 'Slight'-vowel in such cases usually agrees with the Compound Shva following it. We have another instance of such NON-agreement in אֲחֲזִי (Ruth iii. 15) *K.* Imper. 2 s. *f.* fr. אחז,—for which however some read אֱחֲזִי in which there is the usual agreement.

(iii.) In זֹעֲמָה (Nu. xxiii. 7) *K.* Imper. 2 s. *m.* w. ה fr. זעם, the 1ˢᵗ Rt-letter has ⸺ and the 2ᵈ Rt-letter ⸺; this is a very unusual form—instead of זַעֲמָה or זְעָמָה.

(ε) In יִדְּחוּ (Jer. xxiii. 12) *Nφ.* Fut. 3 pl. *m.* fr. דחה, there is ⸺ before the ח instead of the ⸺ of the form יִגְלוּ fr. גלה —because the ח prefers ⸺ before it. Owing to this preference of the ח for ⸺, the Compensation for Dagesh F. is thus often not made in the case of ח in order that a ⸺ may be retained before it—as the Student already knows.

---

* There is a similar contraction in מְשָׁרֵת (1 K. 1. 15) *Pi.* Partic. s. *f.* fr. שרת מְשָׁרֶתֶת; and so מַחֲבַת (Ez. iv. 3) has been supposed to be contracted for the *p.* Partic. s. *f.* form מַחֲבֶתֶת fr. חבת.

NOTE (C).

SOME VERB-FORMS OF WHICH THE 3ᴰ RT-LETTER IS ה, ח, OR עַ.

(A) The occurrence of 'Furtive' ◌ֲ under ה consonantal, or ח, or ע, when at the end of a word after any Long Vowel other than ◌ָ, need not be mentioned here.

(B) In many instances the Long Vowel of the 2ᵈ Rt-letter is replaced by ◌ֶ, so that the 'Furtive' ◌ֲ is unneeded.

   (a) This occurs indeed, but only a few times, in the K. Infin. Constr. as שְׁלֹחַ *the putting forth of* [finger], instead of the usual form שְׁלֹחַ,—בְּשִׁלֹחַ, לְשִׁלֹחַ,—and so בִּגְוַע once (Nu. xx. 3), but לִגְוֹעַ in Pause Nu. xvii. 28.

   (b) It occurs also, but only a few times, in the K. Partic (1), as * נֹטַע once in הֲנֹטַע Ps. xciv. 9,—but הַנּוֹטֵעַ (Jer. xi. 17),—and so *רֹגַע twice (Is. li. 15 & Jer. xxxi. 35) instead of רֹגֵעַ, and *רֹקַע three times (Is. xlii. 5, xliv. 24, & Ps. cxxxvi. 6) instead of רֹקֵעַ.   But

N.B. (i.) This shorter vocalization is USUAL in

   (a) The Infin. Constr. of *Nφ.* and *Pı.*,

   (β) The Imper. 2 s. *m.* and the Fut. 3 s. (*m. & f.*), 2 s. *m.*, and 1 s. & pl., of *Nφ.*, *Pı.*,† & *Hφ.*,

   (γ) The *Pı.* Past 3 s. *m.*   And

(ii.) It occurs also sometimes in the *Hθ.*

---

* It may be observed that in each of these instances the Partic. form may be taken to be 'in Construction.'   Comp. p. 85 (δ, iv) & (ε).

† We have also the full יְזַבֵּחַ in Hab. i. 16, and וַיְזַבֵּחַ 2 K. xvi. 4 & 2 Chr. xxviii. 4.

Examples are given in Tab. XVI (3) which need not be repeated here.

[Obs. (i.) The (⟋⟍) form is usual in Pause; but the endings ח⟋ and ע⟋ occur even in Pause sometimes. They must by no means be *limited* to instances in which there is close connection with a word following. They occur not only with Conjunctive Accents, but also with Disjunctives and even with Pause-Accents. See examples in Tab. XVI (3), (*a*)–(δ), and Note (§).

(ii.) For *Hθ*. Pause-forms, see § 166 (*c*) and Note (‖) on Tab. XVI (3).]

(C) In the 2 s. *f*. Past forms, corresponding to פָּקַדְתְּ *K*., נִפְקַדְתְּ, *N*φ., etc., the 3ᵈ Rt-letter (when it is one of those special letters) generally takes a ⟋ instead of the ⟋ of the ד in the termination-form דְתְּ ⟋; thus, לָקַחַתְּ (instead of *לָקַחְתְּ), etc., see Tab. XVI (3) (C).

N.B. This ⟋ may be recognized as *not belonging to the word grammatically* (but merely a mark or sign to help the pronunciation), by the presence of the Dagesh L. in the ת following. This Dagesh L. belongs to the ת as preceded by SHVA QUIESCENT, and its presence shows that the preceding letter is treated as one that has no Vowel. The ⟋ therefore is treated as having no reality there. It is ABSENT, in theory; but the

---

* Some Bibles have וְלָקַחַתְּ in 1 K. xiv. 3; and so some have שָׁבַחַתְּ in Jer. xiii. 25. Comp. Note (¶) on Tab. XVI (3).

Reader adopts it as a help to the pronunciation, practically.*

(D) Instead of the ת ֶ ָ forms of Partic. s. *f.*, as פֹּקְדָת *K.*, נִפְקָדַת *N*φ., etc., these Verbs have ת ַ ָ as שְׁמָעַת (p. שְׁמֶעֶת:) *K.* Partic (1) s. *f.* fr. שמע, and נִשְׁכָּחַת *N*φ. Partic.† s. *f.* fr. שכח, etc.

Note. These Verbs

    (i) Generally are "Verbs Fut (ַ)" [§ 132, N.B. (β)], and

    (ii) Generally take ַ to the 2ᵈ Rt-letter in the 2 s. *m.* & 2 pl. *f.* of the Imper.‡ *K.* and the 3 & 2 pl. *f.* Fut. *Pi.*, *H*φ., and *Hθ.*

[The above is a re-statement of what is concisely given in Tab. XVI (3). The following few remarks may be added here.]

(*a*) A less help than that mentioned in (C) above is sometimes adopted, in place of Shva Quiescent under a Guttural. There a ַ was seen to be adopted. Λ ָ

---

* Similarly a ַ is adopted in the place of *Shva* Quiescent, to aid enunciation of a Guttural, in שְׁמַעַן (Gen. iv. 23) *K.* Imper. 2 pl. *f.*, fr. שְׁמַעְנָה,—p. 86 (є).

† Some take this word in Is. xxiii. 15 as a form of 3 s. *f.* Past *N*φ. ending in ת ָ,. as אָזְלַת 3 s. *f.* Past *K.*—p 82 (γ). It may perhaps be so. But there is no reason why it should not be taken (as others take it) for what it strictly is, *viz.* Partic. *N*φ. s *f.* "*one forgotten* [Tyre shall be]." Comp. § 140 (γ).

‡ This scarcely needs mention here. It follows from (i) since, as the Student knows already, the IMPERATIVE *Kal* generally has

    the (ֵ)-form in Verbs that are 'Fut (ֵ),' and

    the (ַ)-form in Verbs that are 'Fut (ַ).'

As an exception to the usual (ַ)-form for Verbs whose 3ᵈ Rt-letter is Guttural, we have in Gen. xlii. 16 the (ֵ)-form טְבֵחַ *K.* Imper. 2 s. *m.* fr. טבח in the expression וּטְבֹחַ טֶבַח (lit. *and kill a killing*, for "*prepare some meat*"). It will easily be perceived that the form וּטְבַח before the Noun טֶבַח would have been exceedingly inharmonious.

would be impossible there, because there is no syllable following. But, where possible, a ֲ is sometimes adopted; thus, for instance, instead of the Quiescent Shva under the 3ᵈ Rt-letter ע in

יָדַעְתָּ, and (with Affs.) יְדַעְתּוֹ ,יְדַעְתַּנִי ,יְדַעְתָּם,

יָדַעְתִּי, and (with Affs.) יְדַעְתִּיו ,יְדַעְתִּיהָ ,יְדַעְתִּיךָ, etc.,

we find ֲ in the following forms

יְדַעֲנוּךָ (Hos. viii. 2) and יְדַעֲנוּם (Is. lix. 12)—*i.e.* the 1 pl. Past *K.* יָדַעְנוּ with Affs. ךָ *thee (m.)* and ם *them (m.).*

N.B. This help in the case *ע before נ is found also in the 1 pl. Past of some few other Roots,—and not only in the *Kal,* as שְׁמַעֲנוּהָ (Ps. cxxxii. 6) *i.e.* שָׁמַעְנוּ with Aff. *it (f.),* etc., but also in other Voices as בִּלַּעֲנוּהוּ (Ps. xxxv. 25) *Pi.* Past 1 pl. with Aff. *him* fr. בלע, and וְהוֹקַעֲנוּם (2 S. xxi. 6) *Hφ.* Past 1 pl. w. ו pref. & Aff. *them (m.)* fr. יקע.

(*b*) Rarely ֲ is softened and shortened into ֱ before a Guttural 3ᵈ Rt-letter; thus וּבְצַעֱם (Am. ix. 1) *K.* Imper. 2 s. *m.* fr. בצע w. ו pref. and Aff. *them (m.),* instead of וּבְצָעֵם from בְּצַע the 2 s. *m.* Imper. [For the Aff. ם–ֵ, see Note (F) (ɪɪ)—p. 378.]

(*c*) Rarely the characteristic *Khīrik* of the *Hφ.* is replaced by ֱ before a Guttural 3ᵈ Rt-letter having ֲ; thus

---

* We do not mean to limit the occurrence to this special case. On the contrary, we are inclined to consider it but one of many instances of ʜᴇʟᴘ ᴛᴏ ᴛʜᴇ ᴘʀᴏɴᴜɴᴄɪᴀ-ᴛɪᴏɴ by the removal of a Consonant from the end of one syllable to the beginning of the next, with the use of one of the marks of 'Approximation to Vowel-sound.' As other instances of this it may be sufficient to refer merely to cases of a Guttural Fɪʀsᴛ Rt-letter made to begin the second syllable of a word instead of ending the first syllable, as in § 169 (*a,* ii)

וְיִשְׁעֲכֶם: (Is. xxxv. 4) *H*φ. Fut. 3 s. *m.* fr. יִשַׁע w. וֹ pref. and Aff. *you* (*m.*)—for וְיִשְׁעֲכֶם or וִישִׁיעֲכֶם.

(*d*) וְלָקַחַתְּ, Gen. xxx. 15, is supposed by some to be instead of וְלָקַחְתְּ (for וְלָקַחַתְּ) Past *K.* 2 s. *f.* fr. לָקַח, w. וֹ pref. It may perhaps be so. But strictly the word is the Infin. *K.* (קַחַת) with לֹ and וֹ pref.,—see Note (A) on Tab. XIX.

(*e*) So וְנֹכָחַתְּ:, Gen. xx. 16, is supposed by some to be instead of וְנֹכָחְתְּ: (for וְנֹכָחַתְּ:) Past *N*φ. 2 s. *f.* fr. יכח, in Pause, w. וֹ pref. It may be so. But strictly the word is the Partic. *N*φ. s. *f.* fr. יכח, in Pause, with וֹ prefixed.]

Note (D).

A Remark on §§ 230 & 231.

With regard to the two forms of the *K.* Fut. 3 & 2 pl. *f. viz.* תְּקֻמְנָה (§ 230) and תְּקוּמֶינָה (§ 231), it may be sufficient to remark that the former is the one which most strictly belongs to the Class of Verbs עׂו. The י of the ending ‑ֶינָה does not belong to this Class of Verbs, but rather may be said to be borrowed from Verbs of which the 3^d Rt-letter is *Quiescent*.

Note (E).

Remarks on §§ 236 (γ) & 237.

(*a*) In §§ 236 (γ) & 237 we mentioned some Variations in regard to the position of the Accent in the case of certain forms of Verbs עׂו. The Student should observe

carefully the distinctions there pointed out.* We may
add here a brief remark on the VARIATION in the
position of the Accent—which occasions sometimes the
loss of those distinctions.   At the risk of some repetition
of what we have said already, we may perhaps call
attention here to the following Great RULES :

RULE I. The Accent of most Verb-forms is (where
    nothing interferes† with it) on that syllable in
    which the SECOND Rt-letter is involved—comp.
    § 164 (N.B.) and p. 363.

---

* Thus :—

   קָמָה *K.* Past 3 s. *f.*,

   קָמֶה *K.* Partic (1) s. *f.*,—the ה having the Accent as in § 139 (β) ;

   קוּמָה *K.* Imper. 2 s. *m.* with ה (§ 141, γ),

   קוּמֶה *K.* Partic (2) s *f.* :

   קוּמִי *K.* Imper. 2 s. *f.*,

   קוּמִי *K.* Infin. with Aff *my*.

† There are several cases of interference ·—

We must of course except

(i.) The 2 pl. *m.* & *f.* of all Past Tenses;—the Accent is always on the
   תֶּם & תֶּן (or תֶם & תֶן of Tabs. XXII and XXIII) in all Past Tenses
   of all Voices of all Verbs ;—also

(ii.) All forms in which the syllable involving the 2ᵈ Rt-letter is FURTHER
   FROM THE END THAN THE PENULTIMA, comp Pt. I, § 42; for example,
   in הֲקֵמֹתִי or הֲקֵימֹתִי *Hφ.* Past 1 s. fr. קוּם (Tab. XX) the 2ᵈ Rt-letter
   is involved in the *Long K͞hirik* (Pt. I, § 12) attached to the ק .But
   the syllable formed by the ק and that *K͞hirik* being Antepenultimate
   CANNOT bear a Tone-Accent,—and so in סָבֹותִי *K.* Past 1 s. fr. סבב
   (Tab. XXI) the 2ᵈ Rt-letter, which is implied by the Dag. *F.* after the
   ס, is at the end of the *Antepenultimate* syllable.

(iii.) Forms ending in a closed syllable with a LONG Vowel in it have the
   Accent on that final syllable.   Comp. Pt. I, § 55 (9, a).   Thus in such
   forms as קוּמָם, יְקוּמֵם, etc., in Tab. XX, the Accent is on the last
   syllable.   [*continued*]

In Verb-forms whose 2[d] Rt-letter is Quiescent, this 2[d] Rt-letter is involved or implied in the vowel of the FIRST Rt-letter—comp. Tab. XX.—Hence Rule I. has the following SPECIAL FORM for these special Verbs:

RULE II. The Accent of most Verb-forms whose 2[d] Rt-letter is *Quiescent* is (where nothing interferes with it) on that syllable in which the FIRST Rt-letter is involved or implied.[*]

(β) In accordance with RULE II, the Accent is PROPERLY (it may be said) on the PENULTIMA of the 2 s. *m.* Imper. *K.* with the ה of § 141 (γ), thus קוּמָה.   But, in accordance

---

Moreover,

(iv.) ANALOGY rules the position of the Accent in the derived forms קוֹמְמָה, קוֹמְמוּ, etc., and in the Passive forms קוֹמַם, יְקוֹמַם, etc.

N.B. It might however be said that the forms קוֹמֵם, etc., and קוֹמַם, etc., and הִתְקוֹמֵם, etc., of Tab. XX, are "BORROWED" from a Root פֶּ'עֵע, and therefore correspond with forms of Tab. XXI. But in סֹבְבָ, סֹבְבָה, סֹבַב, etc., the Accent is on the syllable in which the 2[d] Rt-letter is involved; and so in סֹבְבָה, סֹבַב, etc., and הִתְגֹּדֵד, etc.

(v.) Some endings, besides those in (i.), always take the Accent; for instance, the הָ of the Partic. s. *f.*, and the Pron-Aff. ךְ when preceded by ָ, and some others. For Verb-forms with Pron-Affs, however, the Student had better refer to the Tables. Such composite words involve something besides the simple Verb-form, and this in itself often causes 'interference' with the Rule for the simple Verb-form.

(vi.) We must except also some Apocopated forms of the Fut. *K.* and *Hθ.* and the Imper. *Hφ.*; thus, יֵבְךְ for יִבְזֶה fr. בזה, יִרָא for יִרָאֶה fr. ראה, יֶגֶל for יַגְלֶה fr. גלה, הֶרֶף for הַרְפֵּה fr. רפה, etc.; and such forms as וַיָּקֶם from יָקוּם, וַיֵּסַב from יָסֹב, תֵּשֶׁב from תָּשִׁיב, etc.

[*] Many forms also of he Verbs whose 2[d] and 3[d] Rt-letters are the same (Tab. XXI.), have the Accent on the syllable to which the FIRST Rt-letter belongs; thus סַבָּה, סַבּוּ, נָסַבָּה, הֵסַבָּה, etc.,—the 1st Rt-letter being then also in the syllable in which the 2[d] Rt-letter is involved or implied.

with RULE I, the Accent is on the LAST SYLLABLE* of the 2 s. *m.* Imper. *K.* of פְּקֹד with ה (§ 141, γ), thus פָּקְדָה in which the ק having Shva *Moving* belongs to that LAST syllable.

Analogy therefore with the corresponding forms of 'Full' Verbs, and general Analogy (it may be said) with all other Verbs, is in favour of the Accent being on the הָ— when attached to these *Kal* forms. And it is perhaps not surprising that, instead of following the special Rule (II) for the 'Verbs whose 2ᵈ Rt-letter is Quiescent,' some forms follow the general Analogy— especially where Rhythm, or Emphasis, or Euphony, may be aided by the Accentuation of the last syllable.

Similarly in the case of the 2 s. *f.* and 2 pl. *m.* Imper. *K.*, †קוּמִי and קוּמוּ, the Accent may be said to be *properly* Penultimate, in accordance with the special Rule (II) for these Verbs. But sometimes the Accent is on the last syllable, as it is in such forms as פְּקִדִי & פְּקִדוּ [Tab. XIV], in accordance with general Analogy [Rule I].

(γ) So also in the 3 s. *f.* and the 3 pl. Past *Kal*, קָמָה and קָמוּ, the Accent may be said to be *properly* Penultimate, in accordance with the special Rule (II) for these Verbs. But sometimes the Accent is on the last syllable, as

---

* We are dealing here with the ordinary simple forms, not Pause-forms. In Pause-forms, when the 2ᵈ Rt-letter has a Vowel, this letter and vowel form a syllable on which the Accent is given (in accordance with Rule I),—unless something inter-feres, as in § 166 (*e*).

† So גִּילִי (comp. § 225), which occurs several times with the Accent on the Penultima, is once (Zech. ix. 9) noted מִלְרַע i.e. *with the Accent on the* LAST *syllable.*

in such forms as פָּקְדָה & פָּקְדוּ in accordance with general Analogy.

(δ) And so too in Past-Tense forms which have the Accent on the Penult. properly, and in which with the וֹ prefixed as in § 160 the Accent is thrown upon the last syllable,— there is the corresponding Variation: thus, from שָׁבָה K. Past 3 s. *f.* of שׁוּב, וְשָׁבָה Is. xxiii. 17, but וְשָׁבָה Is. vi. 13. So קַמְתִּי, קַמְתִּי fr. קַמְתִּי וְקַמְתִּי fr. קָמֵת & קַמְתְּ וְקַמְתְּ fr. שָׁבְתִּי, etc., and so וּבָאת fr. בָּאת; but also וּבָאת, and so וּבָאתִי fr. בָּאתִי.

[Note. In וָמַתִּי׃ Gen. xix. 19 the Accent remains on the Penult. in accordance with the exception in the case of Pause-Accents in § 160.]

NOTE (F).

ON SOME FORMS OF PRON-AFFS. TO VERBS.

I. It is usual to have

(*a*) With PAST-TENSE forms, the Affixes

נִי me, נוּ us, ם (מוֹ) them (*m.*), ן them (*f.*);

(β) With IMPER. & FUT. forms, the Affixes

נִי me, נוּ us, ם (מוֹ) them (*m.*), ן them (*f.*).

II. But sometimes we find an Affix of the former set, viz. (*a*), after an Imper. or a Future form; thus, the unaccented ם of וּבְצַעַם (Am. ix. 1, from the Imper. 2 s. *m.* בְּצַע) may be supposed to be shortened from the accented ם [instead of the

ם‍ַ in what would be the regular form *viz.* וּבְצָעָם, comp.
Tab. XXVII, Notes (*a*) & (*β*)]. And so we have with a
Future-Tense form sometimes

ם‍ָ instead of ם‍ַ,

ן‍ָ (rarely ן‍ָ) instead of ן‍ַ,

נִי‍ָ (p. נִי‍ָ:) instead of נִי‍ַ,

נוּ‍ָ (rarely) instead of נוּ‍ַ.

Comp. Tab. XXVIII, Note (ε, vi–ix).

Thus יִלְבָּשֵׁם (Ex. xxix. 30) *K.* Fut. 3 s. *m.* fr. לבש w. Aff.
hem (*m.*),—instead of יִלְבָּשֵׁם which would be the regular form
Tab. XXVIII, Notes (*a*) & (*β*)]. So יְאָהָבַנִי (Gen. xxix. 32)
K. Fut. 3 s. *m.* fr. אהב w. Aff. *me,*—instead of יֶאֱהָבַנִי which
would be the regular form; and so תִּרְדְּבָּקַנִי (Gen. xix. 19)
K. Fut. 3 s. *f.* fr. דבק w. Aff. *me.* So also יְכִּירָנוּ (Is. lxiii. 16)
Hφ. Fut. 3 s. *m.* fr. נכר w. Aff. *us,* וַיּוֹשִׁעֶן (Ex. ii. 17) *Hφ.*
Fut. 3 s. *m.* w. Aff. *them* (*f.*). יְחִיתָן (Hab. ii. 17) *Hφ.* Fut. 3 s *m.*
fr. חתת [for יַחְתָּן,—or "*borrowed*" in form from an unused
root חות], is a rare form; for which, so far as the ‍ַ is concerned, it might be sufficient to refer merely to § 165 (I, δ).

So fr. ראה, יִרְאָנִי (Ex. xxxiii. 20) *K.* Fut. 3 s. *m.* w. Aff.
me, but also וַיִּרְאָנִי (2 S. i. 7); and וַתִּרְאָנִי (Nu. xxii. 33) *K.*
Fut. 3 s. *f.* w. ו Convers. & Aff. *me,* but also תִּרְאָנִי: (Job x. 18),
and תִּרְאָנִי (Jer. xii. 3) 2 s. *m.*

III. So the PAST has the Aff. נִי‍ַ of the set (*β*) in וַיִּסְּרֵנִי
(Is. viii. 11), but the נִי‍ַ of (*a*) in יִסְּרַנִי (Ps. cxviii. 18); etc.

NOTE (G).

OBJECTIVE PRON-AFFS. USED '*RELATIVELY.*'

(*a*) A Pronoun represented by an Affix attached to a Verb
may stand, in connection with אֲשֶׁר before the Verb-
form, for a Relative Pronoun in English,—as in "A field
אֲשֶׁר בֵּרֲכוֹ* יי *which* The-LORD *hath-blessed,*" lit. *which
it* (*m.*), Gen. xxvii. 27, etc.—Comp. § 27.

(*β*) The Pron-Affix by itself may also be rendered sometimes
by a Relative Pronoun in English,—the אֲשֶׁר being
omitted as in § 31;—thus, "There be three things . . . ,
yea four (לֹא יְדַעְתִּים) *which I-know not*" Prov. xxx. 18,
lit. *I know not them* (*m.*).   So עֲשִׂיתִם (Is. xlii. 16) may
be rendered "*which I-have-done,*"—and Is. xliii. 7 may
stand thus, "Every-one who is called by My Name and
(בְּרָאתִיו) *whom-I-have-created* for My glory; (יְצַרְתִּיו)
whom-I-have-formed, yea (עֲשִׂיתִיו) *whom-I-have-made.*"

NOTE (H).

As was said on page 237 the literal rendering of the words
בָּרָא לַעֲשׂוֹת [Gen. ii. 3],—*viz.* "HE *created to make*" or *for the
purpose of making,*—seems to bear a sufficiently clear and simple
sense.   There is no established phrase-use of the two words
which at all interferes with our rendering the two words
literally.†   All that may fairly be said is that another form

---

* For the ־ see Pt I, § 72.

† The literal rendering must surely be adopted in the somewhat similar expressions
צִוִּיתִי לַעֲשׂוֹת, צָנָה לַעֲשׂוֹת, חָשַׁבְתִּי לַעֲשׂוֹת, זָמַם לַעֲשׂוֹת, etc.

of rendering is POSSIBLE, as we may try to show in this concluding 'NOTE.'

(a) There are some Hebrew expressions consisting of a TENSE-FORM AND AN INFINITIVE (with or without the prefix לְ) which may be rendered by an *English Adverb* AND *Tense-form*,—the English Adverb corresponding with the Hebrew Tense-form, and the English Tense-form with the Hebrew Infinitive;—thus וַיֹּסְפוּ לְדַבֵּר [Deut. xx. 8] *and they shall speak again* (lit. *and they shall add to speak*); לֹא אֹסִף לְקַלֵּל עוֹד [Gen. viii. 21] *I will not again curse any-more* (lit. *I will not add to curse any-more*), and וְלֹא אֹסִף עוֹד לְהַכּוֹת *and I will not again any-more smite* (lit. *and I will not add any-more to smite*); לֹא תָשׁוּב עֵינִי לִרְאוֹת טוֹב [Job vii. 7] *my eye shall no more see good* (lit. *it shall not return to see*); לֹא אָשׁוּב לְשַׁחֵת [Hos. xi. 9] *I will not any-more destroy* (lit. *I will not return to destroy*); לָמָּה נַחְבֵּאתָ לִבְרֹחַ [Gen. xxxi. 27] *why didst thou flee secretly?* (lit. *why wert thou concealed with-regard-to fleeing?*); יַרְבֶּה לִסְלוֹחַ [Is. lv. 7] *He will abundantly pardon* (lit. *He will multiply to pardon*); הֲרֵעֹתֶם לַעֲשׂוֹת [Jer. xvi. 12] *ye have acted evilly* (lit. *ye have caused-evil as-regards acting*); וַתָּרַע לַעֲשׂוֹת [1 K. xiv. 9] *and thou hast acted evilly*, or *dealt ill*; etc.

And so, without the prefix לְ before the Infin., אַל תֹּסֶף רְאוֹת [Ex. x. 28] *see not again* (or *see no more*, lit. *add not to see*); הִסְכַּלְתָּ עֲשׂוֹ [Gen. xxxi. 28] *thou hast acted foolishly* (lit. *thou hast-been-foolish as-regards acting*); etc.

(β) Similarly also in the case of a Participle and Imperative with an Infinitive; thus וּמַפְלִא לַעֲשׂוֹת [Ju. xiii. 19] *and* [*he was*] *acting wondrously*; מֵיטִיב לְנַגֵּן [1 S. xvi. 17] *playing well*; הַמַּעֲמִיקִים לַסְתִּר [Is. xxix. 15] *who are hiding deeply*; and so הַרְבּוּ לִפְשֹׁעַ [Am. iv. 4] *transgress ye abundantly* (lit. *multiply ye to transgress*); etc.*

(γ) So בָּרָא לַעֲשׂוֹת in the expression אֲשֶׁר בָּרָא אֱלֹהִים לַעֲשׂוֹת Gen. ii. 3 MAY PERHAPS be taken to be an instance similar to those in (*a*). As a rendering of the whole expression we might then have "*which* GOD CREATIVELY MADE." But we cannot quite agree with the "*produxit faciendo*" adopted by Gesenius [Thesau. p. 236 (*a*)], nor with the "*He created producing*" given by Dr. Kalisch in his Note on Gen. ii. 3 [*Comment. on Genesis*, p. 83].

We prefer the LITERAL RENDERING given on p. 237.

---

* Sometimes after an IMPERATIVE another Imperative is used, as in שׁוּב שְׁכָב *lie-down again* (lit. *return lie-down*) 1 S. iii. 5 & 6; etc.

N.B. (i.) This may be said to be but an instance of the not uncommon occurrence of TWO SIMILAR VERB-FORMS in Hebrew where a VERB WITH AN ADVERB may seem more natural in English; thus אָשׁוּבָה אֶרְעֶה צֹאנְךָ *I will again feed thy flock* (lit. *I will return I will feed*) Gen. xxx. 31, אוֹסִיף אֲבַקְשֶׁנּוּ עוֹד *I will seek it yet again* (lit. *I will add I will yet seek it*) Prov. xxiii. 35, אַל תַּרְבּוּ תְדַבְּרוּ‥‥ *speak not so-much* (lit. *multiply ye not that ye speak*) 1 S. ii. 3. And so with וConvers. וַיָּשָׁב וַיִּשְׁלַח *and again he sent* (lit. *and he returned and he sent*) 2 K. i. 11, אָשׁוּב וְרִחַמְתִּים *I will again compassionate them* (lit. *I will return and will compassionate them*) Jer. xii. 15.

(ii.) The two Verb-forms, in some few instances, are of different Persons; thus, we have the 2 s. *f.* and the 3 pl. *m.* Future forms in the address to the daughter of Babylon לֹא תוֹסִיפִי יִקְרְאוּ לָךְ‥‥ *they shall no-more call thee f.* (lit. *thou shalt not add that they shall call thee*) Is. xlvii. 1, etc.

VOCABULARY.

[*⁎* This Vocabulary contains merely a few words, some of which are not always given in the Notes to the Exercises. The little that is said about these words here will be sufficient, it is hoped, to enable the Student to work through the Exercises.—Other words, which are sufficiently given in the Notes to the Exercises, need not be repeated here.]

אָב (*m.*) *a father*, Tab. XIII.1.

אַבְרָם *Abram.*

אַבְרָהָם *Abraham.*

אָדָם (*m.*) *Adam, man.*

אֱדֹם (*m.*) *Edom.*

אֲדֹנָי *Lord, The Lord.*

אֲהָהּ *Oh! Alas!* אוֹיֵב seep 92(52).

אוֹר (*m.*) *light.*

אָז (אֲזַי) *then*

אֹזֶן (*f.*) *an ear*, Tab. XI; Dual אָזְנַיִם, Tab. VII.

אָח (*m.*) *a brother*, Tab.XIII.2

אָחוֹת (*f.*) *a sister*, Tab. XIII. Note (†, *a*).

אַחֵר (*m.*) *another.*

אַיִן (p. אֵין) *nothing*, אֵין *there is not*,—Tab. XIII, Note (‡, δ).

אִישׁ (*m.*) *a man, each one, any one.*

אַךְ *but, only.*

אַל *not*, Obs. I & IV, p. 93.

אֶל *to*, Tab. IV.

אֵל (*m.*) *God*, with Aff. אֵלִי *my God.*

אֵלֶּה *these* (*m & f.*), p. 28.

אֱלֹהִים (*m.*) *God*, a plur. Noun, (also *gods*), w. Affs. אֱלֹהָיו *his*, etc.

אֶלֶף (*m.*) *a thousand*, Tab. X. 1, Dual אֲלְפַּיִם.   (אם *f.*)

אֵם (*f.*) *a mother*, w. Affs. אִמּוֹ, etc.—Plu. אָמוֹת.

אָמַר *to say.*

אָנוּ *Kthiv*, Tab. I. Note 6.

אֲנַחְנוּ *we*, p. אֲנַחְנוּ, Tab. I.

אֲנִי *I*, p. אָנִי, Tab. I.

אָנֹכִי *I.*

אַף *also, moreover.*

אַף (*m.*) *anger*, i.c. the same, w. Affs. אַפּוֹ, etc.⁕

אֵפוֹא *now.*

אֶרֶז (*m.*) *a cedar.*

אֹרֶךְ *length.*

⁕ Also *a nose, nostril*, Dual אַפַּיִם *nostrils.*

אֶרֶץ (f.) *earth, land,* (p. אֶרֶץ, and הָאָרֶץ w. ה 'def.'), see Tab. X. 1 for the Sing., and Tab. XII. 1 for the Plu.

אִשָּׁה *a woman, a wife,* pl. נָשִׁים.

אֲשֶׁר *who, which, that.*

אַתְּ *thou* (*f.*), p. אַתְּ, Tab. I.

אַתְּ (& את *Kthiv*) for אַתָּה, Tab. I. Note 2.

אֵת (אֶת־) Tab. III. 1.

אֵת (אֶת־) Tab. III. 2.

אֶת־מִי *whom?* (Objective).

אַתָּה *thou* (*m.*), p. אַתָּה, Tab. I.

אתי *Kthiv* for אַתְּ, Tab. I. Note 3.

אַתֶּם *ye* (*m.*) Tab. I.

אַתֵּן once *ye* (*f.*) Tab. I. Note 5.

אַתֵּנָה *ye* (*f.*) Tab. I.

בְּאֵר *a well,* i.c. the same.

באר שֶׁבַע *Beersheba* (p. שֶׁ).

בָּבֶל (*f.*) *Babylon.*

בֶּגֶד (*m.*) *a garment,* pl. בְּגָדִים.

בְּגוִֹי (p. 91) see גוֹי.

בּוֹר (*m.*) *a pit,* 'i.c.' the same.

בַּיִת (*m.*) *a house,* Tab. X. 3.

בְּמַיִם (p. 92) see מַיִם.

בֵּן (*m.*) *a son,* Tab. XIII. 4.

ברך *Pi. to bless, Pu. to be blessed.*
N.B. The only part of the *Kal* that is used in this

sense is the Partic (2), *viz.*

בָּרוּךְ *blessed* s. *m.* (i.c. בָּרוּךְ),

בְּרוּכָה s. *f.*,

בְּרוּכִים & בְּרֻכִים pl. *m.* (i.c. בְּרוּכֵי).

* Also the Infin. Absol בָּרוֹךְ (*to bless*) occurs once (Josh. xxiv. 10).

בְּשֵׁם (p. 92) see שֵׁם.

בָּשָׁן *Bashan.*

בֹּשֶׁת (*f.*) *shame.*

בַּת (*f.*) *a daughter,* pl. בָּנוֹת i.c. בְּנוֹת, Tab. XIII. 5.

גַּאֲוָה (*f.*) *pride.*

גִּבּוֹר (*m.*) *mighty, a mighty one.*

גְּבוּרָה (*f.*) *might.*

גְּבִיר (*m.*) *a lord.*

גֹּדֶל (*m.*) *greatness,* Tab. XI.

גָּדוֹל (*m.*) *great,* etc.,—§ 76, ii.

גּוֹי (*m.*) *a nation,* pl. גּוֹיִם *nations, Gentiles, heathen.*

גַּיְא *a valley,* i.c. the same.

גַּם *also, even.*

גַּם כִּי *although.*

גַּן (*m.*) *a garden* (p. גָּן), i.c. גַּן, w. Aff. גַּנּוֹ, etc.

דבר *Pi. to speak.*

דָּבָר (*m.*) *a word, a thing,* Tab. IX.

דֶּרֶךְ (*m. & f.*) *a way,* Tab. X. 1.

דֶּשֶׁא *grass.*

---

* This is perhaps best taken to be a *Kal* form, like פָּקוֹד. Some, however, think it to be a *Pi-él* Infin. like פַּקֵּד, but with ◌ to compensate for the Dagesh which the ר cannot receive—וּלְבָרְכוֹ is Infin. PI-ÉL (with ל pref. & Aff. *him*) in 2 S viii. 10 & 1 Chr xviii. 10, and so it is best to take it in 1 S. xiii. 10, but the omission of *Metheg* there (in some Bibles) might be claimed by some as supporting their opinion that the word is Infin. KAL.

דֶשֶׁן (m.) *fat, rich food,* Tab. X. 2.

הֶבֶל (m.) *Abel, a breath.*

הַבָּשָׁן *the [country] Bashan.*

הָגָר (f.) *Hagar.*

הֲדֹם *a footstool,* 'i.c.' the same.

הוּא *he,* Tab. I.

הִוא *she,* Tab. I, Note (1).

הוֹי *Ho !*

הִיא *she,* Tab. I; § 32 (II), § 94.

היה *to be,* etc., pp. 276–278.

הֵם, הֵמָּה *they* (m.), Tab. I.

הָמוֹן (m.) *a multitude,* i.c. הֲמוֹן.

הן הנה *behold !, lo !.*

הֵנָּה *they* (f.), Tab. I.

הֵנָּה *hither.*

הַר (הָר) (m.) *a mountain,* i.c. הַר, pl. הָרִים, i.c. הָרֵי.

וַיְּבֶךְ
וַיְּמַךְ
וַיִּתַר
וַיַּתַר
וַתֵּבַךְ
נִתְּכָה
וַתְכַּס
וַתֵּתַע
etc.
} See 'Analytical Index,' for references.

זֹאת *this* (f.), p. 28.

זֶה *this* (m.), p. 28.

זָהָב (m.) *gold,* i.c. זְהַב.

זָקֵן (m.) *old, an old man, an elder,* i.c. זְקַן, pl. זְקֵנִים, i.c. זִקְנֵי.

זֶרַע (m.) *seed,* w. Affs. זַרְעוֹ, etc., as in Tab X. 1.

חַיִּים (m.) *life,* a Noun of plural form.

חֶסֶד (m.) *kindness, mercy, goodness,* Tab. X. 1.

חֶרֶב (f.) *a sword,* see Tab. X. 1 for Sing.; pl. חֲרָבוֹת, see Tab. XII. 1.

חֹשֶׁךְ (m.) *darkness,* Tab. XI. 1.

טוֹב (m.) *good,* § 76 (i). Also used as a Noun '*good.*'

טוּב (m.) *goodness, goods.*

טֶרֶף *prey.*

יְבוּל (m.) *produce, increase.*

יָד (f., also m.) *a hand,* i.c. יַד, w. Affs. יָדוֹ, etc., Dual יָדַיִם *hands,* i.c. יְדֵי, w. Affs. יָדָיו, etc.

ידע *to know,* Tab. XVIII.

יְהוּדָה *Juda.*

יוֹם (m.) *a day,* pl. יָמִים, i.c. יְמֵי.

יוֹסֵף (or יֹסֵף) *Joseph.*

יַחְדָּו *together.*

יְיָ stands for The NAME, pronounced אֲדֹנָי. Comp. Pt. I, § 79 (2).

יְיָ stands for The NAME when pronounced אֱלֹהִים. Comp. Pt. I, § 79 (2).

יַיִן (p. יֵיןְ) (m.) *wine,* i.c. יֵין.

יָם (m.) *a sea* (יַם when unaccented), pl. יַמִּים.

יְמֵי see יוֹם.

יָמִין (f.) *a right hand.*

יַעֲקֹב *Jacob.*

יִצְחָק *Isaac.*

יְרוּשָׁלַם (p. ַםִ) *Jerusalem.*

יָרֵחַ (m.) *moon.*

יִשְׂרָאֵל *Israel.*

יִתְרוֹ *Jethro.*

כַּאֲשֶׁר *as,* also *when.*

כָּבוֹד (m.) *honour, glory,* i.c. כְּבוֹד.

כַּד (m.) *a pitcher,* w. Affs. כַּדּוֹ, etc.

כֹּה *thus.*

כֹּהֵן (*m.*) *a priest.*

כּוֹס *a cup.*

כּוּר עֳנִי *the furnace of affliction.*

כֹּחַ (*m.*) *strength* (§ 74, *a*).

כִּי *for, because, that.*

כֹּל *all* (כָּל *when unaccented*), w. Affs. כֻּלּוֹ, etc.

כֵּן *so.*

כְּנַעַן *Canaan* (p. כְּנַעַן).

כָּנָף (*f.*) *a wing,* Dual כְּנָפַיִם.

כִּנּוֹר (*m.*) *a harp.*

כֶּסֶף (*m.*) *silver* (p. כְּסַף) Tab. X. Note (*).

כַּף *a hand,* w. Affs. כַּפּוֹ, etc., Dual כַּפַּיִם.

כֶּרֶם *a vineyard,* Tab. X. 1.

לֹא *not,* Obs. II & III, p. 93.

לְאֹם (*m.*) *a people, nation,* pl. לְאֻמִּים.

לֵב (*m.*) *a heart,* w. Affs. לִבּוֹ, etc., pl. לִבּוֹת.

לֵבָב (*m.*) *a heart,* w. Affs. לְבָבוֹ, etc., pl. לְבָבוֹת.

לַהַב (*m.*) *a flame,* pl. לְהָבִים i.c. לַהֲבֵי.

לֶהָבָה (*f.*) *a flame,* i.c. לַהֶבֶת, pl. לְהָבוֹת i.c. לַהֲבוֹת.

לֶחֶם (*m.*) *bread,* Tab. X. 1 (Sing.).

לַיְלָה (*m.*) *night* (p. לָיְלָה).

לָכֵן *therefore.*

לָמָה *why? wherefore?*

לָמוֹ *to them* (*m.*), Tab. II. 2.

לְעוֹלָם *for ever.*

לְפָנִים *before* (i.e. פָּנִים *face,* with pref. ל), i.c. לִפְנֵי *before,* w. Affs. לְפָנָיו *before him,* etc.

מְאֹד *exceedingly.*

מַאֲכָל (*m.*) *food.*

מִדְבָּר *wilderness,* i.c. מִדְבַּר.

מַה (מָה, מֶה) *what?*, p. 29.

מוּדַעַת (p. 141) *Hoph.* Partic. s. *f.*, fr. ידע, [*a thing*] *made known.* (§ 92, γ).

מוּת *K. to die, Pi. to kill, Hφ. to cause to die, or put to death.*

מַחֲנֶה (*m.*) *a host,* i.c. ה‑.

מִי *who?*, p. 29.

מַיִם (p. מֵימַי) *water, waters,* i.c. מֵי.

מְלָאכָה (*f.*) *work,* w. Affs. מְלַאכְתּוֹ, etc.; מְלֶאכֶת —comp. § 74 (*f.*).

מֶלֶךְ *a king,* Tab. X. 1.

מִנְחָה (*f.*) *an offering.*

מִצְרַיִם *Egypt.*

מַר *bitterness, bitterly.*

מֹשֶׁה *Moses.*

מִשְׁעֶנֶת *a staff;* w. Affs. מִשְׁעַנְתּוֹ, etc.

נָא *now, I pray, we pray.*

נְאֻם *"saith"* (E.V.), lit. [*is*] *said-of* (or *by*).

נֶגֶד *before.*

נְהִי *lamentation.*

נֹחַ *Noah.*

נַחַל (*m.*) *a brook, a valley.*

נָטִיף *comp.* p. 172 (θ).

נַעַר *a boy* (p. נַעֲרִי).

נֶפֶשׁ (*f.*) *a soul,* Tab. X. 1 (for the Sing.); Plu. נְפָשׁוֹת, Tab. XII. 2.

נָקָם *vengeance.*

סֵתֶר *a hiding-place, secret-place.*

עֶבֶד (*m.*) *a servant,* Tab. X. 5.

עבר *to pass, pass over, go beyond, transgress.*

עֻגָב *an organ.*

עַד *unto, until.*

עֵדֶר *(m.) a flock, herd, w. Affs.* עֶדְרוֹ, *etc.*

עוֹד *yet, still, a long while.*

עוֹלָם *eternity, ever.*

עָוֹן *(m.) iniquity, pl.* עֲוֹנוֹת.

עַיִן *(f., rarely m.) an eye* (p. עֵינוֹ),—Tab. XIII. Note (‡, *a* & *β*).

עִיר *(f.) a city, pl.* עָרִים.

עַל *on, upon, over, etc.,* Tab. IV. 2.

עֶלְיוֹן *(m.) most high.*

עִם *with,* Tab. III.

עַם (עָם) *a people, w. Affs.* עַמּוֹ, *etc.,* pl. עַמִּים.

עָמָל *(m.) trouble.*

עֳנִי *(m.) misery* (p. עָנְיִ), *with Affs.* עָנְיִי, *etc.*

עֲנַקְתֵּמוֹ *from* עֲנָקָה *3 s. f. Past K., see* Note (*γ*, iv) *on* Tab. XXV.

עֵץ *(m.) a tree, pl.* עֵצִים, *i.c.* עֲצֵי.

עֵשָׂו *Esau.*

עַתָּה *now* (p. עֵתָה).

פֹּה *here.*

פֶּן *lest.*

פָּנִים *a face (a plural Noun), i.c.* פְּנֵי, *w. Affs.* פָּנָיו, *etc.*

פקד *to visit, etc.*

פַּרְעֹה *Pharaoh* [better, *Pharao*].

פֶּשַׁע *trespass,* Tab. X. 2.

צֹאן *sheep, a flock of sheep.*

צֶדֶק *righteousness,* Tab. X. 2.

צוּר *a rock.*

צִיּוֹן *(f.) Zion.*

צֵל *a shadow.*

צַלְמָוֶת *shadow of death.*

צַר *(m.)* } *a foe,* also *distress.*
צָרָה *(f.)* }

קֹדֶשׁ *(m.) holiness, with Affs.* קָדְשׁוֹ, *etc.* Tab. XI.

קָטֹן *(m.) little.*

קָטָן *(m.) little, etc.,* § 76 (iii).

ראה *to see, look;* ראה ב׳ *to look at* (p. 204).

ראֹשׁ *(m.) a head, plu.* רָאשִׁים.

רְבָבָה *(f.) ten thousand, a myriad,* pl. רְבָבוֹת, *i.c.* רִבְבוֹת.

רַבִּים *(m.) many (plu. of* רַב).

רִבְקָה *Rebekah.*

רֶגֶל *(f.) a foot, Dual* רַגְלַיִם.

רוּחַ *(m. & f.) Spirit,* also *spirit, wind.*

רַע & רָע *m.* / רָעָה *f.* { *bad, evil,*—sometimes used Substantively, " *evil.*"

רַעַם *thunder* (p. רָעַם).

רֶשַׁע *wickedness,* Tab. X. 4 (p. רֶשַׁע).

רָשָׁע *a wicked man, pl.* רְשָׁעִים

שְׁאוֹל *(m. & f.) Sh'ol, the pit, grave, Hades.*

שאר *Nφ. to be left, Hφ. to cause to remain.*

שְׁאֵרִית *(f.) a remnant, i.c. the same.*

שֵׁבֶט *(m.) a sceptre, a rod,* also *a tribe.* Tab. X. 2.

שְׁבִי " *a captivity*" for *a body of captives, i.c. the same* (p. שְׁבִי).

שבע *Nφ. to swear, Hφ. to adjure.*

שֶׁבַע, *see* בְּאֵר שֶׁבַע *Beersheba.*
שָׂדֶה *a field.*

שִׁיר (m.) *a song.*

שֻׁלְחָן (m.) *a table*

שְׁלֹמֹה *Solomon.*

שְׁלָמָה *for why?* [p. 24, Notes (a) & (d)].

שֵׁם (m.) *a name* [Tab. XIII. Note § (a)].

שָׁם *there.*

שָׁמָּה *thither* (sometimes also rendered *there*).

שְׁמוֹ, שְׁמִי,—see שֵׁם.

שָׁמַיִם (m.) *heavens, heaven,* (p. ־ֵים), i.c. שְׁמֵי.

שְׁמוֹ & שִׁמְךָ, שִׂמְכֶם, שָׁמָם,—see שֵׁם.

שֶׁמֶן *oil.*

שֶׁמֶשׁ (m. & f.) *Sun* (p. שְׁמְשֹׁ).

שְׁנַיִם (i.c. שְׁנֵי) *two,* p. ־ֵים.

שָׂפָה *a lip,* i.c. שְׂפַת, Dual שְׂפָתַיִם (p. ־ֵים) i.c. שִׂפְתֵי.

שַׂק (שְׂקִי) (p. שַׂקִּים) } *sackcloth.*

שַׂר *a prince,* pl. שָׂרִים, i.c. שָׂרֵי.

שָׂרָה *Sara.*

תְּהוֹם (m. & f.) *a deep, an abyss,* pl. תְּהֹמֹת.

תָּוֶךְ *midst,* i.c. תּוֹךְ, w. Affs. תּוֹכוֹ, etc.

תּוֹר *a row, series,* and so *a band of things,* as *a string of beads* and such like. Also,

תּוֹר *a turtle-dove.*

תְּפִלָּה (f.) *prayer.*

A BRIEF

ENGLISH-HEBREW VOCABULARY.

[NOTE.—This Vocabulary contains only a few words which are omitted sometimes in the Notes to the English-Hebrew Exercises.]

Abram אַבְרָם.
Abraham אַבְרָהָם.
All כֹּל, see Vocab. p. 386.
And,* וְ prefix (§ 3, pp. 1 & 2).
As, כְּ prefix (§ 4).
  As he (*or* I, thou, etc.)—see Tab. II (3).

Brethren, }
Brother, } see Tab. XIII (2).
By, בְּ prefix (§ 4).

Cast, To, שלך *Hiph.*
Command, A, מִצְוָה.
Command, To, צוה *Pi.* (the וֹ being Consonantal).

Edom אֱדוֹם (*m.*).
Esau עֵשָׂו.

For (Conjunction), כִּי.
For (Preposition), לְ prefix (§ 4).
From, מִ prefix (§ 5), also מִן.
  From him (*or* me, thee, etc.)— see Tab. II (4).

GOD, אֱלֹהִים declined like the Plural שִׁירִים in Tab. V. For the forms with prefixes see pp. 2 (Note ‡, ii) & 3 (Note †, ii).

Hand יָד Vocab. p. 385,—also p. 46 (*t*).
He הוּא Tab. I.
House בַּיִת Tab. XIII (3).

If אִם.
Impress, To, שׁנן *Pi.* as in Tab. XIV
In (Prepos.), בְּ prefix (§ 4).
  In him (*or* me, thee, etc.) Tab. II (1).
Israel יִשְׂרָאֵל.
It (*f.*) הִיא.
It (*m.*) הוּא.

Jacob יַעֲקֹב.
Joseph יוֹסֵף.

Like, כְּ prefix (§ 4).
  Like him (*or* me, thee, etc.), Tab. II (3).

Many, Much, רַב (Sing.), רַבִּים (Plu.).
Mischief רָעָה (*f.*), [for p. 220, line 4].
More-than, מִ pref. (§ 5),—also מוֹ.
  More-than he (*or* I, thou, etc.) מִ Tab. II (4).
Moses מֹשֶׁה.

---

* N.B.—The only means of rendering into Hebrew an ENGLISH PAST-TENSE preceded by "AND" (as in "*And he visited*") is by means of a HEBREW FUTURE with וֹ Conversive (thus וַיִּפְקֹד)—§§ 154 Rule III (p 101) & 161 (2) (p 104).

No לֹא.
Not לֹא.
Not (Deprecative) אַל, Obs. IV
p. 93.

On עַל.—With Pron.-Affs. see
Tab. IV (2).

Pass, Pass-over, To, עבר (Fut. -‑-).
People, A, עַם Vocab. p. 387.
Pharaoh פַּרְעֹה.

Say, To, אמר p. 128, etc. Comp.
Tab. XVII.
Saying (לֵאמֹר see Tab. XVII,
Note †, ii).
Sell, To, מכר (Fut. -‑).
Send, To, שׁלח Kal (Fut. —).
Send-away, To, שׁלח Pi.
She הִיא Tab. I.
Soul נֶפֶשׁ Vocab. p. 386.

Take, To, לקח Tab. XIX. Note (A).
Than he (or I, thou, etc.) מ (Tab.
II, 4).
That (Conjunction) כִּי.
That } (Demonstrative). See § 32,
    & } p. 28 ; and (Adjectivally-
This } Demonstrative) § 94, p. 58.

They הֵם (m.) & הֵן (f.), Tab. I.
Thou אַתָּה (m.) & אַתְּ (f.), Tab. I.
Thus כֹּה.
To, לְ prefix (§ 4).
    To him (or me, thee, etc.) Tab.
    II (2).
To-day, (Hebrew the day) הַיּוֹם.
Two, see p. 62.

Upon, עַל,—with Pron.-Affs. Tab.
IV (2).

Voice קוֹל.

Water מַיִם, Vocab. p. 386.
What? מַה p. 29.
Where? אַיֵּה.
Where (§ 30), p. 23.
Whether? הֲ prefix (§ 7).
Who? מִי, p. 29.
Who, whom (Relative) אֲשֶׁר, pp.
21–23.
Whose? See p. 29.
Whose (Relatively). See pp. 22,
etc.
Word דָּבָר Tab. IX.

INDEX

OF PASSAGES OF THE HEBREW BIBLE WHICH ARE CITED IN THE PRECEDING PAGES.

NOTE.

In this 'Index' the Chapters and Verses are those of the 'Hebrew' Bible.—Also

The order in which the Books are arranged here is the order in which they stand in the 'Hebrew' Bible. It may be well for the Student to be familiarized with this order. A Table of the 'Order of the Books' is given on the following page.

392

TABLE

OF THE

ORDER OF THE BOOKS

IN THE 'HEBREW' BIBLE.

(I) Pᴇɴᴛᴀᴛᴇᴜᴄʜ.

1 Genesis
2. Exodus.
3. Leviticus.
4. Numbers.
5. Deuteronomy.

(II.) Pʀᴏᴘʜᴇᴛs (earlier and later).

6. Joshua.
7. Judges.
8 and 9.   Samuel (1 and 2).
10 and 11.   Kings (1 and 2).
12. Isaiah.
13. Jeremiah.
14. Ezekiel

[*Minor Prophets* (xii)].

-15. Hosea.
16. Joel.
17. Amos.
18. Obadiah.
19. Jonah.
20. Micah.

21. Nahum.
22. Habakkuk.
23. Zephaniah.
24. Haggai.
25. Zechariah.
26. Malachi.

(III.) Hᴀɢɪᴏɢʀᴀᴘʜᴀ.

27 Psalms.
28. Proverbs.
29. Job

30. Song of Songs. ⎫
31. Ruth.   ⎬ *The*
32. Lamentations.   ⎪ *five*
33. Ecclesiastes.   ⎬ *Rolls.*
34. Esther.   ⎭

35. Daniel.
36. Ezra.
37. Nehemiah.
38 and 39.   Chronicles (1 and 2).

INDEX.

Genesis	PAGE		Genesis	PAGE
i. 1	43, 226, 230		ii. 15	241, 242
2	226, 230		16	242
3	226		17	242, 243, xviii. (of Tables)
4	221, 226		18	243
5	227, 234, 235 (twice)		19	136, 243
6	225, 227		20	243
7	227, 228		21	243, 244
8	228, 234		22	244
9	65, 228, 312		23	244
10	228		24	244
11	221, 228		25	245
12	229		iii. 1	237, 245, 253
13	229, 234		2	245
14	229		3	245
15	229		4	245
16	230		5	245, 246, 256, xviii. (of Tables)
17	230		6	128, 246, 247
18	230		7	248
19	230, 234		8	237, 248
20	230 (twice)		9	248
21	230 (twice), 231		10	248
22	231		11	249
23	231, 234		12	249
24	231, 232		13	249, 305
25	232		14	249, 250
26	232, 255		15	250
27	230, 232, 255		16	250, 324
28	233		17	250, 251
29	233		18	251, 252
30	233		19	252
31	227, 234		20	252
ii. 1	236		21	252
2	236		22	224, 253, 257, 258, 259
3	236, 380		23	259
4	237, 238		24	237, 259, 260
5	238, 239 (twice)		iv. 23	86, 122, 372
6	238, 239, 240		v. 1	79
7	135, 240		5	65
8	240		29	271
9	240		vi. 3	155
10	241		19	5
11	23, 84, 241		viii. 3	78
12	2 [Note (i, iv)]		5	78, 234 (twice)
13	241			
14	241			

394

Genesis		PAGE
viii.	7	... 322
	12	139
	13	. 234 (twice)
	17	... 139, 286
	21	. 381
	22	. 224
ix.	24	... 135
x.	25	. 229
xi.	1, 6	. . 65
	3	... 88
	7	. 24, xxx (of Tables)
xii.	1	. . 260
	2	..., 261
	3	... 261, 262
	4	262
	5	.. 262, 263
	6	.. 263
	7	.. 263, 264
	8	.. 264
	9	.. 78, 264
	10	... 264
	11	.. 264, 265
	12	. 265
	13	... 265
	14	... 265
	15	... 265, 266
	16	.. 266
	17	. 266
	18	266
	19	. 266
	20	... 266
xiii.	3	. 253
	15	.. 23
xiv.	18	... 139, 232
xvi.	10	... 324
	11	.. 178
	12	... 54
xvii.	4, 5	. xii. (of Tables)
	16	.. 255
xix.	4	.. 113, 238
	8	... 58
	9	. . 78
	15	. 59
	19	... 378, 379
xx.	7	. 279
	13	... 129
	16	. 374
xxi.	23	.. 23
xxii.	2	. 23, 67
	12	... 103
	17	324
xxiii.	6	. . xxxii (of Tables)
xxiv.	5	... 6, 23
	15	.. 239
	16	. 50
	30	105
	43	... 59
	45	... 239 (twice)
	59	. 135

Genesis		PAGE
xxiv.	61	... 137
xxv.	8	... 129
	16	. 59
	23	... 3
	26	... 35
xxvi.	3	... 260
	13	. 78, 81, 319
xxvii.	19	... xxiii (of Tables)
	27	... 22, 380
	29	... 191
	37	.. iii. (of Tables)
	41	... 117
xxviii.	13	... 23
xxix.	20	.. 65
	32	... 379
xxx.	15	.. 374
	30	... 255
	31	... 382
xxxi.	5	... 253
	7	. 346, 354
	27	... 381
	28	. 381
	30	. 82, 338
	39	.. 84, 346, xvii. (of Tables)
	40	... 292
	42	... 253, 255
xxxii.	1	iv. (of Tables)
	5	.. 128
	11	255
	18	... 29
	20	... xviii. (of Tables)
xxxiii.	11	. 169, 275
	13	... 179
xxxiv.	27	.. 43
	28	... 43
xxxv.	15	... 105
xxxvii.	33	.. xxxvi. (of Tables)
xl.	20	. 323
xli.	23	... 51
	34	... 105
	43	... 78, 350
	50	. 229
	51	.. 306
	56	... 229
xlii.	28	. 23
xliii.	16	... 24, 372
	18	.. 365
xliv.	16	... 315
	33	... 137
	61	... 137
xlvi.	3	... 323
xlvii.	11	... 137, xxiv. (of Tables)
	21	... 350
xlviii.	9	... xxxviii. (of Tables)
	22	.. 67
xlix.	10	... 342
	11	... 84, 232, xii. and xvii. (of Tables)
	12	... 54

Genesis   PAGE
xlix. 22 ... 173

Exodus
i. 10 ... 88
16 .. 173, 278, 364
17 ... 287
19 .. 173, 279, 364
ii. 3 .. xl. (of Tables)
4 ... 133, 323, xxiv. (of Tables)
9 ... 295
17 . 379
iii. 2 . 83, 330, xv. (of Tables), xvii. (of Tables)
18 ... 54
iv. 11 .. 154
v. 21 ... xxvi. (of Tables)
vi. 28 342
vii. 18 . 101
27 .. 330
ix. 3 ... 277
23 ... 116
x. 3 . 340
8 .. 29
28 137, 381
xii. 9 .. 319
21 . 86
22 .. 101
xiii. 21 ... 296
xiv. 3 ... 160
4 .. 88
21 . 137
xv. 2 .. 293
5 .. xliii. (of Tables)
11 . iii. (of Tables)
17 ... 275
20 ... 285
xvi. 14 . 176
23 . 170
xviii. 26 .. 85, 336
xix. 13 ... 288
xx 13, 17 ... 103
19 93
25 . 161
xxi. 19 .. 342
28 . 78
37 114
xxii. 8 .. 89
xxiii. 4 . 328
25 . 102
xxv. 5 ... 347
31 . 171
xxix. 30 ... 379
35 ... iv. (of Tables)
xxxiii. 3 ... xliii. (of Tables)
20 379
xxxiv. 33 ... 80
xxxv. 25 ... 280
26 .. 280, iv. (of Tables)

Exodus   PAGE
xxxvi. 1 ... iii. (of Tables)
xl. 32 . 80

Leviticus
iv. 13 . 67
23 .. 281, 288
28 .. 288
v. 22 .. iii. (of Tables)
vii. 14 ... 67
23 .. 179
xi. 44 .. 326
xii. 2 . 275
xiii. 2 ... 67
55 . 178, 318
56 ... 178, 318
xiv. 41 ... 100
42 . 162
43 .. 342
xv. 31 ... 368
xvi. 1 . 80
29 ... 234
xvii. 13 .. 100
xviii. 25 . 311
28 . 311 (twice)
xx. 7 326
xxi. 5 88
xxiii. 22 ... 81
xxv. 18 ... 101
21 . 172
48 . 67
xxvi. 18 ... 342
34 . 211, 356
35 . 356
43 . 356

Numbers
i. 18 .. 358
47 ... 358
iii. 16 ... 104
iv. 23 ... 123
v. 22 ... 79
vii. 2 .. 85
viii. 7 ... 316
24 ... 123
ix. 13 .. 253
xi. 12 ... 6
15 ... i. (of Tables)
16 ... xxiii. (of Tables)
xii. 19 ... iii. (of Tables)
27 ... 23
xiv. 16 ... 322
24 ... 23
31 ... 274
45 ... 355
xv. 35 .. 78
xvi. 5 ... 138
26 ... 58
xvii. 28 ... 370, xxii. (of Tables)
xx. 3 ... 370

Numbers   PAGE

xx. 5 ... 58
xxi. 27   317
    30   288, xliii (of Tables)
xxii. 11   xxx (of Tables)
    12   iv. (of Tables)
    17 ... xxx. (of Tables)
    18   55
    28 . 298
    30   23
    33   379
xxiii 7   86, 369
    12 ... 59
    13 . xxxviii (of Tables)
    26   93
xxiv. 3 .. 83, xvii. (of Tables)
    7 .. 304, 317
    17   101
xxv. 11 . 346
xxvii. 16 .. 105
xxxii. 7 ... 293
    11   346
    12 .. 346
    17 .. 163, 274
    30 . 129
    42   iii. (of Tables)
xxxiv. 7 .. 313
    8 ... 313
    10   314
xxxv. 8   5
    16 . 156
    20 ... 334

Deuteronomy

i. 19   58
    38 .. 85
    44   355
ii. 9 . 158
    21   179
iv. 1 .. 324
    8 . 21
    10   88
    15 . 342
    16 . 89
    34 . 300
v. 24   i. (of Tables)
vi. 17   88
vii. 8 . 80
    24   350
viii. 3 . 82
    9   22
    14 . 59, 285
    16   59, 82
ix 19   113
    21   105
    28 .. 322
x. 19 . 102
xi. 14   288
xiii. 4 .. xii. (of Tables)
    11 . 285

Deuteronomy   PAGE

xiv. 21 .. 225
    1 . 78
xv. 2   306
    18 .. 89
xvii. 12 . 85
xix. 5   67
xx. 2   xviii. (of Tables)
    8 . 381
xxi. 7 .. 82
    8 . 178, 318
    11 .. 46
xxii. 1 . xii. (of Tables)
    14 ... 285
    24   179
xxiv. 4 . 178
xxvi. 1 ... 104
    12   66, 79, 120, 349
xxviii. 25   362
    48   350
    52 .. 51
    57   284
    59 . vi (of Tables), xxxii (of Tables)
xxxi 27   277
xxxii. 6   211 (twice)
    8   349
    13 . 135
    18 . 306
    21 . 346
    28   327
    36   82
    41 . 54
xxxiii 8 .. 300
    16   273
    21 .. 271

Joshua

ii. 6 ... 211
    8 . 238
    13   xii (of Tables)
iii. 17 .. 349
iv. 3   349
    24 .. 287
v. 5   163
vi. 17 .. 82, 352
    22   85
    23 . 85
vii. 7 . 119, 349, 352
ix. 4 .. 315
    12 ... 315
x. 13   59
    17 ... 341
    24   59, 82
xi 14 .. 350
xiv. 8 .. 172
xviii. 20 . 114
xxii. 9 . 129
    25 .. 286
xxiii. 5 ... 334
    15 .. iv. (of Tables)

Joshua   PAGE
xxiv. 8 ... 275
10 . 384

Judges
ii. 2 ... 103
iii. 16 . xii. (of Tables)
iv. 4 ... 366
v. 4 ... 322
8, 12 .. 86
14 .. iii. (of Tables)
26 ... 88
28 . 280, 344
vi. 15 .. 52
32 157
vii. 4 ... 53
viii. 2 .. 3
16 43
22 . xv. (of Tables)
ix. 10 .. 86
53 .. 104
xi. 25 ... 338
xiii. 2 .. 42
6, 7 . 178
8 .. 348
19 ... 382
xiv. 8 158
xvi. 10 . 346, 354
13, 15 . 346, 354
16 346
xvii. 2 i. (of Tables)
3 ... 78
xviii. 22 . 355
xix. 5 ... 85, 113, 332
8 ... 332
11 .. 133
13 . 160
20 .. 154
25 ... 286
xx. 39 . 338
45 .. 355

1 Samuel
i. 1 ... 42
14 . 89
20 ... iv. (of Tables)
28 ... 325
ii. 3 382
13 ... 32
15 ... 88
16 ... 78, 88
22 ... 89
28 ... 78
iii. 5, 6 . 382
7 ... 239
vi 9 .. 255
10 .. 300
12 .. 178
vii. 2 ... 293
14 ... 155

1 Samuel   PAGE
vii 17 81, 113
x. 6 291, 317
7 . 273
13 .. 291, 317
xii. 1 .. 105
13 ... 325
xiii. 10 384
15 ... 341
19 ... 82
21 xii. (of Tables)
xiv 22 355
24 .. 269
27 .. 155
34 ... xii. (of Tables)
xv. 23 . 350
xvi. 15 ... 369
17 274, 382
xvii. 11 . 58
25 355
35 . 120, 326
35 326
47 . 138
55 .. 46
58 .. 29
xviii 3 . 80
29 .. 286
xix 24 . 104
xx. 6 .. 77, 338
28 .. 338
40 .. 227
xxi. 3 329, 366
10 ... 28
14 . 313
xxii. 2 .. 173
xxiii. 28 4
20 46
xxiv. 19 1 (of Tables, twice)
21 ... 78
xxv. 5 ... 325
7 . 351
8 ... 272
18 .. 297
34 ... 273 (twice)
xxvi. 13 53
xxviii. 7 ... 46
8 ... 86
15 ... 335
24 ... 270
xxx. 22 .. 110
xxxi. 2 ... 355

2 Samuel
i. 7 ... 379
26 ... 82
ii. 22 ... 299
iii. 11 ... 80, 286
iv. 8 ... 328
10 .. 253, 254
v. 12 ... 304, 344

2 Samuel   PAGE
vi. 1 ... xxiii. (of Tables)
6, 9 ... 129
20 ... 170
viii. 10 .. 384
xi. 24 .. 289 (twice)
xii. 8 .. 137
14 ... 342
xiii. 8 ... 156
18 . 88
xiv. 2 ... 277
3 ... 272
6 ... 299
11 .. 324
13 ... 82
xvii. 11 ... 129, 340
16 ... 154
22 67
xviii. 1 . 104
8 ... 163
16 .. 4
25 . 81
xix. 38 .. 157
xx. 10 ... 101
13 281
xxi. 6 ... 373
xxii. 2 ... 346
26 ... 316
27 361
41 ... xxvi. (of Tables)
xxiii. 1 161
6 ... 292
xxiv. 10 .. 353

1 Kings
1 15 ... 369
ii. 20 ... 157
27 . 4
iii. 12 ... 253
15 ... 135
26 ... 104
vi. 19 .. xxvi. (of Tables)
vii 16 .. 134
viii. 9 ... 294
37 ... 158
ix. 11 .. 344
28 .. 105
39 ... 345
xii. 3, 12 ... 272
xiii. 7 ... 331
33 .. 229
xiv. 2 .. i. (of Tables)
3 371, xxii. (of Tables)
5, 6 .. 330
9 ... 381
12 .. 272
xv. 25 ... 235
xvii. 14 ... xxvi. (of Tables)
13 ... 285
xviii. 27 ... 346

1 Kings   PAGE
xix. 14 ... 342
20 ... 144, 333
xx. 27 ... 358
31 ... 54
41 ... 158
xxi. 29 ... 275
xxii. 41 .. 235

2 Kings
i. 11 ... 382
ii. 10 ... 83, 330, xv. (of Tables),
xvii. (of Tables)
iii. 14 ... 260
iv. 2 ... iii. (of Tables)
16 . i. (of Tables)
22 ... 67
v. 18 .. 324
vi. 7 ... 157
19 ... 137
viii. 1 ... i. (of Tables)
ix. 2 .. 274
18 ... v. (of Tables)
33 ... 296
xi. 2 ... 135
xii. 1 .. 139
xiii. 17 289
xiv. 22 ... 79
xv. 16 . 5
xvi. 4 .. 370
7 . 163
15 ... 310
xvii. 4 ... 118
15 .. 113
33 .. 103
xviii. 32 .. 103
xix. 2 . 274
xxi. 3 ... 343
xxii. 20 328
xxiv. 20 ... 350
xxv. 1 ... 235

Isaiah
i. 2 . 105
3 ... 105
15 89**
16 ... 316, xv. (of Tables)
20 ... 105
21 ... 84, xvii. (of Tables)
30 ... v. (of Tables)
iii. 6 ... iii. (of Tables)
16 ... 297, 345
v. 19 ... 88
vi. 9 ... 78
10 ... 113
13 . 378
vii. 9 .. 78
11 ... 312
14 ... xxxii. (of Tables)
15 ... 78

Isaiah   PAGE
viii. 11 ... 379
17 ... 312
23 ... 41
ix. 9 .. 113
19 .. 104
x. 13 .. 368
17 ... xii. (of Tables)
32 ... 295
xi. 9 .. 323
xiii. 18 .. 345
xiv. 3 ... 4
8 .. 85
23 .. 280
26 . 5
27 .. 113
xv. 5 ... 113, 176
xvi. 13 . 105
14 ... 105, 153
xvii. 8 .. 5
10 .. 336
xviii. 2 . 347
4 ... 88, 334
7 ... 347
xix. 3 ... xxx. (of Tables)
5 . 351
6 .. 177
16 ... 101
xx. 2 .. 105
xxi. 3 . 330
12 . 271
17 ... 105
xxii. 3 ... 341
xxiii. 8 .. 341
9 . 341
11 . 79
15 .. 234, 372
17 . 378
xxiv. 2 ... 3, 55
3 .. 105
xxv. 6 .. 173
xxvi. 7 . 139
19 .. 179
xxvii. 4 ... 88, 334 (twice)
8   281, 307, 308
10 ... 113
12 . 105
xxviii. 12 ... 267
17 . 283
19 .. 362
27 .. 356
xxix. 6 ... 329
9 ... 176
14 ... 328
15 ... 382
xxx. 1 ... lii (of Tables)
2 .. lii. (of Tables)
6 .. 179
12 ... xviii. (of Tables)
28 ... 295

Isaiah   PAGE
xxx. 29 ... xv. (of Tables)
30 .. 329
33 ... 329
xxxi. 4 . 123
5 .. 349
xxxii. 2 .. 320
3 ... 110
9 . 122
11 ... 320
xxxiii. 1   356
9 ... 253
10   318
12 . 145
14 .. 329
20 .. 113
xxxiv. 9 ... 329
xxxv. 1 . 154
4 .. 374
xxxvi. 11 ... 93
14 ... 305
xxxviii. 5 ... 328
19 .. 282
xl. 5 .. 105
24   365
xli. 5   271
7 .. 114
15 ... xii. (of Tables)
23 ... 173
25 . 271
xlii. 5 .. 370
16 .. 380
18 ... 46
20 ... 170
xliii. 7 ... 380
8 .. 286
xliv. 3 ... 134
8 ... 289
18 .. 162
21 ... 306
24 .. 370
27 ... 118
xlvi. 1 ... 303
8 ... 268
xlvii. 1 ... 382
2 ... 86, 118
13 ... 24
14 ... 116
xlix. 3 ... 21
21 ... 163
23 ... 23, 311
26 ... 283
l. 1 ... 306
li. 6 ... 113
15 ... 370
16 ... 342
23 ... 281
lii. 5 ... 138, 318, 367
7 ... 290
15 ... 296

Isaiah   PAGE

liii. 3 ... 353
9 .. xii. (of Tables)
liv. 14 . 317
lv. 7 .. 381
lvi. 3 . 290
4 ... 24
lviii. 9 xv. (of Tables)
11 211
lix. 3 178, 368
4 368
5 .. 163, 335
12 . 373
13 .. 368
19 . 295
lx. 4 ... 122
5 .. 287
7 . xxxix. (of Tables)
lxiii. 3 177, 296, 351
16 . 379
lxiv. 8 . 103
10 . 54
lxv. 12 . 24
24 . 238
lxvi. 4 ... 24

Jeremiah

ii 12 . 86
36 ... 128
iii. 5 . 82
17 .. 312
iv. 7 .. 301
30 ... i. (of Tables)
v. 17 .. iii. (of Tables)
24 .. 288
22 .. xxxix., xl (of Tables)
29 .. 93
vi. 2 291
22 .. 160
vii. 10 .. 110
22 ... 285
34 . 4
ix. 2 . 355
4 .. 346, 354
x. 2 ... iii. (of Tables)
5 304
7 ... 280, 287
17 .. 86, xxiii. (of Tables)
20 284
xi 7 .. 161
xii. 2 366 (twice)
3 ... 379
15 .. 382
xiii. 19 ... 211
25 371, xxii. (of Tables)
xiv. 16 iii. (of Tables)
xvi. 4 . xii. (of Tables)
12 381
13 ... 161
16 . 154

Jeremiah   PAGE

xvii. 18 ... 274
xxii. 20 331
24 ... xl. (of Tables)
xxiii. 12 .. 369
13 ... 291, 317
14 .. 272
17 ... 78
xxv. 3 .. 350
16 .. 366, xxx. (of Tables)
38 ... 283
xxvi 5 .. 350
9 . 291
xxvii. 18 .. 272
22 ... 275
xxix. 8 ... 353
xxxi. 21 ... 82, 154
32 . 350
35 ... 370
xxxii 9 ... 88
44 78
xxxvi. 32 . lii. (of Tables)
xxxvii. 12 .. 349
xxxviii. 17 ... 278
22 ... 161
xxxix. 7 . 273
xlii. 16 ... 342
xliii. 6 . l. (of Tables)
20 ... xxiv. (of Tables)
xliv. 4 .. 350
25 . 151, xxviii. (of Tables)
xlvi. 8 .. 129, 367
xlix. 3 . 89
4 ... 358
10 .. 339
l. 5 .. 272
8. 285
14 ... 281
21 . 118
22 .. 340
34 . 349
li. 9 . xxxii. (of Tables)
33 350

Ezekiel

i. 5 ... iii. (of Tables)
7 .. 301
iii. 15 . 357
20 ... 88
iv. 3 .. 369
12 ... 251
v. 11 153
13 . 317
viii 16 ... 178
xi. 17 .. 160
xiii. 18 iii. (of Tables)
19 . 156, 345
xiv. 3 ... 340, xv. (of Tables)
xvi 4 . 323, 347
5 .. 323

Ezekiel — PAGE

xvi 13 .. 283
31 .. 277
34 277
51 ... xii. (of Tables)
52 323, xii. (of Tables), xvi. (of Tables)
54 ... iv. (of Tables)
55 155, xii. (of Tables), 156
61 xii. (of Tables)
xvii 15 . 85, 113
23 .. 122
xviii. 14 iii. (of Tables)
xx. 30, 31 .. 341
43 . 160
xxi. 19 ... 66
21 . 134
29 351
xxii. 4 . 273 (twice)
7 179
xxiii. 16 88
20 . 88
39 . 81
45 iv. (of Tables)
46 ... 362
47 iv. (of Tables)
48 .. 318
xxiv. 12 211
xxv. 6 81
xxvi 8 100
15 . 340
16 . 104
18 117
xxviii. 8 . xii. (of Tables)
9 6
14 . l. (of Tables)
xxxi. 5 .. 121
7 174, 283
14 v. (of Tables)
xxxii. 19 87
20 86
30 ... 3
xxxiii 13 88
xxxiv 21 . 116
31 ... i. (of Tables)
xxxv. 9 155
11 vi. (of Tables)
xxxvii 7 337
10 291, 317
17 . 345
xxxviii. 23 326
xxxix 26 302
xl. 3 274
4 275
xlii. 9 ... iii. (of Tables)
xliv. 5 .. 113

Hosea — PAGE

i 2 342
ii 2 xii. (of Tables)

Hosea — PAGE

ii. 5 . 326
iv. 2 . 78
13, 14 ... 345
vi. 9 . 343 (twice)
viii 2 . 373
x. 4 ... 319
9 . 362
10 ... 334
11 84, xvii. (of Tables)
14 151, 356
xi. 3 . 177
4 . 129
9 . 381
xiii. 15 .. 161

Joel

i. 2 6
iv. 3 281
6 5
11 . 353

Amos

i 11 82
ii. 4 . xviii. (of Tables)
iv. 2 . 344
3 ... 82
4 382
v. 11 366
ix. 1 373, 378
5 ... 156
8 77

Obadiah

3 305
11 ... 281
12 . 76
13 .. 88

Jonah

i 7, 8, 12 24

Micah

i. 6 336
8 . 136
10 ... 112
15 ... 275
ii. 7 .. 5
8 .. 163
13 ... xxviii. (of Tables)
iv. 6, 7 .. 330
8 ... 271
vii. 8 ... 269
10 ... 269
16 110

Nahum

i. 3 .. 50
ii 4 . 347
9 ... 112

Nahum   PAGE
iii. 2 ... 330
    5 ... 352
    7 ... 292, 347
    10 ... 281
    11 .. 277

Habakkuk
i. 16 ... iii (of Tables)
ii. 17 ... 379
iii. 6 .. 365

Zephaniah
i. 14   330
ii. 13 .. 174

Haggai
ii. 16 . 4

Zechariah
i. 9 ... 260
ii. 4   281
    17 .. 160
iv. 5 .. 59
    10 ... 162
v. 4   160, 211, 335
    11 .. 145, iii. (of Tables)
ix. 2 . 114
    9 . 377
    17 . 293
xi. 5 ... 355
    8 . 105
    10 .. 349
xiii. 4 ... 291

Malachi
i. 14 ... 369
iii. 2 . 272
    9 . 271
    20   324

Psalms
i. 3 ... v. (of Tables)
ii. 5 .. v. (of Tables)
    12 . 193
iii. 6   135
iv. 7 .. 303
v. 9 . 139, 286, 353
    12 . 117, v. (of Tables)
vi. 4 .. i. (of Tables)
vii. 6 . 177, 363
viii. 2 .. xxvi. (of Tables)
ix. 15 .. vi (of Tables)
x. 12   303
xii 4 ... 55
    9 .. 150
xiv. 5 ... 228
xvi. 5 . 328
xviii. 3 . 24, 346
    23 ... iii. (of Tables)

Psalms   PAGE
xviii. 26 .. 316
    27 . 361
xix. 9 .. 268
    14 .. xxx. (of Tables)
xx. 4 . 88, 335
xxii. 15 . 253
xxv. 2 ... 117
    9 .. 101
xxvi. 7 ... 79
xxviii. 2 ... 302
    7 .. 282
xxix. 9 . 116
xxxi. 8 .. 82
xxxii. 1 .. 24, 303
    8 .. 247, 289
xxxv. 14 ... 327
    25 .. 373
xxxix. 2 . 88
xli. 5 .. 335
xlii. 7 .. xxx. (of Tables)
xliv. 8 . 161
    11 ... iii. (of Tables)
    18 .. 272
    19 .. iii. (of Tables)
xlv. 3 .. 176, 284
    5 .. 55
    6 .. 113
    9 .. iii. (of Tables)
    18 . 88, 138, 282
xlvii. 4 . 76
xlviii. 5 . 113
    16 .. 113
xlix 19   282
l. 5 . 85
li. 6 . xviii. (of Tables)
    7 . 344
lii. 7 . 366
lv. 10 ... 345
    16 .. 305, v. (of Tables)
lvii. 5 . 88
lviii. 7 . 362
    9 .. 46
    10 .. 55
lix. 5 ... 317
lx. 6 .. 36, 295
    8 ... 105
lxiii. 4 .. 52
lxiv. 5 . 289
lxv. 10 .. 355
lxvi 3 ... 55
lxviii. 3 ... 340
    4 ... 117
    8   322
    13 ... 292
    18 . 64
    24 . iii. (of Tables)
    26 .. 330
    28 .. xliii. (of Tables)
lxix. 18 .. 105

Psalms   PAGE
    lxix. 21   295
          24   110
    lxxi. 19 .. 55
          20 . 280
          23 ... 122
    lxxii. 5 ... 32
           13 . 153
           17   295
           20 .. 347
    lxxiii. 2 . 82, 297
            9 ... 116
            28 ... 55
    lxxiv. 8 ... 283, xliii. (of Tables)
    lxxvi. 6 .. 177
    lxxviii. 18 .. xv. (of Tables)
             41 .. 314
    lxxx. 11 .. 173, 347
          13 ... 270
          14 ... 177
          16 ... 82
    lxxxi. 6 ... 138
    lxxxiii. 19 .. 24
    lxxxviii. 14 ... 110
    lxxxix. 8   119
            10 ... 302
            42 . 253
            45 .. 110
    xc. 2   239
        12   xxii. (of Tables)
    xci. 12 . 303
    xciii. 5 ... 290
    xciv. 1   354
          5 ... 113
          9   370, xxii. (of Tables)
          20 .. 348, 367 (twice)
    xcv. 4 . 22, 54
         5 . 21, 211
         9 ... 300
    ci. 5 ... 367
    cii. 5 ... 299
         25 ... 32
         26 . 110
    civ. 22, 28 . 112
         26, 27 . 113
         29 ... 112, xxiii. (of Tables)
         30   101, 112
    cvi 22 ... 55
    cxiii. 6 .. 84, xvii. (of Tables)
    cxiv. 8 ... 59, 232
    cxvi. 6 . 138
          7 ... v. (of Tables)
          16 ... 113
    cxviii. 18 ... 342, 379
    cxix. 50 ... 279
          65 .. 113
    cxxx. 4 ... 287
          6 ... 85
    cxxxii. 6 ... 373
            12 ... vi. (of Tables)

Psalms   PAGE
    cxxxiii. 1 ... 29
    cxxxv. 7 .. 285
    cxxxvi. 6 .. 370
    cxxxviii. 6 .. 137
    cxxxix. 18 ... 161
            20 .. 302
    cxl. 13 ... 82
    cxli. 3 ... 86
          5 . 293
          8 ... iii. (of Tables
    cxliii. 3 ... 344
    cxlv. 8 ... 50
    cxlvii. 1 ... 342
    cxlix. 6 ... xii (of Tables)

Proverbs
    i. 10 ... 267
       28 . xxxix. (of Tables)
    ii. 13 .. 5
    iii. 30 . 157
    iv. 11 ... 288
        24 .. 353
    v. 4 ... xii. (of Tables)
       22   xxxix. (of Tables)
    vii. 17 ... 295
    viii. 6   55
          17 .. 128
          24 .. 341
          25 . 239
    ix. 9 .. 137
    x. 3 ... 116
    xi 25 . 288
    xiv. 3 .. 337
    xv. 20   54
    xvii. 4 ... 130
    xix. 11 . 350
         19 .. 50
         23   114
    xx. 22 ... 138
    xxii. 21 . 36
    xxiii 13, 14 .. 299
          35 .. 382
    xxiv. 3 .. 317
          7 .. 163
          14 ... 335 (twice), xxiv. (of
                 Tables)
          31 . 173
    xxv. 4 .. 281
         19 .. 348
    xxvi. 26 ... 317
    xxvii. 15 ... 360—364
    xxx. 6 ... 137
         17 ... 342
         18 ... 380

Job
    i. 4 .. xii. (of Tables)
       10 ... i. (of Tables)
       21 ... 284

Job

		PAGE
iii.	25 ...	271
iv.	2 .	300
	4	160
	12	iii. (of Tables)
	19 .	23
v.	5 ...	22
	25	53
vi.	16 .	v. (of Tables)
	22 ..	369
vii.	7 ..	381
ix.	15 .	176, 366
x.	18 ..	379
xi	17 ...	88
	20 .	iii. (of Tables)
xiii	9 ..	346, 354
	21 .	353
xv.	22	173
	35	78
xvi	5 .	210
	21	138
xvii.	2 ..	154
xix.	2 .	173, 281
xx	23 ...	v. (of Tables)
	26	367
xxi.	4 ...	6
	5 ..	356
	16 .	iii. (of Tables)
	29 .	325
xxii.	8 ..	137
	20 ..	163
	21 ..	273
	23	x (of Tables)
	28 .	157
xxiv	21 .	135
	24 .	356
xxvi.	9 .	177
xxvii.	21 .	137
xxviii.	11 .	286
xxix.	17 .	362
	25	24
xxx.	8 .	298
	15	120
	22.	313
xxxi	8	366
	11 .	i. (of Tables)
	21	295
xxxii	11 .	130
	12 ..	v. (of Tables)
xxxiii.	4 .	211
	13 ..	154
	25 .	177
	30	160
xxxiv.	13 ...	41
	22	114
xxxv.	11 ...	130
xxxvi.	2 ...	345
	18 .	297
xxxvii.	12 .	41
xxxix.	17 ...	306

Job

		PAGE
xl.	32 ...	137
xli.	3 ...	345
	17 ..	302
	25 .	173
xlii.	5 ...	xliii. (of Tables)
	7 .	342
	11	xii (of Tables)

Song of Solomon

i.	6	330
	10	290
iii	4 ...	274
iv.	6	137
v.	2 ..	152
viii.	5 .	xxxvi. (of Tables)

Ruth

i.	1	79
	13 ..	122
ii.	8	338
	14 ..	iii. (of Tables)
	21	89
iii.	15	369, xxiii. (of Tables)
iv	5 ..	82

Lamentations

i.	4	330
	12	365
	16	330
ii.	11 .	79, 340
	13 .	46
iii.	1	24
	2 ...	137
	6 .	211
	25 ..	311
	33	281
	53 .	133, 281
iv.	14	368
	15 ...	300, 301 (twice)

Ecclesiastes

ii.	1 .	300
	18 .	294
iii.	18 ..	223
iv.	2 ..	330
v.	8	116
vii	22 ..	i. (of Tables)
viii.	15	290
	17 .	24
ix.	12 ...	348
x.	1 ...	284
	10 .	310 (twice)
xi.	3 ..	276
xii.	4 ...	123
	5 ..	151, 295
	12 .	iii. (of Tables)

Esther

i.	5 ...	341
iii.	13 ..	338

Esther PAGE
iv. 4 .. 273
v. 2 101
viii. 6 ... 322
8 339
ix. 1 .. 339

Daniel
i. 1 ... 235
21 .. 235
ii 9 316
viii. 13 .. 334
ix. 1 235
2 ... 154, 235
4 ... 88
19 ... 113
24 ... 343
xi. 14 .. 304, 317

Ezra
vii 8 ... 235
viii. 25 .. 334, 341
x. 14 ... 5
16 .. 234, 322
17 . 234

Nehemiah
iv. 9 156
v. 7 .. 173, 305

Nehemiah PAGE
ix. 6 . i (of Tables)
19 296
x. 39 .. 120, 349
xi 17 . 282
xiii. 21 .. 152

1 Chronicles
ii 16 .. xii. (of Tables)
v. 20 . 339
x. 2 . 355
xv. 26 .. 116
27 . 177
xviii. 10 384
xxix. 23 . xxii. (of Tables)

2 Chronicles
ii 16 . 163
xiv 4 ... 5
xx. 35 177
xxi. 17 ... 50
xxvi. 15 ... 288
xxviii. 4 . 370
33 . 353
xxix. 19 161
xxxi. 7 ... 342
xxxiv. 4 . 5
7 . 5
28 ... 328

INDEX OF HEBREW WORDS.

א

	PAGE
אֶאֱמָצְכֶם	...210
אָאֹר	...262, 271
אָאָרְבָה	Tab. XVII (Pdgm)
אָב	...31, Tab. XIII. 1
אַב	Tab. XIII (Note 1)
אָבָא	...273
אַבָּא	...275
אָבָאָה	...273
אֹבֵד	327, App^x (C) to Tab. XIV (Note *)
אָבֵּד	...343, Tab. XIV (Note *e*)
אָבְדְךָ	comp. Tab. XV (Note *)
אבה	...267
אָבוֹא	...267
אָבוֹא	...273 (Note *)
אָבוֹאָה	...273 (Note *)
אֲבשׁ (=אֲבשׁ)	... see p. 153, Tab. XX
אֲבשָׂה (=אֲבשָׂה)	... see p. 153, Tab. XX
אָבוֹת (i.c. אֲבוֹת)	31, Tab. XIII. 1
אֲבִי	...Tab. XIII. 1
אבי	...275
אָבִי	275; also Tab. XIII. 1
אָבִיא	...275
אֲבִיאֵנוּ	...275
אָבִי, אָבִיחוּ etc.	... Tab. XIII. 1
אַבִּיטָה	see § 211 (p. 145)
אבִיעָה	see § 211 (p. 145)
אָבֵל (& אֲבֵל)	... 327
אֲבַלַּע	... Tab. XVI (3) (Note §)
אַבְרֵךְ	...350
אֲבְרֵךְ (& אַבְרֵךְ)	p. xxi of Tabs.
וַאֲבָרְכְךָ (p. ־ְ ־ְ ־ְ)	...261
אֲבַשָׂה	...153
אָבֹת (אֲבֹתַי, etc.)	Tab. XIII. 1
אֲבֹתָם	......Tab. XIII (Note 4)
אֶגְאָלְתִּי	...351
אַגִּידָה	...145
אַגִּישׁ	Tab. XIX
אַגֵּל	...190
אֶגְלֶה	...Tab. XXIII
אֲגַלֶּה	...Tab. XXIII
אַגְלֶה	...Tab. XXIII
אֲדֹנָי	...2, 3, 4, (in Notes)
אַדַע (& אֵדַע)	... 137
אֶדְעָה (& אֵדְעָה)	... 138
אֶדְרֹשׁ (in הָאֶדְרֹשׁ)	340, Tab. XIV (Note *d*)
אֶדְרֹשׁ	...340
אֹהַב (like אֹכַל, Tab. XVII)	
אֶהֱב	130*
אֹהָב	128, 130**
אֲהֲבָה	......Tab. XXV (Note *a*)
אֲהֲבָךְ	...Tab. XXVII (Note β
אֲהֵבוּ	209, Tab. XXV (Note *a*)
אֲהֲבוּךְ	...209
אֲהֵבוּ	... Tab. XVII

	PAGE
אֲהֵבֶךָ	209, Tab. XXV (Note *a*)
אֲהֵבֶךָ	329
אֲהַבְתִּי	84, 269
אֶהְגֶּה	...see page 191
אֲהוֹרִגֶנּוּ	282, 354
אֲהִי	...277
אֶחְיֶה	...277
אֹהֱלֹה	see Tabs. XI (3) & VIII
אֲהָלוֹת	33
אָהֳלִי	...Tab. XI (Note §)
אֹהָלִים	etc. ... Tab. XI (Note §)
אָהֳלֵיהֶם	etc. ... Tab. XI (Note §)
אֹהָלִים	33
אֵהֵלֵךְ	...117
אֲהַלְלָה	...346
אהמה	...191
אֲהַמְיָה	172, Tab. XXIII (Note 6)
אֶהְפֹּךְ	...117
אַהֲרֹנָה	...117
אֶהְרְגֵנְהוּ	...208
אוֹבֵדָה	...129
אוֹרֶה	...282
אוֹדְךָ	...282
אוֹדֶךָ	...210, 282
אוֹדֶנּוּ	...282
אֲוֶה	...267
אִוִּיתִי	...267
אוּכִיל	...129
אֹכְלָה	329, also Tab. XVII (Pdgm)
אוֹלִיכָה	...137
אֹמְרָה	130**
אוֹר (Verb)	...268
אוֹרַח	...289
אוּרוּ	...271
אוֹרִי	...268
אוֹדְךָ	...289
אֶנְשֵׁב	... Tab. XVIII
אוֹשֵׁב	... Tab. XVIII
אֹלִיֵּיב	... Tab. XVIII
	PAGE
אוֹתָהּ	...267
אוֹתָהֶם	...Tab. III (Note 2)
אוֹתְהֶן	...Tab. III (Note 3)
אוֹתְכֶם	...Tab. III (Note 4)
אַיִן	...130
אַזְכִּירָה	88, 334
אָזְלַת	82
אָזְנַיִם with Affs.	...... Tab. VII
אָח with Affs	Tab. XIII (2)
אֶחֱבֹשׁ	...117
אֶחָד (& אַחַד)	62, etc.
אֲחֵרִים	65
אַחַת (& אֶחָת)	62, etc.
אֲחֻזָּה	...278
אֲחֻזּוֹ (& ־הֶ)	...278
אָחוֹת w. Affs.	...Tab. XIII (Note †, *a*)
אֶחֱזוּ (like אֶעֱלֶה on p. 192)	
אָחַז	130**
אֲחַזְתָּה (like פְּקַדְתָּה, fr. פָּקַד, Tab. XXV)	
אֲחַזְתָּם (like פְּקַדְתָּם, fr. פָּקַד, Tab. XXV)	
אֶחְטָם	...117
אֲחִי	Tab. XIII (2)
אֲחִי	Tab. XIII (Note 5)
אָחִיהָ	...279
אֲחֻיָה	...280
אָחִיו (& אָחִיהוּ)	...Tab. XIII (2)
אֶחְסַר	...117
אֶחְפֹּץ	...117
אַחַר	...343
אַחַר see (אַ וְ)	...128
אַחֲרֵי	...344
אַט (& אָט) (a Particle, "*gently*")	
אַט & אָט	...297
אַטָּה	...297
אֵיבְךָ	269, 328, App.x (B) to Tab. IX
אֵיבְכֶם	App.x (B) to Tab. IX
אֵיבָה	...269

PAGE

אֹיַבְתִּי 269
אֹיֵב ... ... Tab. XVIII
אֵיטְבָה comp. Tab. XVIII
אֵיטִיב ... ... Tab. XVIII
אֵיטִיבָה (the preceding with ה)
אֵיכָה 248
אֱלִיל 136, 282
אֵילְכָה 136
אֵילְלָה 136, 282
(אֵין) אֵין w. Affs. .. Tab. XIII (Note ‡, δ)
אִיעָצָה 135
אִירָא 287
אִירָאֶנּוּ 287
אִיתָם ... Tab. XXI (Note 4)
אַךְ (a Particle, "but, only")
אַךְ 299
אֶכְבְּדָה 88
אֶכְבְּרָה Pause-form of the preceding
אַכֶּה 299
אַכֵּהוּ 299
אַכְּכָה 299
אֲכָל־ 249
אָכָל ... Tab. XIV (Note f)
(אֹכֵל &) אֹכַל ... ... Tab. XVII
אַכַּל (like אֲגַל in Tab. XXIII)
אכלה 335, Tab. XVII (Pdgm)
אֹכְלָה 329
אֲכָלְךָ ...242, Tab. XV (Note *)
אַכְלְךָ ...Tab. XXX (Note β, 9)
אֲכַלְכֵּל ... ... see p. 175
אֲכָלְכֶם ...245, Tab. XV (Note ‡)
(אָכַלְתָּ &) תְ 110
אֲכָלַתְהוּ ... ... Tab. XXV (γ)
אַכֶנּוּ 299
אַכַּף ... Tab. XXI (Note 9)
אֶכְתָּבְנָה comp (ζ) on pp. 333 & 334
אֶל (for אֵלֶה, in הָאֵל) 58 (Note*)

PAGE

אַל (with Fut., to express "Do not") 93
אֶל w. Affs. ... ... Tab. IV
אֵלֶה 78, 269
אֲלֵהֶם ... ... Tab. IV (Note 1)
אֵלוֹת 269
אֵלַי 269
אֲלֵיהֶם ... ... Tab IV (Note 1)
אֵלֵימוֹ ... ... Tab. IV (Note 1)
אַלְיַת 269
אֵלֵךְ 137
אֵלְכָה (& כָה־) 136
אֲלֵיכֶם=אֲלֵכֶם ... ...Tab. IV
אָנָה 270
אֲנֹוהוּ 293
אֲנוּשָׁה 295
(אֲנַחֵהוּ & נִי־) 296
אֲנַחְנוּ (אֲנַחְנוּ .p)... ...9, Tab. I
אַנִּיחַ 294
אֲנַסֶּה 300
אֲנַסְּכָה 300
אֲנַסְנוּ 300
אֲנַקֵּךְ 302
אֲנַשֵּׂא 304
אָסֹב etc. ... 180, Tab. XXI
(אֲסֹבֵב & ב־) ... ... Tab. XXI
אֲסַבְּבָה ... ... Tab. XXI
אָסֹבָה ... ... Tab. XXI
אֹסְפָה 137
אֶסְפָּה ... ... 86 (Note *), 335, Tab. XVII (3, iii)
אֶסְפִּי 86 (ζ), Tab. XVII (Note §)
אֹסְרִי 84
אָסְרֵם 334
אֶעְבְּרָה 117
אֶעֱזֹבָה 117
אֶעַל (אֶעֱלֶה p) ...171, 192, 193
אֶעֱלֶה 171, 191

PAGE

אַצְלָה 171, 192
אֶעֱלֹוֶה 118
אעלצה 117
אֶעֶרְכֶה 117
אֹפְּהֶם 270
אַפִּי 270
אַפִּי 270
אֹפֶל ... ... Tab. XIX
אֲפֵלָה (p. אֲפֵלָה:)... ...144, 335
אֹפֶן ... ... Tab. XXIII
אֶפְקֹד w. Affs. Tab. XXVIII
אֶפְשָׂעָה 88, 334
אַצּוּ 310
אֲצַוֶּה 310
אֲצַוְּךָ 310
אֲצַוֶּךָ 210, 310
אֲצַוְּךָ 310
אֲצַוֶּנּוּ 310
(אֲצָק) אָצֶק 134
אֲקַוֶּה 312
אָקוּם ... ... Tab. XX
אָקוּמָה 158
אֲקוֹמֵם ... ... Tab. XX
אֶקַּח ... Tab. XIX (Note (A)
אֶקָּחֶה ... Tab. XIX (Note (A)
(אָקֵם &) אָקִים ... Tab. XX
אַקֵּל ... Tab. XXI (Note 4)
אֶקְרָאֶה 335
אֶרֶא 191
אֲרֶא ... ... Tab. XXIII
אֶרְאָךְ 260
אֶרְאָךְ 260
אֲרֶה־ 271, Tab. XXI (Note *, β)
אָרוּ 270
אֹרוּ 268, 271
אֲרוֹטֵם 318
אָרוֹר 270
אָרוּר 249, 271
אֲרוּרָה 251, 271

PAGE

אֲרוּגִים 271
אֲרוֹתִי 271, Tab. XXI (Note i)
אֹרֶךְ w. Affs. ... ...Tab. XI
אֲרָנֶה 312
אֲרִיתִי 270
אֲרֻקָּה ... Tab. XXII (Note 7)
אֲרָרֶה 271
אֲרֶשׁ 343
אֶשָּׂא 303
אֶשָּׂאֵנּוּ 303
אֵשֶׁב ... ... Tab. XVIII
אֶשְׁבָּה (p. בָּהּ —, comp. p.136) 335
אִשֶּׁה 46
אֲשֻׁוֶּה 313
אֲשַׁוֶּה 313
אָשִׁית 250
אֶשְׁכְּבָה 88
אַשְׁכִּילָךְ 247
אַשְׁכִּים 350
אֶשְׁלַחַךְ 210
אֶשְׁלָחֲךָ 210
אֶשְׁמְרָה 88
אַשְׁקֶה 144, 333
אֲשְׁקוֹטָה 88, 334
אֶשְׁקוֹלָה 334
אֶשְׁכְּלָה 88
אֲשֶׁר 21–24
אֵשֶׁת 190, Tab. XXIII (Note 7)
אֵשֶׁת 46
אֶשְׁתּוֹלְלוּ 177
אֶשְׁתַּחֲוֶה ... Tab. XXIII (Note ¶)
אֶשְׁתַּעְשַׁע ... ... 176 (Note †, 3)
אֵת w. Pron.-Affs. ... ... Tab. III (1 & 2)
אֵתֶיוֹ ... ... Tab. XXIII
אֶתֶּן (נָה — & אִתְּנָה, ו —)... Tab. XIX (Note B)
אֶתְּנִי 271, Tab XXII (Note g)
אֶתְּקֶנֵךְ Tab. XXVIII (Note δ)

ב

PAGE

ב w. Pron.-Affs. Tab. II

בָּא, בָּאָה, בָּאוּ ... 272

בָּא, בָּאָה, בָּאוּ (twice), בָּאִי ... 272

בָּאָבְדַן ... 322

בְּאַהֲבָתוֹ ... 80

בָּאֱחֹז ...130*

בָּאִי ... 272

בֹּאָנָה ... 272

בָּאנוּ ... 272

בְּאֵר ... 343

בָּאתָ (in וּבָאתָ, Pt. I. § 29, Note), 272

בָּאת, בָּאתָ, בָּאתָה, בָּאתִי ... 272

בָּאתְנוּ ... 272

בְּנֹגַע ... 370

בְּנֹעַת Tab. XIX (Note a)

בְּרֹנֶת ... 232

בְּדַעַת ... 133

בְּהִבָּרְאָם ... 238

בְּהַדְּרֶךְ ... 6

בָּהַכּוֹת ... 298

בָּהַנַּחַל ... 349

בְּהִעָוֹתוֹ ... 309

בָּהַעֲלֹות ... 192

בְּהַפְרִידוֹ ... 80

בְּהִצַּוֹתוֹ ... 301

בְּהִצֹּתָם ... 301

בְּהַקְרִיבְכֶם ... 80

בָּהָרֵג ... 340

בְּהִשָּׁפַח ... 356

בְּהַשָּׁמַיִם ... 6

בְּהִשָּׁפְטוֹ ... 80

בְּהִתְוַדַּע ... 133

בּוֹאָנָה ... 272

בּוֹכִיָה ... 173

בֻּשַּׁקְכֶם ... 366

בַּז ... 161

(בְּזֹאת &) בְּזֹאת ... 28

(בַּזֶּה &) בָּזֶה ... 28

בִּזְכְרֵנוּ ... 80

בְּחֻרַי ... 321

בְּטֶרֶם ... 239

בִּיהוֹכֶף ... 138

בִּינָתִי ... 154

בַּיִת w. Affs. Tab. XIII (3)

בִּיתָה ... 42

בְּכָשְׁלוֹ ... 80

בְּכָתוֹב ... 123

בָּלַע, & בִּלַע Tab. XVI (3) (B, γ)

בִּלְעָדִי

בִּלְעָדַי } Tab. IV (4)

בִּלְעָדֶיךָ

בָּמוֹת ... 151

בְּמָלְכוֹ ... 80, 139

בְּמֹצַאֲכֶם ... Tab. XV (Note ‡)

בֵּן w. Affs. Tab. XIII

בֶּן שֶׁבַע שָׁנִים ... 139

בְּנוֹ ... 232

בָּאנוּ for בָּנוּ ... 272

בְּנָטֹתִי ... 297

בְּנָפֹל ... 123, 144

בְּנָשָׂאִי ... 302

בָּנַת ... Tab. XXIII

בָּנְתָה like קָמָה Tab. XX, with ה (p. 82, i)

בְּסָאסְאָה ... 307 & 308

בְּעָבְרְכֶם ... 80

בְּעָטֵף ... 79 (Note †), 340

בְּעָיוּ ... 172, Tab. XXIII

בֹּעֲרָה & בִּעֲרָה ... 329

בַּעֲשֹׂר (cp. p. 79), 120, 349

בְּפָתְחִי ... 81

בְּצֵאתוֹ ... 262

בְּצִדְקָתֶךָ 323, 343, App[x] (A) to Tab. XIV (3)

בְּצֹותוֹ ... 309

בְּצַעְדְךָ ... 322

בְּקָנְאוֹ ... 346

PAGE

בְּקַעְם 81
בְּקָצְרֶךָ 80
בְּקָרְבָתָם 80
בָּרָא לַעֲשׂוֹת 236, 380–382
ברבות 123
בתך (& בְּרֶךְ) 343, and App^x to 'Tab. XVI (2)'
בִּרְךָ Tab. XXI (Note *, a)
בֹּשׁ׳ (& בֹּשׁ׳)... 24 (Note f)
בשאת 302
בֹּשׁ, בֹּשָׁה, etc. ... 152, Tab. XX
בְּשֶׁבֶת 133
בֹּשׁוּ, etc. ... 153, Tab. XX
בִּשּׂוֹא 302
בְּשַׁחֲטָם 81
בְּשָׁכְבָה 81
בָּשָׁכְבוֹ 81
בְּשָׁכְבְךָ 80
בְּשָׁכֵן 123
בִּשֵׁל ... ... 24 (Note g)
בְּשַׁלַּח Tab. XVI (3) (B, a)
בְּשָׁלְחִי 80
בְּשַׁלְחֲךָ ... Tab. XV (Note †)
בִּשֵּׁלִי ... ... 24 (Note g)
בִּשֵּׁלָמִי ... ... 24 (Note g)
בְּשָׁמְעֵךְ 80
בשנו ... ... Tab. XX
בְּשָׁפֵּר 123
בשפג 123
בשתי ... ... Tab. XX
בָּשְׁתָּם ... ... Tab. XX

ג

גָּאֲלָה ... Tab. XXVII (β)
גָּבַה 121, 190
גָּבְהָא 121
נִבְהַת ... ... 121, 190, etc.

PAGE

נָבְרוּ 81
גָּדוֹל 50
גְּדָל- ... ...50 (Note)
גָּדְלָה 50
גָּדְלוּת 50
גָּדְלִי 328
(& גָּדְלוּ) Tab. XI (Note *)
גְּדֵלִים 328
גְּדֵלִים 50
גָּדַלְךָ ... Tab. XI (Note *)
גּוֹאֵל w. Affs. App^x (B) to Tab IX
גּוֹלָה, etc. 173
גָּוַע ... ... 150 (Note)
גָּוַע ... ... 150 (Note)
גָּוַעְנוּ ... ... 150 (Note)
גִּידִים 163
גַּל 170, 190
גָּלוּי, etc. 173
גָּמָל w. Affs. Tab. IX (Note *, β)
גְּמַלִּים, etc. Tab. IX (Note *, β)
גָּנַבְתִּי 84
גֵּשׁ ... ... Tab. XIX
גָּשָׁה 335
גֶּשֶׁת 143

ד

דָּבָר w. Affs. ... Tab. IX
דִּבֶּר 342, 343
דבר ... ...121, 342, 343, Tab. XIV (Note e)
דָּבָר ... 83, 'App^x (B) to Tab. XIV' (a)
דבשי 40
דּוֹחָה 275
רִינֵג 154
דִּכָּא 344

PAGE

דִּכְאָה Tab. XXII (Note o)
דַּלְיוֹ ... ... Tab. XXIII
דַּע 133
דֵּעָה 323
דְּעֶה & דֵּעָה ... 335 (Note)
דְּעוּ 133
דְּעִי 133
דַּעַת 133
דְּעַת 133
דֵּעְתוֹ 133

ה

ה for the 'Def. Art.' 4, 5
ה Interrog. 5, 6
ה for the Vocative ' O,' 46
הָ— towards... ... 42
הָאָדְרֵשׁ 340
הַאֲזֵנָּה 122
הָאֲנִיחוּ 177
הָאֲחָתֶ 279
הָאִיר 268
הָאָכֵל 129, 340
הָאָנַח ... Tab. XVI (3)
(B, β & Note §)
הָאָסֹף 129, 340
(Tab. XIV, Note d)
הָאֵר 268
הָאֲרִיךְ 350
הָאִירָה 268
הַב 133
הֵבֵאת 169, 185, 275
הֵבֵאתָ (& w. Affs.) ... 274
הֵבֵאתָה 275
הֵבֵאתִי 274
הָבַח 133

הָבוּ 133
הָבִי 133
הָבִיא 274
הֵבִיאֲךָ, etc. 274
הֲבִיאֹתְ, etc. 274
הֱבִיאַנִי 274
הֲבִיאֹתָ w. Affs. 274
הֹבִישָׁה 161
הֲבִישׁוֹתָ 161
הֻגַּדְתָּ 266
הֹגָה 281
הֹגוּ 368, Tab. XXIII (1)
הִגִּישׁ ... ... Tab. XIX
הַגִּישָׁה Tab. XIX (Note β)
הֶגְלָ 190
הַגְלָה 190
הָגְלָה 352
הֶגְלָה ... 352, Tab. XXIII
הִגְלִיתָ 352
הָגְלָם 352
הֶגְלַת (form) 211
הָגְלַת 211
הֻגַּשְׁתָּ ... Tab. XVI (3) (C)
הָגַשׁ 143
הַגִּשָׁה Tab. XIX (Note β)
הַדַּעַת 240
הִדְרִיכָה 349
הָהָיְתָה 277
הַהֹלֵךְ 241
הוּא ... Tab. I (Note 1)
הֵוֵא 276
הוֹבִישׁ 161
הוֹבִישׁוּ 161
הוֹבַשְׁתָּ 161
הוֹגָה 281
הוֹגָה 281

PAGE

חֹונָעֲנוּ 110

הֹודַע 138, Tab. XVI (3) (B, β)

הֹודַעְתָּ 110

הֶֹה 276

הֶנֹה 276

הֶוִי 276

הֹוֶה 277

הוּפָּה 299

הֹוכַח 138

הֻגְּלָדֶת 323

(הֹולָם &) הֹולָם 114

הֻגֶּף 295

הֹוצֵא 286

הֹוצֵא 286

הֹוצֵיא, etc. 285

הֹוצֵאת see והו' p. 285

הֹוצִיאָהג 285

הֹורֻגֵנִי 289

הֹורֵיתִי 288

הֹורֵנִי 289

הֹורֻתָנִי 288

הֹושֵׁיב ... 134, Tab. XVIII

הֹושֵׁב ... 134, Tab. XVIII

הֹושִׁישָׁה 138

הֹושֵׁע 138

הֹושֵׁר Kthv (for הַיָשֵׁר Kri, p. 139) ... 353

הַנֵּח 296

הֻגֵּה 296

הֻגֵּית 296

הֻגֵּג 316

הֻזְבַּרְכֶה 351

הֻזְנֵית ... ... Tab. XXIII

הֶחְבָּאתָה 82, 352

הֶחֱזֻקִי 350

הֻתִּיתָם 279

PAGE

הֹחֲלֹותְ Tab. XXI (Note ‡)

הָחֳלֵיתִי 193

הָחֳלָם Tab. XXI (Note ‡)

הָחֳרֻבָה 120

הָחֳרַמְתָּם 119

הֻט 297

הֻטֶּה 297

הֻטֻהג 297

הֻטֻהֲרֻי 316

הֻטֻהֲרֻי 112, 316

הֻטֻהֲרֻנו 316

הֻטֻג 297

הֻטֻוֹח 342

הֻטֻי 297

הֻטֻיתֶם 297

הֻטֻלְתִּי 161

הֻטֻמְאָה 178

הֻטֻתג 297

הָיֹו 276

הָיֹה & הָיֹו Tab. XXIII (1)

הֻיֻּלֵד 348

הֻיֻּוֹנָה 283

הֻיֻּוצֵת 284

הֲיֹות 243, 276

הֻיֻחֻבָרֻד 348

הֻיֻטֵב 134

הֻיֻטֵיב 134, 266, Tab. XVIII

הָיִיתָ (Pt. I. § 21, Note) in וה' p. 277

הָיִיתִי 277

הֱיִיתֶם 277

הֵילִיכִי ... ... 135 (ζ)

הֵילֵל 136

הֵילֵל 136, 282

הֵילִילוּ 136, 282

הֵילִילִי 136, 282

PAGE

הֵינִיק 135
הִיָּצֵא (*Kri*) ... 139, 286
הֵיִצְלָח 113
הֵיָּשֵׁר (*Kri*) ... 139, 353
הָיְתָה 226
הֲיִתָם 277
הַךְ 299
הֻכַּבֵּם 178, 318
הֻכָּה 174, 298, 299
הִכָּה 174, 298, 342
הֻכָּה 299
הֻכָּהוּ 298
הֻכָּהוּ 298
הֻכָּהוּ 299
הֻכּוּ 298
הֻכּוּ 299
הַכּוּ 299
הֻכּוּם 298
הֻכּוּם 299
הֻכּוּנִי 298
הֻכּוֹת 174, 298
הֻכּוֹתוֹ 298
הָכִין 349
הֻכֵּינִי 299
הִכִּיתָ 298
הִכִּיתָה 298
הִכִּיתוֹ 298
הִכִּיתִי 298
הֻכֵּיתִי 299
הִכִּיתִיךָ (&ךְ) 298
הֻכֵּיתָם 298
הִכִּיתֶם 298
הִכִּיתָנוּ 298
הִכִּיתָנִי 298
הֻכַּךְ 298
הֲכַלְמָנוּם 351
הֻכַּם 298

PAGE

הֻלְמַפַּת *i.e.* מַכָּה *a stroke* 'i.c.,' with prefixes ה & כ 139
הָכֵן (Infin. Absol. *H*φ. fr. כון) ... 349
הֲכַנּוּ 161
הַפְּנִי (p. נִי—) 298
הֻכְּרַת 85
הָכְּתָה 299
הַכְּתָה 298
הֻכְּתוֹ 298
הֻכְּתִי 298
הֻכְּתִיו 298
הֻכְּתִיךְ 298
הַכְּתָךְ (p. הֻכְּתָךְ) 298
הֻכְּתָם 298
הָלְאִיתִיךְ 352
הָלְאָנִי 352, Tab. XXX (3)
הָלְאָת 211, 352
הִלְבִּישׁ 123
הִלְבִּישָׁה 123
הִלְבִּישִׁי 124
הִלְבַּשׁ 123, 124
הִלְבַּשְׁתָּ 123
הֶלְקָרַת 323
הָלוֹךְ 78, 264
הֲלִילוֹ (*Kri*) 282
הֲלִילִי 282
הָלְכּוּא 82
הִלְכָּתִי 110
הֻלְקַח Tab. XVI (3) (B, *a*)
הַמְאָרָדִים see מא, p. 271
הַמּוּצִיאֶךָ 285
הַמְּוָתָה [Pt. I. § 55 (7, Note*)] 41
הִמְטִיר 239
הָמְלַחַת 355, Tab. XVI (3) (C)
הִמְלִיט 349

	PAGE
הַמְסִיו	172
הַמְעָד	110, 353
הַמְעַט	5, 6
הַפְּעַמְקִים	382
הַמְרֻגָּלִים	85
הַמִּשְׁנָה	78
הַמַּשְׁפִּילִי	84
הַמַּתָּה	161
הַמְּתַהַפֶּכֶת	260
הֵמַתִּי	161
הֵמַתָּם	161, 326
הֵמַתָּן	161, 326
הִנָּבֵא	291
הִנָּבֵאוֹ	291
הִנָּבְאוּ	291, 317
הִנָּבְאוֹ	291
הַנְּבִאִי	291
הִנַּבֵּאתִי	291, 317
הַנֵּרֹף (in כְּתָגְרֹף)	340
הַנֵּם	145
הַנַּח	242, 294
הַנַּחוּ	294
הִנַּחְתָּמְתִּי	317
הַנַּחַת	353
הַנִּיא	293
הַנִּיחַ	242
הִנִּיחַ	145, 242, 294
הֱנִיחָה	294
הַנִּיחָה	145, 294
הֲנִיפוֹתִי	295
הַנִּלְנָה	290
הַנִּמְצָאָה	341
הַנִּמְצָאִים (& צ)	341
הַנִּמְצָאת	341
הֲנִסָּה	300
הֻנַּפְתָ	161, 295, Tab. XX (Note)
הַגְּצֹּ	295
הֻנְּקָה	301
הֻנְּקִי	301
הַנִּרְאָה	264
הֻנְּתוֹ	340, Tab. XIV (Note d)
הַסֹּבֵב	84, 241
הַסְּבִיב	328
הַפִּיתוּף	161
הַסְּכַלַת עֵשׂוֹ	381
הֶעֱבִיר	119, 349, 350
הַעֲבִיר	349
הַעֲבֵר	353
הַעֲבַרְתָּ	119, 351
הֶעֱבַרְתִּי	119
הֶעֱרַתִּי	161
הֶעֱנָה	309
הֶעֱוֵח	309
הֶעֱוּג	309
הֶעֱיֵנוּ	309
הֶעֱנִיתִי	309
הַעֲנֶה	Tab. XXI (Note iii)
הֶעֱל	170, 193
הֶעֱלָה, etc.	192
הַעֲלָה	351
הֶעֱלָה (twice)	192
הֹעֲלָה	193
הַעֲלוֹת	192
הַעֲלִי	192
הֹעֲלָתָה	193
הֶעֱלַם	211
הָעֹמְדִים	85
הֶעֱמַדְתָּה	82
הֶעֱשֹׂוּ	173
הֶעָתִיקוּ	119
הֶפְחַתִּי	110
הַפְלָה	Tab. XXII (Note ‖)
הַפְצַר	350

	PAGE
הַפְקִדוּ	208
הַפְרֵף	Tab. XXI
הִפְרַחְתִּי	Tab. XXIII
הַצֵּג	145
הַצֵּו	301
הִצְטַיַּדְנוּ	150, 315
הִצִּיב	134, 145
הִצִּיג	145
הִצִּיל	349
הִצִּית	145
הִצַּלְנוּ	110
הִצַּלַח	Tab. XVI (3) (B, β)
הִצַּתִּי	145
הַקְדֵּשׁ	78
הָקֵם	151
הֵקִים	151
הֲקִימוֹ	209
הֲקִיצֹתִי	161
הָקַם	151
הֲקֵמֹת	Tab. XX
הֲקֵמֹתִי	Tab. XX
הֻקַם	161
הִקְצוֹת	342, 350
הִקְרִיב	264
הַקְשִׁיבָה	86, 334
הִרְאָה	352
הִרְאֵיתָ	352
הִרְאֵיתִי	352, Tab. XXIII (11)
הִרְאִיתִיךָ	352
הִרְאִיתִים	352
הִרְאִיתָם	352
הִרְאִיתָנוּ	352
הִרְאִיתַנִי	352
הִרְאָךָ	352
הִרְאָנוּ	352
(הַרְאֵנִי p.) הַרְאַנִי	352

	PAGE
הָרַף (fr. רבה,—like חָרֵב p. 190, etc.)	
הַרְבָּה (Infin.)	250
הַרְבּוּ לְפֶשַׁע	382
הָרְבִיעִית	235
הִרְבֵּית	Tab. XXIII
הִרְגִּיז	349
הִרְגִּיעַ	349
הָרָה	78
הוֹרַחֵהוּ	288
הֹרוּ	368
הִרְוֵיתִי	312
הִרְוִיתַנִי	312
הִרְנַנִי	312
הַרְחֵק	353
הָרִימָה	158
הֲרִימוֹת	Tab XX (Note)
הֲרִימוֹתִי	Tab. XX (Note)
הָרֵם (& ס״ם—)	157
הָרְמֵשׁ	232
הָרְמֵשֶׁת	231
הֹרֵנִי	288
הַרְעֹתָם (like הַסֻבֹּתָם, Tab. XXI, with Compensⁿ for Dagesh).	
הרף	170, 190, 193, Tab. XXIII
הָרְפָּא	121
הַרְפֵּה	Tab. XXII (Note t)
הִרְצַת	211, Tab. XXIII
הִרְתִּיךְ	288
הִשְׁאִלְתִּיהוּ	325
הִשָּׁבְעָה	86
הִשַּׁבַּתָּ	122
הֲשַׁבֹּתָם	Tab. XX (Note)
הִשִּׁיאֻךָ	305
הִשִּׁיאֻךָ	305

<table>
<tr><td colspan="2" align="right">PAGE</td><td colspan="2" align="right">PAGE</td></tr>
<tr><td align="right">הִשִּׁיאַנִי</td><td align="right">249, 305</td><td align="right">הִתְאָשֹׁשׁוּ (or א)</td><td align="right">268</td></tr>
<tr><td align="right">הֲשִׁיבֻנוּ</td><td align="right">Tab. XX (Note)</td><td align="right">הִתְבּוֹנֵן</td><td align="right">162</td></tr>
<tr><td align="right">הֲשִׁיבֹתֶם</td><td align="right">Tab. XX (Note)</td><td align="right">הִתְבּוֹנֵנוּ</td><td align="right">162</td></tr>
<tr><td align="right">הַשְּׁבִיעִית</td><td align="right">235</td><td align="right">הִתְנַגֵּל</td><td align="right">190, Tab. XXIII (14)</td></tr>
<tr><td align="right">הִשְׁבַּתִּי</td><td align="right">122</td><td align="right">הִתְנַגְּלָה</td><td align="right">190</td></tr>
<tr><td align="right">הִשְׁבַּתֶּם</td><td align="right">122</td><td align="right">הִתְנַגַּע</td><td align="right">Tab. XVI (3) (B, δ)</td></tr>
<tr><td align="right">הִשְׁחַתִּי</td><td align="right">122</td><td align="right">הִתְנַעֲשׂוּ</td><td align="right">366</td></tr>
<tr><td align="right">הַשְׁכִּים</td><td align="right">350</td><td align="right">הִתְהַלְלוּ</td><td align="right">Tab. XXI (Note iv)</td></tr>
<tr><td align="right">הַשְׁכֵּם</td><td align="right">350</td><td align="right">הִתְהַלַּכְתָּ</td><td align="right">110</td></tr>
<tr><td align="right">הִשְׁלַחְתָּנָה</td><td align="right">82</td><td align="right">הִתְהַלַּכְתִּי</td><td align="right">110</td></tr>
<tr><td align="right">הִשְׁלַךְ</td><td align="right">355</td><td align="right">הִתְוַדַּע</td><td align="right">Tab. XVI (3) (B, δ)</td></tr>
<tr><td align="right">הִשְׁלִכוּ</td><td align="right">350</td><td align="right">הִתְווּ</td><td align="right">314</td></tr>
<tr><td align="right">הָשְׁלְכָה</td><td align="right">355</td><td align="right">הִתְוֵיתָ</td><td align="right">314</td></tr>
<tr><td align="right">הָשְׁמָה</td><td align="right">356</td><td align="right">הֶחְתְּחָיֶנָה</td><td align="right">279</td></tr>
<tr><td align="right">הַשְׁמִידוֹ (הֵ' &)</td><td align="right">350</td><td align="right">הִתְחַל (ל- &)</td><td align="right">170</td></tr>
<tr><td align="right">הִשְׁמִידָךְ</td><td align="right">350</td><td align="right">הִתְחַל</td><td align="right">190</td></tr>
<tr><td align="right">הַשְׁמִידָם</td><td align="right">350</td><td align="right">הִתְחַלְחַל</td><td align="right">175</td></tr>
<tr><td align="right">הַשִּׁשִּׁי</td><td align="right">234</td><td align="right">הִתְחִיוּ</td><td align="right">271</td></tr>
<tr><td align="right">הִשְׁתַּחֲוָה, etc.</td><td align="right">315</td><td align="right">הִתְיַצֵּב</td><td align="right">133</td></tr>
<tr><td align="right">הִשְׁתַּחֲוֶנָה</td><td align="right">Tab. XXIII (Note †)</td><td align="right">חֵתַל</td><td align="right">346</td></tr>
<tr><td align="right">הִשְׁתַּחֲווּ</td><td align="right">(IIθ. Past, or Imper., 2 pl. m.) Tab. XXIII (Notes † and ‖)</td><td align="right">הַחְלָף</td><td align="right">346, 347</td></tr>
<tr><td align="right">הִשְׁתַּחֲווּ</td><td align="right">Tab. XXIII (Note §)</td><td align="right">הִתַּמַּם</td><td align="right">316</td></tr>
<tr><td align="right">הִשְׁתַּחֲוֵיתָ</td><td align="right">(Hθ. Past 2 s. m.) Tab. XXIII (Note †)</td><td align="right">הִתְנַבּוֹת</td><td align="right">291, 317, Tab. XXII (Note c)</td></tr>
<tr><td align="right">הִשְׁתַּחֲוֵיתֶם</td><td align="right">(IIθ. Past 2 pl. m.) Tab. XXIII (Note †)</td><td align="right">הִתְנַבִּיתָ</td><td align="right">291, 317</td></tr>
<tr><td align="right">הִשְׁתַּחֲוֵיתִי</td><td align="right">(Hθ. Past 1 s.) Tab. XXIII (Note †)</td><td align="right">הִתְיַעֲתָם</td><td align="right">Tab. XXIII (12)</td></tr>
<tr><td align="right">הִשְׁתַּעֲשֵׁעוּ</td><td align="right">176</td><td align="right">הִתְעַנַּג</td><td align="right">Tab. XIV (Note h, a)</td></tr>
<tr><td align="right">הִשְׁתַּפֵּךְ</td><td align="right">315</td><td align="right">הִתְפּוֹלֵל forms</td><td align="right">152</td></tr>
<tr><td align="right">הִתְאַנָּה</td><td align="right">267</td><td align="right">הִתְפַּלְפֵּל</td><td align="right">175</td></tr>
<tr><td align="right">הִתְאַוּוּ</td><td align="right">267</td><td align="right">חִתְפַּלְשִׁי</td><td align="right">112</td></tr>
<tr><td align="right">הִתְאַוֵּיתִי</td><td align="right">267</td><td align="right">הִתְפַּקְרוּ</td><td align="right">358</td></tr>
<tr><td align="right">הִתְאַוִּיתֶם</td><td align="right">314</td><td align="right">הָתְפַּקְרַג</td><td align="right">358</td></tr>
<tr><td align="right">הִתְאַוֵּר</td><td align="right">112, Tab. XIV (Note h, a)</td><td align="right">הִתְרוֹעֵעִי</td><td align="right">162</td></tr>
<tr><td align="right"></td><td align="right"></td><td align="right">הִתְשׁוֹטַטְנָה</td><td align="right">162</td></tr>
<tr><td align="right"></td><td align="right"></td><td align="right">הַתְּשִׁיעִית</td><td align="right">235</td></tr>
<tr><td align="right"></td><td align="right"></td><td align="right">הִתְפַּעְפַּע</td><td align="right">176</td></tr>
<tr><td align="right"></td><td align="right"></td><td align="right">הִתְפַּעְפַּע</td><td align="right">176</td></tr>
</table>

ו

	PAGE
ו before Past Tense,	100
ו CONJUNCTIVE, before a Future Tense ...	101
ו CONVERSIVE, before a Future Tense ...	101
ו ordinary prefix,	1 & 2
וֹ prefix ...	179, 223–225
וָאֲבָרְכָה ...	261
וָאֲבָרֶכְךָ ...	261
וָאֲבָרְכֶךָ ...	260
וָאַגִּדְלָה ...	261
וַאדֹנָי ...	2
וָאֹהַב ...	130**
וָאוֹרֵד ...	289
וָאֶחְבָּא ...	248
וָאַחַר ...	128
וָאָט (see אָט ...174, 297)	
וְאָיַבְתִּי ...	150
וָאִירָא ...	248
וָאִישָׁנָה ...	135
וָאַךְ ...	299
וָאַכֶּה ...	299
וְאָכַל ...	259
וָאֹכַל ...	249
וְאָכַלְתְּ [comp. § 160] ...	252
וֵאלֹהִים ...	2
וְאִם ...	179
וָאֹמְרָ ...	265
וָאָנֻ ...	270
וָאֱנוֹשָׁה ...	295
וְאֶחֱרַם ...	334
וָאַעֲנֶה ...	345
וָאָעַד ...	157
וָאָעִיד ...	157
וָאֶעֱשִׁיר ...	355

	PAGE
וָאֶעְשֹׂף ...	261
וָאֶפְקֹד ...	101
וַאֲקוּת ...	312
וָאֲקַנֶּה ...	312
וָאָקוּם ...	150, 157
וָאֶקַּח ...	266
וָאָקִים ...	157
וָאֲקַיְּמָה ...	150
וָאָקָם ...	150
וָאֶקְרָאֶה ...	335
וָאֵרָא ...	191
וָאֶרְאֶה ...	171
וָאָרוּהָ ...	270
וָאָרֶץ ...	179
וָאֵשֵׁב ...	137
וָאָשִׂים ...	157
וָאֶשְׁלַךְ ...	105
וָאֶשְׁמְעָה ...	334
וָאֶשְׁקוּלָה ...	334
וּבָאת ...	272
וּבָחוּר ...	78
וּבְצֶעַם ...	378
וּבְקָצְרְכֶם ...	81
וּבְשַׁחֲטָם ...	81
וּבָשֵׁל ...	319
וְגָנַב ...	78
וַדְּבֵק ...	244
ודיגום ...	154
וְהַאֲזִנִיחוּ ...	351
וְהֹגֹ ...	368
וְהִגְלָם ...	352
וְהוֹצֵאת ...	285
וְהוֹקַעֲנוּם ...	373
וְהַזֹּארֵה (see וו', 163) ...	335
וְהֶחֱזַקְתִּי ...	120
וְהֹרַתָּם ...	368

	PAGE
וְהַחֲרַמְתֶּם	119
וְהִטֳּהָרוּ	112
וְהָיָה	241, 265
וֶהָיָה	171, 261, 267
וְהָיִי	229, 243
וְהָיוּ	171, 277
וִהְיִיתֶם	171, 246, 277
וַהֲמִיתִיו	326
וְהָמַכּוּ	356
וַהֲמִתִּיהָ	326
וְהַעֲבַרְתִּי	119
וְהַעֲלִיתָ (or ל)	192
וְהַעֲלָתָה	192
וַהֲמֵאתוֹ	311
וְהִקְדַּשְׁנֻ	110
וְהִרְאֵיתִי	352
וְהָרְגוּ	265
וַהֲרִנִּיז	349
וְהִרְצָת	211
(וְהָשַׁמּוּ &)	356
וְהִשְׁקָה	240
וְהִתְגּוֹדַלְתִּי	326
וְהִתְגָּעֲשׁוּ	366
וְהִתְהֹלְלוּ	366
וְהִתְקַדִּשְׁתִּי	110
וְהִתְקֻדְּשָׁתֶּם	326
וְחַי	225, 259, 278
וָחָי	278
וְחָיָה	278
וֶחָיָה	171
וְהָיוּ	171, 279
וְחָיִיתֶם	171, 278
וְחָיִתָה	265
וְחָיְתָה	278
וְחָתוֹם	78
וּטְבֹחַ טֶבַח	372
וְטָאטֵאתִיהָ	280
וַיֹּאחֶז	129
וַיֹּאכַל	247
וַיֵּאֶל	269
וַיֹּאמֶר	129, 226
וַיַּאֲצֶל	130**
וַיָּאֶר	268
וַיֵּאת	271
וַיַּאֲתִיוּן	271
וַיַּאֲתָגֵנִי	271
וַיָּבֹא	272
וַיָּבֹא	242
וַיָּבֹאוּ	263
ויבאו (Kthiv)	272
וִיבָאֵנִי	273
וַיַּבְדֵּל	226
ויבו (Kthiv)	272
וַיָּבוֹא	272
וַיְבִיאָהּ	244
וַיִּבֶן	244, 263
וַיְבָרֶךְ	231
וַיִּגַּל	222
וַיַּגַּל	222
וַיֶּגַּל	222
וַיִּגְרֶשׁ	259
וַיִּדָּבְקוּ	355
וַיְדַבֵּר	101
וַיְדַבְּרוּ	101
וַיֵּדוּ	133, 281
וַיֵּדַע	138
וַיֵּדַע	138
וַיֵּדְעוּ	248
וַיִּזָּר	144
וַיִּדְרְכוּ	355
וַיָּהֲבְלוּ	113
וַיְהִי	227

	PAGE
וַיְהִי	222, 226, 277
וַיְהִי	277
וַיִּהְיוּ	244, 277
וַיְהַלְלוּ	265
וְיוֹכַח	138
וַיּוּכַח	138
וַיֵּלֶךְ	137
וַיּוֹצֵא	286
וַיּוּר	289
וַיֵּשֶׁב	137, Tab. XVIII
וַיּוֹשֶׁב (once)	137 (Note *)
וַיּוֹשַׁע	138
וַיֵּזֶן	296
וַיָּזֶן	296
וַיֶּזֶן	296
וַיִּזְבַּח	370
(וַיְחִי &) וִיחִי	279
(וַיְחִי &) וִיחִי	279
וַיְחַיֶּה	280
וִיחַיְּחוּ	280
וַיִּחְיוּ	279
וַיָּחֶל	192
יָחֶן) וַיִּחַן	192)
וְיֵט	174
וַיֵּט	264
וַיֵּט	174
וַיִּטֲהֲרוּ	316
וַיִּטַּע	240
וַיָּחֶל	139
וַיֵּיטֶב	135
וַיֵּיטֶב	136
וַיִּיֶן	139
וַיִּיף	174, 283
וַיִּיצֶר	135, 240
וַיִּיקַץ	135
וַיִּיקֶץ	135

	PAGE
וַיַּךְ	299
וַיַּךְ	299
וַיַּכֶּה	299
וַיַּכּוּ	299
וַיְכַל	236
וַיְכַלּוּ	236
וַיִּכְתּוּ	355
וַיִּכְתּוֹם	355
וַיַּלְבִּישֵׁם	252
וַיְיֶלֶד	78
וַיֵּלֶךְ	262
וַיֵּלֶךְ	137
מֶּלֶךְ	137
וַיֵּלֶךְ	137
וַיֵּלֶד	137
וַיִּלְמַד	101
וַיָּלֶן	154
וַיִּמְרֹד	365
וַיָּמָת	156
וַיִּגַּע	266
וַיַּנְחֵהוּ	241
וַיַּנִּחֵהוּ see 'נ	294
וַיַּנַּח	157
וַיַּנִּיחֵהוּ see 'נ	294
וַיִּנָּסֵם	300
וַיִּגַּע	158
וַיָּסָב	Tab. XXI (Note *)
וַיִּסְגֹּר	244
וַיִּסַּע	264
וַיֵּסֶף	130**
וַיִּסְפוּ	381
וַיִּסָּר	158
וַיַּעֲבֹר	263
וַיַּעֲשֶׂה	283
וַיִּעַף	156

	PAGE
וַיָּעַף	156
וַיַּעַצְרֻהוּ	118
וַיַּעַשׂ	222, 227
וַיַּעֲשׂוּ	248
וַיַּעְתַּק	119, 264
וַיִּפַּח	240
וַיִּפֹּל	243
וַיִּפְקֹד	105, 222
וַיִּפְשַׁט	104
וַיֵּצֵא	285
וַיֵּצֵא	286
וַיֵּצֵא	286
וַיֵּצְאוּ	262
וַיְצַו	242, 266
וַיָּצֻם	156
וַיַּצְמִירוּ	150, 315
וַיָּצַם	156
וַיַּצְמַח	240
וַיֵּצֶר	135, 248
וַיַּצֶּת	145
וַיִּקְאֻנּוּ	311
וַיִּקֻדֹּשׁ	236
וַיִּקְו	312
וַיִּקַּח	241
וַיָּקָם	156
וַיָּקֶם	157
וַיָּקָם	156, 157
וַיָּקֶם	157
וַיִּקַץ	135
וַיִּקֶץ	135
וַיִּקְרָא	227
וַיַּרְא	171, 191, 226
וַיֵּרָא	171, 263
וַיִּרְאֶה	191
וַיַּרְאֶה	191
וַיִּרְאוּ	265
וַיִּרְאַנִי	379
וַיִּרֶב	130**
וַיֵּרֶד	264
וַיִּרְדּוּ	232
וַיָּרֶץ	156
וַיָּרָץ	156
וִירִשׁוּהָ	209
וִירֵשׁוּךְ	209
וִירִשְׁתָּהּ	209, 324
וִירִשְׁתֶּם	209, 324
וִירִשְׁתָּם	209, 324
וַיֵּשֶׁב	136
וַיֵּשֶׁב	137
וַיֵּשֶׁב	156, 382
וַיֵּשֶׁב	157
וַיִּשָּׁבַע	Tab. XVI (3) (B, β)
וַיִּשָּׁבְךָ	110
וַיִּשְׁבֹּת	236
וַיִּשְׁבֵּם	101
וַיִּשְׁכֹּן	260
וַיִּשְׁלַח	104
וַיְשַׁלְּחוּ	266
וַיְשַׁלְּחֻהוּ	259
וַיַּשְׁלִיכֵם	212
וַיָּשֶׂם	157, 240
וַיֹּשַׁע	138
וַיִּשַׁע	138
וַיַּשְׁעֵכֶם	374
וַיִּשְׁפֹּט	78
וַיִּשְׁפֹּךְ	101
וישתחו (Kthiv.)	191
וַיִּשְׁתַּחֲווּ	191
וַיִּשְׁתַּחֲוֶן (for וּ)	191
וַיֵּתֵא	271
וַיֵּתְוּ	313
וַיִּתְחַבֵּא	248

	PAGE
וַיִּתֵּן	230
וְכִבֵּס	343
וְכִבְשֻׁהָ	233
וּכְחִכִּי	343
וְכִלֹּתוּ	211, Tab. XXX (5)
וְכִפֶּר	343
נֵלֵךְ	266
וְלָנָה	160, 335
וְלָנוּ	160
וְלִנְפֹּל	79
וְלָקַחַת	374
(וְלָקַחְתָּ &) see	371
וּמִפְלָא	382
וּמִפַלְטִי	346
וּמְקַלֵּל	262
וּמִשְׁמַרֹו	80
וְנֹאחֲזוּ	129
וַנְהִי	277
וְנֹטֵיהֶם see	297
וְנֵחַף	211, 296
וַנִּירָם	288
comp. Tab. XXX (7)	
וְנֵךְ	299
וְנִכְחַת	374
וְנִכַּפֵּר	178, comp. 318
וַנָּסָב	Tab. XXI (Note*)
וְנָשֵׁב & וַנֵּשֶׁב	136 & 137
וְנָשׁוּב, וַנֵּשֶׁב	156
וַנֵּשֶׁב	157
וְנִשְׁלוֹחַ	338
וְנָחוֹן	78
וּסְעָרָה	331, 332
וְעָשֹׁת	172
וּפָרַת	319
וּפְשַׁתֶּם	159, 324
	PAGE
וְצֶעֱקִי	331, 332
וְקַמְתָּ	378
וְקָרָאת	Tab. XXII (Note*)
וְרֻחַמְתִּים	382
וְשָׁבָה	378
וְשָׁרֵשְׁךָ	366
וַתְּאַלְצֵהוּ	346
וַתֹּאמֶר	129, 245
וַתֹּאנָה	155
(Kthiv) וַתָּבֵאת, ותבאתי	273
(תֻּבַּד) .. וַתֻּבַּד	292
וַתְּדַר	144
וַתְּהִי	222, 277
וַתַּחַר	192
וַתּוּשָׁב	137
וַתֵּחַז	130**
וַתְּחִי & וּתְחִי	279
וַתְּחַלְּנָה	345
וַתַּחְמֹרָה	Tab. XXVIII (ε)
וַתֵּיטֶב	135
וַתִּמְטָב	136
וַתִּינָק	136
וַתְּחִיפִי	283
וַתַּךְ	299
וַתֻּכֶּה	192
וַתָּלָה	192
וַתָּמָג	156
וַתִּנִיקֻהוּ	295
וַתָּסָב	Tab. XXI (Note*)
וַתַּעֲשׂ	171
וַתֻּפַּחוּ	270
וַתִּקְרָא	311
וַתִּקַּח	247
וַתִּקַּח	265
וַתָּקָם & וַתָּקֻם	156 & 157

	PAGE
וַתֵּרֶא	191, 246
וַתִּרְאֶה	228
וַתֵּרָאנָה	155
וַתִּרְאֵנִי	379
וַתֵּשֶׁב	136, 139
וְתָשֹׁבְנָה	155
וַתַּשְׁק	171
וַתִּתְחַלְחַל	175
וַתִּתֵּן	247
וַתֵּתַע (for וַתִּתְעֶה)	171, 222 Tab. XXIII (5)
וַתִּתְצַּב	133

ז

זֹאת	28, 58
זֶבַח	Tab. XVI (3) (B, γ)
זֶה	28, 58
זַיִת (pl. of זֵיתִים & זֵיתֵיהֶם fr. כֶּם)	Tab. XIII (Note ‡, β)
זְעֵמָה	86
זַעְפוֹ	322
זִמְרָה	342
זֵן w. Affs.	App. (A) to Tab. IX

ח

חֲגֹרַת	320, 321
חָדַל & חָדֵל	326
חָדְלוּ	111
חוֹסִי	193
חַי & חֵי	173, 278, 279
חָיָה f. (in וְחָיָה) & חַי m.,	278
חָיָה	173, 279
חָיָה	279

	PAGE
חָיוֹ	278
חָיוֹ	278
חָיִוּ	279
חָיוּ	279
חָיוֹת	278
חָיוֹת & חַיּוֹת	173, 279
חַיֵּי	279
חָיִיהֻ	279
חַיִּים	173, 279
חָיִיתָ	278
חֱיִיתֶם	278
חִיִּיתָם	279
חִיִּיתֻנִי	279
מַיְלִים	Tab. XIII (Note ‡, a)
חַיַּי	279
חִיִּתַנִי	279
חָיְתָה	278
חָיְתוּ	231, 232
חֻבֵּי (in וְכְחֻבֵּי)	343
חַל	190
חֳלִי (p. חֳלִיוֹ), etc.	40
חָלָץ	342
חָלַק w. Affs.	Tab. X
חֲמוֹתָה	Tab. XIII (Note †, β)
חֲמַרְמָרוּ	176
חָסָיָה	172, Tab. XXIII
חָסִיּוּ	172
חָסַר & חָסֵר	327
חָפְצָה	Tab. XIV (Note †, a)
חֲפֵצִי	327
חָצוֹת	66 (Note ¶)
חֲצִי (& חֵצִי)	40, 66
חצִיוֹ	66
חָצֵר w. Affs.	Appˣ (A) to Tab. IX

	PAGE
חֲצֵרֹת etc App* (A) to Tab. IX	
חֳרָבוֹת, חָרְבָּה, etc.	41
הָרבג (ד, ס)	86
חַרְבִּי	118, 331
חֳרָשִׁים, etc.	Tab. IX (Note)
חָשַׁבְתָּה	82
חֲשִׁים	163
חֶשְׂפִּי	86, 118
חַתִּים	Tab. XXI (Note 2)

ט

	PAGE
טָאטֵאתִי	280
טָוּ	280
טָח for טָח	162
טֻמְאַת, טָמֵא, טָמֵא	328
טֶרֶם with Fut. & Past	238, 239

י

	PAGE
יֹאבַד (ד &)	128
יֹאבֶה	267
יֶאֱהָבֵנִי	Tab. XXVIII (β)
יֶאְוֶה	267
יָאוֹר	268
יֵאוֹת	269
יֹאחֵז	128
יָאִירוּ, יָאִיר	268
יֹאכַל, יֹאכֵל	Tab. XVII.
יֶאֱתֶה	270
יֵאָנַח	Tab. XVI (3) (B, β)
יֵאָסְפוּן	112
יֶאְסֹר	130**
יֵאָפֶז	270
יָאָר	268
יַאַרְגוּ	Cp. Tab. XVII [Paradigm, Note (†)]

	PAGE
יַאַרְכוּ	130**
יַאְשְׁמוּ	130**
יָאָתָה	280
יָאָתָיוּ, יֵאָתָת	271
יָבֹאוּ	272
יְבִאָנוּ, ...נִי &	273
יְבִאָנִי	273
יָבוֹא	see 272
יִיבַשׁ for יְבוֹשׁ	161
יְבֵן	192, Tab. XXIII
יַבְטַח	Tab. XVI (3) (B, β)
יִבֶךְ	190, Tab. XXIII (4)
יִבְכָּיוֹן	Tab. XXIII (8)
יָבֵשׁ	135
יִיבְשׁוּ or יָבְשׁוּ	134
יָבְשֶׁת	322
יְפַּח	292
יַגִּיחַ	292
יָגִיל	155
יָגֵל, יָגֶל, יָגַל	170, 190 (cp. 222)
יַגַּשׁ	143, 144
יַדְבְּקוּ	see 355
יְדֹרוֹן & יַדֵּד	292
יָדוּ & יָדוּ	281
יָדִין & יָדוֹן	155
יְדַכֶּם	46
יֵדַע (ד &)	137
יְדַעַת	138
יָדַעְתָּ	Tab. XVI (3) (C)
יְדֹר	144
יַדְרְכוּ	see 355
יְדַשְּׁנָה	335
יֶהְגֶּה	191
יֶהְדֹּף	116
יֶהְדְּפֵם & ...נִי	334

	PAGE
יְהוּא	276
יְהוּדָה	282, 354
יְהוֹדוּד	138, 282, 354
יְהוֹסֵף	138
יְהוֹשֻׁעַ	138, 354
יְהִי	170, 222, 226, 277 Tab. XXIII (3)
יְחִי	170, 277
יְהֵילִילוּ	138, 282, 354
יַהֲמֶה	191
יַהֲסִיּוֹן	172, Tab. XXIII (8)
יַחַרְגְּהוּ	208
יָהַתַּל	346
לוֹ_ & יָהַתֲלוּ	346, 354
יוּאָר	271
יוֹדַעְתִּי	366
יוֹלֵדָה	330
יוֹלֵךְ	Tab. XVIII
יוֹסֵב	356
יוֹסֵף	328
יוֹסֵף	137
יוֹצִיאוּם	286
יוֹקְשִׁים	348
יוֹרָא	288 (Note)
יוֹרֵהוּ	289
יוֹרוּךָ, יוֹרוּ	289
נוּ_ & יוֹרֵנוּ	289
יוֹשֵׁד	356
יוֹשִׁיב	134
יֻזֶּה (יֻו, יֻו,) & יֻזֶּה (יֻו)	296
יַחְבְּרוּךְ	see 348
יַחֵךְ	170, 192
יַחְדְּלוּ	116
יַחֹם & יָחֹם	153
יֶחֱנָרוּ	150 (Note)
יֶחֱזֶה	191

	PAGE
יְחִי & יְחִי	171, 279
יִחְיֶה	279
יְחַיֻּהוּ	280
יִהְיוּ	279
יְחִיּ	265, 280
יְחַיֵּנוּ, יְחַיֵּנִי, יְחַיֶּה	280
יְחִישָׁה	88
יֶחֱמַתְנִי	344
יַחַן & יַחֲנֶה	191 & 192
יִחַץ	192
יַחַר & יִחַר	170 (cp. 192)
יֶחֶרְדוּ	117
יֶחֶרְדוּ	118
יֶחֱשֹׁף	116 (Note ‡)
יֵחַת	144
יֵט (יֵיט׳), יֵט	174, 297
יִיטַב	134
יָפֶה, יִפֶּה	174, 297
יַפֵּחֻהוּ	297
יָפוּ	297
יְפֹור	144
יַפְגִּנוּ, יַפְגֶּךָ	297
יְפוֹשׁ	144
שׁ_ & יִיבַשׁ	135
יִיבְשׁוּ	135
יֵיָדַע	137 (Note ‖)
יֵיטַב	135, 265
יֵיטְב	Tab. XVIII
יֵיטִיב	134, Tab. XVIII
יֵיטִיב	135 (Note ‡, ii)
יֵילִילוּ, יֵילִיל	136, 282
יֵינִיק	135
יִיף (נָיִיף)	174
יִיפְּחוּ	284
יִירְאָנִי	287
יֵירְאָנִי	288

	PAGE
יָרֵחַ	288
יַךְ, יַכָּה	174, 299
יַכֵּהוּ, יַכְּחוּ, יַכָּה	299
יָכֹו, יָכוּ & יַכֹו	299
יַכֻּם, יַפֻּךְ, יַכֹּותָ	299
יְכֹונֵנוּ	317
יָכְכָה, יַכְכָה	299
יָכֹל, etc.	84
יְכַלֶּה	Tab. XXII (Note v)
יָכַלּוּ	Tab. XIV (Note †, β)
יְכַלְכֵּל	175
יְכַלֵּת	322
יְכָלְתָיו	210
יְכָלְתֻם (& תָּן—)	325
יָכְנוּ, יַכֶם	299
יְכַסְיְמוּ	Tab. XXX (8)
יְכַרְסְמֶנָּה	177
יֶכָּת	356, Tab. XXI (Note ¶)
יֶכָּתוּ (& תוּ—)	357
יַכַתֻּם	see 355
יִלְבָּשׁוּ	see 111
יַלְבִּשֵׁם (שְׁנוּ—, & שְׁנִי—)	208 & 209
יְלִדְתִּיהוּ (—תִּי, —תָנוּ , —תִיךְ)	
	Tab. XXV (β)
יִלָּוֶה (& וּ—)	290
יַלְוּךְ	290
יַלְוֻנוּ	290
יָלִיזוּ	161
יָלִין	154
יִלְכְּדֻנוּ	Tab. XXVIII (γ)
יַלְקְטוּן	112
יְמוּתוּן	160
יַמַּח	192, Tab. XXIII
יִמָּלֵה	Tab. XXII (Note u)
יִמְשָׁל	250
יָמֻתוּן	160
יָנָאֵץ	151, 295
יַנְדְּהוּ	292
יַנְהוּ	293
יִגְוֶה	293
יָנֹון	295
יַנַּח	145
יַנְחֵהוּ & הוּ—	294
יַנְחוּנִי	296
יַנְחֵם	296
יַנַחֵם	294
יְנַחֲנוּ (& נִי—)	296
יְנִיאוּ, יְנִיא & יְנִי	293
יָנִים	145, 241
יַנִּיחֵהוּ, וּם—, ־ם	294
יָנִין	295
יָנֵסוּ	300
יָנַע	see 157 (Note §)
יַנְקֵף	295
יָנַעוּ	301
יָנֵשׁוּ	Tab. XXII (Note i)
יַנְשׂוּא	304
יָסַךְ	356
יָסְעוּ	143
יַעַבְרֶנָּהוּ & נְהוּ—	Tab. XXVIII (δ & γ)
יְעֻנַּת	150 (Note)
יְעֹור	160
יָעַל, יַעַל	171, 192, 193
יַעֲלֶה	171, 191, 192
יְעַרְעַר	176
יָעַץ	113
יַעֲצֹר (twice)	116
יַעֲרֹב	116
יַעַרְבוּ	117
יַעֲשֶׂה	171
יַעֲשַׁן (twice)	116

PAGE

יַעְשֹׁר 120

יַעְשְׂרַנּוּ 355

יְפִיפִיתָ 176, 284

יִפְקֹד 114

יִפְקְדוּ ... ... see 111

יִפָּקְדוּ ... ... see 111

יִפְקָדְךָ, —ךָ, —כֶם ... 210

יִפְקְדֶךָ 210

יִפָּק׳ & יִפָּקְדֵנוּ ... 208, 210

יַפְקִידֵנוּ 208

יִפְשְׁטוּ ... ... 104 (Note ¶)

יַפְתְּ 50

יַפְתְּ (fr. יַפְתֶּה) ... 171, 191

יְצָאֻהוּ, יצא 286

יְצָאִי 284

יְצָאֻ 286

יְצָאָנִי 284

יַצֵּב, יַצֶּב 145

יָצֵג, יַצֵּג, יַצֶּג 145

יְצַוֶּה, יְצַוֶּה, יְצַו 310

יְצַוּוּ, יְצַוֻהוּ 310

יְצַנְּחוּ ... ... 150 (Note)

יְצַוֵּנוּ, —ֵם, יְצַוְּךָ ... 310

יְצִיאֻהוּ 286

יַצִּית, יַצִּיעַ, יַצִּיג, יַצִּיב ... 145

יַצְלִחַ ... ... see 113

יַצְלִחַ see Tab. XVI (3) [B, β]

יַצַּע 145

יַצִּתּוּ, יַצֶּת 145

יָצָתִי 284

יְקַוֶּו, יְקַוּוּ, יְקַנֶּה, יְקַו 312

יִקַּח (& חַ—) Tab. XIX (Note γ, vi)

יִקָּחָהּ (& הוּ) Tab. XXVIII (β)

יִקָּחֻהוּ, etc Tab. XIX (Note A)

יַקְטִירוֹן 88

PAGE

יָקִיא 311

יְקִימוֹן 160

יִקַּל ...Tab. XXI (Note 3)

יָקָם 157

יָקֻמוּ 150

יִקְרָאֻ K. Fut 3 pl. m.
Pause-form, fr. קרא 238

יִקְרָאֻנְנִי ... Tab. XXVIII (γ)

יְרֵא ... 191, Tab. XXIII

יִרְאָ ... 171, Tab. XXIII

יְרָא 185

יִרְאָה, יְרֵא, יְרָא 328

יַר׳, יַרְ׳, יִרְאָה 171

יִרְאֻ ... ... Tab. XXII

יראֻ 289

יְרָאוֹהֻ, —ֻי, —ךְ 287

—ֶ׳יךְ & יְרָאָיו, יִלְאִי ... 287

יִרָאָךְ 287

יְרֵאתִי, יָרֵאתָ 287 (cp. 185,
Obs. XXV. N.B.

יְרֵאת 287

יְרָאתָם & יְרֵאתָם 287

יָרֵב 157

יָרֵב 231

יְרַבְּצֻן 112

יַרְד ... ... Tab. XXIII

יַרְדֹּף 177

יֶרַח, —ִים & יָרַח, יָרֵחַ ... 288

ירוד, יָרְהֻ, ירוּ 289

יְרַמֵּחַ ... ... 150 (Note)

יְרִוְיֻן 312, Tab. XXIII (8)

יְרַוְוּד 312

יָרוֹן ...Tab. XXI (Note 3)

יָרֵחַ ... ... 157 (Note §)

יָרֵם 155

יֹרֵנִי, יָרֵם 289

PAGE

וְרִפּוּ Tab. XXII (Note *j*)

ד— & יְרְשׁוּךְ Tab. XXV (*a*)

יְרְשִׁיעַ 89

יְרִשְׁתֶּם 159

יֵשׁ (יֵשׁ־) w. Affs. Tab. XIII (Note §, δ)

יִשָּׂא, יִשָּׂאוּךְ 305

יִשָּׂא (ָם־ , דְ־ , הוּ־ , ךָ־) 303

יִשָּׂאוּ (אָהוּ־, אֹם־ & אָם־) 303

יִשָּׂאוּנְךָ 303

יִשָּׂאֶנָה (ני־ , נִי־) ... 303

יֵשֵׁב (twice) 137

יָשֵׁב 151, 155

יָשֵׁב 157

יֵשֵׁךְ ... ...170, 190, 192, Tab. XXIII (3)

יֵשַׁח (twice) 306

יֵשׁוּעַ , יֵשׁוּעַ 313

יְשׁוּעָתָה 353

יִשִּׂיא (twice), יַשִּׂיא ... 305

יָשִׂים 155, 156, 157

יִשָּׁכְבוּ 238

יִשְׁכְּבֻן 89

יִשַּׁל 171, 192

יִשְׁלַח Tab. XVI (3) (B, β)

יִשְׁלָחֵהוּ (חַזְּ— , חֵנוּ— , חֵנִי—) Tab. XXVIII (β)

יִשְׁלָיוּ ... 172, Tab. XXIII

יָשֵׂם , יַשֵׂם 154, 155

יַשְׁמִיעֵנוּ 212

יֵשַׁע 170, 192

יְשַׁעֲשֵׁעוּ ... ... 176 (Note †)

יִשְׁפּוּטוּ 85, 336

יַשְׁק 191, Tab. XXIII (13)

יְשָׁרֵשׁוּ ... ... 366 (Note)

יְשָׁרְתוּנְךָ ... Tab. XXVIII (γ)

PAGE

יְשָׁרַתִּי 110

יְשֵׁשׁוּם 154

יִשְׁתַּחוּ (חוּ— &) ... 191, 315 Tab. XXIII (¶)

יִשְׁתַּחֲוֶה 315, Tab. XXIII (¶)

יִשְׁתַּחֲווּ ...Tab. XXIII (Note)

יִתְאָו 267, Tab. XXIII (15)

יִתְאַוֶּה (אוּ— &) 267

יִתְאוֹנֵן 268

יִתְבֹשָׁשׁוּ 245

יִתְגַּל ... ...170, 191, Tab. XXIII (15)

יִתְגַּלָּע Tab. XVI (3) (B, ii)

יִתְגָּעֲשׁוּ 367

יִתְהַלָּךְ (דְ— , כוֹ—) ... 358

יִתְוּ 313

יִתְוַכָּח ... ... 133 (‡, *b*), Tab. XVI (3) (B, ii)

יִמֵּן ,etc. Tab. XIX (Note B)

יִתְנַבֵּא (או— &) 317

יִתְנַגַּח Tab. XVI (3) (B, δ)

יִתְנֶחָם 112, 317

יִתְעֹרָר 162

יִתְפַּקֵּד (דוּ— &) 358

יִתְקַדְּשׁוּ 112

כ

כ the prefix... ... ... 2, 3

כ w. Affs. Tab. II (& Notes)

כַּאֲבֹל 327

כְּבָרִי , כָּבֵד , כָּבֵד... ... 327

כָּבוֹא 272

כְּבַלַּע Tab. XVI (3) (B, *a*)

כִּנְבַה 123

	PAGE
כִּדְבָרְכֶם	80
כַּיּוֹם, כְּהָחִלּוֹת, בְּהֶחָכָם ..	6
כְּהִגָּנַע Tab. XVI (3) (B, a)	
כְּהֵן	343
כְּהִנָּדֹף	340
כְּהָחֵל	346, 347
כִּזְכֹּר	123
כְּלֹאתִי Tab. XXII (Note n)	
כָּלוּ Tab. XXII (Note h)	
כָּלוּ	347
כְּלִי, כְּלִי	40
כָּלְכַּל (—לָךְ, —לָךְ ,(—), כִּלְכֵּל, כַּלְכֵּל	
כָּלְכְּלוּ &	175
כְּלָנוּ ... Tab. XXX (2)	
כְּמוֹת	151
כִּמְלֹאת Tab. XXII (Note a)	
כִּנְטוֹתוֹ	297
כַּנְלֹתֶךָ	300
כִּנְפֹל	123, 144
כָּסֹג	173, 347
כִּפְנֹשׁ	123
כִּקְרֹחַ	123
כְּקָרְבְכֶם ... Tab. XV (Note ‡)	
כְּרֶם	150
כָּרֵת	347
כָּרַתִּי, כָּרַת	122
כְּשַׁבֵּב	123
כְּשַׁבֵּת	133
כְּשָׁמְעָם	80
כִּתֵּר	345

ל

ל the prefix	2, 3
ל w. Affs. Tab. II (& Notes)	
ל for '3d Rt-letter' ...	69

	PAGE
לֹא ordinary negative	93
לֹא PRECEDES	93
לֹא Prohibitive	93, 103
לֶאֱהֹב (& לַאֲהֹב) ...	130*
לְאַהֲבָה	80, 322
לָאוֹר	160, 268
לְאָכְלָה	233
לֵאסֹר & לֵאמֹר ...	130*
לָבוֹא, לָבוֹא	272
לָבִיא (for לְהָבִיא) ...	273
לִבְרָם	323
לָנוֹעַ	150 (Note)
לָגֶשֶׁת	Tab. XIX
לָגַעַת ...Tab. XIX (Note a)	
לִרְעֶה	Tab. XVIII
לָרַעַת	133 (§), 259
לִדְרִיוֹשׁ	322
לְהָאִיר	268
לְהַאֲלֹתוֹ	269
לְהָבִיא	273
לַחֲגֹרִים, לַחֲגוֹר	6
לְהוֹנֹתָם	283
לְהוֹצִאָהוּ	285
לְהוֹרֹתָם	288
לְהַחוֹפָה	6
לָהֶם	343 (†)
לִהְיוֹת	276
לְהַכּוֹת	298
לְהָבִיל	130**
לְהָנִיחַ	145
לַהֲנָפָה, לְהָנִיף	295
לְהִסָּתֵר	114
לְהָעָם	6
לְהָפִיר	349
לְהַצִּיב	145
לְהָקִיטוֹ ... Tab. XXIV (δ, 4)	

PAGE

לְהֵרָאֹה ... Tab. XXIII (10)

לְהִתְגֹּלֵל 365

לְחִי (& לֶחָיו, לְחָי) ... 40

לִחְיֹות 278

לִחְיֹות (—ֹו, —ֶם, נוּ—)... 279

לַחֲלֹק ... ... 349 (Note *)

לְחָמְלָה 80

לַחְמָם 116

לַחֲנֹנְכֶם & לַחֲנֹנֵנוּ Tab. XXIV (a)

לַחְתֹּם, לַחְשֹׁב, לַחְקֹר, לַחְצֹב ... 116

לָטַעַת 143

לִידֹות 281

לִיסֹוד & לִיסֹוד 342

לִיסְרָה 342

לִיקֲהַת ... ... 342(‡)

לְיִרְאָה 80, 286

לְיִרְאָם (& —גִי) 288

לֵירֹות, לֵירֹוא 288

לֵךְ & לֶךְ 133

לֵךְ Tab. II (2) & Note (6)

לְכָה 133, Tab. II (Note 6)

לְכָה 133, 136

לְכִי & לְכִי, לְכוּ & לְכוּ ... 136(†)

לְכִי ... Tab. II (Note 7)

לְכַלֵּא, לְכַלֵּה 343

לְכָתּוֹ ... ... 133 (Note ‖)

לָלֶכֶת 263

לְמַיִם 225

לְמִלֹּאֹות [Cp. Pt I, § 58 (Note*)]
Tab. XXII (Note b)

לְמַלֹּאת ...Tab. XXII (Note b)

לְמָלְכוֹ 80

לְמִשְׁפָּטַי 176, 366

לָנוּ Tab. II (2) & Note (§)

לָנוּ 160

לָנִים ... ... 152 (Note)

PAGE

לַנְחֹתָם 296

לְנַסֹּות 300

לִנְפֹּל 123, 144

לִנְפֹּל 79

לִנְתֹשׁ & לִנְתֹץ 123

לְסַבּוֹ ... Tab. XXIV (δ, 5)

לְסַעֲדֹו (—ֶך, & עָרְכָם) Tab.
XXIV (a)

לִסְתֹּר [Cp. 79 (Note †), 382]

לְעֻגֹּת 150

לְעָזְבֹך ... Tab. XXIV (δ)

לְעַנֹּות 340

לַעֲשֹׂות 236, 381 (twice), 382

לַעְשֵׂר 79, 120, 349

לְפָעֳלָם 322

לִצְבֹּא & לַצָּבָא 123

לְקֹנִי 311

לֹקֵחַ ... ...Tab. XIX (A)

לָקַחָה 244, Tab. XIX (Note γ, v)

לְקָחִי Tab. XIX (Note A, 3)

לָקַחַת ... ...Tab. XIX (A)

לְקַחְתְּ ... Tab. XVI (3) (C)

לְקַחְתּוֹ ... Tab. XXIV (δ, 3)

לָקֵם ... ... 150 (Note)

לְקָרְבָה 80

לִרֹא 286

לִרְאֹות 340

לְרַאֹתְכֶם ... ... 349 (Note)

לְרָחְצָה 322

לְרָחְקָה 321

לְרִשְׁתֹּו ... Tab. XXIV (δ, 2)

לְשֵׂאֵת 302

לְשֹׁומֹו ... Tab. XXIV (δ, 4)

לְשֶׁבֶת ... 133, Tab. XVIII

לִשְׂרֹד 123

לְשִׁטְנֵו ...Tab. XXIV (a, iii)

לְשִׂימוֹ ... Tab. XXIV (δ, 4)
לְשָׁכֵב (ב ־ &)...79 (Note *)
לְשָׁמֵד ... ... 79 (†)
לְשָׁמֵץ ... ... 79 (†)
לָתֵת (ת־) Tab. XIX (B)
לְתִמ ...Tab. XIX (Note 5)

מ

מ ordinary prefix 3, 4, 6
מ (or מִן) w. Affs. Tab. II (& Notes)
מֵאָדָם 347
מֵאַהֲבַת 80
מְאִירַת, מְאִירוֹת, מֵאִיר ... 268
מֵאֵן 330
־וּ & מֵאֲנָה 344
מָאָסְכֶם, מָאֲסָם 321, Tab. XV (Note ‡)
מְאַסְפָיו 347
מְאָרְרִים 271
מָבוֹא & מָבֹא 272
מְבְעֶטֶּךָ 369
מִנְבוּרֹתָם, מִבְצִיר ... 3
מְנֻרָתָה 110
־וֹת & מִהְיוֹת 276
מְחַבֹּות 298
מַהֵר 330
מָחֳרָה 344
מַחֲרֶבֶת 324
מוֹנַיִךְ 281
מוֹרַשַׁת 138
מוֹנַיִךְ 283
מוֹעֶדֶת 348
מוֹצָאוֹת 286
מוֹצָאַי 285
הֶן & מוֹצָאֵיהֶם, מוֹצָאַי ... 336
מוֹצִי' & מוֹצָאִים 285

מוֹצָאת & מוֹצָאִים 286
מוֹצָאתָיו 336
מ־מוֹת, ־מָיִם, ־מָה, מוּקָם ... 163
מוֹרָאִים 289
מוֹרָט 347
מוֹרִים, ־י, ־יךָ 289
מָוֶת w. Affs. Tab. XIII (Note ‡, ε)
מוֹת 151, 243
מוֹתֵנוּ, מוֹתִי, מוּתָה, מוֹתוֹ ... 151
מוֹתַי Tab. XIII (Note ‡, ε)
מֵזֶו 130
מַחְאָד 81
מָחוֹן 4
מָחָיָה 279
מַחְלְמִים 353
מָחְסָפַס 176
מַחֲצָה (ת־ &) 66
מְטַחֲנִי 172
מֵינִק, ־יָקָה, ־קַת ... 135
מֵינִקְתוֹ (ה־ &) ... 135, Tab. XXVI (§)
מְיֻרָאִים 288
מְיֻרָאתוֹ 80, 286
מַכֶּה (ה־ , ־הוּ &), and מַכֶּה (ה־ , & ־ה) ... 298
מַכִּים, מָכִים, (וֹת־ &) ... 298
מַכֵּךְ 298
מְכַלְכֵּל 175
מְכַרְבָּל 177
מִכְרֶה 86
מִכְתֵּשׁ 353
מָלֵא (מ' &) 327
מָלֵא, מִלֵּא 344
מִלְאוּ 346
מְלֵאת Tab. XXII (Note a)
מִלֵּאתִי 84

	PAGE
מַלְוֶה	290
מְלוּכָה, מלוכי	86
מָלוֹשִׁגִי	367
מָלִים	163
מַלִינִים (נם &—)	161
מַלְכִּי צֶדֶק	232
סָלֹךְ תִּמְלֹךְ	78
מֶלֶךְ w. Affs. ... Tab. X	
מַלְכָּה w. Affs. ...Tab. XII	
מָלְכִּי, מַלְכָּה...	86
מַלְכֵּנוּ	130
מַלְתָּעוֹת	362
מְמוֹתֵי Tab. XIII (Note ‡, ε)	
מְמַחִים	173
מִנְאָץ 318,	367
מָנָד & מֵנַד	292
מְנַדֵּיכֶ	292
מְנַדִּים	292
מְנוּשִׁי	306
מָנֵחַ	145
מִנְקִתּוֹ & ה‍ָ‍	135
מַסִּית	161
מַסְתֵּר	353
מְעָדוֹת ... ... 134 (‡)	
מַעְזְרִים	353
מַעְיֵנוּ	232
מַעֲלֶה (ח‍ָ &—)	192
מְעָצְבְּךָ	4
מַעֲשֵׂה w. affs.	44
מַעֲשֵׂה	85
מַעֲתִיק	119
מָפְקָד, מִפְקָד	83
מִפְתָּח	353
מָצָא, etc.	185
מָצָּב 134,	145
מָצַק	134

	PAGE
מָצָתִי Tab. XXII (Note d)	
מְקוֹמָם, מ‍ָ‍, מ‍ָ‍, etc.	163
מְקִיצָה, מָקִים, etc. ...	163
מָרְבָּע	67
מַרְגִּז	4
מִרְדָּה	323
מִרְדֹּף	4
מְרוֹמְמִי	162
מְרַקֵּדָה	330
מִשָּׂאתוֹ	302
מִשְׁבָּת	133
מִשְׁגַּבּוֹ, etc. Appˣ (B) to Tab IX	
מִשְׂהַהוּ ... Tab. XXVII (β)	
מִשְׁחַת	369
מָשְׁכוּ & מִשְׁכּוּ	86
מְשֻׁלָּשׁ	67
מִשְׁמָרִים	85
מִשְׁפָּט w. Affs. Appˣ (B) to Tab. IX	
מְשָׁרֵת	369
מָשָׁאתוֹ	302
מִשְׁתַּחֲוֶה ... Tab. XXIII (‡)	
כְּשְׁתַּחֲוִיתָם	178
מֵת, etc. ... 152, Tab. XX	
מַת, etc. ... 152, Tab. XX	
מִתְאַוֶּה, י‍ִ‍ם	267
מִתְאַנֶּה	270
מִתְאוֹנְנִים	268
מַתָּה, מְתָה & מֵתָה ...	152
מִתְהַלֵּךְ	248
מָתַי, מֵתוּ ...152, Tab. XX	
מֹתָיו (in מְבֹתָיו) Tab. XIII (Note ‡, ε)	
מְתִיד	162
מַתָּם & מֵתִים	152
מְתַלְעוֹת	362
כְּתַמֵּם	316

	PAGE
מָתְנוּ & מָתַן	... 151
מִתְנַכְּרָה	... 330
מִתְקוֹמֵם, etc.	... 163
מִתְקוֹמְמִי	... 162

נ

	PAGE
נָאוָה, נָאֲוָה	... 291
נָאווּ, נָאֲווּ	... 290, 291
נָאוֹר	... 268
נָאוָתָה, נָאוֹת	... 269
נֹאחֲזוּ	... 129
(—לָה & נֹאכְלָה)	...130 (add¹ Note)
נָאץ נָאַצְתָּ	... 342
נֶאֱצוּ	... 344
נֵאַר	... 343
נֹאֲרִים	... 271
נָבָא	... 273
נָבוּהַ	...Tab. XXI (Note 6)
נָבִיא	... 275
נְבִכִים	... 160
נִבְלָה	...Tab. XXI (Note 6)
נָבְקָה	...Tab. XXI (Note 8)
נִנְאֲלוּ	... 178, 368
נֶגְבָּה	... 42
(—יְ, יִ—דוֹ)...	... 39
נִגְדַּע & נֶגְדַּע	... 340
נָגוֹף	... 338
נִגְזַרְתִּי	... 110
נָגִידָה	... 145
נָגַל	... 190
נִגְלָה, etc.	... 173
נִגְלוֹת	...170 & 173
נֶגַע w. Affs.	Tab. X
נִדְמָה	...Tab. XXI (Note 7)
ע & גֶּרַע—	... 137

	PAGE
שָׂ & גֶּרְעָה—	... 138
נֶגֶר (or גֶּרֶר) w. Affs. Tab. X	
נְהִי, נִהְיָה 277, Cp. Tab. XXIII (9)	
נִהְיָה & —יָתָה, —יָתָ, —יִית, (—יֵיתִי)	... 278
נֶחָמָה	... 191
נֶהֶפְכוּ & נֶהֶפְכוּ	... 119
נוּגֵי, נוּגוֹת	... 281
נוֹדִיעָה	... 137
נֻסְּרוּ	... 318
נוֹצִיא	... 286
נוֹרָאֹתֶיךָ, —אָה & גוֹרָא 287	
נוֹרָאֹת	... 55, 287
נוּבִּידָה	... 334
נַעֲקָף	... 110
נֶחְבָּאִים	... 341
נֶחְבֵּאת	... 119, 381
נֶחְפָּה	... 339
נֶחְבְּאֻם	...Tab. XXII (Note f)
נֶחֱזֶה	... 191
נִחְיֶה	... 279
(—וֹת &), נַחֲלָה	... 193
נָחַלְתִּי, נָחֲלוּ	... 193
נַחְלְמָה	... 118
נֶחָם	... 296
נֶחָם, נָחָם	...144 (Cp. 343)
נֶחְמְדֵהוּ	... 116
נֶחֱמָדִים	... 119
תָּם & נֶחֱמָתִי—	... 144
נֶחֱנָה	... 191
נָחֲנִי & נָחַנִי	... 296
נֶחְסָף	...Tab. XXI (Note i)
נֶחְפָּה	... 193
נַחְפְּשָׂה	... 118
נִחַר	...Tab. XXI (Note ii)
נַחֲרָבוֹת, נֶחֱרָבְתָּ, נָחֶרְכוּ	... 119

	PAGE
נֶחֱרִים, נֶחֱרוּ	193
‎־בוּ & נֶחְשָׁבוּ	119
נֶחְתּוּ	144
נֶחְתּוֹם	339
נָטֶה, נטווֹת & נטוי (Kthiv), נָטוּי, etc.	297
נְטִיַי	297, Tab. XXIII
נִטְמָאִים	341
נִטַמֵּם	Tab. XXII (Note f)
נֹטֵעַ	370
נֹטְרָה	330
נִיכָם	283, Tab. XXX (7)
‎־שָׁה & נִירְשָׁה	135
נִכְּאוּ	298
נִכְבַּדִּי, נִכְבַּדֵּי	341
נִכְבַּדֶּיהָ, נִכְבַּדֵּיהֶם	341
נַבֵּהַ, נַבֵּחוּ	299
נָכוּ, נִכְבָּה	298
נֹכַחַת	138
נָכֵם, נִכְּנוּ	297
נִכְסֹף	338
נִכְסַפְתָּה	82
נִכַּפֵּר	318
נִכְרַתָּ	122
נִפְתַּח	298
‎־יִם & נִלְווּ	290
נִלְחֹם	338
נָלִין	154 (Note *)
‎־כָה & גִלְקְחָה	136
נִמְלְחוּ	113
נִמְצָא (thrice)	Tab. XXII
‎־אַךְ, ‎־אִים, נִמְצָאִים	341
נָכַר	160 (Note)
נֵס	300
נָסֹב	180
נָסָה	303

	PAGE
נָסַח (‎־וּי—, ‎־הוּ—)	300
‎־תֶם, ‎־תִי—, נְסִיתוֹ, נְסוֹת	300
נַסֵּנִי	300
נָסְעָה & נָסְעָה, נָסְעָה	144
נַסַּתוֹ & נִסְתָה	300
נֶעְבַּד	116 (†)
נַעֲבְרָה & נַעֲבָדָה, נַעֲבְרָה	118
נֶעְבַּר	116, 119, 340
נֵעוֹר	160 (Note)
נֶעֱזָב Nφ. Past 3 s. m.	119
(& נָעַל) נָעַל	192, 193 (cp. 171)
נַעֲלָה	171, 191
נֶעְלָם	116
נֶעֱלָמָה	119 (Note *)
נָעֳמָת	110
נַעֲנֵיתִי	193
נֶעֱנְשׁוּ	119
נֶעֱצָרָה	119
נַעַר w. Affs.	Tab. X
נֶעֱרַח w. Affs.	Tab. XII
נֶעֶרְמוּ	119
נֶעֱרָץ	119 (Note *)
נַעֲשָׂה	193
נֶעֶשְׂתָה & נֶעֶשְׂתָה, נֶעֶשׂוּ	193
נַעְתּוֹר	339
נָפוֹצֶת	163 (‡)
נִפְלָאת	185
נִפְלָאַתָה	82, Tab. XXII
נִפְלָה, & נִפְלָה & נִפְלָה	144
נָפְלוּ	113
נָפְלִינוּ	Tab. XXII (Note l)
נֵפֶן	Tab. XXIII
נפצות	163
נִפְצוֹתָם	160
נִפְתִּי	295
נָצָא	300, 801

	PAGE
‎ַ‎ב‎—‎ & נָצַב	145
‎ָ‎בָה‎—‎ & נִצְּבָה	134, 145
נָצוּ	300, 301
נִצְטַדָּק	89*, 315
נֵצִים	301
נִצַּלְנוּ	110
נֹצְצִים	301
נָצְרָה	86
נָצְרַח	83
נַקֵּה, נִקָּה, נָקֹה	301
נִקְוֶה, נָקוּ	312
נָקוּמָה	158
נִקְטָתָם & נקומתם	160
‎יתִי‎—‎, נְקִיתָ	301
נַקֹּנִי	302
‎ָתָה‎—‎ & נִקְתָה	301
נָרִיעָה	158
עָרְבָאוּ [Pt. I, § 58 (Note *)] Tab. XXII	
נִרְפָּתָה Tab. XXII (Note w)	
נשׂא	173, 305
נָשָׂא	305
נָשָׂא & נְשָׂא, נָשׂא	302
נְשָׂא, נָשָׂא, נשׂא	303
נָשָׂא	303
נשׂא, נְשָׂא	304, 344
נְשָׂאוֹם, נְשָׂאוֹ	302
נְשָׂאֵי & נשׂאות	303
נשׂאים	173, 305
נְשָׂאִים & נשׂאים	303
נִשָּׂאֲךָ	302
נשׂאל נשׂאל	77, 338
נשׂאת, נָשָׂאתָ &	302
נָשָׂאת (twice)	304
‎תִי‎—‎ & נְשָׂאתָה	302
נְשָׂאתִיכֶם	303
	PAGE
נְשָׂאתִים‎-‎	302
נְשָׂאתַנִי & נִשָּׂאתָנִי	302
נִשְׁבָּח	335
‎רָה‎—‎ & נִשְׁבְּרָה, ‎ר‎—‎ & נִשְׁבַּר	123
‎נָשׂוּא‎—‎, נָשׂוּא, נָשׂוֹא	303
נָשׂוֹא & נָשׂוּ	302
משׂוּי	303
נָשִׁים (& נְשֵׁי), etc.	46
נִשְׁלוֹחַ 338, Tab. XIV (Note d)	
נִשֵּׁכִי	306
נָשְׁעֲגֻ	122
נִשְׂרְפָה	88
נשׁתָּנָה	360—364
נִשְׁתַּחֲוֶה ...Tab. XXIII (Note)	
נִשְׁתָּעֶה ... Tab. XXIII (17)	
נְתַנֵּל ... Tab. XXIII (17)	
נִתְחַכְּמָה	88
נָתַנּוּ	122, 146
נְתַנּוּ Tab. XIX (Note δ, ii)	
נתנך	329
‎תִּי‎—‎, ‎תְּ‎—‎, ‎תִּי‎—‎, נָתַתָּ 146, Tab. XIX (B)	
‎ן‎—‎ & נְתַתֶּם 146, Tab. XIX (B)	
נְתַתָּם Tab. XIX (Note δ, ii)	

ס

סֹבִי, סָבוֹ, סַבוּ, סֹב, סַב 180, Tab. XXI	
סבב ... Tab. XXI	
סֹבוּ ... Tab. XXI	
סָבוּנִי	180
סַבּוֹתִי 180, Tab. XXI	
סֹבִיב	328
סָבֵּךְ	180
סַבְנִי (i.e. סָבוּ, Tab. XXI, w. Aff. me) 180	
סָבֹתֶם, סַבֹתִי 180, Tab. XXI	

PAGE

סוּרָה ... 163 (Note *, *d*)

סָעַד ... 113, 332 & Note *

סְעָדֵנִי ... Tab. XXVII (β)

סַפְּרָה 86

סָרִיסִים, etc. App˟ (A) to Tab. IX (Note §)

ע

עֶבֶד w. Affs. ... Tab. X

עַבְרִי 118

עַד w. Affs. ... Tab. IV (3)

עֲדָי (& עָדִי), עָדָיו, עֲדָיִם 40

עוֹלֵל 365

עֹמְיָה ... ... 173 (†)

עֲנוּת 32

עִירֹה [Cp. Tab. VIII] Tab. XIII (Note ‡, γ)

עַל w. Affs. ... Tab. IV

עָלָה, עָלֵהוּ Tab. IV (Note 2)

עֲלֵהֶם ... Tab. IV (Note 4)

עָלָיו ... ... 362 (Note)

עָלַי Tab. IV (2) & Note (2)

עָלֵימוֹ & עָלַיְכִי Tab. IV (Notes 3 & 4)

עֲלֵיכֶם = עֲלֵכֶם in Tab. IV

עִם w. Affs. ... Tab. III

עָמְדוּ 112, 118

עִמָּדִי (*with me*) Tab. III (Note)

עִמָּדִי 118

עִמָּהֶם *with them* (m.) Tab. III

עִמְּכָה ... Tab. III (Note 5)

עִמָּכֶם ... ... Tab. III

עֲמָקִי 328

עֻנָּבִי App˟ (A) to Tab. IX

עֲנִי (& עָנִי), עָנָיו 40

עֲנִקְתָּמוֹ ... ...Tab. XXV (γ)

PAGE

עֵץ w. Affs. ... Tab. XIII (Note §, β)

עֲקָבַי & עֲקֵבִי App˟ (A) to Tab. IX (†, ii)

עַר 151

עֹרָה 321

עֲבֵל & עָרֵל 327

עֲשָׂהוּ 211

עֲשׂוֹ & עֲשָׂהוּ Tab. XXVI (‡)

עֲשׂוֹ ... ... 173 (Note §)

עֲשׂוֹ 381, Tab. XXIII (2)

עֲשׂוֹת 238

עֲשִׂית, עֲשִׂיתָ 249

עֲשֵׂךְ 211

עֲשֵׂנִי (& דָּ—), עֲשֵׂךְ Tab. XXVI (‡)

עֲשָׂת 172

עֲשָׂתַנִי, עֲשָׂתְהוּ, עֲשָׂתָה 211

פ

פֶּה w. Affs. Tab. XIII, 6

פִּי (twice), פִּיהֶם, פִּיהָ, פִּיהוּ Tab. XIII, 6

פִּיּוֹת, פִּיו ... ...Tab. XIII (6)

פִּיּוֹת ... Tab. XIII (††)

פִּים, פִּיךָ ... Tab. XIII, 6

פִּימוֹ ...Tab. XIII (Note 9)

פִּיפִיּוֹת ... Tab. XIII (††)

פֶּלֶג 345

פִּלַּלְתִּי 110

פִּלְפֵּל & פַּלְפַּל forms 175

פֹּעַל w. Affs. Tab. XI (3)

פֹּעַל & פֹּעַל forms ... 365–368

פְּעַלְעַל & פְּעַלְעַל, etc., forms ... 176

פָּקַדְךָ 210

PAGE

פָּקִיד w. Affs. App^x (A) to Tab. IX

כְּרִי (& פְּרִי), פִּרְיוֹ etc. ... 40

פְּרִיכֶם, פֶּרְיֶךְ ... 40

פְּרִיהֶם & פְּרָיָם ... 40

פַּרְשֵׁז ... 177

פָּרָשָׁיו ... Tab. IX (Note δ)

פְּשֻׂטָה ... 320, 321

פֶּתַח ...Tab. XVI (3)(B, γ)

צ

צֵאתְךָ, צֵאתוֹ, צֵאת ... 262, 284

צָבָא w. Affs. Tab. IX (Note *)

צְדָקָה w Affs. App^x (C) to Tab. IX.

צָוָה, etc. ... 309

צִוִּיתִיךָ ... 249, 251

צִוַּתָה ... 211

צֵלָעָה ... 330

צְמָדַי ... p. x* of Tabs.

צָמַת Tab. XXII (Note r)

צָמַתִי Tab. XXII (Note e)

צְעָקָה w. Affs. App^x (C) to Tab. IX.

צפו (Kthiv), צָפוּי (Kri) ... 173

צָרִים ...Tab. XXI (Note 2)

ק

קָאָה ... 311

קָאם ... 151 (†)

קָבְהּ Tab. XXI (Note *, β)

קָבְנוּ ... Tab. XXVII (γ)

קָנָה ... 310

קָוָה (twice) & קַוּ ... 312

PAGE

קֹוֶיךָ, קֹוֵי, קֹוָי ... 311

(נוּך, קֹוֶינָהוּ &) קֹוִינוּ ... 312

—תִיךְ & קֹוִיתִי, קְוִיתִי ... 312

קוּם, etc. ...163, Tab. XX

קוֹם ...151, Tab. XX

קוּמָה & קוּמָה 158 (Cp. 377)

קוּמִי & קוּמִי 159 (Cp. 377)

קוֹמֵם (& ◌ֵם) ...Tab. XX

קֹותָה ... 312

קָחִי, קְחָה, קַח, קַח Tab XIX (Note A)

נּוּ & קָחֲנָה, ◌ֵם & קָחֵם Tab. XXVII (β)

קַחַת ...Tab. XIX (Note A)

קְטַנּוֹת, קְטַנָּה ... 50

נָם, ◌ֵם, ◌ִים, קְטַנֵּי Tab. IX(Note *, β)

קִיג ... 311

קָמוּ, קָם ... 150 (Note)

קִימָנוּ ... 163

קָם, etc. 151 (twice), 163, Tab. XX

קָמוּ, קָמָה ... 151, 159, 377

קָמְה ... 151, 159, 163

קָמוּ ... 150

קָמִי ... 162

קְמוֹ, etc. ... Tab. XX

קְמָנָה ... 155, Tab. XX

קַמְתִּי, קַמְתָ ... Tab. XX

קָמְצוֹ ... Tab. XI (Note)

קְנַאוּנִי ... 346 (Note)

קָנֹה ... Tab. XXIII (2)

קָנֶךָ & ◌ֶ"ד, קָנָהוּ ... 211

קָנִיתָ (Kri), קָנִיתִי (Kthiv) 81

קָנֵנִי ...Tab. XXX (1)

קַצְרֵי ... 328

קְרָאוֹת [Pt I, § 58 (Note *)] Tab. XXII (Note a)

PAGE

קְרָאָנָה, קְרָאֻהוּ Tab. XXVII (β)

קְרָאת 169, 185

קָרְבָה 81

קָרְבָה 112, 331

קָרְבָה 112

קָרוּא w. Affs. App^x (A) to Tab. IX

קָרוֹב w. Affs. App^x (A) to Tab. IX

ל

רָאוּ (Pŭ. Past 3 pl.) Pt I, § 49 (Note)

רָאוֹת 170

רָאֻמוֹת 163

רֹאנִי ... Tab. XXVI (‡)

רָאֻתְךָ ... Tab. XXX (4)

רְבוּ ... ... Tab. XXI (†)

רֻגְּזָה 320, 321

רְגָלִים & רַגְלַיִם ... 32

רֹגַע 370

רֻדַּם ... Tab. XXX (6)

רֹחַב w. Affs. ... Tab. XI

רְטֻפַּשׁ 177

רִיבוֹת 154

רָנִּי & רָנּוּ Tab. XXI (Note *, γ)

רְפָאָה 335

רְפָאתִי & רְפָאנוּ Tab. XXII (q & p)

רְפָה ... Tab. XXII (s)

רָצֹאתִי ... Tab. XXIII

רקע 370

רֻקַּעָה 81

רִשְׁפֵּי ... p. x* of Tabs.

ש

שַ, שָ, שֶ, as Prefixes ... 24

שָׁאֻנִי, שָׁאֻ, שָׁאֵהוּ, שָׁא ... 303

שָׁאטִים & שָׁאטוֹת 163

שָׁאִי 303

שְׁאֵלָה ... ... 322 (Note *)

שְׁאֵלָתָיו & שְׁאֵלָתִיהוּ Tab. XXV (β)

שְׁאֵלְתָם 159, 325

שָׁאֲנִיחֲנוּ 294

שָׂאתִי, שָׂאתוֹ, שְׂאֵת 302

שְׁבָה & שֵׁב ... 133, Tab. XVIII

שָׂבֵעַ i.e. שָׂבֵעַ ... 327

שִׁבְעָם etc., & שִׁבְעִים App^x (A) to Tab. IX

תָּ, —תִי, שְׁבְתוֹ, (שָׁבָת &)שָׁבָת— 133

שָׁבַר 121

שָׁדְדָה, שָׁדְדָה 347

שְׁדָדְנוּ, שָׁדְדוּ 347

שׁוֹבִי 163

שׁוֹם & שֹׁם 154

שׁוֹמְמִין 330

שׁוֹמֵר w. Affs. App^x B (4) to Tab. IX

שׁוֹעָל w. Affs App^x B (2) to Tab. IX

שֻׁנְקִים fr. שׁוּק p. x** of Tabs. (θ)

שְׁנָרִים fr. שׁוּד p. x** of Tabs. (θ)

שׁוֹשַׁתִּי 368

שׁחֲרוּ 369

שֶׁחֲטָה 322

שָׁחַתָּ 122

שִׁחֲתוּ 344

שָׁחֹתִי ... Tab. XXI (Note ii)

שִׁחַתֶם 122

שִׁיָהוּ & שִׁיוֹ ... Tab. XIII (¶)

שִׂים —מִי, —מוּ, שִׂימָה (twice), ... 154

שָׁיָצָא 284

שִׁיר w. Affs. Tab. V

שִׁית, (שִׁיתִי and so שִׁיתוֹ) ... 154

	PAGE
שִׂיחוֹ Tab. XIII (Note ‡, γ)	
שָׁכַב ... ... 79 (Note *)	
שְׁכָב (*K* Imper. 2 s. *m.*, in p.) 382	
שְׁבַחַת ... Tab. XVI (3) (C)	
מֶךְ שְׁכְמוֹ ,שְׁכָם (& שְׁכֶם)— 40	
שְׁכִנְתָּה Appˣ (C) to Tab. IX. (Note ‡)	
שְׁלַוְתִּי 172	
שָׁלַח & שְׁלַח Tab. XVI (3)	
שָׁלְחָה 83, 120	
שָׁלְחַךְ 329	
שְׁלִישׁוֹ, etc. Appˣ (A) to Tab. IX	
שֵׁת & שְׁלִשָׁה, שָׁלֹשׁ, שְׁלֹשׁ— 62, etc.	
שְׁלַחְתְּ Appˣ (C) to Tab. IX (4, β)	
שֵׁם ... ...154 twice	
שֵׁם (שֶׁם-) w. Affs. Tab. XIII (Note §, a)	
שָׁמָה 23	
שְׁמִי & שְׁמוֹ, שְׁמָה & שָׁמָה ... 154	
(שִׂמְחֵי &) שִׂמְחַי 328, Appˣ (A) to Tab. IX	
שָׁמַנְתָּ ... ... 62, etc.	
שָׁמַע 112, 113	
שָׁמְעָה 86	
שָׁמְעוּ & שִׁמְעוּ 112	
שְׁמָעוּנִי ... Tab. XXVII (β)	
שְׁמַעַן 86, 372	
שְׁמַעֲנוּךְ 373	
עַת & שָׁמַעַת 372	
שָׁמְרָה 86	
שִׁמְרָה 112	
שָׁמְרָה 82	
שָׂמֵחַ & שָׂמֵחַ 154	
שְׂמָחָם Tab. XIII (Note §, a)	
שָׂנֵאתָ, שָׂנֵא, etc. ... 185	

	PAGE
שֶׁעֲשַׁעְתִּי, שִׁעֲשַׁע ... 176 (†)	
pl. of שִׁפְחָה שְׁפָחוֹת ... 40	
שָׁפַט 81, 113	
שִׁפְטָה 366	
שְׁפָמֶךְ ... Tab. XV (Note *)	
שפכה *Kthiv* (twice), שָׁפְכוּ *Kri*, & שָׁפְכוּ 82	
שְׂרָפִים 83	
שֹׁרֶשׁ 365	
שָׁרְשׁוּ 366	
שָׁתוֹת ... Tab. XXIII (1)	
שְׁתִי 154	
שְׁתָם 83	

ת

	PAGE
תֹּאבֶן 128	
תֹּאבוּ, תֹּאבֵה 267	
תֵּאָבֵל 130**	
תֵּאָהֵב 130**	
תֵּאָנַח 267	
תֵּאָחֵז 130**	
תֹּאחֵז 128, 130**	
תֵּאָטֵר 130**	
תָּאִירוּ, תָּאִיר 268	
ל-ְ & תֹּאכַל 242, Tab. XVII. 2 (a & γ)	
תֹּאכְלֻחוּ 367	
תֹּאכְלוּ 245	
נוּ- & תֹּאכְלֶנָּה 251	
תֹּאלֶף 130**	
תֵּאָמַנָה ... ... 122 (Note *)	
תֹּאטֵף 130**	
תָּאְנֶה 270	
תֵּאָפֶינָה & תֵּאָפֶה, תֵּאפֹג ... 270	
תָּאֹר 271	

PAGE

תָּאֱרָב 130**
תָּאׇרְנָה 155, 268
תָּאְשֵׁם 130**
תָּאתָה 271
תֹּבָא 267
תְּבוֹאֵהוּ, תְּבֹאֵנּוּ, תָּבֹא 273
תָּבוֹאנָה & תְּבֹאֵינָה 156
תְּבֹאֵמוֹ 275
תָּבֹאן, תָּבֹאנָה, תְּבֹאֶינָה ... 156, 273
תְּבֹאֵנִי 273
תְּבֹאָתְךָ, תָּבֹאתָה 273
תְּבוֹאֶינָה 156
תְּבוֹאֵךְ 273
תְּבוֹאֵנּוּ 273
תִּבְעָיוּן (K. Fut. 2 pl. m. fr.
   בעה) ... ... Cp. 172
תְּבַקֵּשֶׁנָּה 346
תֶּבְשִׁי, תַּבְשׁוּ, תֶּבַשׁ 153
תִּנָּבֵּל ... ... 114 (†)
תִּנְגְיוּן 173, 281
תָּגִיל 155
תֵּגֶל, תָּגֵל, תִּגַּל, תִּגָּל ...191 & 192
תִּגְּעוּ 245
תַּגֵּשׁ 143
תִּדְבָּקוּן 89
תָּדִין 155
—ע & תֶּזְרַע 137
תֶּדְעִי 138
תֵּדֹר 144
תָּהְגֶּה 191
תֶּהְדֹּפוּ 116
תְּהִי 222, 277,
   Tab. XXIII (5)
תִּהְיֶה (—יִי, —יֶנָה, —יֶין, —יֶנָה) 277
תַּהֲלֹךְ ... ... 116 (§)
תֶּהֱמִי, תֶּהֱמֶה 191

PAGE

תְּהַרְגֻּנּוּ 208
תְּהָחֵלוּ or תְּהַחֲלוּ 346 (†), 354
תּוֹמִיךְ 328
תּוֹנֵנּוּ 283
תּוֹסֵף 137
תּוֹסָף [Hφ. Fut. 2 s. m. fr.
   יסף], Pt. I. § 47 (Note)
תּוֹפְפוֹת 330
תּוֹגְּרָא 287
תּוֹרָה w. Affs. ... Tab. VI
—תָו & תּוֹרוֹתָם ... 47 (u)
תּוֹרֶם (& ־ךָ), ... 289
—כֶן & תּוֹרַתְכֶם ... see 46 (t)
—ו & תּוֹרָתָם ... 46 & 47
תְּעַבְרֻן 88
תִּזְלִי (תָּאָזְלִי or תָּאֱזְלִי for) 128
תָּחוֹם 153
—זִי & תֶּחֱזֶה 191
—יוּן & תִּחְיוּ, תִּחְיֶה, תְּחִי,
   (—יִי, —יֶנָה) ... 279
תַּחֲנָה 191
תֶּחְפָּץ, תַּחְפֹּץ 117
תֵּחַת (fr. נחת) 144
תֵּחַת (fr. חתת), Tab. XXI (Note v)
תַּט, תַּם, תִּשֶּׁה, תַּשֶּׁה .. 174, 297
תַּמְחוּ 297
תִּפֹּר 144
תִּיבֵשׁ 135
תִּיטַב & תִּיטְבִי 134
תְּיֵלִילוּ 136, 282
תֵּינַק & תֵּינִיק 135
תֵּיעָשֶׂה 171
(& תִּירָאוּן, (—ָאִי &) תִּירָאוּ
   (—ָאִם) 287
תִּירָאןְ 287
תַּד, תִּכָּה — ... 174, 299

	PAGE
תַּכַּח	171, 192
תִּכְּנֶינָה & תִּכָּנֶה	289
תִּכּוֹנְנִי & תִּכּוֹנֵן	317
תַּכְּנוּ	299
תִּכַּסֶּה	317
תִּלְבְּשָׁן	88
תֵּלַח	192
תַּלְוֻנוּ ,תִּלְוֶה	290
תֵּלִינוּ	161
תָּלֶן ,תָּלוּ ,מְלִיץ	154
תַּלְכִּי ,תֵּלְכוּ	136
תְּמוּטֶינָה	156
תָּמֵתוּן & תְּמוּתוּן	160
תְּמוּתְנָה	156 (†)
תְּנָאֶפְנָה	345
תָּנֹד	293
תנואון (Kthiv)	293
תְּנַחֲנִי ,תְּנַחֵם ,תַּנְחָה	296
תְּנִיאוּן (Krî)	293
תְּנִיחֵנִי & —חֲנִי	294
תַּנְשָׁא	317
תַּנְקְשֵׁנִי	306
תָּסֹב	180
תִּסְעוּ	143 (‡)
תֹּסֶף	130**
תֹּסֶף	137, 381
תִּסְמַּתֵּר	315
תַּעֲבוּרִי	337
תַּעֲבֹרוּ	112
תַּעֲנֻבָה	88
תְּעוּפֶינָה	156
תַּעֲנֶנָּה	122
תְּעַבְּסְנָה	345
תַּעֲלֶה ,(תַּעַל &) תַּעַל	171, 191-193
תַּעֲלִי	191
תַּעֲמְדוּ & —דִי	117
תַּעֲשֶׂה	171
תָּפוּצֶנָה & תְּפוּצֶינָה	156
תְּפַלַּחְנָה	345
תֵּפֶן	222
מֵצֵאנָה ,תֵּצֵאן	285
תְּצֻנֵּי ,תֵּצֶם	310
תֵּצֵינָה	301
תֵּצֵת	145
תָּקֹמְנָה	155
תֵּרָא	191
תְּרַבַּאי	287 (Note)
תִּרְגַּלְתִּי	177
תֵּרְחוּ	289
חרוב (Kthiv)	157 (‡)
תָּרוּם	155
תַּרְטֶשְׁנָה	345
תָּרֻם	155
תְּרַמַּסְנָה	110
תִּשְׁבִּי	136, Tab. XVIII
תִּשָּׁאנָה	303
תֵּשֵׁב ,תֵּשְׁבִי	134, 136
תֵּשֵׁב	157 (‡)
תְּשַׁבֵּינָה	156
תָּשֹׁבְנָה & תָּשֹׁבֶן	155
תֵּשֵׁה	306
תְּשׁוֹכֶם	318
תְּשׁוּפֶנּוּ	250
תִּשְׁחְתוּן	89
תֵּשִׁי	306
תָּשִׂים	154, 155
תִּשְׁלִיכֻהוּ (Hφ. Fut. 2 pl. *m.* w. Aff. *him*)	212
תִּשְׁמוּרֵם	337
תִּשְׁמְרוּן	88
תִּשָׁעַשְׁעוּ	176
תִּשְׁתַּבְּרִין	89

	PAGE			PAGE
תְּתָא	313	תִּתְכַּם	317
תִּתְאָו, הִתְאַוה ...	267	תִּתְמַּם	316
תִּתְגַּל	191	(תֵּעַע *K.* Fut. 3 s. *f.* fr.)	171
תִּתְחַלְחַל	175	תִּתְפַּתָּל & תִּתַּפָּל	361
תִּתְיַפִּי	284	תִּתְעַצֵּב	133 (‡)
תִּתְיַצֵּב	133 (‡)		

END OF INDEX OF WORDS.

INDEX.

Accent, ordinarily on syllable involving 2ᵈ Rt-letter in Verb-forms 109

Accent, thrown forward in some Past-Tense forms with *Váv* prefixed 104

Accents, Introductory remarks on, Pt. I. §§ 37–46.

Accents, Table of, Pt. I. §§ 65–69.

Adjectives 50–55

A'-leph [Pt. I. §§ 2 (i) and 9 (Note)], Quiescent [Pt. I. § 30], cannot have Dagesh [Pt. I. § 49].

A'-leph prefix for 1 s. Fut. *Kal* takes *Segol* generally ...76, 116

A'-leph, Verbs having, as 1ˢᵗ Rt-letter ...128–130**, Tab. XVII

A'-leph, Verbs having, as 3ᵈ Rt-letter ... 169, 185, Tab. XXII

A'-leph, Kaumets (⎺) not dropped before, sometimes 336

Alphabet, Pt. I. § 8.

Analysis of Verb-forms in Gen. i.–iii. and xii. ... 226–266

Apocopated forms of Verbs ל״ה 170, 171, 190–193

Apocopated forms generally [but not always—Note (‡) on p. 171] used with *Váv* Convers., and with אַל *Deprecative*, and in a *Positive* wish 222

"Become, To" (for ל׳ היה)... 254 & 255 (latter part of Note)

B'gad-k'phath letters, Pt. I. §§ 47 & 48.

—————— Verbs whose Root has any of the ... 123

'Borrowed' forms... 161, 162, etc.

Classification of Verbs which are sometimes called 'Irregular' 124

'Compaginis' (Yód) 232

Compensation for Dagesh-F. 115 (comp. § 6*b*)

Compound Shva [Pt. I. §§ 22–24], always *Moving* 117

—————— sometimes under other letters than those in Pt. I. § 24 [Pt. I. Appˣ D] 346

'Construct form,' 'Construct State,' or 'State of Construction' 33–36, 45

—————— before a Preposition, [See Obs. XXX]... 193

Couple, *Váv* with *Kaumets* before second word of a ... 223–225

"Created to make" (for "created and made" of E.V.) [Gen. ii. 3] 380–382

Dagesh 'Conjunctivum,' 'Dirimens,' 'Euphonic,' 'Forte Euphonicum,' 'Intermediate,' [See Pt. I. § 71, Note (‡)].

DAGESH-FORTE [Pt. I. §§ 49, 53 & 54].

———— after 'Hé for the Def. Art.' ... 4
(cases in which it is NOT put) 4, 5

———— after the prefix מ from, ... 3
(cases in which it is NOT put) 3, 4

———— for an omitted Rt-letter נ or ח 121, 122

———— in 1st Rt-letter for Nún of Niph-ăl 71, 76, 79, 87

———— in 1st Rt-letter sometimes for ח of Hithpă-él 89*, 316–318

———— in 2d Rt-letter of Pĭ-él, Pŭ-ăl, and Hithpă-él ... 71

———— often omitted over Shva 346

DAGESH-LENE [Pt. I. § 47], sometimes omitted [Pt. I. § 48], cannot stand after 'Shva-Moving,' or after a Vowel [Pt. I. § 47 N.B.]

DAGESH-LENE when in Rt-letters (B'gad-k'phăth) of Verb-forms 122–124, 'Suppᵗ to Tab. XIV'

"Day," "first," "second," etc., of the E.V. in Gen. i. 234–236

DEFECTIVE 'Long-Khĕrik and Shŭ-rik' [Pt. I. §§ 12 & 14].

DEFICIENT rather than FULL Khou-lem' used with ו Convers. and with אל Deprec. and in expression of a Positive wish 105, 222

'Definite-Article,' Hé for, not to be placed before a Noun which is 'i.e.', etc. 43

DIACRITIC POINT of שׁ and שׂ [Pt. I. § 61 Note].

'Doubly-Irregular' Verbs, so called by some, ... 174, 267–314

"Evening and Morning" [Gen. i. 5] 227

'FURTIVE' PATHAKH [Pt. I. § 60] 114

———— dropped (of course) when any addition is made to the word ... 44, 120

FUTURE-TENSE 75, 76, 85–89, 333 –337

———— forms, with Hé at end of the more common forms, 88, 105, 111, 117, 118, 334 (η), 335

———— Kal, Shūrik (or ú) form of, 336 & 337

———— usages, Some, 99

———— with Negative Particle, 93, 103, 105, 222

———— with 'Váv Conversive' ... 101, 102

———— with 'Váv Conversive' precedes its Subject... 104

'Fut. (—)' Verbs 85 (Note ‡), 104 116, 118

———— with — to prefixes ית of Fut. K. before חט 116

'Fut. (—)' Verbs 85 (Note §), 104 116, 117

———— often 'Intransitive' ... 10

———— with — to prefixes ית of Fut. K. before חט 11

"Has become as one of Us" [Gen iii. 22], Note on, ... 252–25

Hê at the end of a word to express "*towards*" ... 42

—— at the end of some Future forms ... ... 88 etc.

—— at the end of some Imperative forms ... ... 86 etc.

—— at the end of some Infinitive forms 80

—— at the end of Past forms 82, etc.

—— for 'Interrogation' ... 56

—— stands before the *first word* of Interrogative clause ... 93

—— for the 'Definite Article' 4, 5, 6

——————————— NOT to be placed before a Noun 'i.e.' etc. 43

Hê, The, to be prefixed to Adjectives with '*Definite*' words . 51

Hê, The, to be prefixed to Demonstrative Pronouns *when used Adjectively* 58

Hê of *Hiph.*, and of *Hithpǎ.*, sometimes replaced by *A'-leph* 177

Hê preceded by *Segol* sometimes at the end of forms 335 (Note *)

Hê Quiescent [Pt. I. §§ 29, 31].

——————— Verbs having as 3ᵈ Rt-letter 170–173, 190–193, Tab. XXIII

Hê when Consonantal at the end of a word has *Mappêk* [Pt. I. § 31].

Hê Consonantal, Verbs having, as 3ᵈ Rt-letter .. 190 (Note *)

Hê where a 'Relative Pronoun' is required in English ... 59

Hiph-îl 71, 74, 76, 79 (& Note), 83, 86, 119, etc.

Hiph-îl forms, Some, ... 348–355

Hithpǎ-êl (see also below) 71, 74, 76, 83, 89 & 89*, 112, 133 (Note ‡, *b*), etc.

—————— forms, Some, 357–364

—————— forms transposing the *Thâv* ... 89, 315

—————— forms which drop the *Thâv* 89*, 316–318

Hoph-ǎl ... ... 71, 76, 83, etc.

—————— forms, Some, 355–357

—————— Imperative found rarely 87 (Note)

Huph-ǎl 72, 143

Imperative connected with Future 87

—————— forms 86, 87, 331–335

—————————— with *Hê* at the end 86, 87, 111, 112, 330, 335

Imperative Negative, expressed by Future with Negative Particle 93, 103

Imperative NOT TO BE USED WITH a Negative Particle 93

Imperative only in 'Second-Person' forms 93

Infinitive Absolute 77, 78, 319

—————— Construct and with Prefixes ... ... 79, 80, 320–324, Tab. XIV (Appˣ A thereto)

—————— forms 77, 81, 319–324

—————— with *Hê* (and *Thâv*) at the end, 80, 320, 321, 323

—————— with Pron.-Affs. 80, Tabs. XV & XXIV (see also Tabs. XVII, etc.)

Interrogation marked by *Hê* prefixed, 5, (see also p. 91, Voc. 2)

Kaumets in place of *Pathakh* in certain instances ... 185, 209

KAUMETS retained sometimes where it is usually dropped 335, 336
KAUMETS-KHAUTUPH [Pt. I. § 15 (& Note), §23 (Note), §55 (10)]
KHOULEM 'Full' and 'Deficient' [Pt. I. § 13]
KIBBÚTS sometimes in the form of *Shŭrik* [Pt. I. § 14, N.B.]
————, The usual form of, (*viz.*⸗), sometimes used for Shŭrik [Pt. I. § 14]

LONG-Khērik sometimes in the form of *Short*-Khērik [Pt. I. § 12]
LONG-Khērik, The usual form of (viz. '—), sometimes used for *Short*-Khērik [Pt. I. §12, N.B.]
LONG-VOWEL in an Open syllable, sometimes, *in place of a Short-vowel in a Closed syllable* (Obs. XXIII) 185

MAKKĒPH [Pt. I. § 37 (2)].
MAPPĒK [Pt. I. §§ 31, 34]... 121
METHEG [Pt. I. §§ 43–45].
MIXED-VOICE forms and MIXED-TENSE forms 177, 178
MUTE 'Yod' [Pt. I. § 35].

Negative Particles אַל & לֹא *precede Tense* 93
NIPH-ĂL 71, 76, 77, 79 Note, 83, 87, 119, etc.
NIPH-ĂL forms, Some, 338–341
NUN Final at end of some Future forms ... 88 (twice), 89, 160

OBSERVATIONS I–XI 93
———— XII–XV ... 139
———— XVI–XXII 179 & 180

OBSERVATIONS XXIII–XXV 185
———— XXVI–XXX 190–193
———— XXXI & XXXII 202
———— XXXIII–L 208–212

PARTICIPLES 82–85, 326–330, Appˣ (B) & (C) to Tab. XIV
PAST-TENSE (K.), ordinary forms 73 & 74
————, other forms 81, 324, 325
PAST-TENSE with *Váv* prefixed 100, 104
————must precede its Subject... ... 104
PAUSE-FORMS [Pt. I. § 41].
———— of Nouns with Pron.-Affs. see Tabs. V–XIII.
———— of Particles with Pron.-Affs. see Tabs. II–IV
———— of Personal Pronouns 9, Tab. I
———— of Verbs 110–113*
PAUSE-FORMS NOT in Pause 113*
PÍ-ĔL ... ... 71, 76, 83, etc.
———— forms, Some, ... 342–347
PLURAL-FEM. form of Nouns (and Adjectives & Participles) 31
PLURAL-MASC. form of Nouns (and Adjectives & Participles) 31
PO-ĔL & Po-ĂL Voice-forms 365–368
PRESENT ... ... 72, 84, 99 (III)
PRONOUNS, Absolute forms, 9, Tab. I
———— Adjective ... 58, 59
————, Affix-forms 13, etc., Tabs. VIII & XXXI

PRONOUNS, Demonstrative ... 28
———— Interrogative ... 29
———— Relative ... 21-24
PRONOUN-AFFIXES to Nouns, Tabs. V-XIII.
———————— to Particles, Tabs. II-IV
———————— to Verbs, Tabs. XXIV-XXXI & Obs. XXXIII-L (on pp. 208-212), also Note (F) on pp. 378 & 379
PRONOUN-AFFIXES used Relatively 24, 380
PŬ-ĂL ... ... 71, 76, 83, etc.
——— forms, Some, ... 347, 348

Relative Pronoun 21-24

Sequence of events often marked by use of Tenses (Past & Future) simply 100
SHORT-Khîrik sometimes in the form of Long-Khîrik [Pt. I. § 12 (N.B.)]
SHORTENING of a Long Vowel in a closed syllable, Examples of, (1) when the Accent is *removed* (see ' Note ' in ' Notes on Tab. XIV '), (2) when the Accent is ' *drawn back* ' 124
SHVA [Pt. I. §§ 2 (ii), 3]; *understood* under *one* vowelless letter at end of a word [Pt. I. § 4], but *put* under *two* such [Pt. I. § 6]
SHVA ' *Medium* ' (of Dr. Ewald) [Pt. I. § 57]
——— ' Moving ' & ' Quiescent,' Definitions [Pt. I. § 21], Rules for [Pt. I. § 55 (1-9 & 11-14)]
SHVA-MOVING always takes a Com-

pound form under certain letters, [Pt. I. § 24]
Simple Shva under the letters ע ח ה א [Pt. I. § 55 (6)] 117, 118, 119 (*N*φ. & H φ.), 120
SHURIK sometimes in the form of *Kibbúts* [Pt. I. § 14]
———, The usual form of (viz. ו), sometimes used for *Kibbúts* [Pt. I. § 14 (N.B.)]
' SLIGHT '-Vowel [Pt. I. § 56] 35-38, 115, 117-119

TENSES 72-74
——— precede Subject except there be Emphasis on the Subject 105
TENSE-USAGES 97-103 (& § 162)
Three forms of Past *Kal* ... 81
TSAYRE (—) rather than '— in Fut. Hiph. in certain cases 222

VÁV-CONSONANTAL as 2d Rt-letter, Verbs having, ... 150
VÁV CONVERSIVE 101, 102, 128, 135, 136 (twice), 137, 156-158, 171
VÁV with *Kaumets* 179, 223-225, [but see also p. 101 (Obs. 1)]
Verb and Noun together from the same Root, for Emphasis, 228 & 229
Verbs ' Doubly Irregular ' (so called by some) ... 174, 267-314
' Verbs Fut. (—),' and ' Verbs Fut. (—),' ... 85 (Notes ‡ & §)
VERBS, Introductory remarks on, 69-89**
——— ' Med. A,' ' Med. E,' and ' Med. O,'[bad terms for ' ע,' ' ע,' and ' ע'] 81

VERBS, Names of the Seven ordinary Voices 69–72

VERBS are not always used in all
the Voices 221

VERBS of which the Root has *Nun*
for 3ᵈ letter ... 121 & 122

—— of which the Root has *Résh*
in it... 121

—— of which the Root has *Tháv*
for 3ᵈ letter 121 & 122

—— whose 1ˢᵗ Rt-letter is *A-leph*,
128–130**, Tab. XVII &
Paradigm

—— whose 1ˢᵗ Rt-letter is *Yod*
133–139, Tab. XVIII

—— whose 1ˢᵗ Rt-letter is *Nun*
143–146, Tab. XIX

—— whose 2ᵈ Rt-letter is *Váv* or
Yod ... 150–163, Tab. XX

—— whose 2ᵈ and 3ᵈ Rt-letters
are the same, 179 & 180, Tab.
XXI

(ע'ע a bad designation for
these Verbs... ... ... 179)

VERBS whose 3ᵈ Rt-letter is *A-leph*
169, 185, Tab. XXII

—— whose 3ᵈ Rt-letter is *Hé
Consonantal* ... 190 (Note *)

—— whose 3ᵈ Rt-letter is *Hé
Non-consonantal* 170–173, 190–
193, Tab. XXIII

—— with Pron.-Affs. 175, 208–
212, Tabs. XXIV etc

VOICE-forms, Ordinary ... 69–72

——————— Other ... 175–177

——————— which are called
Poél and *Po-ăl* ... 365–368

VOCABULARY Heb.-Eng....383–388

——————— Eng.-Heb., 389 & 390

N.B. (α) The 'Pt. I.' referred to in these Tables is the FIRST PART (PART I.) of the 'INTRODUCTORY HEBREW GRAMMAR.'

(β) The § § referred to are those of the Exercise-book if Pt. I. be not mentioned.

TABLE I.

PERSONAL PRONOUNS. — ABSOLUTE FORMS.

[N.B.—p. stands for 'Pause-form.' Pt. I., § 41.]

Singular.	I {	אֲנִי or אָנֹכִי p. אֲנִי ׃ אָנֹכִי ׃	thou {	m. (p. ׃ אָתָּה) ²אַתָּה f. (p. ׃ אַתְּ) ³אַתְּ	he (or it) she (or it)	הוּא הִיא, הוּא ¹
Plural.	we {	(אֲנַחְנוּ & ⁶אֲנַחְנוּ) p. (אֲנַחְנוּ ׃ & נַחְנוּ׃)	ye {	m. אַתֶּם f. ⁵אַתֵּנָה	they {	m. הֵמָּה, הֵם f. ⁴הֵנָּה

1. הוּא in the Pentateuch; — הִיא, the usual form elsewhere, is comparatively rare in the Pentateuch. The הוּא is 'read' as הִיא [see Pt. I., § 79 (3).]

[Note.—In Job xxxi. 11, הוּא is *Kthiv* for הִיא *Krí* [Pt. I., § 74 (3)], and in the same verse וְהִיא is *Kthiv* for וְהוּא *Krí*.]

2. אָתָּ, in Nu. xi. 15, Deut. v. 24, for Euphony; and, in Ez. xxviii. 14, for shortness. In 1 S. xxiv. 19, Ps. vi. 4, Job i. 10, Eccles. vii. 22, Neh. ix. 6, אַתְּ is *Kthiv* for אַתָּה *Krí* [Pt. I., § 74 (3)]. Gesenius [Thesaurus, p. 129 (a)] gives אָתָּ for 1 S. xxiv. 19, Ps. vi. 4; but this is a mistake, as in each case it is merely אַתְּ *Kthiv* there. — The Reader should be put on his guard against the very great mistake (made by some) of mixing up the *Kthiv* and *Krí* together, and speaking of this *incongruous mixture* as being "*written*" and "*read*," — whereas the truth is that such is neither "*written*" nor "*read*" at all, in the technical sense. Needless and great confusion is caused by the *misuse* of technical terms.

3. אֹתִי is *Kthiv* (Ju. xvii. 2, 1 Ki. xiv. 2, 2 Ki. iv. 16, 23, viii. 1, Jer. iv. 30) for אַתְּ *Krí*, and (Ez. xxxvi. 13) for אַתָּ *Krí* [Pt. I., § 74 (3)].

4. There is *another* word, הֵנָּה, *hither*, to be distinguished from this by the context only.

5. אַתֵּן, Ez. xxxiv. 31.—The forms אַתֵּן (and אַתֵּנָה), which some give, should not be adopted.

6. אָנוּ is *Kthiv* (Jer. xlii. 6) for אֲנַחְנוּ *Krí* [Pt. I., § 74 (3)].

1

TABLE II.

Pronoun-marks attached to *Prefixes*—

N.B.—p. stands for 'Pause-form.' Words in [ ] are not in the Bible.

(i.) בְּ *in*, לְ *to* or *for* :—

In / בְ	**Singular.**	in me בִּי §	in thee { (m.) (p. : בָּךְ*) בְּךָ¹ / (f.) בָּךְ*	in { him בּוֹ / her בָּהּ	(1)
	Plural.	in us בָּנוּ §	in you { (m.) בָּכֶם / (f.) [וּבָכֶן]	in them { (m.) בָּהֶם, בָּם ² / (f.) בָּהֵן, בָּהֶן ³	
To / לְ	**Singular.**	to me לִי	to thee { (m.) (p. : לָךְ†) לְךָ ⁶ / (f.) לָךְ† ⁷	to { him לוֹ ⁴ / her לָהּ ⁵	(2)
	Plural.	to us לָנוּ §	to you { (m.) לָכֶם / (f.) [וְלָכֶן] לָכֶנָה ¹⁰	to them { (m.) לָהֶם, לָמוֹ ⁸ / (f.) לָהֶן, לָהֵנָה ⁹	

(ii.) כְּ (or, כְּמוֹ) *as* or *like*, מ (מִנִּי, מִן) *from* :—

As or Like. / כְּ (or כְּמוֹ)	**Singular.**	like me כָּמוֹנִי	like thee { (m.) כָּמוֹךָ ¹¹ / (f.) כָּמוֹךְ	like { him כָּמוֹהוּ / her כָּמוֹהָ	(3)
	Plural.	like us כָּמוֹנוּ	like you { (m.) כְּמוֹכֶם, כָּכֶם / (f.) [כְּמוֹכֶן, כָּכֶן]	like them { (m.) כְּמוֹהֶם, כָּהֶם, כְּהֵם ¹² / (f.) [כְּמוֹהֶן], כָּהֵן ¹³	

In the place of the ◌ָ given above, there may also be וֹ ; thus כָּמוֹנִי, 1 K. xxii. 4, etc.

From / מ (or מִן)	**Singular.**	from me מִמֶּנִּי ¹⁵	from thee { (m.) (p. : מִמֶּךָ) מִמְּךָ / (f.) מִמֵּךְ	from { him מִמֶּנּוּ ‡ ¹⁴ / her מִמֶּנָּה	(4)
	Plural.	from us מִמֶּנּוּ ‡	from you { (m.) מִכֶּם / (f.) [מִכֶּן]	from them { (m.) מֵהֶם, מֵהֵמָּה ¹⁶ / (f.) מֵהֶן, מֵהֵנָּה	

For the Notes see next page (3).

NOTES ON TABLE II.

* The *two* words marked thus are the same in form. They can be distinguished from each other by the context only.

† See Note *.

‡ See Note *.

§ Somewhat like each of the words thus marked, there is another word (to be distinguished therefrom), viz , בִּי, *prithee;* בָּנוּ (not בְּנוּ), *they built;* לָהֶן (not לָהֵן) Ruth i 13, which is either *for them* or (according to some) *therefore;* לָהֵנָּה *on this side, on that side;* לָכֵן *therefore;* לָנוּ *they lodged.*

1 Also בְּכָה, Ps. cxli. 8.

2 Also בְּהֵמָה, Ex. xxxvi. 1; Hab. i. 16.

3 Also בָּהֵנָּה, Lev. v. 22; Jer. v. 17; also in Nu. xiii. 19, where the accent is *wrongly* placed on the last syllable in several editions.

4 לֹא is *Kthiv* sometimes for לוֹ *Kri* [Pt. I , § 74 (3)]

5 לָהּ, Nu. xxxii. 42, is for לָהּ; the (–) marks the ה as רפה [Pt. I., § 48, ‡ i., ii.]. So לָה, Zech. v. 11, Ruth ii 14, in some copies.

6 לְכָה, Gen. xxvii. 37, Is. iii 6. This is distinguished by the context only from לְכָה, *go thou* (m.), with ה added; and this last, dropping the ה, is sometimes לְךָ.

7 לכי (2 K. iv. 2) is *Kthiv* for לָךְ *Kri* [Pt. I., § 74 (3).]

8 לָהֶמָּה, Jer. xiv. 16.

9 Ez. i. 5; xlii. 9.

10 Ez. xiii. 18.

11 כָּמֹכָה, Ex. xv. 11.

12 Also ‡ בָּהֵמָּה, Jer. xxxvi. 32.

13 Ez. xviii. 14.

14 ‡ מִנְהוּ Job iv. 12. Also ‡ מִנְהוּ (Ps. lxviii. 24) according to some.

15 Also מָנִי, as Is. xxx. 1. (Also ‡ מֶנִּי Ps. xviii. 23[a], Job xxi. 16.) [There is another word מִנִּי (and, twice, מִנֵּי Is. xxx. 11), which means merely *from* (= מִן), as Ju. v. 14, Ps. xliv. 11, 19, etc. — The מִנִּי of Ps. xlv. 9 is taken by some for מִנִּים *musical instruments,* and by others supposed to mean *a band of musicians.*]

16 Jer. x. 2; Eccles. xii. 12. Also מִנְּהֶם, Job xi. 20.

---

a Also Ps. lxv. 4.

TABLE III.

(1) אֵת (אֵת־) the mark of the 'Definite Object,' (2) אֵת (אֵת־) *with*, (3) עִם *with*.

			(1)
me אֹתִי	thee { m. (p.: אֹתָךְ [1]) אֹתְךָ / f. אֹתָךְ	him אֹתוֹ / her אֹתָהּ	אֵת
us אֹתָנוּ	you { m. אֶתְכֶם [4] / f. [אֶתְכֶן]	them { m. אֹתָם [2] / f. אֶתְהֶן [3]	אֶת־

(*α.*) Forms of (1) are sometimes given for those of (2). — (*β.*) In place of the ֹ given above, there may be the full וֹ; thus, אוֹתִי Deut. xxxii. 51, etc.

with			(2)
with me אִתִּי	with thee { m. (p.: אִתָּךְ) אִתְּךָ / f. אִתָּךְ	with { him אִתּוֹ / her אִתָּהּ	אֵת
with us אִתָּנוּ	with you { m. אִתְּכֶם / f. [אִתְּכֶן]	with them { m. אִתָּם / f. [אִתָּן]	אֶת־

with			(3)
with me עִמִּי [7]	with thee { m. (p.: עִמָּךְ) עִמְּךָ [5] / f. עִמָּךְ	with { him עִמּוֹ / her עִמָּהּ	עִם
with us עִמָּנוּ	with you { m. עִמָּכֶם / f. [עִמָּכֶן]	with them { m. עִמָּם [6] / f. [עִמָּן]	

---

1 Also אֹתְכָה Ex. xxix. 35.

2 Also אֶתְהֶם Gen. xxxii. 1; אוֹתָהֶם Ez. xxiii. 45.

3 Also אֹתָנָה Ex. xxxv. 26; אֹתָן Ez. xvi. 54; אוֹתָהֶן Ez. xxiii. 47.

4 Also אוֹתְכֶם Josh. xxiii. 15.

5 Also עִמָּכָה 1 S. i. 26.

6 Also עִמָּהֶם Nu. xxii. 12.

7 Also עִמָּדִי (fr. עמד).

Table IV.

(1) אֶל *to*, (2) עַל *on*, or *upon*, [(3), and (4), below].

to			
to me (p. :אֵי‑) אֵלַי	to thee { m. אֵלֶיךָ / f. (p. :יִךְ‑) אֵלַיִךְ	to { him אֵלָיו / her אֵלֶיהָ	(1) אֶל [also וְאֶלָ]
to us אֵלֵינוּ	to you { m. אֲלֵיכֶם* / f. אֲלֵיכֶן*	to them { m.[1] אֲלֵיהֶם / f. אֲלֵיהֶן	

on			
on me (p. :יִ‑) עָלַי	on thee { m. עָלֶיךָ / f. (p. :יִךְ‑)[3] עָלַיִךְ	on { him עָלָיו / her[2] עָלֶיהָ	(2) עַל also עֲלֵי
on us עָלֵינוּ	on you { m. עֲלֵיכֶם* / f. עֲלֵיכֶן*	on them { m.[4] עֲלֵיהֶם / f. עֲלֵיהֶן	

(3) From עַד [also עֲדֵי] *unto, even to*, etc., the following occur,—
עָדַי *unto me*, עָדֶיךָ *unto thee* (m.), עָדָיו *unto him*, עָדֶיהָ *unto her*,
and עֲדֵיכֶם with עַ [Job xxxii. 12], *unto you* (m.), עָדֵיהֶם [2 K. ix. 18]
for *unto them* (m.). } (3)

(4) From בִּלְעֲדֵי [the Construct form—(there is no בִּלְעַד) besides, the
following occur,—
בִּלְעָדֶיךָ , בִּלְעָדַי (p. :יִ‑) , } (4)

---

[1] Often אֲלֵהֶם.—אֵלֵימוֹ Ps. ii. 5.—[אֱלֵיהֶם (Ez. xxxi. 14), which some take to
mean "*to them* (m.)," strictly means "*their* (m.) *strong ones*," i.e. *the strong ones
among them*].

[2] The following words, עֲלֵי *leaves-of* (Neh. viii. 15, etc.), עָלֵהוּ *his leaf* (Ps. i. 3,
etc.), עָלֶהָ *her leaf*, or *leafage* (Is. i. 30), are from עָלֶה *a leaf*.

[3] Also :עָלֵיְכִי Ps. cxvi. 7.

[4] Often עֲלֵהֶם.—Also עָלֵימוֹ Ps. v. 12, lv. 16; Job vi. 16, xx. 23, etc.

* Also without the יִ; לֵ instead of לָ.

Table V. (i.) Singular.

my שִׁירִי	thy {	m. (p. ‎ֶךָ‎ :) שִׁירְךָ	his	שִׁירוֹ	שִׁיר
		f. שִׁירֵךְ	her	שִׁירָהּ	
our שִׁירֵנוּ	your {	m. שִׁירְכֶם	their {	m. שִׁירָם	song
		f. שִׁירְכֶן		f. שִׁירָן	i. c. שִׁיר (§ 52)

(ii.) Plural.

my { שִׁירַי (p. ‎ֶי‎ :)	thy {	m. שִׁירֶיךָ	his	שִׁירָיו	שִׁירִים
		f. (p. ‎ַיִךְ‎ :) שִׁירַיִךְ	her	שִׁירֶיהָ	
our שִׁירֵינוּ	your {	m. שִׁירֵיכֶם	their {	m. שִׁירֵיהֶם	songs
		f. שִׁירֵיכֶן		f. שִׁירֵיהֶן	i. c. שִׁירֵי (§ 56 ix.)

Table VI. (i.) Singular.

my תּוֹרָתִי	thy {	m. (p. ‎ֶךָ‎ :)[1] תּוֹרָתְךָ	his	תּוֹרָתוֹ	תּוֹרָה
		f. תּוֹרָתֵךְ	her	תּוֹרָתָהּ	
our תּוֹרָתֵנוּ	your {	m. תּוֹרַתְכֶם	their {	m. תּוֹרָתָם	law
		f. תּוֹרַתְכֶן		f. תּוֹרָתָן	i. c. תּוֹרַת (§ 56 v.)

(ii.) Plural.

my { תּוֹרֹתַי[3] (p. ‎ֶי‎ :)	thy {	m. תּוֹרֹתֶיךָ[2]	his	תּוֹרֹתָיו	תּוֹרוֹת
		f. (p. ‎ַיִךְ‎ :) תּוֹרֹתַיִךְ	her	תּוֹרֹתֶיהָ	
our תּוֹרֹתֵינוּ	your {	m. תּוֹרֹתֵיכֶם	their {	m. תּוֹרֹתֵיהֶם[4]	laws
		f. תּוֹרֹתֵיכֶן		f. תּוֹרֹתֵיהֶן[5]	i. c. תּוֹרֹת

The ‎ י ‎ is sometimes dropped in (ii.).

---

[1] ‎ָתֶיךָ‎ Ez. xxxv. 11; Ps. ix. 15.
[2] Rarely ‎תָךְ‎, as Deut. xxviii. 59.
[3] ‎תַי‎ Ps. cxxxii. 12, as some say.
[4] By Contraction ‎ָתָם‎.
[5] ‎ָתָן‎.

TABLE VII.

A Noun of Dual Form.

my { אָזְנִי / p. : אָזְנַי	thy { *m.* אָזְנֶיךָ / *f.* (p. : אָזְנֵיךְ) אָזְנַיִךְ	his אָזְנָיו / her אָזְנֶיהָ	*אָזְנַיִם (p. : ־יִם) ears [i.c. אָזְנֵי]
our אָזְנֵינוּ	your { *m.* אָזְנֵיכֶם / *f.* אָזְנֵיכֶן	their { *m.* אָזְנֵיהֶם / *f.* אָזְנֵיהֶן	

* The ־ָ to the א is ŏ.

TABLE VIII.

Various Forms of these Pronoun Affixes.*

[Those within ( ) are not for Composition.]

(i.) For a Noun in the Singular,

First Person.	Second Person.	Third Person.	
rare ־ִי, ־ַי	־ְךָ, ־ֶיךָ, ־ֶךָ (־ָךְ) [p.(־ְכָה), ־ֶכָה]	־וֹ, ־ֶהוּ, ־ֵהוּ (־ָה), ־ָו	M.
	־ֵךְ, ־ָךְ, ־ֶךָ (־ֵכִי, ־ָכִי) ־ֶיךָ [*rare,*]	־ָהּ, ־ֶהָ, ־ָהֶ, ־ָיהָ (rare, ־ָא, ־ֶנָּה)	F.
־ָנוּ, ־ֵנוּ, ־ִינוּ	־ֶכֶם, ־ְכֶם, ־ִיכֶם	־ָם, ־ֶהֶם, ־ָהֶם, ־ֵמוֹ, (־ָהֶם)	M.
	־ְכֶן, ־ְכֶנָה (־ָכֶן), ־ֶן	־ָן, ־ֶהֶן (־ָהֶן‡, ־ָהֵנָּה, ־ַתָּנ־)	F.

(ii.) For a Noun in the Plural or Dual,

First Person.	Second Person.	Third Person.	
־ַי [p.: ־ָי] (־ָיִ)	־ֶיךָ (־ֶיךְ)	־ָיו, ־ֵיהוּ (־ָיהוּ ; ־ָי, ־ֹהִי)	M.
	־ַיִךְ (rare ־ַיְכִי), ־ַיְךְ [p.:	־ֶיהָ (rare ־ָא)	F.
־ֵינוּ (־ֵנוּ)	־ֵיכֶם (־ֵכֶם)	־ֵיהֶם, ־ֵימוֹ, ־ֶהֶם (rare ־ֵהֵמָה)	M.
	־ֵיכֶן (־ֵכֶן ; ־ֵיכֶנָה rare)	־ֵיהֶן (־ֶהֶן ; ־ֵהֵנָּה rare)	F.

* Excluding some few which are peculiar to Tab. II. (3, 4). [Objective Aff⁸. hereafter.]

† Also ־ֶנּוּ.   ‡ Also ־ָה, ־ֶנָּה.

TABLE IX.

(i.) Singular.

my	דְּבָרִי	thy	m. (p. :ךְָ) דְּבָרְךָ f. דְּבָרֵךְ	his her	דְּבָרוֹ דְּבָרָהּ	*דָּבָר word (i.c. דְּבַר)
our	דְּבָרֵנוּ	your	m. דְּבַרְכֶם f. דְּבַרְכֶן	their	m. דְּבָרָם f. דְּבָרָן	

(ii.) Plural.

my (p. :הָ) דְּבָרַי	thy	m. דְּבָרֶיךָ f. (p. :יִךְ) דְּבָרַיִךְ	his her	דְּבָרָיו דְּבָרֶיהָ	דְּבָרִים words (i. c. דִּבְרֵי)
our דְּבָרֵינוּ	your	m. דִּבְרֵיכֶם f. דִּבְרֵיכֶן	their	m. דִּבְרֵיהֶם f. דִּבְרֵיהֶן	

* (a.) When the last letter is א, the ַ is retained before it when ‹ i. c.;' thus, צָבָא *a host*, i. c., צְבָא. [When the first letter of the word is one of the four א ה ח ע, there must be a compound Shva under it in the place of the ְ in דְּבַר (cp. γ.)].

(β.) Some words of the form פָּעֵל replace, in declension, their second ַ by ַ *followed by Dagesh Forte;* thus, קָטֹן *little* (or *a little one*) gives קְטַנָּם, and Plu. קְטַנִּים (i. c. קְטַנֵּי).

So גָּמָל *a camel* gives Plu. גְּמַלִּים (i. c. גְּמַלֵּי) גְּמַלָּיו, גְּמַלֵּיהֶם,...:

(γ.) When the first letter of the word is one of the four א ה ח ע,

    (i.) It must have a Compound Shva wherever the ד in (Tab. IX.) has Shva-Moving; thus, from חָתָן *a son-in-law*, חֲתַן (i. c.), חֲתָנוּ, etc.;—

    (ii.) It will have a ‹Slight' Vowel (where necessary) agreeing with the Compound Shva of (i.); thus, from חָכָם, *a wise man*, Plu. חֲכָמִים, i. c. חַכְמֵי, etc.

(δ.) Such Nouns as חָרָשׁ *a smith*, פָּרָשׁ *a horseman* (§ 60), (which really belong to the class of words like גַּנָּב *a thief*, with Dagesh Forte in their middle letter), *retain* the ַ of their first letter; thus, חָרַשׁ (i. c.), חָרָשִׁים Plu. (חָרָשֵׁי i. c.);— the forms with Pron. Affixes being (Sing.) וֹ ַ ַ, etc., (Plu.) יָ ַ ַ, etc., as in פָּרָשָׁיו (from פָּרָשִׁים).

(ε) The Dual Decl. of a פָּעֵל Noun, as כָּנָף *a wing*, Du. כְּנָפַיִם (i.c. כַּנְפֵי), is כְּנָפַיִו (ֶיהָ), כְּנָפֶיד (ֶיךְ), כְּנָפַי, כַּנְפֵיהֶם (— ֶהֶן), כַּנְפֵיכֶם (כֶן), כְּנָפֵינוּ.

	our	f.	m. your.	f.	m. their.	my.	f.	m. thy.	her.	his.	i.o.
elder	זְקֵנֵנוּ	־ְכֶן	זְקֵנְכֶם	־ָן	זְקֵנָם	זְקֵנִי	־ֵךְ	זְקֵנְךָ[1]	־ֶה	זְקֵנוֹ	s. (1) זָקֵן (זְקַן*)
elders	זְקֵנֵינוּ	־ֵיכֶן	זְקֵנֵיכֶם	־ֵיהֶן	זְקֵנֵיהֶם	זְקֵנַי[3]	־ַיִךְ[2]	זְקֵנֶיךָ	־ֶיהָ	זְקֵנָיו	pl. זְקֵנִים (זִקְנֵי†)
court	חֲצֵרֵנוּ	־ְכֶן	חֲצֵרְכֶם	־ָן	חֲצֵרָם	חֲצֵרִי	־ֵךְ	חֲצֵרְךָ[1]	־ָה	חֲצֵרוֹ	s. (2) חָצֵר (חֲצַר)
courts	חֲצֵרֵינוּ	־ֵיכֶן	חֲצֵרֵיכֶם	־ֵיהֶן	חֲצֵרֵיהֶם	חֲצֵרַי[3]	־ַיִךְ[2]	חֲצֵרֶיךָ	־ֶיהָ	חֲצֵרָיו	pl. חֲצֵרִים‡ (חַצְרֵי†)
officer	פְּקִידֵנוּ	־ְכֶן	פְּקִידְכֶם	־ָן	פְּקִידָם	פְּקִידִי	־ֵךְ	פְּקִידְךָ[1]	־ָה	פְּקִידוֹ	s. (3) פָּקִיד§ (פְּקִיד)
officers	פְּקִידֵינוּ	־ֵיכֶן	פְּקִידֵיכֶם	־ֵיהֶן	פְּקִידֵיהֶם	פְּקִידַי[3]	־ַיִךְ[2]	פְּקִידֶיךָ	־ֶיהָ	פְּקִידָיו	pl. פְּקִידִים (פְּקִידֵי)
kinsman	קְרוֹבֵנוּ	־ְכֶן	קְרוֹבְכֶם	־ָן	קְרוֹבָם	קְרוֹבִי	־ֵךְ	קְרוֹבְךָ[1]	־ָה	קְרוֹבוֹ	s. (4) קָרוֹב§ (קְרֹב)
kinsmen	קְרוֹבֵינוּ	־ֵיכֶן	קְרוֹבֵיכֶם	־ֵיהֶן	קְרוֹבֵיהֶם	קְרוֹבַי[3]	־ַיִךְ[2]	קְרוֹבֶיךָ	־ֶיהָ	קְרוֹבָיו	pl. קְרוֹבִים (קְרוֹבֵי)
guest	קְרוּאֵנוּ	־ְכֶן	קְרוּאֲכֶם	־ָן	קְרוּאָם	קְרוּאִי	־ֵךְ	קְרוּאֲךָ[1]	־ָה	קְרוּאוֹ	s. (5) קָרוּא§ (קְרוּא)
guests	קְרוּאֵינוּ	־ֵיכֶן	קְרוּאֵיכֶם	־ֵיהֶן	קְרוּאֵיהֶם	קְרוּאַי[3]	־ַיִךְ[2]	קְרוּאֶיךָ	־ֶיהָ	קְרוּאָיו	pl. קְרוּאִים (קְרוּאֵי)

Note. (α) The Declension of פֶּעֶל is like Tab. IX; and (β) that of פָּעוֹל is like (5) here. (γ) ־ַ may stand for ־ֲ, Pt. I, § 14. (δ) Under one of ע ח ה א a Moving ־ַ must of course take a Compound form.

* (i) A 'Borrowed' פֶּעֶל form. But (ii) אֲבָל (for אָבָל) fr. אָבַל, יָגֵן fr. יָגֹן, etc., are the strictly proper forms. (iii) Some פֶּעֶל words 'borrow' 'i.c.' a פָּעֵל (and, rarely, פֶּעֶל) form; thus גָּדֵר, 'i.c.' גְּדֵר; so יָרֵךְ, 'i.c.' יְרֵךְ; etc.—† (i) Some RETAIN the ־ֵ; thus אֲבֵלִים fr. אָבֵל (pl. of אָבֵל), שְׂמֵחַי as well שְׂמֵחִים fr. שְׂמֵחִים (pl. of שָׂמֵחַ), etc. (ii) עִנְּבֵי fr. עֲנָבִים (pl. of עֵנָב) is a 'Euphonic' irregular form. So עָקְבֵי from pl. of עָקֵב (besides עִקְּבֵי the regular form).—‡ חֲצֵרוֹת, the f. form of this, is 'i.c.' חַצְרוֹת, and w. Affs. חַצְרוֹתָיו—also חֲצֵרוֹתָיו Comp. Note (†), and so חֲצֵרוֹתַי ('p.' for ־ַי).—§ The ־ֵ is sometimes retained in the Pl. and w. Affs.; thus סָרִים 'i.c.' סָרִים, pl. סָרִיסִים ('i.c.' סָרִיסַי), and סָרִיסָיו etc.; so, fr. שָׁלִישׁ שְׁלִישִׁי, שְׁלִישָׁיו, & pl. שְׁלִישִׁים, שְׁלִישָׁיו; and so fr. שָׁבוּעַ ('i.c.' שְׁבוּעַ) or w. ־ַ, and dual שְׁבֻעַיִם, pl. שָׁבֻעִים & שָׁבֻעוֹת ('i.c.' שְׁבֻעַת), etc.

[1] p. ־ֶךָ. [2] p. ־ַיִךְ. [3] p. ־ָי.

App.ˣ (B) to Tab. IX :—Declension-forms of some words mĭ-l'rä—with only LAST VOWEL liable to change.

	our.	f.	m. your.	f.	m. their.	my.	f.	m. thy.	her.	his.	i.c.	
star	כּוֹכָבֵנוּ	־ְכֶן,	כּוֹכַבְכֶם,	־ֶן	כּוֹכָבָם,	כּוֹכָבִי	כּוֹכָבֵךְ,	כּוֹכָבְךָ,	־ָה	כּוֹכָבוֹ	(כּוֹכַב)	כּוֹכָב s. (1)
stars	כּוֹכָבֵינוּ	־ֵיכֶן,	כּוֹכָבֵיכֶם,	־ֵיהֶן,	כּוֹכָבֵיהֶם,	³כּוֹכָבַי	²כּוֹכָבַיִךְ,	כּוֹכָבֶיךָ,	־ֶיהָ	כּוֹכָבָיו,	(כּוֹכָבֵי)	(a) כּוֹכָבִים pl.
fox	שׁוּעָלֵנוּ	־ְכֶן,	שׁוּעַלְכֶם,	־ֶן	שׁוּעָלָם,	שׁוּעָלִי	שׁוּעָלֵךְ,	¹שׁוּעָלְךָ,	־ָה	שׁוּעָלוֹ,	(שׁוּעָל)	שׁוּעָל s. (2)
foxes	שׁוּעָלֵינוּ	־ֵיכֶן,	שׁוּעָלֵיכֶם,	־ֵיהֶן,	שׁוּעָלֵיהֶם,	³שׁוּעָלַי	²שׁוּעָלַיִךְ,	שׁוּעָלֶיךָ,	־ֶיהָ	שׁוּעָלָיו	(שׁוּעָלֵי)	שׁוּעָלִים pl.
judgment	מִשְׁפָּטֵנוּ	־ְכֶן,	מִשְׁפַּטְכֶם,	־ֶן	מִשְׁפָּטָם,	מִשְׁפָּטִי	מִשְׁפָּטֵךְ,	¹מִשְׁפָּטְךָ,	־ָה	מִשְׁפָּטוֹ,	(מִשְׁפַּט)	מִשְׁפָּט s. (3)
judgments	מִשְׁפָּטֵינוּ	־ֵיכֶן,	מִשְׁפָּטֵיכֶם,	־ֵיהֶן,	מִשְׁפָּטֵיהֶם,	³מִשְׁפָּטַי	²מִשְׁפָּטַיִךְ,	מִשְׁפָּטֶיךָ,	־ֶיהָ	מִשְׁפָּטָיו,	(מִשְׁפָּטֵי)	מִשְׁפָּטִים pl.

N.B. (α) The מ prefixed in Nouns of this form is NOT A 'ROOT'-letter. The Form is מִפְעָל.

(β) Sometimes the ־ְ is replaced by ־ַ followed by *Dagesh*; thus fr. מִשְׂגָּב (i.e. מִשְׂגַּב) מִשְׂגַּבּוֹ *his....,* etc. So in other Forms also, sometimes.

	our.	f.	m. your.	f.	m. their.	my.	f.	m. thy.	her.	his.	i.c.	
preserver	שׁוֹמְרֵנוּ	־ְכֶן,	שׁוֹמֶרְכֶם,	־ֶן	שׁוֹמְרָם,	שׁוֹמְרִי	־ֵרְךְ,	¹שׁוֹמֶרְךָ,	־ָה	שׁוֹמְרוֹ,	(שׁוֹמֵר)	שׁוֹמֵר s. (4) †
preservers	שׁוֹמְרֵינוּ	־ֵיכֶן,	שׁוֹמְרֵיכֶם,	־ֵיהֶן,	שׁוֹמְרֵיהֶם,	³שׁוֹמְרַי	²שׁוֹמְרַיִךְ,	שׁוֹמְרֶיךָ,	־ֶיהָ	שׁוֹמְרָיו,	(שׁוֹמְרֵי)	שׁוֹמְרִים pl.
Redeemer	גּוֹאֲלֵנוּ	־ְכֶן,	גּוֹאַלְכֶם,	־ֶן	גּוֹאֲלָם,	גּוֹאֲלִי	־ֵלֵךְ,	גּוֹאַלְךָ,	־ָה	גּוֹאֲלוֹ,	(גּוֹאֵל)	גּוֹאֵל s. (5) †
redeemers	גּוֹאֲלֵינוּ	־ֵיכֶן,	גּוֹאֲלֵיכֶם,	־ֵיהֶן,	גּוֹאֲלֵיהֶם,	³גּוֹאֲלַי	²גּוֹאֲלַיִךְ,	גּוֹאֲלֶיךָ,	־ֶיהָ	גּוֹאֲלָיו,	(גּוֹאֲלֵי)	גּוֹאֲלִים pl.

(a) אוֹצָר *treasure* (like כּוֹכָב in the Sing.) has the *f.* Plu. אוֹצָרוֹת ('i.e.' אוֹצְרוֹת), w. Affs. אוֹצְרוֹתָיו, etc.

* Also with ־ַ for 'Slight'-vowel, as in אוֹיְבָהּ & אוֹיַבְכֶם fr. אוֹיֵב; and, with ־ַ, as in שׂנֵאָהּ & שׂנַאֲכֶם fr. שׂוֹנֵא.   † There may be ־ֵ for the ־ָ.

¹ p. ־ְךָ.   ² p. ־ַיִךְ.   ³ p. ־ַיְ.   ⁴ p. ־ְךָ.   ⁵ p. ־ֵיְ.

App[X] (C) to Tab. IX:—Declension of some Feminine Nouns, פְּעֻלָה, פְּעָלָה, etc.

	our.	f.	m. your.	f.	m. their.	my.	f.	m. thy.	her.	his.	i.c.		
righteousness	צִדְקָתֵנוּ	־ְכֶן	צִדְקַתְכֶם	־ָן	צִדְקָתָם	צִדְקָתִי	־ֵךְ	צִדְקָתְךָ [1]	־ָהּ	צִדְקָתוֹ	(צִדְקָת׳)	צְדָקָה	s. (1)
righteousnesses	צִדְקֹתֵינוּ	־ֵיכֶן	צִדְקֹתֵיכֶם [5]	־ָן	צִדְקֹתָם [4]	צִדְקֹתַי [3]	־ַיִךְ [2]	צִדְקֹתֶיךָ	־ֶיהָ	צִדְקֹתָיו	(צִדְקוֹת)	צְדָקוֹת	pl.
sighing	אַנְחָתֵנוּ	־ְכֶן	אַנְחַתְכֶם	־ָן	אַנְחָתָם	אַנְחָתִי	־ֵךְ	אַנְחָתְךָ [1]	־ָהּ	אַנְחָתוֹ	(אַנְחַת)	אֲנָחָה	s. (2)
sighings	אַנְחֹתֵינוּ	־ֵיכֶן	אַנְחֹתֵיכֶם [5]	־ָן	אַנְחֹתָם [4]	אַנְחֹתַי [3]	־ַיִךְ [2]	אַנְחֹתֶיךָ	־ֶיהָ	אַנְחֹתָיו	(אַנְחוֹת)	אֲנָחוֹת	pl.
cry	צַעֲקָתֵנוּ	־ְכֶן	צַעֲקַתְכֶם	־ָן	צַעֲקָתָם	צַעֲקָתִי	־ֵךְ	צַעֲקָתְךָ [1]	־ָהּ	צַעֲקָתוֹ	(צְעָקַת†)	צְעָקָה	s. (3)
cries	צַעֲקֹתֵינוּ	־ֵיכֶן	צַעֲקֹתֵיכֶם [5]	־ָן	צַעֲקֹתָם [4]	צַעֲקֹתַי [3]	־ַיִךְ [2]	צַעֲקֹתֶיךָ	־ֶיהָ †	צַעֲקֹתָיו †	(צְעָקוֹת)	צְעָקוֹת	pl.

(4) פְּעֻלָה is declined (α) sometimes as the פְּעֻלָה forms above—the ־ being dropped‡; thus (i.) fr. נְבֵלָה ('i.c.' ‡ נִבְלַת), נִבְלָתוֹ & נִבְלָתָהּ etc.; and so (ii.), fr. the Plu. חֲצֵרוֹת ('i.c.' ‡ חַצְרוֹת), חַצְרֹתָיו & חַצְרֹתֶיהָ [Cp. (2) above]; but (β) sometimes the ־ is retained as in the 'Constr.' forms שְׂרֵפַת & אֲבֵדַת of שְׂרֵפָה & אֲבֵדָה and in such Aff.-forms as שְׁאֵלָתִי (or, contracted, שְׁאֵלָתְךָ 1 S i. 17) & שְׁאֵלָתָם (besides שְׁאֵלָתֶם, the ־ dropped as in α); and so (iii.), fr. the Plu. חֲצֵרוֹת, חֲצֵרֹתַי & חֲצֵרֹתָיו besides the forms in α. ii.), and similarly גְּדֵרֹתֶיהָ fr. גְּדֵרוֹת (which is 'i.c.' גִּדְרֹת, the ־ dropped as in α).

(5) PLU. Fem. forms פְּעֻלוֹת & פְּעָלוֹת, fr. a Sing. פָּעֵל or פָּעַל & פָּעֵל, are declined as the Plurals above in (1-4).

(6) Some Nouns in ־ֶה (several in ־ֶה ־ֶ) have for the Sing. 'i.c.,' & w. Pron.-Affs., forms fr. ־ַת ־ֶ: comp. 'N.B.' in Note (‡) below and 'Notes on Tab. X' [VI (α-ε)].

(7) For the Decl. of Plurals in ־ִים fr. Sings. in ־ֶה (Cp. § 44, etc.), see Tables of Masc. forms—as Tab. V, IX, etc.

* בְּרָכָה has בִּרְכַּת (a borrowed form) 'i.c.' So חֲרָדָה has חֶרְדַּת 'i.c.' The Plu. בְּרָכוֹת is 'i.c.' בִּרְכוֹת regularly.   † ־ is sometimes retained in תְּעָלָה 'i.c.,' & in תְּעָלָתֶיהָ, fr. Plu. of תְּעָלָה. So in קְעָרֹתָיו fr. קְעָרָה ('i.c.' קְעָרַת) Plu. of קְעָרָה ('i.c.' קְעָרַת).   ‡ So in בֶּהֱמַת 'Constr.' form of בֶּהֱמָה & בַּהֲמוֹת of the Plu. בְּהֵמוֹת. N.B. The Decl.-forms Sing. of בֶּהֱמָה are בֶּהֱמָתוֹ (־ָה, ־ֶה־) etc. [fr. an unused בַּהֲמַת]; & so שְׁכֶנְתָּה fr. שְׁכֵנָה = שְׁכֶנַת a neighbour (f.)]; & גְּבֶרֶת = גְּבִירָה fr. (גְּבִירַת): See 'Notes on Tab. X-XII' [VI. 2).

¹ p. ־ֶהָ.   ² p. ־ָיִךְ.   ³ p. ־ָיַ.   ⁴ Or ־ֵיהֶם.   ⁵ Or ־ֵיהֶן.

TABLE X.

	our.	f.,	m., your.	f.,	m., their.	my.	f.,	m., thy.	her,	his.	(i. c.)		
king	מַלְכֵּנוּ	־ְכֶן	מַלְכְּכֶם	־ָן	מַלְכָּם	מַלְכִּי	־ֵךְ	מַלְכְּךָ¹	־ָהּ	מַלְכּוֹ	(מֶלֶךְ) מֶלֶךְ*	s.	1.
kings	מְלָכֵינוּ	־ֵיכֶן	מַלְכֵיכֶם	־ֵיהֶן	מַלְכֵיהֶם	מְלָכַי²	־ַיִךְ²	מְלָכֶיךָ	־ֶיהָ	מְלָכָיו	(מַלְכֵי) מְלָכִים	pl.	
vow	נִדְרֵנוּ	־ְכֶן	נִדְרְכֶם	־ָן	נִדְרָם	נִדְרִי	־ֵךְ	נִדְרְךָ¹	־ָהּ	נִדְרוֹ	(נֵדֶר) נֶדֶר*	s.	2.
											(נֶדֶר) נֶדֶר	s.	
vows	נְדָרֵינוּ	־ֵיכֶן	נִדְרֵיכֶם	־ֵיהֶן	נִדְרֵיהֶם	נְדָרַי³	־ַיִךְ²	נְדָרֶיךָ	־ֶיהָ	נְדָרָיו	(נִדְרֵי) נְדָרִים	pl.	
part	חֶלְקֵנוּ	־ְכֶן	חֶלְקְכֶם	־ָן	חֶלְקָם	חֶלְקִי	־ֵךְ	חֶלְקְךָ¹	־ָהּ	חֶלְקוֹ	(חֵלֶק) חֵלֶק*	s.	3.
parts	חֲלָקֵינוּ	־ֵיכֶן	חֶלְקֵיכֶם	־ֵיהֶן	חֶלְקֵיהֶם	חֲלָקַי²	־ַיִךְ²	חֲלָקֶיךָ	־ֶיהָ	חֲלָקָיו	(חֶלְקֵי) חֲלָקִים	pl.	
blow	נִגְעֵנוּ	־ְכֶן	נִגְעֲכֶם	־ָן	נִגְעָם	נִגְעִי	־ֵךְ	נִגְעֲךָ¹	־ָהּ	נִגְעוֹ	(נֶגַע) נֶגַע*⁴	s.	4.
blows	נְגָעֵינוּ	־ֵיכֶן	נִגְעֵיכֶם	־ֵיהֶן	נִגְעֵיהֶם	נְגָעַי³	־ַיִךְ²	נְגָעֶיךָ	־ֶיהָ	נְגָעָיו	(נִגְעֵי) נְגָעִים	pl.	
boy	נַעֲרֵנוּ	־ְכֶן	נַעַרְכֶם	־ָן	נַעֲרָם	נַעֲרִי	־ֵךְ	נַעַרְךָ†	־ָהּ	נַעֲרוֹ	(נַעַר) נַעַר*	s.	5.
boys	נְעָרֵינוּ	־ֵיכֶן	נַעֲרֵיכֶם	־ֵיהֶן	נַעֲרֵיהֶם	נְעָרַי³	־ַיִךְ²	נְעָרֶיךָ	־ֶיהָ	נְעָרָיו	(נַעֲרֵי) נְעָרִים	pl.	
servant	עֲבָדֵנוּ	־ְכֶן	עַבְדְּכֶם	־ָן	עַבְדָּם	עַבְדִּי	־ֵךְ	עַבְדְּךָ¹	־ָהּ	עַבְדּוֹ	(עֶבֶד) עֶבֶד*	s.	6.
servants	עֲבָדֵינוּ	־ֵיכֶן	עַבְדֵיכֶם	־ֵיהֶן	עַבְדֵיהֶם	עֲבָדַי³	־ַיִךְ²	עֲבָדֶיךָ	־ֶיהָ	עֲבָדָיו	(עַבְדֵי) עֲבָדִים	pl.	

* Some of these take, in Pause, ־ָ instead of the Penultimate ־ֶ; thus, שֶׁבַע (from שֶׁבַע, זֶבַח, נַחַל, עֶבֶד) : נֶחַל : עֶבֶד : זֶבַח. | † In Pause נַעֲרֶךָ. — ¹ In Pause ־ֶךָ. — ² In Pause ־ָיִךְ. | ³ In Pause ־ָי. — ⁴ As in (2). — Or, as in (1), צֶלַע w. Affs. צַלְעִי etc. (= Decl.).

TABLE XI.

	our.	f.,	m., your.	f.,	m., their.	my.	f.,	m., thy.	her.	his.	(i. c.)	
length	אָרְכֵּנוּ	־כֶן ,	אָרְכְּכֶם	־ן ,	אָרְכָּם	אָרְכִּי	־ךְ ,	אָרְכְּךָ¹	־הָ ,	*אָרְכּוֹ	(אֹרֶךְ)	אֹרֶךְ s. 1.
breadth	רָחְבֵּנוּ	־כֶן ,	רָחְבְּכֶם	־ן ,	רָחְבָּם	רָחְבִּי	־ךְ ,	רָחְבְּךָ¹	־הָ ,	*רָחְבּוֹ	(רֹחַב)	רֹחַב s. 2.
work	פָּעֳלֵנוּ	־כֶן ,	פָּעָלְכֶם	־ן ,	פָּעֳלָם	פָּעֳלִי	פָּעָלֵךְ	פָּעָלְךָ †	־הָ ,	*פָּעֳלוֹ	(פֹּעַל)	פֹּעַל s. 3.
works	פְּעָלֵינוּ	־יכֶן ,	פְּעָלֵיכֶם	־יהֶן ,	פְּעָלֵיהֶם	פְּעָלַי³	־יִךְ² ,	פְּעָלֶיךָ	־יהָ ,	פְּעָלָיו	(פְּעָלַי)	פְּעָלִים‡ pl.

N.B.—Those beginning with א, ה, or ע, take *properly* ־ֲ for the ־ְ in pl., as in חֳדָשִׁים *months*, etc., from חֹדֶשׁ.§

TABLE XII.

	our.	f.,	m., your.	f.,	m., their.	my.	f.,	m., thy.	her.	his.	(i. c.)	
queen	מַלְכָּתֵנוּ	־כֶן ,	מַלְכַּתְכֶם	־ן ,	מַלְכָּתָם	מַלְכָּתִי	־ךְ¹ ,	מַלְכָּתְךָ	־הָ ,	מַלְכָּתוֹ	(מַלְכַּת)	מַלְכָּה s. 1.
queens	מַלְכֹתֵינוּ	־יכֶן ,	מַלְכֹתֵיכֶם	־יהֶן³ ,	מַלְכֹתֵיהֶם	מַלְכֹתַי	־יִךְ² ,	מַלְכֹתֶיךָ	־יהָ ,	מַלְכֹתָיו	(מַלְכוֹת)	מַלְכוֹת pl.
								[With שׁ where there is מ in 1.—See § 69 (a.)]		(שִׁפְחָתוֹ)]	(שִׁפְחַת)	שִׁפְחָה s. 2.
girl	נַעֲרָתֵנוּ	־כֶן ,	נַעֲרַתְכֶם	־ן ,	נַעֲרָתָם	נַעֲרָתִי	־ךְ ,	נַעֲרָתְךָ	־הָ ,	נַעֲרָתוֹ	(נַעֲרַת)	נַעֲרָה s. 3.
girls	נַעֲרֹתֵינוּ	־יכֶן ,	נַעֲרֹתֵיכֶם	־יהֶן³ ,	נַעֲרֹתֵיהֶם	נַעֲרֹתַי	־יִךְ² ,	נַעֲרֹתֶיךָ	־יהָ ,	נַעֲרֹתָיו	(נַעֲרֹת)	נְעָרוֹת pl.
								[The ח having ŏ where there is ־ to the מ in 1 above. Cf. § 69 (β.)]		(חָכְמָתוֹ)]	(חָכְמַת)	חָכְמָה s. 4.

---

* The ־ָ under the first letter is ŏ. Some Nouns of this Class have ־ֳ instead of the ־ָ (ŏ); thus, קָמְצוֹ fr. קֹמֶץ.—From גֹּדֶל we have once גָּדְלוֹ (with ־ָ), but also גָּדְלוֹ and גָּדְלְךָ (with ־ָ, ŏ).

† In Pause : פָּעֳלֶךָ.   ¹ In Pause : ־ָךְ.   ² In Pause : ־ָיִךְ.   ³ In Pause : ־ָהּ.   ⁴ Contracted ־ָתָם.   ⁵ Contracted ־ָתָן.

‡ But קְדָשִׁים and הַקֳּדָשִׁים (from קֹדֶשׁ), [קֳדָשָׁיו *his..* וְקֳדָשָׁיו *and his...*]. Similarly שָׁרָשָׁיו, from שֶׁרֶשׁ *a root*.

§ From אֹהֶל *a tent*, Plu. אֹהָלִים [אֹהָלַי, אֹהָלֶיךָ, בְּאֹהָלֶיךָ, לְאֹהָלֶיךָ, מֵאֹהָלֶיךָ, אָהֳלֵיהֶם, אָהֳלֵיכֶם i.c., אֹהָלִים besides בְּאֹהָלִים [לְאֹהָלָיו], Job xxii. 23)].

(I) 'Constr.' forms, (II) Affix-forms, (III) Various forms.

I. The forms פְּעָל, מֶעָל, פֹּעָל, etc. [see Rule vii. on p. 36], in the Sing., undergo no change 'i.c.' But

(1) Some פֶּעַל or פֹּעַל words borrow 'i.c.' a form from פָּעָל or כְּעָל; thus חֶדֶר for חָדָר 'i.c.,'—הֶבֶל for הָבֶל 'i.c.,'—זֶרַע Nu. xi. 7 (but *many times* זָרַע) 'i.c.'—שֶׁגַר as well as שְׁגַר 'i c,'—נֶטַע for נְטַע 'i.c.,' etc.

(2) Some Plu. forms 'i.c.,' w. ◌ֵ Quiescent (to 2ᵈ Rt.-letter) followed by Dag. L., are Irreg.; as חַסִּדֵי* (4 times, but also the Regʳ חֲסִדֵי twice) & צַמְדֵי* Is. v. 10, רְשָׁפֵי Song viii. 6 (but also רְשָׁפֵי Ps. lxxvi. 4) from the Plurals of צֶמֶד & חֶסֶד.

II. Some Decl.-forms are Irreg.:—(1) Sing. forms w. Moving Shva (to 2ᵈ Rt.-letter), as (α) בִּגְדוֹ (*his*) & בגדי (*my*) fr. בֶּגֶד. (β) For גֶּלְלוֹ fr. גָּלָל Comp. Pt. I. § 55 (11). (γ) So סָבְכוֹ (w. 'Euphᶜ' D., Pt. I. § 70) Jer. iv. 7, fr. the פֹּעַל form סְבַךְ. (δ) Besides תָּאֳרֶם & תָּאֳרוֹ (fr. תֹּאַר) as in Tab. XI. 3, there is also the form תָּאֳרוֹ Is. lii. 14; and so (according to some) פֹּעֳלוֹ Is. i. 31.

(2) Plu. forms (w. Affs. 2 pl. & 3 pl.) w. ◌ֵ Quiescent to 2ᵈ Rt.-letter follᵈ by Dag. L.; as נִסְכֵּיהֶם* & כַּסְפֵּיהֶם* fr. the Plurals of נֶסֶךְ & כֶּסֶף.

III. Some פֶּעַל or פֹּעַל Nouns vary slightly in Decl.-vowel. Thus, fr. יֵשַׁע or יֶשַׁע we have once יֵשְׁעָה (w. ◌ֵ), but also יִשְׁעִי & יִשְׁעֲךָ & יִשְׁעֶךָ & יִשְׁעוֹ: & יִשְׁעֵנוּ (w. ◌ֵ); and so, fr. קֶצֶף, we have קִצְפָּה (w. ◌ִ), but also קִצְפּוֹ & קִצְפְּךָ: & קִצְפִּי (w. ◌ִ).

IV. (1) The 'Slight'-vowel for the Plu. ('i c.,' and w. Affs. for 2 pl. & 3 pl) is generally the same as the Decl.-vowel of the Sing, as seen in Tab. X. 1–6. But

(2) There are some slight Variations; thus הֶבֶל has הֶבְלוֹ in the Sing. (w. ◌ֶ), but הַבְלֵי & הַבְלֵיהֶם in the Plu. (w. ◌ַ direct fr. the ◌ֲ of הֲבָלִים), so חֶדֶר has חֶדְרוֹ as in Tab. X. 3, but חַדְרֵי the Plu. 'i.c.' (w. ◌ַ direct fr. the ◌ֲ of חֲדָרִים).

Obs. (α) חֶבֶל *a cord* has ◌ַ in חַבְלוֹ *his cord* Job xviii. 10, and so חַבְלֵי *cords of* (6 times); and

(β) חֶבֶל or חֵבֶל *a pain* (perhaps from '*contortion*'), which does not occur in the Sing. w. Pron.-Affs., has ◌ֶ in חֶבְלִי *pains of* Hos. xiii. 13 & חֶבְלֵיהֶם *their pains* Job xxxix. 3.

(γ) חבלי in 5 other places is the same as in (β). Some take it in these 5 places to be the same as חַבְלִי in (α)—badly.

---

* These are *strictly* fr. Plurals of unused פֶּעֳלָה or פֶּעֳלָה forms. So בְּטָנִים is Plu. of בִּטְנָה (◌ָ δ) rather than of בֶּטֶן.

V. (1) Some פֶּעֶל or בֶּעֶל Nouns have a FEM. FORM OF PLU. (in ־ות). Thus (a) אֶרֶץ, pl. אֲרָצוֹת, and (β) נֶפֶשׁ pl. נְפָשׁוֹת, are declined in the Sing. as in Tab. X. 1—and in the Plu. as in Tab. XII.

VI. Words* in תָ־ ־ֻ [§74 (e), p. 45], or תָ־ ־ֶ with a Guttural, (1) are UNCHANGED 'I.C.' IN THE SING., (2) are DECLINED IN THE SING. as in Tab. X, (3) have Plurals from the corresponding הָ־ form : † thus [for (2) & (3)],

(α) אֹמֶנֶת *a nursing-mother* has Decl.-form אֹמַנְתּוֹ, אֹמַנְתָּהּ, etc.; & Plu. אֹמְנוֹת (fr. אֹמְנָה) unchanged 'i.c.' & w. Affs.;

(β) מֵינֶקֶת *a nurse* has Decl.-form מֵינַקְתָּהּ, מֵינַקְתּוֹ, etc.; & Plu. מֵינִיקוֹת (fr. מֵינִיקָה) unchanged 'i.c.' & w. Affs.; so

(γ) שְׁכֵנֶת *a neighbour* (f.) has Decl.-form שְׁכֶנְתּוֹ, etc.; & Plu. שְׁכֵנוֹת (fr. שְׁכֵנָה) unchanged 'i.c.' & w. Affs.;

(δ) [בְהֵמֵת] *cattle* has Decl.-form בְהֶמְתּוֹ etc.; & Plu. בְהֵמוֹת, 'i.c.' (fr. בְּהֵמָה 'i.c.'). Cp. 'App^x C to Tab IX' [4].

(ε) תּוֹכַחַת *reproof* has Decl.-form תּוֹכַחְתּוֹ etc.; & Plu. תּוֹכָחוֹת, 'i.c.' (fr. תּוֹכַחָה, & תּוֹכֵחֹת fr. תּוֹכֵחָה).

(ζ) The תָ־ ־ֶ Decl.-form, in Sing., is used for several Nouns in הָ־ ־ֶ (which are undeclined in הָ־ ־ֶ); thus מִלְחַמְתּוֹ etc. fr. מִלְחָמָת for מִלְחָמָה, מַמְלַכְתּ etc. fr. מַמְלָכָה for מַמְלָכָה, מֶמְשַׁלְתּוֹ etc. fr. מֶמְשָׁלָה, מֶרְכַּבְתּ etc. fr. מֶרְכֶּבֶת for מֶרְכָּבָה for מֶרְכָּבָה, etc.

(η) The Plurals of the Nouns in (ζ) are from the הָ־ form; thus מַרְכְּבֹתָיו & 'i.c.' מַרְכְּבוֹת & מֶרְכָּבוֹת (etc); מִלְחָמוֹת 'i.c.' מַרְכְּבֹתָיו (*his*) are fr. an unused Sing. [מַרְכָּבָה].

(θ) Some contracted פֶּעֶל (or פֵּעֶל) & פָּעֵל forms have Decl.-forms as in Tabs. X & XI; thus חֵטְאוֹ etc. (as in Tab. X. 3) fr. חֵטְא [for חֵטְא or 'חֵ], & יְפִיוֹ etc. (as in Tab. XI. 1) fr. יְפִי p.: 'יָפִי § 63. So צֵל, & תַּךְ, [contracted for צְלַל (or צְלַל), & תְּכַךְ] have the Plurals צְלָלִים, & תְּכָכִים; and so דּוּד *a pot* has Plu. דְּוָדִים, שׁוּק *a street* has Plu. שׁוּקִים, & שׁוֹר *an ox* has Plu. שְׁוָרִים—as fr. form פֶּעֶל (or 'פֶּ) or 'פָּ.

---

* So some Infinitives in תָ־ ־ֶ and תֶ־ ־ֶ, as שֶׁבֶת [Tab. XVIII] w. Decl.-form שִׁבְתּוֹ etc., & קַחַת [Tab. XIX, Note (A)] w. Decl.-form קַחְתּוֹ etc.

† So Contracted forms in ־וֹת (for ־יָת, =־יָה), and in ־יָת (for ־יָת, =־יָה), have their Pl. from ־יָה and ־יָה. Thus מַלְכִיּוֹת *kingdoms* is Plu. of מַלְכוּת (as also חֲנִיּוֹת *cells* Plu. of חָנוּת), and תַּחְתִּיּוֹת *lower parts* Plu. of תַּחְתִּית (as also דָּלִיּוֹת *boughs* Plu. of דָּלִית, & זָוִיּת *corners* Plu. of זָוִית).

TABLE XIII.

Of some Irregular Nouns.

	our.	f.,	m., your.	f.,	m., their.	my	f.,	m., thy.	her,	his.	(i.c.)			
father	אָבִינוּ	־יכֶן	אֲבִיכֶם	־יהֶן	אֲבִיהֶם	אָבִי	־יךְ	אָבִיךְ	־יהָ	אָבִיו (& ־יהוּ)	(אֲבִי 1)	אָב *	s.	1
fathers	אֲבֹתֵינוּ	־יכֶן	אֲבֹתֵיכֶם	־יהֶן	אֲבֹתֵיהֶם'	אֲבֹתַי	־יךְ	אֲבֹתֶיךָ	־יהָ	אֲבֹתָיו	(אֲבוֹת)	אָבוֹת	pl.	
brother	אָחִינוּ	־יכֶן	אֲחִיכֶם	־יהֶן	אֲחִיהֶם	אָחִי	־יךְ	אָחִיךְ	־יהָ	אָחִיו (& ־יהוּ)	(אֲחִי)	אָח †	s.	2.
brothers	אָחִינוּ	־יכֶן	אֲחֵיכֶם	־יהֶן	אֲחֵיהֶם	אַחַי	־יךְ	אַחֶיךָ	־יהָ	אֶחָיו	(אֲחֵי)	אַחִים	pl.	
house	בֵּיתֵנוּ	־כֶן	בֵּיתְכֶם	־הֶן	בֵּיתָם	בֵּיתִי	־ךְ	בֵּיתְךָ	־הָ	בֵּיתוֹ	(בֵּית)	בַּיִת ‡	s.	3.
houses	בָּתֵּינוּ	־יכֶן	בָּתֵּיכֶם	־יהֶן	בָּתֵּיהֶם	בָּתַּי	־יךְ	בָּתֶּיךָ	־יהָ	בָּתָּיו	(בָּתֵּי)	בָּתִּים	pl.	
son	בְּנֵנוּ	־יכֶן	בִּנְכֶם	־הֶן	בְּנָם	בְּנִי	־ךְ	בִּנְךָ	־הָ	בְּנוֹ	(בֵּן)	בֵּן §	s.	4.
sons	בָּנֵינוּ	־יכֶן	בְּנֵיכֶם	־יהֶן	בְּנֵיהֶם	בָּנַי	־יךְ	בָּנֶיךָ	־יהָ	בָּנָיו	(בְּנֵי)	בָּנִים	pl.	
daughter	בִּתֵּנוּ	־כֶן	בִּתְּכֶם	־הֶן	בִּתָּם	בִּתִּי	־ךְ	בִּתְּךָ	־הָ	בִּתּוֹ	(בַּת)	בַּת ‖	s.	5.
daughters	בְּנֹתֵינוּ	־יכֶן	בְּנוֹתֵיכֶם	־יהֶן	בְּנֹתֵיהֶם	בְּנֹתַי	־יךְ	בְּנֹתֶיךָ	־יהָ	בְּנֹתָיו	(בְּנוֹת)	בַּת ‖	s.	5.
mouth	פִּינוּ	פִּיכֶן	פִּיכֶם	פִּיהֶן	פִּיהֶם'	פִּי	פִּיךְ	פִּיךָ	פִּיהָ	פִּיו or פִּיהוּ, פִּיו	(פִּי)	פֶּה ¶	s.	6.
										[not declined] [(f.) ††פִּיּוֹת and] (m.) **פִּים			pl.	

For the Notes 1, 2, 3, etc., and * † ‡, etc., see next page.

1 אָב G. xvii. 4, 5. 2 p.: ־ךָ. 3 p.: ־ךָ. 4 And אֲבֹתָם. 5 p.: אָחִי. 6 p.: ־ךָ. 7 And בֵּן (& בְּנִי & בְּנוֹ). 8 p.: בְּנֵךְ. 9 Also פִּימוֹ.

* A father.—So, from the imaginary חָם a father-in-law, we have חָמִיהָ her.., and חָמִיךְ thy (f.)..

† A brother.—(a.) אָחוֹת a sister (·i. c.· אֲחוֹת) has the regular SINGULAR Declension

אֲחֹתוֹ | ־הּ | אֲחֹתְךָ | ־ךְ | אֲחֹתִי | אֲחֹתָם | ־ן, אֲחֹתְכֶם | ־ן, אֲחֹתֵנוּ

But the PLURAL forms that occur are

אַחְיוֹתַי [Krî, and אַחוֹתַי Kthiv] Josh. ii. 13.

אַחְיוֹתֵךְ [Ez. xvi. 52, and אֲחוֹתָיִךְ v. 51, 55, 61] אֲחוֹתֵיכֶם [Hos. ii. 2]

אַחְיוֹתַי [Job xlii. 11] אַחְיוֹתֵיהֶם [Job i. 4, 1 Chr. ii. 16].

(β.) From the imaginary חָמוֹת a mother-in-law, we have חֲמוֹתֵךְ thy (f.).., חֲמוֹתָהּ her... .

‡ A house.—(a.) Nouns of the form פּוּל [p.: פִּיל] are regularly declined like this IN THE SINGULAR. The regular PLURAL is of the form פִּילִים (m.), or פִּילוֹת (f.); [thus from חַיִל, Pl. חֲיָלִים, (for עַיִן, see § 48)—but זַיִת has Pl. זֵיתִים.]

(β.) In the 'Construct' and 'Declension' forms, the י regularly becomes Quiescent in ־ given to the first letter, as in the Sing. of (3) above, and in the Plu. forms זֵיתֵיהֶם, זֵיתֵיכֶם,—and (from the Dual עֵינַיִם eyes), עֵינַי, עֵינֶיךָ, עֵינָיו, etc.

(γ.) Some Nouns of this Class take ־ instead of ־; thus, שִׁיתוֹ Is. x. 17 (from שַׁיִת), and עִירֹה his colt, Gen. xlix. 11 (from עַיִר).

(δ.) אַיִן (אַיִ 'Constr. form') there is not, or none, takes Pronoun-Affs. thus, I am not אֵינֶנִּי, thou art not (m.) אֵינְךָ & (f.) אֵינֵךְ, he is (or was) not אֵינֶנּוּ (& she... ־נָּה), they m. are not אֵינָם (אֵינֵמוֹ & אֵינֵימוֹ),

(ε.) Similarly, the ו of some Nouns of the form פּוּל becomes Quiescent in י; thus (from מָוֶת death, ·i. c.· מוֹת), מוֹתִי, מוֹתוֹ (or מֹתוֹ), and (from an imaginary Plural מוֹתִים) מוֹתַי deaths of, Is. liii. 9 (though some have a different opinion about this word). [From an imaginary מָמוֹת,—מְמוֹתִי (Plu. ·i. c.·) Jer. xvi. 4, Ez. xxviii. 8.]

§ A son.—(a.) שֵׁם a name (·i. c.· שֶׁם, שֵׁם־) is, in the Singular, declined with Affixes like בֵּן, but has Pl. שֵׁמוֹת (·i. c.· שְׁמוֹת), with affixes (־ך) שְׁמֹתָם.

(β.) עֵץ a tree (·i. c.· עֵץ), retains its ־; thus, עֵצְךָ, עֵצוֹ, Pl. עֵצִים (·i. c.· עֲצֵי), עֵצָיו, עֵצֶיךָ.

(γ.) Some Nouns, like this in appearance, belong to a different Class, and retain their ־ throughout.

[(δ.) יֵשׁ (יֵשׁ־) there is, takes Pron.-Affixes, thus, יֶשְׁךָ thou (m.) art, יֶשְׁכֶם (יֶשְׁבָם) Deut. xiii. 4) ye (m.) are, יֶשְׁנוֹ he is.]

‖ A daughter. [Contracted from בֵּנֶת; whence would come בִּנְתוֹ contracted into בַּתּוֹ, and so the others.]

¶ A mouth.—פֶּה [·i. c.· פֶּה] has פִּיו Deut. xxii. 1, פִּיהוּ 1 S. xiv. 34.
** 1 Sa. xiii. 21.
†† Pro. v. 4. Also פֵּיוֹת Ju. iii. 16. [פִּיפִיוֹת (redupl.) Is. xli. 15, Ps. cxlix. 6.]

VII. Hithpă-êl.	VI. Hoph-ăl.	V. Hiph-îl.	IV. Pŭ-ăl.
הִתְפָּקֵד { בְּ־, כְּ־, לְ־, מֵהִתְפָּקֵד הִתְפָּקְדוֹ,...*	הָפְקַד (־ֵד) { בְּ־, כְּ־, לְ־, מֵהָפְקַד, הָפְקְדוֹ,...*	הַפְקֵד (־יד) { בְּ־, כְּ־, לְ־, מֵהַפְקִיד הַפְקִידוֹ,...*	פֻּקַד (־ֵד) { בְּפֻ, כְּפֻ, לְפֻ, מְפֻקַד פֻּקְדוֹ,...*
(or ק) הִתְפָּקֵד הִתְפָּקְדָה הִתְפָּקַדְתָּ הִתְפָּקַדְתְּ הִתְפָּקַדְתִּי הִתְפָּקְדוּ הִתְפָּקַדְתֶּם הִתְפָּקַדְתֶּן הִתְפָּקַדְנוּ	הָפְקַד הָפְקְדָה הָפְקַדְתָּ הָפְקַדְתְּ הָפְקַדְתִּי הָפְקְדוּ הָפְקַדְתֶּם הָפְקַדְתֶּן הָפְקַדְנוּ	הִפְקִיד הִפְקִידָה הִפְקַדְתָּ הִפְקַדְתְּ הִפְקַדְתִּי הִפְקִידוּ הִפְקַדְתֶּם הִפְקַדְתֶּן הִפְקַדְנוּ	§ פֻּקַד פֻּקְדָה פֻּקַדְתָּ פֻּקַדְתְּ פֻּקַדְתִּי פֻּקְדוּ פֻּקַדְתֶּם פֻּקַדְתֶּן פֻּקַדְנוּ §
מִתְפָּקֵד	מָפְקָד	מַפְקִיד	מְפֻקָד
(or ק) הִתְפָּקֵד הִתְפָּקְדִי הִתְפָּקְדוּ (or ק) הִתְפָּקֵדְנָה	None.	הַפְקֵד הַפְקִידִי הַפְקִידוּ הַפְקֵדְנָה	None.
(or ק) יִתְפָּקֵד (or ק) תִּתְפָּקֵד (or ק) תִּתְפָּקֵד תִּתְפָּקְדִי (or ק) אֶתְפָּקֵד יִתְפָּקְדוּ (or ק) תִּתְפָּקֵדְנָה תִּתְפָּקְדוּ (or ק) תִּתְפָּקֵדְנָה (or ק) נִתְפָּקֵד	§ יָפְקַד תָּפְקַד תָּפְקַד תָּפְקְדִי אָפְקַד יָפְקְדוּ תָּפְקַדְנָה תָּפְקְדוּ תָּפְקַדְנָה נָפְקַד	יַפְקִיד (־ֵד) תַּפְקִיד (־ֵד) תַּפְקִיד (־ֵד) תַּפְקִידִי אַפְקִיד (־ֵד) יַפְקִידוּ תַּפְקֵדְנָה תַּפְקִידוּ תַּפְקֵדְנָה נַפְקִיד (־ֵד)	§ יְפֻקַד תְּפֻקַד תְּפֻקַד תְּפֻקְדִי אֲפֻקַד יְפֻקְדוּ תְּפֻקַדְנָה תְּפֻקְדוּ תְּפֻקַדְנָה נְפֻקַד

For the Notes see next pages.

III. PÏ-ÊL.	II. NIPH-ÂL.	I. KAL.	
פַּקֵּד (ד׳)	[a]הֻפְקַד & נִפְקַד	(const.) פְּקֹד, (abs.) פָּקוֹד	INFINITIVE.
בְּפַ׳, כְּפַ׳, לְפַ׳, מְפַקֵּד }	בְּ׳, כְּ׳, לְ׳, מֵהִפָּקֵד }	בִּפְ׳, כִּפְ׳, לִפְ׳, מִפְקֹד	With ב כ ל מ
פַּקְּדוֹ,...*	הִפָּקְדוֹ,...*	פָּקְדוֹ,...* (p. xviii infra)	W. Pron. Aff[s].
			PAST TENSE.
פִּקֵּד	נִפְקַד	‡פָּקַד [נָגַּה, יָכֹל]	3 m. }
פִּקְּדָה	נִפְקְדָה	פָּקְדָה, יָכְלָה	3 f. }
פִּקַּדְתָּ	נִפְקַדְתָּ	פָּקַדְתָּ, ־ה, יָכֹלְתָּ	2 m. } Sing.
פִּקַּדְתְּ	נִפְקַדְתְּ	פָּקַדְתְּ, יָכֹלְתְּ	2 f. }
פִּקַּדְתִּי	נִפְקַדְתִּי	פָּקַדְתִּי, יָכֹלְתִּי	1. }
פִּקְּדוּ	נִפְקְדוּ	פָּקְדוּ, יָכְלוּ	3 m. & f. }
פִּקַּדְתֶּם	נִפְקַדְתֶּם	פְּקַדְתֶּם, יְכָלְתֶּם	2 m. }
פִּקַּדְתֶּן	נִפְקַדְתֶּן	פְּקַדְתֶּן, יְכָלְתֶּן	2 f. } Plu.
פִּקַּדְנוּ	נִפְקַדְנוּ	פָּקַדְנוּ, יָכֹלְנוּ	1. }
			PARTICIPLES.
מְפַקֵּד	נִפְקָד	פֹּקֵד [נֹגַהּ, יָכֹל] (1) } (p. xvii)	
		פָּקוּד (2) }	
			IMPERATIVE.
פַּקֵּד (or קַ)	הִפָּקֵד	‡פְּקֹד, יְ־ [לְבַשׁ] (& p. 86)	2 m. }
פַּקְּדִי	הִפָּקְדִי	פִּקְדִי, לִבְשִׁי	2 f. } Sing.
פַּקְּדוּ	הִפָּקְדוּ	פִּקְדוּ, לִבְשׁוּ	2 m. } Plu.
פַּקֵּדְנָה	הִפָּקַדְנָה	פְּקֹדְנָה, לְבַשְׁנָה	2 f. }
			FUTURE.
יְפַקֵּד	יִפָּקֵד (or קַ)	יִפְקֹד, יִלְבַּשׁ	3 m. }
תְּפַקֵּד	תִּפָּקֵד (or קַ)	תִּפְקֹד, תִּלְבַּשׁ	3 f. }
תְּפַקֵּד	תִּפָּקֵד (or קַ)	תִּפְקֹד, תִּלְבַּשׁ	2 m. } Sing.
תְּפַקְּדִי	תִּפָּקְדִי	תִּפְקְדִי, תִּלְבְּשִׁי	2 f. }
אֲפַקֵּד	אֶפָּקֵד (or אַ)	אֶפְקֹד, אֶלְבַּשׁ	1. }
יְפַקְּדוּ	יִפָּקְדוּ	יִפְקְדוּ, יִלְבְּשׁוּ	3 m. }
תְּפַקֵּדְנָה (or קַ)	תִּפָּקַדְנָה (or קַ)	תִּפְקֹדְנָה, תִּלְבַּשְׁנָה	3 f. }
תְּפַקְּדוּ	תִּפָּקְדוּ	תִּפְקְדוּ, תִּלְבְּשׁוּ	2 m. } Plu.
תְּפַקֵּדְנָה (or קַ)	תִּפָּקַדְנָה (or קַ)	תִּפְקֹדְנָה, תִּלְבַּשְׁנָה	2 f. }
נְפַקֵּד	נִפָּקֵד	נִפְקֹד [נִלְבַּשׁ]	1. }

For some other forms see pp. 115 etc.

* For INFIN. WITH PRON.-AFFS. see § 137 (4) and Tab. XV.

† פָּקַד is of the form פָּעַל.

There are two other forms of the Past KAL, viz., [(a) & (β)],

(a) The פָּעֵל form, as כָּבֵד *he was heavy,* of which the other Person-forms are the same as those in the first column of Tab. XIV, thus—

כָּבֵד, כָּבְדָה, כָּבַדְתָּ, כָּבַדְתְּ, כָּבַדְתִּי, כָּבְדוּ, כְּבַדְתֶּם, כְּבַדְתֶן, כָּבַדְנוּ.

N.B. In Pause the 2ᵈ Rt.-letter in 3 s. *f.* & 3 pl. of these has ־ָ ; as in כָּבֵדָה 3 s. *f.*, כָּבֵדוּ 3 pl. ;—and

(β) The פָּעֵל form, as יָכֹל *he was able,* which is given in small type in the Table. Also

N.B. (i) The 2ᵈ Rt.-letter in 3 s. *f.* & 3 pl. of these has ־ֹ ; as in יָכֹלָה 3 s. *f.*, יָכֹלוּ 3 pl.

(ii) The ־ָ in the 2 pl. m. & 2 pl. f. of this Tense is ŏ [Pt. I. § 55 (9, *b*)]. Moreover,

OBS. Of Past-Tense forms belonging to this Table,—IN PAUSE,—

(1) The 3 s. & 3 pl. forms [except those in (a) & (β) above] have, under their 2ᵈ Rt.-letter,—in Pause,—

(i) ־ָ in *Kăl, Niph-ăl, Pŭ-ăl, Hŏph-ăl, Hĭthpă-êl* [see h (a, ii) below];

(ii) ־ֵ in *Pĭ-êl.*—See more on pp. 111 & 112.

(2) The 2 s. *m.* & 2 s. *f.,* and the 1 s. & 1 pl, of all Voices, may have ־ָ in Pause [see p. 110 (Note *)]. But

(3) The 2 pl. *m.* & 2 pl *f.* are unchanged in Pause, and have always the ACCENT ON THE FINAL תֶּם־ & תֶן־ in all VOICES ;

(4) The 3 s. *f.* & 3 pl. in the *Hiph-îl* are unchanged in Pause.

‡ IN PAUSE, the 2ᵈ Rt-letter has ־ֵ in these. Then, in the Imperative *Kal* 2 s. *f.* & 2 pl. *m.,* the ־ֵ returns to the 1ˢᵗ Rt-letter—as in לְבֵשִׁי 2 s. *f.* & לְבֵשׁוּ 2 pl. *m* (Imper. *Kal*).

§ In Pause, the 2ᵈ Rt.-letter has ־ֵ in these forms.

(a) For Variations when the Root has in it one of the 5 letters א ח ה ע ר see Tabs. XVI (1)–XVI (3) (and pp. 115–121 & 368–374).

(b) In Pause the 2ᵈ Rt-letter has ־ֹ. Then, in Imper. *Kal* 2 s. *f.* & 2 pl. *m.,* ־ֹ returns to the 1ˢᵗ Rt.-letter as in פְּקֹדִי 2 s. *f.* & פְּקֹדוּ 2 pl. *m.*

(c) In Pause the 2ᵈ Rt.-letter has ־ֵ.

(d) For the two forms of Infin. Absol. *Niph-ăl* see pp 338 & 339. The ב form occurs in נִכְסֹף, נִלְחֹם, נִשְׁאֹל, נִשְׁלוֹחַ [Pt. I. § 60], and a few others. Also we find הִנָּתֹן and הֵאָכֹל (the ־ֵ to compensate for the Dag. F. which א cannot receive) ; and once אִדָּרֹשׁ Ez. xiv. 3.

(e) Sometimes the 2ᵈ Rt.-letter has ־ֵ in *Pĭ-êl* Past 3 s. *m.* ; thus, אִבַּד 2 K. xxi 3 ;—and sometimes ־ָ , thus, דִּבָּר & וְכִבֶּס often (as well as דָּבַר & כִּבֵּס sometimes), and וְכִפֶּר.

(f) In a few instances the מ is omitted. Thus some give שַׁבֵּחַ Eccles. iv. 2 as Partic. s. *m. Pĭ-êl* (for מְשַׁבֵּחַ), see also p. 330. Similarly we have as *Pŭ-ăl* Partic. s. *m.* אֻכָּל Ex. iii 2 (wrongly taken as Past 3 s. *m.* by some), and לֻקַח 2 K. ii. 10 ; and so a few others.

(g) Also with ־ (ŭ), instead of ־ (ŏ), Comp. p. 72; thus הֻשְׁלַךְ & הֻשְׁכַּב Past 3 s. m.,—מֻשְׁלָךְ Partic. s. m.,—and so the Fut. יֻשְׁלַךְ 3 s. m. תֻּשְׁלַךְ 3 s. f. & 2 s. m., etc.

(h) (α) In the *Hithpă-ĕl* Past, Imper. and Fut., (i) the 2ᵈ Rt.-letter often has ־, as given within () in the Table, thus, הִתְחַזַּק Past 3 s. m. (& Imper. 2 s. m.) fr. חזק, הִתְעַנַּג Imper. 2 s. m. fr. ענג, and so the Fut. forms יִתְחַזַּק 3 s. m. twice and נִתְחַזַּק 1 pl. once (but also יִתְחַזֵּק 3 s. m. several times, with ־) fr. חזק, and תִּתְחַכַּם 2 s. m. fr. חכם, תִּתְעַלַּפְנָה 3 pl. f. fr. עלף, etc., and (ii) the PAUSE-vowel is ־ (lengthened from the ־ **) in the Past, Imper. & Fut., as in הִתְנַלָּח & הִתְאַזָּר (Lev. xiii. 33, comp. p. 113) Past 3 s. m. fr. אזר & נלח, and so in הִתְיַצָּבָה: (Job xxxiii. 5) Imper. 2 s. m. w. ה as in § 141 (γ) [p. 86], and in the Fut. forms יִתְאַדָּם: 3 s. m. fr. אדם, תִּתְעַנָּג: 2 s. m. & תִּתְעַנָּגִ: 3 s. m. & תִּתְעַנַּגְנּוּ: 2 pl. m. fr. ענג, יִתְקַדָּשׁוּ: 3 pl. m. fr. קדש, etc.; and (iii) as examples of both the ־ and the ־ (or ־) form from the same Root we have also, fr. הלך, both יִתְהַלֵּךְ and יִתְהַלָּךְ: Fut. 3 s. m. & יִתְהַלָּכוּ: Fut. 3 pl. m., and so fr. קדש not only הִתְקַדְּשׁוּ: Past 3 pl. & Imper. 2 pl. m. and יִתְקַדָּשׁוּ: Fut. 3 pl. m., but also הִתְקַדֶּשׁ־ [for הִתְקַדֵּשׁ, the ־ for ־ because of the *Makkĕph*—Pt. I. § 55 (9, b)] which some take as Past 3 s. m.,—but it may be Inf. Constr.

(β) Some few times the 1ˢᵗ Rt.-letter has ־ (instead of ־ followed by Dag. F.), thus יִתְפָּקֵד, הִתְפָּקְדוּ, יִתְפָּקְדוּ [No other *Hithpă-ĕl* forms fr. פקד occur, but only these three. Those in the Table are Paradigm-forms.]

(j) In all Voices, ה־ often occurs at the end of the Imper. 2 s. m. [see § 141 (γ), p. 86] and the Fut. 1 s. & 1 pl. [see § 144, p. 88]

ₐ With a first Rt.-letter either (1) ††שׂ, (2) שׁ, (3) ס, (4) צ, (5) ד, ט, or ת [pp. 89 & 89*]—the *Hithpă-ĕl* form is (1) הִשְׁתַּפֵּךְ of (שפך), (2) הִשְׁתַּבֵּר (of שׁבר), (3) הִסְתַּתֵּר (of סתר) the [ת of הָת being transposed], (4) הִצְטַדֵּק (of צדק) (the ת of הָת transposed and replaced by ט], (5) הַדַּבֵּר (of דבר), הַטַּהֵר (of טהר), הַתַּמֵּם (of תמם). So, with ז, הִזַּנְבּוּ (of זכה) Is. i. 16 (for הִתְזַכּוּ, as in Tab. XXIII), and a few others.

[Note—Sometimes, from removal of the Accent, a SHORT-Vowel is found where in the Table there is a LONG-Vowel *in a closed final syllable*,—Pt. I. § 55 (9, b). Thus לִשְׁאָל־אָכֶל [Pt. I. § 37 (2)] Ps. lxxviii. 18, with ־ (ŭ) for the ־ of לִשְׁאָל; so מְשָׁל־בָּנוּ Ju. viii. 22, with ־ (ŏ) for the ־ of מְשָׁל, and יִמְשָׁל־בָּךְ Gen. iii. 16, with ־ (ŏ) for the ־ of יִמְשָׁל. So with ־ for ־, וְדַבֶּר־אָוֶן Is. lviii. 9, הִתְקַדֶּשׁ־חָג Is. xxx. 29, and many others]. So, when the Accent is *drawn back* [Pt. I. § 46], as in הִשָּׁמֶר לְךָ Gen. xxxi. 29

** The name and form *Hithpă-ĕl* (with ־) are now too generally adopted, or one would be glad to give the ־ form in the body of the Table and the ־ within the (), and to call the Voice הִתְפָּעַל (*Hithpă-ăl*).

†† With one exception Jer. xlix. 3, for which see § 246 [p. 162].

APPENDIX (A) TO TABLE XIV.—Inf*. with בּ כּ לּ מּ.

מִפְקֹד	לִפְקֹד,	כִּפְקֹד,	בִּפְקֹד,	(i.) *Kal.*
מֵהִפָּקֵד	לְהִפָּקֵד,	כְּהִפָּקֵד,	בְּהִפָּקֵד,	(ii.) *Niph-ăl.*
מִפַּקֵּד	לְפַקֵּד,	כְּפַקֵּד,	בְּפַקֵּד,	(iii.) *Pī-êl.*
מִפֻּקַּד	לְפֻקַּד,	כְּפֻקַּד,	בְּפֻקַּד,	(iv.) *Pŭ-ăl.*
מֵהַפְקִיד	לְהַפְקִיד,	כְּהַפְקִיד,	בְּהַפְקִיד,	(v.) *Hiph-îl.*
מֵהָפְקַד	לְהָפְקַד,	כְּהָפְקַד,	בְּהָפְקַד,	(vi.) *Hoph-ăl.*
מֵהִתְפַּקֵּד	לְהִתְפַּקֵּד,	כְּהִתְפַּקֵּד,	בְּהִתְפַּקֵּד,	(vii.) *Hithpă-êl.*

⁂ (1) For Inf*. with ח added, see § 137 (4, iii.).

(2) The Inf*. are declined with Pron. Aff*. like those in Tab. V. 1, see (4).

(3) The ending תָ֫ for הָ֫ is not limited to Participles s. *f.*, (as פֹּקֶרֶת, פֹּקְרַת, etc.). Thus, from a form צִדְקַת for צְדָקָה [Inf. *Pī.* of צדק, with הָ], we find בְּצַדְקָתֵךְ *through thy (f.) justifying*, Ez. xvi. 52.

(4) For the ordinary Inf*. with Pron. Aff*., see Tab. XV.

APP*. (B) TO TABLE XIV.—Participles. [*NEXT PAGE.*]

APP*. (C) TO TABLE XIV.—Partic*. (*m.*) with Aff*.

Plural.		Singular.		
&c., his	i. c.	&c., his	i. c.	
פֹּקְדָיו,...	פֹּקְדִים, פֹּקְדֵי	פֹּקְדוֹ,...	(same*) פֹּקֵד	(1) ⎱ ⎰ (i.)
פְּקוּדָיו,...	פְּקוּדִים, פְּקוּדֵי	פְּקוּדוֹ,...	פָּקוּד, פְּקֻד	(2)
נִפְקָדָיו,...	נִפְקָדִים, נִפְקְדֵי	נִפְקָדוֹ,...	נִפְקָד, נִפְקַד	(ii.)
מְפֻקָּדָיו,...	מְפֻקָּדִים, מְפֻקְּדֵי	מְפֻקָּדוֹ,...	(same) מְפֻקָּה,	(iii.)
מְפֻקָּדָיו,...	מְפֻקָּדִים, מְפֻקְּדֵי	מְפֻקָּדוֹ,...	מְפֻקָּד, מְפֻקַּד	(iv.)
מַפְקִידָיו,...	מַפְקִידִים, מַפְקִידֵי	מַפְקִידוֹ,...	(same) מַפְקִיד†	(v.)
מָפְקָדָיו,...	מָפְקָדִים, מָפְקְדֵי	מָפְקָדוֹ,...	מָפְקָד, מָפְקַד	(vi.)
מִתְפַּקְּדָיו,...	מִתְפַּקְּדִים, מִתְפַּקְּדֵי	מִתְפַּקְּדוֹ,...	(same) מִתְפַּקֵּד,	(vii.)

---

* Also אֹבֵד, D. xxxii. 28.

† Also דֶ֫יךָ, i. c. דֵ֫יךָ.

APPENDIX (B) TO TABLE XIV.—PARTICIPLES.

Plu. f.	Plu. m.	Sing. f.	Sing. m.	
פֹּקְדוֹת	פֹּקְדִים	*פֹּקְדָה (or פֹּקֶדֶת†)	פֹּקֵד (1)	} (I.) *Kal.*
פְּקוּדוֹת	פְּקוּדִים	פְּקוּדָה	פָּקוּד (2)	
נִפְקָדוֹת	נִפְקָדִים	נִפְקָדָה (or נִפְקֶדֶת)	נִפְקָד	(II.) *Niph.*
מְפַקְּדוֹת	מְפַקְּדִים	*מְפַקְּדָה (or מְפַקֶּדֶת)	מְפַקֵּד	(III.) *Pi-él*
מְפֻקָּדוֹת	מְפֻקָּדִים	מְפֻקָּדָה (or מְפֻקֶּדֶת)	מְפֻקָּד‡	(IV.) *Pŭ-ăl.*
מַפְקִידוֹת	מַפְקִידִים	*מַפְקִידָה (or מַפְקֶדֶת)	מַפְקִיד	(V.) *Hiph.*
מָפְקָדוֹת	מָפְקָדִים	מָפְקָדָה (or מָפְקֶדֶת)	מָפְקָד§	(VI.) *Hŏph.*
מִתְפַּקְּדוֹת	מִתְפַּקְּדִים	*מִתְפַּקְּדָה(or מִתְפַּקֶּדֶת)	מִתְפַּקֵּד	(VII.) *Hithpă.*

(α.) (i.) For the ו of (2) there is often ⸺ [Pt. I., § 14], as in דָּבָר m., נְצָרַת f. (i.c.), שְׂרָפִים pl. m., etc. שְׁלָחָה f.,

(ii.) The Construct form of פָּעוּל is פְּעוּל or פְּעָל, as in שְׁתֻם Nu. xxiv. 3.

(β.) Participles of the Passive Voices (II., IV., VI.) generally retain the ⸺ of the 2ᵈ Root-letter (except when 'i.c.,' and in the ⸺ ⸺ form).

(γ.) The *Hiph.* Partic. sometimes drops the י⸺. See Appendix, p. 353.

(δ.) (i.) The Participle יָכֹל *able* (Sing. m.) given in Tab. XIV., is the Participle *Kal* of פָּעֹל form, [יְכֹלָה Sing. f., יְכֹלִים Plu. m., יְכֹלוֹת Plu. f.], whence

(ii.) Constr. forms—פְּעָל s. m., [פְּעֹלַת s. f., פְּעֹלֵי pl. m., פְּעֹלוֹת pl. f.].

(iii.) There is also the Participle *Kal* of פָּעֵל form, as מָלֵא *full, full of,* (Sing. m.), [מְלֵאָה Sing. f., מְלֵאִים Pl. m., מְלֵאֹת Pl. f.], whence

(iv.) Constr. forms—פְּעֵל‖ s. m. [‖ פְּעֹלַת s. f. ‖ פְּעֹלֵי pl. m., פְּעֹלוֹת pl. f.]

(ε.) The Singular Participle sometimes receives an 'added' י, as in אֹסְרִי *binding* (Sing. m.) [from אֹסֵר], Gen. xlix. 11; so in הַמַּשְׁפִּילִי [from מַשְׁפִּיל] Ps. cxiii. 6; אֹהַבְתִּי [from אֹהֶבֶת] Hos. x. 11, and מְלֵאָתִי [from מְלֵאַת, Constr. form of מָלֵאָה (δ. iii.)] Is. i. 21; גְּנֻבְתִּי [from גְּנֻבַת (for גְּנוּבָה Pt. I. § 14) Constr. form of גְּנוּבָה] Gen. xxxi. 39.

---

* Or with ⸺ as in מִתְנַבְּרָה, מְרַקְּדָה, בֹּעֵרָה. [בֹּעֵרָה is s. m. with ה.]

† In Pause, sometimes the same (thus, נֹפֶלֶת, אֹמֶנֶת:); and sometimes ⸺תָ: as in עֹמֶדֶת:, יוֹשֶׁבֶת:.

‡ Also, some few times *without* the מ; thus, אֻכָּל Ex. iii. 2; לֻקַּח 2 K. ii. 10.

§ Also מִ instead of מָ (δ).

‖ Also [§ 56 (i.)] יְרֵאת s. f., יְרֵאִי pl. m., (fr. יָרֵא); so קְצֵרִי (fr. קָצֵר).

¶ And פָּעֵל,—thus פָּעֵא when the 3ᵈ Rt-letter is א, as יָרֵא fr. יָרֵא.

SUPPLEMENT TO TABLE XIV.

N.B. DAGESH LENE is to be put in a 2d Rt-letter which is one of the 6 בגדכפת, WHENEVER THE 1st RT-LETTER HAS SHVA-QUIESCENT [Pt. I, § 47 (2)];—as in the following FUTURE forms of *Kal*, *Hiph-îl* and *Hoph-ăl*, and in the PAST-TENSE forms of *Niph-ăl*, *Hiph-îl* and *Hoph-ăl*, as also in the INFIN., PARTIC., and IMPER. forms given below.

HOPH-ĂL. Past.	HIPH-ÎL. Past.	NIPH-ĂL. Past.	HOPH-ĂL. Future.	HIPH-ÎL. Future.	KAL. Future.	
הָכְתַּב	הִכְתִּיב	נִכְתַּב	יָכְתַּב	יַכְתִּיב (בַּ)	יִכְתֹּב	3 s. *m.*
הָכְתְּבָה	הִכְתִּיבָה	נִכְתְּבָה	תָּכְתַּב	תַּכְתִּיב (בְּ)	תִּכְתֹּב	3 s. *f.*
הָכְתַּבְתָּ	הִכְתַּבְתָּ	נִכְתַּבְתָּ	תָּכְתַּב	תַּכְתִּיב (בְ)	תִּכְתֹּב	2 s. *m.*
הָכְתַּבְתְּ	הִכְתַּבְתְּ	נִכְתַּבְתְּ	תָּכְתְּבִי	תַּכְתִּיבִי	תִּכְתְּבִי	2 s. *f.*
הָכְתַּבְתִּי	הִכְתַּבְתִּי	נִכְתַּבְתִּי	אָכְתַּב	אַכְתִּיב (בְ, יבָה §144. *a*)	אֶכְתֹּב (אֶכְתְּבָה §144. *a*)	1 s.
הָכְתְּבוּ	הִכְתִּיבוּ	נִכְתְּבוּ	יָכְתְּבוּ	יַכְתִּיבוּ	יִכְתְּבוּ	3 pl. *m.*
			תָּכְתַּבְנָה	תַּכְתֵּבְנָה	תִּכְתֹּבְנָה	3 pl. *f.*
הָכְתַּבְתֶּם	הִכְתַּבְתֶּם	נִכְתַּבְתֶּם	תָּכְתְּבוּ	תַּכְתִּיבוּ	תִּכְתְּבוּ	2 pl. *m.*
הָכְתַּבְתֶּן	הִכְתַּבְתֶּן	נִכְתַּבְתֶּן	תָּכְתֵּבְנָה	תַּכְתֵּבְנָה	תִּכְתֹּבְנָה	2 pl. *f.*
הָכְתַּבְנוּ	הִכְתַּבְנוּ	נִכְתַּבְנוּ	נָכְתַּב	נַכְתִּיב (בְ, יבָה §144. β)	נִכְתֹּב (נִכְתְּבָה §144. β)	1 pl.

INFINITIVES:— הַכְתֵּב (& הַכְתִּיב etc.) *Hiph-îl*, הָכְתֵּב etc. *Hoph-ăl.*

PARTICIPLES (s. *m.*):— נִכְתָּב *Niph-ăl*, מַכְתִּיב *Hiph-îl*, מָכְתָּב *Hoph-ăl;*

IMPERATIVE:—*Hiph-îl* הַכְתֵּב 2 s. *m.* (& הַכְתִּיבָה § 141·γ), הַכְתִּיבִי 2 s. *f.*, הַכְתִּיבוּ 2 pl. *m.*, הַכְתֵּבְנָה **2 pl.** *f.*

TABLE XV.

The INFIN. with Pronoun-Affixes (*Possessive*); (i.) KAL, (ii.) NIPH-ĂL, (iii.) PĬ-ÊL, (iv.) PŬ-ĂL, (v.) HIPH-ÎL, (vi) HOPH-ĂL, (vii.) HITHPĂ-ÊL.

our	f.	m. your	f.	m. their	my	f.	m. thy	her	his	
פָּקְדֵנוּ	־כֶן	‡ ,פָּקְדְכֶם	־ן	,פָּקְדָם	פָּקְרִי	פָּקְרֵךְ	* ,פָּקְדְךָ	־הָ	,פָּקְדוֹ	(i.) visiting.
הִפָּקְדֵנוּ	־כֶן	,הִפָּקֶדְכֶם	־ן	,הִפָּקְדָם	הִפָּקְרִי	הִפָּקְרֵךְ	† ,הִפָּקֶדְךָ	־הָ	,הִפָּקְדוֹ	(ii.) being visited.
פַּקְּדֵנוּ	־כֶן	,פַּקֶּדְכֶם	־ן	,פַּקְּדָם	פַּקְּרִי	פַּקְּרֵךְ	† ,פַּקֶּדְךָ	־הָ	,פַּקְּדוֹ	(iii.) visiting (Intens.).
פֻּקְּדֵנוּ	־כֶן	,פֻּקַּדְכֶם	־ן	,פֻּקְּדָם	פֻּקְּרִי	פֻּקְּרֵךְ	,פֻּקַּדְךָ	־הָ	,פֻּקְּדוֹ	(iv.) being visited. (Int.)
הַפְקִידֵנוּ	־כֶן	,הַפְקִידְכֶם	־ן	,הַפְקִידָם	הַפְקִידִי	(p. ; ־ךְ) ,הַפְקִידְךָ	,הַפְקִידוֹ	־הָ	,הַפְקִידוֹ	(v.) causing to visit.
הָפְקְדֵנוּ	־כֶן	,הָפְקַדְכֶם	־ן	,הָפְקְדָם	הָפְקְרִי	הָפְקְרֵךְ	,הָפְקֶדְךָ	־הָ	,הָפְקְדוֹ	(vi.) being caused to visit.
הִתְפַּקְּדֵנוּ	־כֶן	,הִתְפַּקֶּדְכֶם	־ן	,הִתְפַּקְּדָם	הִתְפַּקְּרִי	־קְּרֵךְ	† ,הִתְפַּקֶּדְךָ	־הָ	,הִתְפַּקְּדוֹ	(vii.) visiting himself.

25

*** For the ‘SLIGHT’-vowel under the פ sometimes, in the above, see Note (II.) on page 89.—For other *Affix*-forms see Tab. VIII.

* [Also אָכְלְךָ *thy* (m.) *eating*, Gen. ii. 17, (the ־ under א as in Pt. I., § 24). So others].—In Pause, ־ךָ as in שָׁפְטֶךָ *Thy judging*, Ps. li. 6.

† [Instead of ־ךָ, there is sometimes ־ךָ before a Guttural; thus ־חָךָ, as in בְּשִׁלְחָךָ]. In Pause : ־ךָ.

‡ [Also אָכָלְכֶם *your* (m.) *eating*, Gen. iii. 5; and so others]. Also בְּקָרָבְכֶם *at your* (m.) *approaching*, D. xx. 2; מָאָסְכֶם *your* (m.) *refusing*, Is. xxx. 12 (and so מָאֲסָם *their* (m.) *refusing*, Am. ii. 4). Also בְּמֹצַאֲכֶם *on your* (m.) *meeting* [lit., *finding*], Gen. xxxii. 20.

TABLE XVI (1).   Variations when the First Rt-letter is ה, ח, or ע [§§ 169–179 (pp. 115–120)].

N.B. *Some of the words below are merely Paradigm-forms.*

[*⁎* The PĪ-ĒL, PŬ-ĂL, & HĬTHPĂ-ĒL, are as in Tab. XIV.]

	(I.) KAL.	(II.) NIPH-ĂL.	(V.) HIPH-ÎL.	(VI.) HOPH-ĂL.
INF. ABS.	עָמֹד	נֶעְתּוֹר, הֵעָמֵר	הַעֲמֵד	הָעֳמֵד
Const., and	עֲמֹד, בּ׳, כּ׳	הֵעָמֵר, בּ׳, כּ׳	הַעֲמִיד, בְּ׳, כְּ׳	הָעֳמַד, בְּ׳, כְּ׳
with ב כ ל מ	לְ, מֵעֲמֹד	לְ, מֵהֵעָמֵר	לְ, מֵהַעֲמִיד	לְ, מֵהָעֳמַד
w. Pron. Affs.	עָמְדָן, ···	הֵעָמְדָן, ···	הַעֲמִידָן, ···	הָעֳמְדָן ···
PAST 3 s. *m.*	עָמַד	נֶ׳ נֶעֱמַר	הֶ׳ הֶעֱמִיד	הָעֳמַד
3 s. *f.*	עָמְדָה	נֶעֶמְרָה	הֶעֱמִידָה	הָעֳמְדָה
2 s. *m.*	עָמַדְתָּ	נֶעֱמַרְתָּ	‡ הֶעֱמַדְתָּ	הָעֳמַדְתָּ
2 s. *f.*	עָמַדְתְּ	נֶעֱמַרְתְּ	הֶעֱמַדְתְּ	הָעֳמַדְתְּ
1 s.	עָמַדְתִּי	נֶעֱמַרְתִּי	‡ הֶעֱמַדְתִּי	הָעֳמַדְתִּי
3 pl.	עָמְדוּ	נֶעֶמְרוּ	הֶעֱמִידוּ	הָעֳמְדוּ
2 pl. *m.*	עֲמַדְתֶּם	נֶעֱמַרְתֶּם	‡ הֶעֱמַדְתֶּם	הָעֳמַדְתֶּם
2 pl. *f.*	עֲמַדְתֶּן	נֶעֱמַרְתֶּן	‡ הֶעֱמַדְתֶּן	הָעֳמַדְתֶּן
1 pl.	עָמַדְנוּ	נֶעֱמַרְנוּ	הֶעֱמַדְנוּ	הָעֳמַדְנוּ
(1) PARTICIPLES. (2)	עֹמֵד, עָמוּד	נֶ׳ נֶעֱמָר	מֶ׳ מַעֲמִיד	מָעֳמָד

XIX*

	Imp. / Fut.	Qal (עָמֹד)	Qal (עָצֹר)	Qal (עָרֹב)	Qal (עָתַר)	Niph.	Hiph.	(in pause)	Hoph.
Imperative									
2 s. m.		עֲמֹד,	חֲזַק			הֵעָמֵד	הַעֲמֵד		
2 s. f.		עִמְדִי,	חִזְקִי			הֵעָמְדִי	הַעֲמִידִי		
2 pl. m.		עִמְדוּ,	חִזְקוּ			הֵעָמְדוּ	הַעֲמִידוּ		
2 pl. f.		עֲמֹדְנָה,	חֲזַקְנָה			הֵעָמַדְנָה	הַעֲמֵדְנָה		
Future									
3 s. m.		יַעֲמֹד,	יַעֲצֹר,	יַעֲרֹב,	יֶעְתַּר	יֵעָמֵד	יַעֲמִיד (or ־ד),	יַ'	יָעֳמַד
3 s. f.		תַּעֲמֹד,	תַּעֲצֹר,	תַּעֲרֹב,	תֶּעְתַּר	תֵּעָמֵד	תַּעֲמִיד,	פַּ'	תָּעֳמַד
2 s. m.		תַּעֲמֹד,	תַּעֲצֹר,	תַּעֲרֹב,	תֶּעְתַּר	תֵּעָמֵד	תַּעֲמִיד,	פַּ'	תָּעֳמַד
2 s. f.		תַּעַמְדִי,[1]	תַּעַצְרִי,	תַּעַרְבִי,[6]	תֶּעְתְּרִי	תֵּעָמְדִי	תַּעֲמִידִי,	פַּ'	תָּעֳמְדִי
1 s.		אֶעֱמֹד,[2]	אֶעֱצֹר,*	אֶעֱרֹב,[7]	אֶעְתַּר†	אֵעָמֵד	אַעֲמִיד,	אַ'	אָעֳמַד
3 pl. m.		יַעַמְדוּ,[3]	יַעַצְרוּ,	יַעַרְבוּ,[8]	יֶעְתְּרוּ	יֵעָמְדוּ	יַעֲמִידוּ,	יַ'	יָעֳמְדוּ
3 pl. f.		תַּעֲמֹדְנָה,	תַּעֲצֹרְנָה	תַּעֲרֹבְנָה	תֶּעְתַּרְנָה	תֵּעָמַדְנָה	תַּעֲמֵדְנָה,	פַּ'	תָּעֳמַדְנָה
2 pl. m.		תַּעַמְדוּ,[4]	תַּעַצְרוּ,	תַּעַרְבוּ,[9]	תֶּעְתְּרוּ	תֵּעָמְדוּ	תַּעֲמִידוּ,	פַּ'	תָּעֳמְדוּ
2 pl. f.		תַּעֲמֹדְנָה,	תַּעֲצֹרְנָה	תַּעֲרֹבְנָה	תֶּעְתַּרְנָה	תֵּעָמַדְנָה	תַּעֲמֵדְנָה,	פַּ'	תָּעֳמַדְנָה
1 pl.		נַעֲמֹד,[5]	נַעֲצֹר,**	נַעֲרֹב,[10]	נֶעְתַּר††	נֵעָמֵד	נַעֲמִיד,	נַ'	נָעֳמַד

[1] p. תַּעַמְדִי.   [2] With ה, עָמְדָה (p. אֶעֶמְדָה).   [3] p. יַעַמְדוּ.   [4] p. תַּעַמְדוּ.   [5] With ה, נַעַמְדָה (p. נַעַמְדָה).

[6] p. תַּעַרְבִי.   [7] With ה, עָרְבָה (p. אֶעֶרְבָה).   [8] p. יַעַרְבוּ.   [9] p. תַּעַרְבוּ.   [10] With ה, נַעַרְבָה (p. נַעַרְבָה).

* Also with ה like אֶפְקֹרָה (p. אֶפְקֹרָה).   ** And w. ה, נַעֲצֹרָה (p. נַעֲצֹרָה).   † Also with ח like אֶלְבְּשָׁה (p. אֶלְבְּשָׁה).   †† And, w. ה, נֶעְתְּרָה (p. נֶעְתְּרָה).

‡ Often, with ו, וָעַ'; thus וְהַעֲמַדְתָּ, comp. § 160. So, fr. חרם, הַחֲרַמְתִּי but וְהַחֲרַמְתִּי, and הַחֲרַמְתֶּם but וְהַחֲרַמְתֶּם, etc.—This is not so in

[ס] וְהֶחֱזַקְתָּ Lev. xxv. 35, and וְהֶחֱזַקְתִּי 1 S. xvii. 35.

TABLE XVI (2).

Variations when the 2d Root-letter is א, ה, ח, or ע:—[ר, next page].

(a.) The forms are the same as in Tab. XIV., except as regards—

    (1) the COMPOUND form of *Shva Moving* under 2d Root-letter [§ 168 (iv.)];

    (2) a 'Slight'-vowel under the 1st Root-letter which may agree with the Compound Shva following it [§ 168 (v.)].

    (3) the absence of Dag. F. from 2d Root-letter in *Pi.*, *Pŭ.*, *Hithp.*; and

    (4) the 'Compensation' *sometimes* made for that Dagesh Forte [§ 168 (iii.)];

(β.) The Vowel-change referred to in (4) above is—

    (i.) (a) generally made before א, as in יְתָאֵר [פֻּקַּד], מֵאֵן [לְפֻקַּד] לְפָאֵר [מְפֻקַּד], כִּנְאֵל [וַיְפַקֵּר], etc.; but (b) sometimes not made, as נִאֵץ, etc.;

    (ii.) (a) often NOT made before ה or ע in *Pi.* & *Hithp.*; but (b) generally made before those two letters in *Pŭ.*;

    (iii.) GENERALLY NOT MADE before ח in *Pi.*, *Pŭ.*, *Hithp.*

(γ.) The following illustrate sufficiently the peculiarities of these Verbs.

[Obs.—Some of the forms below are merely *Paradigm-forms*.

N.B.—For the 'Compensation,' of (4) above, see the forms within ( )].

HITHP. (of נֵעֵר).	PŬ-ĂL (of רֻחַם).	PÏ-ÊL.	NIPH-ĂL.	KAL.	
(Tab. XIV.)		צַעֵק (צַ)	(Tab. XIV.)	(Tab. XIV.)	INF.
הִתְנַעֲרוּ (נַ),...	רֻחֲמוּ (‑עֻ‑)	צַעֲקוּ (צַ),...	הִצָּעֲקוּ,...	צַעֲקוּ,...	w. Aff. PAST.
הִתְנַעֵר (נַ)	רֻחַם (‑עֻ‑)	צִעֵק (צִ)	נִצְעַק	צָעַק	3 s. m.
הִתְנַעֲרָה (נַ)	רֻחֲמָה (‑עֻ‑)	צִעֲקָה (צִ)	נִצְעֲקָה	צָעֲקָה	3 s. f.
הִתְנַעֲרוּ (נַ)	רֻחֲמוּ (‑עֻ‑)	צִעֲקוּ (צִ)	נִצְעֲקוּ	צָעֲקוּ	3 pl.
מִתְנַעֵר (נַ)	מְרֻחָם (‑עֻ‑)	מְצַעֵק (צַ)	(Tab. XIV.)	(Tab. XIV.)	PARTIC. IMPER.
הִתְנַעֵר (נַ)		צַעֵק (צַ)	(Tab. XIV.)	(Tab. XIV.)	2 s. m.
הִתְנַעֲרִי (נַ)		צַעֲקִי (צַ)	הִצָּעֲקִי	צַעֲקִי	2 s. f.
הִתְנַעֲרוּ (נַ)		צַעֲקוּ (צַ)	הִצָּעֲקוּ	צַעֲקוּ	2 pl. m. FUT.
יִתְנַעֵר (נַ)	יְרֻחַם (‑עֻ‑)	יְצַעֵק (צַ)	(Tab. XIV.)	(Tab. XIV.)	3 s. m.
תִּתְנַעֲרִי (נַ)	תְּרֻחֲמִי (‑עֻ‑)	תְּצַעֲקִי (צַ)	תִּצָּעֲקִי	תִּצְעֲקִי	2 s. f.
יִתְנַעֲרוּ (נַ)	יְרֻחֲמוּ (‑עֻ‑)	יְצַעֲקוּ (צַ)	יִצָּעֲקוּ	יִצְעֲקוּ	3 pl. m.
תִּתְנַעֲרוּ (נַ)	תְּרֻחֲמוּ (‑עֻ‑)	תְּצַעֲקוּ (צַ)	תִּצָּעֲקוּ	תִּצְעֲקוּ	2 pl. m.

⁎ For ‑ֶ before ח (& ה) in *Hithp.* Pause-forms, see § 166 (c, d). Thus, יִתְנֶחָם : 3 s. m. Fut., and וָאֶתְנֶחָם : 1 s. with ו Conv. So, וְהִנֶּחָמְתִּי : 1 s. (ת dropped), and וְהִטֶּהֲרוּ : 3 pl. (2d Root-letter ה), Past with ו Conv.

Appendix to TABLE XVI (2).

VARIATIONS WHEN THE 2nd ROOT-LETTER IS רּ.

The forms are as in Tab. XVI., except in *Pĭ-êl*, *Pŭ-ăl*, and *Hithpă-êl.*

(VII.) Hithpă-êl.	(IV.) Pŭ-ăl.	(III.) Pĭ-êl.	
הִתְבָּרֵךְ, בְּ׳, כְּ׳, לְ׳, מֵהִתְבָּרֵךְ הִתְבָּרְכוֹ,...		בָּרֵךְ, בְּ׳, כְּ׳, לְבָרֵךְ, מְבָרֵךְ בֵּרְכוֹ,...	Inf. Abs. & Constr., & with בכלמ. With Pron. Aff.
			Past.
הִתְבָּרֵךְ (or בר)	בֹּרַךְ	בֵּרֵךְ, בֵּרַךְ	3 s. m.
הִתְבָּרְכָה	בֹּרְכָה	בֵּרְכָה	3 s. f.
הִתְבָּרַכְתָּ	בֹּרַכְתָּ	בֵּרַכְתָּ	2 s. m.
הִתְבָּרַכְתְּ	בֹּרַכְתְּ	בֵּרַכְתְּ	2 s. f.
הִתְבָּרַכְתִּי	בֹּרַכְתִּי	בֵּרַכְתִּי	1 s.
הִתְבָּרְכוּ	בֹּרְכוּ	בֵּרְכוּ	3 pl.
הִתְבָּרַכְתֶּם	בֹּרַכְתֶּם	בֵּרַכְתֶּם	2 pl. m.
הִתְבָּרַכְתֶּן	בֹּרַכְתֶּן	בֵּרַכְתֶּן	2 pl. f.
הִתְבָּרַכְנוּ	בֹּרַכְנוּ	בֵּרַכְנוּ	1 pl.
			Participle.
מִתְבָּרֵךְ	מְבֹרָךְ	מְבָרֵךְ	
			Imperative.
הִתְבָּרֵךְ		בָּרֵךְ	2 s. m.
הִתְבָּרְכִי		בָּרְכִי	2 s. f.
הִתְבָּרְכוּ		בָּרְכוּ	2 pl. m.
הִתְבָּרֵכְנָה		בָּרֵכְנָה	2 pl. f.
			Future.
יִתְבָּרֵךְ	יְבֹרַךְ	יְבָרֵךְ	3 s. m.
תִּתְבָּרֵךְ	תְּבֹרַךְ	תְּבָרֵךְ	3 s. f.
תִּתְבָּרֵךְ	תְּבֹרַךְ	תְּבָרֵךְ	2 s. m.
תִּתְבָּרְכִי	תְּבֹרְכִי	תְּבָרְכִי	2 s. f.
אֶתְבָּרֵךְ	אֲבֹרַךְ	אֲבָרֵךְ	1 s.
יִתְבָּרְכוּ	יְבֹרְכוּ	יְבָרְכוּ	3 pl. m.
תִּתְבָּרֵכְנָה	תְּבֹרַכְנָה	תְּבָרֵכְנָה	3 pl. f.
תִּתְבָּרְכוּ	תְּבֹרְכוּ	תְּבָרְכוּ	2 pl. m.
תִּתְבָּרֵכְנָה	תְּבֹרַכְנָה	תְּבָרֵכְנָה	2 pl. f.
נִתְבָּרֵךְ	נְבֹרַךְ	נְבָרֵךְ	1 pl.

TABLE XVI (3). [§ 181].

The forms are as in Tab. XIV., except as regards—

(A) the 'Furtive' ◌ַ (§ 168, ii.; & Pt. I., § 60) at the end of a word after any Long Vowel except ◌ֵ; thus, e g., in the Infin. forms, (i) K. שָׁלֹחַ, לִשְׁלֹחַ, (ii.) Nφ.* לְהִבָּקֵעַ, (iii) Pĭ. לְנַבֵּחַ, (v.) Hφ.* הַכְרֵעַ, לְהַשְׁמִיעַ, (vi.) Hŏ.* הָמְלָח, (vii) Hθ* לְהִשְׁתַּבֵּחַ†; and so in the Partic⁸. K. שֹׁלֵחַ (1), מַנְבִּיחַ (2),—& שָׂמֵחַ [§ 139 (γ) & (δ, iii)], Pĭ. מְשַׁלֵּחַ, Hφ. מַנְבִּיהַ, Hθ. מִשְׁתַּגֵּעַ†;

(B) the replacing, sometimes, a Long Vowel by ◌ַ so as to dispense with the 'Furtive' ◌ַ. This is not very common in K. Inf. Constr., as שְׁלַח once (usually שְׁלֹח), בִּגְוַע Nu. xx 3 (but, p. : לִגְוֹעַ Nu. xvii. 28), and in Partic. (1) [§ 139 (γ)] as נֹטַע once (Ps. xciv. 9), רֹגַע twice, רֹקַע three times [עַ◌ for עֵ◌]. But there is

N.B. generally ◌ַ [for ◌ֵ followed by 'Furtive' ◌ַ] in the

(a.) Inf. Constr. Nφ. & Pĭ.; as בְּשַׁלַּח, שַׁלַּח, הַלְקַח, כְּהִכָּנַע, כְּבַלַּע, etc.;

(β.) Imper. & Fut. Nφ., Pĭ. & Hφ.; as יְשַׁלַּח, שַׁלַּח, וַיֵּאָנַח, הֵאָנַח, הוֹדַע, הַצְלַח (& ◌ַ Ps. xc. 12), וַיַּצְלַח (& ◌ַ 1 Chr. xxix 23), אַל תַּשְׁמַע, וַיִּשְׁבַּע, אַל יַבַּח [for the ◌ַ form of fut. Hφ., see § 162 (e, ii)];

(γ.) Pĭ Past, as בִּלַּע, פִּתַּח, זִבַּח, etc. [In p., ◌ֵ returns, as in בִּלֵּעַ :, פִּתֵּחַ :].

(δ) We find הִתְוַדַּע, הִתְנַגַּע, Hθ. Inf. (but also לְהִשְׁתַּבֵּחַ†, לְהִשְׁתַּגֵּעַ†, מְהִסְתַּפֵּחַ†), and Fut. יִתְנַגַּח.

[Obs. (i) (◌ֵ ◌ַ) remains in Inf⁸ Abs , Partic⁸., and in Pause generally.§

(ii.) Hθ. Pause-forms‖ have ◌ֵ to the 2d Root-letter regularly; see § 166 (c); thus, תִּתְבַּלָּע :, יִתְנַגָּעַ :, יִתְוַכָּח : [Sect. XVI], etc.]. Also,

(C) 2 s. f. Past forms (cp פָּקַדְתְּ, etc). Here 3rd Root-letter generally¶ takes ◌ַ instead of ◌ְ, the תְּ remaining unchanged, thus, שָׁבַחַתְּ, לָקַחַתְּ, שְׁמַעַתְּ, יָדַעַתְּ, etc.; and so in other Voices, as in Hφ.* הִגַּעַתְּ (for הִגַּעְתְּ, see Sect. XVI.), Hŏ. הֻמְלַחַתְּ; and, lastly,

(D) instead of the תֶ◌ ◌ֶ form of the Participles s. f. [see § 139 (β), p. 83], these Verbs have תַ◌ ◌ַ; thus, שֹׁמַעַת, פֹּרַחַת (p. : שֹׁמָעַת), etc.

Note—These Verbs generally take ◌ַ to 2nd Root-letter in Imp. & Fut. Kal; and in 2 pl. f. Imp (3 & 2 pl. f. Fut) Pĭ, Hφ., & Hθ.

---

* Nφ., Hφ., Hŏ., Hθ., are abbrev. terms for Niph-ăl, Hiph-ĭl, Hoph-ăl, Hithpă-êl.

† For transposition of ת (of הִת) & 1st Root-letter, see Tab. XIV. (*͙*).

‡ So in זָרֻעַ (for זָרוּעַ), the ◌ֻ being Defective Shurik [Pt. I., § 14].

§ But חַ◌ & עַ◌ occur sometimes in Pause, and often with less Disjunctive (besides Conjunctive) Accents. See (a—δ) & הֵאָנַח (Imper. Nφ), נִגְרַע, תֵּאָנַח, תִּזְרַע, יִכָּנַע, וַיִּשָּׁבַע, and נֹחַ (Pĭ Past), וַיְּנַתַּח, וַיְּפַלַּח, תְּפַתַּח, אֲבַלַּע, etc.

‖ Except Inf⁸. and Partic⁸. s. m. These always have the (◌ֵ ◌ַ) form in Pause.

¶ Some Bibles have ◌ַ to the 3d Root-letter, as in וְלָקַחַתְּ 1 K. xiv. 3, שָׁבַחַתְּ Jer. xiii. 25.

NOTE.

The Student will be better able to understand the concise
statements of the preceding page by reference to the

PARADIGM

on the following two pages.

TABLE XVI (3) PARADIGM.—[The 3d Bi-letter ה, ח, or ע]. *Some of the words are merely Paradigm-forms.*

VII. Hithpā-ēl.	VI. Hoph-al.	V. Hiph-il.	IV. Pu-al.	III. Py-el.	II. Niph-al.	I. Kal.	
*הִשְׁתַּלֵּחַ	הָשְׁלֵחַ	הַשְׁלֵחַ	שֻׁלַּח (—חַ)	שַׁלֵּחַ	הִשָּׁלֵחַ, נִשְׁלוֹחַ	שָׁלֹחַ	Inf. Abs.
הִשְׁתַּלֵּחַ (—חַ)	הָשְׁלֵחַ	הַשְׁלִיחַ	שֻׁלַּח	שַׁלֵּחַ (—חַ)	הִשָּׁלֵחַ	שְׁלֹחַ (שְׁלַח)	Inf. Constr.
בְּ׳, כְּ׳, לְ׳, מֵהִשְׁתַּלֵּחַ (—חַ)	בָּ׳, כָּ׳, לָ׳, מָהְשְׁלַח	בְּ׳, כְּ׳, לְ׳, מַהְשְׁלִיחַ	בְּ׳, כְּ׳, לְ׳, מְשֻׁלָּח	בְּ׳, כְּ׳, לְ׳, מְשַׁלֵּחַ (—חַ)	בְּ׳, כְּ׳, לְ׳, מֵהִשָּׁלֵחַ (—חַ)	בִּשְׁ׳, כִּשְׁ׳, לִשְׁ׳, מִשְׁלֹחַ (—לֹחַ)	w. ב כ ל מ
הִשְׁתַּלְּחוֹ,…	הָשְׁלְחוֹ,…	הַשְׁלִיחוֹ,…	שֻׁלְּחוֹ,…	שַׁלְּחוֹ,…	הִשָּׁלְחוֹ,…	שָׁלְחוֹ,…	w. Pron. Affs.
*הִשְׁתַּלֵּחַ	הָשְׁלַח	הִשְׁלִיחַ	שֻׁלַּח	שִׁלַּח (—ם)	נִשְׁלַח	שָׁלַח	Past. 3 s. m.
הִשְׁתַּלְּחָה	הָשְׁלְחָה	הִשְׁלִיחָה	שֻׁלְּחָה	שִׁלְּחָה	נִשְׁלְחָה	שָׁלְחָה	3 s. f.
הִשְׁתַּלַּחְתָּ	הָשְׁלַחְתָּ	הִשְׁלַחְתָּ	שֻׁלַּחְתָּ	שִׁלַּחְתָּ	נִשְׁלַחְתָּ	שָׁלַחְתָּ	2 s. m.
הִשְׁתַּלַּחַתְּ	הָשְׁלַחַתְּ	הִשְׁלַחַתְּ	שֻׁלַּחַתְּ	שִׁלַּחַתְּ	נִשְׁלַחַתְּ	שָׁלַחַתְּ	2 s. f.
הִשְׁתַּלַּחְתִּי	הָשְׁלַחְתִּי	הִשְׁלַחְתִּי	שֻׁלַּחְתִּי	שִׁלַּחְתִּי	נִשְׁלַחְתִּי	שָׁלַחְתִּי	1 s.
הִשְׁתַּלְּחוּ	הָשְׁלְחוּ	הִשְׁלִיחוּ	שֻׁלְּחוּ	שִׁלְּחוּ	נִשְׁלְחוּ	שָׁלְחוּ	3 pl.
הִשְׁתַּלַּחְתֶּם	הָשְׁלַחְתֶּם	הִשְׁלַחְתֶּם	שֻׁלַּחְתֶּם	שִׁלַּחְתֶּם	נִשְׁלַחְתֶּם	שְׁלַחְתֶּם	2 pl m.
הִשְׁתַּלַּחְתֶּן	הָשְׁלַחְתֶּן	הִשְׁלַחְתֶּן	שֻׁלַּחְתֶּן	שִׁלַּחְתֶּן	נִשְׁלַחְתֶּן	שְׁלַחְתֶּן	2 pl. f.
הִשְׁתַּלַּחְנוּ	הָשְׁלַחְנוּ	הִשְׁלַחְנוּ	שֻׁלַּחְנוּ	שִׁלַּחְנוּ	נִשְׁלַחְנוּ	שָׁלַחְנוּ	1 pl.

32

XXII**

XXII***

Form	שֹׁלֵחַ (1), שָׁלוּחַ (2) [וּשְׁלַח]	נִשְׁלָח	מְשַׁלֵּחַ [־ֵחַ]	מְשֻׁלָּח	מַשְׁלִיחַ	מֻשְׁלָח	*מִשְׁתַּלֵּחַ
IMPER. 2 s. m.	שְׁלַח	הִשָּׁלַח (־ַח)	שַׁלַּח		הַשְׁלַח (־ֵחַ)		*הִשְׁתַּלֵּחַ (־ֵי)
2 s. f.	שִׁלְחִי	הִשָּׁלְחִי	שַׁלְּחִי		הַשְׁלִיחִי		הִשְׁתַּלְּחִי
2 pl. m.	שִׁלְחוּ	הִשָּׁלְחוּ	שַׁלְּחוּ		הַשְׁלִיחוּ		הִשְׁתַּלְּחוּ
2 pl. f.	שְׁלַחְנָה	הִשָּׁלַחְנָה	שַׁלַּחְנָה		הַשְׁלַחְנָה		הִשְׁתַּלַּחְנָה
FUTURE 3 s. m.	יִשְׁלַח	יִשָּׁלַח (־ַח)	יְשַׁלַּח (־ֵחַ)	יְשֻׁלַּח	יַשְׁלִיחַ (־ֵחַ)	יֻשְׁלַח	*יִשְׁתַּלֵּחַ (־ֵי)
3 s. f.	תִּשְׁלַח	תִּשָּׁלַח (־ַח)	תְּשַׁלַּח (־ֵחַ)	תְּשֻׁלַּח	תַּשְׁלִיחַ (־ֵחַ)	תֻּשְׁלַח	תִּשְׁתַּלֵּחַ (־ֵי)
2 s. m.	תִּשְׁלַח	תִּשָּׁלַח (־ַח)	תְּשַׁלַּח (־ֵחַ)	תְּשֻׁלַּח	תַּשְׁלִיחַ (־ֵחַ)	תֻּשְׁלַח	תִּשְׁתַּלֵּחַ (־ֵי)
2 s. f.	תִּשְׁלְחִי	תִּשָּׁלְחִי	תְּשַׁלְּחִי	תְּשֻׁלְּחִי	תַּשְׁלִיחִי	תֻּשְׁלְחִי	תִּשְׁתַּלְּחִי
1 s.	אֶשְׁלַח	אֶשָּׁלַח (־ַח)	אֲשַׁלַּח (־ֵחַ)	אֲשֻׁלַּח	אַשְׁלִיחַ (־ֵחַ)	אֻשְׁלַח	אֶשְׁתַּלֵּחַ (־ֵי)
3 pl. m.	יִשְׁלְחוּ	יִשָּׁלְחוּ	יְשַׁלְּחוּ	יְשֻׁלְּחוּ	יַשְׁלִיחוּ	יֻשְׁלְחוּ	יִשְׁתַּלְּחוּ
3 pl. f.	תִּשְׁלַחְנָה	תִּשָּׁלַחְנָה	תְּשַׁלַּחְנָה	תְּשֻׁלַּחְנָה	תַּשְׁלַחְנָה	תֻּשְׁלַחְנָה	תִּשְׁתַּלַּחְנָה
2 pl. m.	תִּשְׁלְחוּ	תִּשָּׁלְחוּ	תְּשַׁלְּחוּ	תְּשֻׁלְּחוּ	תַּשְׁלִיחוּ	תֻּשְׁלְחוּ	תִּשְׁתַּלְּחוּ
2 pl. f.	תִּשְׁלַחְנָה	תִּשָּׁלַחְנָה	תְּשַׁלַּחְנָה	תְּשֻׁלַּחְנָה	תַּשְׁלַחְנָה	תֻּשְׁלַחְנָה	תִּשְׁתַּלַּחְנָה
1 pl.	נִשְׁלַח	נִשָּׁלַח (־ַח)	נְשַׁלַּח (־ֵחַ)	נְשֻׁלַּח	נַשְׁלִיחַ (־ֵחַ)	נֻשְׁלַח	נִשְׁתַּלֵּחַ (־ֵי)

* For the transposition of the שׁ and the ת, see ‘Note (I), pp. 89 & 89*.’

*** For (A), (B), (C), (D), and Note,—see page 30.

TABLE XVII.

Verbs א"פ, *i.e.* whose 1st Root-letter is א [See also next page].

These are generally as in Tab. XVI (1), with the following exceptions:—

(1) The INF. Construct *Kal* often has $-$ under the 1st Root-letter, as in—

אֱחֹז, *בֶּאֱחֹז, כֶּאֱכֹל, לֶאֱכֹל,† מֵאֱכֹל,

(2) The FUTURE *Kal*, of some of them,

    (α.) has the א Quiescent after $\div$ given to the prefixes י ת ן; thus,—

יֹאכַל, תֹּאכַל, תֹּאכְלִי, יֹאכְלוּ, תֹּאכַלְנָה, נֹאכַל,

    (β.) In the case of the 1 s. Fut. *K.*, the א of the Root is *dropped* (after the prefix א bearing $\div$); thus, אֹכַל instead of אֹאכַל.

        N.B.—The א of the Root is also dropped (rarely) in other forms, thus, וַיֹּסֶף for וַיֹּאסֶף [(δ)] 2 S. vi. 1, תֹּסֶף for תֹּאסֵף [(γ)] Ps. civ. 29, etc.

    (γ.) We have $-$ in יֹאחֵז 3 s. *m.*, תֹּאחֵז 3 s. *f.*, אֹחֵז 1 s. So in Pause, יֹאכֵל : תֹּאכֵל :‡ אֹכֵל : נֹאכֵל :, and & אֹכֵלָה : נֹאכֵלָה (fr. אֹכְלָה 1 s. & נֹאכְלָה 1 pl.) with ה, and יֹאכֵלוּ : 3 pl. *m.*, etc.

    (δ.) The $-$ in such forms as וַיֹּאמֶר, is for the $-$ of (γ.); for,

        N.B.—the Long-Vowel $-$ is shortened when the Accent is removed from the $-$ of יֹאמַר etc.

    (ε.) Many Verbs whose 1st Root-letter is א are conjugated according to Tab. XIV., rather than as above, except that the א of the Root takes $-$ and the prefixes א י ת ן take $-$ generally. This is so in Verbs 'Fut. ($\div$)' as well as in Verbs 'Fut. ($-$),' [p. 85 (‡, §)] ; thus,—

        (i.) יֶאֱסֹף, תֶּאֱסֹף, נֶאֱסֹף ; (ii.) יֶאֱהַב, תֶּאֱהַב, etc.

        N.B.—The Fut. forms in (β, N.B.) and (ε, i.) are of the same Verb. So those of אחז in (γ.) and יֶאֱחֹז 3 s. *m.*, תֶּאֱחֹז 3 s. *f.*; also of אהב we find אֹהַב 1 s., and אֶהֱהַב: (for אֶאֱהַב) 1 s. in Pause.

(3) In the IMPER. *K.*—(i.) the א generally has $-$ in 2 s. *m.*, as in אֱמֹר, אֱהַב, etc.; but, (ii.) in the 2 s. *f.*, and 2 pl. *m.*, the 'Slight'-vowel is, generally, $-$ as in Tab. XIV.; thus, אִמְרִי, §אִמְרוּ, etc. But $-$ before ה or ח, as in אֱחֹזוּ, אֱהַבוּ.‖ (iii.) The 2 s. *m.* Imper. *K.* with the ה of § 141 (γ) generally takes $-$ (δ) as in אָכְלָה *eat thou* (*m.*) G. xxvii. 19; but also $-$, as in אִסְפָה Nu. xi. 16.

---

* Also with א, as in אֱכֹל בֶּאֱכֹל. So in אֱמֹר ($-$, δ), and הֶאֱמֹר; but also בֶּאֱמֹר, and כֶּאֱמֹר.

† Also (i.) לֶאֱסֹר (as well as לֶאֱסוֹר). (ii.) The common word לֵאמֹר is Inf. *Kal* of אמר with ל prefixed (for לֶאֱמֹר). This word is rendered "saying" in the E.V.; thus, G. xxiii. 8, "And he communed with them (לֵאמֹר) *saying*; etc."

‡ This 1 s. Fut. *K.* is the same in form as אֹכֵל, the s. *m.* Partic. *K.*, and the context alone can decide between them.

§ Once אִסְפִּי Jer. x. 17, with a Real short-vowel followed by $-$ Quiescent.

‖ אֶחֱזִי 2 s. *f.* (Ruth iii. 15. Other Bibles have אֲחֳזִי.)

(TABLE XVII). PARADIGM. VERBS פ"א [pp. 128–130**.]

Form	III. PI-ĒL, IV. PŬ-ĂL, VII. HITHPĂ-ĒL, &c.	II. NIPH-ĂL.	I. KAL.
INFIN. Abs.		הֵאָכֹל (הֵאָכֵל)	אָכוֹל
Infin. Constr. & w. ב כ ל מ	III. PI-ĒL, IV. PŬ-ĂL, VII. HITHPĂ-ĒL, are the same as in Tab. XIV.	הֵאָכֵל, בְּ, כְּ, / לְ מֵהֵאָכֵל	אֲכֹל, בְּ, כְּ, לְ, מֵאֲכֹל (Also בֶּאֱכֹל, אֱכֹל,….See also p. xxiii, Notes (*) & (†).)
w. Pron. Affs.		הֵאָכְלוֹ, …	אָכְלוֹ, …
PAST 3 s. m.	V. HIPH-ÎL, VI. HOPH-ĂL, are as in Tab. XVI (1). ‖	נֶאֱכַל	אָכַל
3 s. f.		נֶאֶכְלָה	אָכְלָה
2 s. m.		נֶאֱכַלְתָּ	אָכַלְתָּ
2 s. f.		נֶאֱכַלְתְּ	אָכַלְתְּ
1 s.		נֶאֱכַלְתִּי	אָכַלְתִּי
3 pl.		נֶאֶכְלוּ (נֶאֶכָֽזוּ) §	אָכְלוּ
2 pl. m.		נֶאֱכַלְתֶּם	אֲכַלְתֶּם
2 pl. f.		נֶאֱכַלְתֶּן	אֲכַלְתֶּן
1 pl.	These forms and the *Imper. & Fut. Nφ.* are as in Tab. XVI (1).	נֶאֱכַלְנוּ	אָכַלְנוּ
PARTIC. (1) s. m.		נֶאֱכָל	אֹכֵל
(2) s. f.			אָכוּל
IMPER. 2 s. m.	אֱהֶב §	(p. xxiii (3), (אֶסְפָּה) † אֱכֹלה	אֱכֹל, אֱכֹלה † (אֶסְפָּה)
2 s. f.	אֱהֲבִי §	(p. xxiii, Note (§), (אִסְפִּי)	אִכְלִי §
2 pl. m.	אֱהֲבוּ §		אִכְלוּ
2 pl. f.	אֱהַבְנָה		אֱכֹלְנָה
FUTURE 3 s. m.	(Pr. xv. 9 ¶ (וְאֶהֱבוּ:) § יֶאֱהַב (etc. (יֶאֱ')	יֶאֱרַב	(ל‍ֶָ) יֹאכַל
3 s. f.	תֶּאֱהַב §	תֶּאֱרַב	(ל‍ֶָ) תֹּאכַל
2 s. m.	תֶּאֱהַב §	תֶּאֱרַב	(ל‍ֶָ) תֹּאכַל
2 s. f.	תֶּאֱהֲבִי † (תֶּאֱ')	תֶּאֱרְבִי † (תֶּאֱ')	(p. ל‍ִָ) תֹּאכְלִי
1 s.	(אֱהֲב‍.fr. אֱהַב .ft‍‍. אֶהֱבֶ)§אֶאֱהַב (וָאֹהַר, אֶהֱבוּ,וָאֹהַב)	אֶאֱרַב אֶאֱרֲבָה †	אֹכַל (ל‍ֶָ, ל‍ֶָ)
3 pl. m.	יֶאֱהֲבוּ † (יֶאֱ')	יֶאֱרְבוּ †	(p. ל‍ִָ) יֹאכְלוּ
3 pl. f.	תֶּאֱהַבְנָה	תֶּאֱרַבְנָה	תֹּאכַלְנָה
2 pl. m.	(Pr. i. 22 ¶ (תְּאֵהֲבוּ:) תֶּאֱהֲבוּ † (תֶּאֱ')	תֶּאֱרְבוּ † (תֶּאֱ')	(p. ל‍ִָ) תֹּאכְלוּ
2 pl. f.	תֶּאֱהַבְנָה	תֶּאֱרַבְנָה	תֹּאכַלְנָה
1 pl.	נֶאֱהַב §	נֶאֱרַב, נֶאֱרֲבָה †	נֹאכַל, ל‍ֶָ (ל‍ֶָ, ל‍ֶָ)

* With ה,—אָכְלָה, אַהֲבָה, comp. § 137 (4, iii) [p. 80]. † p. (—ָ֑). ‡ p. (—ָ). § p. (—ָ).
‖ For some contracted forms see § 191, & p. 130**. For some irregular, or 'borrowed,' forms see § 190 (β, ii), and p. 130**. ¶ In some copies. Others give אֲהַב:.

For (III.) PI-ĒL, (IV.) PŬ-ĀL, (VII.) HITHP. see § 193 (iii) w. Notes † & ‡.	(VI.) HOPH.	[fr. יטב]	(V.) HIPH.	(II.) NIPH-ĀL.	[For הֵעֵר etc., & הֵעָתוֹ etc., see Notes (a) & (c) below.]	(I.) KAL.
		הֵיטֵב	הוֹשֵׁב	הִוָּשֵׁב		יָשֹׁב INF. ABS.
		(הֵיטִיב, כ’, כ’, ל’, מֵהֵיטִיב הֵיטִיבוֹ,···)	(הוֹשִׁיב, כ’, כ’, ל’, מֵהוֹשִׁיב הוֹשִׁיבוֹ,···)	(הִוָּשֵׁב, כ’, כ’, ל’, מֵהִוָּשֵׁב הִוָּשְׁבוֹ,···)		שֶׁבֶת‘, ‘, כ’, כ’ Constr. and לָשֶׁבֶת‘, מֹשֶׁבֶת w. ב כ ל מ שִׁבְתּוֹ‘,·· w. Pron. Affs.
						PAST.
	הוּשַׁב	הֵיטִיב	הוֹשִׁיב	נוֹשַׁב		יָשַׁב 3 s. m.
	הוּשְׁבָה	הֵיטִיבָה	הוֹשִׁיבָה	נוֹשְׁבָה		יָשְׁבָה 3 s. f.
	הוּשַׁבְתָּ	הֵיטַבְתָּ	הוֹשַׁבְתָּ	נוֹשַׁבְתָּ		יָשַׁבְתָּ 2 s. m.
	הוּשַׁבְתְּ	הֵיטַבְתְּ	הוֹשַׁבְתְּ	נוֹשַׁבְתְּ		יָשַׁבְתְּ 2 s. f.
	הוּשַׁבְתִּי	הֵיטַבְתִּי	הוֹשַׁבְתִּי	נוֹשַׁבְתִּי		יָשַׁבְתִּי 1 s.
	הוּשְׁבוּ	הֵיטִיבוּ	הוֹשִׁיבוּ	נוֹשְׁבוּ	(As in Table XIV.)	יָשְׁבוּ 3 pl.
	הוּשַׁבְתֶּם	הֵיטַבְתֶּם	הוֹשַׁבְתֶּם	נוֹשַׁבְתֶּם		יְשַׁבְתֶּם² 2 pl. m.
	הוּשַׁבְתֶּן	הֵיטַבְתֶּן	הוֹשַׁבְתֶּן	נוֹשַׁבְתֶּן		יְשַׁבְתֶּן 2 pl. f.
	הוּשַׁבְנוּ	הֵיטַבְנוּ	הוֹשַׁבְנוּ	נוֹשַׁבְנוּ		יָשַׁבְנוּ 1 pl.
	מוּשָׁב	מֵיטִיב	מוֹשִׁיב	נוֹשָׁב		(As in Table XIV). PARTICIPLES.

XXIV

[For דַּע etc., see Note d. So רֵשׁ (p. רֵשׁ) fr. יְרֹשׁ.]   [fr. יטב § 197 (a–ε)] ³

	ישב	יטב	(Tab. XIV.)	הֹושֵׁב[5], (הוֹדַע) § 199.e	הֵיטֵב	יֹושֵׁב
2 s. m.	שֵׁב[d], שֵׁב־, שְׁבָה†		הֻושַׁב	הֹושֵׁב[5]	הֵיטֵב, ־יבָה	
2 s. f.	שְׁבִי (p. שֵׁבִי)			הֹושִׁיבִי	הֵיטִיבִי	
2 pl. m.	שְׁבוּ (p. שֵׁבוּ)			הֹושִׁיבוּ	הֵיטִיבוּ	
2 pl. f.	שֵׁבְנָה, שֹׁבְן			הֹושֵׁבְנָה	הֵיטֵבְנָה	
FUTURE.						
3 s. m.	יֵשֵׁב*[e] (יֵדַע etc., Note e)	יֵטֵב	יֻושַׁב*, (יֻוָדַע etc.)	יֹושֵׁב*[4]	יֵיטִיב*[4], {ב ־ֵ, (וַיֵּ־)}	יֹושֵׁב
3 s. f.	תֵּשֵׁב*	תֵּיטַב	תֻּושַׁב*	תֹּושֵׁב*	תֵּיטִיב*	תֹּושֵׁב
2 s. m.	תֵּשֵׁב*	תֵּיטַב	תֻּושַׁב*	תֹּושִׁיב*	תֵּיטִיב*	תֹּושֵׁב
2 s. f.	תֵּשְׁבִי†	תֵּיטְבִי, תֵּי'	תֻּושְׁבִי	תֹּושִׁיבִי	תֵּיטִיבִי	תֹּושִׁיבִי
1 s.	אֵשֵׁב, אֶשְׁבָה†	אֵיטַב§	אֻושַׁב, ־בָה[7]	אֹושִׁיב[5]	אֵיטִיב[5]	אֹושֵׁב
3 pl. m.	יֵשְׁבוּ†	יֵיטְבוּ	יֻושְׁבוּ	יֹושִׁיבוּ	יֵיטִיבוּ	יֹושְׁבוּ
3 pl. f.	תֵּשֵׁבְנָה‡	תֵּיטֵבְנָה	תֻּושַׁבְנָה	תֹּושֵׁבְנָה	תֵּיטֵבְנָה	תֹּושֵׁבְנָה
2 pl. m.	תֵּשְׁבוּ†	תֵּיטְבוּ	תֻּושְׁבוּ	תֹּושִׁיבוּ	תֵּיטִיבוּ	תֹּושְׁבוּ
2 pl. f.	תֵּשֵׁבְנָה‡	תֵּיטֵבְנָה	תֻּושַׁבְנָה	תֹּושֵׁבְנָה	תֵּיטֵבְנָה	תֹּושֵׁבְנָה
1 pl.	נֵשֵׁב*, נֵשְׁבָה†	נֵיטַב§	נֻושַׁב*, ־בָה	נֹושִׁיב*[5]	נֵיטִיב*[5]	נֹושֵׁב

---

[1] p. שַׁבְתְּ.   [a] Also, fr. ידע, דֵּעַת (p. דַּעְתּ) & בְּרֵעַת & לָרֵעַת etc. [§ 194 (Note ƒ, δ)]; also דֵּעָה (&, w. ל, לָדֵעָה) Ex. ii. 4).   [b] לָשֶׁבֶת in direct Constr. as in G. xvi. 3. For לָרֵעַת see (a).   [c] דֵּעָתֵו etc., fr. דֵּעַת of ידע.   [d] Fr. ידע, דֵּע & (w. ה) דֵּעָה or דְּעֵה Prov. xxiv. 14.   [e] Fr. ידע, יְדַע (p. יָדַע), and once יְדַע Ps. cxxxviii. 6), Cp. § 199 (a–δ).   [2] יְרֵשְׁתֶּם fr. ירש.   [3] טֶ in Pause, as in § 197 (β, ε). [For 'Defective' Long-Khirik, as in יטב, see Pt. I, § 12].   [4] Also w. ־ to 2ᵈ Rt-letter as in יֹושֵׁב (so יֵלֵךְ & יֹלֵךְ 3 s. m., אֹולַךְ 1 s., fr. ילך (יֵלֵךְ), יֵיטֵב etc. For ־חַ & ־עַ— see § 199 (η).   [5] And ־יבָה w. ה at the end.

✳ The 2ᵈ Rt-letter has ־ֶ when the accent is removed; thus יֵשֵׁב, and so יֵדַע, וַיֵּשֶׁב, וַיִּישַׁב, וַיֵּשֶׁב, etc.   † 2ᵈ Rt-letter has ־ֶ in Pause; thus, Imp. לְכָה § 194 (Note ¶, a), Fut. תֵּלְכִי & תֵּלֵכְנָה etc. § 198 (β), and נֵלְכָה & אֵלְכָה § 198 (γ).   ‡ תֵּלַכְנָה fr. ילך.   § ־בָה (p. ־בָה) w. ה, as in § 197 (ε).   ¶ יֵדַע אֵדְעַ fr. ידע.

TABLE XIX.

Variations in the case of Verbs פ״נ [Sect. XVI.].

The Voices (III.) Pī-ĕl, (IV.) Pŭ-ăl, (VII.) Hithpă-ĕl, are as in Tab. XIV.

	(I.) Kal.	(II.) Niph.	(V.) Hiph.	(VI.) Hoph.
Inf. Abs.	נָגוֹשׁ		הִגֵּשׁ (הַ—ישׁ)	הֻגֵּשׁ
Const., & with בכלמ	גֶּשֶׁת בְּ׳, כִּגְשֶׁת / לָגֶשֶׁת, מִגֶּשֶׁת	As in Tab. XIV.	(הַגִּישׁ, בְּ׳, כִּ׳, / לְ׳, מֵהַגִּישׁ	(הֻגַּשׁ, בְּ׳, כְּ׳, / לְ׳, מֵהֻגַּשׁ
W. Pron. Aff.	גִּשְׁתּוֹ ,...		הַגִּישׁוֹ ,...	הֻגְּשׁוֹ ,...
Past.				
3 s. m.		נִגַּשׁ	הִגִּישׁ	הֻגַּשׁ
3 s. f.		נִגְּשָׁה	הִגִּישָׁה	הֻגְּשָׁה
2 s. m.		נִגַּשְׁתָּ	הִגַּשְׁתָּ	הֻגַּשְׁתָּ
2 s. f.	As in Tab. XIV.	נִגַּשְׁתְּ	הִגַּשְׁתְּ	הֻגַּשְׁתְּ
1 s.		נִגַּשְׁתִּי	הִגַּשְׁתִּי	הֻגַּשְׁתִּי
3 pl.		נִגְּשׁוּ	הִגִּישׁוּ	הֻגְּשׁוּ
2 pl. m.		נִגַּשְׁתֶּם	הִגַּשְׁתֶּם	הֻגַּשְׁתֶּם
2 pl. f.		נִגַּשְׁתֶּן	הִגַּשְׁתֶּן	הֻגַּשְׁתֶּן
1 pl.		נִגַּשְׁנוּ	הִגַּשְׁנוּ	הֻגַּשְׁנוּ
Participles.	(As in Tab. XIV.)	נִגָּשׁ	מַגִּישׁ	מֻגָּשׁ
Imperative.				
2 s. m.	גַּשׁ, גֶּשׁ- גְּשָׁה		הַגֵּשׁ ¶	
2 s. f.	גְּשִׁי, גְּשִׁי		הַגִּישִׁי	
2 pl. m.	גְּשׁוּ, גְּשׁוּ		הַגִּישׁוּ	
2 pl. f.	גֵּשְׁנָה		הַגֵּשְׁנָה	
Future.				
3 s. m.	יִגַּשׁ, יִפֹּל *		יַגִּישׁ (—ֵשׁ)	יֻגַּשׁ
3 s. f.	תִּגַּשׁ, תִּפֹּל		תַּגִּישׁ ,,	תֻּגַּשׁ
2 s. m.	תִּגַּשׁ, תִּפֹּל		תַּגִּישׁ ,,	תֻּגַּשׁ
2 s. f.	תִּגְּשִׁי, תִּפְּלִי ‡	As in Tab. XIV.	תַּגִּישִׁי ,,	תֻּגְּשִׁי
1 s.	אֶגַּשׁ †, אֶפֹּל §		אַגִּישׁ ¶	אֻגַּשׁ
3 pl. m.	יִגְּשׁוּ, יִפְּלוּ ‡		יַגִּישׁוּ	יֻגְּשׁוּ
3 pl. f.	תִּגַּשְׁנָה, תִּפֹּלְנָה		תַּגֵּשְׁנָה	תֻּגַּשְׁנָה
2 pl. m.	תִּגְּשׁוּ, תִּפְּלוּ ‡		תַּגִּישׁוּ	תֻּגְּשׁוּ
2 pl. f.	תִּגַּשְׁנָה, תִּפֹּלְנָה		תַּגֵּשְׁנָה	תֻּגַּשְׁנָה
1 pl.	נִגַּשׁ *†, נִפֹּל §		נַגִּישׁ ¶	נֻגַּשׁ

For Verbs of this class with ע for 3rd Root-letter, and for some forms ending in ה◌ and for the Verbs לקח and נתן,— see ‹ Notes on Tab. XIX.› [next page].

* § in p. [§ 165 (I. β & II. ii)].   † w. ה, עָשָׂה (p. עָשָׂה).
‡ § in p. [§ 165 (II, i)].   § w. ה, לָה (p. :לָה).   ¶ w. ת, יָשַׂת.

	(B.) KAL	(A.) KAL
INF. ABS.	נָתֹן	לָקֹחַ
Constr. and w. ב כ ל מ	‎(תֵּת, בְּ, כְּ, / לָתֵת, מִתֵּת	‎(קַחַת, בְּ, כְּ, / לָקַחַת, מִקַּחַת
W. Pron. Affs.	תִּתּוֹ, …	קַחְתּוֹ, …
PAST		
3 s. m.	נָתַן (p.: ⟨ תֵּן ⟩)	לָקַח (p.: ⟨ קָח ⟩)
3 s. f.	נָתְנָה (p.: ⟨ נָה ⟩)	לָקְחָה
2 s. m.	נָתַתָּ, נָתַתָּה &	לָקַחְתָּ
2 s. f.	נָתַתְּ	לָקַחַתְּ
1 s.	נָתַתִּי (p.: ⟨ תִּי ⟩)	לָקַחְתִּי (p.: ⟨ תִּי ⟩)
3 pl.	נָתְנוּ	לָקְחוּ (p.: ⟨ חוּ ⟩)
2 pl. m.	נְתַתֶּם	לְקַחְתֶּם
2 pl. f.	[נְתַתֶּן]	[לְקַחְתֶּן]
1 pl.	נָתַנּוּ	לָקַחְנוּ
PARTICIPLE		
(1)	נֹתֵן	לֹקֵחַ
(2)	נָתוּן	לָקוּחַ
IMPERATIVE		
2 s. m.	תֵּן, תֶּן־, תְּנָה	קַח (p.: ⟨ קָח ⟩), קְחָה
2 s. f.	תְּנִי (p.: ⟨ נִי ⟩)	קְחִי
2 pl. m.	תְּנוּ	קְחוּ (p.: ⟨ חוּ ⟩)
2 pl. f.	[תֵּנָּה]	[קַחְנָה]
FUTURE		
3 s. m.	יִתֵּן, יִתֶּן־	יִקַּח
3 s. f.	תִּתֵּן, תִּתֶּן־	תִּקַּח
2 s. m.	תִּתֵּן	תִּקַּח
2 s. f.	תִּתְּנִי	תִּקְּחִי
1 s.	אֶתֵּן, אֶתֶּן־, אֶתְּנָה (p.: ⟨ נָה ⟩)	אֶקַּח אֶקָּחָה
3 pl. m.	יִתְּנוּ (p.: ⟨ נוּ ⟩)	יִקְּחוּ (p.: ⟨ חוּ ⟩)
3 pl. f.	[תִּתֵּנָּה]	[תִּקַּחְנָה]
2 pl. m.	תִּתְּנוּ	תִּקְּחוּ (p.: ⟨ חוּ ⟩)
2 pl. f.	[תִּתֵּנָּה]	[תִּקַּחְנָה]
1 pl.	נִתֵּן, נִתְּנָה	נִקַּח, נִקְּחָה

(α.) Verbs פ״נ, and with ע for 3rd Rt.-letter, take —— — instead of —— — in the Inf. Constr. *K.*; thus (fr. נגע) לָגַעַת in בְּגַעַת. [But also נְגֹע, לִנְגֹּעַ.] See also Tab. XVI (3).

(β.) The 2 s. *m.* Imper. *Hφ.* הַגֵּשׁ with the ה of § 141 (γ, δ) is הִגָּשֵׁה (or הַגָּשָׁה, Pt. I., § 12). For the 1 s. and 1 pl. Fut. *K.*, etc., w. the ה of § 144, see § 211.

(γ.) (i.) The Verb לקח *to take* drops its ל, as the נ of נגש is dropped in Tab. XIX. [See col. A.]. (ii.) This is not so in other Verbs beginning with ל. (iii.) The Dagesh Forte placed in the ק after a vowel, to stand for the omitted 1st Rt.-letter, is dropped (see column A) when the ק has —. (iv.) But the Dagesh Forte reappears in the ק when the word is in Pause. (v.) This Verb in *Niph.* and *Pû.* is like Tab. XIV., [except that in לֻקֳחָה Gen. ii. 23 3 s. *f.* Past *Pû.*) the ק is without Dagesh Forte, and has — instead of —]. (vi.) In *Hoph.*, יֻקַּח (p.: יֻקָּח) and תֻּקַּח, the 3 s. *m.* and 3 s. *f.* Fut., are as in Tab. XIX.

(δ.) (i.) Col. B exhibits the *Kal* of נתן *to give*. (ii.) This Verb has *Niph.* as in Tab. XIX.; also הִנָּתֹן Inf. (Abs.) (w. ל, לְהִנָּתֶן), Past 2 pl. *m.* נִתַּתֶּם, 1 pl. נִתַּנּוּ, cp. § 188 & § 216] *Hoph.* Fut. 3 s. *m.* יֻתַּן.

[1] Also קַח twice, (probably). [2] Also לָקַח three times. [3] Also לָקֵח once. [4] נָתַן once, and נָתַן־ once.—תֵּת even before (ׁ); [תִּתֶּן K. xvii. 14, is *Kthiv* for תֵּת *Krî*]; but לָתֵת when the Accent is removed from last syllable, as in Gen. xv. 7, Ex. v. 21. לָתֵן (with ן added) K. vi. 19. [6] תִּתָּה 2 S. xxii. 41. תֶּנָה Ps. viii. 2 (by many supposed to be Inf.) must be Imper., there is elsewhere. [8] נָתַן־ once.

TABLE XX. Variations for ע"ו & ע"י [pp. 150–163]

Form	(I.) Kal	Kal (fr. מוּת)	Kal (fr. בּוּשׁ)	(II.) Niph. Given merely as a Paradigm.	(III.) Pi-êl.	(IV.) Pŭ-al.	(V.) Hiph-îl.	(VI.) Hoph.	(VII.) Hithp.
Inf. Abs.	קוֹם			הִקּוֹם	קוֹמֵם	קוֹמַם	הָקֵם		הִתְקוֹמֵם
Constr. and w. ב כ ל מ	קוּם, בְּ, כְּ, / לָקוּם, מָקוּם [Also בְּמֹת, etc., (but לָמֹת), and with Aff. מֹתוֹ, etc.; fr. מֹת]			הִקּוֹם, בְּ, כְּ, / לְ, מֵהִקּוֹם	קוֹמֵם, בְּ, כְּ, / לְ, מְקוֹמֵם		הָקִים, בְּ, כְּ, / לְ, מֵהָקִים		
W. Pron. Aff.	קוּמוֹ,... (§ 220. ii, etc.)			הִקּוֹמוֹ...	קוֹמְמוֹ,...	קֻמְמוֹ,...	הֲקִימוֹ,...		הִתְקוֹמְמוֹ,...
Past		(fr. מוּת)	(fr. בּוּשׁ)						
3 s. m.	קָם	מֵת	בֹּשׁ	נָקוֹם	קוֹמֵם	קוֹמַם	הֵקִים	הוּקַם	הִתְקוֹמֵם,—ֶם
3 s. f.	קָמָה	מֵתָה	בֹּשָׁה	נָקוֹמָה	קוֹמְמָה	קוֹמְמָה	הֵקִימָה	הוּקְמָה	הִתְקוֹמְמָה
2 s. m.	קַמְתָּ,—תָּה	מַתָּ, מֵתָה	בֹּשְׁתָּ	נָקוּמֹתָ	קוֹמַמְתָּ	קוֹמַמְתָּ	הֲקֵמֹתָ[2] (־ֹי)[3]	הוּקַמְתָּ	הִתְקוֹמַמְתָּ
2 s. f.	קַמְתְּ	[מַתְּ]	בֹּשְׁתְּ	נָקוּמֹת	קוֹמַמְתְּ	קוֹמַמְתְּ	הֲקֵמֹת	הוּקַמְתְּ	הִתְקוֹמַמְתְּ
1 s.	קַמְתִּי	מַתִּי	בֹּשְׁתִּי	נָקוּמֹתִי	קוֹמַמְתִּי	קוֹמַמְתִּי	הֲקֵמֹתִי[2] (־ֹי)[3]	הוּקַמְתִּי	הִתְקוֹמַמְתִּי
3 pl.	קָמוּ	מֵתוּ	בֹּשׁוּ	נָקוֹמוּ	קוֹמְמוּ	קוֹמְמוּ	הֵקִימוּ	הוּקְמוּ	הִתְקוֹמְמוּ
2 pl. m.	קַמְתֶּם	מַתֶּם	בָּשְׁתֶּם	נְקוּמֹתֶם	קוֹמַמְתֶּם	קוֹמַמְתֶּם	הֲקֵמֹתֶם (־ֹ,—ֶ)[4]	הוּקַמְתֶּם	הִתְקוֹמַמְתֶּם
2 pl. f.	קַמְתֶּן	מַתֶּן	בָּשְׁתֶּן	נְקוּמֹתֶן	קוֹמַמְתֶּן	קוֹמַמְתֶּן	הֲקֵמֹתֶן[2]	הוּקַמְתֶּן	הִתְקוֹמַמְתֶּן
1 pl.	קַמְנוּ	מַתְנוּ	בֹּשְׁנוּ	נְקוּמֹנוּ	קוֹמַמְנוּ	קוֹמַמְנוּ	הֲקֵמֹנוּ[3] (־ֹ)	הוּקַמְנוּ	הִתְקוֹמַמְנוּ
Participles.									
(1)	קָם	מֵת	בֹּשׁ	נָקוֹם	מְקוֹמֵם	מְקוֹמָם	מֵקִים	מוּקָם	מִתְקוֹמֵם
(2)	קוּם (see also § 248)								

(V.) Hiph-îl: (see also § 241.)   (VI.) Hoph.: 6 (see also § 241.)

	Qal (קוּם)	Qal (בּוֹשׁ)	Niphal	Polel	Hiphil	Hophal	Hithpolel
IMPERATIVE.							
2 s. m.	קוּם ,מָה—	בֹּשׁ ,ה—	הִקּוֹם	קוֹמֵם ,מָה—	הָקֵם, הָקִימָה		הִתְקוֹמֵם ,מָה—
2 s. f.	קוּמִי	בֹּשִׁי	הִקּוֹמִי	קוֹמְמִי	הָקִימִי		הִתְקוֹמְמִי
2 pl. m.	קוּמוּ	בֹּשׁוּ	הִקּוֹמוּ	קוֹמְמוּ	הָקִימוּ		הִתְקוֹמְמוּ
2 pl. f.	קֹמְנָה	בֹּשְׁנָה	הִקּוֹמְנָה	קוֹמֵמְנָה	הֲקֵמְנָה		הִתְקוֹמֵמְנָה [§ 245]
FUTURE.							
3 s. m.	יָקוּם*	יֵבוֹשׁ	יִקּוֹם ,יֵעוֹר	יְקוֹמֵם	יָקִים (קֵם)+	יוּקַם	יִתְקוֹמֵם (מָם—) [Pause-forms, § 245]
3 s. f.	תָּקוּם* (Also ־ֹם § 224)	תֵּבוֹשׁ	תִּקּוֹם	תְּקוֹמֵם	תָּקֵם (קֵם)+	תּוּקַם	תִּתְקוֹמֵם
2 s. m.	תָּקוּם*	תֵּבוֹשׁ	תִּקּוֹם	תְּקוֹמֵם	תָּקֵם (קֵם)+	תּוּקַם	תִּתְקוֹמֵם
2 s. f.	תָּקוּמִי	תֵּבֹשִׁי	תִּקּוֹמִי	תְּקוֹמְמִי	תָּקִימִי	תּוּקְמִי	תִּתְקוֹמְמִי
1 s.	אָקוּם ,מָה—	אֵבוֹשׁ ,ה—	אֶקּוֹם	אֲקוֹמֵם ,מָה—	אָקֵם (קֵם)	אוּקַם	אֶתְקוֹמֵם ,מָה—
3 pl. m. (§ 239)	יָקוּמוּ	יֵבֹשׁוּ	יִקּוֹמוּ	יְקוֹמְמוּ	יָקִימוּ	יוּקְמוּ	יִתְקוֹמְמוּ
3 pl. f.	תָּקֹמְנָה[1] / תָּקוּמֶינָה	תֵּבֹשְׁנָה	תִּקּוֹמְנָה	תְּקוֹמֵמְנָה	תָּקֵמְנָה[5]	תּוּקַמְנָה	תִּתְקוֹמֵמְנָה [§ 245]
2 pl. m. (§ 239)	תָּקוּמוּ	תֵּבֹשׁוּ	תִּקּוֹמוּ	תְּקוֹמְמוּ	תָּקִימוּ	תּוּקְמוּ	תִּתְקוֹמְמוּ
2 pl. f.	תָּקֹמְנָה[1] / תָּקוּמֶינָה	תֵּבֹשְׁנָה	תִּקּוֹמְנָה	תְּקוֹמֵמְנָה	תָּקֵמְנָה[5]	תּוּקַמְנָה	תִּתְקוֹמֵמְנָה
1 pl.	נָקוּם* ,מָה—	נֵבוֹשׁ ,ה—	נִקּוֹם	נְקוֹמֵם ,מָה—	נָקֵם (קֵם)+	נוּקַם[6]	נִתְקוֹמֵם ,מָה—

* The וּ, on losing the Accent, becomes — (ŏ); thus, יָקֹם ,וַיָּקָם ,וַתָּקָם, etc.   † For the — in יָקֹם ,וַיָּקָם, etc., see § 232 (ii.).

1 As in תָּשֹׁבְנָה (fr. שׁוּב, as well as תְּשׁוּבֶינָה). See § 230.   2 Also הֲנִחַ, etc., § 242.   3 As in הֲרִימוֹת ,הֲרִימֹתִי ,הֲשִׁיבֹנוּ.

4 As in הֲשִׁיבֹתֶם ,הֲשִׁיבֹתָם.   5 תְּקִימֶנָה Jer. xliv. 25.   Also תָּהִימֶנָה Mi. ii. 13, fr. הוּם; which is for תְּהִימֶינָה, analogous to תְּקוּמֶינָה in Kal.   6 ק in Pause.   7 Or הֲקֻם, as in בְּהִדְרֹשׁ Isai. xxv. 10.

a For the ע"י forms שִׂים, בָּשִׂים, etc., and Imper. שִׂים s. m. (ה שִׂימָה w. ה), שִׂימִי s. f., שִׂימוּ 2 pl. m., see § 225.

TABLE XXI. Variations when the 2nd & 3rd Rt.-letters are the same (כְּפוּלִים). [p. 180].

N.B.—(1) It will be understood that some words given here, as from סבב, are merely Paradigm-forms. (2) So for נדד. (3) וּ may occur where ־ֻ is given below, and conversely. (4) Forms like those in Table XIV need not be given here.

(VII.) Hith. (of נדד)	(VI.) Hŏph-ăl.	(V.) Hiphîl.	(IV.) Pŭ̆ăl.	(III.) Pĭ-ēl.	(II.) Niph.	(I.) Kal (of סבב)	
הִתְגֹּרֵד		הָסֵב	סֹבֵב	סֹבֵב	הִסֵּב, הִסּוֹב	סָב	Inf. Abs.
(same.)		הָסֵב, בְּ, כְּ, / לְ, מֵהָסֵב	סֹבֵב, בְּ, כְּ, / לְ, מְסֹבֵב	סֹבֵב, בְּ, כְּ, / לְ, מְסֹבֵב	הִסֵּב, בְּ, כְּ, / לְ, מֵהִסֵּב	*סָב, בְּ, כְּ, / לְ, מְסָב	Constr. and w. ב כ ל מ
הִתְגֹּרְדוֹ,...		וַהֲסִבּוֹ,...	סֹבְבוֹ,...	סֹבְבוֹ,...	הִסַּבּוֹ,...	סַבּוֹ,...	W. Pron. Aff.
							Past.
הִתְגֹּרֵד	הוּסַב	הֵסֵב, ־ךְ-ב	סֹבַב	סֹבֵב	נָסַב,** ־ךְ-ב	†סַב, סָב	3 s. m.
הִתְגֹּרְדָה	הוּסַבָּה	הֵסַבָּה	סֹבְבָה	סֹבְבָה	נָסַבָּה,8 ־ךְ-בָּה	†סַבָּה	3 s. f.
הִתְגֹּרַדְתָּ	הוּסַבְתָּ	וַהֲסִבֹּתָ & הִפַרְתָּ & הִקַלֹּתָ	סֹבַבְתָּ	סֹבַבְתָּ	נְסַבֹּתָ	סַבֹּתָ	2 s. m.
הִתְגֹּרַדְתְּ	הוּסַבְתְּ	וַהֲסִבֹּת	סֹבַבְתְּ	סֹבַבְתְּ	נְסַבֹּת	סַבֹּת	2 s. f.
הִתְגֹּרַדְתִּי	הוּסַבְתִּי	וַהֲסִבֹּתִי §	סֹבַבְתִּי	סֹבַבְתִּי	נְסַבֹּתִי	סַבֹּתִי	1 s.
הִתְגֹּרְדוּ	הוּסַבּוּ	הֵסַבּוּ, ־ךְ-בּוּ	סֹבְבוּ	סֹבְבוּ	נָסַבּוּ, ־ךְ-בּוּ	†סַבּוּ, סַבּוּ :	3 pl.
הִתְגֹּרַדְתֶּם	הוּסַבֹּתֶם	וַהֲסִבֹּתֶם §	סֹבַבְתֶּם	סֹבַבְתֶּם	נְסַבֹּתֶם	סַבּוֹתֶם	2 pl. m.
הִתְגֹּרַדְתֶּן	הוּסַבְתֶּן	וַהֲסִבֹּתֶן	סֹבַבְתֶּן	סֹבַבְתֶּן	נְסַבֹּתֶן	סַבּוֹתֶן	2 pl. f.
הִתְגֹּרַדְנוּ	הוּסַבְנוּ	וַהֲסִבֹּנוּ	סֹבַבְנוּ	סֹבַבְנוּ	נְסַבֹּנוּ	סַבּוֹנוּ	1 pl.
מִתְגֹּרֵד	מוּסַב	מֵסֵב, ־ךְ-ב	מְסֹבָב	מְסֹבֵב	נָסַב, ־ךְ-ב (נְסַבִּי)	(Tab. XIV.)²	Participles.
							Imperative.
הִתְגֹּרֵד, ־דָה		הָסֵב, ־בָּה, הֲסֵרָה		סֹבֵב	הִסֵּב, ־ב	*סֹב (נַל, once?)	2 s. m.
הִתְגֹּרְדִי		הָסֵבִּי, ־בִּי		סֹבְבִי	הִסֵּבִּי, ־בִּי	*סֹבִּי, סָבִּי	2 s. f.
הִתְגֹּרְדוּ		הָסֵבּוּ, ־בּוּ		סֹבְבוּ	הִסֵּבּוּ, ־בּוּ	*סֹבּוּ, סָבּוּ	2 pl. m.
הִתְגֹּרֵדְנָה		הֲסִבֶּינָה		סֹבֵבְנָה	הִסַּבֶּינָה	סַבֶּינָה	2 pl. f.

[See also iv, below.]

	Qal		(Poel)	(Poel)	(also)	Hophal	Hithpoel
3 s. m.	*יָסֹב[11], [וַיָּסָב]	יָסֵב, ־ֹב	יְסֹבֵב	יְסֹבֵב	(also) יָסֵב, יַסֵב, (־ֵיב)	יוּסַב	יִתְגֹּדֵד
3 s. f.	*תָּסֹב[3]	תָּסֵב, ־ֹב	תְּסֹבֵב	תְּסֹבֵב	תָּסֵב	תּוּסַב	תִּתְגֹּדֵד
2 s. m	*תָּסֹב	תָּסֵב, ־ֹב	תְּסֹבֵב	תְּסֹבֵב	תָּסֵב	תּוּסַב	תִּתְגֹּדֵד
2 s. f.	תָּסֹבִּי	תָּסֵבִּי, ־ְבִי	תְּסֹבְבִי	תְּסֹבְבִי	תָּסֵבִּי	תּוּסַבִּי	תִּתְגֹּדְדִי
1 s.	אָסֹב[4]	אָסֵב[9], ־ֹב	אֲסֹבֵב	אֲסֹבֵב, אֲסֹבְבָה	אָסֵב, ־ָבָה	אוּסַב	אֶתְגֹּדֵד, ־ְדָה
3 pl. m.	יָסֹבּוּ	יָסֵבּוּ, ־בּוּ	יְסֹבְבוּ	יְסֹבְבוּ	יָסֵבּוּ	יוּסַבּוּ	יִתְגֹּדְדוּ
3 pl. f.	תָּסֻבֶּינָה[5]	־ֶינָה[10]	תְּסֹבֵבְנָה	תְּסֹבֵבְנָה	תָּסֵבְנָה, ־ֶינָה	תּוּסַבֶּינָה	תִּתְגֹּדַדְנָה
2 pl. m.	תָּסֹבּוּ	תָּסֵבּוּ, ־בּוּ	תְּסֹבְבוּ	תְּסֹבְבוּ	תָּסֵבּוּ	תּוּסַבּוּ	תִּתְגֹּדְדוּ
2 pl. f.	תָּסֻבֶּינָה[5]	־ֶינָה[10]	תְּסֹבֵבְנָה	תְּסֹבֵבְנָה	תָּסֵבְנָה, ־ֶינָה	תּוּסַבֶּינָה	תִּתְגֹּדַדְנָה
1 pl.	*נָסֹב[6], [נָסֵב]	נָסֵב, ־ב	נְסֹבֵב	נְסֹבֵב, נְסֹבְבָה	נָסֵב, ־בָּה	נוּסַב	נִתְגֹּדֵד, ־ְדָה

[See also iv. below.]

1 Also (α.) w. ־ֵ, פְּשֵׂךְ fr. שׂכך, לָרַד fr. רדד; (β.) w. ־וֹת, as in חַנּוֹת fr. חנן. (γ.) The ä-form, in לִבּוּר fr. ברר, is borrowed from עו״י.
2 Also תַּם (once תָּם, ־תָּם) from תמם (תַּמָּה) s. f., and so הַתַּים pl. m. of חַת fr. חתת, צָרִים pl. m. of צַר or צָר fr, צרר). 3 Also (יָרֹון rare),
תֵּקַל, יֵקַל. 4 אֵקַל (אֵיתָם Ps. xix. 14). 5 תְּסֹבְנָה (thus תְּרֹנָּה), תְּסֻבֶּינָה. 6 נָבְוֹחַ with ה (for נָבֹחָה); also נָבְקָה Gen. xi. 7 (for נָבֹקָה).
7 With ה, נִדְמֶה fr. דמם. [These words within the [ ] are merely *Paradigm-forms*, which may be said to be 'borrowed' from the פ״נ].
8 נָבְקָה Is. xix. 3 (for נָבֹקָּה). 9 אָף. 10 Also תְּצֻקַּנָה, תְּצֶלֶּינָה; [תִּסֹּבְנָה]. 11 Also תָּסֹב, יָסֹב, etc. (as in Nφ.).

* The ־ֵ is shortened into ־ֶ (ĕ) when the Accent is removed from the ־ֵ; thus (α.) בְּרֹךְ Inf. *Kal* w. ב; (β.) אֱרֹד Imper. K. 2 s. m. with ה (for אֱרֹה, fr. ארד) and so in קָבָה Nu. xxii. 11 & 17, for קָבָה fr. קבב. So also (γ.) in רָנִּי 2 s. f., רָנּוּ 2 pl. m. fr. רנן; and (δ.) Fut. K. with ו Conversive וַיָּסָב 3 s. m., וַתָּסָב 3 s. f., וַנָּסָב 1 pl.

† 1st Root-letter has ־ַ in Pause; thus, סָב׃ 3 s. m. Past K., and רָבּוּ׃ 3 pl. Past K. fr. רבב *to be many*, etc.
‡ The ה has ־ַ before a Guttural; thus, הַחֵל (*i.e.* הָחֵל Inf., with ־ַם *their m.*), הַחֲלוֹת 2 s. m. Past, etc.

§ Or with ־ַ for ־ֵ, as in הֵרַעְתָ (or הֲרֵעֹתָ־ֶ), הֲרֵעֹתֶם, הֲרֵעֹתִי, for Compensation. ¶ Also יַבְתֵּי fr. כתת [Cp. p. 355].
‖ Also ־ַ ם, as in יַבֵּת 3 s. m. & יַבֵּתוּ (p. ־תּוּ,) 3 pl. m. fr. כתת [Cp. p. 357]. ** Rarely נָסֵב.

Note (i.) Compensation for a Dagesh Forte is sometimes made, as in אֲרוֹתִי (like סַבֹּתִי) 1 s. Past K. fr. ארר, נֵחַנְתְּ 2 s. f. Nφ. of חנן, etc. But (ii.) sometimes it is not made, especially before ה, as in שַׁחוֹתִי fr. שחח, נֵחַר fr. חרר, etc. (iii.) Dagesh Forte is sometimes dropped (cp. 6, above). So in הֵעֹזֶה fr. עזז, etc. (iv.) Hθ. Pause-forms have ־ָ, as in הִתְהַלָּלוּ Jer. xxv. 16, תִּשְׁתּוֹחָח Ps. xlii. 7, etc.

(v.) Fr. חתת, תֵּחַת & יֵחַת (p. ־תַ), אָחַת (w. ה, אֶחְתָּה), יֵחַתּוּ & תֵּחַתּוּ (p. ־תּוּ,), (like יָסֹב etc., w. Compens. for D.) may be of K. or Nφ. Fcz.

TABLE XXII. VERBS ל״א. [See also pp. 169 (I) & 185-189].—*Some of the words here are merely Paradigm-forms.*

(VII.) HITHP.	(VI.) HOPH.	(V.) HIPH.	(IV.) PŬ-AL.	(III.) PI-ÊL.	(II.) NIPH-AL.	(I.) KAL.	
הִתְמַצֵּא	הֻמְצֵא	הַמְצֵא	מֻצָּא, מְצֹא	מַצֵּא, קַנֹּא	הִמָּצֵא	מָצֹא	INF. ABS.
הִתְמַצֵּא,[1][e] בְּ, כְּ		הַמְצִיא, בְּ, כְּ,		מַצֵּא,[1] בְּ, כְּ,	הִמָּצֵא,[1] בְּ, כְּ,	מְצֹא,[1][a] בְּמ׳, כְמ׳,	Constr. and
לְ, מֵהִתְמַצֵּא		לְ, מֵהַמְצִיא		לְ, מִמַּצֵּא[b]	לְ, מֵהִמָּצֵא	לִמְצֹא, מִמְּצֹא	w. ב כ ל מ
הִתְמַצְאוֹ,...	הֻמְצְאוֹ,...	הַמְצִיאוֹ,...	מַצְאוֹ,...		הִמָּצְאוֹ,...	מָצְאוֹ,...	w. Pron. Affs.
							PAST.
הִתְמַצֵּא	הֻמְצָא	הִמְצִיא[||]	מֻצָּא	מִצֵּא, קִנֵּא	נִמְצָא	מָצָא, יָרֵא	3 s. m.
הִתְמַצְּאָה	הֻמְצְאָה	הִמְצִיאָה[¶]	מֻצְּאָה	מִצְּאָה	נִמְצְאָה,[w] נִפְלָאתָה[f]	מָצְאָה,[*] יָרְאָה	3 s. f.
הִתְמַצֵּאתָ	הֻמְצֵאתָ (־תָה)	הִמְצֵאתָ	מֻצֵּאתָ	מִצֵּאתָ[o]	נִמְצֵאתָ, וְנֶחְבֵּאתָ	מָצָאתָ, יָרֵאתָ	2 s. m.
הִתְמַצֵּאת	הֻמְצֵאת	הִמְצֵאת	מֻצֵּאת	מִצֵּאת	נִמְצֵאת	מָצָאת,[r] יָרֵאת	2 s. f.
הִתְמַצֵּאתִי	הֻמְצֵאתִי	הִמְצֵאתִי	מֻצֵּאתִי	מִצֵּאתִי[p]	נִמְצֵאתִי	מָצָאתִי,[d] יָרֵאתִי[n,e]	1 s.
הִתְמַצְּאוּ	הֻמְצְאוּ[†]	הִמְצִיאוּ	מֻצְּאוּ[†]	מִצְּאוּ[†]	נִמְצְאוּ,[†] נִרְפְּאוּ	מָצְאוּ,[h] יָרְאוּ[‡]	3 pl.
הִתְמַצֵּאתֶם	הֻמְצֵאתֶם	הִמְצֵאתֶם	מֻצֵּאתֶם	מִצֵּאתֶם	נִמְצֵאתֶם[f]	מְצָאתֶם, יְרֵאתֶם[g]	2 pl. m.
הִתְמַצֵּאתֶן	הֻמְצֵאתֶן	הִמְצֵאתֶן	מֻצֵּאתֶן	מִצֵּאתֶן	נִמְצֵאתֶן	מְצָאתֶן, יְרֵאתֶן	2 pl. f.
הִתְמַצֵּאנוּ	הֻמְצֵאנוּ	הִמְצֵאנוּ	מֻצֵּאנוּ	מִצֵּאנוּ[q]	נִמְצֵאנוּ[1]	מָצָאנוּ,[g] יָרֵאנוּ	1 pl.
							PARTICIPLE
מִתְמַצֵּא	מֻמְצָא	מַמְצִיא	מְמֻצָּא	מְמַצֵּא	נִמְצָא	מֹצֵא (צֵ), יָרֵא	(1) s. m.
						מָצוּא	(2) s. m.

	Kal	Niphal	Piel	Pual	Hiphil	Hophal	Hithpael
2 s. m.	מְצָא	הִמָּצֵא	מַצֵּא	—	הַמְצֵא	—	הִתְמַצֵּא
2 s. f.	מְצָאִי	הִמָּצְאִי	מַצֵּאִי	—	הַמְצִיאִי	—	הִתְמַצְּאִי
2 pl. m.	מְצָאוּ, יְראוּ	הִמָּצְאוּ	מַצְּאוּ	—	הַמְצִיאוּ	—	הִתְמַצְּאוּ
2 pl. f.	מְצֶאנָה	הִמָּצֶאנָה	מַצֶּאנָה	—	הַמְצֶאנָה	—	הִתְמַצֶּאנָה
Future.							
3 s. m.	יִמְצָא [v]	יִמָּצֵא	יְמַצֵּא	יְמֻצָּא (אֻ—) [u]	יַמְצִיא	יֻמְצָא	יִתְמַצֵּא
3 s. f.	תִּמְצָא	תִּמָּצֵא	תְּמַצֵּא	תְּמֻצָּא	תַּמְצִיא	תֻּמְצָא	תִּתְמַצֵּא
2 s. m.	תִּמְצָא	תִּמָּצֵא	תְּמַצֵּא	תְּמֻצָּא	תַּמְצִיא	תֻּמְצָא	תִּתְמַצֵּא
2 s. f.	תִּמְצְאִי	תִּמָּצְאִי	תְּמַצְּאִי	תְּמֻצְּאִי	תַּמְצִיאִי	תֻּמְצְאִי	תִּתְמַצְּאִי
1 s.	אֶמְצָא [s]	אֶמָּצֵא	אֲמַצֵּא	אֲמֻצָּא	אַמְצִיא	אֻמְצָא	אֶתְמַצֵּא
3 pl. m.	יִמְצְאוּ [†]	יִמָּצְאוּ [‡]	יְמַצְּאוּ [†]	יְמֻצְּאוּ	יַמְצִיאוּ	יֻמְצְאוּ	יִתְמַצְּאוּ
3 pl. f.	תִּמְצֶאנָה [k] (תֶּ—אֶי)	תִּמָּצֶאנָה [m] (תֵּ—אֶי)	תְּמַצֶּאנָה	תְּמֻצֶּאנָה	תַּמְצֶאנָה	תֻּמְצֶאנָה	תִּתְמַצֶּאנָה
2 pl. m.	תִּמְצְאוּ [†]	תִּמָּצְאוּ [‡]	תְּמַצְּאוּ [†]	תְּמֻצְּאוּ	תַּמְצִיאוּ	תֻּמְצְאוּ	תִּתְמַצְּאוּ
2 pl. f.	תִּמְצֶאנָה	תִּמָּצֶאנָה	תְּמַצֶּאנָה	תְּמֻצֶּאנָה	תַּמְצֶאנָה	תֻּמְצֶאנָה	תִּתְמַצֶּאנָה
1 pl.	נִמְצָא	נִמָּצֵא	נְמַצֵּא	נְמֻצָּא	נַמְצִיא	נֻמְצָא	נִתְמַצֵּא

Note:—(1) There are some Inf⁵ in ת ־ֶ (cp. Tab. XXIII) as [a] מְלֹאת (בִּמְלֹאת), קְרֹאות, etc.; [b] לִמְלֹאת (& ־ֹא—), as well as לִמְלָא [c]; [o] הִתְנַבּוֹת. (2) א is dropped in [d] נִפְלֵינוּ, [e] תִּרְפֶּינָה, [f] נַחְבְּתֶם, נִטְמְתֶם, [g] אֶתְגוּ, etc. N.B. (3) א elided in [h] כֻּלֵּא for כֻּלְאוּ, [i] יַנְשִׁוּ for יַנְשִׁאוּ, [l] יֵרַפְּאוּ for יֵרָפְאוּ, etc. (4) י for א in [k] תֵּרָפֶינָה, [l] נִשְׁאֵנוּ, etc. (5) א ־ֶ in [n] כִּלֵּאתִי, [o] דִּכֵּאת, [p] רִפֵּאתִי, [q] רִפֵּאנוּ; (6) ־ֶ in [r] צָמֵת, etc. (7) [s] ה for א in רָפֵה, רָפָה, [t] הַרְפֵּה, [u] יָמְצָה, etc. (8) Forms borrowed from Tab. XXIII, [v] יְכֻלֶּה, G. xxiii. 6, [w] נִרְפְּתֶה (Pause-form of נִרְפְּתָה = נִרְפְּאָה) Jer. li. 9, etc.

* וְקָרָאת Is. vii. 14, comp. p. 185 (Note). † p. ־ֶא—. ‡ p. ־ֶא—. § וְרָאתָם Josh. iv. 24 is like מְצָאתֶם. ‖ הַפְלֵא D. xxviii. 59. ¶ See also § 138 (B) (ii, β).

** 1 Sam. vi. 10. So נָשֹׁו Ezek. xxxix. 26 (for נָשְׁאוּ); and, as some say, with א added נָשֹׁוא Ps. cxxxix. 20.

Table XXIII. Variations for ל״ה [pp. 170–173, & 190–193].

	VII. Hithpaêl.	VI. Hoph-al.	V. Hiph-îl.	IV. Pŭ-al.	III. Pi-êl.	II. Niph-al.	I. Kal.
Inf. Abs.	הִתְגַּלֵּה	הָגְלֵה	הַגְלֵה, [נַ־ֹּה], הַרְבֵּה	גֻּלֶּה	גַּלֵּה, ־ֵי [נַ־ֹּה]	הִגָּלֵה, נִגְלֹה	גָּלֹה, בָּכֹו, נָצֹא
Constr. & w. בכלם	הִתְגַּלֹּות, etc.		הַגְלֹות, etc.	גֻּלֹּות, etc	גַּלֹּות, בְּגַ, כְּגַ, לְגַלֹּות, מְגַלֹּות	הִגָּלֹות[10], בְּ, כְּ, [10]לְ, מֵהִגָּלֹות	גְּלֹות[2], בִּגְ, כִּגְ, לִגְ, מִגְּלֹות
w. Pron. Affs.			הִגְלֹתֹו, …	גֻּלְּתֹו, …	גִּלְּתֹו, …	הִגָּלְתֹו, …	גָּלֹתֹו, …
Past.							
3 s. m.	+הִתְגַּלָּה	הָגְלָה	הִגְלָה, הֶגְלָה	גֻּלָּה	גִּלָּה	נִגְלָה	גָּלָה
3 s. f.	הִתְגַּלְּתָה	הָגְלְתָה	הִגְלְתָה[a], הִרְצָת	גֻּלְּתָה	גִּלְּתָה	נִגְלְתָה[a]	גָּלְתָה[a], חָסְיָה, גָּלָת
2 s. m.	הִתְגַּלִּיתָ	הָגְלֵיתָ	הִגְלֵיתָ, הִנְגֵיתָ	גֻּלֵּיתָ	גִּלִּיתָ	נִגְלֵיתָ	גָּלִיתָ, בָּנְתָה
2 s. f.	הִתְגַּלִּית	הָגְלֵית	הִגְלֵית, הִרְבֵּית	גֻּלֵּית	גִּלִּית	נִגְלֵית	גָּלִית
1 s.	הִתְגַּלִּיתִי	הָגְלֵיתִי	[11]הִגְלֵיתִי, הִפְרֵתִי	גֻּלֵּיתִי, ־ֵיתִי	גִּלִּיתִי, ־ֵיתִי	נִגְלֵיתִי	גָּלִיתִי, בָּנְתִי, רָאֹתִי
3 pl.	הִתְגַּלּוּ	הָגְלוּ	הִגְלוּ	גֻּלּוּ	גִּלּוּ	נִגְלוּ	גָּלוּ, נָסְיָג, דָּלְיָג
2 pl. m.	הִתְגַּלִּיתֶם	הָגְלֵיתֶם	הִגְלֵיתֶם, הִתְעֵיתֶם[12]	גֻּלֵּיתֶם	גִּלִּיתֶם	נִגְלֵיתֶם	גְּלִיתֶם
2 pl. f.	הִתְגַּלִּיתֶן	הָגְלֵיתֶן	הִגְלֵיתֶן	גֻּלֵּיתֶן	גִּלִּיתֶן	נִגְלֵיתֶן	גְּלִיתֶן
1 pl.	הִתְגַּלִּינוּ	הָגְלֵינוּ	הִגְלֵינוּ	גֻּלֵּינוּ	גִּלִּינוּ	נִגְלֵינוּ	גָּלִינוּ
Participle.							
(1) s. m.	+מִתְגַּלֶּה	מָגְלֶה	מַגְלֶה	מְגֻלֶּה	מְגַלֶּה	נִגְלֶה	גֹּלֶה (גֹּלֶה) l.c.

For apocopated forms see p. 49 below.

Paradigm of the ל״ה verb גָּלָה (Imperative continued, and Future). Columns run right-to-left on the page as Qal, Niphal, Piel, Pual, Hiphil, Hophal, Hithpael; asterisked (*) forms are the apocopated forms used with ו Conversive. Dashes mark stems with no form.

Person	Qal	Niphal	Piel	Pual	Hiphil	Hophal	Hithpael
2 s. m.	גְּלֵה	הִגָּלֵה	גַּל	—	הַגְלֵה, חֶרֶף	—	הִתְגַּלֵּה[14]
2 s. f.	גְּלִי	הִגָּלִי	—	—	הַגְלִי	—	§הִתְגַּלִּי
2 pl. m.	גְּלוּ; בְּעֵי, אֱתָיו	הִגָּלוּ	—	—	הַגְלוּ	—	‖הִתְגַּלּוּ
2 pl. f.	גְּלֶינָה	הִגָּלֶינָה	—	—	הַגְלֶינָה	—	הִתְגַּלֶּינָה
FUTURE.							
3 s. m.	יִגְלֶה; {*יִבֶן[3], יֵשַׁע}, *יָרֶא[4]	יִגָּלֶה, *יָגֶל, *יִמַּח, *יֵרָא	יְגַלֶּה, *יְגַל	יְגֻלֶּה	יַגְלֶה, *יֶגֶל, יֵרֶד[13]	יָגְלֶה	יִתְגַּלֶּה[15]
3 s. f.	תִּגְלֶה; *תְּבֶן, *תֶּרֶא[5]	תִּגָּלֶה, *תָּרֵא, *תִּגַּל	תְּגַלֶּה, *תְּגַל	תְּגֻלֶּה	תַּגְלֶה, *תֶּגֶל	תָּגְלֶה	תִּתְגַּלֶּה[16]
2 s. m.	תִּגְלֶה; *תְּבֶן, *תֶּרֶא[5]	תִּגָּלֶה, *תָּרֵא, *תִּגַּל	תְּגַלֶּה, *תְּגַל	תְּגֻלֶּה	תַּגְלֶה, *תֶּגֶל	תָּגְלֶה	תִּתְגַּלֶּה[16]
2 s. f.	תִּגְלִי	תִּגָּלִי	תְּגַלִּי	תְּגֻלִּי	תַּגְלִי	תָּגְלִי	תִּתְגַּלִּי
1 s.	אֶגְלֶה; *אֵפֶן[7]	אֶגָּלֶה, (א), *אֶגַּל, *אֵרָא	אֲגַלֶּה, *אֲגַל	אֲגֻלֶּה	אַגְלֶה	אָגְלֶה	אֶתְגַּלֶּה
3 pl. m.	יִגְלוּ; *יִשְׁלָיוּ[8]	יִגָּלוּ	יְגַלּוּ	יְגֻלּוּ	יַגְלוּ	יָגְלוּ	יִתְגַּלּוּ
3 pl. f.	תִּגְלֶינָה	תִּגָּלֶינָה	תְּגַלֶּינָה	תְּגֻלֶּינָה	תַּגְלֶינָה	תָּגְלֶינָה	תִּתְגַּלֶּינָה
2 pl. m.	תִּגְלוּ	תִּגָּלוּ	תְּגַלּוּ	תְּגֻלּוּ	תַּגְלוּ	תָּגְלוּ	תִּתְגַּלּוּ
2 pl. f.	תִּגְלֶינָה	תִּגָּלֶינָה	תְּגַלֶּינָה	תְּגֻלֶּינָה	תַּגְלֶינָה	תָּגְלֶינָה	תִּתְגַּלֶּינָה
1 pl.	נִגְלֶה; *נֶפֶן[9]	נִגָּלֶה, נֵרָא, נָגֶל	נְגַלֶּה	נְגֻלֶּה	נַגְלֶה	נָגְלֶה	נִתְגַּלֶּה[17]

[1] הָיוּ fr. הָיָה, etc. (הֱגִי fr. הָגָה); & שָׁתוֹת fr. שָׁתָה, etc. [2] Also הֶ⸱, as in קְנֵה; ו as in עֲשׂוּ. [3] יֵשֵׁב [יְהִי (fr. הָיָה), יְהִי (fr. הָיָה)]. [4] יֵרֵד, תֵּבְךְּ, תְּחִי (fr. חָיָה), תְּחִי [fr. הָיָה]. [5] תְּבֶן. [6] אֶחֱמְיָה. [7] אֵשֵׁת. [8] יַבְּיוּן (fr. בכה). [9] נְקִי (fr. הָיָה). [10] לְהֵרָאֶה. [11] וַיִּרְאֵתִי & הֵרָאוּ. [12] Krî Jer. xlii. 20. [13] יַעַשׂ, יֵרֶא, יֵרֶד. [14] הִתְגַּל. [15] יִתְגַּל (p. [illegible]). [16] תִּשְׁתַּע, תֵּשְׁתְּ, וַיֵּתַע. [17] נִתְגַּל. [60] יַמְרוּ (fr. רוה), יֶהֱמָיוּן.

* With ו Conversive this 'Apocopated' form is used generally. † הִשְׁתַּחֲוֵה (וַתֵּן— 2 s. m., הֵן— 1 s.), הִשְׁתַּחֲוֵיתִי 3 pl. (וֹתֵּן— 2 pl. m.) ‡ מִשְׁתַּחֲוֶה. § הִשְׁתַּחֲוִי. ‖ הִשְׁתַּחֲווּ. ¶ תִּשְׁתַּחֲוֶה. הִשְׁתַּחֲו (וַתְּ—) 3 s. f., הִשְׁתַּחֲוִיתָ 2 s. m., הִשְׁתַּחֲוֵיתִי 1 s., הִשְׁתַּחֲוֵיתָ 3 pl. יִשְׁתַּחֲווּ (וַתְּ— p. וַתְּ—) 3 pl. f., תִּשְׁתַּחֲווּ 2 pl. m., נִשְׁתַּחֲוֶה 1 pl.

⸱ תֶה in Pause.

Note A on Table XXIII.

Participle Forms.

Plu. (*f.*)	i.c.	Plu. (*m.*)	i.c.	Sing. (*f.*)	i.c.	Sing. (*m.*)
גֹּלוֹת‡	־ֵי	גּוֹלִים	־ַת	גֹּולָה†	־ֶה	גֹּולָה* (1) (I) *Kal.*
גְּלוּיוֹת	־ֻיֵ	גְּלוּיִים	־ֻיַת	גְּלוּיָה	נְלוּי	גָּלוּי § (2)
נִגְלוֹת	־ֵי	נִגְלִים	־ַת	נִגְלָה	־ֶה	נִגְלָה (II) *Niph.*

₊ In other Voices the only change from the s. *m.* forms (given in Tab. XXIII) is in the endings—which are

Plu. (*f.*)	i.c.	Plu. (*m.*)	i.c.	Sing. (*f.*)	i.c.	Sing. (*m.*)
־וֹת	־ֵי	־ִים	־ַת	־ָה	־ֶה	־ָה

Obs. (i) The Plu. (*f.*) Partic.-forms are the same in Constr.

   (ii) The *K.* Partic.-forms חַי (p. חָי׃) *living* s. *m.*, חַיָּה s. *f.*, חַיִּים pl. *m.*, חַיּוֹת pl. *f.*, are "borrowed" from a Root חיי (=חיה), being like סַב s. *m.*, סַבָּה s. *f.*, from סבב.

   (iii) חָיוֹת *K.* Partic. pl. *f.*, Ex. i. 19, is "borrowed" from a Root עו׳.

   (iv) The word מְמֻחָיִם in Is. xxv. 6 is *Pŭ.* Partic. pl. *m.* of מחה=מחי. (See also p. 173.)

---

* נֹשֵׁא s. *m.* (with א standing for the ה) 1 S. xxii. 2 ;—נֹשְׁאִים Neh. v. 7 has א ' superfluous.'

† עֹמְיָה fr. בֹּכִיָה ,עטה fr. בכה, etc.—פֹּרָת Gen. xlix. 22.

‡ אֹתָיוֹת, Is. xli. 23, fr. אתה.

§ עָשׂוּ in הֶעָשׂוּי Job xli. 25 (§ 6, *d.* ii). In Job xv. 22 צָפוּי is *Krî* for צפו Kthv.

   N.B. As in Pt. I, § 14, we may have ־ֻ for ו before the י.

יִתְגַּלֶּה, יִתְגַּל[α], יִשְׁתַּחוּ[γ] (p.חֻ)	{ יָגֶל[η] / יֶגֶל[θ] }	יִגְלֶה, יִגֵל[ε]	יִגְלֶה, יִגֵל[ε]	יִגְלֶה { יָגֶל[α] / יָגֵל[β] // יָגֶל[γ] / יָגֵל[δ] } יְחִי[1]	3 s. m.
תִּתְגַּלֶּה, תִּתְגַּל[α], תִּשְׁתַּחוּ[γ] (p.חֻ)	{ תָּגֶל[η] / תֶּגֶל }	תִּגְלֶה, תִּגֵל[ε]	תִּגְלֶה, תִּגֵל[ε]	תִּגְלֶה { תָּגֶל / תָּגֵל[β] // תָּגֶל[γ] / תָּגֵל[δ] } תְּחִי[1]	3 s. f. & 2 s. m.
אֶתְגַּלֶּה, אֶתְגַּל	{ אָגֵל[η] / אֶגֵל }	אֶגְלֶה, אֶגֵל[ε]	אֶגְלֶה, אֶגֵל[ε]	אֶגְלֶה { אָגֵל[γ] / אָגֵל[δ] }, אֶחְיִ[1]	1 sing.

(1 plu. forms have נ for the ' of 3 s. m.)

(α) So *יָפְתְּ 3 s. m. (פתה), *יָשֹׁב (שבה); and יִיף (יפה), and יֶחַד (חדה) with ח instead of ה as in C on p. 30 of Tabs., and יָאת (אתה).—N.B. (α) יָרֵא (ראה) is a special form, as also in η below, (only in וַיִּרְא, otherwise יָרֵא as in δ).

(b) יַן and יֵן are direct contracted forms of יִנֶּה (נזה).

(β) i. So 3 s. m. יֶרֶב (רבה), יָפֶן (פנה), יָבֶן (בנה), etc.; and so יַחַן† (חנה), יַחַר† (חרה), etc.; besides יַעַל† p. יַ (חלה), יַשַׁע† (שעה), etc. as p. 51 of Tabs.:—ii. So 3 s. f. or 2 s. m. תֶּבֶן (בנה), etc.; and תַּחַר† (חרה), תַּעַל† p. תַּ (עלה), etc. as p. 51 of Tabs.

(γ) i. So 3 s. m. *יֵשְׁתְּ (שתה), יֵשְׁל (שלה), יֵרֶד (רדה), יָבֶךְ (בכה), etc.; but יַן & יֵן are direct contracted forms of יִנֶּה (נזה) & יָפֶה (נטה):—ii. so 3 s. f. and 2 s. m. *תֵּשְׁתְּ (שתה), תֵּבְךְ (בכה), etc.; but תַּט is a direct contracted form of תִּנֶּה (נטה):—and iii. so 1 Sing. *אֶשְׁתְּ (שתה).

(δ) i. So 3 s. m. יֵשֵׁל (שלה), יֶרַע† (רעה), יֵרָא (ראה):—ii. so 3 s. f. and 2 s. m. תֶּפֶן (פנה), תֵּרֶא (ראה), etc.; and תֶּכַה† (כהה), תֵּלֶה† (להה), etc.:—and iii. so 1 Sing. אֶפֶן (פנה), אֶרֶא (ראה); but יַחַז† (חזה), and תֵּעַ† (תעה), etc.

(עלה), etc. [of form אֶגַל not used in Kal]. And iv. so 1 Plu. נָפֶן (פנה), אֶעַל† (עלה), etc. [of form נֶגַל not used]. but נַעַל† (עלה), נַעַשׂ† (עשה), גְּרָא (ראה).

(ε) i. So 3 s. m. יֵקֶר (קרה), and יָפֶח (מחה), יִרָא‡ (ראה):—ii. so 3 s. f. or 2 s. m. תֵּעַשׂ‡ (עשה) like תִּגַל;—and iii. so 1 Sing. אָפֶת (פתה), אֶרָא‡ (ראה).

(ζ) i. So 3 s. m. יָקֶו (קוה), יָקֻו (קוה), יְמָן (מנה), יְצַו (צוה), etc.; and יָתֵו with Euph. ־ (תוה):—and ii. so 3 s. f. or 2 s. m. תֶּכֶם (כסה), תֵּעַר (ערה), etc.:—and iii. so 1 Sing. אֶצַו (צוה), etc.

(η) i. So *יַפְתְּ (פתה), וַיִּרְא (ראה), יֵרְדְּ† (רדה), יֵשְׁקְ (שקה); is a special form as in (α):—ii. so 3 s. f. or 2 s. m. *תֵּשְׁקְ (שקה). iii. The 1 Sing. אָט (נטה) and אָךְ (נכה), and iv. the 1 Plu. נָךְ (נכה) may be of this form or merely direct contractions of נֶכֶּה and אֶכֶּה and אֶפֶּה.

(θ) i. So יֵעַל† p. יָ (עלה), יֶרֶב (רבה), יָחַר† (חרה), יָפֶן (פנה), etc. as p. 51 of Tabs.:—ii. So 3 s. f. or 2 s. m. תֵּרֶף (רפה), תֵּמַח† (מחה), etc.; and תַּעַל† (עלה) etc., as p. 51 of Tabs.

(κ) i. So 3 s. m. יִתְכַּם (כסה), יִתְאוּ with Euph. ־ (אוה), etc.:—ii. so 3 s. f. or 2 s. m. תֶּכַס p. כָ (כסה), תִּתְחָר (חרה), תִּתְכַּם p. תִּ (כסה), etc.

(λ) For חָוָה—from שחה (p. 89, I. i.).

---

[1] Fr. היה; the full forms being אֶהְיֶה, תִּהְיֶה, יֶהְיֶה, Comp. p. 277. So יְחִי, תְּחִי, from חיה, p. 279. Obs. יֶהִי and יֶחִי are Pause-forms of יְהִי and יְחִי.

* The usual form when the second Rt-letter is one of the בגד כפת, i.e. one of the seven letters ב, ג, ד, כ, פ, ת.
† With ־ because of one of the החע.
‡ With compensation for Dagesh F.

SUPPLEMENT TO TABLE XXIII.—N.B. *Several of the words below are merely Paradigm-forms.*

	I. KAL.	II. NIPH-AL.	III. PI-EL, IV. PU-AL, VII. HITHPA-EL	V. HIPH-IL.	VI. HOPH-AL.
INFIN. ABS.	עֲלֹה, ־ֹה	הֵעָלֹה, הֵרָאֹה	are as in Table XXIII.	הַעֲלֵה, ־ֵה, ־ֵה	הָעֲלֵה (־ֵה)
Constr. & w. בכלמ	עֲלוֹת (־וֹ), בְּ׳, כְּ׳, ל׳, מֵעֲלוֹת	הֵעָלוֹת בְּ׳, כְּ׳, ל׳, מֵהֵעָלוֹת		הַעֲלוֹת בְּ׳, כְּ׳, ל׳, מֵהַעֲלוֹת	הָעֲלוֹת בְּ׳, כְּ׳, ל׳, מֵהָעֲלוֹת
	(הֱיוֹת, בִּהְיוֹת), etc., see p. 276.				
w. Pron. Affs.	עֲלֹתוֹ, ...	הֵעָלֹתוֹ, ...		הַעֲלֹתוֹ, ...	הָעֲלֹתוֹ, ...
PAST. 3 s. m.	עָלָה	נַעֲלָה¹ נִהְיָה		הֶעֱלָה⁶ הֶעֱלָה	הָעֲלָה
3 s. f.	עָלְתָה, עָשָׂת	נַעֲלָתָה² נִהְיְתָה³		הֶעֱלָתָה⁷ הַעֲלָתָה²	הָעֲלָתָה, הָעַלְתָה׃
2 s. m.	עָלִיתָ, ־ֹיתָה	נַעֲלֵיתָ נִהְיֵיתָ		הֶעֱלֵיתָ⁸ (or לֹ)	הָעֲלֵיתָ
2 s. f.	עָלִית	נַעֲלֵית		הֶעֱלֵית⁸	הָעֲלֵית
1 s.	עָלִיתִי	נַעֲלֵיתִי נִהְיֵיתִי⁴		הֶעֱלֵיתִי⁸ (or לֹ)	הָעֲלֵיתִי
3 pl.	עָלוּ	נַעֲלוּ⁵ נָחֵלוּ		הֶעֱלוּ	הָעֲלוּ, הָעֲלוּ
2 pl. m.	עֲלִיתֶם, הֱיִיתֶם (p. 277)	נַעֲלֵיתֶם		הֶעֱלֵיתֶם⁹	הָעֲלֵיתֶם
2 pl. f.	עֲלִיתֶן	נַעֲלֵיתֶן		הֶעֱלֵיתֶן	הָעֲלֵיתֶן
1 pl.	עָלִינוּ	נַעֲלֵינוּ		הֶעֱלֵינוּ	הָעֲלֵינוּ
PARTIC. (1).	עֹלֶה (i.e. עֹלֶה)	נַעֲלֶה (i.e. ־ֶה)		מַעֲלֶה (i.e. ־ֶה)	מָעֲלֶה (i.e. ־ֶה)

Paradigm of the verb עָלָה (ל״ה), continued — Imperative (concluded) and Future, through Kal, Niphal, Hiphil and Hophal. Each conjugation shows the full form and (in the narrow columns) the apocopated / jussive and comparison forms.

	Kal		Niphal		Hiphil		Hophal
2 s. m.	עֲלֵה,	חֲיֵה	הֵעָלֵה		הַעֲלֵה,	קַל	
2 s. f.	עֲלִי,	הֱיִי [חֲיִי]	הֵעָלִי		הַעֲלִי		
2 pl. m.	עֲלוּ,	הֱיוּ	הֵעָלוּ		הַעֲלוּ		
2 pl. f.	עֲלֶינָה,	[הֱיֶינָה]	הֵעָלֶינָה		הַעֲלֶינָה		
FUTURE.							
*** 3 s. m.**	יַעֲלֶה,	‡יַעַל	יֵעָלֶה	יֵעָל	יַעֲלֶה	+יַעַל, יָסֻר	יָעֳלֶה
3 s. f.	תַּעֲלֶה,	+תַּעַל	תֵּעָלֶה	תֵּעָל	תַּעֲלֶה,	+תַּעַל	תָּעֳלֶה
2 s. m.	תַּעֲלֶה,	+תַּעַל	תֵּעָלֶה	תֵּעָל	תַּעֲלֶה,	+תַּעַל	תָּעֳלֶה
2 s. f.	תַּעֲלִי		תֵּעָלִי		תַּעֲלִי		תָּעֳלִי
1 s.	אֶעֱלֶה,	+אֶעַל	אֵעָלֶה	אֵעָל	אַעֲלֶה,	+אַעַל	אָעֳלֶה
3 pl. m.	יַעֲלוּ		יֵעָלוּ		יַעֲלוּ		יָעֳלוּ
3 pl. f.	תַּעֲלֶינָה		תֵּעָלֶינָה		תַּעֲלֶינָה		תָּעֳלֶינָה
2 pl. m.	תַּעֲלוּ		תֵּעָלוּ		תַּעֲלוּ		תָּעֳלוּ
2 pl. f.	תַּעֲלֶינָה		תֵּעָלֶינָה		תַּעֲלֶינָה		תָּעֳלֶינָה
1 pl.	נַעֲלֶה,	+נַעַל	נֵעָלֶה	נֵעָל	נַעֲלֶה	+נַעַל	נָעֳלֶה

---

[1] See (i) on p. 193. [2] In Pause: תָּה‎ — ֶ — ֵ — ָ or :תָּה‎ — ֶ — ֵ — ַ —

[3] In Pause: נֶחְיָתָה‎. [4] Also מָחֳלִיתִי. [5] נֶחֱרוּ Song i. 6. [6] הֶחֱלִי fr. חלה, Is. liii. 10.— הֶעֱלְךָ with Aff. *thee* (*m.*), הֶעֱלָנוּ with Aff. *us.* [7] הֶעֱלָם with Aff. *them* (*m.*). [8] וְהֶעֱ with ו Convers. [9] הֶעֱלִיתַנִי with Aff. *me.*

* Also יֶחֱרֶה fr. חרה, יֶהְגֶּה fr. הגה; Comp. (β) & (γ) on p. 191; יֶחְיֶה fr. חיה (p. 277), יִחְיֶה fr. היה (p. 279).

† In Pause (: — ֶ — ֵ).

‡ Also יַחַר fr. חרה, and יָחַד fr. חדד; Comp. (ζ, δ) and 'Note' on p. 192.— יֶחִי fr. יִחְיֶה, etc., p. 277; יְחִי fr. יִהְיֶה, etc. (p. 279).

TABLE XXIV.—INFINS. WITH PRON.-AFFS. (OBJECTIVE, ETC.).

(*₀* Each Infin. here has the pref. לְ of בכלם).

Pronouns Obj. etc.	HIPH-ÎL. לְהַפְקִיד *to cause to visit.*	PI-ÊL. לְפַקֵּד *to visit* (Intens.)	KAL. לִפְקֹד *to visit·*
him	לְהַפְקִידוֹ	לְפַקְּדוֹ	לְפָקְדוֹ
her	לְהַפְקִידָהּ	לְפַקְּדָהּ	לְפָקְדָהּ
thee (m.)	{ לְהַפְקִידְךָ / ־דְךָ	{ לְפַקֶּדְךָ / לְפַקֶּדְךָ	{ לְפָקְדְךָ / (־קָדְ)
thee (f.)	לְהַפְקִידֵךְ	לְפַקְּדֵךְ	לְפָקְדֵךְ
me	לְהַפְקִידֵנִי	לְפַקְּדֵנִי	{ לְפָקְדֵנִי / לְפָקְרִי (־נִי)
them (m.)	לְהַפְקִידָם	לְפַקְּדָם	לְפָקְדָם
them (f.)	לְהַפְקִידָן	לְפַקְּדָן	לְפָקְדָן
you (m.)	לְהַפְקִידְכֶם	לְפַקֶּדְכֶם	{ לְפָקֶדְכֶם / לְפָקְדְכֶם
you (f.)	לְהַפְקִידְכֶן	לְפַקֶּדְכֶן	{ לְפָקֶדְכֶן / לְפָקְדְכֶן
us	לְהַפְקִידֵנוּ	לְפַקְּדֵנוּ	לְפָקְדֵנוּ (־נִי)

NOTE :—(α) Instead of the ־ָ (ŏ) of the 1st (and sometimes the 2d) Rt-letter in the *Kal*, there may be (i) ־ַ as in such forms as לְסַעֲדָה, לְסַעֲדוֹ, לְשָׂטְנוּ ; (ii) ־ָ as in לְחָנְנָה ; (iii) ־ֶ as in לְשָׂטְנוּ.

(β) The few forms from other Voices will be understood from those above.

(γ) So for forms from some other Verbs. But we may add those in (δ) :—

(δ) (1) לַעֲזֹב *to forsake,* (*him*) לְעָזְבוֹ, (*thee* m.) לְעָזְבְךָ, etc.

    (2) לָרֶשֶׁת *to possess,* (*him*) לְרִשְׁתּוֹ, etc.

    (3) לָקַחַת *to take,* (*him*) לְקַחְתּוֹ, etc.

    (4) לָשׂוּם *to put,* (*him*) לְשׂוּמוֹ, etc. [לְשִׂימוֹ, לָשִׂים, etc.]

        לְהָקִים *to raise,* (*him*) לַהֲקִימוֹ, etc.

    (5) לָסֹב *to go round,* (*him*) לְסֻבּוֹ, etc. — [לְסוֹבְבוֹ, לְסוֹבֵב, etc.—לַהֲסִבּוֹ, לְהָסֵב, etc.].

    (6) לִקְנוֹת *to buy,* (*him*) לִקְנֹתוֹ, etc. [לַעֲשֹׂתוֹ, לַעֲשׂוֹת, etc.].

(TABLE XXV) PAST *K.*, WITH PRON.-AFFIXES (OBJECTIVE, ETC.)

Pronouns Obj., etc.	פָּקַדְנוּ *we visited.*	פְּקַדְתֶּם &—תֶּן *ye (f.) & ye (m.) visited.*	פָּקְדוּ *they visited.*	פָּקַדְתִּי *I visited.*	פָּקַדְתְּ *thou (f.) visitedst.*	פָּקַדְתָּ *thou (m.) visitedst.*	פָּקְדָה *she visited.*	פָּקַד *he visited.*
him	פְּקַדְנוּהוּ	פְּקַדְתּוּהוּ	פְּקָדוּהוּ	{ פְּקַדְתִּיו / פְּקַדְתִּיהוּ }	{ פְּקַדְתִּיו / פְּקַדְתִּיהוּ }	{ פְּקַדְתּוֹ / פְּקַדְתָּהוּ }	{ פְּקָדָתוּ / פְּקָדַתְהוּ }	{ פְּקָדוֹ / פְּקָדָהוּ }
her	פְּקַדְנוּהָ	פְּקַדְתּוּהָ	פְּקָדוּהָ	פְּקַדְתִּיהָ	פְּקַדְתִּיהָ	פְּקַדְתָּהּ	פְּקָדַתָּה	פְּקָדָהּ
thee (m.)	פְּקַדְנוּךָ	—	פְּקָדוּךָ	פְּקַדְתִּיךָ	—	—	פְּקָדָתְךָ	פְּקָדְךָ (־ְךָ)
thee (f.)	פְּקַדְנוּךְ	—	פְּקָדוּךְ	פְּקַדְתִּיךְ	—	—	פְּקָדָתֵךְ (ד)	פְּקָדֵךְ (־ָךְ)
me	—	פְּקַדְתּוּנִי	פְּקָדוּנִי	—	פְּקַדְתִּינִי	פְּקַדְתַּנִי (־נִי)	פְּקָדַתְנִי	פְּקָדַנִי (־נִי)
them (m.)	פְּקַדְנוּם	פְּקַדְתּוּם	פְּקָדוּם	פְּקַדְתִּים	פְּקַדְתִּים	פְּקַדְתָּם (־מֹו) γ. iv	פְּקָדָתַם	פְּקָדָם (־מֹו)
them (f.)	פְּקַדְנוּן	פְּקַדְתּוּן	פְּקָדוּן	פְּקַדְתִּין	פְּקַדְתִּין	פְּקַדְתָּן	פְּקָדָתַן	פְּקָדָן
you (m.)	פְּקַדְנוּכֶם	—	פְּקָדוּכֶם (?)	פְּקַדְתִּיכֶם	—	—	פְּקָדַתְכֶם	פְּקָדְכֶם
you (f.)	פְּקַדְנוּכֶן	—	פְּקָדוּכֶן (?)	פְּקַדְתִּיכֶן	—	—	פְּקָדַתְכֶן	פְּקָדְכֶן
us	—	פְּקַדְתּוּנוּ	פְּקָדוּנוּ	—	פְּקַדְתִּינוּ	פְּקַדְתָּנוּ	פְּקָדָתְנוּ	פְּקָדָנוּ

Note:—(α) The פָּעֵל forms [§ 138 (A)] retain the ־ַ as in אֲהֵבוֹ, אֲהֵבָהּ, אֲהֵבַנִי, etc., fr. אָהֵב.—So יְרֵשׁוּךָ, יְרֵשׁוּךָ, fr. יָרֵשׁ, which belong to a פָּעֵל form [יָרֵשׁ].—(β) As belonging to the פָּעֵל form, some take such forms as אֲהֵבְתִּיהוּ *I have begotten him*, יְלִדְתִּיךָ *I have begotten thee (m.)*, יְלִדְתָּנוּ *thou (m.) hast begotten us*, יְלִדְתִּינִי *thou (f.) hast born me* ; and שְׁאִלְתִּיהוּ & שְׁאִלְתִּיו *I asked him* (cp. הִשְׁאִלְתִּיהוּ 1 s. Past Hφ., with ־יהוּ *him*).—(γ) There are a few other forms of Affixes ; thus (i) ־נִי *me*, (ii) ־תְהוּ (for ־תוּ in p.) as in אֲבֵלָתְהוּ G. xxxvii. 33, (iii) ־תֶךְ (־תֵךְ) Song viii. 5), (iv) ־תְמוֹ as in עֲנָתָמוֹ for עֲנָתָם.

* Also ־ְךָ, in Pause.

(Table XXVI) Participles with Pron.-Affixes.

The Student may make *complete* Tables by replacing

(i)   דָן־ in 'Appˣ (C) to Tab. XIV' by the forms in column (i) below;

(ii) דָת־ in 'Appˣ (B) to Tab. XIV' by the forms in column (ii) below,

(iii) דִים־ in 'Appˣ (B) to Tab. XIV' by the forms in column (iii) below,

(iv) וֹת־ in 'Appˣ (B) to Tab. XIV' by the forms in column (iv) below :-

Partic. Plu.		Partic. Sing.	
(iv.) (*f.*)	(iii.) (*m.*)	(ii.) (*f.*)	(i.) (*m.*)
־תָיו	־דָיו	§־דְתָּו (־דְהוּ)	־דָו (־דָהוּ)
־תָיה	־דֶיה	־דָתָה	־דָה (־דָם)
*־תָיךְ	־דֶיךְ	־דָתְךָ (־דוּ)	־דְךָ (־גָדוּ)
†(־יהָ) ־תָיךְ (־יהָ) ־דֶיךְ	־דָתֵךְ	־דֵךְ (־דֵכִי)
(־יִ) ־תָי (־יִ) ־דָי	־דָתִי (־יִ)	‡־דִי (־גִי)
(־תָם) ־תֵיהֶם	־דֵיהֶם	־דָתָם	־דָם (־דָמוֹ)
(־תָן) ־תֵיהֶן	־דֵיהֶן	־דָתָן	־דָן
*־תֵיכֶם	־דֵיכֶם	־דְתְכֶם	*־דְכֶם
*־תֵיכֶן	־דֵיכֶן	־דְתְכֶן	*־דְכֶן
־תֵינוּ	־דֵינוּ	־דְתֵנוּ	־דֵנוּ

Note :—(α) The Passive Participles in 'Appˣ (B) to Tab. XIV' cannot strictly have *Objective* Affixes. [For Decl. of forms in דֶה־ see Tab. VI (i).]

(β) The Hebrew Participles, *as Nouns*, may be 'in Constr.', and may have *Possessive* Pron. Affixes. For instance,

(γ) the Partic. (of פָּעֵל form) יָרֵא *one* (*m.*) *fearing*, or *a fearer*, 'in Constr.' is יְרֵא *a fearer of* (and so יְרֵאִים *fearers* (*m.*) is i.c. יִרְאֵי *fearers of*).— Of יְרֵאָה *one* (*f.*) *fearing*, or *a fearer* (*f.*), the Construct form would be יִרְאַת (and that of יְרֵאֹת would be יִרְאֹת). [See also § 139 (δ, iv.]

(δ) The Partic. of פָּעֵל form takes the Affs. thus,—Sing. פְּעֵלְוֹ, פְּעֵלָה, etc., Plu. (פְּעֵלִים) פְּעֵלָיו, פְּעֵלֶיךָ, etc. So we have יְרֵאָיו *those* (*m.*) *fearing him*, or *his fearers*, יְרֵאֶיךָ *those fearing thee* (*m.*), or *thy fearers*.

* The '*Slight*'-*vowel* of 2ᵈ Rt-letter here is ־ֱ (־ֲ or ־ֳ); thus, נֹתְנָה (אֹיְבָה, אֹהֲבָה).

† Also דְךָ־.

‡ ־ֶנִי, ־ֵנִי׳. עֹשֵׂנִי fr. עָשָׂה, & רֹאֵנִי (once) fr. רָאָה,—in which the ח״ה is dropped as, also, in עֹשׂוֹ and עֹשֵׂהוּ, עֹשָׂה (p. עֹשֵׂהוּ), etc., fr. עָשָׂה.

§ Also with ־ָ. Thus, fr. מֵינֶקֶת,—מֵינַקְתּוֹ, מֵינִקְתָּהּ, etc.

(TABLE XXVII) IMPERATIVES *K.* WITH PRON.-AFFIXES.

Pronouns Obj., etc.	פְּקֹדְנָה visit ye (f.)	פִּקְדוּ visit ye (m.)	פִּקְדִי visit thou (f.)	פְּקֹד visit thou (m.)
him		פְּקָדֻהוּ	פִּקְדִיהוּ	פְּקָדֵהוּ (־ֶנּוּ) / פָּקְדוֹ
her		פְּקָדוּהָ	פִּקְדִיהָ	פְּקָדֶהָ (־ֶנָּה) / פָּקְדָהּ
me		פְּקָדוּנִי	פִּקְדִינִי	פָּקְדֵנִי
them (m.)		פְּקָדוּם	פִּקְדִים	פָּקְדֵם (־ֵמוֹ)
them (f.)		פְּקָדוּן	פִּקְדִין	פָּקְדֵן
us		פְּקָדוּנוּ	פִּקְדִינוּ	פָּקְדֵנוּ

˟˟˟ The forms given above are for Verbs 'Fut (־ֹ־)' [§§ 141 (*a*, ‡), & 162 (*b*, §)].

Note:—(*a*) In Verbs 'Fut (־ַ־),' the 2ᵈ Rt-letter has ־ָ (lengthened from ־ַ); and so

(β) with one of the letters אחע (or ה consonantal) as 3ᵈ or 2ᵈ Rt-letter, we have מְשָׁחֵהוּ *anoint thou* (m.) *him,* אֱהָבֶהָ *love thou* (m.) *her,* גְּאָלָהּ *redeem thou* (m.) *her* (or *it f.*), סְעָדֵנִי *support Thou me;* and so קְרָאֶנָּה *proclaim thou* (m.) *it* (*f.*), קְרָאֻהוּ *call ye upon Him,* שְׁמָעֵנִי *hear ye me,* etc.; and so from קַח (r. לקח), קָחֶנּוּ *take* (or *fetch*) *thou* (m.) *him,* קָחֶנָּה *take thou* (m.) *it* (*f.*), קָחֵם *take* (or *fetch*) *them* (m.)—whence קָחֶם־ G. xlviii. 9.

(γ) In Nu. xxiii. 13 קָבְנוֹ *curse thou* (m.) *him* is an irregular form from קבב with 'Epenthetic נ' (as it is called) between the Verb and the Affix.

(δ) In other Voices, the only change is in the 'syllable of junction'; thus,

the *Pi.* פַּקֵּד gives פִּקְּדֵהוּ, etc.,

the *Hφ.* הַפְקֵד gives הַפְקִידֵהוּ, etc.

Pronouns Obj., etc.	נִפְקֹד *we will visit.*	תִּפְקְדוּ } ־ֹדְנָה *ye (f.) ye (m.) will visit.*	תִּפְקֹדְנָה *they (f.) will visit.*	יִפְקְדוּ *they (m.) will visit.*
him	(נִפְקְדֶנּוּ) נִפְקְדֵהוּ נִפְקְדוֹ	תִּפְקְדוּהוּ	תִּפְקְדוּהוּ	יִפְקְדוּהוּ
her	נִפְקְדֶנָּה נִפְקְדֶהָ נִפְקְדָהּ	תִּפְקְדוּהָ	תִּפְקְדוּהָ	יִפְקְדוּהָ
thee (m.)	נִפְקָדְךָ נִפְקָדֶךָּ	—	תִּפְקָדוּךָ	יִפְקָדוּךָ
thee (f.)	נִפְקְדֵךְ	—	תִּפְקְדוּךְ	יִפְקְדוּךְ
me	—	תִּפְקְדוּנִי	תִּפְקְדוּנִי	יִפְקְדוּנִי
them (m.)	נִפְקְדֵם	תִּפְקְדֵם	תִּפְקְדֵם	יִפְקְדֵם
them (f.)	נִפְקְדֵן	תִּפְקְדֵן	תִּפְקְדֵן	יִפְקְדֵן
you (m.)	נִפְקָדְכֶם	—	תִּפְקְדוּכֶם	יִפְקְדוּכֶם
you (f.)	נִפְקָדְכֶן	—	תִּפְקְדוּכֶן	יִפְקְדוּכֶן
us	—	תִּפְקְדוּנוּ	תִּפְקְדוּנוּ	יִפְקְדוּנוּ

*** The forms given above are for Verbs 'Fut (–ֹ–)' [§ 141 (α, ‡)].

Note:—(α) In Verbs 'Fut (–ֵ–)' the 2d Rt-letter has ֵ (lengthened from ֶ); thus, from יִלְבַּשׁ, יִלְבָּשֵׁנִי *he* (or *it m.*) *will clothe me*, יִלְבָּשֵׁם [see ε (vii, a)] *he shall put on them* (m.) [*as clothes*]; and so,

(β) with one of the letters אחע, or ה consonantal, for 3d or 2d Rt-letter we have יִשְׁלָחֵהוּ & יִשְׁלָחֶנּוּ *he will send him*, יִשְׁלָחֲךָ *he will send thee* (m.), יִשְׁלָחֵנִי *he will send me*, יֶאֱהָבֵנִי [ε, vi] *he will love me*, etc.; and so, from יַקַּח (r. לקח) יִקָּחֵהוּ *he will take him*, יִקָּחֶהָ *he will take her*, etc.

(γ) The נ of § 145 stands sometimes between the Verb and a Pron.-Affix; thus יַעֲבָרֶנְהוּ Jer. v. 22 *they* (m.) *shall pass over it* (m.) from יַעֲבֹרֻן, יִלְכְּדֻנּוּ Pr. v. 22 *they* (m.) *will take him* from יִלְכְּדוּ, יִקְרָאֻנְנִי (etc.) Pr. i. 28 *they* (m.) *shall call-upon me* from יִקְרָאוּ (etc.). So also in the *Pi-él* יְשָׁרְתוּנֶךְ Is. lx. 7 *they* (m.) *shall minister-unto thee* (f.). [ֶךְ for ֵךְ as in Pt. I, § 55 (9, b)].

I will visit.	thou (f.) wilt visit.	thou (m.) wilt visit.	she will visit.	he will visit.	For Fut. see (α) below.
(אֶפְקְדֶנּוּ)		(תִּפְקְדֶנּוּ)	(תִּפְקְדֶנּוּ)	(יִפְקְדֶנּוּ)	
אֶפְקְדֵהוּ	תִּפְקְדִיהוּ	תִּפְקְדֵהוּ	תִּפְקְדֵהוּ	יִפְקְדֵהוּ	
אֶפְקְדוֹ		תִּפְקְדוֹ	תִּפְקְדוֹ	יִפְקְדוֹ	
אֶפְקְדֶנָּה		תִּפְקְדֶנָּה	תִּפְקְדֶנָּה	יִפְקְדֶנָּה	
אֶפְקְדָהּ	תִּפְקְדִיהָ	תִּפְקְדָהּ	תִּפְקְדָהּ	יִפְקְדָהּ	
אֶפְקְדֶהָ		תִּפְקְדֶהָ	תִּפְקְדֶהָ	יִפְקְדֶהָ	
אֶפְקָדְךָ	—	—	תִּפְקָדְךָ	יִפְקָדְךָ	
אֶפְקָדְךָ׃			תִּפְקָדְךָ׃	יִפְקָדְךָ׃	
אֶפְקָדֶךָ	—	—	תִּפְקָדֶךָ	יִפְקָדֶךָ	
—	תִּפְקְדִינִי	תִּפְקְדֵנִי	תִּפְקְדֵנִי	יִפְקְדֵנִי	
אֶפְקְדֵם	תִּפְקְדִים	תִּפְקְדֵם	תִּפְקְדֵם	יִפְקְדֵם	
אֶפְקְדֵן	תִּפְקְדִין	תִּפְקְדֵן	תִּפְקְדֵן	יִפְקְדֵן	
אֶפְקָדְכֶם	—	—	תִּפְקָדְכֶם	יִפְקָדְכֶם	
אֶפְקָדְכֶן	—	—	תִּפְקָדְכֶן	יִפְקָדְכֶן	
—	תִּפְקְדִינוּ	תִּפְקְדֵנוּ	תִּפְקְדֵנוּ	יִפְקְדֵנוּ	

(δ) We find the נ (called 'Epenthetic נ'), between Verb and Affix, also in other Persons; thus, יַעֲבָרֶנְהוּ Jer. v. 22 *he* (or *it m.*) *will pass-over it* (*m.*) from עבר; אֶתְּקֶנְךָ ,יַעֲבָר Jer. xxii. 24 *I will pluck thee* (*m.*) from נתק [the Dag. L. in ך is in accordance with Pt. I, § 47 (2) & § 55 (7)].

(e) Besides the Affix-forms given above, there are some others. Thus (i) ־ֶהָ instead of ־ָהּ *her*, as in וַתַּחְמְרָה Ex. ii. 3 *and she daubed it* (*f.*). (ii) The ־ְךָ *thee* (*m.*) is in Pause ־ֶךָ׃ (also ־ֶךָ:); and (iv) the Affix ־ְךָ, with ה after it, has the form ־ֶכָה. (v) The 2 s. f. ־ֵךְ has י sometimes after it, thus ־ֵכִי. (vi) Instead of ־ֵנִי *me*, we have sometimes ־ֵנִי (p.־ֵנִי). (vii) Instead of ־ֵם *them* (*m.*), we have (1) sometimes ־ֵמוֹ and (2) sometimes ־ֶם, and so (viii) ־ֶן (rarely ־ֶן) for ־ֶן *them* (*f.*). Rarely (ix) ־ֶנּוּ for ־ֶנוּ *us*. (x) ־ֵנִי *me*, has Dagesh for the נ of (δ).

(ζ) For the 'Slight'-vowel in some forms see Obs. XLIII (p. 210).

---

* So ־ֵנִי (Ps. L. 23), with the נ of (δ), in Pause.

TABLE XXIX.

From Tables XXV & XXVIII, which give the Past & Future *Kal* with Pron.-Affixes, the Past & Future forms of other Voices, with such Affixes, will be easily recognized. It may be useful, however, to give here the following:—

(I.) (α) PAST PĬ-ÊL WITH PRON.-AFFIXES (OBJECTIVE, ETC.).

פָּקַדְנוּ	פְּקַדְתֶּם &—תֶּן	פָּקְדוּ	פְּקַדְתִּי	פָּקַדְתְּ	פָּקַדְתָּ	פָּקְדָה	פָּקַד
פְּקַדְנוּהוּ	פְּקַדְתּוּהוּ	פְּקָדוּהוּ	פְּקַדְתִּיו	פְּקַדְתִּיו	פְּקַדְתָּהוּ ⇐תּוֹ· פְּקַדְתּוֹ		פְּקָדוֹ
פְּקַדְנוּהָ	פְּקַדְתּוּהָ	פְּקָדוּהָ	פְּקַדְתִּיהָ	פְּקַדְתִּיהָ	פְּקַדְתָּהּ	פְּקַדְתָּהּ	פָּקְדָהּ
פְּקַדְנוּךָ	——	פְּקָדוּךָ	פְּקַדְתִּיךָ	——	——	פְּקַדְתְּךָ	(←דֶ) פְּקָדְךָ
פְּקַדְנוּךְ	——	פְּקָדוּךְ	פְּקַדְתִּיךְ	——	——	(נ) פְּקַדְתֵּךְ	(←ךְ) פְּקָדֵךְ
etc.	etc.	etc.	etc.	etc.	etc.	etc.	etc.

(β) PAST HIPH-ÎL.

הִפְקַדְנוּ	הִפְקַדְתֶּם &—תֶּן	הִפְקִידוּ	הִפְקַדְתִּי	הִפְקַדְתְּ	הִפְקַדְתָּ	הִפְקִידָה	הִפְקִיד
הִפְקַדְנוּהוּ	הִפְקַדְתּוּהוּ	הִפְקִידוּהוּ	הִפְקַדְתִּיו	הִפְקַדְתִּיו	הִפְקַדְתּוֹ	הִפְקִידָתְהוּ	הִפְקִידוֹ
הִפְקַדְנוּהָ	הִפְקַדְתּוּהָ	הִפְקִידוּהָ	הִפְקַדְתִּיהָ	הִפְקַדְתִּיהָ	הִפְקַדְתָּהּ	הִפְקִידָתָהּ	הִפְקִידָהּ
הִפְקַדְנוּךְ	——	הִפְקִידוּךָ	הִפְקַדְתִּיךָ	הִפְקַדְתִּיךָ	——	——	(←דֶ) הִפְקִידְךָ
etc.	etc.	etc.	etc.	etc.	etc.	etc.	etc.

(II.) (a) FUTURE PÎ-ÊL WITH PRON.-AFFIXES (OBJECTIVE, ETC.).

נְפַקֵּד	תְּפַקְּדוּ (=דְנָה)	תְּפַקֵּדְנָה	יְפַקְּדוּ	אֲפַקֵּד	תְּפַקְּדִי	תְּפַקֵּד	תְּפַקֵּד	יְפַקֵּד
נְפַקְּדֵנוּ נְפַקְּדֵהוּ נְפַקְּדוֹ	תְּפַקְּדוּהוּ	תְּפַקְּדוּהוּ	יְפַקְּדוּהוּ	אֲפַקְּדֵנוּ אֲפַקְּדֵהוּ אֲפַקְּדוֹ	תְּפַקְּדִיהוּ	תְּפַקְּדֵנוּ תְּפַקְּדֵהוּ תְּפַקְּדוֹ	תְּפַקְּדֵנוּ תְּפַקְּדֵהוּ תְּפַקְּדוֹ	יְפַקְּדֵנוּ יְפַקְּדֵהוּ יְפַקְּדוֹ
נְפַקְּדֶנָּה נְפַקְּדָהּ נְפַקְּדֶהָ	תְּפַקְּדוּהָ	תְּפַקְּדוּהָ	יְפַקְּדוּהָ	אֲפַקְּדֶנָּה אֲפַקְּדָהּ אֲפַקְּדֶהָ	תְּפַקְּדִיהָ	תְּפַקְּדֶנָּה תְּפַקְּדָהּ תְּפַקְּדֶהָ	תְּפַקְּדֶנָּה תְּפַקְּדָהּ תְּפַקְּדֶהָ	יְפַקְּדֶנָּה יְפַקְּדָהּ יְפַקְּדֶהָ
נְפַקֶּדְךָ נְפַקְּדֵךְ נְפַקֶּדְךָ etc.	—	תְּפַקְּדוּךְ תְּפַקְּדוּךָ	יְפַקְּדוּךְ יְפַקְּדוּךָ	אֲפַקֶּדְךָ אֲפַקְּדֵךְ אֲפַקֶּדְךָ		—	תְּפַקֶּדְךָ תְּפַקְּדֵךְ תְּפַקֶּדְךָ etc.	יְפַקֶּדְךָ יְפַקְּדֵךְ יְפַקֶּדְךָ etc.

(β) FUTURE HIPH-ÎL WITH PRON.-AFFIXES (OBJECTIVE, ETC.).

נַפְקִיד	תַּפְקִידוּ (=דְנָה)	תַּפְקֵדְנָה	יַפְקִידוּ	אַפְקִיד	תַּפְקִידִי	תַּפְקִיד	תַּפְקִיד	יַפְקִיד
נַפְקִידֵנוּ נַפְקִידֵהוּ	תַּפְקִידוּהוּ	תַּפְקִידוּהוּ	יַפְקִידוּהוּ	אַפְקִידֵנוּ אַפְקִידֵהוּ	תַּפְקִידִיהוּ	תַּפְקִידֵנוּ תַּפְקִידֵהוּ	תַּפְקִידֵנוּ תַּפְקִידֵהוּ	יַפְקִידֵנוּ יַפְקִידֵהוּ
etc.	etc.	etc.	etc.	etc.	etc.	etc.	etc.	etc.

N.B. (i) Some of the 'varying' forms of the Affixes, at the foot of Tables XXV and XXVIII, may be found with Verb-forms of other Voices.

(ii) It is scarcely necessary to remind the student again here of Pt. I, §§ 12 & 14,—i.e. of Defective Long-*Khērik* and Defective *Shurik*.

(TABLE XXX).   PAST *K.* OF עשׂה WITH PRON.-AFFIXES (OBJECTIVE, ETC.).

we made.	ye (f.) ye (m.) made.	they made.	I made.	thou (f.) madest.	thou (m.) madest.	she made.	he made.
עָשִׂינוּ	עֲשִׂיתֶם { ־תֶן }	עָשׂוּ	עָשִׂיתִי	עָשִׂית	עָשִׂיתָ	עָשְׂתָה	עָשָׂה
עֲשִׂינוּהוּ	עֲשִׂיתּוּהוּ	עָשׂוּהוּ	{ עָשִׂיתִיהוּ / עָשִׂיתִיו }	{ עָשִׂיתִיהוּ / עָשִׂיתִיו }	{ עָשִׂיתָהוּ / עָשִׂיתוֹ }	{ עָשָׂתְהוּ / עָשָׂתּוּ }	עָשָׂהוּ
עֲשִׂינוּהָ	עֲשִׂיתּוּהָ	עָשׂוּהָ	עָשִׂיתִיהָ	עָשִׂיתִיהָ	עָשִׂיתָה	עָשָׂתָה	עָשָׂה
עֲשִׂינוּךָ	—	עָשׂוּךָ	עָשִׂיתִיךָ	—	—	עָשָׂתְךָ	(־הוּ) עָשְׂךָ
עֲשִׂינוּךְ	—	עָשׂוּךְ	עָשִׂיתִיךְ	—	—	עָשָׂתְךָ	עָשְׂךָ
etc.	etc.	etc.	etc.	etc.	etc.	etc.	etc.

FUT. *K.* OF עשה WITH PRON.-AFFIXES (OBJECTIVE, ETC.).

נַעֲשֶׂה	תַּעֲשׂוּ (־שֶׂינָה)	תַּעֲשֶׂינָה	יַעֲשׂוּ	אֶעֱשֶׂה	תַּעֲשִׂי	תַּעֲשֶׂה	תַּעֲשֶׂה	יַעֲשֶׂה
(־נִי) נַעֲשֵׂהוּ	תַּעֲשׂוּהוּ	תַּעֲשׂוּהוּ	(־נִי) יַעֲשׂוּהוּ	(־נִי) אֶעֱשֵׂהוּ	(־נִי) תַּעֲשִׂיהוּ	(־נִי) תַּעֲשֵׂהוּ	(־נִי) תַּעֲשֵׂהוּ	(־נִי) יַעֲשֵׂהוּ
(־נָּה) נַעֲשֶׂהָ	תַּעֲשׂוּהָ	תַּעֲשׂוּהָ	(־נָּה) יַעֲשׂוּהָ	(־נָּה) אֶעֱשֶׂהָ	(־נָּה) תַּעֲשִׂיהָ	(־נָּה) תַּעֲשֶׂהָ	(־נָּה) תַּעֲשֶׂהָ	(־נָּה) יַעֲשֶׂהָ
{ נַעֲשְׂךָ / נַעֲשְׂךָ: }	—	תַּעֲשׂוּךְ	יַעֲשׂוּךְ	{ אֶעֶשְׂךָ / אֶעֶשְׂךָ: }	—	—	{ תַּעֶשְׂךָ / תַּעֶשְׂךָ: }	{ יַעֶשְׂךָ / יַעֶשְׂךָ: }
etc.	etc.	etc.	etc.	etc.	etc.	etc.	etc.	etc.

Note:—(α) Some of the above are merely Paradigm-forms. (β) It may perhaps be well to add here the following few forms—(1) קָנָנִי 3 s. *m.* Past *K.* of קנה, w. aff. for *me*; (2) כִּלָּנוּ 3 s. *m.* Past *Pi.*; w. aff. for *us*; (3) הֶלְאָנִי 3 s. *m.* Past IIφ. of לאה, w. aff. for *me*; (4) רְאִתְךָ Job xlii. 5 (cp. Tab. XXV, Note γ, iii) 3 s. *f.* Past *K.* of ראה, w. aff. for *thee* (*m.*); (5) וְכִלַּתּוּ 3 s. *f.* Past *Pi.* of כלה, w. pref. 1 and aff. for *him*; (6) רֹדֵם Ps. lxviii. 28 (if from רדה *) Partic. *K.* s. *m.*, w. aff. for *them* (*m.*); (7) נִינֵם Ps. lxxiv. 8 (cp. וַנִּירָם Nu. xxi. 30, fr. ירה) 1 pl. Fut. *K.* of ינה, w. aff. for *them* (*m.*); (8) יְכַסְיָמוּ Ex. xv. 5 (ַ for וֹ) 3 pl. *m.* Fut. *Pi.* of כסה, w. aff. for *them* (*m.*), cp. p. 172 (θ); (9) אֲכַלֶּךָ Ex. xxxiii. 3 is 1 s. Fut. *Pi.* of כלה with aff. for *thee* (*m.*), the ַ being instead of the ֶ of אֲכַלֶּה (and the Dag. F. of ל omitted over the ַ) for Euphony.—Some other forms will be given elsewhere.—[* The LXX ἐν ἐκστάσει points to the Root רדם].

XLIII.

Note.

The forms of the Future *K.* of עָשָׂה w. Pron. Affs. (Obj. etc.)
which *actually occur* are

יַעֲשֵׂהוּ   *he will make him* (or *it m.*),

יַעֲשֶׂה
יַעֲשֶׂנָּה   } *he will make her* (or *it f.*),

יַעֲשֵׂם   *he will make them* (*m.*),

תַּעֲשֶׂנּוּ   *thou* (*m.*) *shalt make it* (*m.*),

תַּעֲשֶׂהָ   *thou* (*m.*) *shalt make it* (*f.*),

אֶעֱשֶׂנָּה   *I will make, or do, it* (*f.*),

אֶעֶשְׂךָ   *I will make thee* (*m.*),

יַעֲשׂוּהָ   *they* (*m.*) *will do it* (*f.*),

יַעֲשׂוּנִי   *they* (*m.*) *will make me*,

נַעֲשֶׂנָּה   *we will do it* (*f.*).

Many of the words given in Tab. XXX are, therefore, merely
Paradigm-forms. The proper form to begin with would, in
accordance with Tab. XXVIII, have been the נוּ— form [יַעֲשֶׂנּוּ].
As this word does not occur, we preferred to begin with יַעֲשֵׂהוּ
Then, for the sake of the uniformity which is necessary in a
Paradigm, the *corresponding* forms had to be given first in
other places.

TABLE XXXI.

FORMS OF PRON.-AFFIXES (OBJECTIVE) ATTACHED TO VERBS.

	First Person.	Second Person.	Third Person.
Sing. m.		[9] ־ךָ (־כָה), ־ךָ ׃ ־ךָ (׃־כָה)	[1] ־וֹ, [2] ־וֹ, [3] ־הוּ
		[10] ־ךָ (׃־כָה), ־נְךָ	[4] ־נּוּ (־נֵהוּ), ־נּוֹ
Sing. f.			[6] ־ֵהוּ (־ָהּ), [7] ־ָהּ
		[11] ־ךְ	־נָּהּ
Plu. m.	[12] ־נִי, [13] ־נִי	כֶם	[17] ־ם, [16] ־ם, ־מוֹ, ־מוֹ
	[14] ־נֵנִי (־נִי), [15] ־נִי, [16] ־נִי		־הֶם (־יהֶם), Tab. XXX, β.8), ־מוֹ
Plu. f.	־נוּ	כֶן	[19] ־ן, [20] ־ן

*_** Attention may also be directed to Note (F) on pages 378 & 379.

[1] As in Tabs. XXIV (Inf.), XXV (Past), XXVI (Partic.).

[2] ו CONSONANTAL:—as in (α) יו֫ (ו֫) Tab. XXV, (β) יו֫ for *Plu.* Participles [Tab. XXVI].

[3] הו UNACCENTED:—as in (α) הו֫ Tab. XXV (Past); (β) הו֫ (יהו֫) Tabs. XXVII (Imper.) & XXVIII (Fut.); (γ) יהו֫ (הו֫) Tabs. XXV (2 s. *f.* & 1 s.), XXVII & XXVIII; (δ) והו֫ (הו֫) Tabs. XXV, XXVII & XXVIII; (ε) תהו֫ (תהו֫) & contracted תו֫ (׃תו֫) Tab. XXV.

[4] Tabs. XXVII & XXVIII.

[5] Tab. XXVIII, Note (δ).

[6] Tabs. XXVII Note (γ), & XXVIII Note (γ).

[7] Rare, as in וַתַּחְמְרָה [Ex. ii. 3] *K.* Fut. 3 s. *f.* w. ו Conv. & Aft. it (*f.*) fr. חמר.

[8] UNACCENTED:—as in (α) ־ךָ Tabs. XXVII & XXVIII; (β) ־יךָ Tab. XXVI; (γ) ־יךָ (־ךָ) Tabs. XXV, XXVII & XXVIII; (δ) ־ךָ (־ךָ); Tabs. XXV, XXVII & XXVIII; (ε) [For ־תָה וְ־תָה (׃־תָה) Tab. XXV.

9 Either (A) ACCENTED after ־ַ, ordinarily [see Tabs. XXIV, XXV (3 s. m. & f.), XXVII & XXVIII], but see also below (B, γ & δ) ; Or (B) UNACCENTED:—as in (a) דֶ֫יךָ (דֶ֫יךָ*) Tab. XXV, (β) דֶ֫יךָ (דֶ֫יךָ†) Tabs. XXV & XXVIII ; (γ) וּדֶ֫יךָ (וּדֶ֫יךָ†), thus יִשָּׁא֫וּנְךָ Ps. xci. 12 [Comp. Tab. XXVIII, Note (γ)], and (δ) ־ֶ֫תְךָ thus יֶלְדַּ֫תְךָ Song viii. 5, rarely ; (ε) ־ֶ֫יךָ ; and (ζ) ־ֶ֫יךְ Tab. XXVI.

10 Jer. xxii. 24 ; Comp. Tab. XXVIII, Note (δ).

11 Either (A) at the end of an ACCENTED syllable, as in (a) דֶ֫ Tab. XXV (sometimes) ; (β) דֶ֫ Tabs. XXIV, XXV, XXVI & XXVIII ; (γ) דֶ֫י (דֶ֫י*) Tab. XXV ; (δ) דֶ֫וּ (דֶ֫וּ†) Tabs. XXV & XXVIII ;
Or (B) at the end of an UNACCENTED syllable, as in (a) תְךָ֫ (תְךָ֫) Tab. XXV ; (β) וּדֶ֫ (וּדֶ֫†) Tab. XXVIII, Note (γ) ; (γ) דֶ֫י (דֶ֫י) Tab. XXVI.

12 This ־ַי is not often used Objectively [Tabs. XXIV & XXVI], but rather ־ַנ (see Notes 13-16, below). The ־ַ after Partic. s. f., and the ־ַ (־ַי) after Partic. pl., Tab. XXVI, may be as in Tab. VIII.

13 UNACCENTED:—as in (a) נִי֫ (נִי֫) & נִי֫ Tabs. XXIV & XXV ; (β) נִי֫ (נִי֫) Tabs. XXIV, XXVI, XXVII & XXVIII ; (γ) יִ֫נִי (נִי֫*) and (δ) יִ֫נִי (נִי֫†) Tabs. XXV, XXVII & XXVIII ; (ε) תָנִי֫ (תָנִי֫) Tab. XXV.

14 Thus in תְּבָרֲכַ֫נִּי (Gen. xxvii. 19) Pĭ. Fut. 3 s. f. fr. ברך, and תְּבַעֲתַ֫נִּי (Job vii. 14) Pĭ. Fut. 2 s. m. fr. בעת, each w. Aff. me. [For the ־ַ of רֵ see Pt. I. § 72. The Dagesh in the נ, in these two words, is supposed to imply the נ of Tab. XXVIII, Note (δ).]

15 In תֶּדְכָּא֫וּנַנִי (Job xix. 2) Pĭ. Fut. 2 pl. m. w. Aff. me fr. דכא [Comp. Tab. XXVIII, Note (γ)].

16 As in יְכַבְּדָ֫נְנִי (Ps. l. 23) Pĭ. Fut. 3 s. m. w. Aff. me fr. כבד [Comp. Tab. XXVIII. ε, vi)]. For נְנִי see T. XXVIII, γ.

17 ACCENTED :—as in (a) סֶ֫ Tabs. XXIV, XXV, XXVI ; (β) סֶ֫ Tabs. XXVII & XXVIII ; (γ) סֶ֫ים (סֶ֫*) Tab. XXV, XXVII & XXVIII ; (δ) סֶ֫וּ (סֶ֫†) Tabs. XXV, XXVII & XXVIII.

18 UNACCENTED :—in (a) תָם֫ Tab. XXV, and (β) סֶ֫ in צֶעֳסָם see p. 378.

19 ACCENTED :—as in (a) נֶ֫ Tabs. XXIV, XXV, XXVI ; (β) נֶ֫ Tabs. XXVII & XXVIII ; (γ) נֶ֫י (נֶ֫*) Tabs. XXV, XXVII & XXVIII ; (δ) נֶ֫וּ (נֶ֫†) Tabs. XXV, XXVII & XXVIII ; (ε) נֶ֫ (rare).

20 UNACCENTED :—in תָ֫ Tab. XXV.

21 UNACCENTED :—as in (a) נוּ֫ Tabs. XXIV, XXV ; (β) נוּ֫ (נוּ֫) Tabs. XXIV, XXVI, XXVII & XXVIII ; (γ) יְנוּ (נוּ֫*), and (δ) יְנוּ֫ (נוּ֫†), Tabs. XXV, XXVII & XXVIII.

---

* Defective LONG-KHIRIK (Pt. I. § 12).　　† Defective SHURIK (Pt. I. § 14).